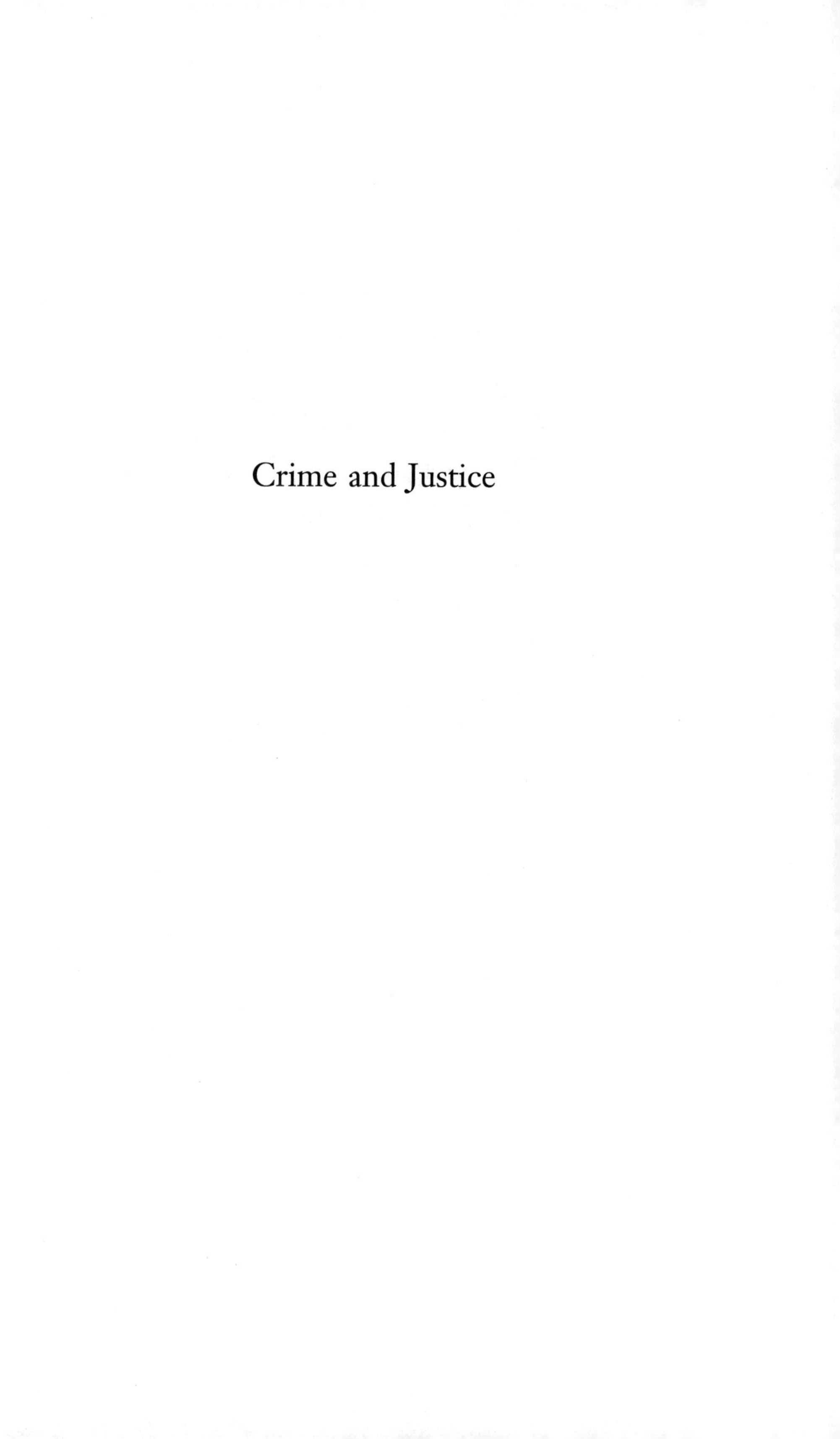

Crime and Justice

Crime and Justice

A Review of Research

Edited by Michael Tonry

VOLUME 28

The University of Chicago Press, Chicago and London

This volume was prepared under Grant Number 92-IJ-CX-K044 awarded to the Castine Research Corporation by the National Institute of Justice, U.S. Department of Justice, under the Omnibus Crime Control and Safe Streets Act of 1968 as amended. Points of view or opinions expressed in this volume are those of the editors or authors and do not necessarily represent the official position or policies of the U.S. Department of Justice.

The University of Chicago Press, Chicago 60637
The University of Chicago Press, Ltd., London

Printed in the United States of America

ISSN: 0192-3234

ISBN: 0-226-80860-2

LCN: 80-642217

The paper used in this publication meets the minimum requirements of American National Standard for Information Sciences—Permanence of Paper for Printed Library Materials, ANSI Z39.48-1984. ♾

Contents

Preface

These are interesting times for criminal justice practitioners, policy makers, and researchers. In the United States, crime rates have been falling for nearly a decade, the prison population is stabilizing in most states and declining in some, and prominent policy initiatives are as likely to be about treatment programs as about toughness. Outside the United States, crime rates have been falling in most countries since at least the mid-1990s, and both treatment and restorative justice programs are receiving heightened attention and support. Crime and criminal justice played but minor parts in the recent campaigns that produced a new U.S. president and a reelected British prime minister. Crime trends and political attitudes importantly shape crime policies, people's thinking about crime and punishment, and, for researchers, what's new and what's interesting.

Fifteen years ago, when crime rates were rising rapidly in most Western countries, and particularly so in the United States, crime policy focused on ways in which more vigorous policing, longer prison sentences, and more closely monitored community penalties might reduce crime rates. Against that backdrop, it is not surprising that subjects such as criminal careers, deterrence and incapacitation, prison population trends, and policy experiments preoccupied researchers and funding agencies. Against the current backdrop, the hot topics include restorative justice, rehabilitation research, human development, and crime prevention strategies.

Social scientists have been studying crime, criminals, and the criminal justice system for more than a century. Academic disciplines have developed, methods have advanced, and analytic techniques have become more sophisticated, but the subjects studied have changed little. Nothing fundamental in the human condition has changed, and the institutions and ideologies of the criminal justice system have long been in place. The details of crimes of fraud, theft, sex, and violence have changed, but only the details. The conditions of life, biography, biology, and circumstance that make one person more likely than another to be a criminal or a victim are the same as they have always been. The apparatus of the criminal justice system has not changed much in a quarter century, or a century. Police, prosecutors, probation, prisons, and courts perform the functions they have always performed. Techniques and technologies have changed, but that's all.

And yet, most of the essays in this volume could not have been written much before this. That is true in a trivial sense—research findings now available were not available earlier—but that is not what we mean. The thoughts underlying most of the essays had not taken shape until recently, even though the subjects they address are familiar. Social, economic, and normative developments of our times have made questions evident that were not evident before, or did not seem interesting. The sensibilities of a time shape what people think and believe, and consequently what they find sufficiently interesting or important to be worth the investment of time, money, and careers.

Of the seven essays in this volume, only one, Richard Harding's survey of prison privatization, covers much the same though updated ground as an earlier essay (Douglas McDonald's "Private Penal Institutions," *Crime and Justice* 16 [1992]). And only one of the others treads ground formerly covered in significant part. John Laub and Robert Sampson's examination of research on desistance from criminality deals with issues akin to those Jeffrey Fagan covered in "Cessation of Family Violence: Deterrence and Desistance" (*Crime and Justice* 11 [1989]), but more widely.

Of the rest, only one, Grant Harris, Tracy Skilling, and Marnie Rice's comprehensive overview of research on psychopathy, is on a topic *Crime and Justice* could have covered substantially earlier (and we tried: two earlier efforts to commission such an essay came to nought).

The remainder of the essays address topics not previously addressed except tangentially. Sometimes this is because contemporary scholars have only recently begun investigating new facets of old subjects. Michael Bellesiles's essay on the history of gun regulation from Elizabethan times to 1968 tells a story only recently brought to light. Daniel Nagin considers analytical and substantive issues at the intersection between the emerging literature on cost-effectiveness and cost-benefit studies of crime prevention policies and the burgeoning literature on developmental crime prevention. David Boerner and Roxanne Lieb's case study of the evolution of sentencing policy in Washington State exemplifies a genre—policy histories—that is almost unknown for the criminal justice system.

Leena Kurki and Norval Morris's preliminary look at supermaximum security prisons required the establishment of such prisons before they could be described. Though prisons have always had high-security areas, and there have long been maximum security prisons, supermax prisons provide ultrahigh security, movement controls, and degrees of isolation that are unprecedented for whole prisons.

Crime and Justice essays do not emerge from ether or grow like weeds, so editorial comments on inferences that might be drawn from their subjects may seem narcissistic. Most *Crime and Justice* essays are commissioned in the aftermath of editorial board suggestions (though a small minority are commissioned in response to proposals from authors). More are commissioned than can be published. Publication decisions are importantly influenced by comments from editorial board members and independent specialist referees.

Crime and Justice is a collective effort. The writers are the volumes and, nearly always gracefully and patiently, they put up with complicated and time-consuming editorial processes. The editorial board picks topics, suggests writers, reviews drafts, and gives *Crime and Justice* the benefit of eleven shaping minds. Many people help out as referees. The series would not exist without support from the National Institute of Justice (NIJ), which has funded it for a quarter century, under seven presidential administrations and larger numbers of Attorneys General and NIJ directors. Judy Reardon oversees all matters affecting *Crime and Justice* for NIJ, and we greatly appreciate her kind attentions and efficient help. The series would not exist except for all the participation of all these people, and we are enormously grateful to them. Readers will decide whether all this effort is worthwhile.

Michael Tonry
Norval Morris

John H. Laub and Robert J. Sampson

Understanding Desistance from Crime

ABSTRACT

The study of desistance from crime is hampered by definitional, measurement, and theoretical incoherence. A unifying framework can distinguish termination of offending from the process of desistance. Termination is the point when criminal activity stops and desistance is the underlying causal process. A small number of factors are sturdy correlates of desistance (e.g., good marriages, stable work, transformation of identity, and aging). The processes of desistance from crime and other forms of problem behavior appear to be similar. Several theoretical frameworks can be employed to explain the process of desistance, including maturation and aging, developmental, life-course, rational choice, and social learning theories. A life-course perspective provides the most compelling framework, and it can be used to identify institutional sources of desistance and the dynamic social processes inherent in stopping crime.

Why do they stop? Although the vast majority of criminal offenders stop committing crimes, desistance is not well understood. Criminology has been far more interested in the question, Why do individuals start? Most criminological research consists of cross-sectional "snapshots" or short-term panel studies of offending. There have been few long-term longitudinal studies of crime over the full life span. As a consequence, relatively little is known about desistance and, for that matter, the processes of persistent criminal behavior throughout the

John H. Laub, professor of criminology at the University of Maryland, College Park, and Robert J. Sampson, professor of sociology at the University of Chicago, gratefully acknowledge the research assistance of Elaine Eggleston and Chris Kenaszchuk and thank Frank Cullen, Jeffrey Fagan, Shadd Maruna, Alex Piquero, Michael Tonry, Chris Uggen, and two anonymous reviewers for their insights and suggestions.

0192-3234/2001/0028-0001$2.00

life course. Indeed, the characteristics that distinguish persistence in a life of crime from desistance within any group of high-risk offenders are generally unknown.

Criminological theories are not silent on why most offenders usually stop. For example, Akers argues, "other than one's own prior deviant behavior, the best single predictor of the onset, continuation, or desistance of delinquency is differential association with law-violating or norm-violating peers" (1998, p. 164). Despite a lack of systematic research, there is no shortage of theoretical speculations (see also Agnew 1997; Matsueda and Heimer 1997). This has not always been the case. One of the most powerful critiques of criminological theory was offered by David Matza in his classic book, *Delinquency and Drift* (1964), in which he introduced the idea of "maturational reform" to explain why most delinquency was transient and situational and why, as adolescents grew up, they simply left delinquency behind. He concluded that "most theories of delinquency take no account of maturational reform; those that do often do so at the expense of violating their own assumptions regarding the constrained delinquent" (Matza 1964, p. 22).

In this essay we examine theory and both quantitative and qualitative research on desistance from crime and other problem behaviors (such as alcohol and drug abuse). From this body of knowledge, it is clear that a number of factors are associated with desistance from crime. Elements such as family formation and gaining employment, for example, appear to predict desistance from crime in adulthood. But the research evidence is not strong or convincing. To cite but one example, in an extensive review of the literature, Wright and Wright (1992, p. 54) concluded that "no clearly confirming set of findings has emerged from research to date that demonstrates that getting married and having children reduces the likelihood of criminal offense." In order to make sense of this small but growing line of research, we organize our overview within several explanatory frameworks. We believe this strategy offers the best hope of making sense of the accumulated research literature. We also present a life-course perspective on desistance based on our long-term study of crime and deviance over the life span. The goal is not to present a full-blown theory but to offer a theoretical framework that identifies the key sources of change in the desistance process and begins to specify the causal mechanism involved. We also examine the implications of the life-course framework as a guide to future research on desistance.

From a theoretical standpoint, understanding desistance from crime requires a theory of crime and the criminal "offender." Desistance cannot be understood apart from the onset of criminal activity and possible continuation in offending over time. Whether or not one embraces the criminal career paradigm (Blumstein et al. 1986), good theories of crime ought to account for the onset, continuation, and desistance from criminal behavior across the life span. We believe a life-course perspective offers the most compelling framework for understanding the processes underlying desistance and the role of social context in shaping the dynamics of desistance. Specifically, we advance a life-course theory of age-graded informal social control as a means of understanding both the onset of and desistance from criminal behavior (Sampson and Laub 1993). Without a theory of crime, researchers and policy makers would be better off dropping the term "desistance" from their lexicon and focusing on the presence or absence of recidivism (Hoffman and Beck 1984).

Some researchers have argued that the policy ramifications from the study of desistance are clear and direct. For example, Uggen and Piliavin assert that desistance researchers have a "more legitimate and expansive license to intervene in the lives of participants" (1998, p. 1413). Moreover, they insist that the conditions of desistance are "much more amenable" to manipulation compared with the conditions of offending. Understanding the factors that lead to desistance is important in shaping interventions that reduce reoffending among those already involved in crime. This moves the field away from the narrow but now fashionable idea that prevention strategies administered early in the life course are the only feasible strategies to reduce criminal behavior.

We reach several conclusions. More attention should be devoted to the conceptualization and measurement of desistance. It is useful to distinguish desistance as a process from termination of criminal activity as an event, and we offer examples of its confounding in current research. On the basis of our review of the literature, desistance stems from a variety of complex processes—developmental, psychological, and sociological—and thus there are several factors associated with it. The key elements seem to be aging; a good marriage; securing legal, stable work; and deciding to "go straight," including a reorientation of the costs and benefits of crime. Processes of desistance from crime in general, specific types of crime, and multiple forms of problem behavior seem to be quite similar.

Although several theoretical frameworks provide a plausible explanation of desistance, the life-course perspective provides the most beneficial approach to understanding both persistence in and desistance from crime because of its explicit focus on the unfolding of lives in social context. To buttress this argument, we highlight new findings from our long-term follow-up study (Laub and Sampson 2001) of 500 delinquents at age seventy. Our life-history, narrative data underscore the need to examine desistance as a process consisting of interactions between human agency, salient life events, and historical context.

We conclude the essay by offering explicit ideas to guide future research and by considering the implications of our survey for crime control policies. We discuss ways to better identify, specify, and eventually understand the causal mechanisms supporting the desistance process. Integrating quantitative and qualitative methods offers the best strategy for furthering this agenda. With respect to policy concerns, and consistent with our life-course framework, current policies of incarceration are unlikely to foster desistance from crime in the long run.

These themes are organized as follows. Section I examines the conceptual, definitional, and measurement issues relating to desistance from crime. Both quantitative and qualitative studies of desistance are considered in Section II, including research on criminal careers, studies of recidivism, and studies with a specific emphasis on desistance from crime. Section III summarizes research on desistance from domestic violence and other problem-related behaviors. We organize the small, but growing body of literature on desistance into several explanatory frameworks in Section IV. These conceptual accounts include maturation and aging, developmental, life course, rational choice, and social learning. In Section V, we present a life-course perspective on desistance from crime drawing on our long-term follow-up study of juvenile delinquents. Using life-history narratives we address processes of desistance over the full life span, with a focus on middle age. Section VI discusses the implications for future research and policy on desistance from crime.

I. Desistance and Pornography: Do We Know It When We See It?

Although desistance is a major component of the criminal career model (Blumstein et al. 1986), it is the "least studied process" (Loeber and LeBlanc 1990, p. 407; see also Farrington 1986, pp. 221–23) compared with research on onset, persistence, and escalation in criminal offending.

A. Conceptual Issues

Defined as ceasing to do something, "desistance" from crime is commonly acknowledged in the research literature. Most offenders, after all, eventually stop offending. Yet there is relatively little theoretical conceptualization about crime cessation, the various reasons for desistance, and the mechanisms underlying the desistance process. As Maruna noted, "Desistance from crime is an unusual dependent variable for criminologists because it is not an event that happens, but rather it is the sustained *absence* of a certain type of event (in this case, crime)" (2001, p. 17). Compounding this lack of conceptualization is the confounding of desistance with aging. It is well known that crime declines with age in the aggregate population (Gottfredson and Hirschi 1990). The decline of recidivism with age led Hoffman and Beck to argue for the existence of an age-related "burnout" phenomenon (1984, p. 621). These authors found that rates of recidivism decline with increasing age and that this relationship maintains, controlling for other factors linked to recidivism such as prior criminal record. Moreover, there is evidence that offenders change as they age (see, e.g., Shover 1985, 1996; Cusson and Pinsonneault 1986). It appears that both formal and informal social controls become more salient with age. For example, fear of doing time in prison becomes especially acute with age (see Shover 1996).

As Rutter (1988, p. 3) has pointed out, one question is whether predictors of desistance are unique or simply the opposite of predictors leading to offending. To date, it appears that most predictors of desistance are the reverse of risk factors predicting offending (LeBlanc and Loeber 1993, p. 247). For example, Farrington (1992) contends that the onset of antisocial behavior is due to changes in social influence from parents to peers and that desistance is due to changes in social influence from peers to spouses. This indicates that the predictors of desistance are distinguished from the predictors of the onset of crime. This finding was evident in the Gluecks' research on criminal careers conducted in the 1930s and 1940s (see, e.g., Glueck and Glueck 1943). Recently, Uggen and Piliavin (1998) referred to this idea as "asymmetrical causation."

According to Loeber and LeBlanc, desistance does not occur "merely as a function of individuals' chronological age" (1990, p. 452). One reason for this is that desistance can take place at any time during the life span. The factors involved in desistance are different at different ages. That is, early desistance, before age eighteen, is likely to be different from late desistance, after age thirty (Weitekamp and Kerner 1994). Also, it may be that desistance at the same age is different for those with early versus late onset of criminal offending (Tremblay 1994). Nevertheless, based on the available data, desistance occurs most often during and after adolescence. Based on the evidence, desistance is normative for most offenders. Moffitt, for example, has written, "Indeed, numerous rigorous self-report studies have now documented that it is statistically aberrant to refrain from crime during adolescence" (1994, p. 29). This makes the lack of conceptualization of desistance from crime even more of a mystery.

Several serious conceptual questions remain unanswered. For example, Can desistance occur after one act of crime? If so, are the processes of desistance from a single act of crime different from desistance after several acts of crime? Is there such a thing as "spontaneous remission" and, if so, can the term be precisely defined? For example, Stall and Biernacki (1986) define spontaneous remission as desistance that occurs absent any external intervention. How can "genuine desistance" be distinguished from "false desistance"? How long a follow-up period is needed to establish desistance? Baskin and Sommers argue that a two-year hiatus indicates "temporary cessation" and is a long enough period to consider the "processes that initiate and sustain desistance" (1998, p. 143). How can "intermittency in offending" be distinguished from "true desistance"? For instance, Elliott, Huizinga, and Menard (1989, p. 118) employ the term "suspension" because suspension implies either temporary or permanent cessation. Farrington has stated, "even a five-year or ten-year crime-free period is no guarantee that offending has terminated" (1986, p. 201). Barnett, Blumstein, and Farrington (1989) found a small group of offenders who stopped offending and then restarted after a long time. What role does death or serious physical injury play in the study of desistance? Reiss (1989, pp. 229–39) has emphasized that criminologists tend mistakenly to assume that desistance is always a voluntary decision. The fact is that high-rate offenders are more likely to exit the risk pool through death (see, e.g., Lattimore, Linster, and MacDonald 1997). Should de-escalation to less serious offending be seen as an indication of desistance? In a similar vein, if offending ceases, but problem behavior remains or increases, what does that say about desistance? Weitekamp and Kerner note, "Desistance of crime could quite contrarily be considered as a process which may lead to other forms of socially deviant, unwanted or personally dreadful problems" (1994, p. 448). All of these issues raise fundamental questions about the meaning of desistance.[1] Answers to these and other questions are not found in the research literature.

At the heart of the conceptual questions is a conception of stability and change over the life course. Does desistance occur when there is a change in one or more of the following domains: crime, criminality, or opportunity? Is desistance related to one, two, or all three indicators? Defining criminality as the propensity to offend, Gottfredson and Hirschi (1990) argue that desistance occurs when there is a change in crime or opportunity. In their view, propensities to crime are stable over the life course and thus could not account for desistance from crime. Like Gottfredson and Hirschi, we maintain that crime changes over time (Sampson and Laub 1993), but we also contend that opportunities for crime are ubiquitous (Sampson and Laub 1995). However, so far we have been silent as to whether criminality (propensity) changes or remains stable over time, although we imply that traits like self-control can change over time as a consequence of changes in the quality or strength of social ties.

Ultimately, the concern with propensity (assuming that such an entity exists) may not be an important issue. LeBlanc and Loeber, for example, recognize that "manifestations of deviancy in the course of individuals' lives may change, while the underlying propensity for deviancy may remain stable" (1998, p. 179). Perhaps the focus ought to be on the heterogeneity of criminal behavior over the life span and not some unobserved latent concept.[2]

[1] Similar questions have been raised regarding the vocabulary and conceptualization of "displacement" and crime. For example, Barr and Pease (1990) have suggested that "deflection of crime from a target" is a better and more accurate formulation than displacement.

[2] Bushway et al. (2001) take a purely empirical approach to studying desistance as a process by offering a statistical model for changes in the rate of offending over time. They argue that "to study change (i.e., change that can be explained), we need to explicitly shift our focus from observed behavior to the underlying propensity to offend" (Bushway et al. 2001, p. 6). In their paper, Bushway and his colleagues endorse semiparametric trajectory models (Nagin and Land 1993) as the best method to capture changes in propensity to offend. Whether their statistical conceptualization of desistance offers a new approach compared with earlier conceptualizations remains to be seen. To us, the implications of their paper for qualitative research on desistance from crime are not readily apparent. Moreover, a strict focus on a latent (or unobserved) propensity to offend—the road taken by Bushway et al. (2001)—assumes but does not articulate a particular kind of individual-level theory.

B. Definitional Issues

A clear and precise definition of desistance cannot be developed that is separate from a clear and precise research question.[3] Developing a definition of desistance for the sake of having a definition is not worth the effort. Currently, there is no agreed-upon definition of desistance (see Bushway et al. 2001).[4] Some definitions are vague. For example, Shover defined desistance as the "voluntary termination of serious criminal participation" (1996, p. 121). Other definitions are arbitrary. For instance, Farrington and Hawkins (1991) defined desistance as having no convictions between ages twenty-one and thirty-two following a conviction before age twenty-one. Others are so idiosyncratic to a study or a data set that they are hard to defend. For example, Warr (1998) defined desistance as reporting smoking marijuana during the year preceding wave 5 interviews in the National Youth Survey but not reporting any such incidents in the year preceding wave 6. Other definitions do not sound like desistance at all. Clarke and Cornish write, "Desistance is, in any case, not necessarily permanent and may simply be part of a continuing process of lulls in the offending of persistent criminals . . . or even, perhaps, of a more casual drifting in and out of particular crimes" (1985, p. 173). Finally, some researchers do not define desistance but purport to study it (see, e.g., Trasler 1979)!

Weitekamp and Kerner (1994) have tried to disentangle the various components of desistance. They define termination as the time when the criminal or delinquent behavior stops permanently. In contrast, suspension is defined as a break in offending behavior. These authors also view desistance as a process (not an event) by which frequency of offending decelerates and exhibits less variety (see Maruna [2001] and Bushway et al. [2001], who also take the position that desistance is a process, not an event). Weitekamp and Kerner (1994) recommend abandoning the notion of "spontaneous remission" in the study of desistance, arguing that the concept is unclear and theoretically barren.

In a similar vein, Loeber and LeBlanc (1990, p. 409) tried to disentangle desistance by specifying four components of the term: a slowing down in the frequency of offending (deceleration); a reduction in the

[3] Defining persistence in crime suffers the same problem, for there is no standard agreed-upon definition. For example, Wolfgang defined persistent offenders as those having an arrest as a juvenile and as an adult (1995, p. 143). Definitions should not be distinct from research questions.

[4] In fact, an editor of a leading journal once asked us to remove the term from our paper. He argued that "desistance" was not a word. There appears to be no agreed-upon spelling either.

variety of offending (specialization); a reduction in the seriousness of offending (de-escalation); and remaining at a certain level of seriousness in offending without escalating to more serious acts (reaching a ceiling).

C. *Measurement Issues*

There are, of course, serious measurement problems inherent in assessing desistance if for no other reason than that there is ambiguity and imprecision in the study of crime in general. Even though some offenders desist from criminal activity, they may continue to engage in a variety of acts that are considered "deviant" or the functional equivalents of crime (Gottfredson and Hirschi 1990). For example, they may drink alcohol excessively, have children out of wedlock, "loaf" instead of work, gamble, and congregate in bars. Can such actors accurately be called desisters? Perhaps from the narrow confines of the criminal justice system they are, but from a theoretical vantage point, they display behaviors that imply little change in their antisocial trajectory.

As Barnett and Lofaso (1985) have argued, the paucity of data on criminal behavior in later life means that findings on desistance (or the age of termination) may reflect the cutoff of observations at a specific age (i.e., "false desistance") rather than a true cessation of criminal activity. Termination that is followed by criminal involvement can be considered "false" desistance as well (Blumstein, Farrington, and Moitra 1985). The length of follow-up in the measurement period thus seems crucial. Vaillant (1996) noted that in research on alcohol treatment the typical follow-up period is six months to a year. In his long-term follow-up study of male alcohol abuse over a thirty-year period, Vaillant (1996) concluded that two years of abstinence is inadequate to provide a basis for long-term prognosis. He also reported data from a follow-up study of alcohol-dependent men and women showing that 45 percent relapsed after two years of abstinence. Yet only 9 percent relapsed after five years of abstinence. The standard in research on narcotic drug users seems to be a three-year follow-up period; research on cancer typically examines remission five years after onset (Vaillant 1996). In criminological studies the follow-up periods vary considerably, but most are fairly short—six months to a year or two.

An important paper by Nagin, Farrington, and Moffitt (1995) bears on this issue. They found, based on official records of conviction from the Cambridge Study of Delinquent Development, that a group of offenders desisted from crime (starting at age twenty) even though self-reported data from these same subjects revealed continued involvement in drugs, alcohol, and violence outside of the home at age thirty-two. Like Nagin, Farrington, and Moffitt (1995), LeBlanc and Frechette (1989) found varying rates of desistance depending on the source of information. Using official records as the criterion, 62 percent of the official delinquents desisted from crime. However, using self-report data, only 11 percent of the males desisted by age thirty.

D. *Summary Framework*

Like many criminological topics, the topic of desistance elicits conceptual, definitional, and measurement concerns. These are important and demand further theoretical and research attention. In order to increase clarity and provide guidance, we believe two issues stand out.

First, the concepts of desistance and termination of offending cannot be meaningfully studied independent of a conception of crime and the offender. Crime is typically defined as a violation of societal rules of behavior that are embodied in law. When officially recognized, such violations may evoke sanctions by the state. Deviance is typically defined as violations of social norms or generally accepted standards of society (i.e., institutionalized expectations). Even given these definitions, the operational definition of an "offender" remains ambiguous, as does the point at which desistance occurs. How much offending must ensue before one is defined as an "offender"—one, five, ten, twenty acts? And over what period of time must a former offender be "free" of crime before we say that he or she has desisted—a year, ten years?

Although answers to these questions are difficult, some ground rules are possible. Because low-rate offending is normative, especially during adolescence, criminologists should not spend much time or energy theorizing why everyone seems to commit crime during their teen years. Following this logic, criminologists should also not spend much time or energy studying termination and desistance for low-rate offenders (defined as involvement in a single event or a series of relatively isolated events over a long period of time). Furthermore, termination and desistance should be studied among those who reach some reasonable threshold of frequent and serious criminal offending. The precise details of measurement depend on the data set and the research question under investigation. For example, in previous research we have argued for a focus on desistance from persistent and serious delinquency, operationalized as a group of 500 formerly incarcerated juveniles with lengthy and serious criminal records (Sampson and Laub 1993). We return to these definitional issues below, for their resolution is crucial to advancement of research.

Second, once an operational definition of the offender pool has been constructed and defended, we believe it is important to distinguish termination of offending from the concept of desistance. Termination is the time at which criminal activity stops. Desistance, by contrast, is the causal process that supports the termination of offending. While it is difficult to ascertain when the process of desistance begins, it is apparent that it continues after the termination of offending. In our view, the process of desistance maintains the continued state of nonoffending. Thus, both termination and the process of desistance need to be considered in understanding cessation from offending. By using different terms for these distinct phenomena, we separate termination (the outcome) from the dynamics underlying the process of desistance (the cause), which have been confounded in the literature to date.[5]

Perhaps an analogy would be helpful. Marriage is an institution that is marked by a time when it officially starts (date of marriage) and, in many cases, ends (date of divorce). One may thus be said to enter the state of marriage at a discrete point. In this regard, marriage is like offending, which is also marked by an event (the commission of a crime) that occurs at a point in time. Divorce is likewise an event and can be viewed as analogous to termination from offending. One difference, however, is that divorce is fixed in time (e.g., the date of legal separation), whereas termination of offending is characterized by the absence of continued offending (a nonevent). Unlike, say, stopping smoking, where setting a specific quit date is often important, criminal offenders typically do not set a date to quit offending. The period of time necessary to establish that termination has occurred is a sticky issue but one that is possible to overcome. For example, in the criminal career literature, the end of the criminal career is defined as the age at which the last crime is committed (Blumstein et al. 1986). In this case

[5] In a similar vein, Hirschi and Gottfredson (1986) developed the distinction between crime and criminality to capture the idea that crime declines with age while criminality remains stable. They argue, "those concerned with maturational reform appear to confuse change in crime (which declines) with change in criminality (which may not change at all). Part of the reason for this confusion is that we tend to use the same indicator for both concepts. A count of criminal acts serves as a measure of crime and as a measure of criminality" (Hirschi and Gottfredson 1986, p. 58). With respect to stopping offending, the same indicators and processes are used to describe both termination and desistance.

it seems reasonable to specify the date of last crime as the point of termination of offending.

Following Vaughan (1986), we consider the concept of "uncoupling" to be clarifying. Vaughan defined uncoupling as the process of divorce and separation, which occurs prior to, during, and after the event of divorce. Like desistance, uncoupling is not abrupt but a gradual transition out of an intimate relationship. We believe that, just like quitting smoking or uncoupling (Vaughan 1986; Fisher et al. 1993), desistance is best viewed as a process rather than a discrete event. The process is a social transition that entails identity transformation, as from a smoker to a nonsmoker, from a married or coupled person to a divorced or uncoupled person, or from an offender to a nonoffender. Also, like quitting smoking or uncoupling, desistance is not an irreversible transition.

In short, by focusing attention on the conceptual, definitional, and measurement issues surrounding termination and desistance from crime, we urge researchers to make their definitions more explicit and provide details regarding the measurement of these concepts. For purposes of this essay, we focus on research that is directed toward discovering the predictors of termination from persistent offending and "unpacking" the causal dynamics of the processes of desistance. To the extent possible, we examine the multiple social contexts of desistance. LeBlanc and Loeber point out that desistance is embedded in developmental contexts as well, such as a decrease in physical strength and fitness with age (1998, p. 166). We thus emphasize the variety of contexts—developmental, historical, and environmental—that bear on termination and the processes of desistance from crime.

II. Predictors and Processes of Desistance: What Do We Know?

We draw on three bodies of literature—criminal careers research, recidivism studies, and qualitative studies of offenders and ex-offenders—to frame what we know about the predictors and processes of desistance from crime. To the extent possible, special attention is devoted to differences in desistance across offender characteristics (e.g., males vs. females) and by crime type (e.g., robbery vs. burglary vs. spouse assault). Relevant literature pertaining to cessation from other problem behavior and deviance (e.g., illicit drug use and alcohol abuse) is incorporated where appropriate. It is important to point out that we do not systematically review the research literature that focuses solely on the prevalence of desistance. It is our assessment that desistance rates vary so much across sampling and measurement conditions that they are virtually meaningless when taken out of context.

Despite clear limitations in data and serious weaknesses in study designs, several important findings in the previous research relating to the predictors and processes of desistance from crime should be underscored. First, the prevalence of crime declines with age, although there appears to be more variability in the age distribution across offense types than is commonly believed (see Steffensmeier et al. 1989). Thus, desistance is part and parcel of the natural history of offending. Second, the incidence of offending does not necessarily decline with age and may increase with age for certain types of criminal activity and subgroups of offenders (Blumstein et al. [1986]; Farrington [1986]; for an opposite view, see Hirschi and Gottfredson [1983]). Third, there is substantial continuity in offending from childhood to adolescence and into adulthood, and the earlier the onset of criminal activity, the longer the criminal career. Fourth, despite patterns of continuity, there is a great deal of heterogeneity in criminal behavior over the life span because "many juvenile offenders do not become career offenders" (Cline 1980, p. 670). From a theoretical perspective, rather than thinking in simplistic, rigid offender/nonoffender categories, Glaser (1969) suggests that it is more appropriate to view criminality dynamically as a "zigzag path" consisting of crime and noncrime cycles. Along similar lines, Matza (1964) offers the image of "drift" to capture the instability of offending over time. Finally, the literature focusing directly on desistance indicates that there are multiple pathways to desistance. Some of the most important seem to be attachment to a conventional other such as a spouse, stable employment, transformation of personal identity, and the aging process. These predictors and processes of desistance do not seem to vary much by offender characteristics or type of crime.

A. Studies of Criminal Careers and Desistance

Sheldon and Eleanor Glueck may have been the first researchers to examine the relationship between age and criminal behavior over the life span, including age at termination of offending. In their fifteen-year follow-up of 510 male reformatory inmates, they found that the proportion of subjects arrested decreased from 71 percent in the first five-year follow-up period to 57 percent in the third five-year follow-up period (Glueck and Glueck 1943, p. 109). However, the average number of arrests among those arrested increased from 3.3 to 3.6 across the same follow-up periods. Arrests for property crimes declined, but they were replaced by arrests for drunkenness. The average age of the subjects at the end of the fifteen-year follow-up was forty (Glueck and Glueck 1943, p. 3). Similar patterns can be found in the Gluecks' fifteen-year follow-up of 1,000 juvenile delinquents referred to the Judge Baker Clinic (Glueck and Glueck 1940) and their follow-up of 500 juvenile delinquents from the *Unraveling Juvenile Delinquency* study (Glueck and Glueck 1950, 1968).

The Gluecks did not systematically investigate the causes of the decrease in offending over time, although they did compare the reformed and unreformed as well as those who remained serious offenders compared with those who de-escalated to minor offending.[6] The Gluecks concluded that those who reformed "were better circumstanced than those who continued to recidivate over the long-term follow-up span" (Glueck and Glueck 1974, p. 141). Many of these differences were due to varying experiences, personal traits, and circumstances before the onset of offending. From these findings, the Gluecks developed the hypothesis of "delayed maturation" to explain desistance from crime, which we discuss below.

In another seminal research project, subjects from the Cambridge-Somerville Youth Study have been followed into their forties (median age, forty-seven). McCord (1980) found that while the vast majority of juvenile delinquents committed a crime as an adult, the majority of the adult offenders had no history of offending as juveniles. McCord also reported that the earlier the age of onset, the greater the likelihood of recidivism in adulthood.

Lee Robins's (1966) follow-up study of child guidance clinic patients is also pertinent to the topic of continuity and change in offending over time. Robins found that 72 percent of the male children referred to the clinic for antisocial behavior were arrested between the ages of eighteen and thirty. Of those arrested between age eighteen and thirty, 59 percent were arrested after age thirty. Conversely, of those not arrested between age eighteen and thirty, 18 percent were arrested after age thirty (Robins 1966, p. 47). Thus, while these data show continuity of offending well into middle age, they also suggest that "the effect of the early experience begins to diminish after age thirty and recent experiences become more significant" (Cline 1980, p. 666).

[6] The Gluecks defined reform as an absence of criminal activity during follow-up.

Wolfgang, Thornberry, and Figlio (1987) followed a sample from the 1945 Philadelphia birth cohort study (Wolfgang, Figlio, and Sellin 1972) to age thirty. They reported strong continuity in offending across the juvenile and adult years. The peak age of offending is sixteen, and thereafter the rate of offending declines into adulthood. Wolfgang, Thornberry, and Figlio also found that "the average number of offenses committed at each age is relatively constant from ages ten to thirty" (1987, p. 41). In the successor study to Wolfgang, Figlio, and Sellin (1972), Tracy and Kempf-Leonard (1996) collected criminal records up to age twenty-six for 27,160 males and females from a 1958 Philadelphia birth cohort (see also Tracy, Wolfgang, and Figlio 1985). The vast majority of cohort subjects had no record of delinquency or adult crime (71 percent). Six percent committed crimes only as adults and 8 percent committed criminal acts in both the juvenile and adult period. Sixteen percent of the cohort had a record of delinquency but no official contact in adulthood. About two-thirds (68 percent) of the cohort delinquents did not continue offending in adulthood (Tracy and Kempf-Leonard 1996, pp. 80–81).

There is empirical evidence that similar criminal career patterns exist in European countries. In the Cambridge Study in Delinquent Development, Farrington and his colleagues (1988) reported considerable continuity in offending from adolescence to adulthood (defined as age thirty-two). As in the U.S. studies, age of onset predicted persistence in offending. Farrington et al. (1988) also reported that the prevalence of convictions peaked at age seventeen and then declined. It is interesting to note that they found that the sample as a group committed as many offenses between ages twenty-one and thirty-two as in the juvenile and young adulthood periods. The prevalence of certain offenses (e.g., theft from work, assault, drug use, and fraud) did not decline with age.

Stattin and Magnusson (1991) studied a Swedish cohort of 709 males and found a strong connection between criminal activity in childhood (up to age fourteen), adolescence (from fifteen to twenty), and early adulthood (twenty-one to thirty). They also found little onset of offending during the adult period (see also Stattin, Magnusson, and Reichel 1989). These findings of continuity in offending are consistent with the results of another study of the criminal activity of Swedish males in adolescence and adulthood from an older cohort (see Sarnecki 1985).

Overall, criminal career research leads to the clear and nonsurprising conclusion that juvenile delinquency is linked to adult crime. The percentage of juvenile delinquents known to the police that persist as adult offenders ranges from 31 to 71 percent (Blumstein et al. 1986, p. 87). Hence, the juvenile record is a strong predictor of later offending, and this relationship increases as the juvenile record becomes longer (Blumstein et al. 1986, pp. 86–88). At the same time, and perhaps surprisingly, "40 to 50 percent of adult offenders do not have records of juvenile police contacts" (Blumstein et al. 1986, p. 88). There is an apparent paradox at work here. While studies we reviewed show that "antisocial" behavior in children is one of the best predictors of antisocial behavior in adults, "most antisocial children do not become antisocial as adults" (Gove 1985, p. 123).[7] Cline states that although there is "more constancy than change . . . there is sufficient change in all the data to preclude simple conclusions concerning criminal career progressions" (1980, p. 665). He concludes, rightfully, we suggest, that there is far more heterogeneity in criminal behavior than previous work has suggested, and that many juvenile offenders do not become career offenders (Cline 1980, pp. 669–70). Loeber and LeBlanc make a similar point: "Against the backdrop of continuity, studies also show large within-individual changes in offending" (1990, p. 390).

A focus on parameters of the criminal career—onset, participation, incidence, and career length—is the essence of a criminal career approach to the study of crime and criminals. Most important, the criminal career model recognizes that there is a mixture of offending patterns and highlights the need to disaggregate the offender population. The criminal career model takes as a given that causal factors explaining participation in crime, the frequency of offending, and the termination of a criminal career are different. Indeed, a key idea of this approach is that high-rate offenders are distinctive; namely, they have a stable rate of offending and hence do not desist from crime. As

[7] We set aside a detailed discussion of the problematic notion of the concept of "antisocial" behavior. We would emphasize two points, however, that bear on desistance. First, antisocial behavior is in fact social in the sense that it is group or interactional behavior. Second, our understanding of antisocial behavior cannot be considered independent of societal reactions and definitions. For example, the major contributing factor to the dramatic rise in imprisonment rates in the United States and many other countries over the past twenty years, especially of minority groups, has been drug arrests. This has resulted from a shift over time in how the same behavior (taking drugs) is labeled by society. Is drug use (and hence lack of desistance) inherently antisocial? Moreover, the State decision to label and incarcerate someone for drug use bears on the life course of that individual, which may contribute in turn to further "antisocial" behavior or lack of desistance. For these reasons sociologists have been reluctant to embrace antisocial behavior as a concept (see Sampson 2000).

Blumstein and Cohen state, "The common belief that offenders who remain in their criminal careers into their 30s will imminently terminate their careers is not empirically justified. On the contrary, those offenders who are still actively involved in crime at age 30 have survived the more typical early termination of criminal careers, and so are more likely to be the more persistent offenders. After their early 40s, however, their termination rates are quite high" (1987, p. 991; see also Piquero et al. 2001). These offenders are characterized by early onset of offending, high frequency of prior offending, drug use, and unstable employment.

Desistance is referred to as age of termination or career length in the criminal career lexicon, with the fundamental finding that early onset is linked to a longer career. Existing research on the length of criminal careers indicates that most careers are short—five years for offenders who are active in index offenses as young adults (Blumstein et al. 1986, p. 94, but see Farrington, Lambert, and West 1998). For offenders who are still active in their thirties, the residual career length is about ten years (Blumstein et al. 1986, p. 94). Yet the data supporting these conclusions are not without problems. Because of the separation of juvenile and adult record-keeping systems in the United States, many studies of criminal careers have focused on either juveniles or adults. Even more concerning is that the bulk of this research reflects the cutoff of observations at a given age, thus artificially marking the length of criminal careers. Almost all criminal career research has also limited itself to officially defined data on crime.

Overall, the criminal career approach represents a significant movement in criminology, but it appears to have reached a point of stagnation. The reasons are many, but our diagnosis is that the approach faltered because of its narrow focus on measurement and policy. The focus on desistance has been used to enhance the predictive accuracy of criminal career models to identify high-rate offenders prospectively for purposes of incapacitation (see, e.g., Blumstein, Farrington, and Moitra 1985; Barnett, Blumstein, and Farrington 1989). As a result, theoretical accounts of desistance stemming from this body of research (with few exceptions) have been sorely lacking.

B. Studies of Recidivism and Desistance

Although not necessarily within the criminal career paradigm, a small number of investigators have explicitly examined recidivism and desistance using longitudinal data. A follow-up of 200 Borstal boys found that marriage led to "increasing social stability" (Gibbens 1984, p. 61). Knight, Osborn, and West (1977) discovered that while marriage did not reduce criminality, it reduced antisocial behavior such as drinking and drug use (see also Osborn and West 1979; West 1982). Osborn (1980) examined the effect on delinquency of leaving London and found that subjects who moved had a lower risk of reoffending when compared with a similar group who stayed (see also West 1982). There is some evidence that episodes of unemployment lead to higher crime rates (Farrington et al. 1986). Along similar lines, Glaser's extensive study of parolees and recidivism showed that "men in prison have expectations of extremely rapid occupational advancement during the years immediately following their release, expectations which are unrealistic in light of their limited work experience and lack of vocational skills" (Glaser 1969, p. 238). Glaser found that lack of skill and work experience were the major obstacles to finding a good job and that job instability was in turn linked to criminal recidivism.

Trasler (1979) examined the idea of "spontaneous desistance" from crime. For Trasler, desistance stems from a response to changes in the contingencies of reinforcement. In other words, situational changes led to desistance. These adult reinforcers included a job, an adequate income, a home, a wife, children, and adult friends (Trasler 1979, p. 316).

In an effort to assess the effect of several transitional life events on desistance from crime, Rand examined data for 106 male offenders from the follow-up study of the 1945 birth cohort in Philadelphia. Rand (1987) found no effect on desistance for fatherhood, serving in the military, vocational training, or going to college. Moreover, other transitional life events (e.g., cohabitation) were positively related to crime. Marriage, completing high school, and receiving vocational training in the military were related to reduced criminal involvement, but the results varied considerably by offender characteristics as well as crime-related characteristics.

Farrington and Hawkins (1991) analyzed data from the Cambridge Study of Delinquent Development to assess the characteristics of desisters compared with persisters in adulthood. From this prospective longitudinal study of 411 London males that started when the boys were eight or nine, they found no relationship between factors influencing prevalence, early onset, and desistance. For example, early troublesome behavior was an important predictor of both participation in offending and early onset of crime, yet this variable was not strongly related to persistence in criminal behavior in adulthood (Farrington and Hawkins 1991, p. 28). However, father's participation with the boy in leisure activities was associated with a later onset and desistance from crime even when controlling for parental criminality (Farrington and Hawkins 1991, p. 19). Along with parental involvement, commitment to school was also associated with desistance from crime.

Loeber et al. (1991) studied desistance in juvenile offending using data from the Pittsburgh Youth Study, a longitudinal study of boys and their primary caretakers. They found several variables that were associated with desistance in offending, including low social withdrawal or shyness, low disruptive behavior, and positive motivational and attitudinal factors (Loeber et al. 1991, p. 37). Even more intriguing was the finding that different factors emerged for early desistance (prior to age twelve) and later desistance (ages thirteen to fourteen) (Loeber et al. 1991, pp. 73, 81). Unlike other researchers, Loeber et al. (1991, p. 81) found that most factors associated with initiation were also associated with desistance. Loeber and his colleagues concluded, "Initiation and desistance appear to reflect the positive and negative aspects of a similar process" (1991, p. 81). LeBlanc and Loeber (1998) also showed that rates of desistance varied by crime type as well as type of problem behavior. In addition, age at termination was associated with age of onset and seriousness of the offense, with the most serious offenses ceasing at an advanced age and less serious offenses ceasing at earlier ages.

In our book, *Crime in the Making* (Sampson and Laub 1993), we developed an age-graded theory of informal social control to explain crime and deviance over the life course. Most relevant for the study of desistance is the idea that salient life events and social ties in adulthood can counteract, at least to some extent, the trajectories apparently set in early child development. Our thesis is that social bonds in adulthood—especially attachment to the labor force and cohesive marriage—explained criminal behavior independent of prior differences in criminal propensity. In other words, pathways to both crime and conformity were modified by key institutions of social control in the transition to adulthood (e.g., employment, military service, and marriage). Thus, strong social bonds could explain desistance from criminal behavior in adulthood, despite a background of delinquent behavior.

We tested these ideas using data from the Gluecks' classic study of juvenile delinquency and adult crime (Glueck and Glueck 1950, 1968). We found that despite differences in early childhood experiences, adult social bonds to work and family had similar consequences for the life trajectories of the 500 delinquents and 500 nondelinquent controls. That is, job stability and marital attachment in adulthood were significantly related to changes in adult crime—the stronger the adult ties to work and family, the less crime and deviance among both delinquents and controls. We conceptualized various types of change and argued that social control and turning points were crucial in understanding processes of change in the adult life course (see Laub and Sampson 1993). These concepts were portrayed by examining person-based, life-history data drawn from the Gluecks' longitudinal study of 1,000 men (Glueck and Glueck 1968). Although adult crime was clearly connected to childhood behavior, these qualitative data suggested that both incremental and abrupt change were structured by changes in adult social bonds. Integrating divergent sources of life-history data (e.g., narratives, interviews), our qualitative analysis was consistent with the hypothesis that the major turning points in the life course for men who refrained from crime and deviance in adulthood were stable employment and good marriages.

Building on our earlier work (Laub and Sampson 1993; Sampson and Laub 1993) and the work of Nagin and Paternoster (1994), we, along with Daniel Nagin, drew an analogy between changes in criminal offending spurred by the formation of social bonds and an investment process (Laub, Nagin, and Sampson 1998). This conceptualization suggests that because investment in social relationships is gradual and cumulative, resulting desistance will be gradual and cumulative. Using a dynamic statistical model developed by Nagin and Land (1993), we tested these ideas about change using yearly longitudinal data from the Gluecks' (1968) study of criminal careers (Laub, Nagin, and Sampson 1998). The results showed that desistance from crime was facilitated by the development of quality marital bonds, and that this influence was gradual and cumulative over time. Thus, the timing and quality of marriage matters: early marriages characterized by social cohesiveness led to a growing preventive effect. The effect of a good marriage takes time to appear, and it grows slowly over time until it inhibits crime.

Another finding from this study was that individual characteristics and family circumstances measured in childhood that are known to predict delinquency and adult criminality have a limited capacity to predict desistance.[8] That is, conditional on juvenile delinquency, our

[8] Similarly, Vaillant and Milofsky (1982) showed that the three childhood variables that most clearly predicted alcoholism failed to predict remission. For comparable findings from a study of narcotic addicts, see Vaillant (1973).

study (Laub, Nagin, and Sampson 1998) found that a host of traditional individual-difference factors were at best weakly predictive of eventual desistance. Nagin, Farrington, and Moffitt (1995) also found that similar background variables had a limited capacity to predict desistance among active offenders in a more contemporary sample of 411 British males born in 1951–54. This line of research further supports the contention that adult social bonds may be important in understanding changes in criminal trajectories.

The idea that desistance from crime is gradual and accompanied by the accumulation of social bonds is supported in research by Horney, Osgood, and Marshall (1995, p. 671). Analyzing month-to-month data over a two- to three-year period for a sample of high-rate convicted felons, Horney, Osgood, and Marshall (1995) showed that large within-individual variations in criminal offending were systematically associated with local life circumstances (e.g., employment and marriage). "Moving in with one's wife doubles the odds of stopping offending (compared to moving away), and moving away from one's wife doubles the odds of starting to offend (compared to moving in)" (Horney, Osgood, and Marshall 1995, p. 665). It is interesting to note that the effect of cohabitation was different—living with a girlfriend was associated with higher rates of offending. As Horney, Osgood, and Marshall (1995) have noted, some of the time, some high-rate offenders enter into circumstances like marriage that provide the potential for informal social control. This confirmation of our marriage results is important because the Horney, Osgood, and Marshall (1995) sample contained a sizable proportion of minorities in a contemporary setting.

Using data from the Cambridge Study in Delinquent Development, Farrington and West (1995) examined the effects of three life events—getting married, having a first child, and becoming separated—on offending patterns among working-class males from central London. Part of their analytical strategy was to compare offending before and after marriage within subjects as well as using a more traditional between-subjects analysis. In both the between- and within-subject analyses, Farrington and West (1995) found that marriage decreased offending compared with remaining single. Conversely, separation from a wife and having a child outside of marriage were associated with later offending.

Using data from the National Youth Survey, a longitudinal survey of a nationally representative probability sample of youth in the United States relying on self-reports of criminal involvement, Warr (1998) examined whether desistance from crime was due to marriage or a reduction in exposure to delinquent peers that results from marriage. To ensure variability in both rates of marriage and delinquent behavior, data were drawn from waves 5 and 6, when the respondents were ages fifteen to twenty-one and eighteen to twenty-four, respectively. Warr found that marriage leads to a dramatic decline in time spent with friends as well as reduced exposure to delinquent peers. Warr concluded that his findings provide support for differential association/ social learning theory because peer relations appear to account for the effect of marriage on desistance.

Pezzin (1995) used data from the National Longitudinal Survey of Youth (NLSY) (a nationally representative survey of over 12,000 individuals between fourteen and twenty-two years of age) to investigate the decision to terminate criminal involvement as a function of current and future earnings prospects. She found that the effects of current and future expected criminal earnings significantly reduced the likelihood of offending. Moreover, individuals with higher current legal earnings were more likely to terminate their criminal careers. This study suggests that the benefits of legal behavior need to be considered along with the opportunity costs of illegal behavior in the decision to give up crime.

Shover and Thompson (1992) reanalyzed data from the Rand Inmate Survey in a study of age, differential expectations, and desistance. They outlined two possible explanations of the link between desistance and age. The first was a direct, positive relationship between the aging organism and desistance. The second model emphasized the indirect effects of age on desistance, whereby age interacts with past experiences to alter the assessment of risks and rewards of crime, which in turn leads to desistance from criminal behavior. Shover and Thompson argued that "increasing age and past performance in straight and criminal pursuits determine the offender's differential expectations" (1992, p. 92). Their study revealed support for both the direct and indirect effects of age on desistance from crime.

Selection. Of course, it could be argued that the association between desistance and adult social factors is attributable to a selection process (Gottfredson and Hirschi 1990). A large body of research documents an association between enduring individual characteristics, such as low intelligence and impulsiveness, and criminality. The distribution of these persistent individual differences, which has been referred to as "persistent heterogeneity," is highly skewed to the right (Nagin and Paternoster 1991). It may be that those who desist from crime as young adults are in the middle range of the skewed tail: They are sufficiently prone to crime to be delinquent and unattached in their youth, but not so crime-prone to persist in criminal activity and detachment in their adult years. Selection is thus a threat to the interpretation of any desistance study.

Although not experimental in nature, analyses of desistance have addressed this argument in a number of ways. For example, criminal career researchers have explicitly recognized and modeled offender heterogeneity. Blumstein, Farrington, and Moitra (1985) divided the London sample into innocents, persisters, and desisters and estimated the probabilities of offending for each group. Persisters and desisters are present at each stage of arrest, although at each successive arrest the proportion of persisters will increase. These authors applied this approach to the 1945 Philadelphia birth cohort data; data from Lyle Shannon's cohort studies in Racine, Wisconsin; data from Kenneth Polk's cohort studies in Marion County, Oregon; and the London data from the Cambridge Study in Delinquent Development (Blumstein, Farrington, and Moitra 1985, p. 208). Although each of these studies revealed very different prevalence rates, the general pattern of increasing recidivism rates over time was confirmed in each data set. Using the London data, Blumstein, Farrington, and Moitra found seven factors measured at age eight to ten years of age (early conviction, low family income, troublesomeness, poor school attainment, psychomotor clumsiness, low nonverbal IQ, and having a convicted sibling) that discriminated reasonably well between chronic offenders (six or more convictions) and nonchronic offenders (fewer than six convictions) (1985, p. 216).

Many of these enduring individual differences in offender heterogeneity have been explicitly used as controls in analyses attempting to assess the adult predictors of desistance from crime. In our analyses of the Glueck data, for example, the results seem clear that, conditional on a wide variety of individual differences, marriage and labor market experiences predict rates of desistance. We have thus concluded that the process of selection does not account for the association of social bonds and desistance (see especially Sampson and Laub 1993; Laub and Sampson 1993; Laub, Nagin, and Sampson 1998). What happens in the adult life course matters—a conclusion we believe modifies, but does not deny, the importance of childhood factors.

Perhaps the most convincing attempt to counteract selection bias comes from a recent analysis of data from a national work experiment that drew participants from poor ghetto areas in nine U.S. cities. Uggen (2000) found that, overall, those given jobs showed no reduction in crime relative to those in a control group. However, age significantly interacted with employment to affect the timing of illegal earnings and arrest. Those age twenty-seven or older were more likely to desist when provided marginal employment. Among those younger, the experimental job treatment had no effect on desistance. This is an important finding because the experimental nature of the data addresses the selectivity that has plagued much research in this area. By specifying event history models accounting for assignment to, eligibility for, and participation in the National Supported Work Demonstration Project, Uggen provides more refined estimates of the effects of work as a turning point in the lives of criminal offenders.[9] Moreover, the effect of work on facilitating desistance appears to be age graded; that is, marginal work (defined as minimum wage jobs) leads to desistance among those offenders over the age of twenty-six.

Subgroup Differences. Few studies of desistance have examined differential effects by race. Elliott (1994) examined the National Youth Survey data through wave 8, when the subjects were between ages twenty-four and thirty. Elliott found race differences in desistance over time, with whites desisting earlier than blacks. Elliott speculated that contextual differences—where one was living or working—might explain these differences.

One of the other unexplored issues in desistance research is gender. Most delinquents are male and desistance appears to result from the formation of social bonds with persons of the opposite sex who are far less likely to be delinquent and deviant. What is the process of desistance for females? We know that the age-crime distribution is virtually identical for males and females, although females commit crime at a much lower rate than males (Gove 1985). Nevertheless, with increasing age, there are sharp drop-offs for both males and females.

Uggen and Kruttschnitt (1998) are among the few researchers to study gender differences in desistance. These authors have argued that not only have the vast majority of studies of desistance involved male samples, but also the legal response to crime has been ignored as well. Uggen and Kruttschnitt developed a theoretical perspective on desistance drawing on rational choice theories, social control theories,

[9] Uggen (1999) also found that job quality was related to economic and noneconomic criminal behavior, taking into account sample selection, prior criminality, and other personal characteristics.

and opportunity theories, and they used data from the National Supported Work Demonstration Project to assess patterns of desistance by gender. They found that while women were more likely to desist than men (using both self-report and arrest data), the factors of desistance were the same among men and women. At the same time, they found gender differences in official desistance compared with self-report data (Uggen and Kruttschnitt 1998, p. 361). Unfortunately, there were too few female offenders to disaggregate by crime type. Moreover, this study provides little insight into the underlying mechanisms of desistance by gender.

C. Qualitative Studies of Offenders and Ex-offenders

Qualitative studies of offenders and ex-offenders provide another window from which to view the desistance process. Much of this research involves asking detailed, probing questions to subjects, mainly men, who have desisted from crime. This research strategy has been hampered by the use of small, unrepresentative samples, a heavy reliance on retrospective accounts, and an inability to distinguish among competing hypotheses regarding the desistance process. Nevertheless, this line of inquiry has produced important insights into the underlying processes of desistance from crime that are unobtainable from the typical survey.

A common theme in studying offender accounts is that desistance refers to "successful" disengagement from criminal behavior (Meisenhelder 1977). The idea of desistance or "exiting" in this context refers to the subjective experiences of the offender. For example, on the basis of interviews with twenty felons convicted of property offenses, Meisenhelder (1977, p. 325) found that "successful exiting projects include the development of meaningful expressive attachments and behavioral investments that bind the individuals to conformity and that provide them with significant reasons not to deviate." Along similar lines, Irwin (1970) identified three important components of desistance from a criminal career. The first is finding a good job (Irwin 1970, pp. 134–35). The second is an "adequate and satisfying relationship with a woman, usually in a family context" (Irwin 1970, p. 203). The third is involvement in extravocational, extradomestic activities such as sports or hobbies (Irwin 1970, p. 203).

Societal reactions to crime also appear to interact with age (Shover 1985, 1996; Gartner and Piliavin 1988, p. 302; Shover and Thompson 1992). For example, Shover (1985) reported that aging interacts with the stigma of a criminal record; for those offenders in his sample who desisted in later life, there was an erosion of the original stigma, while for others the process of aging compounded the effect of the original stigma. In this study of fifty aging criminals, Shover (1985) examined two types of experiential change that accompany aging—orientational and interpersonal change. According to Shover, orientational changes included a new perspective on the self, a growing awareness of time changing aspirations and goals, and a growing sense of tiredness. Interpersonal contingencies included the establishment of ties to another person (e.g., a wife) or ties to a line of activity such as a good job (1985, pp. 92–96). Successful participation in a personal relationship, a job, or some other conventional line of activity appeared to reinforce a noncriminal identity.

Recently, Shover (1996) has written one of the most extensive accounts of desistance from crime drawing on qualitative interviews with persistent thieves. As in his earlier work, Shover contended that changes in offending were linked to age and aging, especially the changing calculus of decision making. This process was similar to age-related changes in the lives of nonoffenders. Variation in criminal careers is associated with objective and subjective career contingencies. According to Shover, two classes of contingencies significantly influenced criminal careers: the development of conventional social bonds, activities, and rewards; and strengthened resolve and determination to abandon crime (1996, p. 124). The first could result from a satisfying relationship with a woman, a religious experience, and a satisfying job. Shover argued that "successful creation of bonds with conventional others and lines of legitimate activity indisputably is the most important contingency that causes men to alter or terminate their criminal careers" (1996, p. 129). Aging also influenced subjective contingencies or what Shover called "orientational, resolve-enhancing contingencies" (1996, p. 130). Men turned away from crime because they were less risky and more rational, gained a new perspective on self, had a growing awareness of time as a diminishing resource, and experienced a change in their aspirations and goals (Shover 1996, p. 131). In addition, Shover's main idea was that the meaning of crime and the calculus of crime changed over the life course. However, Shover painfully noted that many men who desist were successes in "only the narrowest, most bureaucratic meaning of non-recidivism. Most ex-convicts live menial or derelict lives and many die early of alcoholism or drug use, or by suicide" (1996, p. 146).

Like Shover, Maruna (2001) provides another important focus on subjective orientations in the desistance process in an effort to understand how desistance works. Maruna sought to bring the person back into the picture to supplement the positivist line of research on desistance. Maruna contended that maturation occurred independent of age and led to subjective changes that were essential to sustain desistance from crime. Simply put, people who are going straight—indicating desistance is a process, not an event—undergo a change in personality and self-concept. Thus, phrases like "new person" or a "new outlook on life" apply to those who desist from crime. Using data from life-history narratives for fifty-five men and ten women drawn from a "targeted" and "snowball" sampling frame, Maruna found that reformed offenders were more other-centered and found fulfillment in generative behaviors, felt a greater control over their destiny and took responsibility for shaping their future, and found a "silver lining" in the negative situation resulting from crime and found meaning and purpose in life.[10] As Maruna (2001) has pointed out, this pattern fits the essential elements of the "prototypical reform story," and this reform tale may be an important part of the desistance process (see also Maruna 1997).

It is noteworthy that Maruna questions the value of the turning point idea to understanding desistance, arguing that it has "probably been overstated" because "nothing inherent in a situation makes it a turning point" (2001, p. 25). For Maruna, a more promising strategy is to focus on individuals as agents of their own change. This view underscores that desistance is a process, not an event, that is initiated by a "disorienting episode" (Lofland 1969) or a "triggering event" (Laub, Nagin, and Sampson 1998) that may or may not lead to a change or turning point in a behavioral trajectory.

Graham and Bowling's (1995) study of desistance had two parts. The first part was an analysis of self-report data drawn from a larger study of offending in England and Wales. The overall sample for this study was over 2,500 individuals ages fourteen to twenty-five. The full sample was used to assess the correlates of persistence and desistance from crime. The second part entailed in-depth life-history interviews with twenty-one desisters (ten males and eleven females, ages sixteen to twenty-seven) to learn more about the influences that led them to de-

[10] Employment was not a factor in the desistance process in Maruna's (2001) study. Because of the dire employment situation in Liverpool (the site of his study), only five of the thirty desisting offenders were employed full-time (Maruna 2001).

sist from crime. These subjects were a subsample drawn from the larger project. Desisters were defined as those having committed three offenses in the past (or one serious offense) and self-reporting no new offenses in the twelve-month period prior to the interview. A total of 166 desisters were identified.

For young women, desistance seemed to occur abruptly as they moved into adulthood (e.g., leaving school, leaving home, forming partnerships, and having children). For male offenders, desistance was a more gradual, intermittent process. The social development variables that appeared important for explaining female desisters were far less useful for explaining male desisters. Simply put, males were less likely to make the transition from adolescence to adulthood, and when they did, it had a different effect (or no effect) compared with the effect it had on females. A major component of desistance for men was disengagement from their deviant peers. Graham and Bowling (1995, p. 84) argued that this is a "precondition" for desistance from crime. In addition, male desisters were more likely to live at home and perceive that their schoolwork was above average. From the life-history interviews, along with disassociation with delinquent peers, Graham and Bowling found that changes in identity and maturity were also important. For example, a sense of direction, recognition of the consequences of crime, and learning that crime does not pay were all identified as important factors in interviews with desisters. For women, having children had the greatest influence on desistance, according to interview data.

Mischkowitz (1994) studied desistance with data from the Tubingen Comparative Study of Young Offenders. This is a longitudinal study of 200 males who were incarcerated in prison along with a control group of 200 men the same age drawn from the general population. All of the men were born between 1935 and 1949 and were between the ages of twenty and thirty years at the time of the study. Desistance was defined as having one's last conviction before the age of thirty-one and not being convicted or incarcerated for the last ten years. Fifty-two case studies of desisters formed the basis of this study. The major finding was that desistance resulted from changes toward a more conventional lifestyle across a variety of domains (e.g., residential, work, family). Although there were different types of desisters (permanent conformists, permanent deviationists, disintegrationists, and reintegrationists), the reintegrationists—those subjects that changed their lifestyle—were the largest group of desisters (Mischkowitz 1994, pp. 321–

22). The other groups may not offend again but may be involved in "hidden crime"; engage in serious alcohol abuse; or generally lead unproductive, socially isolating, unhappy lives.

To probe further the processes underlying desistance, self-report data were collected on the reasons for desistance from the ex-offenders. These reports were supplemented with social worker reports as to what they saw as the reasons for desistance. It is interesting to note that the subjects thought that "free will" to break with the past was the most important reason, followed by a good marriage, and an interest in an occupational career. Social workers, by contrast, discounted free will and emphasized marriage, jobs, and changing one's milieu. It is important to note that, with respect to personal qualities, social workers mentioned "intelligence and certain skills, occupational ambitions, and sociability and adaptability" (Mischkowitz 1994, p. 325). Like many of the studies reviewed here, religious conversion was not a primary cause of desistance among these fifty-two men.

Baskin and Sommers (1998) conducted in-depth, life-history interviews with 170 women who committed a variety of violent crimes (robbery, assault, and homicide) in New York City. They examined desistance from violent crime for thirty women in their sample. It is not clear how these thirty women were selected or whether they represented the population of desisters among the 170 women. Desistance was defined as no criminal involvement for at least two years prior to the interview. Criminal activity was determined through official arrest record checks as well as interviews with program staff for women who participated in treatment programs. Baskin and Sommers uncovered a number of factors related to the decision to stop offending among their sample of female offenders (e.g., criminal justice sanctions, the pains of imprisonment, isolation from family and friends, and physical and mental "wear and tear" of crime and "living the life" on the street, among others). These same factors were uncovered in Shover's work examining male property crime offenders (see also Cusson and Pinsonneault 1986).

Following Fagan (1989) and Sommers, Baskin, and Fagan (1994), Baskin and Sommers outline a three-step process of desistance (1998, pp. 140–43). The first stage is "forming a commitment to change" (Baskin and Sommers 1998, p. 133). This stage is often triggered by a shock or crisis (see Cusson and Pinsonneault 1986). These catalysts for change may include "socially disjunctive experiences" (e.g., hitting rock bottom) or simply may reflect "delayed deterrence" (Baskin and

Sommers 1998, p. 141, fig. 6.1). The second stage is called discontinuance. This stage requires a public announcement or "certification" (Meisenhelder 1977, p. 329) that offending will stop. This stage entailed both objective changes (e.g., new social networks) and subjective changes (e.g., new social identity) (see Shover 1996). The women adopted "social avoidance strategies" in the desistance process; separation from persons and places that facilitate continued involvement in crime and drug use (see Graham and Bowling 1995). The third stage of desistance is maintenance of the decision to stop. A key component in stage 3 is building and maintaining a "network of primary relations who accept and support their nondeviant identity" (Baskin and Sommers 1998, p. 136). Thus, new stakes in conformity need to be developed, and the process of identity reformation in turn strengthens these stakes in conformity. From this perspective, desistance is an outcome of a complex, interactional reciprocal process (see also Thornberry 1987).

In one of the only qualitative studies to examine desistance among African-American and Latino American inner-city young men, Hughes (1998) conducted in-depth interviews with twenty subjects who desisted after a long period of criminal activity. Hughes found four significant factors influencing the move of offenders away from antisocial behavior. These factors included respect and concern for children, especially their own children; fear of physical harm, incarceration, or both; contemplation time away from one's immediate environment; and support and modeling from a dedicated person (e.g., a counselor or mentor). Although derived from a small, convenience sample, these findings are generally consistent with the findings from qualitative studies focusing on white men.

D. *Summary*

It is apparent that desistance stems from a variety of complex processes—developmental, psychological, and sociological. In addition, the context in which desistance occurs (or does not occur) seems important in understanding the particular processes of desistance. However, most explanations of desistance have a "post hoc" feel to them. What is not well developed is a coherent framework or theoretical account for explaining desistance. We thus take the next step of formulating the beginnings of a life-course framework to explain desistance from crime. Before we turn to a full discussion of our life-course perspective on desistance, however, it is useful to assess the similarities and differences in patterns of desistance from domestic violence, illicit drug use, and alcohol abuse.

III. Domestic Violence and Other Problem Behaviors

The question we address here is whether insights into the desistance process can be gleaned by investigating disparate forms of criminal behavior (e.g., domestic violence) as well as other problem behaviors (e.g., drug use and alcohol abuse). Although the evidence is somewhat sketchy, it does appear that domestic violence declines with age (see, e.g., Suitor, Pillemer, and Straus 1990). The evidence is even stronger that drug and alcohol use declines with age (see, e.g., Chen and Kandel 1995). Less is known about the predictors and processes of desistance from domestic violence and other problem behaviors.

A. Domestic Violence

Conventional wisdom holds that there is little cessation from domestic violence over time. The image is that marital conflict involving physical aggression escalates in frequency and severity of violence. However, studies using nonclinical- or nonshelter-based samples show that while there is some evidence for escalation, there is much more discontinuity in offending patterns, especially minor forms of violence, than expected (see, e.g., Feld and Straus 1989). For instance, using data from the National Youth Survey, Woffordt, Elliott, and Menard (1994) found that a considerable number of offenders (48 percent) "suspended" violence in their marital relationships three years later. In an interesting study using data from a community-based sample, Quigley and Leonard (1996) examined desistance in husband aggression in the first three years of marriage. Desistance was defined as the complete cessation of husband aggression at year 2 and year 3 as reported by both members of the couple. The rate of desistance in this sample was 24 percent. That is, forty-five of the 188 couples that reported husband aggression in the first year of marriage reported no further aggression in year 2 or 3. Desistance was also associated with better marital and emotional functioning. Those engaging in serious aggression at year 1 were much less likely to desist in years 2 and 3 (14 percent). Thus, there is evidence for desistance in marital violence. The key question is, What are the factors that lead to desistance, and are the processes of desistance the same or different compared with other offenders?[11]

[11] One of the major concerns in studies of desistance from domestic violence is sample attrition. It is not known to what extent separation and divorce influences rates of partic-

In a significant essay appearing in an earlier volume of the *Crime and Justice* series, Fagan (1989) analyzed desistance from family violence. Like many of the works reviewed above, Fagan argued that the causes of onset might not be relevant for understanding desistance. "What is important to the initiation of violence [and other problem behaviors] may be irrelevant to its cessation," wrote Fagan (1989, p. 414). This implies that although problem behaviors (e.g., family violence, substance abuse, and crime) may have different origins, the processes of cessation may be quite similar. For Fagan, desistance is the outcome of processes that begin with aversive experiences leading to a decision to stop offending. In the case of spouse abuse, desistance follows legal sanctions. This suggests an interesting linkage between specific deterrence and desistance that has been generally overlooked in the literature on desistance from crime (but see Paternoster 1989). Fagan distinguishes cessation, remission, and desistance in the context of family violence, but the terms are germane to criminology as a whole. "Desistance refers to a process of reduction in the frequency and severity of family violence, leading to its eventual end when 'true desistance' or 'quitting' occurs" (Fagan 1989, p. 380). For Fagan, desistance implies a "conscious behavioral intent to reduce the incidence of violence" (1989, p. 380), although is it is not clear why "conscious behavioral intent" is necessary in this or any definition of desistance, nor is there any mention whether this concept can even be measured. Cessation refers to "abstention from family violence, either permanent or temporary, often because of legal or other interventions external to the individual [and] remission is a natural process. It describes a temporary state where there is an episodic lull in violent behavior" (Fagan 1989, p. 380).[12] Although these lulls in offending may become permanent, the notion of remission implies that backsliding is likely (Fagan 1989, p. 380). In his review, Fagan also noted three varieties of cessation: deterrence in response to legal sanctions; dissuasion in response to victim-initiated strategies; and displacement—taking it elsewhere.

ipation in these studies. Research in this area is also hampered by small sample sizes, short follow-up periods, and varying definitions of both domestic violence and desistance.

[12] This is comparable to the intermittency parameter in Nagin and Land (1993). Barnett, Blumstein, and Farrington (1989) developed a model of criminal career patterns among multiple offenders and tested their model prospectively using data up to age thirty for offenders in the Cambridge study of delinquent development. Although their model was generally satisfactory, they did find a small group of offenders who stopped offending and then restarted after a long period of time.

Fagan's model of desistance from family violence has three distinct stages. Stage 1 entails "building resolve or discovering the motivation to stop." Stage 2 involves "making and publicly disclosing the decision to stop." There must be some catalyst to initiate change. This could be the result of increasing the negative consequences and attendant stigma stemming from acts of family violence (e.g., legal sanctions) or by removing the positive rewards stemming from acts of family violence. Fagan makes the crucial point that the processes that initiate the decision to stop may not be sufficient for desistance to occur (1989, p. 409). Stage 3 entails "maintenance of the new behaviors and integration into new social networks" (Fagan 1989, p. 404). Whether desistance can be maintained without changing social networks and identities is a question for future research. Fagan contends that the "substitution" of new networks and supports for old ones and the "stabilization" of those networks and supports is crucial to the long-term success of desistance.

B. *Illicit Drug Use and Alcohol Abuse*

In contrast to research on crime and family violence, there has been some attention devoted to describing the natural history of illicit drug use and alcohol abuse. There is evidence, for example, that most forms of drug use and alcohol abuse decline with age. The exception appears to be cigarette use (see Chen and Kandel 1995). Information is also available regarding the predictors of desistance from illicit drug use and alcohol abuse.

Esbensen and Elliott (1994) used data from eight waves of the National Youth Survey and found that salient life events like marriage and becoming a parent were major factors in discontinuing drug use (i.e., alcohol and marijuana use). Social learning variables that were important in explaining initiation were not significantly related to termination of drug use. However, the relationship between salient life events (e.g., getting married, having a child) may be related to changes in social networks (the number of drug-using friends) (see Warr 1998).

Using a representative sample of over 700 marijuana users, Chen and Kandel (1998) found that the two most important predictors of cessation of marijuana use were frequency of use and age. Infrequent users and those in their late twenties were more likely to stop using. Supporting the notion that life events are important in the cessation of marijuana use, Chen and Kandel (1998) found that first-time pregnancy and parenthood had a significant effect on cessation of marijuana use for women but not for men. Getting married did have an inhibitory effect for men, but it appeared to be anticipatory. For example, men were more likely to stop using marijuana one month prior to their marriage, and women were more likely to stop using marijuana nine months before the birth of their first child. Along similar lines, Yamaguchi and Kandel (1985), emphasizing the idea of social role incompatibility, found that in early adulthood marijuana users stopped using after marriage and child bearing. Instability in marital status and employment was related to continued use (see also Kandel and Yamaguchi 1987). Whether these effects are the consequences or determinants of desistance of use of marijuana is debatable, although the evidence appears to be in favor of selection effects (Yamaguchi and Kandel 1985; Kandel and Yamaguchi 1987; Chen and Kandel 1998).

In a study of cessation from cocaine use, White and Bates (1995) found that those who stopped using were more likely to be older, married, and have children. They also found that friends' use of cocaine and negative consequences stemming from using cocaine were most strongly related to cessation. Whether these findings are due to selection effects is not known.

Supporting the idea of negative consequences in cocaine cessation, Waldorf, Reinarman, and Murphy (1991) found that heavy users of cocaine cited health problems (both physical and psychological), financial problems, work problems, and relationship problems as the most important reasons for quitting use. These findings were based on interview data drawn from 106 quitters derived from a snowball sample of present and past cocaine users. In addition to the negative effects of the cocaine experience, a stake in conventional identity and a commitment to conventional life formed the "social-psychological and social-organizational context within which control and cessation were possible" (Waldorf, Reinarman, and Murphy 1991, p. 222).

In a study of untreated and treated heroin addicts, Biernacki (1986) found that experience of "natural recovery" varied depending on the extent of immersion and identification in the subculture of addiction. Breaking away from the drug and the addict world—both symbolically and literally—is a crucial part of the desistance process. At the same time, addicts need to forge new relationships, new interests, and new investments in order to maintain cessation from drugs. The result of this process is an identity transformation. The course of identity transformation could involve the forging of a new identity, could entail reverting to an old identity that was not spoiled during addiction, or could extend an old identity to replace the primacy of the addict identity (Biernacki 1986, pp. 141–60). Biernacki concluded, "A successful transformation of identity requires the availability of identity materials with which the nonaddict identity can be fashioned. Identity materials are those aspects of social settings and relationships (e.g., social roles, vocabularies) that can provide the substance to construct a nonaddict identity and a positive sense of self" (1986, p. 179).[13]

In a meta-analysis of twenty-seven studies of variations in drinking over the life course, Fillmore and her colleagues (1991) found declines in drinking with age. Temple and his colleagues (1991) found that getting married was negatively associated with consumption for younger and older persons across sex. In contrast, becoming employed was positively related to consumption of alcohol, although the relationship was not significant across all age or sex groups. This study involved a meta-analysis of twelve longitudinal studies. Unfortunately, only two data points were used, and there was no information available on the timing of changes in role status.

In a similar vein, using data from the NLSY, Miller-Tutzauer, Leonard, and Windle (1991) found that young adults who became married exhibited larger decreases of alcohol use compared with those who remained unmarried. Since the declines began in the year prior to marriage, the authors attributed the change to the role transition phase rather than a constraint of marriage itself. As indicated above, whether these declines are due to self-selection (e.g., declines in drinking facilitate marriage) or the effects of courtship and marriage (e.g., alteration in the opportunities to drink) is not clear from this study.

Furthermore, Labouvie (1996), using data from a longitudinal study of two birth cohorts totaling 933 young adults, found evidence for "maturing out" of substance use. Reductions in use were more pronounced for those individuals who became married, became parents, or both, controlling for past use and friends' concurrent use. The benefits of marriage and parenthood appeared the strongest at ages

[13] Adler (1992) has conducted a study of the reintegration of former drug dealers into conventional society. She found that "push" factors were more important than "pull" factors in the desistance process. One of the difficulties former dealers face in the reintegration process is finding legitimate work. Moreover, former dealers find adjustment in the "straight world" particularly difficult because they miss the "level of disposable income, excitement, flexibility, and the pleasure, spontaneity, and freedom they experienced during their halcyon days of drug trafficking" (Adler 1992, p. 124). Adler concludes that her subjects are "postdealers, but not completely reformed deviants" (1992, p. 125; see Adler and Adler 1983).

twenty-eight to thirty-one, which suggests that the timing of events is important. In addition, declines in use were also associated with perceived decreases in friends' use of alcohol, cigarettes, and illicit drugs, which were more likely to occur after age twenty-five. These findings held for both men and women in the study. Labouvie (1996) concluded that "maturing out" is due to selection and self-correction.

Vaillant (1995) has studied the pathways to abstinence in the context of the natural history of alcoholism. Vaillant (1995) found that recovery was anything but spontaneous. The important factors in fostering desistance from alcohol abuse were new relationships, enhanced hope resulting from increased involvement in religion or Alcoholics Anonymous, supervision and monitoring by formal authorities or informal others such as employers or spouses, and finding a substitute dependency. It is surprising that stable abstinence was not predicted by good premorbid adjustment. In Vaillant's study, sociopaths were as likely to desist from alcohol abuse as those with good mental health. As described in detail in Valliant's 1995 study, data were drawn from two samples—268 former Harvard University undergraduates from the Grant study and 456 nondelinquent controls from the Gluecks' *Unraveling Juvenile Delinquency* study.

Little is known about desistance from alcohol abuse without treatment. Using a convenience sample of 182 males, Sobell et al. (1993) found that the majority of "natural recoveries" from drinking problems involved a "cognitive evaluation" of the pros and cons of drinking. Seemingly trivial or mundane events often precipitated changes in drinking behavior. These events seemed to "trigger" a need for change that led to a "major reorientation of the person's frame of reference and perspective" (Sobell et al. 1993, p. 223). Spousal support was reported to be the most helpful factor in maintaining cessation from alcohol abuse.

C. *Summary*

As Fagan (1989) has noted, common processes of desistance have emerged across a variety of problem behavior areas, including crime. First, the decision to stop appears to be preceded by a variety of negative consequences, both formal and informal. Second, multiple processes appear to be involved in sustaining and reinforcing the decision to change. Similarly, examining research on the addictive disorders of alcoholism, smoking, and obesity, Brownell et al. (1986) discovered commonalities in the process of relapse that indicate three basic stages of behavior change—motivation and commitment, initial behavior change, and maintenance of change. These authors make the important distinction between lapses (slips) and relapse and argue that much could be learned about the processes of change if we knew which slips lead to relapses and which do not. Information on the timing of lapses in the change process would also be quite helpful. There is some evidence to suggest that the determinants of lapses are different from the determinants of relapses. For instance, lapses are more commonly associated with situational factors, whereas relapses are related to individual factors such as negative emotional states or stress events.

Stall and Biernacki (1986) have examined spontaneous remission with respect to four substances—opiates, alcohol, food/obesity, and tobacco. They identified common processes of spontaneous remission across these four domains. Spontaneous remission is defined as cessation of problematic substance use for one year without formal treatment. What is compelling about this topic is that these substances are generally considered "addictive." Although the data are limited, key factors in the cessation process included health problems, social sanctions, significant others, financial problems, significant accidents, management of cravings, positive reinforcements for quitting, internal psychic change or motivation, and change in lifestyle. Like others, Stall and Biernacki (1986) propose a three-stage model of spontaneous remission behavior. The first stage concerns building resolve or motivation to quit. The second stage involves a public pronouncement to quit problematic substance use. The third stage is the maintenance of the resolution to quit the problem behavior. This includes the acceptance of a new identity as a nonuser, support from significant others, and successful integration into new, nonusing social networks.

Finally, Prochaska, DiClemente, and Norcross have concluded that the processes of change across a variety of life domains (addictive and other problem behaviors) reveal "robust commonalities in how people modify their behavior. From our perspective, the underlying structure of change is neither technique-oriented nor problem specific" (1992, p. 1110). Prochaska and Velicer (1997) propose what they call a "transtheoretical model" that posits that behavior change occurs through six specific stages of change—precontemplation, contemplation, preparation, action, maintenance, and termination. These stages of change were found across twelve different health behaviors, and they help us to understand "when particular shifts in attitudes, intentions, and behaviors occur" (Prochaska, DiClemente, and Norcross 1992, p. 1107).

In addition to the stages of changes, Prochaska and Velicer (1997) identified a common set of processes of change that also occur across a wide range of health behaviors. These processes of change can be generally characterized as two factors—experiential processes (e.g., self-reevaluation) and behavioral processes (e.g., helping relationships). The processes of change allow us to understand how these shifts occur. The prospects for change are most likely when there is a successful integration of the stages and processes of change. Like Brownell et al. (1986), Prochaska, DiClemente, and Norcross (1992) argue that because relapse is expected, a spiral pattern (rather than linear progression) best captures how people move through the stages of change.

In short, there appear to be commonalities when desisting from several behaviors, including those thought to be addictive. What is striking is that the processes of desistance from problem behaviors such as alcohol dependency are quite similar to the processes of desistance from predatory crime. The significant elements to date are the decision or motivation to change, cognitive restructuring, coping skills, continued monitoring, social support, and general lifestyle change, especially new social networks.

IV. Frameworks for Understanding the Desistance Process

We believe that there are several theoretical accounts of desistance that can provide a framework for classifying and interpreting the individual studies we reviewed above. While there is overlap across these frameworks, we highlight what we see as the differing elements of emphasis within each particular framework. All of these accounts point to promising leads in the desistance process. At the same time, none of the accounts are fully satisfying, and in the end they raise more questions than they answer. We review each of these frameworks and then conclude that the life-course framework is the most promising approach for advancing the state of knowledge regarding desistance from crime and other problem behavior.

A. Maturation and Aging Accounts of Desistance

Framework I. The Gluecks developed the idea of maturation as the key factor in explaining desistance from crime. Their theory was that "the physical and mental changes which enter into the natural process of *maturation* offer a chief explanation of improvement of conduct with the passing of years" (Glueck and Glueck 1974, p. 149). Desistance occurred with the passage of time, specifically, there was a "decline in recidivism during the late twenties and early thirties" (Glueck and Glueck 1974, p. 175).[14] Thus, for the Gluecks desistance was normative and expected, unless an offender had serious biological and environmental deficits (Glueck and Glueck 1943). At the same time, the Gluecks argued that persistent recidivism could be explained by a lack of maturity; offenders who eventually desisted experienced delayed or belated maturation. Although perhaps tautological in nature, the Gluecks argued that the men under study "finally achieved enough integration and stability to make their intelligence and emotional-volitional equipment effective in convincing them that crime does not lead to satisfaction and in enhancing their capacity for self-control" (Glueck and Glueck 1974, p. 170).

The Gluecks believed that maturation was a complex concept and process. They wrote that maturation "embraces the development of a stage of physical, intellectual, and affective capacity and stability, and a sufficient degree of integration of all major constituents of temperament, personality and intelligence to be adequate to the demands and restrictions of life in organized society" (Glueck and Glueck 1974, p. 170). The Gluecks were quite clear that desistance "cannot be attributed to external environmental transformations" (1974, p. 173). The Gluecks called for more research into the "striking maturation" phenomenon from biological, psychological, and sociological perspectives with the goal to "dissect maturation into its components" (1940, p. 270). It is interesting that for the Gluecks age and maturation were not one and the same. It was the case that as age increased, recidivism declined. But age alone was not enough to explain maturation. "It was not the achievement of any particular age, but rather the achievement of adequate maturation regardless of the chronological age at which it occurred that was the significant influence in the behavior change of our criminals" (Glueck and Glueck 1945, p. 81). Nonetheless, the basic idea of this approach is that desistance is the result of offenders growing out of crime and settling down.

Framework II. A variation of the Gluecks' approach is found in Gottfredson and Hirschi's *A General Theory of Crime* (1990). Like the Gluecks, Gottfredson and Hirschi argue that crime declines with age

[14] One idea offered by the Gluecks that has not been supported is that regardless of the age of onset, crime and delinquency run a "fairly steady and predictable course" (Glueck and Glueck 1974, p. 150). Most research shows early onset is linked to a longer criminal career.

for all offenders (see also Hirschi and Gottfredson 1983). Gottfredson and Hirschi contend that the age distribution of crime—onset, frequency, and desistance—is invariant across time, space, and historical context and that this relationship cannot be explained by any variables available in criminology. Gottfredson and Hirschi state, "This explanation suggests that maturational reform is just that, change in behavior that comes with maturation; it suggests that spontaneous desistance is just that, change in behavior that cannot be explained and change that occurs regardless of what else happens" (1990, p. 136).

A fundamental aspect of the Gottfredson and Hirschi account of desistance is the distinction between crime and criminality (1990). According to Gottfredson and Hirschi, crimes are short-term, circumscribed events that presuppose a set of conditions. In contrast, criminality refers to relatively stable differences across individuals in the propensity to commit crime. Gottfredson and Hirschi go on to argue that while crime everywhere declines with age, criminality—differences in propensities, like self-control—remains relatively stable over the life course. They write, "Desistance theory asserts that crime declines with age because of factors associated with age that reduce or change the criminality of the actor. The age theory asserts that crime, independent of criminality, declines with age" (Gottfredson and Hirschi 1990, p. 137). For Gottfredson and Hirschi, criminality is impervious to institutional involvement and impact.

Unlike the Gluecks, Gottfredson and Hirschi do not invoke the process of maturation but rather see a direct effect of age on crime. Decreases in offending over time are "due to the inexorable aging of the organism" (Gottfredson and Hirschi 1990, p. 141). From this theoretical perspective, it follows that criminal behavior is largely unaffected by life-course events—marriage, employment, education, and so forth—or any situational or institutional influences. The basic idea is that desistance "just happens" and that the age effect cannot be explained with the available terms and concepts.[15]

B. Developmental Accounts of Desistance

Framework I. The first developmental account of desistance we present focuses on change in objective and subjective contingencies that accompany aging (Neugarten 1996). For example, identity changes

[15] In a variation of the Gottfredson and Hirschi (1990) position, Wilson and Herrnstein contend that aging leads to a lowering of propensity for crime (1985, p. 145). Both support the notion that declines in crime over the life span are due to aging.

may account for reductions and cessation in crime (see Maruna 2001; see also Gartner and Piliavin 1988; Shover 1996). To illustrate, Mulvey and LaRosa (1986) focus on the period from age seventeen to twenty, the period they call the time of natural recovery. They argue that desistance is the result of shifts in behavioral patterns that characterize adolescence, especially late adolescence (see Mulvey and Aber [1988] for details on this developmental perspective).[16] This process is similar to the one uncovered by Shover in his study of behavioral shifts in response to aging among men.

This account of desistance suggests two themes. First, desistance is normative and expected across the life span. Some "rough-and-tumble" toddlers will desist from antisocial behavior as they enter school, some adolescent delinquents will desist while in high school, and some older delinquents will desist as they make the transition to young adulthood, and so on. Second, cognitive change is a precursor to behavioral change. What Maruna (2001) calls "identity deconstruction" is necessary to begin the long-term process of desistance.[17]

Framework II. A second developmental account of desistance is offered by Gove (1985). Gove argues that explanations of the cessation of various forms of crime and deviance must incorporate biological, psychological, and sociological variables. Thus, Gove seeks to merge elements of both ontogenetic and sociogenic models. Like Hirschi and Gottfredson (1983), Gove maintains that sociological theories of crime are unable to explain patterns of desistance revealed in the data. Gove reviewed six theories of deviance—labeling theory, conflict theory, differential association theory, control theory, anomie theory, and functional theory—and concluded that "all of these theoretical perspectives either explicitly or implicitly suggest that deviant behavior is an amplifying process leading to further and more serious deviance" (1985,

[16] In a series of interviews with delinquent youth, Mulvey and Aber (1988) found that fear of adult sanctions was not an important factor in explaining desistance (but see Glassner et al. [1983] for the opposite finding). However, Mulvey and Aber (1988) did find that youths' social competence in taking advantage of opportunities to "straighten out" was an important, but overlooked, element in the desistance process.

[17] This raises a thorny methodological point. As Gartner and Piliavin have noted, "when an event such as taking a job, marrying, or having a child occurs prior to desistance from crime, it may be viewed as a sign of orientational change. The orientational change, rather than the event itself, is seen as the true cause of desistance. It may be, however, that the event limits the opportunities, time, and energy available for crime even while subjective motivations remain constant, and that objective constraints are directly responsible for changes in behavior" (1988, p. 302). There is currently no way to disentangle the role of subjective vs. objective change as the cause of desistance. It is probably the case that both are present in the change process.

p. 118). However, changes in socially structured roles, psychological well-being, psychological maturation, and biological factors such as physical strength, physical energy, psychological drive, and the need for stimulation provide reasonable accounts of desistance from crime with age. Gove concludes that "biological and psychological factors appear to play a critical role in the termination of deviant behavior" (1985, p. 136). The peak and decline in physical strength, energy, psychological drive, and the need for stimulation maps fairly well the peak and decline in deviant behavior.

Framework III. A third developmental account of crime and desistance from crime is offered by Moffitt (1994). Moffitt spells out two distinct categories of individuals, each possessing a unique natural history of antisocial behavior over the life course. From a desistance standpoint, what is important is that these two antisocial trajectories have unique etiologies that in part account for the differences in desistance.

Life-course-persistent offenders start early in childhood and persist in offending well into adulthood. For this small group of offenders, neuropsychological deficits in conjunction with disrupted attachment relationships and academic failure drive long-term antisocial behaviors. Thus, life-course-persistent offenders do not desist from crime. As Moffitt states, it is not the traits or the environment per se that account for continuity. Rather, her theory of continuous antisocial behavior (and by definition, no desistance) "emphasizes the constant *process* of reciprocal interaction between personal traits and environmental reactions to them" (Moffitt 1994, p. 28). Antisocial dispositions infiltrate into all domains of adolescence and adulthood, and this "diminishes the likelihood of change" (Moffitt 1994, p. 28).

The adolescence-limited offenders are involved in antisocial behavior only during adolescence. This large group of offenders has no history of antisocial behavior in childhood. The delinquency of the adolescence-limited group is situational, and, as a result, virtually all of these offenders desist from criminal behavior over time. Adolescence-limited offenders seek to enjoy the spoils of adulthood (what Moffitt calls the maturity gap), and they mimic the antisocial styles of life-course persisters, and, in turn, they are socially reinforced by the "negative consequences" of delinquent behavior (Moffitt 1994, pp. 30–33). Adolescence-limited offenders desist from crime in response to changing contingencies and reinforcements. For the adolescence-limited group, desistance, like delinquency, is normative. Because adolescence-limited offenders have no history of childhood antisocial behavior resulting in large part because of neuropsychological deficits, the forces of cumulative continuity are much weaker for this group of offenders. Simultaneously, adolescence-limited offenders have more prosocial skills, more academic achievement, and stronger attachments than their life-course-persistent counterparts, characteristics that facilitate desistance from crime.

In sum, Moffitt argues that "the age of desistance from criminal offending will be a function of age of onset of antisocial behavior, mastery of conventional prosocial skills, and the number and severity of 'snares' encountered during the foray into delinquency. Snares are consequences of crime, such as incarceration or injury, that constrain conventional behavior" (Moffitt 1994, p. 45). "Adolescence-Limited delinquents can profit from opportunities for desistance, because they retain the option of successfully resuming a conventional lifestyle. Life-Course-Persistent delinquents may make transitions into marriage or work, but their injurious childhoods make it less likely that they can leave their past selves behind" (Moffitt 1994, p. 45). In contrast to our work (Sampson and Laub [1993], discussed below), Moffitt sees life-course events as conditional determinants of desistance.[18]

C. A Life-Course Account of Desistance

Applying the life-course framework to the study of desistance leads to a focus on continuity and change in criminal behavior over time, especially its embeddedness in historical and other contextual features of social life. The starting point for this account is the large within-individual variations in antisocial behavior over time. Antisocial behavior appears to be highly stable and consistent only for a relatively small number of males whose behavior problems are quite extreme. Even Moffitt (1994) builds on this information to argue that stability is a trait only among "life-course-persistent" delinquents. Whereas change is the norm for the majority of adolescents, stability characterizes those at the extremes of the antisocial-conduct distribution.

In support of this idea, recent criminological research suggests that

[18] Cohen and Vila (1996) have made a similar argument with respect to the different categories of chronic offenders. At one end of the continuum of high rate offenders are "sociopaths." At the other end of the continuum are "competitively disadvantaged" offenders (Cohen and Vila 1996, pp. 144–47). See also Nagin and Land (1993) and D'Unger et al. (1998) for more discussion of typologies of criminal offending over time. The implication is that not all offenders will desist and the processes of desistance may be unique to each distinct offender category.

salient life events influence behavior and modify trajectories—a key thesis of the life-course framework. Specifically, in our earlier work (Sampson and Laub 1993), we have argued that changes in crime (desistance) are due to variations in informal social control or social bonds that are independent of age. Thus, like the developmental accounts of cessation of offending, we maintain that other factors besides age influence the desistance process. The key point here is that salient life events in the life course may or may not change criminal trajectories. What is important is how these salient life events—work, marriage, and military—affect social bonds and informal social control. It may be that crime, criminality, and opportunities for crime vary in response to changes in informal social control. Regardless of the exact reasons for the change, we contend that life-course events matter in the onset, continuation, and desistance process. That is, the life-course events help explain stability and change in behavior over time (see also Rutter, Quinton, and Hill 1990; Thornberry 1987, pp. 881–82).

Despite their similarity, we wish to distinguish the life-course framework from developmental perspectives on crime and desistance. Developmental accounts flow mainly from psychology and focus on regular or lawlike individual development over the life span. Implicit in developmental approaches are the notions of stages, progressions, growth, and evolution (Lewontin 2000). Thus, the resulting emphasis is on systematic pathways of development over time, with the imagery being of the execution of a program written at an earlier point in time. In contrast, life-course approaches, while incorporating notions of individual development such as aging, emphasize variability and exogenous influences on the course of development over time that cannot be predicted by focusing solely on enduring individual traits or even past experiences. Flowing mainly from sociology, life-course accounts embrace the notion that lives are often unpredictable and dynamic and that exogenous changes are ever present. Some changes in life course result from chance or random events, while other changes stem from macrolevel "exogenous shocks" largely beyond the pale of individual choice (e.g., war, depression, natural disasters, revolutions, plant closings, industrial restructuring). Another important aspect of life-course criminology is a focus on situations—time-varying social contexts—that impede or facilitate criminal events. But the bottom-line difference from developmental (especially psychological) accounts is the theoretical commitment to the idea of social malleability across the life course and the focus on the constancy of change, including the dynamic processes that serve to reproduce stability.

D. Rational Choice Accounts of Desistance

The main idea of the rational choice framework of desistance is that the decision to give up crime is based on a conscious reappraisal of the costs and benefits of crime (see Clarke and Cornish 1985; Cornish and Clarke 1986; Gartner and Piliavin 1988). In this perspective, the desisters, like the persisters, are seen as "reasoning decisionmakers" (Cornish and Clarke 1986, p. 13). One important component of this decision is the increasing fear of punishment with aging (see also Cromwell, Olson, and Avary 1991). However, aging is not necessarily tied to the decision to give up crime.

Some researchers have tried to understand the context of rational decisions to stop offending. For example, Cusson and Pinsonneault (1986) contend that the decision to give up crime is triggered by a "shock" of some sort (e.g., a shoot-out during a crime) or "delayed deterrence" (e.g., increased fear of doing more time) or both. Cusson and Pinsonneault found the decision to give up crime was "voluntary and autonomous" (1986, p. 78). These findings are highly speculative—as conceded by the authors—since the study was based primarily on interviews with seventeen ex-robbers in Canada. In a similar vein, Leibrich (1996) studied thirty-seven men and women in New Zealand who were on probation and in the process of going straight. She found that shame was the primary factor in the desistance process in that it was the most commonly identified cost of offending. Three kinds of shame were reported: public humiliation, personal disgrace, and private remorse. As Leibrich stated, "shame was the thing which most often dissuaded people from offending and the growth of self-respect was the thing which most often persuaded them to go straight" (1996, p. 297).

In an interesting study, Paternoster (1989) integrated deterrence and rational choice perspectives in an attempt to understand decisions to participate in and desist from delinquency (i.e., marijuana use, drinking liquor, petty theft, and vandalism). Drawing on data from 1,250 high school students surveyed at three times, Paternoster found that the decision to desist was not related to formal sanction threats (e.g., the perceived severity and certainty of punishment). However, in support of a rational choice perspective, decisions to desist were related to changes in moral tolerance of the delinquent act. Those offenders who made a decision to stop offending began to have stronger moral reservations about the illegal acts in question. This finding held for all four delinquent offenses. It is noteworthy that changes in moral beliefs were associated with changes in peer involvement.

E. Social Learning Accounts of Desistance

Social learning frameworks have been offered to provide explanations of desistance from crime and other forms of problem behavior. Akers (1990) has forcefully argued that social learning accounts incorporate all of the major elements of rational choice and deterrence frameworks. One of the strengths of the social learning approach is its application to all crime types as well as illicit drug use, alcohol abuse, and other problem behaviors (see Akers [1998] for an extensive review of the research literature). In the social learning framework, the basic variables that explain initiation into crime are the same variables that account for cessation from crime. Therefore, for the most part, the account of desistance is the account of initiation in reverse. For example, differential association with noncriminal friends and significant others, less exposure to or opportunities to model or imitate criminal behavior, developing definitions and attitudes favorable to conformity and abiding by the law, and differential reinforcement (social and nonsocial) discouraging continued involvement in crime are all part of the desistance story. Imitation appears less important after onset, while social and nonsocial reinforcements become more important (see Akers 1998). As for onset and continuation, the most important factor in desistance is peer associations.

In support of the social learning framework, Warr (1993) presented data that showed differential association can account for the decline in crime with age. Using data from the first five waves of the National Youth Survey for respondents ages eleven to twenty-one, Warr (1993) found that peer associations (e.g., exposure to delinquent peers, time spent with peers, and loyalty to peers) changed dramatically with age. With respect to desistance, declines in crime were linked with declines in peer associations. When peer variables were controlled, "the association between age and crime is substantially weakened and, for some offenses, disappears entirely" (Warr 1993, p. 35).

Warr (1998) also contended that reduced exposure to delinquent peers accounts for the association between marital status and delinquent behavior. For Warr, marriage is important in desistance from crime because marriage reduces, weakens, and severs ties with delinquent associates. What is not established in Warr's analysis is the mechanism explaining desistance from crime. For instance, an alternative explanation for desistance of crime resulting from marriage focuses on changes in routine activities and opportunities for crime and deviance. Marriage changes one's routine activities, especially with regard to leisure time activities. With Warr's analysis, as with our own (Sampson and Laub 1993), there is no way to distinguish between differential association and routine activity or opportunity explanations of the marriage effect. It is also possible that social control theory can account for Warr's findings. It may well be that friendships change as the result of spouses exerting social control on their mates. For example, wives may limit the husband's number of nights out with the guys. Also, it is possible for new friends to replace old friends as the result of marriage. Marriage often leads to a residential move and exposure to new friends and family. These friends and family can exert social control as well.

F. Summary

According to Elder (1998), the life-course perspective contains several principles: a focus on historical time and place that recognizes that lives are embedded and shaped by context; the recognition that the developmental effects of life events are contingent on when they occur in a person's life—that is, timing matters; the acknowledgment of intergenerational transmission of social patterns—the notion of linked lives and interdependency; and the view that human agency plays a key role in choice making and constructing one's life course. In short, the major objective of the life-course perspective is to link social history and social structure to the unfolding of human lives. A life-course perspective thus looks to explain variations in crime within individuals over time, regardless of whether one is interested in understanding persistence or desistance. Moreover, the life-course perspective is compatible with several criminological theories—social control, social learning, and rational choice. Consistent with this dynamic perspective, an integrative approach to the study of desistance was recently offered by Farrall and Bowling (1999). Arguing that the literature is polarized along the agency-structure divide, these authors seek to integrate structuration and human development theories and thus examine individual decisions, structural constraints, and life events as they lead to change in behavior.

In the next section, we draw on the life-course framework to distinguish the event of terminating offending behavior from the process of desistance from crime. Our framework focuses on the structural sources of change and their role in the process of desistance from crime. The idea of "turning points" frames our discussion. Furthermore, we emphasize the interaction of human agency, life-course events, and context in this process.

V. A Life-Course Framework for Understanding Desistance

In this section we draw on material from our forthcoming book, *Boys in Trouble and How They Age* (Laub and Sampson 2001). In this book, we present and analyze newly collected data on crime and development from birth to age seventy among a group of 500 men with troubled backgrounds. Remanded to reform schools in Massachusetts during their adolescence, these 500 men were the original subjects of a classic study by Sheldon and Eleanor Glueck (1950). Followed to age thirty-two by the Gluecks (Glueck and Glueck 1968) and also studied in our previous work (Sampson and Laub 1993), these men's early lives are known to us in unusual detail.

Our book updates these men's lives at the close of the twentieth century. We tracked, located, and conducted personal life-history interviews with fifty-two men as they approached age seventy. Cases were selected on the basis of their trajectories of adult offending (e.g., persisters, desisters, and intermittent offenders). Overall, fourteen of the men we interviewed were persistent offenders, nineteen were classified as desisters, and nineteen displayed patterns of intermittent offending. The fifty-two life-history interviews were combined with our collection of criminal histories and death records for all 500 original delinquents to age seventy. Integrating these diverse data on lives over seven decades, we present a theory of crime that unites the simultaneous unfolding of personal choice, situational context, and social control. By emphasizing within-individual patterns of variability across the full life course, we illuminate the natural history of crime and its control. We present some illustrative findings from our in-depth, life-history narratives for the group of the men who desisted from crime.

From our analysis it appears that offenders desist as a result of a combination of individual actions (choice) in conjunction with situational contexts and structural influences linked to important institutions. This fundamental theme underscores the need to examine individual motivation and the social context in which individuals are embedded. The processes of desistance operate simultaneously at different levels (individual, situational, and community) and across different contextual environments (family, work, and military). The process of desistance is more than mere aging or "maturational reform" (Matza 1964), and we believe that life-history narratives are useful for unpacking complex interactions between individuals and their environments.

The idea of "turning points" is one way of thinking about change processes. Abbott contends that "turning points are narrative concepts, referring to two points in time at once" (1997, p. 85). Turning points are often retrospective constructions, but Abbott claims that they do not have to be. Abbott identifies several types of turning points—focal, randomizing, and contingent (1997, p. 94)—but all turning points are "shifts that redirect a process" (1997, p. 101). In a similar vein, Denzin emphasizes "epiphanies," and these are defined as a "moment of problematic experience that illuminates personal character, and often signifies a turning point in a person's life" (1989, p. 141). Like Abbott, Denzin identifies several types of epiphanies—major, cumulative, illuminative, and relived (see Denzin 1989, pp. 129–31). Turning points and epiphanies are implicated in the desistance process and reveal the interactive nature of human agency and life events such as marriage, work, and serving in the military. Of course, these individual-level processes take place in a larger structural context. Group processes and structural determinants (e.g., race and ethnicity, social class, and neighborhood) also need to be considered in the desistance process (see also Sullivan 1989).

It thus appears that successful cessation from crime occurs when the proximate causes of crime are affected. A central element in the desistance process is the "knifing off" of individual offenders from their immediate environment and offering them a new script for the future (Caspi and Moffitt 1995). Institutions like the military have this knifing-off potential, as does marriage, although the knifing-off effect of marriage may not be as dramatic.

Another component in the desistance process is the "structured role stability" that emerges across various life domains (e.g., marriage, work, residences). The men who desisted from crime shared a daily routine that provided both structure and meaningful activity. The structure was fully embraced by the men, and one result was a disassociation from delinquent peers in adulthood, a major factor in explaining their desistance from crime (see Graham and Bowling 1995;

Warr 1998). Osgood et al. (1996) have shown that participation in unstructured socializing activities with peers increased the frequency of deviant behaviors among those ages eighteen to twenty-six. Marriage has the potential to radically change routine activities, especially with regard to one's peer group. As Osgood and Lee (1993) argued, marriage entails obligations that tend to reduce leisure activities outside of the family. It is reasonable to assume that married people will spend more time together than with their same-sex peers. Marriage, therefore, has the potential to cut off an ex-offender from his delinquent peer group (see Warr 1998).

The routine activities of work and family life and the resulting informal social ties have two functions. One is to provide social support (Cullen 1994) or emotional "attachment" (Hirschi 1969). The other function is monitoring and control by providing a set of activities and obligations that often are repeated each day. Many habits are mundane, but they nonetheless give structure to one's time and restrict opportunities for crime. Moreover, these activities result from shifts in role expectations that are not fully explained by age (Osgood and Lee 1993).

What is also notable in the desistance process is human agency. A vital feature that emerged from our qualitative data is that personal conceptions about the past and future are apparently transformed as men maneuver through the transition from adolescence to adulthood (Emirbayer and Mische 1998, p. 992; see also Cohler 1982; Maruna 2001). The men engage in what can be called "transformative action." Although informed by the past, agency is also oriented toward the future (see Emirbayer and Mische 1998; Maruna 2001). Thus, projective actions in the transition from adolescence to adulthood advance a new sense of self and a new identity as a desister from crime or, more aptly, as a family man, hard worker, good provider, and so forth. Thus, the men we studied were "active" participants in the desistance process.[19]

As we observed in our life-history narratives, the men who desisted from crime seem to have acquired a degree of maturity by taking on family and work responsibilities. They forged new commitments, made a fresh start, and found new direction and meaning in life. These com-

[19] Using detailed narrative data from a follow-up study of a sample of adolescent female and male offenders, Giordano, Cernkovich, and Rudolf (2000) find a reciprocal relationship between the actors' own cognition and their subsequent behavior. In this study, human agency is an important element in the desistance process for both female and male offenders. (For more details, see Giordano, Cernkovich, and Rudolph [2000].)

mitments were not necessarily made consciously or deliberately but rather were "by default"—the result of "side bets" (Becker 1960, p. 38). The men made a commitment to go straight without even realizing it. Before they knew it, they had invested so much in a marriage or a job that they did not want to risk losing their investment (Becker 1960). Involvement in these institutions—work and marriage—reorders short-term situational inducements to crime and, over time, redirects long-term commitments to conformity (Briar and Piliavin 1965).

It seems that men who desisted changed their identity as well, and this in turn affected their outlook and sense of maturity and responsibility. From our life-history narratives, for example, we sense that certain roles and certain behaviors are seen as "age inappropriate" (see also Hill 1971; Shover 1996). One former delinquent linked the role of "party boy" to being young and single. In response to the question, "What about your marriage? Has that changed you?" Richard said with a hearty laugh, "Oh yeah. I mean that's when you really had to settle down." He continued, "Especially when John [his oldest son] came." Remaining a delinquent or a party boy or a hell-raiser would signify a state of "arrested development" and be incompatible with an adult status (see Gove 1985, p. 129). This notion is consistent with Hill (1971), who discussed changes in identity over the life cycle as one moves from "a hell-raiser to a family man."

We are by no means claiming an absence of regret in the process of desistance. In his study of the transformation from being a hell-raiser to being a family man, Hill presented evidence of the ambivalence that men sense regarding their new role and identity as "family men" (1971). This is not surprising because, as Smelser pointed out, bonded relations are fused with ambivalence—dependence, even when welcomed, "entails a certain entrapment" (1998, p. 8). For example, William told us that if he were not married he would be "wandering" around. He said ruefully, "There's many times I wanted to go back to Alaska to see what it was like now. But we can't do that. We're hoping to go to Disney next March." We heard many such bittersweet remembrances of deviant lives left behind—of exciting moments given up.

Thus, both objective and subjective contingencies are important in the desistance process (Shover 1996). Cohler (1982) noted that a subjective reconstruction of the self is especially likely at times of transition. The basic idea relates to "the double constitution of agency and structure: temporal-relational contexts support particular agentic orientations, which in turn constitute different structuring relationships of actors toward their environments. It is the constitution of such orientations within particular structural contexts that gives form to effort and allows actors to assume greater or lesser degrees of transformative leverage in relation to the structuring contexts of action" (Emirbayer and Mische 1998, p. 1004).

The lessons we learned about desistance from our life-history narratives are consistent with the research literature on drug and alcohol relapse. In a study of 100 hospital-treated heroin addicts and 100 hospital-treated alcohol-dependent individuals, Vaillant (1988) found that external interventions that restructure a drug addict's or an alcoholic's life in the community were often associated with sustained abstinence. The main factors are compulsory supervision, finding a substitute dependence to compete with drug or alcohol consumption, obtaining new social supports, and membership in an inspirational group and discovery of a sustained source of hope and inspiration (see also Vaillant and Milofsky 1982). Culling the recent literature on treatment, especially from Canada, produces some hopeful signs that offenders can be rehabilitated when proximate causes of crime are targeted. Programs that address dynamic attributes of offenders and their circumstances (e.g., antisocial attitudes, involvement with delinquent peers, and employment status) that can change during and after the treatment process appear to be more successful than programs that focus on static factors or background characteristics (Andrews, Bonta, and Hoge 1990; Andrews and Bonta 1994; Gendreau, Cullen, and Bonta 1994; Bonta 1996; Gendreau 1996).

What is also striking from our life-history narratives is that there appear to be no major differences in the process of desistance for nonviolent and violent juvenile offenders. Despite contrary expectations from many criminological theories, this finding is consistent with empirical research showing that violent offenders have the same background characteristics as frequent but nonviolent offenders (Farrington 1991; Capaldi and Patterson 1996; Piquero 2000). In fact, Farrington concluded that "the causes of aggression and violence must be essentially the same as the causes of persistent and extreme antisocial, delinquent, and criminal behavior" (1991, p. 25). Our life-history narratives reveal that the processes of desistance across a wide variety of crime types are very similar.

Of course, an important caveat in our research concerns what we have called the "favored historical context" in which the Glueck men came of age. This period of history was marked by less alienation and social deviance than today, low unemployment, increasing national wealth, and expansion of the occupational structure. In contrast, the level of training and education required for most employment today has changed dramatically. In this context, William Julius Wilson (1996) has documented the decline of work, especially in disadvantaged neighborhoods in U.S. cities. As noted by Wilson and others, the consequences of joblessness are severe with respect to a variety of outcomes, including crime, family life, and community organization.

One other important aspect of the historical context for this cohort concerns the military. Military service in the World War II era provided American men from economically disadvantaged backgrounds with an unprecedented opportunity to better their lives through on-the-job training and further education, especially the G.I. Bill of Rights (see Sampson and Laub 1996). In contrast, the military as a vehicle for escaping poverty has stalled in the 1990s for persons disadvantaged economically and socially (e.g., high school dropouts, members of minority groups, young people with criminal records). There is evidence that nearly half of those who try to join today's military do not get in and that the military has virtually abandoned recruiting in disadvantaged neighborhoods in inner cities (Ricks 1997).

VI. Directions for Theory, Research, and Policy

What are the implications of our review for future theory, research, and policy? Although there is a developing body of research in this area, there is still much to learn, especially regarding the causal mechanisms in the desistance process. Combining our review with our newer work on desistance from crime, we conclude with an agenda that is broad based yet focused on targeted areas that we believe are most promising.

A. Theoretical Considerations

Several theoretical considerations are worth emphasizing at the outset. First, questions about the processes of desistance must be linked to a theory of crime. Because studies of desistance are also studies of persistent and intermittent offending, we need more theoretical consideration of the natural history of crime.

Second, our understanding of desistance has been hampered by the lack of long-term studies, especially of those involved with the criminal justice system and other systems of formal social control. What we have are "short-term snapshots" and these need to be replaced by "long-term patterns" that convey the dynamic interplay between behavior and temporal variables.

Third, dichotomies such as desister/persister should be used only as heuristic devices. There is substantial heterogeneity in offending patterns—dichotomies (like means) ignore too much variation and have the potential to reify arbitrary groupings. Failing to recognize the inherent artificiality of groups and arbitrary constructions of the "offender" threaten to undermine the program of desistance research altogether. To our mind, the most fruitful desistance theory will focus on the causes of variability in within-individual offending patterns. Following Daniel Glaser, we underscore a theoretical appreciation for the concept of a zigzag path. "Criminals go from noncrime to crime and to noncrime again. Sometimes this sequence is repeated many times, but sometimes criminals clearly go to crime only once; sometimes these shifts are for long durations or even permanent, and sometimes they are short-lived" (Glaser 1969, p. 58). We thus believe that theory should focus not on arbitrary designations between individuals but on what accounts for the variation in offending trajectories within individuals. From a developmental, life-course perspective, within-person change is ongoing and ever present.

B. *Future Research*

A major issue in the study of desistance concerns the availability of data. Much of what we know about desistance—stable noncriminal behavior—is drawn from official data. Are the declines in "official crime" that we see real? Do offenders become more skillful in eluding arrest over time? Do offenders shift to crimes that are less risky with respect to detection and arrest? Do serious offenders drop out because of high mortality or other forms of attrition (see also Gartner and Piliavin 1988)? Much more research is needed on nonofficial sources of data, ranging from self-reports to ethnography to systematic social observation.

From a methodological standpoint, it has been said that one can truly know whether a given offender has truly desisted only in retrospect. Another key issue, then, is, how do we study desistance prospectively? One way would be to study the natural history of crime and provide a better description of the processes of offending over time. Along the same lines, Brownell et al. (1986, p. 778) recommend a research focus on lapses and relapses with respect to problem behavior. Since drinkers, smokers, and binge eaters quit their problem behavior more than once, the idea of understanding relapse is compelling. For instance, what is the effect of lapse and relapse on significant others? What are the determinants and predictors of lapse and relapse? What are the consequences of lapse and relapse? Can lapse and relapse be prevented?

Another potentially useful topic would be to study desistance at all phases of life, especially early in the life course as well as later. Conversely, we need to learn more about "off time" onset of criminal activity. Both will provide insights into the desistance process.

Finally, given the role of human agency in the desistance process, we need to find a way to measure individual motivation, free will, and ultimately the decision to initiate and embrace the process of change. From our data, men who desisted were "active participants" in the desistance process, and we need to capture changes in decision making, shifts in the perceptions of the risks and rewards of crime, and fluctuations in the meanings of "doing crime" versus "going straight." A creative integration of quantitative and qualitative research methods in this area could lead to a major contribution to our understanding desistance.

Subgroup Differences and Secular Change. There are several research questions about stability and change in crime over the life course. In our view, the central issue concerns the underlying mechanisms or processes that lead to desistance from crime and other problem behavior, and whether these processes have shifted over time. In our research examining the lives of disadvantaged men who experienced the transition from adolescence to young adulthood in the 1950s and 1960s, we found that desistance from crime was related to job stability, marital attachment, and successful military experiences. However, the extent to which these mechanisms explain desistance from crime today is not known, although the evidence suggests that they do. Linking historical shifts to individual transitions is a central theme of the life course.

Another important question is whether the mechanisms of desistance differ by race, gender, and social class. Although limited, there is some evidence to suggest that there are differential rates of desistance by race (Elliott 1994). More research is needed to determine how the predictors and processes of desistance differ across various subgroups in the population. We expect that variations by race, ethnicity, and structural context in promoting successful transitions to young adulthood will have effects on the desistance process. We know that rates of marriage and employment vary by race and social class. We also know neighborhood contexts vary as well, and it is expected that these neighborhood differences will interact with individual differences to increase the probability of crime and violence (Moffitt 1997). But exactly how these interactions between person and context affect the desistance process is the key research question.

Gangs. Thornberry (1998) found that gangs facilitate delinquent behavior, especially violent behavior. Thus, one would expect that gang members would have more difficulty desisting from crime compared with non–gang members. Compared with the literature on joining gangs, the literature on leaving gangs is sparse (see Spergel 1990, pp. 222–26). For those who do leave, the story appears similar to what we learned for non–gang members leaving crime. For example, Curry and Decker (1998, p. 72) reported that in addition to experiencing or witnessing violence, life-course events like employment, marriage, and becoming a parent were the key reasons for leaving a gang. According to Spergel (1990, p. 225), there is growing evidence that gang membership does not end with adolescence. Hagedorn (1988) has also argued that changes in the macrolevel opportunity structure vis-à-vis jobs and marriage have led to continued involvement in gangs among adults and subsequently less desistance from crime. More research is needed on desistance with respect to specific crime types and criminal organizations.

Alcohol. Many studies have established a link between alcohol abuse and serious criminal behavior, including violent crime (see Reiss and Roth 1993). More research is needed to ascertain the role of alcohol abuse in perpetuating crime beyond adolescence. Recently, Nielsen (1999) examined racial/ethnic differences in drunkenness using data from the 1991 National Household Survey on Drug Abuse. She found that whites "aged out" of drunkenness, but African-Americans and Hispanics did not. This is consistent with other literature on the topic (see e.g., Fillmore et al. 1991; but cf. Neff and Dassori 1998). For the overall sample, being employed, going to school, or being married was associated with less frequent drunkenness. This finding is also consistent with other literature indicating that participation in adult social roles is associated with decreased substance abuse (see e.g., Miller-Tutzauer, Leonard, and Windle 1991; Labouvie 1996). However, perhaps even more important, Nielsen (1999) found differential effects by race/ethnicity. Marriage, for instance, inhibited drunkenness for whites but had no effect for African-Americans. The marriage effect for Hispanics was not especially strong. Further study of this issue will provide a better understanding of the linkage between alcohol use, violent behavior, and desistance from crime (see also Fagan 1990, pp. 270–76).

C. *Future Policy*

One of the major policy issues of the day concerns whether criminal justice sanctions foster recidivism or help lead to the termination of offending. This issue has had a long and protracted history in criminology, and we cannot hope to do it justice here. Still, we believe that desistance research has yielded some sturdy findings that offer sobering implications for many taken-for-granted assumptions that pervade the policy arena.

Perhaps the most salient finding concerns the possible counterproductive effects of punitive sanctions when considered in the long run of individual lives. In our research program analyzing the Gluecks' data, for example, we examined the role of criminal behavior and reactions to it by the criminal justice system over the course of adolescence and young and middle adulthood. We found that delinquent behavior has a systematic attenuating effect on the social and institutional bonds that normally link adults to society (e.g., labor force attachment, marital cohesion). More specifically, we found that social bonds to employment were directly influenced by criminal sanctions—incarceration as a juvenile and as a young adult had a negative effect on later job stability, which in turn was negatively related to continued involvement in crime over the life course (see also Fagan and Freeman 1999).

From this finding as well as other suggestive evidence (see Freeman 1991; Nagin and Waldfogel 1995) we have pursued the idea of "cumulative continuity," which posits that delinquency incrementally mortgages the future by generating negative consequences for the life chances of stigmatized and institutionalized youth (see Sampson and Laub 1997). Arrest and especially incarceration may spark failure in school, unemployment, and weak community bonds, which in turn increase adult crime. Serious delinquency in particular leads to the "knifing off" of future opportunities such that participants have fewer options for a conventional life. Our analysis of the Gluecks' data showed that the effects of long periods of incarceration were most severe when manifested in early adolescence—many of the Glueck juveniles were simply cut off from the most promising avenues for later desistance from crime. This finding is consistent with Western and

Beckett's recent study of a contemporary sample showing that the negative effects of youth incarceration on adult employment time exceeds the large negative effects for dropping out of high school and living in an area with high unemployment (1999, p. 1048).

There is, of course, a long line of criminological research focusing on the potential backfiring of official sanctions and the role of stigma in generating further crime and deviance (for a review, see Paternoster and Iovanni [1989]; Sampson and Laub [1997]). More recently, Sherman (1993) has developed the idea of defiance as a possible response to the formal sanctioning process. In the arena of substance abuse, Biernacki (1986, p. 185) has argued that the acceptance of ex-addicts into normal social worlds is essential for the recovery process. This line of inquiry in criminology is relevant to policies based on deterrence and other forms of punitive intervention; simply put, we need to take into account the potential negative side effects of sanctioning for fostering desistance, along with factors that facilitate offender reintegration.

Perhaps the silver lining can be found in another of the major conclusions from our long-term study of the Glueck delinquents: intra-individual change is widespread even among a large group of individuals labeled as serious, persistent juvenile delinquents and possessing all the risk characteristics that many believe are enduring and stable across the life course. From a policy standpoint, the message is that change is possible, and therefore it is critical that individuals are given the opportunity to reconnect to institutions like family, school, and work after a period of incarceration or any criminal justice contact for that matter (Cook 1975; Braithwaite 1989). This is not to say that rehabilitation efforts or other forms of therapeutic intervention necessarily foster desistance. In many instances, they do not. What we are urging is that policy makers consider the risks and benefits of interventions for other domains of life that in an indirect way affect later outcomes. Much as for criminals who lack self-control, incarceration policies that appear to policy makers to be a wise move in the short run may appear less so over the long haul.

REFERENCES

Abbott, Andrew. 1997. "On the Concept of Turning Point." *Comparative Social Research* 16:85–105.

Adler, Patricia A. 1992. "The 'Post' Phase of Deviant Careers: Reintegrating Drug Traffickers." *Deviant Behavior* 13:103–26.

Adler, Patricia A., and Peter Adler. 1983. "Shifts and Oscillations in Deviant Careers: The Case of Upper-Level Drug Dealers and Smugglers." *Social Problems* 31:195–207.

Agnew, Robert. 1997. "Stability and Change in Crime over the Life Course: A Strain Theory Explanation." In *Developmental Theories of Crime and Delinquency*, edited by Terence P. Thornberry. New Brunswick, N.J.: Transaction.

Akers, Ronald L. 1990. "Rational Choice, Deterrence, and Social Learning in Criminology: The Path Not Taken." *Journal of Criminal Law and Criminology* 81:653–76.

———. 1998. *Social Learning and Social Structure: A General Theory of Crime and Deviance.* Boston: Northeastern University Press.

Andrews, D. A., and James Bonta. 1994. *The Psychology of Criminal Conduct.* Cincinnati: Anderson.

Andrews, D. A., James Bonta, and Robert D. Hoge. 1990. "Classification for Effective Rehabilitation: Rediscovering Psychology." *Criminal Justice and Behavior* 17:19–52.

Barnett, Arnold, Alfred Blumstein, and David P. Farrington. 1989. "A Prospective Test of a Criminal Career Model." *Criminology* 27:373–85.

Barnett, Arnold, and Anthony J. Lofaso. 1985. "Selective Incapacitation and the Philadelphia Cohort Data." *Journal of Quantitative Criminology* 1:3–36.

Barr, Robert, and Ken Pease. 1990. "Crime Placement, Displacement, and Deflection." In *Crime and Justice: A Review of Research*, vol. 12, edited by Michael Tonry and Norval Morris. Chicago: University of Chicago Press.

Baskin, Deborah R., and Ira B. Sommers. 1998. *Casualties of Community Disorder: Women's Careers in Violent Crime.* Boulder, Colo.: Westview Press.

Becker, Howard S. 1960. "Notes on the Concept of Commitment." *American Journal of Sociology* 66:32–40.

Biernacki, Patrick. 1986. *Pathways from Heroin Addiction Recovery without Treatment.* Philadelphia: Temple University Press.

Blumstein, Alfred, and Jacqueline Cohen. 1987. "Characterizing Criminal Careers." *Science* 237:985–91.

Blumstein, Alfred, Jacqueline Cohen, Jeffrey Roth, and Christy Visher, eds. 1986. *Criminal Careers and "Career Criminals."* Washington, D.C.: National Academy Press.

Blumstein, Alfred, David P. Farrington, and Soumyo Moitra. 1985. "Delinquency Careers: Innocents, Desisters, and Persisters." In *Crime and Justice: An Annual Review of Research*, vol. 6, edited by Michael Tonry and Norval Morris. Chicago: University of Chicago Press.

Bonta, James. 1996. "Risk-Needs Assessment and Treatment." In *Choosing Correctional Options That Work*, edited by Alan Harland. Thousand Oaks, Calif.: Sage.

Braithwaite, John. 1989. *Crime, Shame, and Reintegration.* Cambridge: Cambridge University Press.

Briar, Scott, and Irving Piliavin. 1965. "Delinquency, Situational Inducements, and Commitment to Conformity." *Social Problems* 13:35–45.

Brownell, Kelly D., G. Alan Marlatt, Edward Lichtenstein, and G. Terence Wilson. 1986. "Understanding and Preventing Relapse." *American Psychologist* 41:765–82.

Bushway, Shawn, Alex Piquero, Lisa Briody, Elizabeth Cauffman, and Paul Mazerolle. 2001. "An Empirical Framework for Studying Desistance as a Process." *Criminology* (forthcoming).

Capaldi, Deborah M., and Gerald R. Patterson. 1996. "Can Violent Offenders Be Distinguished from Frequent Offenders? Prediction from Childhood to Adolescence." *Journal of Research in Crime and Delinquency* 33:206–31.

Caspi, Avshalom, and Terrie E. Moffitt. 1995. "The Continuity of Maladaptive Behavior: From Description to Understanding in the Study of Antisocial Behavior." In *Developmental Psychopathology*, vol. 2, *Risk Disorder, and Adaptation*, edited by Dante Cicchetti and Donald J. Cohen. New York: Wiley.

Chen, Kevin, and Denise B. Kandel. 1995. "The Natural History of Drug Use from Adolescence to the Mid-Thirties in a General Population Sample." *American Journal of Public Health* 85:41–47.

———. 1998. "Predictors of Cessation of Marijuana Use: An Event History Analysis." *Drug and Alcohol Dependence* 50:109–21.

Clarke, Ronald V., and Derek B. Cornish. 1985. "Modeling Offenders' Decisions: A Framework for Research and Policy." In *Crime and Justice: An Annual Review of Research*, vol. 6, edited by Michael Tonry and Norval Morris. Chicago: University of Chicago Press.

Cline, Hugh F. 1980. "Criminal Behavior over the Life Span." In *Constancy and Change in Human Development*, edited by Orville G. Brim, Jr., and Jerome Kagan. Cambridge, Mass.: Harvard University Press.

Cohen, Lawrence E., and Bryan J. Vila. 1996. "Self-Control and Social Control: An Exposition of the Gottfredson-Hirschi/Sampson-Laub Debate." *Studies on Crime and Crime Prevention* 5:125–50.

Cohler, Bertram. 1982. "Personal Narrative and Life Course." In *Life Span Development and Behavior*, vol. 4, edited by Paul B. Baltes and Orville G. Brim, Jr. New York: Academic Press.

Cook, Philip. 1975. "The Correctional Carrot: Better Jobs for Parolees." *Policy Analysis* 1:11–54.

Cornish, Derek B., and Ronald V. Clarke. 1986. *The Reasoning Criminal: Rational Choice Perspectives on Offending*. New York: Springer.

Cromwell, Paul F., James N. Olson, and D'Aunn Wester Avary. 1991. *Breaking and Entering: An Ethnographic Analysis of Burglary*. Newbury Park, Calif.: Sage.

Cullen, Francis. 1994. "Social Support as an Organizing Concept for Criminology: Presidential Address to the Academy of Criminal Justice Sciences." *Justice Quarterly* 11:527–59.

Curry, G. David, and Scott H. Decker. 1998. *Confronting Gangs: Crime and Community*. Los Angeles: Roxbury.

Cusson, Maurice, and Pierre Pinsonneault. 1986. "The Decision to Give Up Crime." In *The Reasoning Criminal: Rational Choice Perspectives on Offending*, edited by Derek B. Cornish and Ronald V. Clarke. New York: Springer.

Denzin, Norman K. 1989. *Interpretive Interactionism.* Newbury Park, Calif.: Sage.

D'Unger, Amy, Kenneth C. Land, Patricia McCall, and Daniel S. Nagin. 1998. "How Many Latent Classes of Delinquent/Criminal Careers? Results from Mixed Poisson Regression Analyses." *American Journal of Sociology* 103:1593–1630.

Elder, Glen H., Jr. 1998. "The Life Course as Developmental Theory." *Child Development* 69:1–12.

Elliott, Delbert S. 1994. "Serious Violent Offenders: Onset, Developmental Course, and Termination." *Criminology* 32:1–22.

Elliott, Delbert S., David Huizinga, and Scott Menard. 1989. *Multiple Problem Youth: Delinquency, Substance Use, and Mental Health Problems.* New York: Springer.

Emirbayer, Mustafa, and Ann Mische. 1998. "What Is Agency?" *American Journal of Sociology* 103:962–1023.

Esbensen, Finn-Age, and Delbert S. Elliott. 1994. "Continuity and Discontinuity in Illicit Drug Use: Patterns and Antecedents." *Journal of Drug Issues* 24:75–97.

Fagan, Jeffrey. 1989. "Cessation of Family Violence: Deterrence and Dissuasion. In *Family Violence*, edited by Lloyd Ohlin and Michael Tonry. Vol. 11 of *Crime and Justice: A Review of Research*, edited by Michael Tonry and Norval Morris. Chicago: University of Chicago Press.

———. 1990. "Intoxication and Aggression." In *Drugs and Crime*, edited by Michael Tonry and James Q. Wilson. Vol. 13 of *Crime and Justice: A Review of Research*, edited by Michael Tonry. Chicago: University of Chicago Press.

Fagan, Jeffrey, and Richard B. Freeman. 1999. "Crime and Work." In *Crime and Justice: A Review of Research*, vol. 25, edited by Michael Tonry. Chicago: University of Chicago Press.

Farrall, Stephen, and Benjamin Bowling. 1999. "Structuration, Human Development, and Desistance from Crime." *British Journal of Criminology* 39:253–68.

Farrington, David P. 1986. "Age and Crime." In *Crime and Justice: An Annual Review of Research*, vol. 7, edited by Michael Tonry and Norval Morris. Chicago: University of Chicago Press.

———. 1991. "Childhood Aggression and Adult Violence: Early Precursors and Later Life Outcomes." In *The Development and Treatment of Childhood Aggression*, edited by Daniel J. Pepler and Kenneth H. Rubin. Hillsdale, N.J.: Erlbaum.

———. 1992. "Explaining the Beginning, Progress, and Ending of Antisocial Behavior from Birth to Adulthood." In *Facts, Frameworks, and Forecasts*, edited by Joan McCord. New Brunswick, N.J.: Transaction.

Farrington, David P., Bernard Gallagher, Lynda Morley, Raymond J. St. Ledger, and Donald J. West. 1986. "Unemployment, School Leaving, and Crime." *British Journal of Criminology* 26:335–56.

———. 1988. "Cambridge Study in Delinquent Development: Long-Term Follow-Up." Unpublished manuscript. Institute of Criminology, Cambridge University.

Farrington, David P., and J. David Hawkins. 1991. "Predicting Participation, Early Onset, and Later Persistence in Officially Recorded Offending." *Criminal Behaviour and Mental Health* 1:1–33.

Farrington, David P., Sandra Lambert, and Donald J. West. 1998. "Criminal Careers of Two Generations of Family Members in the Cambridge Study in Delinquent Development." *Studies on Crime and Crime Prevention* 7:85–106.

Farrington, David P., and Donald J. West. 1995. "Effects of Marriage, Separation, and Children on Offending by Adult Males." In *Current Perspectives on Aging and the Life Cycle*, vol. 4, edited by Zena Blau and John Hagan. Greenwich, Conn.: JAI Press.

Feld, Scott L., and Murray A. Straus. 1989. "Escalation and Desistance of Wife Assault in Marriage." *Criminology* 27:141–61.

Fillmore, Kaye Middleton, Elizabeth Hartka, Bryan M. Johnstone, E. Victor Leino, Michelle Motoyoshi, and Mark T. Temple. 1991. "A Meta-analysis of Life Course Variation in Drinking." *British Journal of Addiction* 86:1221–68.

Fisher, Edwin B., Jr., Edward Lichenstein, Debra Haire-Joshu, Glen D. Morgan, and Heather R. Rehberg. 1993. "Methods, Successes, and Failures of Smoking Cessation Programs." *Annual Review of Medicine* 44:481–513.

Freeman, Richard. 1991. "Crime and the Employment of Disadvantaged Youth." Working Paper. Cambridge, Mass.: Harvard University, National Bureau of Economic Research.

Gartner, Rosemary, and Irving Piliavin. 1988. "The Aging Offender and the Aged Offender." In *Life-Span Development and Behavior*, vol. 9, edited by Paul B. Baltes, David L. Featherman, and Richard M. Lerner. Hillside, N.J.: Erlbaum.

Gendreau, Paul. 1996. "The Principles of Effective Intervention with Offenders." In *Choosing Correctional Options That Work*, edited by Alan Harland. Thousand Oaks, Calif.: Sage.

Gendreau, Paul, Francis T. Cullen, and James Bonta. 1994. "Intensive Rehabilitation Supervision: The Next Generation in Community Corrections?" *Federal Probation* 58:72–78.

Gibbens, T. C. N. 1984. "Borstal Boys after 25 Years." *British Journal of Criminology* 24:49–62.

Giordano, Peggy C., Stephen A. Cernkovich, and Jennifer L. Rudolph. 2000. "Gender, Crime, and Desistance: Toward a Theory of Cognitive Transformation." Unpublished manuscript. Bowling Green, Ohio: Bowling Green State University.

Glaser, Daniel. 1969. *The Effectiveness of a Prison and Parole System*. Abridged ed. Indianapolis: Bobbs-Merrill.

Glassner, Barry, Margaret Ksander, Bruce Berg, and Bruce D. Johnson. 1983. "A Note on the Deterrent Effect of Juvenile vs. Adult Jurisdiction." *Social Problems* 31:219–21.

Glueck, Sheldon, and Eleanor Glueck. 1940. *Juvenile Delinquents Grown Up*. New York: Commonwealth Fund.

———. 1943. *Criminal Careers in Retrospect*. New York: Commonwealth Fund.

———. 1945. *After-Conduct of Discharged Offenders*. London: Macmillan.

———. 1950. *Unraveling Juvenile Delinquency*. New York: Commonwealth Fund.

———. 1968. *Delinquents and Nondelinquents in Perspective*. Cambridge, Mass.: Harvard University Press.

———. 1974. *Of Delinquency and Crime*. Springfield, Ill.: Charles C. Thomas.

Gottfredson, Michael R., and Travis Hirschi. 1990. *A General Theory of Crime*. Stanford, Calif.: Stanford University Press.

Gove, Walter R. 1985. "The Effect of Age and Gender on Deviant Behavior: A Biopsychosocial Perspective." In *Gender and the Life Course*, edited by Alice S. Rossi. New York: Aldine.

Graham, John, and Benjamin Bowling. 1995. *Young People and Crime*. Research Study 145. London: Home Office.

Hagedorn, John M. 1988. *People and Folks: Gangs, Crime, and the Underclass in a Rustbelt City*. Chicago: Lake View Press.

Hill, Thomas W. 1971. "From Hell-Raiser to Family Man." In *Conformity and Conflict: Readings in Cultural Anthropology*, edited by James P. Spradley and David W. McCurdy. Boston: Little, Brown.

Hirschi, Travis. 1969. *Causes of Delinquency*. Berkeley: University of California Press.

Hirschi, Travis, and Michael R. Gottfredson. 1983. "Age and the Explanation of Crime." *American Journal of Sociology* 89:552–84.

———. 1986. "The Distinction between Crime and Criminality." In *Critique and Explanation: Essays in Honor of Gwynne Nettler*, edited by Timothy F. Hartnagel and Robert A. Silverman. New Brunswick, N.J.: Transaction.

Hoffman, Peter B., and James L. Beck. 1984. "Burnout—Age at Release from Prison and Recidivism." *Journal of Criminal Justice* 12:617–23.

Horney, Julie D. Wayne Osgood, and Ineke Haen Marshall. 1995. "Criminal Careers in the Short-Term: Intra-individual Variability in Crime and Its Relation to Local Life Circumstances." *American Sociological Review* 60:655–73.

Hughes, Margaret. 1998. "Turning Points in the Lives of Young Inner-City Men Forgoing Destructive Criminal Behaviors: A Qualitative Study." *Social Work Research* 22:143–51.

Irwin, John. 1970. *The Felon*. Englewood Cliffs, N.J.: Prentice Hall.

Kandel, Denise B., and Kazuo Yamaguchi. 1987. "Job Mobility and Drug Use: An Event History Analysis." *American Journal of Sociology* 92:836–78.

Knight, B. J., S. G. Osborn, and Donald J. West. 1977. "Early Marriage and Criminal Tendency in Males." *British Journal of Criminology* 17:348–60.

Labouvie, Erich. 1996. "Maturing Out of Substance Use: Selection and Self-Correction." *Journal of Drug Issues* 26:457–76.

Lattimore, Pamela K., Richard L. Linster, and John M. MacDonald. 1997. "Risk of Death among Serious Young Offenders." *Journal of Research in Crime and Delinquency* 34:187–209.

Laub, John H., Daniel S. Nagin, and Robert J. Sampson. 1998. "Trajectories of Change in Criminal Offending: Good Marriages and the Desistance Process." *American Sociological Review* 63:225–38.

Laub, John H., and Robert J. Sampson. 1993. "Turning Points in the Life Course: Why Change Matters to the Study of Crime." *Criminology* 31:301–25.

———. 2001. *Boys in Trouble and How They Age.* Cambridge, Mass.: Harvard University Press.

LeBlanc, Marc, and Marcel Frechette. 1989. *Male Criminal Activity from Childhood through Youth: Multilevel and Developmental Perspectives.* New York: Springer.

LeBlanc, Marc, and Rolf Loeber. 1993. "Precursors, Causes, and the Development of Criminal Offending." In *Precursors and Causes in Development and Psychopathology,* edited by Dale F. Hay and Adrian Angold. New York: Wiley.

———. 1998. "Developmental Criminology Updated." In *Crime and Justice: A Review of Research,* vol. 23, edited by Michael Tonry. Chicago: University of Chicago Press.

Leibrich, Julie. 1996. "The Role of Shame in Going Straight: A Study of Former Offenders." In *Restorative Justice: International Perspectives,* edited by Burt Galaway and Joe Hudson. Monsey, N.Y.: Criminal Justice Press.

Lewontin, Richard. 2000. *The Triple Helix: Gene, Organism, and Environment.* Cambridge, Mass.: Harvard University Press.

Loeber, Rolf, and Marc LeBlanc. 1990. "Toward a Developmental Criminology." In *Crime and Justice: A Review of Research,* vol. 12, edited by Michael Tonry and Norval Morris. Chicago: University of Chicago Press.

Loeber, Rolf, Magda Stouthamer-Loeber, Welmoet Van Kammen, and David P. Farrington. 1991. "Initiation, Escalation, and Desistance in Juvenile Offending and Their Correlates." *Journal of Criminal Law and Criminology* 82: 36–82.

Lofland, John. 1969. *Deviance and Identity.* Englewood Cliffs, N.J.: Prentice-Hall.

Maruna, Shadd. 1997. "Going Straight: Desistance from Crime and Life Narratives of Reform." In *The Narrative Study of Lives,* vol. 5, edited by Amia Lieblich and Ruthellen Josselson. Thousand Oaks, Calif.: Sage.

———. 2001. *Making Good: How Ex-offenders Reform and Reclaim Their Lives.* Washington, D.C.: American Psychological Association Books.

Matsueda, Ross L., and Karen Heimer. 1997. "A Symbolic Interactionist Theory of Role-Transitions, Role Commitments, and Delinquency." In *Developmental Theories of Crime and Delinquency,* edited by Terence Thornberry. New Brunswick, N.J.: Transaction.

Matza, David. 1964. *Delinquency and Drift.* New York: Wiley.

McCord, Joan. 1980. "Patterns of Deviance." In *Human Functioning in Longitudinal Perspective,* edited by Saul B. Sells, Rick Crandall, Merrill Roff, John S. Strauss, and William Pollin. Baltimore: Williams & Wilkins.

Meisenhelder, Thomas. 1977. "An Exploratory Study of Exiting from Criminal Careers." *Criminology* 15:319–34.

Miller-Tutzauer, Carol, Kenneth E. Leonard, and Michael Windle. 1991. "Marriage and Alcohol Use: A Longitudinal Study of 'Maturing Out.'" *Journal of Studies on Alcohol* 52:434–40.

Mischkowitz, Robert. 1994. "Desistance from a Delinquent Way of Life?" In *Cross-National Longitudinal Research on Human Development and Criminal Be-*

havior, edited by Elmar G. M. Weitekamp and Hans-Jurgen Kerner. Dordrecht: Kluwer Academic.

Moffitt, Terrie E. 1994. "Natural Histories of Delinquency." In *Cross-National Longitudinal Research on Human Development and Criminal Behavior*, edited by Elmar G. M. Weitekamp and Hans-Jurgen Kerner. Dordrecht: Kluwer Academic.

———. 1997. "Neuropsychology, Antisocial Behavior, and Neighborhood Context." In *Violence and Childhood in the Inner City*, edited by Joan McCord. Cambridge: Cambridge University Press.

Mulvey, Edward P., and Mark Aber. 1988. "Growing Out of Delinquency: Development and Desistance." In *The Abandonment of Delinquent Behavior*, edited by Richard L. Jenkins and Waln K. Brown. New York: Praeger Publishers.

Mulvey, Edward P., and John F. LaRosa. 1986. "Delinquency Cessation and Adolescent Development: Preliminary Data." *American Journal of Orthopsychiatry* 56:212–24.

Nagin, Daniel, David P. Farrington, and Terrie E. Moffitt. 1995. "Life-Course Trajectories of Different Types of Offenders." *Criminology* 33:111–39.

Nagin, Daniel S., and Kenneth C. Land. 1993. "Age, Criminal Careers, and Population Heterogeneity: Specification and Estimation of a Nonparametric, Mixed Poisson Model." *Criminology* 31:327–59.

Nagin, Daniel S., and Raymond Paternoster. 1991. "On the Relationship of Past and Future Participation in Delinquency." *Criminology* 29:163–90.

———. 1994. "Personal Capital and Social Control: The Deterrence Implications of Individual Differences in Criminal Offending." *Criminology* 32:581–606.

Nagin, Daniel S., and Joel Waldfogel. 1995. "The Effects of Criminality and Conviction on the Labor Market Status of Young British Offenders." *International Review of Law and Economics* 15:107–26.

Neff, James Alan, and Albana M. Dassori. 1998. "Age and Maturing Out of Heavy Drinking among Anglo and Minority Male Drinkers: A Comparison of Cross-Sectional Data and Retrospective Drinking History Techniques." *Hispanic Journal of Behavioral Sciences* 20:225–40.

Neugarten, Bernice L. 1996. *The Meanings of Age: Selected Papers of Bernice L. Neugarten.* Chicago: University of Chicago Press.

Nielsen, Amie L. 1999. "Testing Sampson and Laub's Life Course Theory: Age, Race/Ethnicity, and Drunkenness." *Deviant Behavior* 20:129–51.

Osborn, S. G. 1980. "Moving Home, Leaving London, and Delinquent Trends." *British Journal of Criminology* 20:54–61.

Osborn, S. G., and Donald J. West. 1979. "Marriage and Delinquency: A Postscript." *British Journal of Criminology* 19:254–56.

Osgood, D. Wayne, and Hyunkee Lee. 1993. "Leisure Activities, Age, and Adult Roles across the Lifespan." *Society and Leisure* 16:181–208.

Osgood, D. Wayne, Janet K. Wilson, Patrick M. O'Malley, Jerald G. Bachman, and Lloyd D. Johnston. 1996. "Routine Activities and Individual Deviant Behavior." *American Sociological Review* 61:635–55.

Paternoster, Raymond. 1989. "Decisions to Participate in and Desist from Four Types of Common Delinquency: Deterrence and the Rational Choice Perspective." *Law and Society Review* 23:7–40.

Paternoster, Raymond, and Leeann Iovanni. 1989. "The Labeling Perspective and Delinquency: An Elaboration of the Theory and an Assessment of the Evidence." *Justice Quarterly* 6:359–94.

Pezzin, Liliana E. 1995. "Earning Prospects, Matching Effects, and the Decision to Terminate a Criminal Career." *Journal of Quantitative Criminology* 11:29–50.

Piquero, Alex R. 2000. "Frequency, Specialization, and Violence in Offending Careers." *Journal of Research in Crime and Delinquency* 37:392–418.

Piquero, Alex R., Alfred Blumstein, Robert Brame, Rudy Haapanen, Edward P. Mulvey, and Daniel S. Nagin. 2001. "Assessing the Impact of Exposure Time and Incapacitation on Longitudinal Trajectories of Criminal Offending." *Journal of Adolescent Research* 16:54–74.

Prochaska, James, Carlo DiClemente, and John Norcross. 1992. "In Search of How People Change: Applications to Addictive Behaviors." *American Psychologist* 47:1102–14.

Prochaska, James O., and Wayne F. Velicer. 1997. "The Transtheoretical Model of Health Behavior Change." *American Journal of Health Promotion* 12:38–48.

Quigley, Brian M., and Kenneth E. Leonard. 1996. "Desistance of Husband Aggression in the Early Years of Marriage." *Violence and Victims* 11:355–70.

Rand, Alicia. 1987. "Transitional Life Events and Desistance from Delinquency and Crime." In *From Boy to Man, from Delinquency to Crime*, edited by Marvin E. Wolfgang, Terence P. Thornberry, and Robert M. Figlio. Chicago: University of Chicago Press.

Reiss, Albert J., Jr. 1989. "Ending Criminal Careers." Final Report prepared for the Desistance/Persistence Working Group of the Program on Human Development and Criminal Behavior. MacArthur Foundation and National Institute of Justice.

Reiss, Albert J., Jr., and Jeffrey A. Roth. 1993. *Understanding and Preventing Violence*. Washington, D.C.: National Academy Press.

Ricks, Thomas E. 1997. "U.S. Infantry Surprise: It's Now Mostly White; Blacks Hold Office Jobs." *Wall Street Journal* (January 6), pp. A1, A6.

Robins, Lee. 1966. *Deviant Children Grown Up*. Baltimore: Williams & Wilkins.

Rutter, Michael. 1988. "Longitudinal Data in the Study of Causal Processes: Some Uses and Some Pitfalls." In *Studies of Psychosocial Risk: The Power of Longitudinal Data*, edited by Michael Rutter. Cambridge: Cambridge University Press.

Rutter, Michael, David Quinton, and Jonathan Hill. 1990. "Adult Outcomes of Institution-Reared Children: Males and Females Compared." In *Straight and Devious Pathways from Childhood to Adulthood*, edited by Lee Robins and Michael Rutter. Cambridge: Cambridge University Press.

Sampson, Robert, J. 2000. "On the Social Development of Antisocial Behavior: A Review Essay." *Social Development* 9:565–68.

Sampson, Robert J., and John H. Laub. 1993. *Crime in the Making: Pathways and Turning Points through Life.* Cambridge, Mass.: Harvard University Press.

———. 1995. "Understanding Variability in Lives through Time: Contributions of Life-Course Criminology." *Studies on Crime and Crime Prevention* 4:143–58.

———. 1996. "Socioeconomic Achievement in the Life Course of Disadvantaged Men: Military Service as a Turning Point, Circa 1940–1965." *American Sociological Review* 61:347–67.

———. 1997. "A Life-Course Theory of Cumulative Disadvantage and the Stability of Delinquency." In *Developmental Theories of Crime and Delinquency*, edited by Terence P. Thornberry. New Brunswick, N.J.: Transaction.

Sarnecki, Jerzy. 1985. *Predicting Social Maladjustment. Stockholm Boys Grown Up*, 1. Research Report 17. Stockholm: National Council for Crime Prevention.

Sherman, Lawrence W. 1993. "Defiance, Deterrence, and Irrelevance: A Theory of the Criminal Sanction." *Journal of Research in Crime and Delinquency* 30:445–73.

Shover, Neal. 1985. *Aging Criminals.* Beverly Hills, Calif.: Sage.

———. 1996. *Great Pretenders: Pursuits and Careers of Persistent Thieves.* Boulder, Colo.: Westview Press.

Shover, Neal, and Carol Y. Thompson. 1992. "Age, Differential Expectations, and Crime Desistance." *Criminology* 30: 89–104.

Smelser, Neil J. 1998. "The Rational and the Ambivalent in the Social Sciences." *American Sociological Review* 63:1–15.

Sobell, Linda C., Mark B. Sobell, Tony Toneatto, and Gloria I. Leo. 1993. "What Triggers the Resolution of Alcohol Problems without Treatment?" *Alcoholism: Clinical and Experimental Research* 17:217–24.

Sommers, Ira, Deborah R. Baskin, and Jeffrey Fagan. 1994. "Getting Out of the Life: Crime Desistance by Female Street Offenders." *Deviant Behavior* 15:125–49.

Spergel, Irving A. 1990. "Youth Gangs: Continuity and Change." In *Crime and Justice: A Review of Research*, vol. 12, edited by Michael Tonry and Norval Morris. Chicago: University of Chicago Press.

Stall, Robb, and Patrick Biernacki. 1986. "Spontaneous Remission from the Problematic Use of Substances: An Inductive Model Derived from a Comparative Analysis of the Alcohol, Opiate, Tobacco, and Food/Obesity Literatures." *International Journal of the Addictions* 21:1–23.

Stattin, Hakan, and David Magnusson. 1991. "Stability and Change in Criminal Behavior Up to Age 30." *British Journal of Criminology* 31:327–46.

Stattin, Hakan, David Magnusson, and Howard Reichel. 1989. "Criminal Activity at Different Ages." *British Journal of Criminology* 29:368–85.

Steffensmeier, Darrell J., Emile Andersen Allan, Miles D. Harer, and Cathy Streifel. 1989. "Age and the Distribution of Crime." *American Journal of Sociology* 94:803–31.

Suitor, J. Jill, Karl Pillemer, and Murray A. Straus. 1990. "Marital Violence in a Life Course Perspective." In *Physical Violence in American Families*, edited by Murray A. Straus and Richard J. Gelles. New Brunswick, N.J.: Transaction.

Sullivan, Mercer. 1989. *Getting Paid.* Ithaca, N.Y.: Cornell University Press.

Temple, Mark T., Kaye Middleton Fillmore, Elizabeth Hartka, Bryan M. Johnstone, E. Victor Leino, and Michelle Motoyoshi. 1991. "A Meta-analysis of Change in Marital and Employment Status as Predictors of Alcohol Consumption on a Typical Occasion." *British Journal of Addiction* 86:1269–81.

Thornberry, Terence P. 1987. "Toward an Interactional Theory of Delinquency." *Criminology* 25:863–91.

———. 1998. "Membership in Youth Gangs and Involvement in Serious and Violent Offending." In *Serious and Violent Juvenile Offenders: Risk Factors and Successful Interventions*, edited by Rolf Loeber and David P. Farrington. Thousand Oaks, Calif.: Sage.

Tracy, Paul E., and Kimberly Kempf-Leonard. 1996. *Continuity and Discontinuity in Criminal Careers.* New York: Plenum.

Tracy, Paul E., Marvin E. Wolfgang, and Robert M. Figlio. 1985. *Delinquency in Two Birth Cohorts: Executive Summary.* Washington, D.C.: Government Printing Office.

Trasler, Gordon. 1979. "Delinquency, Recidivism, and Desistance." *British Journal of Criminology* 19:314–22.

Tremblay, Richard E. 1994. "Desistance from Crime: Towards a Life-Course Perspective." Discussant Paper presented at the International Society for the Study of Behavioral Development, Amsterdam, June 28–July 2.

Uggen, Christopher. 1999. "Ex-offenders and the Conformist Alternative: A Job Quality Model of Work and Crime." *Social Problems* 46:127–51.

———. 2000. "Work as a Turning Point in the Life Course of Criminals: A Duration Model of Age, Employment, and Recidivism." *American Sociological Review* 65:529–46.

Uggen, Christopher, and Candace Kruttschnitt. 1998. "Crime in the Breaking: Gender Differences in Desistance." *Law and Society Review* 32:339–66.

Uggen, Christopher, and Irving Piliavin. 1998. "Asymmetrical Causation and Criminal Desistance." *Journal of Criminal Law and Criminology* 88:1399–1422.

Vaillant, George E. 1973. "A 20-Year Follow-up of New York Narcotic Addicts." *Archives of General Psychiatry* 29:237–41.

———. 1988. "What Can Long-Term Follow-up Teach Us about Relapse and Prevention of Relapse in Addiction?" *British Journal of Addiction* 83:1147–57.

———. 1995. *The Natural History of Alcoholism Revisited.* Cambridge, Mass.: Harvard University Press.

———. 1996. "A Long-Term Follow-up of Male Alcohol Abuse." *Archives of General Psychiatry* 53:243–49.

Vaillant, George E., and Eva S. Milofsky. 1982. "Natural History of Male Alcoholism. IV. Paths to Recovery." *Archives of General Psychiatry* 39:127–33.

Vaughan, Diane. 1986. *Uncoupling: Turning Points in Intimate Relationships.* New York: Vintage.

Waldorf, Dan, Craig Reinarman, and Sheigla Murphy. 1991. *Cocaine Changes: The Experience of Using and Quitting*. Philadelphia: Temple University Press.

Warr, Mark. 1993. "Age, Peers, and Delinquency." *Criminology* 31:17–40.

———. 1998. "Life-Course Transitions and Desistance from Crime." *Criminology* 36:183–216.

Weitekamp, Elmar G. M., and Hans-Jurgen Kerner. 1994. "Epilogue: Workshop and Plenary Discussions, and Future Directions." In *Cross-National Longitudinal Research on Human Development and Criminal Behavior*, edited by Elmar G. M. Weitekamp and Hans-Jurgen Kerner. Dordrecht: Kluwer Academic.

West, Donald J. 1982. *Delinquency: Its Roots, Careers, and Prospects*. London: Heinemann.

Western, Bruce, and Katherine Beckett. 1999. "How Unregulated Is the U.S. Labor Market? The Penal System as a Labor Market Institution." *American Journal of Sociology* 104:1030–60.

White, Helene Raskin, and Marsha E. Bates. 1995. "Cessation from Cocaine Use." *Addiction* 90:947–57.

Wilson, James Q., and Richard J. Herrnstein. 1985. *Crime and Human Nature*. New York: Simon & Schuster.

Wilson, William Julius. 1996. *When Work Disappears: The World of the New Urban Poor*. New York: Knopf.

Woffordt, Sharon, Delbert Elliott, and Scott Menard. 1994. "Continuities in Marital Violence" *Journal of Family Violence* 9:195–225.

Wolfgang, Marvin E. 1995. "Transitions of Crime in the Aging Process." In *Delinquency and Disrepute in the Life Course: Contextual and Dynamic Analyses*, edited by Zena Smith Blau and John Hagan. Greenwich, Conn.: JAI.

Wolfgang, Marvin, Robert Figlio, and Thorsten Sellin. 1972. *Delinquency in a Birth Cohort*. Chicago: University of Chicago Press.

Wolfgang, Marvin, Terence Thornberry, and Robert Figlio. 1987. *From Boy to Man: From Delinquency to Crime*. Chicago: University of Chicago Press.

Wright, Kevin N., and Karen E. Wright. 1992. "Does Getting Married Reduce the Likelihood of Criminality? A Review of the Literature." *Federal Probation* 56:50–56.

Yamaguchi, Kazuo, and Denise B. Kandel. 1985. "On the Resolution of Role Incompatibility: A Life Event History Analysis of Family Roles and Marijuana Use." *American Journal of Sociology* 90:1284–1325.

David Boerner and Roxanne Lieb

Sentencing Reform in the Other Washington

ABSTRACT

Washington State's sentencing reform in the early 1980s encompassed all felonies, including those resulting in sentences to prison and jail; the state also enacted the first and only sentencing guidelines for juvenile offenders. Several lessons are suggested from Washington's experience: sentencing guidelines can change sentencing patterns and can reduce disparities among offenders who are sentenced for similar crimes and have similar criminal histories; a sentencing commission does not operate as an independent political force, except when such delegation serves the legislature's purpose; guidelines are policy-neutral technologies that can be harnessed to achieve the legislature's will; in states where citizen initiatives are authorized, sentencing issues will appear on the ballot, attract political support, and make significant changes to sentencing policy; guidelines allow a state to set sentences with advance knowledge of the consequences to prison and jail populations; guidelines are likely to become more complex over time as legislators strive to respond to new perceptions of crime seriousness, while simultaneously paying attention to prison and jail costs.

Twenty years ago, Washington State enacted what at that time was the most comprehensive reform of adult sentencing laws in the nation. The Sentencing Reform Act of 1981 rejected many core tenets of indeterminate sentencing, putting into place a sentencing system based on

David Boerner is an associate professor at Seattle University Law School; he previously served as Chief Criminal Deputy with the King County Prosecuting Attorney's Office and currently is chair of the Washington State Sentencing Guidelines Commission. Roxanne Lieb directs the Washington State Institute for Public Policy; she staffed Washington's Sentencing Guidelines Commission from its inception to 1990. Thanks to the anonymous reviewers and to Richard Frase, Michael Tonry, and Janie Maki for their contributions.

0192-3234/2001/0028-0002$02.00

principles of just desert and accountability. Since then, the legislature has not been shy about changing the act; it has been revised each year since its enactment. Sentences in 1999 differ significantly from those imposed in 1984; many are longer and require more conditions. Nevertheless, the act reached the millennium structurally intact.

The American experience with sentencing reform now spans a quarter century (Tonry 1996, chap. 1). Many of the reformers' goals have been achieved in at least some jurisdictions. Some were unrealistic or carried unintended consequences. Washington's reform is of particular interest because of its scope: the legislation encompassed all felonies, including those resulting in sentences to probation and jail; the state also enacted the first and only sentencing guidelines for juvenile offenders.

Washington's story suggests a number of lessons about sentencing guidelines. First, in contrast to mandatory sentences, which are rarely implemented as intended, sentencing guidelines can significantly change sentencing patterns. Second, guidelines can reduce disparities among offenders who are sentenced for similar crimes and have similar criminal histories. Third, unconstrained discretion in sentencing operates to favor whites and disfavor members of minority groups.

Washington's story also suggests lessons about the roles and powers of various institutions. First, sentencing commissions derive their power from the legislature and do not operate as an independent political force, except in circumstances where delegation to this body serves the legislature's purpose. Second, guidelines are policy-neutral technologies that can be harnessed to achieve the legislature's will. The legislature will use its power over sentencing policy in different ways at different times. Third, in states where citizens' initiatives are authorized, initiatives concerning sentencing are likely to appear on the ballot, attract popular support, and effect significant changes. Fourth, guidelines allow a state to set sentences with advance knowledge of the consequences to prison and jail populations and thereby to project necessary correctional resources. Thus, the branch of government setting the sentences also writes the check, increasing the opportunity for prudent resource management. Fifth, guidelines are likely to become increasingly complex over time, as legislators strive to respond to new perceptions of crime seriousness, while simultaneously paying attention to prison and jail costs.

Finally, any change in sentencing laws, procedures, and processes will alter the distribution of discretionary powers. Guidelines shift the allocation of discretion; actors and agencies that lose discretion will work to regain it. Voluntary prosecutorial guidelines at the state level will not control charging and plea-bargaining practices. The idiosyncratic nature of this aspect of prosecutors' work, coupled with the complex patterns of interaction between the prosecutors and defense attorneys, means that outside scrutiny is unattainable.

This essay is divided into six sections. Section I discusses the 1970s reformers' vision and the history of legislative actions leading up to adoption of guidelines legislation (1975–81). The first five years of the work of Washington's guidelines commission are described in Section II, including the development of the sentencing grid and related policies (1981–86). The period 1986–92 is covered in Section III; during this time, the legislature reinstated itself as the source of policy direction. Section IV covers 1993–95, when citizen initiatives dominated state sentencing policy. We review experience since 1995 in Section V and conclude in Section VI.

I. The Reformers' Era, 1975–81

Washington's first sentencing laws were enacted at the turn of the century. The state was an early and enthusiastic convert to the rehabilitative ideal and indeterminacy, and it granted wide and unconstrained discretion to judges and correctional officials (Boerner 1985, pp. 2–3). Judges were authorized to choose between prison and probation with few exceptions, subject only to review for abuse of discretion. Probation could be coupled with a jail term of up to one year, and judges had unrestricted authority to impose conditions of probation. Prison sentences were imposed at the statutory maximum, with the parole board having authority to set release dates for those whose rehabilitation was "complete" and judged a "fit subject for release" (Wash. Rev. Code, title 9, chap. 95, sec. 100 [2001]). Judges made recommendations about minimum terms but had no power to set minimum terms or prescribe parole conditions.

A handful of the most serious crimes carried mandatory terms of imprisonment. In all other matters, the parole board's discretion to release, and to impose parole conditions, was essentially unrestrained. Taken as a whole, Washington fit Zimring's description of a "labyrinthine" sentencing and corrections system that "lacks any principle except unguided discretion" (Zimring 1977, p. 6). This characterization was also valid for the state's juvenile system, which was established in 1913.

Washington's sentencing policies must be understood in the context of the division of power between state and local government. Both historically and at present, many political decisions about sentencing policies are influenced by whether the local or the state government pays the price. Washington's state prison system houses adult felons with sentences over one year; sentences of one year or less are served in jails and are the responsibility of local government. Supervision in the community, to the extent it is authorized, is a state responsibility. In the juvenile system, local authorities operate the diversion and probation programs and the detention centers; the state operates the institutions for those with sentences over a year and administers parole.

A. Options, 1975

Sentencing reform in Washington encompassed both the juvenile and adult sentencing codes. Because they were enacted separately—the juvenile reform in 1977 and the adult in 1981—and because the two systems are typically seen as worlds apart, this story is usually bifurcated. Connecting them, however, reveals their shared philosophical base and the breadth of reformist vision.

The story begins in 1975 with the House of Representatives' creation of a new subcommittee of the Social and Health Services Committee. This subcommittee was given a wide-ranging assignment that encompassed both adult and juvenile correctional systems. Representative Ron Hanna, the chair, had worked in juvenile corrections and was passionate about wanting to change the system. The committee's membership was unusual for the time, in that it was not numerically dominated by legislators representing districts with large correctional institutions. One member, Representative Mary Kay Becker, noted that the group viewed its task differently than did most legislative committees. The clear goal, she noted, was to develop state policy, rather than to review proposals from organizations (Becker 1979, p. 298).

During 1975, the committee visited most of the state's juvenile correctional institutions with two aims: viewing the facilities and hearing from administrators, staff, residents, agencies, and the general public. Everywhere the committee went, meetings were arranged so they could interact with people who spent their days working with juvenile and adult offenders. They focused on a simple, powerful question: How can the state do a better job?

The tour proved invaluable. Committee members gained close-hand knowledge of state facilities and talked with a wide range of people. They developed access to a network of experts outside the state capital, contacts that proved valuable later in testing reactions to proposed legislation.

The tour also revealed that the views and priorities of organizations they typically relied on concerning juvenile issues were out of tune with those of others in the system. The juvenile court administrators and judges became seen by the committee as strongly vested in the status quo and unwilling to examine the effects of their decisions and practices. As the system was constructed, the state paid for juvenile institutions and group home beds, with local government covering other costs. This gave local government representatives a strong financial incentive to decide that youth offenders needed to be institutionalized or removed from their families. The lack of interest of these groups in altering this arrangement caused the reformers to look elsewhere for political support.

The committee also became aware of the national debate that was challenging the rehabilitative underpinnings of sentencing and corrections. The desirability of individualized decision making was a premise of these systems in the United States for most of the 1900s. In the early 1970s, the U.S. Parole Commission challenged this norm by analyzing the patterns of its decision making, then devising a guidelines matrix based largely on past practice (Gottfredson, Wilkins, and Hoffman 1978). This approach did not require agreement ahead of time on sentencing purposes or appropriate penalties. The analysis was descriptive, based on examining past decisions and describing the patterns. From that point, decision makers thinking about sentencing and parole had the option to mirror historical practices or to set new policy directions.

Influential individuals in Washington were reading about the U.S. Parole Commission and studying the works of Marvin Frankel (1972), Norval Morris (1974), and Kenneth Culp Davis (1969), among others. By 1975, the King County prosecutor, Christopher T. Bayley, was advocating a radical departure from the individual treatment model for sentencing. Bayley argued for a fundamental change based on the following philosophy. First, punishment—expressed as a loss of liberty—should follow conviction for every serious crime. Second, the amount of punishment should be determined by the seriousness of the crime the defendant committed. Third, other factors, such as the defendant's need for treatment, his or her attitude, or predictions of future dangerousness, are irrelevant. Fourth, variations must be permitted in individual cases, for it is impossible to foresee every future possibility, but these exceptions must be principled and supported by written reasons (Bayley 1976*a*).

A 1975 Governor's Task Force proposal brought this debate to public attention. The task force's proposal pushed the rehabilitative ideal to its outer limits. It proposed abolishing all distinctions in punishment between crimes, thus severing the proportionality link between crime and punishment. All felonies, regardless of severity, were to be punishable by an indeterminate sentence of not more than five years. A category of "dangerous offenders," subject to an indeterminate life sentence, was to be reserved for the most serious offenders (Governor's Task Force on Decision Making Models in Corrections 1975). The proposal's proponents were articulate advocates of the "rehabilitative ideal" and sought to extend it to its logical conclusion (Allen 1981).

The political response to the proposal was quick and sharp, with prosecutor Bayley leading the charge in the press. The controversy soon evolved into a major public debate on sentencing and its purposes. In December 1975, Bayley sponsored a conference on this topic that included addresses by such national figures as Norval Morris and Robert Martinson. A subsequent *University of Washington Law Review* issue featured articles from a variety of perspectives (Symposium 1976).

The political stakes were revealed in the next election. Two superior court judges in King County, both vocal supporters of the rehabilitative ideal, were defeated in their bids for reelection. Both were well-respected jurists. Incumbent judges were rarely challenged during this period and even more rarely unseated. The election upset was remarkable.

B. The Juvenile System

Starting in the 1970s, pressures to alter the state's juvenile system began to mount from numerous sources, including U.S. Supreme Court decisions, population increases in state juvenile institutions, and concerns about upward trends in juvenile crime rates. Several U.S. Supreme Court decisions had mandated due process and procedural safeguards for juveniles (Feld 1998). In addition, financial incentives from the federal government encouraged states to remove status offenders from juvenile court jurisdiction (Becker 1979, p. 292).

Between 1969 and 1975, the Washington legislature had repeatedly considered comprehensive juvenile justice reform proposals, and although most passed at least one house, all died before passage. The proposals were drafted by a variety of groups, including the Judicial Council, Northwest Washington Legal Services, and superior court judges. The failure of the proposals was caused by the serious polarization of interests: one group's remedy was antithetical to others (Becker 1979, p. 295). A recent increase in commitments to state juvenile institutions added to concerns about the juvenile system, particularly in terms of state budget implications.

By 1976, Representative Hanna's subcommittee reached consensus on changes to the juvenile system. They chose to tackle the juvenile laws first because the sense of political and practical urgency was far greater, thus offering more political opportunity. The subcommittee came to four key conclusions. Expenses for juvenile treatment had increased continuously without a significant increase in the rate of effectiveness. Rather than emphasize treatment, the system should emphasize work as a productive, therapeutic endeavor. Crisis intervention programs for families were the key to keeping children out of the court and institutional system. For the juvenile courts, a pilot project should experiment with the determinate sentencing model proposed by Marvin Wolfgang, in which the "strictness of the sentence would be related to the severity and frequency of the child's criminal behavior" (Substitute House Resolution 46, 44th Legislature, 2d Extraordinary Sess. 1 [1976]).

Committee leaders pressed forward. More "accountability," both by offenders and by the system, emerged as a powerful rallying point. In June 1976, a legislative subcommittee reviewed a document prepared by a nonpartisan staff member that defined three major deficiencies of the existing juvenile system. First, the system was not accountable to citizens. No way had been found to measure its performance. Its ends were unclear, the means inconsistent. Second, the system did not hold youthful offenders accountable. Violent offenders often had their cases handled informally, while misdemeanants and nonviolent offenders went to court. Third, the system was unable to help offenders. The conflict between the punishment and rehabilitation roles of probation workers and institutional officers undermined their ability to help, and juvenile crime had been increasing, undermining the system's effectiveness (Naon 1976, p. 41).

Other aspects of the juvenile code were controversial, particularly concerning responses to truants, runaways, and youth in conflict with their families. Finding political consensus on these issues was an exceptional challenge. When a crime is committed, the state's role is clear:

to restore balance to the social contract. When a juvenile runs to the streets and refuses to return home, the state's role is more ambiguous. Should the state arrest and confine the youth in a detention facility or an institution? Does the answer change if the youth left home because of physical or sexual abuse by a parent? As the elements for reform of the offender side of the law took shape, the political consensus for status offenders was more elusive (Lieb and Brown 1999, p. 274).

1. *Bipartisan Coalition Supports Reform.* By January 1977, a bill to reform the offender side of the juvenile code was introduced, and a broad coalition of supporters testified. A bipartisan coalition spanned the political spectrum, including the American Civil Liberties Union, Legal Services, the defense bar, prosecutors, crime victims, and law enforcement. The King County Prosecutor's Office sent two attorneys to the state capitol to keep the bill alive and help resolve disagreements. A separate bill regarding status offenders was introduced in the Senate; eventually, both bills were combined (House Bill 371, 45th Leg., Extraordinary Sess., 1977). This consolidation increased the political momentum and support base and allowed the leaders to break the previous political logjams.

The "missing links" in the reform coalition were juvenile court administrators and probation staff, some of whom actively lobbied in opposition. Because these groups had become identified as "defenders of the status quo," their resistance was viewed as predictable. Judges did not actively support or oppose the law; a later survey revealed that at the time, many believed the legislation had little chance of passing (Steiger and Doyan 1979).

Because many sections of the bill were drafted quickly, and the system changes were enormous, a clause that delayed implementation for one year helped to garner votes. The plan was to spend the next session perfecting the legislation. For reasons unrelated to the juvenile law, the governor surprised the state in 1978 by not calling a legislative session, something that had rarely occurred in recent history. Thus, the legislation went into effect in 1978 with some internal contradictions (House Bill 371, 45th Leg., 1st Extraordinary Sess. [1977] Codified at Wash. Rev. Code, title 13).

2. *Juvenile Guidelines.* The legislation radically altered the juvenile justice system. Decision making was formalized, with discretion shifted from probation staff to the prosecutor. Previously, probation counselors decided which cases to keep out of court and which to refer to prosecutors; it was a decision-making process described as based often

on "extra-legal factors and idiosyncratic choice" (Schneider and Schram 1983, p. 24). Due process rights and other procedural guarantees were provided to juveniles. Juvenile courts could no longer shift the costs of delinquent youth to the state by committing them to state care and instead the courts were given incentives to use less onerous local sanctions.

The law established standards for a sentencing system based on age, offense, and prior history. Courts were given discretion to depart from the guidelines, if necessary, to impose a just sentence. This provision, labeled a "manifest injustice sentence," could be used to increase or reduce the amount of punishment; written reasons were necessary and the sentence could be appealed.

The 1977 act created a new commission to review and evaluate the sentencing and dispositional aspects of the law. The Washington State Juvenile Disposition Standards Commission was directed to report to the legislature every two years regarding changes to the sentencing grid. The body was given substantial authority—its recommendations went into effect unless modified by the legislature. Although the commission's responsibilities paralleled those of the typical adult sentencing commission, its structure and operations were far less independent. The ten-member panel was chaired by the division director of juvenile institutions.

Implementation moved to the state agency responsible for juvenile institutions, the Department of Social and Health Services. The agency assigned Warren Netherland, an institutional warden, to oversee the task. Netherland was a strong believer in the just deserts philosophy and a strategic thinker. Working with a broad coalition, he solicited the views and suggestions of groups with a stake in the reform. When it came time to draft the guidelines, Netherland worked with a hand-picked group and exercised control over all decisions. The sentencing standards took effect July 1, 1979.

The standards commission early on set operating procedures that required consensus decisions before statutory changes were recommended. Since the membership included prosecutors and the defense bar, it was difficult to reach agreement on major changes in sentencing. During the first decade of the group's operation, revisions to the guidelines were primarily technical in nature. Its recommendations were not controversial and were either adopted as proposed or allowed to take effect without modification (Steiger 1998, p. 343). By the second decade, however, juvenile crime again became a topic of political debate, and key legislators grew frustrated with the body's inaction. Eventually, the juvenile standards commission was eliminated and its functions were transferred in 1996 to the adult sentencing commission.

The political climate that influenced changes in the state's juvenile system was equally focused on adult sentencing. Here, though, the reform process was slower.

C. Voluntary Parole Guidelines Falter

The experiences of the U.S. Parole Commission in developing guidelines influenced Washington's Board of Prison Terms and Paroles. Beginning in 1974, members began discussing matrix guidelines as a possible remedy for perceived disparities. At that time, the board had jurisdiction over more than 12,000 individuals, including approximately 4,000 in the prison system (Petersen and Gearhart 1979).

In 1975, the board agreed to "establish explicit policy and rationale for Board decision-making" (Patrick and Petersen 1979, p. 3). According to a board document, this decision was "undoubtedly activated, if not induced, by the introduction of determinate sentencing legislation in the 1975 legislative session" (Patrick and Petersen 1979, p. 3). Several advantages were envisioned. With explicit criteria, rationales for decisions would be clearer and more understandable to offenders and the public. Disparities in decision making would be reduced. Board practices could be evaluated by comparison with explicit policy (Patrick and Petersen 1979, p. 3).

The board sought and received a three-year grant in 1976 from the Law Enforcement Assistance Administration of the U.S. Department of Justice to develop and implement guidelines. In July 1976, the board adopted a matrix model to fix minimum terms of confinement that divided crimes into thirteen categories. For each offense category, low, medium, and high ranges were set according to the perceived likelihood of parole success.

In fall 1977, researchers concluded that board members were generally ignoring the guidelines (Patrick and Petersen 1979, p. 11). By the following spring, three new members joined the board, including a new chairman. The guidelines fell into disuse. The effort revived in 1978 with a new set of guidelines based on a consensus process in which board members assigned weights to hypothetical cases. This version, however, did not influence decision making to a great extent; overall, the board stayed inside these guidelines only about 63 percent of the time (Patrick and Petersen 1979, p. 17). A similar compliance rate could have been achieved by setting one guideline sentence of thirty-six months. In practice, thirty-six months was the minimum term sentence selected by board members for about 60 percent of offenders (Barnoski 2000).

In January 1979, the board revised the guidelines to reduce the number of crime categories from thirteen to eight and adopted guidelines for parole violations. In June 1979, compliance in minimum term setting was again found to be modest: terms were set within the guidelines in less than two-thirds of cases. The researchers concluded that even though the board as a collective body was committed to the guidelines, the individual practices of members suggested that "the degree of its collective commitment lacks the intensity necessary to realize one of the primary objectives of the guidelines: reduction of disparity in minimum terms set for similar offenses" (Patrick and Petersen 1979, p. 44). Only one of the 163 departures from the guidelines was accompanied by a written justification, even though board policy required justification in each departure. The report concluded that board members, "individually and collectively, *must* decide whether they can and will *totally* support the guideline policy. If the entire membership of the Board agrees to support *and* conduct their decision-making responsibilities under the tenets of the guideline policy, they must be prepared to exercise peer pressure in the prevention of penal philosophy that is in conflict with the collective philosophy" (Patrick and Petersen 1979, p. 44).

The controversy within the board about the guidelines, and the modest levels of compliance, suggested that voluntary guidelines were an unlikely means to control this body's discretion.

D. *Voluntary Sentencing and Prosecution Guidelines*

Also responding to the public debate, the Superior Court Judges Association adopted judicial guidelines in 1978. Like the parole board's initial effort, the judicial guidelines were designed to reflect past practice. The guidelines covered the jail versus prison decision (sentences under a year in Washington are served in jail; others are prison sentences), and maximum sentence length. The guidelines were voluntary; no statute or court rule required compliance or even consideration by individual judges. A 1981 study found that judges used the guidelines in 70 percent of cases, and of those, 66 percent were within the guidelines (State of Washington Superior Court Judges Association and Office of the Administrator for the Courts 1981).

The state's prosecuting attorneys also adopted guidelines. King County developed office policies for filing and disposition decisions in the early 1970s (Bayley 1976*b*, 1978). Several other counties followed, and in 1980, uniform (but voluntary) charging and disposition policies were adopted by the Washington Association of Prosecuting Attorneys (1980).

In some states, similar voluntary restrictions on discretion averted legislative action (e.g., in Maryland and, for a time, Florida; Carrow 1984). It is ironic that Washington's experience with voluntary guidelines adopted by the parole board, the judiciary, and prosecutors taught two lessons: guidelines were a legitimate means to control discretion, and voluntary guidelines were not likely to reduce disparity because compliance will be modest.

E. Adult Sentencing Reform

The leaders in the House of Representatives who championed juvenile sentencing reform applied the same principles to reform of adult sentencing. Legislation drafted in the King County Prosecutor's Office, first introduced in 1977 and based on just deserts principles, passed the House of Representatives but died in the Senate. The same thing happened in 1979.

Reform pressures did not abate, however, and in 1980, a bipartisan select committee on corrections was appointed by the House of Representatives to concentrate on adult sentencing. This committee, led by Representatives Mary Kay Becker and Gene Struthers, spent months conducting hearings across the state and debating alternatives. Representative Becker had been a leader in the juvenile reform legislation. Norm Maleng, who had replaced Christopher Bayley as King County Prosecuting Attorney, became a strong advocate for reform. Maleng's chief of staff, Robert Lasnik, became the principal lobbyist for the proposal.

The committee considered the experiences of other states with sentencing reforms and studied the reform arguments and proposals. Ultimately, the committee drafted legislation that drew on national reform proposals, but selectively. The legislation reflected a consensus of otherwise disparate interests and groups. (Representative Becker jokingly described the unlikely consensus between herself, a liberal Democrat, and Representative Struthers, a conservative Republican, as akin to "Jane Fonda and John Wayne co-authoring a book on the history of the Vietnam War" [*Seattle Post-Intelligencer* 1984, p. 4A].) The coalition of disparate political groups supporting the reform mirrored the state's experiences with juvenile sentencing reform and presaged the consensus that would later be reached in other states and the federal government in adopting sentencing guidelines (Stith and Koh 1993).

Following House passage, the proposed reform legislation moved to the Senate, where it had stalled each session since 1977. No hearing was expected, as the judiciary committee chair was on record as opposing determinate sentencing. Serendipitously, control of the Senate shifted when a Democratic senator switched party affiliation a third of the way through the session. The new Republican chair of the judiciary committee supported sentencing reform, and thus the reform package developed by the House select committee moved quickly, was approved by the Senate, and was passed into law in 1981. Implementation was delayed until 1984; a newly created sentencing guidelines commission was directed to develop the sentencing grid and related policies.

Although the final vote on the Sentencing Reform Act of 1981 was virtually unanimous, this result masked opposition by two key groups—judges and corrections officials. As with the juvenile reform, these opponents played significant roles in the system and had the potential to block legislative action. Judges resented the reform's restrictions on their discretion, but they were a disorganized political force.

The governor, John Spellman, was not a strong proponent, but he had not played a major role on criminal justice issues and chose not to involve himself in the deliberations. Coincidentally, his legal counsel, as a King County deputy prosecutor, had played an instrumental role in the juvenile reform. The secretary of corrections, Amos Reed, did not take a public stand. Later, on April 22, 1983, when the bill-signing ceremony occurred, the governor commented to the secretary, "Well, Amos, we didn't think this bill would ever pass, did we?"

F. The 1981 Reform Bill

The legislature's central role in sentencing reform distinguished, and continues to distinguish, Washington from many other states that enacted commission-centered reforms. Unlike Minnesota's commission, described as having "primary control over the setting of statewide sentencing policy" (Frase 1993, p. 337), the Washington commission's role was advisory from the beginning. Washington's legislature never delegated its power over sentencing. When it revoked its long-standing delegation of sentencing policy to judges and the parole board, the legislature did not redelegate this authority to a commission. The commission was to serve a valuable role by crafting details and providing policy advice, but the legislature intended to control sentencing policy.

When the Washington commission started work, the legislature had already resolved many sentencing policy issues. Their scope and detail were influenced by two factors. First, reformers had worked on the measure for seven years, negotiating and crafting resolutions to concerns from organizations and legislators. Second, the state already had experience with juvenile guidelines and there were aspects of that law that reformers either wanted to duplicate or to avoid in the adult system. To a smaller extent, Minnesota's experiences with sentencing guidelines were known and offered policy makers a chance either to mirror that state's law or to take different approaches.

The legislative framework included the following elements:

Just Deserts Emphasis. The multiple—and often inconsistent—purposes of sentencing were integrated into principled coexistence, with just deserts the primary but not exclusive purpose.

Truth and Certainty. All sentences were to be determinate; that is, both length and conditions were to be known "with exactitude" (Wash. Rev. Code, title 9, chap. 94A, sec. 030[16] [2001]) at the time imposed, with the sole exception of provisions allowing up to a one-third reduction in sentence for good behavior in jail or prison. The power of courts to suspend or defer sentences was abolished, as were parole release and supervision.

Structuring but Not Eliminating Discretion. Sentencing ranges of prescribed—and relatively narrow—width were to be based solely on the crime of conviction and the offender's criminal history (Wash. Rev. Code, title 9, chap. 94A, sec. 40 [2001]). The sentencing ranges were presumptive, not mandatory; judges could depart from the range with written justification, subject to substantive appellate review (Wash. Rev. Code, title 9, chap. 94A, sec. 120[3] [2001]). The commission was to develop the nation's first statewide prosecutorial guidelines covering charging decisions and plea agreements.

Rehabilitation Given a Limited Focus. Sentences intended to rehabilitate offenders were restricted to a defined class of first-time, nonviolent offenders (Wash. Rev. Code, title 9, chap. 94A, sec. 120[5] [2001]). This group was seen as composed of excellent candidates for treatment-oriented sanctions. For all other sentences, sentence conditions were restricted to "crime-related prohibitions," not the performance of affirmative conduct (Wash. Rev. Code, title 9, chap. 94A, sec. 030 [2001]). Crime-related prohibitions were intended to relate specifically to the offense of conviction, for example, for a sex offender, a prohibition against unsupervised contact with minors.

Shift in Priorities. In setting the ranges, the commission was to "emphasize confinement for the violent offender and alternatives to total confinement for the non-violent offender" (Wash. Rev. Code, title 9, chap. 94A, sec. 040[5] [2001]).

Setting the Price Tag. The commission was directed to estimate the impact of the guidelines on prison and jail populations, but current capacity need not dictate sentencing policy.

Legislative Control. The legislature retained its authority over sentencing, with the guidelines commission serving in an advisory capacity.

The commission's task was to develop guidelines that would implement these policy decisions. The legislation called for a fifteen-member body of criminal justice professionals, state agency leaders, and citizens; four legislators served as nonvoting members.

The governor's decisions on commission appointments were greatly influenced by his legal counsel, Marilyn Showalter. Showalter understood the need to appoint members who could tackle the substantive and political challenges ahead. The designated chair, Donna Schram, was a citizen with extensive experience in criminal justice research, including a major evaluation of the state's juvenile justice reform (Schneider et al. 1981). Norm Maleng was appointed as one of the prosecutor's representatives and was later elected by the group as its first vice chair. The judicial, prosecutorial, and defense bar representatives were highly respected by their peers. The commission set to work late in 1981.

II. The Commission's Era, 1981–86

Washington's commission began its work where every sentencing commission begins—by concentrating on the criminal code, crime definitions, and dissecting the degrees of harm represented by various crimes. For several months, commission members worked in subcommittees in which they had ample opportunities to engage in understanding the legislation and each other's experiences and views.

The chair was careful to incorporate extensive discussions into the meetings and for several months took very few votes. She understood that for the commission to succeed, members had eventually to set aside their "representative" statuses and instead to view themselves as part of a body with greater responsibility to the state.

The staff organized research to document past sentencing practices. While the reform was to be prescriptive, not merely descriptive, past practices were seen as an essential baseline. For offenders sent to prison, parole board and Washington State Department of Corrections' records were used. For persons sentenced at the local level (under a year), records were scattered across the state in county jails and probation officers' files.

The commission eventually ranked felonies into fourteen seriousness levels and devised a scoring system for criminal history that assigned variable weights based on the number of convictions, their seriousness, the similarity of the prior conviction to the current offense, and the length of time between convictions. Ranges were set using the "typical" crime as the standard; the King County Prosecutor's staff assisted the commission by providing examples of each. Individual circumstances that fell outside the normal range of conduct were to be addressed by exceptional sentences. The commission's proposed sentencing grid was a matrix with 140 cells (see fig. 1).

Commission members became forceful proponents of the just deserts philosophy; some started with this conviction, and others, particularly the judges, became convinced over time. The legislature's direction was clear—the guidelines were to "apply equally to offenders in all parts of the state, without discrimination as to any element that does not relate to the crime or the previous record of the defendant" (Wash. Rev. Code, title 9, chap. 94A, sec. 340 [2001]). This principle significantly influenced the commission's deliberations and was repeatedly invoked during discussions.

Judicial discretion within the applicable sentence range was unrestricted; judges could impose any sentence within the range for any reason they deemed appropriate, and appellate review was prohibited (Wash. Rev. Code, title 9, chap. 94A, sec. 370 [2001]). For less serious felonies, the range was modest—for serious offenses, it was substantial. Similarly, decisions to use the first-time offender waiver were immune from judicial review. Since the legislature had selected a presumptive sentencing system, the commission needed to set direction on how cases outside the norm were to be recognized and determine the degrees of freedom allowed in setting terms outside the range.

The original legislation defined "exceptional sentences" as warranted when the "imposition of a sentence within the standard range

SERIOUSNESS LEVEL	OFFENDER SCORE									
	0	1	2	3	4	5	6	7	8	9 or more
XV	Life Sentence without Parole/Death Penalty									
XIV	23y 4m 240 - 320	24y 4m 250 - 333	25y 4m 261 - 347	26y 4m 271 - 361	27y 4m 281 - 374	28y 4m 291 - 388	30y 4m 312 - 416	32y 10m 338 - 450	36y 370 - 493	40y 411 - 548
XIII	14y 4m 123 - 220	15y 4m 134 - 234	16y 2m 144 - 244	17y 154 - 254	17y 11m 165 - 265	18y 9m 175 - 275	20y 5m 195 - 295	22y 2m 216 - 316	25y 7m 257 - 357	29y 298 - 397
XII	9y 93 - 123	9y 11m 102 - 136	10y 9m 111 - 147	11y 8m 120 - 160	12y 6m 129 - 171	13y 5m 138 - 184	15y 9m 162 - 216	17y 3m 178 - 236	20y 3m 209 - 277	23y 3m 240 - 318
XI	7y 6m 78 - 102	8y 4m 86 - 114	9y 2m 95 - 125	9y 11m 102 - 136	10y 9m 111 - 147	11y 7m 120 - 158	14y 2m 146 - 194	15y 5m 159 - 211	17y 11m 185 - 245	20y 5m 210 - 280
X	5y 51 - 68	5y 6m 57 - 75	6y 62 - 82	6y 6m 67 - 89	7y 72 - 96	7y 6m 77 - 102	9y 6m 98 - 130	10y 6m 108 - 144	12y 6m 129 - 171	14y 6m 149 - 198
IX	3y 31 - 41	3y 6m 36 - 48	4y 41 - 54	4y 6m 46 - 61	5y 51 - 68	5y 6m 57 - 75	7y 6m 77 - 102	8y 6m 87 - 116	10y 6m 108 - 144	12y 6m 129 - 171
VIII	2y 21 - 27	2y 6m 26 - 34	3y 31 - 41	3y 6m 36 - 48	4y 41 - 54	4y 6m 46 - 61	6y 6m 67 - 89	7y 6m 77 - 102	8y 6m 87 - 116	10y 6m 108 - 144
VII	18m 15 - 20	2y 21 - 27	2y 6m 26 - 34	3y 31 - 41	3y 6m 36 - 48	4y 41 - 54	5y 6m 57 - 75	6y 6m 67 - 89	7y 6m 77 - 102	8y 6m 87 - 116
VI	13m 12+ - 14	18m 15 - 20	2y 21 - 27	2y 6m 26 - 34	3y 31 - 41	3y 6m 36 - 48	4y 6m 46 - 61	5y 6m 57 - 75	6y 6m 67 - 89	7y 6m 77 - 102
V	9m 6 - 12	13m 12+ - 14	15m 13 - 17	18m 15 - 20	2y 2m 22 - 29	3y 2m 33 - 43	4y 41 - 54	5y 51 - 68	6y 62 - 82	7y 72 - 96
IV	6m 3 - 9	9m 6 - 12	13m 12+ - 14	15m 13 - 17	18m 15 - 20	2y 2m 22 - 29	3y 2m 33 - 43	4y 2m 43 - 57	5y 2m 53 - 70	6y 2m 63 - 84
III	2m 1 - 3	5m 3 - 8	8m 4 - 12	11m 9 - 12	14m 12+ - 16	20m 17 - 22	2y 2m 22 - 29	3y 2m 33 - 43	4y 2m 43 - 57	5y 51 - 68
II	0 - 90 Days	4m 2 - 6	6m 3 - 9	8m 4 - 12	13m 12+ - 14	16m 14 - 18	20m 17 - 22	2y 2m 22 - 29	3y 2m 33 - 43	4y 2m 43 - 57
I	0 - 60 Days	0 - 90 Days	3m 2 - 5	4m 2 - 6	5m 3 - 8	8m 4 - 12	13m 12+ - 14	16m 14 - 18	20m 17 - 22	2y 2m 22 - 29

Fig. 1.—Sentencing grid for crimes committed after July 26, 1997, and before July 25, 1999

would impose an excessive punishment on the defendant or would pose an unacceptable threat to community safety" (Laws of 1981, chap. 137, sec. 2[2]). As the commission worked to implement the reform, members studied Minnesota's experience and were impressed with that state's emerging case law interpreting its exceptional sentence provision. The commission decided that Minnesota's appellate decisions would reinforce Washington's reform and assist in creating a "common law of sentencing," one of the stated legislative intents. The commission thus recommended that the legislature replace the original language with Minnesota's provision requiring "substantial and compelling" reasons to justify a departure from the applicable guidelines (Wash. Rev. Code, title 9, chap. 94A, sec. 120[2] [2001]). The legislature concurred in 1983, and the early appellate decisions reviewing exceptional sentences in Washington frequently referred to Minnesota decisions.

The commission chose to guide judicial discretion by creating a set of aggravating and mitigating factors that would justify an exceptional sentence. While careful to state that these factors were "illustrative only and are not intended to be exclusive reasons for exceptional sentences" (Wash. Rev. Code, title 9, chap. 94A, sec. 390 [2001]), the commission reinforced the legislative emphasis on just deserts by selecting only factors relating to the crime. Offender characteristics unrelated to the crime were noticeably absent (Boerner 1985, pp. 2–33).

Washington's commission struggled with whether the guidelines should be based on the statutory definition of the crime or instead should more sensitively measure criminal conduct, varying by elements of the crime or other defined variables (degree of harm to victim, etc.). The eventual decision that sentences were to be based solely on the crime of conviction was reinforced by language that "real facts which establish elements of a higher crime, a more serious crime, or additional crimes cannot be used to go outside the guidelines except upon stipulation" (Wash. Rev. Code, title 9, chap. 94A, sec. 370[2] [2001]). The commission intended to eliminate the former practice of basing sentences on conduct the offender was believed to have done, regardless of whether it was proven or admitted. The commission believed this policy would reinforce the goal that prosecutors charge and accept plea agreements that accurately reflected the crime or crimes that were committed. Crimes that prosecutors either could not or chose not to pursue could not justify an exceptional sentence.

A. Prosecutorial Discretion

The 1981 legislation recognized that sentencing guidelines increased the relative power of prosecutors by increasing the importance of the crime of conviction in determining the ultimate sentence. The legislature thus directed the commission to "devise recommended prosecuting standards in respect to charging of offenses and plea agreements" (Wash. Rev. Code, title 9, chap. 94A, sec. 040[2][c] [2001]). To accomplish this, the commission reviewed earlier efforts of the California District Attorney's Association (1974), the National District Attorney's Association (1977), and the U.S. Justice Department under Attorney General Edward H. Levi (Levi 1978) and Benjamin R. Civiletti (1980), as well as guidelines adopted by the King County (Seattle) Prosecuting Attorney's Office (1980) and the Washington Association of Prosecuting Attorneys (1980).

The commission developed guidelines for charging decisions and plea agreements. When enacted in 1984 they became the most comprehensive set of prosecutorial guidelines ever adopted in the United States (Wash. Rev. Code, title 9, chap. 94A, sec. 430–60 [2001]; Boerner 1985, p. 12-1). Crimes against persons and those against property were distinguished with regard to the necessary evidentiary strength for prosecution, with person crimes set at a lower threshold. A series of nonevidentiary reasons were listed that could support a decision not to prosecute. For the key decisions regarding the number and nature of charges, the direction was that only "charges which adequately describe the nature of the defendant's conduct" were to be filed, and prosecutors should "decline to file charges that are not necessary to such an indication" (Wash. Rev. Code, title 9, chap. 94A, sec. 440 [2001]). Prosecutors were directed not to "overcharge" to obtain a guilty plea; defendants were normally expected to plead guilty to the charge or charges which "adequately describe the nature of his or her conduct" (Wash. Rev. Code, title 9, chap. 94A, sec. 440 [2001]) or go to trial unless one of eight specified situations was present to justify concessions in return for a guilty plea.

The legislation included an enforcement mechanism. When plea agreements were reached, the "nature of the agreement and the reasons" were to be disclosed to the court, and the court "shall determine if the agreement is consistent with the interests of justice and the prosecuting standards" (Wash. Rev. Code, title 9, chap. 94A, sec. 090 [2001]). Once the guidelines were approved by the commission, the key policy decision was whether they were advisory or mandatory. Here, the commission adopted language based on Attorney General Levi's memorandum on federal prosecution standards (Levi 1978; Boerner 1985, p. 12-8): "These standards are intended solely for the guidance of prosecutors in the state of Washington. They are not intended to, do not and may not be relied upon to create a right or benefit, substantive or procedural, enforceable at law by a party in litigation with the state" (Wash. Rev. Code, title 9, chap. 94A, sec. 430 [2001]).

This provision made the prosecutorial guidelines voluntary. Ultimately, they were to join previous voluntary efforts by the state's parole board and judiciary as ineffective efforts to constrain discretion.

B. Retroactivity and Intermediate Sanctions

Guided by what it saw as the difficulty of applying the new guidelines to sentences imposed under the former indeterminate system, the 1981 legislature anticipated prospective application of the guidelines (applied to persons committing crimes on or after July 1, 1984). The parole board was directed to use the guidelines as a benchmark, thus anticipating that the board would operate for some period. Some drafters of the reform anticipated that the board's responsibilities would eventually be taken over by a newly created body, the Clemency and Pardons Board (Lasnik 1981, p. 7).

When the commission considered the paths taken by California and Minnesota in converting from indeterminate to determinate sentences, the two systems' differential premiums on accurate charges was of great concern. Since the conversion could apply constitutionally only when it benefited offenders, sentences would be reduced, in many cases, quite significantly. This choice had few political supporters.

The commission chose to recommend that the 1981 legislative direction to the parole board be supplemented with additional language. The original language directed the board to "consider the purposes, standards and sentencing ranges" of the Sentencing Reform Act and attempt to make decisions that were "reasonably consistent" (Wash. Rev. Code, title 9, chap. 95, sec. 009[2] [2001]). New language was added that the board should also "consider the different charging and disposition practices under the indeterminate sentencing system" and justify sentences outside the range with written reasons (Wash. Rev. Code, title 9, chap. 95, sec. 009[2] [2001]). Washington's transition between systems continues to this day, with a part-time, three-member board remaining to review the terms and releases of approximately

1,000 inmates still in 1999 subject to sentences for pre-July 1, 1984 crimes (Marsh 1999). Other solutions have been considered, but concerns about sentence reductions and implementation burdens have trumped other options. (See Office of Financial Management 1997 and Indeterminate Sentence Review Board 1989.)

The commission spent many hours discussing the legislature's directive that alternatives to total confinement be emphasized for nonviolent crimes. Ultimately, a conversion method was selected: all sentences under one year could be converted to partial confinement (confinement "for a substantial portion of each day with the balance spent in the community"), and up to thirty days of total confinement could be converted to community service at a rate of one day to eight hours (Wash. Rev. Code, title 9, chap. 94A, sec. 380 [2001]). The commission considered day fines but could not reach consensus on this recommendation. Bringing the conversion alternatives to the court's attention, the commission recommended that courts be required to indicate in the sentencing why alternative sanctions were not ordered. This was proposed as a way to learn how the courts viewed alternative sanctions in individual cases and if availability of alternatives in individual counties influenced judges' decisions. (Unfortunately, this requirement is viewed by practitioners and judges as unnecessary and has never been effective in influencing discretion.) These modest alternatives were to be all that were developed. The currency of punishment in Washington was to be confinement, and that judgment was not to change.

C. Population Forecast Shows Sufficient Capacity

By late fall 1983, the commission had a proposed set of guidelines, and its research database was complete, thus allowing the first projections of population impact. Commission members held their breath. The research director announced that the proposed guidelines were reconcilable in projected operation with prison capacity and would, by 1996, decrease the prison population by more than 40 percent to 4,076 (Lange 1982). For jails, the guidelines overall could be implemented within the allocated capacity for felons as long as alternatives to confinement were created (Sentencing Guidelines Commission 1983, p. 42).

For some, the projections seemed too good to be true. Washington had seen prison forecasts in the past "fine tuned" to support various political positions. The governor was the first to challenge the commission's work, telling the news media the forecast represented "blue sky figures" (*Tacoma News Tribune* 1983). The executive branch was worried that the legislature might cancel funding for a planned 500-bed prison. Corrections officials suggested that guidelines would, in fact, increase prison crowding and require even more prison beds than were needed under indeterminate sentencing (*Spokane Chronicle* 1983). The corrections secretary declared that "there's nothing scientific" about the forecast (Lange 1982).

From the other side, a citizen's group argued that the state should immediately cancel its plans for a new 500-bed prison. The commission advanced a more moderate option: continue with the planned new prison, but shelve additional prison construction plans. Here, the commission members' individual credibility was critical, in particular Norm Maleng's. Maleng was known as a prosecutor who would not compromise public safety—in this case, represented by adequate prison space. For Olympia insiders, the reputation of the research director, David Fallen, increased confidence in the prison space projections. Fallen was known to be an exceptional researcher who would never bend science for politics.

In the late fall of 1983, the commission reviewed the draft guidelines and, with the prison forecast showing some room for increases in sentence severity, adjusted some penalties upward. The range for second-degree burglary was increased, as the commission members knew that this felony affected more citizens than any other crime and was not experienced merely as a loss of property but as a personal threat.

The commission appeared before the 1983 legislature with a set of recommendations that could be implemented within existing resources and had been adopted unanimously. Commission leaders came to Olympia on numerous occasions, testifying before committees and meeting informally with the party caucuses. Panels of commission members met with editorial boards throughout the state. Norm Maleng played an active role in legislative negotiations. At a late point in the session, the proposed policy for multiple serious offenses came under scrutiny. Robert Lasnik understood that dissatisfaction with the guidelines on these serious cases could threaten the reform's political viability. He proposed consecutive sentencing for offenders with three or more serious violent offenses, and this amendment was accepted by commission representatives and the bill's sponsors. In April 1983, when the commission's guideline bill was passed, Washington joined the small but growing list of sentencing guidelines states.

D. Implementation

Commission leaders understood that implementation was their next challenge. Major system changes are especially vulnerable to political challenge during their early stages, when the cost of returning to the "old ways" is relatively modest. The commission's first task was to organize the law's complexities into a user-friendly publication. The commission created an implementation manual with individualized sentencing sheets for every major felony. By consulting one sheet, practitioners could identify the applicable scoring rules for criminal history, the sentencing range, and the available sentencing options for each case. This approach resolved concerns about the system's complexities.

Following the advice of staff and members of Minnesota's commission, the commission initiated a proactive media relations campaign (Parent 1988, pp. 136–46). Members met with reporters and editorial boards throughout the state to explain the act, its rationale, and the care with which it had been implemented.

Judicial opposition remained but was significantly moderated by the leadership of the four judges on the commission, all of whom were highly regarded by their peers. While initially skeptical about the wisdom of the Sentencing Reform Act, these judges worked hard to implement the legislature's intent; their support was a significant factor in the act's successful implementation.

Opposition among correctional officials, both state leaders and line staff, remained deep-seated. The reform's proponents believed that shifting from coerced to voluntary rehabilitation was an opportunity to refocus from surveillance to service delivery. The legislature did not increase funding for this purpose, however, and corrections officials did not redirect the state's organizational focus. When commission staff or members spoke to correctional groups and referred to the legislative intent that parolees receive voluntary services, the audiences broke into laughter. The law's emphasis on rehabilitation for first-time, nonviolent offenders was never enthusiastically implemented by the corrections department. Because many offenders in this group were considered at low risk to reoffend, services to this population appeared to many officers as superfluous. Instead, staff concentrated on enforcement of court orders.

In 1984, the department of corrections convinced the legislature that the reform's original provision that all prisoners exit prison through work release was unrealistic. Given that some offenders were poor public safety risks, work release instead became optional (Wash. Rev. Code, title 9, chap. 94A, sec. 150[5] [2001]). In later years, the department repeatedly returned to the legislature, seeking "reform" of the Sentencing Reform Act.

The commission encountered significant challenges in setting sentences for sex crimes, and it concentrated on this issue during the year between legislative adoption of the guidelines in 1983 and the next legislative session. Victim advocates argued that presumptive prison sentences for intrafamily crimes would be viewed as too harsh by the family and would discourage prosecution, and thus they favored an option combining supervision and outpatient treatment. Treatment providers pointed to the compulsive nature of these crimes and argued that without treatment, sex offenders would likely continue to reoffend after release (Lieb and Matson 1997, p. 85).

The commission's resolution exemplified the pragmatism that has characterized sentencing reform in Washington. Working with victim advocates and offender treatment providers, the commission crafted a sentencing option that permitted treatment for sex offenders without prior sex convictions (except those convicted of forcible rape). This "special sexual offender sentencing alternative" included a suspended prison sentence, the only instance in which this centerpiece of the former indeterminate system was authorized (Wash. Rev. Code, title 9, chap. 94A, sec. 120[8] [2001]). This sentencing option, along with more detailed sentencing guidelines for drug offenses, was adopted by the 1984 legislature. Thus, as with the first-time offender provisions in the original act, when state policy makers saw the need, Washington's reform employed the indeterminate system's mechanisms of coerced rehabilitation.

On the eve of implementation, Washington's guidelines received significant statewide and national attention. A columnist in the *Washington Post* noted that "those of us who have been calling for the reform and rationalization of criminal sentencing should just shut up for a while and watch Washington State. Virtually everything the reformers have been demanding is in the new law" (Raspberry 1984).

E. Prison Population

While implementation of the law went smoothly, the consequences for the prison population was dramatic. By 1985, the percent of violent offenders receiving state prison sentences had increased to 65 percent from the 1982 rate of 49 percent, while nonviolent offenders sent to prison declined from 13 percent to 9 percent (Fallen 1986, p. ix). Since 86 percent of all convictions were for nonviolent offenses, this shift reduced the state's overall imprisonment rate from 20 percent in 1982 to 17 percent in 1988 and significantly reduced prison commitments (Fallen 1986, p. 5).

At the same time, parole board releases of prisoners accelerated owing to court rulings in 1986. Prisoners successfully argued that the board was ignoring the legislative mandate that they consider sentencing guidelines in setting release dates, and the court's rulings required the board to reconsider its previous decisions (*In re Myers*, 105 Wn. 2d 257 [Wash. 1986] and *Addleman v. Board of Prison Terms and Paroles*, 107 Wn. 2d 503 [Wash. 1986]). By 1986, the Office of Financial Management estimated that the act had reduced prison inmates by 1,074 (15 percent of the total population) (Fallen 1986, p. 35). This was remarkably close to the commission's 1983 forecast.

Imprisonment rates began to drop. From 156 per 100,000 population in 1984, the rate decreased to 147 in 1986 and reached a low of 124 in 1988, a decrease of 20 percent during a period in which the national average increased by 30 percent, from 188 per 100,000 in 1984 to 244 in 1988. Washington dropped from twenty-fifth in the nation in imprisonment rates in 1984 to thirty-ninth in 1988 (Bureau of Justice Statistics 1998, p. 491).

Washington had the luxury of excess capacity. From 1987 to 1989, the state ran a "rent-a-cell" program with the federal government and other states; approximately 1,000 beds were rented. In this atmosphere, even though the excess capacity was generally known to be short-term, the legislature began to adopt a different attitude. With empty prison beds, the legislative debate on crime and the need to toughen sentences was not tempered by concerns about prison crowding.

Many local government representatives argued that the state had solved its crowding problem by shifting felons to local jails, whose funding was a local responsibility. The commission's research revealed that 20 percent of statewide jail space was dedicated to felons prior to the reform; the majority of jail beds were occupied by misdemeanants. For the first years after the reform, this distribution pattern for the state as a whole remained constant, although the effects varied for individual jails depending on whether they were above or below the state average in sending nonviolent offenders to prison. This research did not convince most local officials, however, nor were they persuaded when the commission found that jail population increases after the reform were primarily influenced by increases in misdemeanor convictions (Bell and Fallen 1990, p. ii). In this political atmosphere, legislative proposals for more severe sentences satisfied two political goals: getting tough on criminals and moving felons from local jails and budgets to state prisons.

F. The Courts Respond

There was a high degree of judicial compliance. In 1985, judges went outside the guidelines in only 3.5 percent of cases. Because the law allowed judicial discretion in the form of sentencing options for first-time and sex offenders, this statistic did not fully describe the exercise of discretion. By combining the decisions involving sentencing options with departure cases, the rate of sentences outside the presumptive range rose to almost 30 percent (Fallen 1986, p. 23). County-to-county variances in sentencing practices were significantly reduced (Fallen 1986, p. 16).

During the legislative debate on the act, critics argued that the state's trial rate would increase dramatically, since defendants no longer had an incentive to plead guilty. This prediction was not realized: the percentage of guilty pleas remained exactly the same in 1985 (90.1 percent) as it had been in 1982. The only changes were a slight decease in jury trials (7.8 percent in 1982, 6.7 percent in 1985) and a slight increase in bench trials (2.1 percent in 1982, 2.8 percent in 1995; Fallen 1986, p. 39; Sentencing Guidelines Commission 1995, p. 18).

G. Charging Practices

With sentencing guidelines, the crime of conviction became far more significant in determining the sentence. Soon after the reform's implementation, conviction patterns shifted (Fallen 1986; see table 1).

For eight of the nine seriousness levels calling for presumptive prison sentences, conviction rates were reduced postreform, supporting the thesis that prosecutors were exercising their discretion to reduce charges. Convictions of offenses with presumptive jail terms, however, reflect a mixed pattern more consistent with the typical variation from year to year. The changes for unranked crime patterns were notable. This category was created for low-frequency crimes whose widely varying nature justified greater judicial discretion. Since unranked crimes have a presumptive sentence range of zero to twelve months, a change of convictions from ranked seriousness levels to this unranked category significantly expanded judicial discretion. Over

TABLE 1

Changes in State Conviction Patterns (in Percent)

Seriousness Level	Fiscal Year 1982	Calendar Year 1985	Difference
Prison sentence:			
XIV	.2	.1	−.1
XIII	.5	.3	−.2
XII	.3	.4	+.1
XI	.1	.2	−.1
X	.9	.5	−.4
IX	5.6	3.5	−2.1
VIII	1.4	.9	−.5
VII	3.4	2.1	−1.3
VI	4.7	5.7	−1.0
Jail sentence:			
V	.8	.9	+.1
IV	10.6	9.5	−1.1
III	8.3	10.7	+2.4
II	34.5	32.2	−2.3
I	28.7	30.6	+1.9
Unranked	0.0	2.5	+2.5
Total	100.0	100.1	

time, this pattern was to become even more pronounced. Prosecutorial discretion was not only unconstrained but arguably increased in comparison to the discretion exercised by other actors in the criminal justice system (Boerner 1997).

H. The Appellate Courts

The first appellate decisions interpreting the reform were awaited with great interest. In its first decision in 1985, an appellate court upheld the act's key principles by reversing an aggravated exceptional sentence that relied on the explanation that an attempted escape had involved "sophisticated and well-planned methods" (*State v. Baker*, 700 P. 2d 1198 [Wash. App. 1985]). Because all attempted escapes involve planning, the court argued, this argument failed to meet the "substantial and compelling test" (*State v. Baker*, 700 P. 2d 1198 [Wash. App. 1985]).

Early decisions also held that factors used in determining the presumptive range (crime and criminal history) could not be used as a justification for an exceptional sentence (*State v. Hartley*, 705 P. 2d 821 [Wash. App. 1985]) and that uncharged conduct could not justify an exceptional sentence (*State v. Harp*, 717 P. 2d 282 [Wash. App. 1986]). In 1986, the Washington Supreme Court unanimously declared the Sentencing Reform Act constitutional, stating that "the trial court's discretion in sentencing is that which is given by the Legislature" (*State v. Ammons*, 718 P. 2d 796 [Wash. App. 1986]). "The legislative wisdom of the Sentencing Reform Act," said the court of appeals, "is not the subject for judicial review" (*State v. Fisher*, 715 P. 2d 530 [Wash. App. 1986]).

By 1986 implementation was complete and the Sentencing Reform Act was an accepted feature of the criminal justice landscape. The reform was widely acknowledged as effective in accomplishing its objectives, even by those who did not share those objectives.

III. The Return of the Legislature, 1986–92

The legislature, which accepted the recommendations of the sentencing commission in every instance from 1983 to 1986, in 1987 began to reassert its primacy. The leaders of the coalition that produced the Sentencing Reform Act in 1981 had left the legislature by this time, and new perspectives became influential. Two issues were prominent: reassessment of sentence lengths for some crimes and reconsideration of postrelease supervision. Washington's experience would prove the prescience of Zimring's assertion that "it takes no more than an eraser" to change sentence lengths in a determinate sentencing system (Zimring 1977, p. 13).

A. Increased Sentence Length

The first change was symbolically important, although it affected few cases. In 1985, the Washington Cattleman's Association approached the commission regarding the sentence range for theft of livestock, "rustling" in the vernacular. The commission had set the presumptive sentence range at Seriousness Level II, the same as Theft in the First Degree (over $1,500). The cattlemen believed this ranking, which called for a presumptive sentence of zero-to-ninety days for first offenders, was a grossly inadequate response to sophisticated armed "rustlers." The commission's initial response was that exceptional sentences could handle these cases, and, thus, no statutory changes were necessary. The cattlemen were not appeased and the debate took on a rural versus urban tension, with the cattlemen arguing that most commission representatives lived in cities and were therefore insensitive to the realities and dangers of rural life.

The commission spent considerable time determining how to respond to the cattlemen without violating the proportionality of the guidelines. Ultimately, the group proposed two degrees of theft of livestock—first degree for theft with the intent to sell and second degree for theft for personal use. Presumptive sentence ranges were increased to three-to-nine months for first degree and one-to-three months for second degree (Wash. Rev. Code, title 9A, chap. 56, sec. 080 [2001]). The impact was small (an average of two convictions per year), but the resolution troubled some commission members who believed the body had sacrificed its principles to political expediency.

1. *Drug Offenses.* Political attention turned in late 1985 toward the harm caused by crack cocaine in particular, and by drug dealers in general. The initial sentence range for delivery of Schedule 1 drugs (heroin, cocaine, and other similar drugs) called for first-time offenders to receive a prison sentence (twelve to fourteen months); the first-time offender waiver allowed a zero-to-ninety-day period of confinement plus a year of supervision. By 1986, commission data showed that many offenders convicted of these crimes were receiving the waiver and avoiding a prison sentence. Norm Maleng led an effort to eliminate this sentencing option for such crimes. He consistently took the position that those who "deal" drugs deserve prison and saw the extensive use of the first-time offender waiver as inconsistent with this goal. It appeared that this adjustment would satisfy the political appetite for increased sentence severity, maintain proportionality within the sentencing grid, and simultaneously reinforce the reform's political viability by adjusting to changed views of crime seriousness.

Not everyone on the commission agreed with Maleng's argument, but all respected his political skills and understood the likely popularity of his position with the legislature. He informed the commission that the prosecutors intended to propose this amendment, but the commission did not formally consider the matter and did not testify. The proposal was adopted by a strong bipartisan majority and took effect in 1987.

The commission's decision to abstain on this issue was, at least to some observers, motivated by a desire to maintain the group's political cohesion and maintain credibility with the legislature. Given the departure of the reform's original legislative proponents, some commission members worried that taking politically unpopular positions would weaken the body's influence in future sentencing debates. As noted by Wright (1998, p. 458), commissions have limited political capital and must select their political battles. In our opinion, the commission accurately assessed its political position; abstaining, however, did not protect the commission's declining political influence.

Concerns about drug offenses did not subside. By 1988, the commission's prosecutors convinced the group to revisit the sentencing ranges for these crimes. The commission recommended that the 1989 legislature increase the seriousness levels (and thus, the presumptive sentence length) for certain drug offenses. Its recommendation was incorporated into an omnibus bill developed and supported by a bipartisan group of legislators. When the legislation passed in 1989, the presumptive sentence ranges for first-offense delivery of drugs increased from 12–14 months to 21–27 months, the offender score points for prior drug convictions were increased, and a twenty-four-month enhancement was added for deliveries occurring within 1,000 feet of a school or a school bus stop or in a public park.

With some penalty increases, the impact on state prison populations is delayed because the increased confinement times show up in the future. In this instance, however, an increased volume of drug convictions occurred in the state at the same time as the penalty change, thus multiplying the population consequences. In combination with the impact of an average one-year sentence for drug deliveries becoming a two-year sentence, the results were dramatic. The number of convictions for drug offenses doubled between 1985 and 1987 and then doubled again between 1987 and 1989. Prison admissions for drug offenses increased from 143 in 1986 to 1,139 in 1989. By 1990, they reached 1,565 and constituted 37 percent of all prison admissions (Washington State Department of Corrections 1996, p. 3).

2. *Sex Offenses.* In 1986, the commission established a subcommittee to reconsider penalties and criminal code definitions for sex offenses. Under the indeterminate system, the wide-ranging discretion of judges and the parole board had been used to adjust penalties to individual circumstances. With determinate sentencing, the criminal code definitions became more critical. The King County Prosecutor's Office had a special assault unit that aggressively prosecuted sex offenses. The unit chief convinced the subcommittee that changes to the criminal code and penalties were necessary, given the harm caused to victims. The commission endorsed the subcommittee's proposed changes. The commission's 1987 legislative proposal was passed in one house but later stalled because of concerns about the need for more

prison beds to accommodate the increased number of prisoners. In 1988, the commission's recommendations were slightly revised and introduced by the legislator who had blocked passage the previous year. This legislation passed without controversy.

In 1989, the legislature again revisited sentencing laws for sex offenders. The kidnapping and mutilation of a child by a released sex offender became a topic of intense public attention, causing the governor to establish a special Task Force on Community Protection. The task force, which included sentencing commission members and was chaired by Norm Maleng, reviewed the state's criminal and mental health laws to determine policy options. The offender involved in the controversial child kidnapping had been released from prison after serving his maximum sentence. His declared intent, before release, to harm children greatly concerned corrections officials, but the threats were considered neither immediate enough to warrant a mental health commitment nor specific enough to warrant criminal prosecution.

The political environment demanded a solution for dangerous offenders about to be released from prison, as well as for sex offenders who would be sentenced in the future. The task force presented a package of proposals to the 1990 legislature, including increases in the presumptive sentence range for sex crimes, reduction of time off for good behavior, and a narrowly focused authorization for indefinite civil commitment for sexually violent predators who completed their prison sentences. Washington's attorney general proposed legislation to enact indeterminate life sentences for all serious violent offenses but did not invest any political capital in promoting his proposal. Task force leaders argued that a return to indeterminate sentencing would leave the state in a powerless position for offenders previously sentenced who exited prison with clear intent to harm and was thus only a partial remedy. The history of the task force's deliberations is detailed in a previous essay (Boerner 1992). The task force's recommendations were unanimously adopted by the legislature in 1990.

Despite these changes, the provisions allowing treatment in the community for sex offenders remained intact. As sentence lengths increased, the eligibility criteria were adjusted so that offenders previously eligible would continue to be eligible. This option retained the strong political support of the victim community, who successfully argued that its availability was essential for successful prosecution of intrafamily sexual abuse.

B. Postrelease Supervision

Washington's 1981 reform legislation abolished both parole and probation. Offenders who completed prison terms were to be released; in instances where work release was a reasonable public safety risk, offenders were to spend time in work release as a transition phase, then exit the system. Three central arguments justified this policy change. First, supervision by parole officers was said not to be helpful in reducing reoffending, but it gave corrections staff extensive discretion to set conditions and impose punishment on selected offenders, with little oversight. Second, parolees were eligible for voluntary services to assist their readjustment. Third, the state must limit its promises to citizens to those that are achievable and realistic. Ex-offenders decide whether to commit new crimes, and the state has relatively little influence on these decisions. The drafters believed that the effectiveness of supervision over released offenders was modest, at best, and highly unlikely to deter crime.

Judges could impose "community supervision" for up to one year, but the authority of courts to order affirmative conditions, such as participation in treatment or school, was severely restricted under the reform. The act authorized only "crime-related prohibitions" (Wash. Rev. Code, title 9, chap. 94A, sec. 030[11] [2001]) and "other sentence conditions authorized by the Act" as conditions of sentence, except with first-time offenders and certain sex offenders. For all other crimes, judges were authorized to impose a one-year term of "community supervision" during which the offender was "subject to crime-related prohibitions and other sentence conditions imposed pursuant" to the act (Wash. Rev. Code, title 9, chap. 94A, sec. 030[8] [2001]). Since those conditions did not include affirmative conduct or the obligation not to commit new crimes, the authority of corrections officers to seek sanctions for violations was substantially reduced. The intent was to replace the "former system of coerced rehabilitation with a system of facilitative rehabilitation" that was "offered but not compelled" (Boerner 1985, pp. 4–6). New crimes were to be prosecuted and charged.

1. *Correctional Officers.* It is not surprising that corrections officials did not share the reformers' views about parole. In 1986, Chase Riveland became secretary of the department of corrections, having previously served as a correctional administrator in Wisconsin and Colorado. Riveland argued that the act seriously restricted correctional

officers' ability to protect the public and left officers powerless as they observed released offenders headed toward criminal acts.

In 1986, a prominent state senator indicated interest in sponsoring a bill that resurrected postrelease supervision. Members of the commission met with him to explain the reformers' rationale for eliminating parole and to try to persuade him to drop the bill. The senator informed the commission that postrelease supervision was essential to public safety and that his judgment on state policy was more in tune with citizens' views than the commission's judgment.

The senator sponsored legislation to reinstate postrelease supervision, which did not pass. He then spearheaded a citizen's initiative drive. The measure did not gather sufficient signatures to appear on the ballot. Following the meeting with the commission, the senator worked assiduously to restrict the body's capacity and political credibility. He proposed numerous amendments to reduce the agency's operating budget, to limit the staff director to a half-time position, and to alter the body's authority. Although the amendments were often withdrawn before a vote, they sent a clear message of disapproval of the agency and of the senator's perception of the commission's arrogance.

2. *Amending the Act.* The senator and the department of corrections crafted a bill for the 1987 session to reauthorize postrelease supervision. The commission realized that opposing the bill altogether was unlikely to stop it, so commission representatives negotiated with the department of corrections to make the proposal as consistent as possible with the act. The result was a bill authorizing a one-year period of postrelease supervision for offenders convicted of serious crimes (offenses committed while armed, sex offenses, and drug offenses). The legislation passed in 1988, with expanded discretion for courts to order offenders to work, not to use or possess controlled substances, and to attend "crime-related treatment or counseling services" (Wash. Rev. Code, title 9, chap. 94A, sec. 120[8] [2001]).

Commission representatives successfully persuaded legislators that requiring offenders to "obey all laws" during this period of supervision was unwise, because prosecutors would lose some incentive to pursue new convictions, knowing that the behavior also qualified as a violation of sentence conditions and therefore the system could far more easily impose punishment under that label. A relatively complex scheme of supervision was developed that differentiated between offenders who did and did not earn good time; those released early because of good time were under administrative rather than court authority.

Thus, once again, Washington's sentencing policies were pragmatically recast. Supervision after release was authorized, but selectively (a third of prison releases initially, rising to 68 percent by 2000), with sanctions for violations limited to the unserved portion of the original sentence (good time could reduce the period of incarceration by up to one-third) or sixty days per violation. The amendments granted no authority to reduce sentence lengths or conditions.

C. Prison Population and Sentence Lengths

By 1992, felony convictions had increased to 18,067, an increase of 127 percent from 7,953 in 1985. Average sentence lengths returned to 1985 levels, with an average prison sentence length of 44 months in 1992 (43.91 months in 1985) and an average jail sentence length of 2.8 months (2.55 months in 1985). The imprisonment rate, which had fallen to 124 per 100,000 population in 1988, began to climb, reaching 192 in 1992. This represented a 23 percent increase over the rate of 156 in 1983, the last preguideline year. This rate of growth, however, was far lower than the national increase of 75 percent from 188 to 330 per 100,000 population in the same period. Prison population continued to increase, reaching 9,930 in 1992 (Sentencing Guidelines Commission 1992*b*, p. iii; Bureau of Justice Statistics 1998, p. 491).

The guidelines' initial success in reducing the prison population provided a climate that enabled the legislature to revisit sentence lengths set in 1984. Significantly, while each change increased sentence length, each change used the guidelines to target particular crimes. This pattern has held; unlike Minnesota and other states (Frase 1993, p. 293), Washington has not had an across-the-board increase—or decrease—in sentence lengths.

IV. The Populist Era, 1992–95

Washington's political system reflects its populist origins. The first provision of the state constitution declares that "All political power is inherent in the people" (Washington Constitution, art. 1, sec. 1). The "people's power" has been jealously guarded and frequently exercised. In 1993 and again in 1995, the people of Washington exercised their "inherent" power to bring back mandatory sentences for certain offenders.

The nation's first "three strikes and you're out" law appeared as an initiative in Washington, along with a second initiative related to felonies committed with a firearm. The 1981 Sentencing Reform Act had repealed Washington's previous broad mandatory minimum provisions and also its habitual criminal act, leaving only three mandatory minimum terms—murder in the first degree (not less than twenty years), assault in the first degree (not less than five years), and rape in the first degree (not less than three years) (Wash. Rev. Code, title 9, chap. 94A, sec. 120[4] [2001]).

A. Three Strikes

Mandatory sentences retained their political popularity in Washington. In 1992, a bill was introduced providing for mandatory life sentences—with release possible only upon a gubernatorial pardon or commutation—following the third conviction of a "most serious offense," which included most crimes of violence. Many leaders in the criminal justice system opposed the proposal; few, however, expressed their opinions openly. Elected officials judged the measure's political support as unstoppable (Wright 1998, pp. 451–53). The sentencing commission offered an alternative, which narrowed the provision's scope considerably. Both proposals failed when the legislature was unable to resolve the differences.

The measure was promoted by a conservative Washington think tank, which turned next to the initiative process. Any proposition may be placed on the ballot with sufficient voter signatures (8 percent of the previous general election's voters). Initiatives are common in Washington, as in most western states—in 1993, for example, voters also adopted measures concerning term limits and freedom of reproductive choice. The "three strikes" initiative easily qualified for the 1992 ballot and passed with over 75 percent of the state vote, carrying each of Washington's thirty-nine counties (Boerner 1997, p. 31).

Washington's "three strikes" law is narrower than those subsequently passed in many other states. It imposes a mandatory life sentence, without reduction by good time or parole, on the third separate conviction of a designated group of "most serious offenses" including homicide, serious assaults, most sex offenses, robbery, any crime committed with a deadly weapon, and repeat drug offenses (Wash. Rev. Code, title 9, chap. 94A, sec. 120[4] [2001]). Because each conviction must meet this criterion, its scope is narrowed considerably. By contrast, Washington's former habitual criminal law applied on the third conviction of any felony.

When the law was passed, state forecasters estimated that it would affect eighty offenders a year. The prison population increases would not appear immediately, however, because such offenders were already subject to long prison terms. The state estimated prison population increases of 134 in 2000, 407 in 2005, and 673 in 2010 (Boerner 1997, p. 31).

These estimates, in fact, proved to be quite high. Convictions have averaged 30 per year (1995 = 36, 1996 = 33, 1997 = 32, 1998 = 25, 1999 = 23, 2000 = 31; Sentencing Guidelines Commission 2000*b*). The average age at conviction was thirty-eight; robbery was the most frequent "third strike" conviction (50 percent), followed by assault (20 percent), and rape (10 percent) (Sentencing Guidelines Commission 1999*a*).

B. "Hard Time for Armed Crime"

Encouraged by the success of "three strikes," the same initiative sponsors returned to the legislature in 1994 with an initiative concerning weapon use in crimes. Titled "Hard Time for Armed Crime," this initiative proposed a two-tiered system of mandatory prison sentence enhancements for felons committing crimes while armed with a deadly weapon. Those armed with a weapon other than a firearm would receive a basic enhancement of six to twenty-four months, depending on the class of felony. For crimes involving firearms, the enhancements would range from eighteen to sixty months. For repeat offenses, enhancements would be doubled. All enhancements were consecutive and to be served without time reductions for good behavior. Sentence ranges for three firearm-related crimes would be increased (reckless endangerment, theft of a firearm, and unlawful possession of a firearm). First-degree burglary would be broadened to include crimes in any building, not just residences.

The initiative also made criminal justice decisions more public. Prosecutors were required to make public their reasons for plea bargains, and the sentencing commission was required to publish sentences imposed by individual judges.

The projected impact of the "hard time" initiative was far greater than the impact of "three strikes." The sentencing commission estimated population increases of 209 in the first year, 810 by the fifth year, and 1,145 by the tenth year. The capital and operating expenditure requirements were estimated at $64 million the first biennium, $57 million the second, $68 million the third, $50 million the fourth, and $55 million the fifth—a total increase of $294 million over the first decade (Boerner 1997, p. 33).

Washington law allows the legislature two choices when initiatives gain the necessary signatures: adopt the initiative as proposed, or adopt an alternative and place both the initiative and the legislative alternative on the ballot. Legislative leaders believed a more moderate alternative would be defeated, and none was proposed. With the memory of the people's overwhelming vote on "three strikes" in mind, by strong bipartisan majorities, the legislature adopted the initiative (Van Wagenen 2001, p. 6).

C. Publication of Judges' Sentencing Decisions

The initiative's direction to the sentencing commission regarding judicial sentencing patterns was very specific. The initiative required that the commission record each judge's sentences for all violent crimes and those involving deadly weapons. When the commission had set up its original database, the group decided not to record judges' names with each sentence. The judicial members successfully argued that such information could be used to unduly pressure judges who were, after all, operating within discretion granted by the legislature. Since there was no requirement for judge-specific data in the original act, this decision had been uncontroversial, both inside the commission and outside.

The commission first responded to the legislative direction by publishing the total number of standard range sentences imposed by individual judges, with detailed information on each exceptional sentence (Sentencing Guidelines Commission 1996). The initiative's chief proponents objected strongly, both to the limitations of the information and to its timing, since it was released after the election cycle. Subsequent reports covered each judge's felony sentences, and publication was advanced to September of each year.

Up to this point, commission publications and data on judicial sentencing patterns have not been the focus of a judicial election campaign. The evidence as to whether judges' decision making has been influenced is more ambiguous. The overall rate of exceptional sentences has increased slightly since the reporting requirement was adopted, but the percentage of mitigated departures steadily declined until recently (Sentencing Guidelines Commission 2000*a;* see fig. 2).

The initiative's requirement that prosecutors make their reasons for plea bargains public has had no discernible effect. No organized system exists for recording plea bargaining reasons, and judges do not routinely require prosecutors to indicate why they enter into bargains.

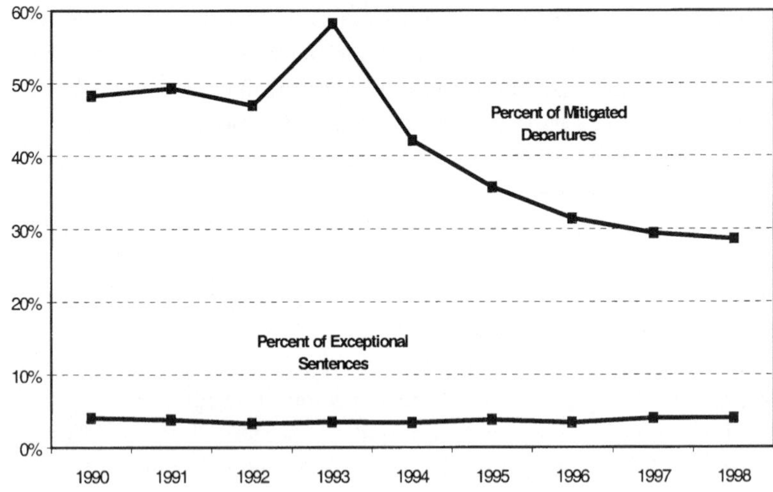

FIG. 2.—Rate of mitigated departures has declined since adoption of reporting requirement.

The sentencing commission's report on judicial sentencing indicates whether the prosecutor agreed with or opposed an exceptional sentence. The nonimplementation of this initiative provision has not attracted criticism. For the initiative sponsors at least, concerns about leniency toward criminals was focused on judges, not prosecutors. Although complaints that judges are "soft on crime" are not uncommon, such criticisms are seldom lodged against prosecutors. Prosecutors are far more likely to be seen as allies in a "get tough" movement (Boerner 1995, p. 198).

Although Washington's citizen initiatives have substantially influenced state sentencing policy, their impact pales in comparison with Oregon's experience. In that state, initiatives directed toward sentencing-related topics have been frequent. Initiatives have become the primary force in Oregon sentencing policy, easily eclipsing the state's sentencing guidelines (Rosenblum 1995, p. 177; Greene 1997, p. 3).

Felony convictions continued to increase during this period, reaching 20,619 in 1995, a 14.1 percent increase over 1992. The average prison sentence length increased to 47.5 months (an 8.2 percent increase over 1992), while the average jail sentence length dropped slightly (from 2.8 months in 1992 to 2.7 months in 1995). The imprisonment rate increased by 10 percent, from 192 per 100,000 in 1992 to 212 per 100,000 in 1995, once again significantly lower than the 25.6

percent increase nationwide from 330 per 100,000 in 1992 to 411 per 100,000 in 1995. Prison population continued to increase, reaching 11,440 (Sentencing Guidelines Commission 1995, p. 10; Bureau of Justice Statistics 1998, p. 491).

V. The Revival of Reform, 1995–2000

The "reform" of the 1981 act has not been limited to changes originated by citizens. Beginning in 1993, the legislature adopted amendments that primarily have increased officials' discretion and authorized sentences that are arguably inconsistent with the core principles of the original act. Three of the changes—boot camp legislation, special provisions (based on drug court rationales) for drug possession offenders, and increased flexibility for non-state-prison sentences—decreased sentence severities and increased judicial discretion. One provision increased the role of risk predictions and increased community corrections officials' discretion. A "two-strikes" provision for serious second sexual offenses increased sentence severity and weakened proportionality protections. Each change, however, employed the structure of the act, and none repealed any portion of the original act.

A. Boot Camps

In 1993, the legislature endorsed the boot camp concept as a means to add structure and discipline to offenders' lives in the hopes of improving their productivity after release. Washington's version became known as a "work ethic camp"; judges could recommend it for those facing prison terms up to three years. If the offender agreed to participate and was accepted by the department of corrections, he or she was credited with three days for each day in the camp, with the balance served on supervised release. Offenders who failed to complete the camp, or did not comply with release conditions, would serve the remainder of the original prison sentence.

While the authorizing legislation did not use the terms "probation" or "parole," the sentence was not determinate. This was the first provision since adoption of the Special Sex Offender Sentencing Alternative in 1984 to authorize indeterminate sentences. It also was the first to reduce penalties.

The program was widely viewed as a desirable option for several years and reached a daily census of 199 in July 1999. By September of 2000, participation was reduced to 57 offenders because offenders and judges preferred a drug sentencing option that we describe in the next subsection (Washington State Department of Corrections FY2000 and 2001, Table 1-A).

B. Drug Sentences

The second change that reduced sentence severity involved drug sentences. The 1987 and 1989 increases in drug sentence severity, combined with a substantial increase in drug convictions, caused drug offenders in the prison population to increase from 16 percent of the prison population in 1990 to 25 percent in 1994. The political discussion about drug crimes reflected a growing awareness that heavy reliance on incarceration for these crimes was expensive and did not resolve some offenders' underlying problems of drug addiction.

In 1991, the Washington State Department of Corrections proposed legislation for a Drug Offender Sentencing Alternative. The legislation was originally supported by the governor as a means to counter the escalating prison population and respond more appropriately to persons with chemical dependencies. The bill was opposed by many people, including prosecutors and members of the sentencing commission, who were concerned that it violated the principles of determinate sentencing. Ultimately, the governor withdrew the proposal and requested that the sentencing commission prepare recommendations for the 1992 legislative session that "provide a renewed emphasis on alternatives to total confinement in jail or prison for non-violent offenders, particularly with respect to strengthening our ability to deal with nonviolent substance abusers whose criminal activity is limited to or caused by that abuse" (Gardner 1991, p. 2). A commission subcommittee spent several months considering options and ultimately proposed creation of a drug offender sentencing option; a separate subcommittee proposed a nonviolent offender option that included an expanded range of alternative sanctions (Sentencing Guidelines Commission 1992*a*, pp. 19–22).

The commission as a whole endorsed the proposals and submitted them to the 1992 legislature. The legislation was opposed by the prosecutors' association and did not move from the assigned legislative committee.

In late 1993 and 1994, the national experiments with drug courts attracted the interest of Washington criminal justice leaders. King County started a drug court in 1994 and was followed by other counties. The judge for King County's drug court, Ricardo Martinez, was a judicial member of the sentencing commission. Judge Martinez earlier served as a deputy prosecutor in King County, where he headed the office's drug unit. Because of his background and his drug court experiences, Judge Martinez was a persuasive advocate for treatment alternatives.

By 1995, Norm Maleng agreed to promote a drug sentencing alternative and organized a diverse coalition of supporters, including law enforcement officials and the sponsors of the "three strikes" and "hard time" initiatives. The proposal for a "Special Drug Offender Sentencing Alternative," modeled loosely on the "Special Sex Offender Sentencing Alternative," combined a drug treatment option for those persons with drug addictions while retaining the concept of "prison sentences for dealers," a consistent feature of Maleng's sentencing priorities. The alternative authorized judges to waive the standard sentence for first-time drug offenders and impose a prison sentence of one-half of the standard range followed by one year of community-based drug treatment. Those who violated conditions of the community portion of the sentence could be returned to prison for the remaining one-half of the standard range (Wash. Rev. Code, title 9, chap. 94A, sec. 120 [2001]).

This alternative sentence was projected to reduce the prison population by 196 in its second year, 240 in its third, 258 in its fourth year, then stabilizing at a reduction of 275. More significant was that this was only the second change to the Sentencing Reform Act since 1984 to reduce the severity of sentences. In practice, use of the alternative initially fell far short of the projections; only 15 percent of eligible cases received the alternative sentence in 1995–96 (Engen and Steiger 1997, p. vii).

In 1999, the legislature modified the provision to expand its use. A sentencing commission study found that judges and prosecutors preferred the work ethic camp option over the drug treatment sentence because it was simple and flexible; defendants and their attorneys preferred it because it involved less confinement time (Du and Phipps 1997, p. 15). The 1999 amendments excluded defendants convicted of drug offenses from the work ethic camp and authorized judges to set conditions prohibiting the offender from using alcohol or controlled substances and requiring performance of other affirmative conditions. In doing so, the legislature created exceptions to several core policies of the Sentencing Reform Act, as had previously been done for first-time offenders and sex offenders. Drug offenders became the third category of offenses exempted from the just deserts philosophy. The amendments immediately increased use of this alternative; in 2000, 895 offenders received this sentencing option.

C. Two Strikes

In 1996, the legislature extended the principle of the "three strikes" initiative to those convicted of a second serious sex offense. This action was not taken in response to a particular case but reflected instead the view that sex recidivists were particularly dangerous and intractable. In 1997, the listed sex offenses were expanded to include serious sex offenses against children. Upon the second conviction of these designated offenses, a mandatory sentence of life imprisonment must be imposed. The "two strikes" provision has been sparingly applied. One defendant received a "two strikes" sentence in 1997, two in 1998, four in 1999, and eight in 2000.

D. Local Discretion

In a little-discussed addition to a bill authorizing drug treatment sentences, the legislature relaxed the strictness of the Sentencing Reform Act on sentences of less than one year. Unlike Minnesota's guidelines, in which the presumptive sentence ranges applied only to prison sentences, Washington's applied to all felony sentences and thus regulated both jail and prison sentences.

The act had always authorized judges to convert any jail sentence (total confinement of one year or less) to partial confinement (work or an education release) and to convert up to thirty days of total confinement to community service at the rate of eight hours of community service for one day of total confinement. Local officials have long believed that the Sentencing Reform Act has caused upward-spiraling jail costs and have argued that meeting those financial obligations leaves them without resources to develop alternative sanctions.

The 1999 legislature added a cryptic but potentially powerful sentence to the provisions of the Sentencing Reform Act governing alternatives to total confinement: "For offenders convicted of non-violent and non-sex offenses, the court may authorize county jails to convert jail confinement to an available county supervised community option and may require the offender to perform affirmative conduct pursuant to RCW 9.94A.129" (Wash. Rev. Code, title 9, chap. 94A, sec. 380[3] [2001]).

No definition of "county supervised community option" was provided, but there is a clear intent to maximize local discretion. Correctional resources at the county level are the fiscal responsibility of county government, and no state funding accompanied the expansion of direction. To date, little implementation has occurred, but planning efforts are under way in several counties.

E. Risk-Based Supervision

The 1999 legislature adopted a more fundamental—and far-reaching—policy change addressing correctional supervision of offenders in the community. The "Offender Accountability Act" was proposed by Joseph Lehman, who became the secretary of the department of corrections after serving as the head of corrections in Pennsylvania and Maine. Motivated by the success of community policing in the United States, as well as calls by some correctional leaders for a "shift in the missions of correctional agencies" (Smith and Dickey 1999, p. 7), the corrections chief argued that public safety could be increased by altering the authority and focus of community corrections staff.

The Offender Accountability Act represents a major shift in policy, primarily by returning discretion to correctional officers, but it does not represent either a return to indeterminate sentencing or a total rejection of just deserts principles. First, no change is made in the term of confinement imposed at sentencing. It retains a determinate term, subject only to reductions based on "good time" calculations. Judges have no greater discretion over the length of confinement than previously under the Sentencing Reform Act, nor over the length of community custody; the judge must impose a sentence within the range of community custody established by the sentencing commission. Judicial discretion is expanded in setting conditions of supervision; conditions can now require affirmative conduct, although they must be "reasonably related to the circumstances of the offense" (Wash. Rev. Code, title 9, chap. 94A, sec. 715 [2001]).

The discretion of corrections officers was substantially increased. For the first time under the Sentencing Reform Act, they have authority to impose conditions without judicial approval, modify or delete conditions without judicial approval (although not with regard to judicially imposed conditions), and reduce, although not lengthen, the term of community custody and discharge the offender without judicial approval.

Coupled with this increase in discretion is a fundamental shift in the basis on which discretion is to be exercised. Prior to the Offender Accountability Act, the only explicit authority for considering risk for reoffending was in the context of exceptional sentences or sex offenders.

In 1991, the Washington Supreme Court had held that "if future dangerousness is to be considered an aggravating factor in determining the sentence for non-sexual offense cases, it is the Legislature's province to make such a decision" (*State v. Barnes*, 818 P. 2d 1088 [1991]).

The legislation directs the department of corrections to concentrate its nonprison resources on higher-risk offenders—those in the top quarter of the risk pool. In authorizing the use of "risk assessment," the legislature accepted the view of the department of corrections—supported by the sentencing commission—that risk prediction accuracy had sufficiently improved since the reform was enacted to warrant a reversal in state policy. The department testified during legislative hearings that actuarial risk prediction is far superior to informal judgments (Grove and Meehl 1996). The state's move toward risk assessment is one of the four conceptions of sentencing and corrections identified by Tonry (1999) as currently coexisting in the United States.

The department plans to implement its new authority aggressively. Pilot projects are under way in which community corrections officers work directly with police officers in a model based on community policing concepts. The department's intent—and the expanded authority granted by the legislature—are in accord with the "new penology" described by Lyons (1999) and Simon and Feeley (1992). At its core, this approach emphasizes surveillance and containment. Its purpose is public safety, not just deserts, although in Washington it will function within boundaries established by just deserts. The expanded discretion in the act will function primarily to increase sentence severity. By increasing the range and nature of allowable sentence conditions, the state also has expanded its authority to intervene when there are violations and impose consequences.

F. Prison Population and Sentence Length

Felony convictions continued to increase, reaching 24,391 in 1999, an 18.3 percent increase over 1995. The average prison sentence length decreased to 44.2 months (a 6.9 percent decrease from 1995), while the average jail sentence length increased slightly (from 2.7 months in 1995 to 2.8 months in 1999). Imprisonment rates increased by 18.4 percent, from 212 per 100,000 population in 1995 to 251 per 100,000 in 1999, slightly more than the 15.8 percent national increase from 411 per 100,000 in 1995 to 476 per 100,000 in 1999 (Sentencing Guidelines Commission 1999*b*, p. 9; Bureau of Justice Statistics 2000, p. 3).

VI. Reflections

In a democracy, resolution of policy issues is inherently political, and sentencing reform in Washington has been a political process in which the legislature reasserted its primacy. The initial reform, now almost two decades old, employed presumptive guidelines to "structure but not eliminate discretionary decisions affecting sentences" (Wash. Rev. Code, title 9, chap. 94A, sec. 010 [2001]). The structure remains intact, and the state continues to operate with a sentencing grid that weighs offense seriousness and an offender score, and produces an applicable sentencing range. Sentencing policies, however, have repeatedly been modified. The central issues do not change, but their resolution, by various decision makers, over time, does change.

Washington's experience has been one of continuous change, with every issue—and its resolution—potentially in political play. This, of course, is neither new nor unique to Washington. Sentencing has always been inherently political. What is distinctive about Washington—and we suggest other guideline states—is that legislative policy direction has shifted from the "big picture" issues to detailed particulars—with rules governing everything from the weight given to prior convictions to the conditions of supervision to determining eligibility for a boot camp.

Pragmatism has always trumped philosophical purity in this state. Washington's initial reform was radical for its time—it rejected the premises of the indeterminate model and adopted a system based on just deserts that significantly constrained the discretion of judges and correctional officials. Subsequent changes exhibit a more complex pattern. Many have resolved issues within the just deserts paradigm, while others have incorporated concepts from other models. However, the fundamental structure of the reform has been retained. Perhaps this approach had political advantages because it involved incremental adjustments and did not threaten institutional stability. Seen this way, the structure of Washington's sentencing guidelines is agnostic as to how fundamental issues of sentencing should be resolved, but it is powerfully effective at implementing whatever resolution is produced by the political process (Boerner 1993).

The effects of so much change have produced a sentencing system far more complex than the original proposal. Changes have focused on particular crimes or groups of crimes and were largely, at least originally, consistent with the legislature's original direction to "emphasize confinement for the violent offender" (Wash. Rev. Code, title 9, chap. 94A, sec. 040[5] [2001]).

A. Prison Population Changes

Since the 1984 guidelines took effect, felony convictions increased by 206.7 percent, from 7,953 in 1985 to 24,391 in 1999. Average prison sentence length remained essentially level (43.9 months in 1985 compared with 44.2 months in 1999), while the percentage of convicted felons receiving prison rather than jail sentences went from 16.6 percent in 1985 to 29.1 percent in 1999, an increase of 75.3 percent. The rate of imprisonment per 100,000 population also increased, but at a lower rate. From a level of 156 per 100,000 population in 1985, imprisonment rates reached a level of 251 per 100,000 in 1999, an increase of 60.9 percent (Sentencing Guidelines Commission 1999*b*, p. 9).

The significance of these increases becomes apparent when the data are compared with national trends. The national imprisonment rate increased by 138 percent, from 200 per 100,000 population in 1985 to 476 per 100,000 in 1999. Washington's increase was less than one-half of the national average increase. The political climate in Washington was not significantly different from that in the rest of the country. Passions ran high and the public mood became increasingly punitive. What was different, we submit, was that the structure of the guidelines focused those punitive instincts on specific categories of crime. Not once during the entire period was there an across-the-board increase in sentence severity. Washington's guidelines thus seem to have moderated the public's punitive passion, not by attempting to deny it, but by channeling it more narrowly than would otherwise have happened. The policy changes aimed at increasing prison use did so, but primarily for the targeted offenses, as figures 3 and 4 show. Figures 3 and 4 display the state's prison admissions over time and the forecasted changes attributed to each sentencing amendment enacted through 1998.

Evaluations of sentencing guidelines nationally have found similar effects in guideline states in which prison populations were explicitly considered (Marvel 1995, p. 707; Reitz 2001, pp. 12–13). Washington's experience, however, is even more striking when compared with its fellow early guideline states, Minnesota and Pennsylvania. The imprisonment rate in Minnesota increased 123 percent from 1985 to 1999 (from 56 per 100,000 population in 1985 to 125 per 100,000 in 1999). In Pennsylvania, the rate increased by 156 percent (from 119 per 100,000 in 1985 to 305 per 100,000 in 1999) (Bureau of Justice

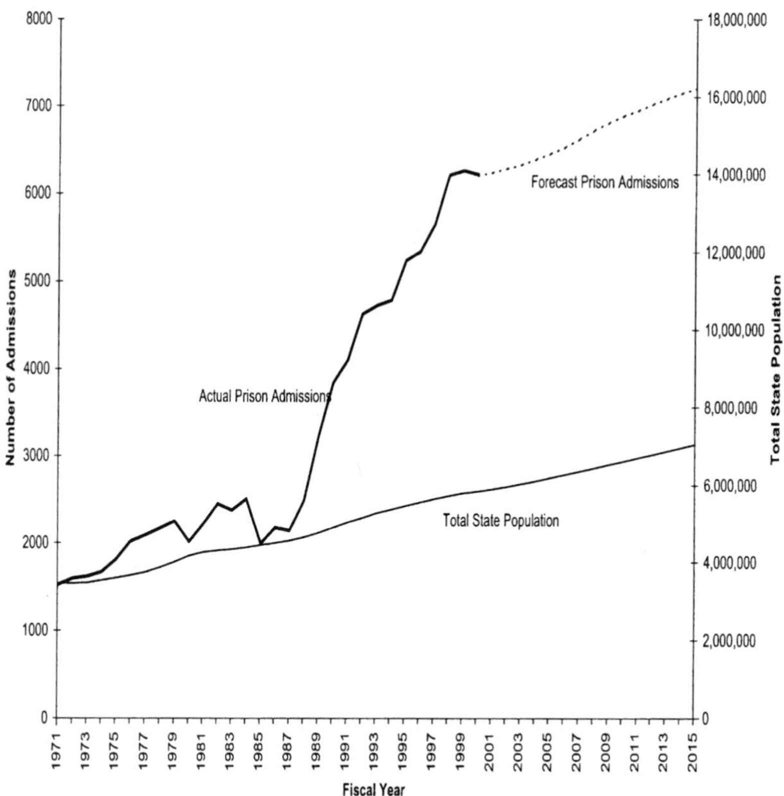

FIG. 3.—Historical and forecast prison admissions

Statistics 1998, p. 491). We do not know why Washington's experience is so different from that of Minnesota and Pennsylvania, but it seems clear that the Washington guidelines have been more effective at channeling the public's passion for punishment.

B. Changes in Discretion

The initial reform altered decision-making authority over sentencing, eliminating parole release, restricting the use of probation conditions, narrowing judges' discretion, and shifting power to prosecutors. The reformers' revised allocation of discretion was not stable, and those parties who lost discretion have pursued legislative avenues to have it returned. The following table outlines the shifts in the allocation of sentencing discretion in Washington (see table 2).

As can be seen in table 2, the legislature did not "structure" all dis-

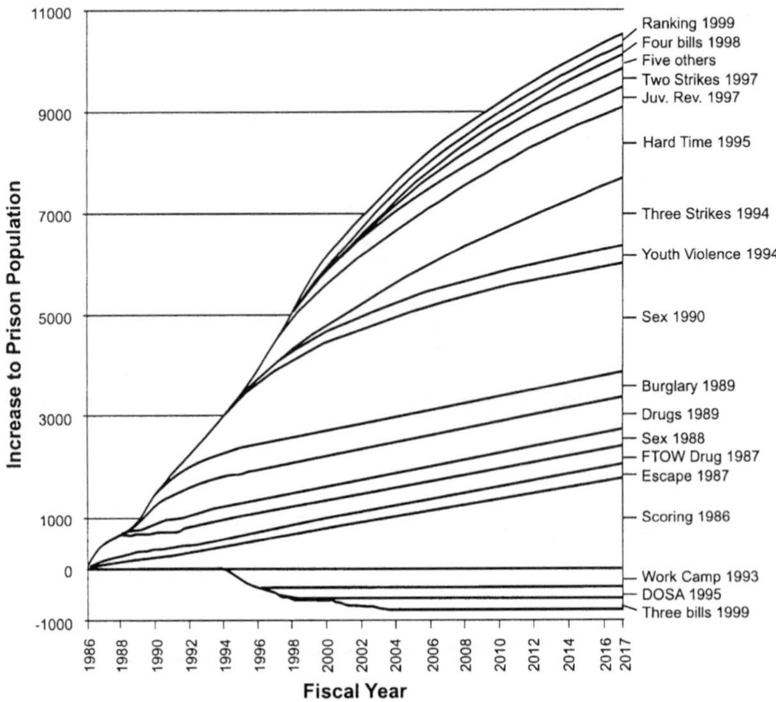

Fig. 4.—Cumulative effects of criminal justice legislation, 1986–2000 sessions

cretionary decisions affecting sentencing in the same manner. In this concluding section, we address Washington's experience in constraining prosecutorial, judicial, and correctional discretion.

1. *Prosecutorial Discretion.* Washington sentencing reformers in the 1970s and early 1980s recognized that prosecutorial discretion was a major portion of the "discretionary decision affecting sentences" that the 1981 act sought to "structure but not eliminate" (Wash. Rev. Code, title 9, chap. 94A, sec. 010 [2001]). Washington's prosecutors were not granted additional discretionary authority, but the restrictions on judicial discretion and elimination of correctional discretion significantly increased the relative power of prosecutors. The legislation took account of this by directing the sentencing commission to "devise recommended prosecuting standards in respect to charging of offenses and plea agreements" (Wash. Rev. Code, title 9, chap. 94A, sec. 040[2][b] [2001]).

The commission took this task seriously and developed the most

TABLE 2

Discretionary Authority

Locus of Discretion	Pre-1984	1984	2000
Legislature	Authority delegated except maximum terms and mandatory minimums for firearms, deadly weapons, and habitual criminal	Delegation revoked; all judicial and correctional discretion subject to legislative decisions	Limited discretion granted to judges and corrections for designated crimes
Prosecutors	Charging and bargaining decisions	Same; however, charging decisions now significantly influence sentence length	No change
Judges	Unguided (except for statutory maximums and mandatory minimums) as to: prison/jail/probation, length of jail, and conditions of probation/revocation. Authorized to impose prison term, but no control over duration.	Limited to length within presumptive range, departure from range if justified, decisions to impose first-time offender waiver and sex offender sentencing options for eligible persons within parameters, and impose sanction for failure to perform sentence conditions	Discretion expanded for certain drug offenders and work ethic camp; more latitude allowed in setting conditions for supervision
Parole board	Unguided (except for mandatory minimums) as to length of prison term, conditions of parole, and revocation of parole	Discretionary authority revoked; directed to take sentencing guidelines into account in setting minimum terms	No change
Corrections	Significant authority to set probation and parole terms and respond to violations	Probation authority greatly restricted; role in parole eliminated	For post-release supervision, granted discretion to impose additional conditions, reduce length, and impose sanctions for violation of conditions

comprehensive set of prosecutorial guidelines ever proposed for legislative adoption. The commission chose to make the guidelines voluntary. Not surprisingly, the courts held that a claim that a prosecutor had not followed the prosecutorial guidelines was not subject to judicial review (*State v. Lee*, 847 P. 2d 25 [Wash. App. 1993]). This meant that the guidelines were effective only insofar as prosecutors chose to follow them. Since the guidelines grew out of earlier collective efforts by prosecutors to articulate policies to guide their own discretionary decisions, that the guidelines were voluntary did not mean they were ignored. The decentralized nature of prosecution in Washington—each of the thirty-nine counties has an independently elected prosecutor and the attorney general has no supervisory or general enforcement powers—meant, however, that regional differences developed, particularly over time, as different prosecutors adopted different policies.

A striking example concerns drug enforcement. The sentencing guidelines call for a presumptive sentence of twenty-one to twenty-seven months for a first offense sale of heroin or cocaine and zero to ninety days for first-offense possession. In King County, Norm Maleng has consistently maintained a policy that drug sales charges are not reduced from sale to possession, even to reward a plea of guilty. As depicted in table 3, of the 1,866 drug cases in King County in 1998, 1,131 (61 percent) were convictions for dealing. This contrasts with only 30 percent in the rest of the state. Now, of course, it may be that this contrast to some degree reflects different behavior patterns, with dealers congregating in King County. However, as prosecutors readily acknowledge, the difference is due to different enforcement, charging,

TABLE 3

Type of Drug Convictions by County

County	Dealing Convictions	Nondealing Convictions	Total
King	1,131 (61%)	735 (39%)	1,866
Pierce	428 (27%)	1,159 (73%)	1,587
Clark	134 (26%)	381 (74%)	515
Snohomish	130 (28%)	339 (72%)	469
Thurston	71 (17%)	340 (78%)	411
Other counties	1,005 (34%)	1,947 (66%)	2,952
Total	2,899 (37%)	4,901 (63%)	7,800
Total less King County	1,768 (30%)	4,166 (70%)	5,934

and plea bargaining policies. In adjacent and demographically similar Pierce County, where prosecutorial policies allow a reduction of dealing charges to possession in return for a guilty plea, of 1,587 drug cases, 428 (27 percent) were convictions for dealing. Policies in both counties are explicit and are publicly defended by the prosecutors who adopted them.

The effect of these policy differences is significant (table 3). Were King County to have adopted the policies followed in the rest of the state, 503 fewer drug offenders would have been committed to prison in 1998. Were King to have followed Pierce County's policy, there would have been 556 fewer prison admissions. However, King County's policies appear more accurately to follow the prosecutorial guidelines adopted by the legislature. They call for prosecutors to "file charges which adequately describe the nature of the defendant's conduct" (Wash. Rev. Code, title 9, chap. 94A, sec. 440 [2001]) and that "a defendant will normally be expected to plead guilty to the charge . . . which adequately describe the nature of his or her conduct or go to trial" (Wash. Rev. Code, title 9, chap. 94A, sec. 450 [2001]).

Were the rest of the state's prosecutors to follow King County's—and the legislature's—policies, however, the effect would have been even more dramatic. Rather than 1,768 drug offenders convicted of dealing—and thus receiving prison sentences—3,572 would have been convicted, an increase of over 1,800 prison admissions. Since the median sentence imposed on dealers in Washington in 1998 was 27.6 months, this shift would significantly have increased the prison population.

The geographical disparity raises significant policy issues. Washington's drug laws are enacted by the state legislature and, in the words of the Sentencing Reform Act, are to be "applied equally throughout the state." However, disparity of this type is the product of Washington's allegiance to local control, with prosecutors being politically accountable only to their local electorate.

Washington's prosecutors' practices (with the exception of Maleng's in King County) demonstrate what Stuart Scheingold termed "policy moderation at the local level," by which he means that symbolic politicization of crime is strongest when furthest removed from the application of the symbolic policies (Scheingold 1991, p. 83). Prosecutors are inherently pragmatists in that they fashion policies that work in their local contexts. Commitment to the principle that every defendant ought to be convicted of what he or she has done, and no less, is much easier when it is disconnected from the reality of managing scarce resources. Maleng, not surprisingly, given his long commitment to sentencing reform, seeks to implement the policies he helped forge. His colleagues do not share his viewpoint. The legislature was, of course, quite aware of the decentralized autonomy of Washington's prosecutors when it chose to make the prosecutorial guidelines aspirational rather than binding. It chose to sanction local decision making and the inevitable geographical disparity it produces (Boerner 1995, pp. 196–200).

What Washington's experience leaves unexplored is whether judicial review could effectively have enforced prosecutorial guidelines. Certainly Washington's experience with judicial review of departures from the sentencing guidelines, which we discuss next, demonstrates the efficacy of judicial review. Prosecutorial decision making, however, involves issues not present at sentencing, when the crime of conviction is set, and defines the starting point. Judicial review of a sentence that departs from the guidelines considers whether the reasons given by the judge for sentencing outside the presumptive range are legally sufficient; there is no review as to whether the starting point was correctly determined. Prosecutorial decision making, however, operates in an environment in which the crime of conviction has not been determined but is the central issue for determination. This determination involves evidentiary sufficiency, so its subjective nature is apparent.

Washington's prosecutorial guidelines recognize that one circumstance that may justify a plea bargain—euphemistically termed a "plea agreement"—is "evidentiary problems which make conviction on the original charges doubtful" (Wash. Rev. Code, title 9, chap. 94A, sec. 450[2] [2001]). The myriad factors that influence a judgment related to likely conviction of a particular crime or crimes, to say nothing of their relative weights, involves polycentric decision making not readily susceptible to judicial review. There is no meaningful external standard against which to measure the subjective discretionary decision. Review of judges' decisions to depart from guidelines, by contrast, involves the comparatively clear-cut question of whether a particular reason justifies an exception.

Reviewing a departure from the prosecutorial guidelines that is said to be justified by "evidentiary problems" would require an intrusive and time-consuming examination of all aspects of the prosecutor's case. This examination can be done—supervisors in prosecutors' offices do it every day—but judges are ill suited to the task. The basis for the determination is subjective—involving the quality of witnesses and the persuasiveness of inferences—and involves the confidential work product of the prosecutor.

In addition, this review must occur in a nonadversarial environment. Once a plea bargain is struck, both the prosecutor and the defense attorneys share an interest in its acceptance. Neither would argue against a position to which they just agreed. Thus, judges would be denied the adversarial testing present in appellate review of judges' sentences, and in nearly all other instances of judicial review. They would be forced to become active investigators of circumstances rather than passive evaluators of arguments—a role most judges are reluctant to undertake.

There may be resolutions to these issues, but Washington's experience does not provide them. Washington's prosecutorial guidelines remain voluntary and thus, as Hobbes put it, "mere words" (Hobbes 1946). The statutory requirement that "the court, at the time of the plea, shall determine if the agreement is consistent with the interests of justice and the prosecuting standards" is routinely satisfied by a preprinted judicial finding in the standard sentencing form that "the agreement is consistent with the interests of justice and the prosecuting standards" (Wash. Rev. Code, title 9, chap. 94A, sec. 090 [2001]).

2. *Judicial Discretion and Appellate Sentencing Review.* Recognizing that the solution to what was perceived as excessive judicial discretion was not to reject discretion entirely, the reformers sought instead the right mix of rule and discretion, the proper balance between the need for articulated principles governing sentencing and for flexibility to depart from the consequences of those principles when necessary to achieve a just result.

The guidelines provide the external standard necessary to constrain discretion. Yet the Washington reformers' intent was to structure, not eliminate, judicial discretion, and thus the guidelines were made presumptive, not mandatory. Departures were permitted when justified by "substantial and compelling reasons" (Wash. Rev. Code, title 9, chap. 94A, sec. 120[2] [2001]). The challenge was to determine which reasons met this standard and which did not. The commission developed, and the legislature adopted a list of aggravating and mitigating factors to guide judicial discretion, but both recognized that they could not anticipate every individual situation deserving a departure. The listed factors were prefaced with the statement that they were "illustrative only and not intended to be exclusive reasons for exceptional sentence" (Wash. Rev. Code, title 9, chap. 94A, sec. 390 [2001]). The intent was for substantive appellate review eventually to develop a "common law of sentencing within the state" (Wash. Rev. Code, title 9, chap. 94A, sec. 210[6] [2001]).

This promise has been realized. A rich body of reported decisions, now numbering in the hundreds, construe and apply the legislative directions. The cases are not all consistent, to be sure, and no single reader will agree with every decision, but the cases are a model of the common law process, an amalgam of principle and policy that brings rationality and consistency to sentencing decisions. An example is illustrative. Sentencing based on predictions of offenders' future behavior was a hallmark of the prior indeterminate sentencing system. Judges sought to protect the public by imposing sentences designed to prevent future criminal behavior through the effects of rehabilitation, deterrence, and incapacitation. Inherent was the problematic practice of prediction. Criticisms of the accuracy of such predictions were at the core of the arguments that led to the adoption of the Sentencing Reform Act (e.g., Morris 1974).

Basing a predictive judgment on past criminal history, which is the most accurate of available predictors, runs afoul of two central precepts of the Sentencing Reform Act—the principle that factors, such as criminal history, used to determine the sentence range cannot be used again as a basis for departing from that range, and the prohibition on use of prior criminal behavior that had not resulted in conviction (Wash. Rev. Code, title 9, chap. 94A, sec. 370 [2001]). In addition, the predictive nature of the enterprise embodies a central tenet of the rejected rehabilitative ideal, that predictions of defendants' future acts can be made.

In the early years, the courts of appeals grappled with these issues in a series of contradictory decisions. In the first, the court stated, "We would uphold an exceptional sentence for one who demonstrates a pattern of predatory sexual offenses upon particularly vulnerable victims, yet who cannot be treated for the deviancy" (*State v. Wood*, 709 P. 2d 1209 [Wash. App. 1985]). The next year, the court of appeals held, without analysis, that "the defendant's lack of amenability to treatment and likelihood of reoffending . . . is a substantial and compelling reason justifying an exception sentence" (*State v. Harp*, 717 P. 2d 282 [Wash. App. 1986]).

Later that year, an aggravated exceptional sentence based solely on "the defendant's propensity to reoffend" was reversed (*State v. Payne*,

726 P. 2d 997 [Wash. App. 1986]). Responding to the argument that exceptional sentences furthered the legislative purpose "to protect the public," the court stated that it "was not persuaded that the Legislature intended preventative detention to further that purpose" (*State v. Payne*, 1000). The court observed that "reliance on a psychologist's prediction of future dangerousness, without any history of similar acts or other corroborating evidence, not only allows wide latitude for abuse, it also undermines those general objectives of proportionality and uniformity" (*State v. Payne*, 1000). Relying on the legislature's direction that the sentencing guidelines be applied without discrimination as to any element not relating to the crime or the defendant's criminal history, the court held that "an offender's personality or predicted dangerousness, standing alone, is not a proper basis for a durational departure" (*State v. Payne*, 1000).

In the next case, however, the court of appeals distinguished *Payne* as holding only that a court should not rely solely on the offender's personality or predicted dangerousness without any history of similar acts or other corroborating evidence and concluded, "given a history of similar acts or other corroborating evidence, the court may enhance the sentence on the basis of a considered assessment of future dangerousness" (*State v. Olive*, 734 P. 2d 36 [Wash. App. 1987]). The court of appeals required that a finding of future dangerousness include both a history of similar acts and proven nonamenability to treatment.

In 1990, the issue first reached the supreme court that affirmed the court of appeals' requirement that "both a history of similar acts *and* lack of amenability to treatment" were necessary (*State v. Pryor*, 779 P. 2d 244 [Wash. 1990]). The court saw the dual requirement as fulfilling "two important considerations. First, it ensures that a defendant's criminal history, which has already been taken into account in determining the appropriate standard sentence range, will not be used again to further enhance the same sentence without further proof of dangerousness. . . . Second, amenability to treatment, or lack thereof, is crucial in assessing the likelihood an individual may pose to the public in the future" (*State v. Pryor*, 248–49).

The supreme court revisited the issue the following year in a review of several cases, not involving sex crimes, where future dangerousness was used to justify an aggravated departure. A three-judge plurality opinion reviewed the goals and structure of the Sentencing Reform Act and found that allowing consideration of future dangerousness generally violated both the principle that factors used in determining the standard range could not be used again and the prohibition on using facts that had not resulted in conviction. Considering the legislative history of the Sentencing Reform Act, the plurality found the different fundamental assumptions governing sentencing of sex offenders provided "authority for this court to consider a defendant's amenability to treatment in sexual offense cases" (*State v. Barnes*, 818 P. 2d 1088 [Wash. 1991], p. 1091) but not others. The plurality stated "if future dangerousness is to be considered an aggravating factor in determining the sentence for non-sexual offense cases, it is the legislature's province to make such a decision" (*State v. Barnes*, 1093). Three concurring justices agreed that extending consideration of future dangerousness to non-sexual offense cases "lies properly within the province of the Legislature" (*State v. Barnes*, 1094).

Subsequent decisions have been faithful to the principles enunciated in *Pryor* and *Barnes*. A series of cases has applied those strictures regardless of the labels used by sentencing judges. Courts have held that findings of "protection of the public" (*State v. Post*, 826 P. 2d 172 [Wash. 1992]), "lack of amenability to treatment and the extraordinary danger the defendant presents to women" (*State v. Ross*, 861 P. 2d 473 [Wash. 1992]), "threat to the community" (*State v. George*, 834 P. 2d 664 [Wash. App. 1992]), and "a strong proclivity to commit these kinds of crimes" (*State v. Hicks*, 888 P. 2d 1235 [1995]) are all functional equivalents of a future dangerousness finding and thus subject to the limitation to sexual offenses required by *Barnes* and the two-prong objective justification required by *Pryor.*

The cases cited above typify the approach taken by Washington's appellate courts in reviewing exceptional sentences. While one can quibble with the result in a particular area, the methodology and the overall results demonstrate that law has come to sentencing in Washington.

3. *Judicial Discretion and Racial Disparity.* There remains the issue of disparity. One main argument in support of guidelines was that they would reduce disparity in general and racial disparity in particular. Here the promise has been achieved, at least in part. While in Washington, like most jurisdictions, members of minority groups, on average, receive more severe sentences than whites, the differences are accounted for by differences in legally relevant variables—the offense of conviction and prior criminal record. There are no significant differences in sentences imposed under the guidelines for those convicted of the same crime with the same offender score (Fallen 1987, pp. 62–64;

TABLE 4

First-Time Offender Departures

	Below Sentence Range	Within or Above Sentence Range	Total
White	408 (33%)	827 (67%)	1,235
Black	26 (15%)	143 (85%)	169
Other	30 (22%)	108 (78%)	138

Source.—Fallen 1987, p. 68.

Sentencing Guidelines Commission 1997, p. II-1; Engen, Gainey, and Steen 1999, p. 2).

Similarly, judicial authority to impose exceptional sentences under the court's departure authority shows little evidence of disparity correlated with race. "Whites and blacks have virtually the same exceptional sentence rates; other minorities are less likely to receive an exceptional sentence" (Fallen 1987, p. 65).

However, significant racial disparity has been found in the use of other alternatives to the presumptive sentence range (i.e., the first-time offender and sex offender sentencing alternatives). Table 4 depicts differences by race in 1987 among eligible defendants who received first-time offender sentences.

Whites were more than twice as likely as blacks to receive sentences less than the presumptive range when such a downward departure was authorized. The pattern is similar, although not as pronounced, for other minorities. Sentences imposed under the sex offender alternative show the same disparities. This alternative authorizes substitution of a community treatment sentence with not more than six months in jail for a prison sentence. Table 5 depicts the differences.

TABLE 5

Sex Offender Alternative Sentences

	Percentage of Eligible Receiving Alternative
White	56
Black	34
Other	38

Source.—Fallen 1987, p. 68.

Data reported by the Sentencing Guidelines Commission in 1997 revealed the same disparities (Sentencing Guidelines Commission 1997, pp. 11-1 to 11-9). In 1998, 37 percent of eligible white offenders received first-time offender sentences, while only 25 percent of eligible black offenders and 22.5 percent of eligible members of other minority groups received such sentences (Sentencing Guidelines Commission 2000*a*, p. 7).

A study of drug sentences imposed between July 1, 1995, and December 31, 1998 demonstrates the same pattern. Both black and Hispanic defendants were found less likely to receive first-time offender sentences than whites (Engen, Gainey, and Steen 1999, p. 51), and the authors concluded that "significant differences by race and ethnicity in the use of alternative sanctions exist even controlling for legal and extra-legal characteristics" (Engen, Gainey, and Steen 1999, p. 3).

What can we learn from these conclusions? Clearly, sentencing guidelines can effectively structure judicial discretion so as to eliminate the influence of race and ethnicity as a variable. Imposing sentences within the presumptive range and granting exceptional sentences are decisions that are constrained by the guidelines. The applicable sentence range is determined solely by the crime of conviction and prior criminal history. Exceptional sentences must be justified by explicit findings of "substantial and compelling circumstances" and are subject to substantive appellate review. The act retains unstructured and unreviewed discretion for sentencing judges in cases in which the offender is eligible for the first-time offender and the sex offender sentencing alternatives. No criteria for use are provided, and the exercise of judicial discretion is not subject to review. In these circumstances, and only in these circumstances, racial disparity emerges. The lesson is powerful: racial disparity is correlated with unstructured and unreviewed discretion.

4. *Correctional Discretion.* Initially, Washington's reform addressed correctional discretion by its partial abolition; parole and probation were prospectively repealed, and correctional officials could vary length or conditions of sentence only by granting or denying good time while in the institution. This decision was, and has remained, deeply resented by many in corrections. Arguing that it is denied the necessary authority to protect the public, the department of corrections has repeatedly pursued the reinstatement of its authority. The 1999 legislature, persuaded by these arguments, returned authority to corrections officials to assess individual risk and to tailor conditions

and supervise offenders in the community pursuant to their risk assessments.

The explicit authority in the Offender Accountability Act to use risk predictions in determining the conditions, intensity, and duration of postrelease supervision raises a series of issues about how the new authority will be exercised. Initially, there is the challenge of implementation. The department of corrections has been granted authority to supervise over 20,000 offenders each year, on the basis of individual assessments of risk, with a staff that for almost two decades has played a comparatively passive role. Converting community corrections officers into the proactive agents of surveillance and intervention contemplated by the "community justice" model presents formidable management challenges (see, e.g., Smith and Dickey 1999). The challenge is greater because essentially no new resources have been provided. Increased surveillance and intervention with high-risk offenders will be possible only by shifting resources from lower-risk offenders. Inevitably, an offender assessed to be medium or low risk will commit an atrocious crime. Retrospective scrutiny, influenced by hindsight bias, will reveal that more intensive supervision was allowed but not undertaken.

The authors of the risk assessment instrument that will be used in Washington are candid about their assessment of its accuracy. False-positive predictors (estimates of failures that do not occur) occur in 30 percent of cases, while false-negative predictions (a risk exists but is not predicted) occur in only 2 to 3 percent of the cases (Andrews and Bonta 1995, p. 49). Such a bias is justified on public safety grounds; it is preferable to overpredict rather than underpredict if the goal is public safety alone. From a just deserts perspective, however, taking control over a person beyond what is deserved for the crime on the basis of a prediction of future behavior is unjust (Morris 1974, pp. 80–84). To do so on the basis of an inaccurate prediction is even more unjust.

This tension is increased when risk is determined, in part, by subjective criteria which are susceptible to racial disparity. Assessments of offender attitudes, both current and past, are part of the determiners of risk. We know that subjective assessments are quite likely to be racially disparate. A recent Washington study illustrates this. In a review of 233 narrative reports from juvenile probation officers, researchers found that probation officers consistently portray the cause of black offenders' delinquency as negative attitudinal and personality traits, while the environment is more frequently used to explain delinquency by white youths. These attributions are not benign; they were found to influence assessments of future dangerousness and served a key role in sentence recommendations (Bridges and Steen 1998, p. 567). We see no reason to believe that similar disparities will not be found in the continuing assessments of risk called for by the Offender Accountability Act.

There remain the consequences of the myriad decentralized discretionary decisions inherent in supervising thousands of offenders. Given the inevitability of scarce supervisory resources, how will those resources be allocated? Will, for example, geographical concentrations of high-risk offenders be targeted for surveillance? Considerations of public safety and efficiency will argue strongly to do so. Surveillance of equal numbers of offenders of equal risk who are dispersed widely through the community would consume significantly greater resources. The choice is obvious, is it not? But, of course, we need not guess; we know the race of those concentrated high-risk offenders just as we know the race of those dispersed equally high-risk offenders. And, we know the race of those offenders who will be found in violation of the conditions of their supervision. We do not suggest that this result is the intended consequence of the grant of discretionary authority. Yet, it is foreseeable and our experience counsels caution (Tonry 1994, pp. 104–15).

Washington's experience with sentencing reform demonstrates that techniques exist that can effectively "structure but not eliminate" discretion. Policy choices can effectively be translated into individual sentencing decisions consistent with those policy choices. Whether these techniques can be applied effectively beyond sentencing is an open question. Certainly, Washington's experience with external constraints on prosecutorial discretion does not offer much hope. Perhaps Washington's correctional administrators will develop techniques to structure and constrain the discretion that has been returned to them. And, of course, there remains the issue of whether constraining discretion is a good idea. For those who see sentencing as an inherently individualized human process, this entire enterprise will remain flawed. For those, however, who see discretion as both inevitable and troubling, Washington's experience has been instructive, and will continue to be.

C. Conclusion

Any evaluation of a sentencing reform must begin with the recognition of its transitory nature. There are no new issues in sentencing, only provisional resolutions of age-old issues. The enduring question is, When will each resolution itself be reformed? As we reflect on the past quarter century of sentencing reform in Washington, we see a continuous process, informed by principle but tempered by pragmatism, with each stage reflecting the consensus of the moment.

This perspective arises from viewing sentencing as a process, not an end, a continuing attempt to reconcile the multiple inconsistent purposes of sentencing and apply them to individual cases in a manner seen as fair by all. The process is collective; sentencing is done in all our names. Since we do not all agree on these issues, the incentive for change is always present. Perhaps not surprisingly, since we were active participants at the time, we favor the consensus of the mid-1980s over that which currently exists, but we also believe the current status to be preferable to that which existed in 1980. These are subjective judgments, of course, and our views are entitled to no more weight than those of any other citizen.

What we believe there can be no doubt about, however, is that the process by which sentencing policy is determined and applied has become visible, resolved for the major part by public debate and not by low-visibility decision makers. Law has come to sentencing in Washington, and law evolves by public, not private decision making. Law's inevitable partner, politics, is a part of that process and inevitably means that there will be winners and losers, step by step, issue by issue. The process is not elegant, and the results are not fully consistent, but the alternatives, in our judgment, are worse. Our experience with sentencing when it was a series of low-visibility discretionary decisions, informed mainly by the values of the decision makers, leaves us with the firm belief that Washington's current sentencing system is more just than the one that preceded it. We are equally firm in our belief that it can be made more just. And so we continue to work.

REFERENCES

Allen, Frances A. 1981. *The Decline of the Rehabilitative Ideal.* New Haven, Conn.: Yale University Press.

Andrews, D. A., and J. L. Bonta. 1995. *The Level of Service Inventory—Revised: User's Manual.* North Tonawanda, N.Y.: Multi-Health Systems.

Barnoski, Robert. 2000. Personal communication to Roxanne Lieb. Washington State Institute for Public Policy, Olympia, March 20.

Bayley, Christopher T. 1976*a*. "Good Intentions Gone Awry: A Proposal for a Fundamental Change in Criminal Sentencing." *Washington Law Review* 51:529–63.

———. 1976*b*. "Plea Bargaining: An Offer a Prosecutor Can Refuse." *Judicature* 60:229–32.

———. 1978. "Plea Bargaining: On Taming the Dragon." *Washington State Bar News* 32(12):14–19.

Becker, Mary Kay. 1979. "Washington State's New Juvenile Code: An Introduction." *Gonzaga Law Review* 14:289–312.

Bell, Merlyn M., and David L. Fallen. 1990. *Changes in Jail Felony Populations: Comparing 1982 to 1988*. Olympia: Sentencing Guidelines Commission, State of Washington.

Boerner, David. 1985. *Sentencing in Washington: A Legal Analysis of the Sentencing Reform Act of 1981*. Seattle: Butterworth Legal Publishers.

———. 1992. "Confronting Violence: In the Act and in the Words." *University of Puget Sound Law Review* 15:525–77.

———. 1993. "The Role of the Legislature in Guidelines Sentencing in the Other Washington." *Wake Forest Law Review* 28:381–420.

———. 1995. "Sentencing Guidelines and Prosecutorial Discretion." *Judicature* 78:196–200.

———. 1997. "Sentencing Policy in Washington." In *Sentencing Reform in Overcrowded Times: A Comparative Perspective*, edited by Michael Tonry and Kathleen Hatlestad. New York: Oxford University Press.

Bridges, George S., and Sara Steen. 1998. "Racial Disparities in Official Assessments of Juvenile Offenders: Attributional Stereotypes as Mediating Mechanisms." *American Sociological Review* 63:554–70.

Bureau of Justice Statistics. 1998. *Sourcebook of Criminal Justice Statistics: 1997*. Washington, D.C.: U.S. Department of Justice, Bureau of Justice Statistics.

———. 2000. *Prisoners in 1999*. Washington, D.C.: U.S. Department of Justice, Bureau of Justice Statistics.

California District Attorney's Association. 1974. *Uniform Crime Charging Standards*. Los Angeles County.

Carrow, Deborah M. 1984. "Judicial Sentencing Guidelines: Hazards of the Middle Ground." *Judicature* 68:161–71.

Civiletti, Benjamin R. 1980. *Principles of Federal Prosecution*. Washington, D.C.: U.S. Department of Justice.

Davis, Kenneth Culp. 1969. *Discretionary Justice: A Preliminary Inquiry*. Urbana: University of Illinois Press.

Du, Can, and Polly Phipps. 1997. *Trading Time for Treatment: Second-Year Evaluation of the Drug Offender Sentencing Alternative (DOSA)*. Olympia: Sentencing Guidelines Commission, State of Washington.

Engen, Rodney L., Randy R. Gainey, and Sara Steen. 1999. *Racial and Ethnic Disparities in Sentencing Outcomes for Drug Offenders in Washington State: FY1996 to FY1999*. Olympia: Washington State Minority and Justice Commission.

Engen, Rodney L., and John C. Steiger. January 1997. *Trading Time for Treatment: Preliminary Evaluation of the Drug Offender Sentencing Alternative (DOSA)*. Olympia: Sentencing Guidelines Commission, State of Washington.

Fallen, David L. 1986. *Preliminary Evaluation of Washington State's Sentencing*

Reform Act. Olympia: Sentencing Guidelines Commission, State of Washington.

———. 1987. *Statistical Summary*. Olympia: Sentencing Guidelines Commission, State of Washington.

Feld, Barry C. 1998. "Juvenile and Criminal Justice Systems' Responses to Youth Violence." In *Youth Violence*, edited by Michael Tonry and Mark H. Moore. Vol. 24 of *Crime and Justice: A Review of Research*, edited by Michael Tonry. Chicago: University of Chicago Press.

Frankel, Marvin E. 1972. *Criminal Sentences: Law without Order*. New York: Hill & Wang.

Frase, Richard S. 1993. "Implementing Commission-Based Sentencing Guidelines: The Lessons of the First Ten Years in Minnesota." *Cornell Journal of Law and Public Policy* 2:279–337.

Gardner, Governor Booth. 1991. Letter to the Sentencing Guidelines Commission, March 4. On file with the Washington State Sentencing Guidelines Commission, Olympia.

Gottfredson, Don M., Leslie T. Wilkins, and Peter B. Hoffman. 1978. *Guidelines for Parole and Sentencing: A Policy Control Method*. Lexington, Mass.: Heath.

Governor's Task Force on Decision Making Models in Corrections. 1975. "Sentencing Act: Final Draft." Prepared for the Governor of the State of Washington. Olympia, Wash.

Greene, Judy. 1997. "Oregon Modifies Mandatory Minimum Laws but Increases Prison Capacity by 125%." *Overcrowded Times* 8(4):3, 8–9.

Grove, W. M., and P. E. Meehl. 1996. "Comparative Efficiency of Informal (Subjective, Impressionistic) and Formal (Mechanical, Algorithmic) Prediction Procedures: The Clinical Statistical Controversy." *Psychology, Public Policy, and Law* 2:293–323.

Hobbes, Thomas. 1946. *Leviathan: or, The Matter, Forme and Power of a Commonwealth, Ecclesiasticall and Civil*. Edited, with an introduction, by Michael Oakeshott. Oxford: Blackwell.

Indeterminate Sentence Review Board, Transfer Study Committee. 1989. *Transfer Study Committee Indeterminate Sentence Review Board: Report to the Legislature*. Olympia, Wash.: Indeterminate Sentence Review Board, January.

King County Prosecuting Attorney's Office. 1980. *Filing and Charging Policies*. Seattle.

Lange, Larry. 1982. "State Panel Offers a Sentencing Plan to Thin Out Prisons." *Seattle Post Intelligencer* (December 7).

Lasnik, Robert. 1981. *The Sentencing Reform Act of 1981*. King County Prosecutor's Office. Seattle.

Levi, Edward H. 1978. Memorandum to U.S. Attorneys, published in the *National Law Journal* 1(9):14–15.

Lieb, Roxanne, and Megan E. Brown. 1999. "Washington State's Solo Path: Juvenile Sentencing Guidelines." *Federal Sentencing Reporter* 11:273–77.

Lieb, Roxanne, and Scott Matson. 1997. "Sex Offender Sentencing in Washington State." *Federal Sentencing Reporter* 10:85–89.

Lyons, Williams. 1999. *The Politics of Community Policing: Rearranging the Power to Punish*. Ann Arbor: University of Michigan Press.

Marsh, Dennis C. 1999. Executive Director, Washington State Indeterminate Sentence Review Board. Personal communication via e-mail to Roxanne Lieb, October 13.

Marvel, Thomas B. 1995. "Sentencing Guidelines and Prison Population Growth." *Journal of Criminal Law and Criminology* 85:696–707.

Morris, Norval. 1974. *The Future of Imprisonment*. Chicago: University of Chicago Press.

Naon, Bob. 1976. "Responding to the Youthful Offender: An Overview and Critique of the Juvenile Justice and Corrections System." Unpublished report. Olympia: Washington State House of Representatives.

National District Attorney's Association. 1977. *National Prosecution Standards*. Chicago: National District Attorney's Association.

Office of Financial Management. 1997. *Governor's Recommendation to Continue the Indeterminate Sentence Review Board*. Olympia, Wash.: Office of Financial Management Executive Policy Division, January.

Parent, Dale. 1988. *Structuring Criminal Sentences*. Seattle: Butterworth Legal Publishers.

Patrick, James Thomas, and Edwin R. Petersen. 1979. *Parole Decisions Projects: Final Report*. Olympia, Wash.: Board of Prison Terms and Paroles.

Petersen, Edwin R., and J. Walter Gearhart. 1979. "Decision-Making Guidelines for Setting Prison Terms and Paroles." Olympia: Parole Decisions Project, Washington State Board of Prison Terms and Paroles.

Raspberry, William. 1984. "Do the Crime, Pay the Price." *Washington Post* (July 27).

Reitz, Kevin R. 2001. "The Status of Sentencing Guidelines Reform in the U.S." In *Penal Reform in Overcrowded Times*, edited by Michael Tonry. New York: Oxford University Press.

Rosenblum, Ellen F. 1995. "Oregon's Sentencing Guidelines." *Judicature* 78:177.

Scheingold, Stuart A. 1991. *The Politics of Street Crime*. Philadelphia: Temple University Press.

Schneider, Anne L., David B. Griswold, Donna D. Schram, and Jill G. McKelvy. 1981. *Executive Summary of Legislative History, Philosophy, and Rationale of the Washington (State) Juvenile Justice Code*. Eugene, Ore.: Institute of Policy Analysis.

Schneider, Anne Larason, and Donna D. Schram. 1983. *Final Report: A Justice Philosophy for the Juvenile Court*. Grant Report no. 79-JN-AX-0028. Washington, D.C.: U.S. National Institute of Justice.

Seattle Post Intelligencer. 1984. July 3.

Sentencing Guidelines Commission. 1983. *Sentencing Guidelines Commission: Report to the Legislature*. Olympia: Sentencing Guidelines Commission, State of Washington.

———. 1992*a*. *A Decade of Sentencing Reform: Washington and Its Guidelines 1981–1991*. Olympia: Sentencing Guidelines Commission, State of Washington.

———. 1992*b*. *Statistical Summary of Adult Felony Sentencing: Fiscal Year 1992*. Olympia: Sentencing Guidelines Commission, State of Washington.

———. 1995. *Statistical Summary of Adult Felony Sentencing: Fiscal Year 1995.* Olympia: Sentencing Guidelines Commission, State of Washington.

———. 1996. *Adult Felony Sentencings: Fiscal Year 1996.* Olympia: Sentencing Guidelines Commission, State of Washington.

———. 1997. *Statistical Summary of Adult Felony Sentencing.* Olympia: Sentencing Guidelines Commission, State of Washington.

———. 1999*a*. *Persistent Offenders Sentence Report.* Updated October 1999. Olympia: Sentencing Guidelines Commission, State of Washington.

———. 1999*b*. *Statistical Summary of Adult Felony Sentencing: Fiscal Year 1999.* Olympia: Sentencing Guidelines Commission, State of Washington.

———. 2000*a*. *The Sentencing Reform Act at Century's End.* Olympia: Sentencing Guidelines Commission, State of Washington.

———. 2000*b*. *Annual Statistical Summary of Adult Felony Sentencing, 1990–2000.* Olympia: Sentencing Guidelines Commission, State of Washington.

Simon, Jonathan, and Malcolm M. Feeley. 1992. "The New Penology: Notes on the Emerging Strategy of Corrections and Its Implications." *Criminology* 30:449–74.

Smith, Michael E., and Walter J. Dickey. 1999. *Reforming Sentencing and Corrections for Just Punishment and Public Safety.* Sentencing and Corrections: Issues for the Twenty-First Century, No. 4. Washington, D.C.: U.S. National Institute of Justice.

Spokane Chronicle. 1983. "Inmate Increase Expected." Spokane, Wash. (January 12).

State of Washington Superior Court Judges Association and Office of Administrator for the Courts. January 1981. *Report of the Sentencing Guidelines Committee.* Olympia, Wash.: Office of the Administrator for the Courts.

Steiger, John C. 1998. "Taking the Law into Our Own Hands: Structured Sentencing, Fear of Violence, and Citizen Initiatives in Washington State." *Law & Policy* 20:333–56.

Steiger, John C., and R. A. Doyan. 1979. *Juvenile Justice and Transition: Changing Philosophies, Changing Laws.* Seattle: University of Washington Center for Law and Justice.

Stith, Kate, and Steve Y. Koh. 1993. "The Politics of Sentencing Reform: The Legislative History of the Federal Sentencing Guidelines." *Wake Forest Law Review* 28:223–90.

"Symposium: Law and the Correctional Process in Washington." 1976. *Washington Law Review* 51:491–696.

Tacoma News Tribune. 1983. "Sentencing Idea Deserves Good Look." (January 10) editorial page.

Tonry, Michael. 1994. *Malign Neglect.* Oxford: Oxford University Press.

———. 1996. *Sentencing Matters.* New York: Oxford University Press.

———. 1999. *The Fragmentation of Sentencing and Corrections in America.* Sentencing and Corrections: Issues for the Twenty-First Century, No. 1. Washington, D.C.: U.S. National Institute of Justice.

Van Wagenen, Richard D. 2001. "Washington State Sentencing Changes, 1994–97." In *Penal Reform in Overcrowded Times,* edited by Michael Tonry. New York: Oxford University Press.

Washington Association of Prosecuting Attorneys. 1980. *Filing and Disposition Guidelines*. Olympia: Washington Association of Prosecuting Attorneys.
Washington State Department of Corrections. 1996. *Washington State County Criminal Justice Databook: 1985 to 1995*. Olympia, Wash.: Department of Corrections.
———. FY2000 and 2001. *Client Characteristics, Population Movement and Custody Report*. Olympia, Wash.: Department of Corrections.
Wright, Ronald F. 1998. "Three Strikes Legislation and Sentencing Commission Objectives." *Law and Policy* 20:429–63.
Zimring, Franklin E. 1977. *Making the Punishment Fit the Crime: A Consumers' Guide to Sentencing Reform*. Occasional Paper no. 12. Chicago: University of Chicago Law School.

Michael A. Bellesiles

Firearms Regulation: A Historical Overview

ABSTRACT

Gun regulation has been a constant component of American law, running from the first settlements in the Chesapeake. Legislatures grappled to reconcile rights and defensive needs against their fear of an unhindered access to firearms. The state's goal of arming some citizens for defense clashed with its effort to prevent the dangerous classes from possessing firearms. Complicating the whole process was a surprising public indifference to firearms prior to the twentieth century. For much of American history, few people contested the state's right to control the possession and use of firearms. In this context, the Second Amendment appeared entirely irrelevant to gun regulation. Until the middle of the twentieth century, American gun laws had a coherent and clear goal of limiting access to firearms to reliable citizens. But since World War II, efforts at gun regulation have usually been prevented by the polarizing enthusiasm for guns among a large segment of the population.

Scholars of the Second Amendment are embroiled in a heated debate over the meaning of that single, ambiguous sentence. The wording is very much a product of the eighteenth century: "A well regulated Militia, being necessary to the security of a free State, the right of the people to keep and bear Arms, shall not be infringed." Those who oppose any form of gun regulation lift up the clause "the right of the people to keep and bear Arms" and insist that the Second Amendment guaranties an undisturbed individual right to gun ownership. Supporters of gun regulations, pointing to the sentence's explanatory opening clause that emphasizes the militia, maintain that the right was granted collec-

Michael Bellesiles is professor of history, Emory University.

0192-3234/2001/0028-0003$02.00

tively for the enhancement of national defense. The argument is clearly presentist in orientation. More troubling is the unwillingness of so many scholars to look closely at the large body of regulatory legislation in early American history and to place the Second Amendment within a precise historical context. Doing so may well disturb both sides in the debate.

Until recently, much of the controversy over the meaning of the Second Amendment has occurred in law reviews. A number of lawyers have argued that the Second Amendment must be understood as upholding an individual right to own guns (Halbrook 1986; Levinson 1989; VanAlstyne 1994). These scholars carry on a careful analysis of the Second Amendment's sentence, supporting their perspective with quotations from a number of key figures from the early republic, many of them antifederalists. So confident were these authors in their position that they declared themselves the upholders of the "Standard Model" of the Second Amendment, declaring "virtual unanimity" among legal scholars for the individualist position (Barnett and Kates 1996, p. 1141). But starting in 1996, a number of historians stepped forth to argue that no part of the constitution could be understood by the deployment of a few quotations, maintaining the necessity for a carefully nuanced appreciation of the historical context in which the Second Amendment was written and ratified (Bellesiles 1996; Higginbotham 1998; Cornell 1999).

There have been many suggestions that the distinction between these two schools of scholarship can be found in differing methodologies. Laura Kalman has drawn attention to the way lawyers rely on quotation hunting, a ransacking of the past for supportive quotations, often yanked out of context, intended to support one absolute position or another (Kalman 1996). Historians, of course, are notorious for avoiding absolute statements about the past, finding previous societies to have been as complex as our own. Single causality arguments are usually rejected as simplistic, and making a case on the authority of a few quotations generally draws a contemptuous dismissal from historians. Probably no scholar has made a more convincing case for the need to understand the constitution in its precise context than Jack Rakove, author of the Pulitzer-award-winning *Original Meanings.* When asked to examine the law review articles on the Second Amendment, he, like most historians, was shocked at the sloppiness of the scholarship and questioned the reliability of articles not subject to peer review (Rakove 2000). In defense of their position, proponents of the individualist perspective have taken a startling postmodernist stance that the precise historical record does not matter; it is the current perspective which is of greatest importance (Mooney 2000).

For those who prize historical context, it may prove useful to trace the development of America's gun laws. This study begins with the English common law heritage and its influence in colonial America. The second section looks to the framing of the Second Amendment before turning to the statute law and judicial decisions that guided legal conduct under this first constitutional system. Section III traces the nature of gun regulation under the revised constitutional system instituted by the Reconstruction era amendments. This period is seen as reaching its apogee with the Supreme Court's decision in *U.S. v. Miller* (307 U.S. 174 [1939]) upholding congressional authority to regulate firearms. The fourth and final section of this essay explores the contested ground of Second Amendment law that began with the indifference toward widespread gun ownership during a period dominated by the Cold War. But that absence of legislative and judicial interest gave way to hot debate following the dramatic rise in the rates of violent crime in the late 1960s and has led to a period of profound legal confusion on the rights and responsibilities of gun ownership by century's end.

Clearly, the United States grants a special cultural power to firearms, yet few historians have bothered to explore the origins or nature of that gun culture (Kennett and Anderson 1975; Bellesiles 2000). Contrary to popular perceptions, the United States has always had gun laws in place, though the level and targets of enforcement have shifted dramatically over time. American gun laws emerged from fear. Through the antebellum period, legislatures acted to prevent access to firearms by those groups identified as most threatening to white social order. At the same time, in order to protect themselves from these dangerous groups, American assemblies passed a variety of gun laws intended to arm the trustworthy—adult, white, male Protestant property owners—with guns that worked. In the aftermath of the Civil War, racist legislators attempted to deny freed blacks access to firearms. These efforts were not significantly different from the efforts of northern and western legislatures to prevent derided immigrant groups, labor unions, and vaguely defined "criminal classes" from possessing guns. Though the Supreme Court has never explicitly incorporated a Second Amendment right to individual gun ownership, states and communities dropped ethnically based restrictions on the possession of firearms by the 1950s. As governments reluctantly extended individual rights to the entire adult population, the perceived right of every American to own an unlimited number and variety of firearms gained acceptance. Though the right of the state to establish restrictions on gun ownership has never been disputed by the federal courts, state regulation became ever less significant. Until the middle of the twentieth century, specific classes of people could be identified as posing a danger to society, and legislatures and local officials could intervene in an attempt to prevent their access to firearms. By the end of the twentieth century, anyone and everyone, from a small child to a spouse, can constitute an armed threat.

I. The English Heritage

From its first appearance in the fourteenth century, the gun aroused government suspicion. Ruling elites refused to accept unnecessary social disorder because of the availability of this new weaponry. Like every European nation, England attempted to limit access to firearms to trained troops in government service and to the elite. There was no doubt that a single company of trained troops could overwhelm and defeat any band of discontented subjects armed with a few guns, but no monarch wanted to test the validity of this theory. Henry VII and Henry VIII both outlawed wheelocks—the first gun to ignite the powder by producing a spark, in this case by a wheel striking a piece of iron. Henry VIII attempted to limit the use of other firearms to the elite, chartering the Fraternity of St. George in London to develop the "Science and Feate of Shootynge" longbows, crossbows, and firearms. This fraternity, which became the Ancient and Honourable Artillery Company of London, was the first group to be granted royal permission to shoot firearms. In the militia act of 1541, Parliament limited the ownership of pistols and crossbows to nobility and freeholders who earned more than £100 a year from their property; a threshold fifty times higher than the forty-shilling freehold needed to vote in county elections. Among the stated justifications of this act was that handguns were easily concealed and therefore more likely to be used in the commission of a crime (For Using of Long Bows, 1503, 19 Henry VII, chap. 4; The Bill for Cross-bows and Hand-guns, 1541, 33 Henry VIII, chap. 6). Later legislation, most of which fell into the category of game or militia laws, followed this model. King James I clearly stated the government's view of gun ownership in dismissing the idea that commoners should enjoy the right to hunt and own firearms: "It is not fit that clowns should have these sports" (Manning 1993, p. 65).

Oliver Cromwell's government did its best to control access to firearms, in spite of, or because of, the increased production of firearms fed by military demand during the English Civil War. Commonwealth agents followed early practices of keeping track of every gun owned within their districts. The Restoration changed little in this regard, except insofar as aristocrats could again purchase as many guns as they desired. Charles II made certain that he knew where every firearm went. In 1660 he ordered gun makers to inform the government of the location of every gun they made and sold (Stern 1954; Neal and Back 1984; Cooper 1993). Charles saw great advantage in centralizing gun making in London, where it could more easily be monitored. In 1671, the Gunmakers' Company of London gained the sole right to proof all firearms made in the London area and all arms made for the government—a privilege they maintained until 1813. In 1685, James II outlawed the importation of foreign firearms, essentially granting the Gunmakers' Company of London a near monopoly on gun making in England (Stern 1954; Hayward 1962; Neal and Back 1984; Blackmore 1986; Cooper 1993).

While the Crown worked to limit the supply side of the equation, Parliament endeavored to undermine the demand. One of the government's most effective means of forestalling the ownership of firearms was the game law. William Blackstone held that the purpose of the game laws was the "prevention of popular insurrections and resistance to the government by disarming the bulk of the people" (Blackstone 1979, 4:175). The game act of 1671, passed unanimously by Parliament, gave gamekeepers the power to seize all weapons used in hunting from those not eligible to hunt, which meant all but large property owners. The law held that the very possession of a gun carried a presumption of the intent to poach. As Blackstone noted, under the game act, the right to hunt—and thus to own a gun without fear of its expropriation—required fifty times as much property as the right to vote. The government intended with its game laws to eliminate guns from the hands of all but the elite; fines for illegal possession were moderate, but the law mandated the confiscation of all firearms employed in violation of the game law. Parliament sought their version of law and order, securing the peace of the realm by eliminating as many weapons of violence as possible (Burn 1836; Kirby 1932; Blackstone 1979; Munsche 1981).[1]

Joyce Lee Malcolm has argued that this monarchical effort to prevent gun ownership came to an end with the Glorious Revolution of 1688 and the Bill of Rights of 1689 (Malcolm 1994). The relevant passage in support of this position is the Bill of Rights' Article 7, which states that "the Subjects, which are Protestants, may have Arms for their Defence suitable to their Conditions and as allowed by Law." Blackstone emphasized the three qualifications to this grant of a "right" to possess a firearm: it is limited by religious belief, social condition, and the law. The English Bill of Rights was thus consistent with preceding arms legislation, which sought to restrict access to all forms of weaponry (Schwoerer 1981). Shortly after finishing the Bill of Rights, Parliament voted to disarm Catholics, declaring that they had no right to bear arms. This act was consistent with the Bill of Rights, as were later acts of Parliament reestablishing levels of property ownership as prerequisites for possessing different kinds of firearms, as well as the militia acts that granted the lords lieutenant the power to disarm anyone whenever they considered it necessary for public peace. Only a specific, reliable group of subjects was allowed access to firearms. When Parliament debated a new game act in 1691, an amendment allowing Protestants to keep guns despite the traditional class-based prohibitions was soundly defeated by a vote of 169 to 65. Sir John Lowther dismissed the proposal as seeking "to arm the mob, which I think is not very safe for any government" (United Kingdom 1764, 9: 67–69).[2]

Given the substantial limitations Parliament imposed on the ability of Englishmen to own a gun under their Bill of Rights, it is difficult to determine the degree to which we can speak of it as a "right." Blackstone's effort to define this "right" basically repeats the limitations he had already stated. He wrote that an "auxiliary right of the subject, . . . is that of having arms for their defence, suitable to their condition and degree, and such as are allowed by law." As with the Bill of Rights, what stands out are the qualifiers—social status and legal restrictions. But Blackstone added a twist, laying down the extraordinary conditions under which this right took on meaning. Owning firearms "is, indeed,

[1] These game laws were generally known as "qualification statutes," as they established strict qualifications for those entitled to take fish and game.

[2] All British rights were similarly restricted. See, e.g., Pocock 1957; Wood 1969; Mayton 1984; Reid 1986.

a publick allowance under due restrictions, of the natural right of resistance and self preservation, when the sanctions of society and laws are found insufficient to restrain the violence of oppression." He leaves many questions unanswered. Who decides "when the sanctions of society and laws are found insufficient to restrain the violence of oppression"? And just how does a right exist only when it is really needed? Put another way, if the government had the authority to prevent gun ownership except when it becomes too tyrannical, then how is the public to arm itself? Since the government has already effected "due restrictions," the people are unarmed at the time that they are supposed to exercise their "auxiliary right" in resisting oppression. It is a perfectly unworkable system (Blackstone 1979, 1:139).[3]

Further complicating Blackstone's view of gun possession was his insistence that the state had the right to place "restrictions" on "the offence of riding or going armed with dangerous or unusual weapons," which constitutes a "crime against the public peace" (Blackstone 1979, 1:104, 4:110). But then the point of gun regulation was state control. Legislation regulating arms production, trade, and ownership increased after passage of the English Bill of Rights, and enforcement of these acts remained rigorous throughout the eighteenth century (United Kingdom 1764; Burn 1836; Greener 1967; Blackstone 1979; Macfarlane 1981; Munsche 1981; Gilmour 1992). Contemporary commentary on every English gun law provides a basic underlying justification: fear. Most members of the elite in England, as elsewhere in the world, feared the common people. It made no sense to allow these commoners access to firearms.

But there were also some intellectuals who feared a standing army (Schwoerer 1974; White 1978). The Commonwealthmen of the late seventeenth and early eighteenth centuries warned, in John Trenchard's words, that "unhappy nations have lost that precious jewell *liberty*" when "their necessities or indiscretion have permitted a standing army to be kept amongst them" (Bailyn 1967, p. 62). Trenchard and his fellow Commonwealthmen called on England to abandon its standing armies—and thus its empire—and rely instead on well-organized militia units for the nation's defense. The English government rejected

[3] Blackstone defined the "auxiliary subordinate rights of the subject" as those "which serve principally as barriers to protect and maintain inviolate the three great primary rights, or personal security, personal liberty, and private property." In order, these five rights are Parliamentary power, the limitations of the king's prerogative, legal redress, petition, and "having arms for their defence" (Blackstone 1979, 1:136–40).

these suggestions as so much academic raving. The English elite, with cause, feared the consequence of telling the lower orders that they were entitled to own a gun. The very idea that such a right existed met with derision and anger from the elite and their government. England placed its trust in its Regulars, not just to defend the Empire, but to expand it (Bailyn 1967; Thompson 1976; Munsche 1981; Shalhope 1982; Robertson 1985; Gilmour 1992; Anderson 2000).

The heart of that expansion lay across the Atlantic in North America. English common law formed the basis for American colonial legislation. From the very first codes of law passed in the Chesapeake and New England colonies, gun ownership was carefully circumscribed. Possession of firearms was not understood as a collective right but rather as a collective duty necessary to the defense of society, with that collectivity precisely defined and far from inclusive. Repeatedly, colonial legislatures passed laws requiring white Protestant, adult male, property holders to own guns as a support for the local militia. Just so there would be no misunderstanding, such laws forbade other groups from owning firearms. Only Protestants could own guns, and not always all Protestants; for instance, in 1637 Massachusetts disarmed the Antinomians. The prohibition on Catholics, indentured servants, and slaves owning guns was maintained in every colony, though the government of Maryland was occasionally lax in its enforcement of the prohibition on Catholics. But in 1756, with the start of the Seven Years' War, the Maryland assembly came into line with the other colonies, expropriating all the arms and ammunition of Catholics and mandating prison terms for any Catholic found concealing arms. In every colony a qualified individual who refused to serve in the militia forfeited any arms and ammunition he might own (Massachusetts 1853–54; Maryland 1883–1972).

In addition to the class and religious divisions that disrupted most European societies, the English settlers of North America had cause for concern from the native Indians, who resisted the conquest of their lands. Not surprisingly, colonial gun laws continually sought to limit Indian access to firearms, legislation supported by the Crown. On several occasions legislatures passed universal bans on Indians purchasing or carrying firearms. In 1619, the Virginia House of Burgesses passed an act that "no man do sell or give any Indians any piece of shott, or poulder, or any other armes offensive or defensive, upon paine of being held a traitor to the colony & of being hanged" (Virginia House of Burgesses 1905–15, 5:13, 91). This law was revised and updated on several occasions over the next century and a half. But the French, Dutch, and Spanish governments, and even English merchants, consistently undermined efforts to keep Indians unarmed. The English reliance on Indian allies in their wars against hostile Indians and competing European powers further complicated matters. As long as colonial governments acknowledged that there were "good Indians" deserving of guns, their efforts to maintain a technological advantage were in jeopardy (South Carolina Commons 1925; Russell 1957; Virginia 1961).

Colonial governments attempted to maintain a distinction between friendly and hostile Indians in terms of the gun trade; one was encouraged, the other forbidden. English merchants repeatedly ignored this legislation. The one check the governments maintained on Indian gun ownership was regulation of gun repair, which was easier to enforce than gun sales. The government of South Carolina was able to keep a close account of Cherokee firearms by requiring that they all be repaired in Charleston, a process that took several months. Since guns were in short supply in North America, and since few people could repair firearms, a broken musket was of little use other than being a clumsy club. The Westos of Virginia discovered the danger of an excessive dependence on firearms in the early 1680s, when the Virginia government cut off their supply of powder and access to repairs and then chased the Westos out of their homelands (North Carolina 1886; Commissioners of the Indian Trade 1955; Crane 1956; Russell 1957; Juricek 1964; Hatley 1993).

To meet the Indian peril, colonial governments required all freemen to own a gun in defense against external dangers. These laws were largely wishful thinking, as few freemen could afford firearms even if they were able to find one for sale. As a consequence, from the very first settlements through the American Revolution, it was necessary for governments to supply firearms to members of the militia. With every military crisis, legislatures passed laws appropriating funds to purchase firearms in Europe for use by the militia (Bellesiles 2000). At the same time, legislators feared that gun-toting freemen might, under special circumstances, pose a threat to the very polity that they were supposed to defend. Colonial legislatures therefore strictly regulated the storage of firearms, with weapons kept in some central place, to be produced only in emergencies or on muster day. Such legislation was on the books of colonies from New Hampshire to South Carolina (Peterson 1956; Novak 1992).

A perception of two potential sources of internal danger underlay legislative efforts to regulate access to firearms. Initially, indentured servants constituted the more dangerous of the two perceived threats. These unfree white laborers had good reason to resist the authority of the English elite, being exploited often unto death and having very little to lose by insurrection. Bacon's Rebellion in 1676 graphically demonstrated the hazard posed by allowing the poor some access to firearms. After receiving their arms from Governor Berkeley, Nathaniel Bacon's forces defeated Virginia's official militia. Most of the colonial legislatures learned from this Virginia uprising and, for the rest of the colonial period, enhanced internal security by outlawing the owning and carrying of firearms by indentured servants (Virginia 1809–23; Morgan 1975).

In several of the colonies the elite came to see slaves and free blacks as posing an even greater danger than indentured servants. An armed slave who knew how to use a firearm was the equal of any white, an inherently dangerous idea. The solution appeared equally obvious: a complete prohibition of gun ownership, strictly enforced. Every southern colony legislated against the ownership of firearms by slaves. They also forbade the carrying of firearms by a slave except when under the direct supervision of his owner. From time to time these laws became rather lax, and favored slaves could be seen hunting with their masters. But legislatures tightened these laws immediately following a slave uprising such as South Carolina's Stono Rebellion of 1740. Such slave uprisings—real and imagined—persuaded colonial legislatures that blacks as a group, slave or free, should not be allowed to own firearms. By the time of the Revolution no concept so aroused white terror as the vision of blacks trained in the use of firearms (Virginia 1809–23; Wood 1974; Breen and Innes 1980; Shea 1983).

Local communities and assemblies passed many kinds of regulatory legislation throughout the colonial period. As in England, American governments sought to regulate the quality, sale, and storage of firearms and munitions; the maintenance of arms used for public purposes; where, when, and by whom firearms could be carried and fired. Legislatures also granted officials the right to expropriate firearms during internal or external crises and to conduct gun censuses. And, most important, legislatures followed the English example in denying the right to own guns to potentially dangerous groups: blacks, slave and free; Indians; unpropertied whites; non-Protestants or potentially unruly Protestants. These laws worked because the political community supported their enforcement, fearing the consequences of unregulated access to firearms and munitions (Bellesiles 1998).

II. The First Constitutional System

The government's authority over firearms remained uncontested in legal venues during the colonial period. Perceived dangers, while distinctive by region, were simply too great and resources too limited for legislatures to render primacy to individual rights. Firearms were held at sufferance, the state reserving the right to limit, regulate, or impress those arms at its discretion. Under common law this "reserved right of the sovereign" differed from eminent domain in that it did not need a special act of Parliament nor did it require just compensation, since firearms were always seen as in the service of the monarch.[4] Forrest McDonald has noted that the "American legislatures had been less squeamish about invading property rights" than Parliament and thus showed little hesitance in exercising this reserved right (McDonald 1985, p. 22). The American Revolution did not change this particular English heritage, as the loyalists discovered when their firearms were confiscated (Flick 1901; Calhoon 1965; Lambert 1987). Nor is it clear that the Second Amendment altered that formulation, as those denied guns because of race, religion, or ethnicity in the new republic could affirm.

Some scholars have argued that the primacy of internal security gave way to libertarian values with the passage of the Bill of Rights in 1791. This conclusion is based on a careful reading of the language and philosophy of the framers of the constitution.[5] Of course, it is not in the least clear that the original intention of the framers of the Constitution and Bill of Rights should guide current thinking on legal issues, especially as there is sufficient evidence that many of the framers felt that their intentions should not determine constitutional interpretation (Berger 1977; Powell 1987; Levy 1988; Rakove 1990, 1997; Scalia 1997). But historians are not supposed to be bothered by these current policy debates; our goal is to discover an accurate narrative to the best of our limited abilities. Within that context, most historians hold that it is far more valuable to establish the social context of the Second

[4] The precise concept of eminent domain was not known under English common law; until the 1770s the taking of property by the sovereign required a special act of Parliament (Blackstone 1979; McDonald 1985).

[5] For different versions of strict constructions of the Second Amendment, see Batey 1986; Halbrook 1986; Malcolm 1994.

Amendment than to devote inordinate energy to parsing the amendment's single sentence (Higginbotham 1998, 1999; Cornell 1999; Bellesiles 1999).

The primary experience guiding the hands of the framers of the Constitution was their collective memory of the American Revolution. They all knew what a near thing it had been. On most occasions the militia had proven a disaster for the American cause. Grossly underarmed, ill trained, and unprepared and unwilling to move into combat, the militia had not lived up to the promise of Bunker Hill. The state governments responsible for arming and training the militia had been loath to spend the money on either goal and had mostly done their best to avoid calling out their units. But for the arms and troops provided by the French, the course of the American Revolution would have been dramatically different (Cress 1982; Carp 1984). Those who framed the Constitution knew of these flaws in the militia and America's military weakness in the absence of a single gun manufactory, so it is no wonder that they passed responsibility for maintaining the nation's defense on to the national government (Washington 1745–99; Hamilton 1961–79). Even the militia was to be the instrument of the federal government, as stated in Article 1, Section 8, which made Congress responsible for "organizing, arming, and disciplining, the Militia."

The other major event that convinced many supporters of the Constitution that the militia must come under federal oversight was Shays' Rebellion in 1786–87. The Shaysites themselves kept insisting that their political protest followed Revolutionary traditions (Taylor 1954; Szatmary 1980), which was precisely what frightened elite leaders like George Washington and James Madison (Washington 1745–99; Continental Congress 1904-37).[6] The whole point for such American political leaders was to establish a government that would guarantee that revolution would not follow upon revolution in the chaotic fashion seemingly endorsed by Thomas Jefferson. The Constitutional Convention convened within this context of feared anarchy and the dissolution of the United States (McDonald 1965; Wood 1969; Rakove 1997).

Starting with Edmund Randolph's opening speech, the convention returned repeatedly to the reform of the militia. In listing the reasons for writing an entirely new government compact to supersede the Arti-

[6] On the impact of Shays' Rebellion on the militia's reputation, see Cress 1982.

cles of Confederation, Randolph gave as his first reason, "1. that the Confederation produced no security agai[nst] foreign invasion; . . . and that neither militia nor draughts being fit for defence on such occasions, enlistments only could be successful." The "common defence" clearly required some sort of national army. The Revolution had adequately demonstrated that "*Volunteers* [are] not to be depended on" in case of war; while "*Militia* [are] difficult to be collected and almost impossible to be kept in the field. . . . Nothing short of a regular military force will answer." None of this was to be taken as an effort to terminate the militia; rather, in Alexander Hamilton's words, "the Militia of all the States [are] to be under the sole and exclusive direction of the United States" (Farrand 1937, 1:19–20, 25, 293; 2:47). "The States neglect their Militia now," Madison went on, "and the more they are consolidated into one nation, the less each will rely on its own interior provisions for its safety. . . . The Discipline of the Militia is evidently a *National* concern, and ought to be provided for in the *National* Constitution" (Farrand 1937, 2:386–87). The majority of those present at the convention agreed that the constitution they were writing should prevent further disorder by bringing the militia under more direct federal control (Farrand 1937).

Some modern observers have argued that the framers perceived the militia as a check on governmental power (Levinson 1989; Malcolm 1994; Reynolds 1995; Barnett and Kates 1996). Yet the Constitution accomplishes the exact opposite, making the militia a potential tool of the central government for the repression of any challenge to federal authority. Article 1, Section 8 granted Congress the authority not only to regulate the militia but also to call "forth the Militia to execute the Laws of the Union, suppress Insurrections and repel Invasions" (Farrand 1937; Higginbotham 1998; Cornell 1999).

Many of the same modern commentators hold that there was an exact correlation between the individual ownership of firearms and the militia, a relationship that informed the Second Amendment (Shalhope 1999). Yet it is difficult to find that attitude in practice during the early national period. The Massachusetts Constitution of 1780 declared that "the people have a right to keep and to bear arms for the common defence." That right did not place the individual beyond the discipline of the state, for the next sentence stated, "And as in time of peace armies are dangerous to liberty, they ought not to be maintained without the consent of the Legislature; and the military power shall always be held in exact subordination to the civil authority, and be governed by it." The Massachusetts Constitution did not end there; Section 1, Article 4 grants the legislature authority to pass laws for the support and regulation of the state's militia, while Article 12 required all militia officers to report to the governor every three months on the number of arms, and so forth, held by the state (Massachusetts 1836, pp. 1–2). It is very difficult to read an "individual" right into such explicit state powers, though some have managed to do so.

Even the most seemingly individualist renderings of gun rights must be matched against the actions of those responsible for these statements. In other words, we need to place these statements of rights within a precise historical context. For instance, the 1776 Pennsylvania Constitution declared that "the people have a right to bear arms for the defense [of] themselves and the State; and as standing armies in time of peace are dangerous to liberty, they ought not to be kept up. And the military should be kept under strict subordination to, and governed by the civil power" (Rakove 1998, pp. 86–87). Again, it is the state's authority that stands out in this declaration, and the state of Pennsylvania did not hesitate to exercise that authority, disarming loyalists and any others who refused to take an oath of allegiance to their government. Gun ownership in Pennsylvania, as in every other state, was premised on the notion that the individual would use that weapon in the state's defense when called upon to do so, and to make the point completely clear, the state required an oath to that effect. The Test Act called for the disarming of those who would not take the oath of allegiance (Pennsylvania 1903; Cornell 1999). As Don Higginbotham points out, "In all the discussions and debates from the Revolution to the eve of the Civil War, there is precious little evidence that advocates of local control of the militia showed an equal or even a secondary concern for gun ownership as a personal right" (Higginbotham 1998, p. 40).

The Constitution's treatment of the militia was in keeping with various state constitutions that aimed to craft a workable militia structure. As the Virginia Declaration of Rights of 1776 stated, "A well-regulated militia, composed of the body of the people trained to arms, is the proper, natural and safe defence of a free state . . . and that in all cases, the military should be under strict subordination to, and governed by, the civil power" (Morison 1929, p. 151). It is hard to miss those opening words, in which Virginia declares its faith in a trained militia. But convincing citizens to submit to that training was the rub, and Virginia, like every other state in the new union, would devote enormous energy over the next eighty years attempting to convince their citizens to perform their martial duties (Brundage 1958; Pitcavage 1995).

The militia provisions of the constitution outraged the antifederalists, who insisted on state control (Wills 1999). After the Philadelphia convention, Luther Martin and other antifederalists imagined every possible scenario of federal tyranny rendering the states impotent. Under the constitution, Martin charged, Congress could decide not to arm the militia, with the result that the militia would have few, if any, guns. Patrick Henry picked up on this reasoning and suggested that Congress could render the states undefended—an issue of real concern in states that actively repressed and enslaved a large minority, or in South Carolina a majority, of their population. "Of what service would militia be to you," Henry asked, "when most probably you will not have a single musket in the State; for as arms are to be provided by congress, they may or may not furnish them?" (Jensen 1976–95, 9: 957.) Apparently Martin and Henry believed the people incapable of acquiring their own firearms. Henry feared what Congress would not do; others suspected the federal government capable of more direct action, using its control over the militia to oppress the states by having the militia of one state invade another (Brundage 1958; Cress 1982).[7] In any formulation, it was not the enhancement of individual rights that the antifederalists sought but limits on the powers of the central government to the benefit of the states.[8]

For the federalists, the Constitution's militia clauses operated within their understanding of concurrent power. State and federal governments shared authority over the militia. The Constitution made Congress responsible for organizing and arming the militia, but nothing in that wording contradicted the states' ability to use their militia as they saw fit when not in active federal service. If an individual state found the militia poorly organized or underarmed, there was no limitation on its right to correct these faults. In this way the militia would neither be so strong as to become a standing army nor so weak as to be ineffec-

[7] For additional antifederalist views on the militia, see Jensen 1976–95, 1:482, 539–40; 2:37–38, 60, 184–85, 290–92, 318–19; 3:20–22, 30–31, 408–12; 4:58. As Higginbotham points out, it is odd that the antifederalists did not quote Blackstone on the militia as "not compellable to march out of their counties, unless in case of invasion or actual rebellion" (Higginbotham 1998, p. 47n.; Blackstone 1979, 1:399).

[8] Federalists ridiculed this argument of a disarmed militia. See, e.g., Farrand 1937, 3: 271–75; Jensen 1976–95, 9:1014, 1074, 1102; 10:1288–96, 1311–12, 1324–25, 1486, 1531; 16:267; Hamilton, Madison, and Jay 1979, pp. 180–86 (no. 29), 313–20 (no. 46). For Luther Martin's response, see Farrand 1937, 3:286–95.

tual against domestic insurrection (Cress 1982; Higginbotham 1998). Most federalists followed the lead of Madison and Randolph at the Virginia ratifying convention in maintaining that a federally regulated militia was the best way of avoiding a standing army. And the real danger of a standing army was not its power, but its expense (Jensen 1976–95).

The federalists were a bit disingenuous in arguing that a well-regulated militia would allow the United States to avoid a standing army. Most federalists had every expectation that the nation would build a more powerful army as soon as the new constitutional government was in place. Few would have disagreed with Gouverneur Morris's later assessment that "an overweening vanity leads the many, each man against the conviction of his own heart, to believe or affect to believe, that militia can beat veteran troops in the open field." At the constitutional convention, "this idle notion, fed by vaunting demagogues, alarmed us" into giving support to the militia. Those present, Morris argued, should have recalled better the revolution, which taught that "to rely on militia was to lean on a broken reed" (Jensen 1976–95, 2: 420). Alexander Hamilton was more succinct in Federalist No. 25: "I expect to be told that the militia of the country is its natural bulwark, and would be at all times equal to the national defence. This doctrine, in substance, had like to have lost us our independence. . . . The facts which, from our own experience, forbid a reliance of this kind, are too recent to permit us to be dupes of such a suggestion." The only sure defense for the nation, the federalists understood, lay in a well-trained and well-supplied national army (Hamilton, Madison, and Jay 1787–88, p. 161).[9]

Though the federalists found little of merit in the antifederalist position on the militia, they did hope to win over their opponents after the Constitution was ratified. The easiest way of assuaging fears without undermining their hard-won social order was to make good on James Madison's promise to consider amendments to the Constitution. In this context, the Second Amendment may be seen as both a political gesture to placate the antifederalists and as an effort to regulate the militia in order to insure against dangerous social upheavals like Shays' Rebellion and slave uprisings (Ellis 1987; Finkelman 1987; Elkins and McKitrick 1993; Patterson 1993). Madison considered a number of

[9] See also Hamilton, Madison, and Jay 1979, pp. 151–56 (no. 24), 180–86 (no. 29), 313–20 (no. 46); Jensen 1976–95, 1:435–36; 3:321–22, 401–2, 457, 508, 532; 4:125, 265–67, 419.

proposals that addressed the structure of the militia. Among the changes recommended were limitations on the number of militia under federal control, the nature and duration of martial law, and the use of militia beyond a state's borders, as well as specific proposals dealing with the training of the militia, the status of conscientious objectors, and the degree of state control over the militia. None became part of the Second Amendment, as Madison preferred simplicity and clarity in all of the amendments he put before Congress (Veit 1991; Higginbotham 1998).

Madison seems to have been authentically open to any suggestions, so long as they did not weaken the federal government. None of the proposed amendments were to undermine the essential authority of the new central government, including its control over the militia. As Madison rhetorically asked, "For whose benefit is the militia organized, armed and disciplined? for the benefit of the United States" (diGiacomantonio 1996, p. 173). In the context of Madison's stated intentions, it is highly significant that in every version of what became the Bill of Rights only one amendment contained a clarifying preamble stating its purpose: the Second Amendment. That purpose, as it was finally worded, was that "a well regulated militia" is "necessary to the security of a free State." The militia would therefore operate as a check against the excesses of the public—precisely its historic use, from putting down slave rebellions to crushing labor unions (Leibiger 1993; Higginbotham 1998).[10]

Madison made plain his understanding of the Second Amendment when he presented it to the House of Representatives in 1789. As is well known, Madison feared the tyranny of the majority and the repressive actions of state governments far more than he did the central government (Banning 1995; Matthews 1995; Rakove 1997; Wills 1999). As he told the House on June 8:

> In our government it is, perhaps, less necessary to guard against the abuse in the executive department than any other, because it is not the stronger branch of the system, but the weaker. . . . But . . . the great danger lies rather in the abuse of the community than in the legislative body. The prescriptions in favor of liberty, ought to be levelled against that quarter where the greatest danger lies,

[10] Roger Sherman's version of the Bill of Rights, which played a key role in the congressional debates, addresses only the militia, with no reference to a right to bear arms; Veit 1991, pp. 266–68.

> namely, that which possesses the highest prerogative of power: But this [is] not found in either the executive or legislative departments of government, but in the body of the people, operating by the majority against the minority. (Rakove 1998, pp. 176–77)

It was an unrestrained citizenry who were to be most feared, and the Bill of Rights should operate to protect liberty against their transgressions.

That most members of the political elite of the United States shared Madison's vision of the Second Amendment's purpose is fairly indicated by the ensuing debate and legislation. The House debate focused on two issues: the "use of the militia" in preventing "the establishment of a standing army" and the wisdom of allowing religious exemptions for service in the militia (Veit 1991, pp. 182–84, 198–99).[11] The leaders of the new nation followed Washington's lead in calling for a standing army backed by a smaller, organized, and better-armed militia. The Constitution provided the framework for such a structure. The first Congress set about giving it shape (Barlow 1956; Millis 1956; Cress 1982; Bellesiles 1999). The legislation that followed uniformly sought to regulate the militia, starting with the first national militia act of 1792, while the state legislatures further revealed their intentions in the limitations they imposed on gun ownership, whether in denying that right to blacks, Catholics, Indians, or the foreign born (Massachusetts 1836; Bellesiles 1998).

Gun ownership in the early national period was clearly a public issue. But it was one subject to a deep tension between federal efforts to arm white male Americans and elite fears that blacks, poor whites, and other dangerous groups might put such weapons to an incorrect use. Much legislation fostered the first while delimiting the latter. Probably the congressmen who framed and approved the Bill of Rights would have been astounded by the argument that gun rights are purely individual; all of them came from states in which the right to own guns was collectively granted to law-abiding white adult Protestant males. Senator Rufus King warned his colleagues in 1790 that "it was dangerous to put Arms into the hands of the Frontier People for their defense, least they should Use them against the United States" (Bowling and Veit 1988, p. 246). States and communities had the authority and responsibility to deny gun possession to those perceived as a threat to

[11] See also Veit 1991, pp. 4, 30, 37–41, 48, 247–48, 293.

social stability, a standard that shifted over time to include nonwhites, workers, the foreign born, and criminals.

The pattern of legislative enactment best indicates the general attitudes of the political classes in America at the time of the Bill of Rights. Every state had gun control legislation on its books at the time the Second Amendment was approved. Every state continued to pass such legislation after the Second Amendment became the law of the land, and they were joined in such regulatory efforts by the federal government, starting with the first national militia act of 1792. State legislatures needed no further argument than public safety, or in constitutional terms, the state's police powers, to justify gun regulation. In this regard they adhered to the English common law heritage and the practice of every European nation. Political thinkers of the eighteenth century perceived the state's primary justification in the preservation of public safety. Legislatures, whether local or national, had a legitimate interest in passing acts to secure that security. Measures that placed precise limitations on the use and possession of firearms aroused amazingly little debate—other than accusations that they were not stringent enough or rigorously enforced (South Carolina 1836–41; Connecticut 1850–90; Maryland 1883–1972; North Carolina 1886–1909; Flick 1901; Calhoon 1965; Lambert 1987). On the one occasion when such legislation was overturned, in *Bliss v. Commonwealth* (1822), the Kentucky Supreme Court ruled that state regulation of firearms violated the state's militia amendment, which granted an explicitly individual right to bear arms (12 Ky. 90). In response, the legislature immediately amended the state constitution to allow such legislation, rewriting the militia amendment to more closely match the federal Constitution's Second Amendment (Kentucky 1835). Otherwise, court after court agreed with the logic of Tennessee's high court in *Aymette v. State* (1840) that since "the object, then, for which the right of keeping and bearing arms is secured is the defence of the public, . . . the Legislature, therefore, have a right to prohibit the wearing or keeping weapons dangerous to the peace and safety of the citizens" (21 Tenn. 154, 1840 WL 1554, 2 Hum. 15).[12]

Such decisions validated a wide variety of gun regulations at the state and federal levels. Congress retained tight control over the sale of firearms and ammunition to the Indians, again needing no further justification than public safety. The Indian Intercourse Act of 1834 placed

[12] See also State v. Reid, 1 Ala. 612 (1840).

strict limitations on those selling any kind of arms to Indians and required a federal license to enter into the Indian trade (United States 1853). States worked to keep firearms out of the hands of those marked as unsafe. As in the past, blacks, slave or free, were included, though in the crisis of the revolution patriot Catholics found themselves able to possess firearms. And as always, political enemies had no right to bear arms. The new U.S. government and several state governments made that abundantly clear in a number of uprisings in the early national period, from the Whiskey Rebellion in 1794 through Fries Rebellion in 1798 to Dorr's Rebellion in 1842, as well as anything approximating a slave uprising (Bellesiles 1999; Cornell 1999).

States also responded to the threat of concealed weapons. Not just pistols, but a variety of small well-made bladed weapons like dirks and Bowie knives, as well as sword canes, could be easily concealed and produced in the midst of an argument to lethal effect. As the early American political scholar Benjamin Oliver wrote in 1832, the "cowardly and disgraceful" act of carrying concealed weapons transformed what might have been a barroom brawl into a deadly encounter. The Second Amendment, which Oliver held relevant only to the militia system, offered nothing "to prevent congress or the legislatures of the different states from enacting laws to prevent citizens from always going armed" (Oliver 1970, pp. 177–78). Most state legislators apparently agreed with Oliver's interpretation. As early as 1801 the Tennessee legislature made it illegal for anyone to "publicly ride or go armed to the terror of the people, or privately carry any dirk, large knife, pistol, or any other dangerous weapon, to the fear or terror of any person" (Tennessee 1821, 1:710). Louisiana's 1813 act outlawing the carrying of concealed firearms allowed police officers to stop and search anyone suspected of carrying a concealed weapon (Louisiana 1813; Greiner 1841), while several state constitutions forbade noncitizens from possessing firearms.[13] This fear of concealed weapons accelerated in the 1830s as pistols became smaller. In 1832 Illinois instituted a $100 fine for anyone caught carrying "upon him any pistol, gun, knife, bludgeon, or other offensive weapon"; Ohio's fine was $200 (Illinois 1833, p. 202; Ohio 1859, pp. 56–57). In 1837 Georgia's legislature forbade shopkeepers from selling or even keeping in stock pistols and concealable bladed weapons (Georgia 1851). The Georgia Supreme Court later de-

[13] See, e.g., the constitutions of Pennsylvania (1790), Kentucky (1792 and 1799), Connecticut (1818), Mississippi (1817), and Maine (1819).

clared this statute unconstitutional in that it prohibited the carrying of weapons but constitutional in its prescription of how they were carried (*Nunn v. Georgia* [1846], 1 Kelly 243).

Many of these concealed weapons acts were written in vague and even contradictory form. Thus the Illinois law would seem to outlaw the carrying of any gun, while a Minnesota law forbade the carrying of any sort of offensive weapon, concealed or in the open, unless the individual had "reasonable cause to fear an assault or other injury or violence to his person, or to his family or property" (Minnesota 1859, p. 742). But it did not establish how such a fear was to be demonstrated under the law.[14]

The fears of white southerners were much more easily defined: armed blacks. Every southern state gave priority to limiting access to firearms among the black population, slave or free. Such legislation was seen as necessary for public safety even when it might interfere with the authority of the slave master over his property (Waldrep 1998). Most had laws like Louisiana's, which strictly forbade slaves from carrying a gun at any time and required free "colored persons" to obtain a permit from a justice of the peace in order to carry a weapon (Greiner 1841). In the northern states, it was the armed immigrant who aroused fears. Several states, including Massachusetts and Connecticut, disarmed immigrant militia companies (Minor 1856; Massachusetts 1856; Williams 1858). Most states also passed laws that attempted to place limits on where and when one could shoot a gun so as to avoid accidents. In the Northwest Territories guns could not be fired within a quarter of a mile of any house or during the night, except in alarm or self-defense, while hunters must always aim their firearms away from any settled community (Ohio 1833–35). Municipal ordinances followed these state laws. Most frontier towns outlawed the firing of a firearm except in cases of self-defense (St. Louis 1843, 1846; Memphis 1857; Jordan 1970).

It is an open question as to how effectively these antebellum gun laws were enforced. Louisiana's concealed weapons act appears to have been rigorously enforced up until the 1850s; the New Orleans police even disarmed and prosecuted a former chief of police for carrying a concealed gun (Rousey 1996). One of the city's editors insisted that no one, not even the police, should be carrying guns: "Dispense with the sword and pistol, the musket and bayonet, in our civil administration

[14] For another obscure act, see Nebraska 1867, p. 624.

of republican laws, and adopt or create a system more congenial to our feelings, to the opinions and interests of a free and prosperous people" (*Louisiana Advertiser* 1834). But the police themselves began violating the law regularly, admitting to carrying concealed pistols in order to defend themselves from civilians carrying concealed pistols. Perhaps as a consequence, the murder rate in New Orleans reached a nineteenth-century high in the years from 1857 to 1860, with the police paying a high price for this change in practice (Rousey 1996). To emphasize their disapproval of the spread of the fashion of carrying a concealed firearm, Louisiana's legislature passed an even stricter concealed carry act in 1855 (Louisiana 1855, 1876), and the state's high court ruled in 1856 that even the partial concealment of a gun remained illegal (*State [of Louisiana] v. J. T. Smith*, 11 La. Ann. Reports 633 [1856]).

Nonetheless, little research has yet been done beyond the legislative level, so it is possible that these acts were mere gestures or, more likely, intended as laws for the convenience of law enforcement officers. A constable who wanted a reason to arrest a suspect could always use the concealed weapons act in the absence of any other evidence of a crime. But far more research is required to make such a statement with any certainty. At the very least, it is evident that state legislatures grappled with the dangers of individual gun ownership in the years after the passage of the Second Amendment.

III. The Revised Constitutional System

During the four years of the Civil War, the United States and Confederate governments succeeded in supplying firearms to the vast majority of men within their respective territories. With the war's end, Congress allowed union veterans to take their guns home, while union commanders did little to prevent confederate soldiers from doing the same. With the wartime demand for tens of thousands of weapons at an end, both the U.S. Army and northern arms makers flooded the market with surplus firearms. The result was a nation saturated with guns.

Few commentators in the North welcomed this development, fearful of the social dangers posed by releasing onto civilian society so many men armed and trained in the use of firearms. In the South, the former leaders of the confederacy wanted to ensure that white men remained armed, fearing the consequences of allowing their former slaves access to guns. These concerns drove legislation that sought to ameliorate the effect of the sudden increase of gun ownership in the United States, some by placing restraints on the sale and carrying of firearms, others by way of racial limitations. With few exceptions, state and federal courts upheld these legal restrictions.

The gun laws of the postwar period break down into regional and urban/rural divisions. Broadly stated, northern cities and western cities and towns worried most about firearms safety and the carrying of guns in public places, while the southern legislatures seemed primarily concerned with which race had access to the most guns. The latter issue is perhaps easiest to understand, as it was basically a continuation of the Civil War under the guise of legislation.

A. South

In the aftermath of the Civil War, many people hoped and thought that the Fourteenth Amendment would extend individual rights further than had previously been the case.[15] For hundreds of thousands of freedmen who had never been allowed to own a firearm, the gun became a symbol of their newly gained freedom and civic rights. If the Second Amendment did indeed protect an individual's right to own guns, then the Fourteenth Amendment's proclamation that "no State shall abridge the privileges or immunities of citizens of the United States" should have secured that right for all American citizens. But once racist whites regained control of the southern legislatures, they passed a series of laws intended to limit the freedmen's access to firearms. This legislation built upon precedent, for all the southern states had race-based restrictions on hunting, militia membership, and gun ownership that had been actively enforced in the antebellum period.

In the immediate aftermath of the war, legislatures still dominated by former confederates passed a series of stringent black codes intended to keep freedmen in a state of peonage. As in the years before the war, militia service and gun ownership were denied to blacks. For instance, Florida's Black Code of 1866 prohibited all blacks from possessing "any Bowie-knife, dirk, sword, firearms or ammunition of any kind." This law applied even if the black person was hunting while in the employ of a white person (Florida 1866, chap. 1468). Violation of this statute would result in forfeiture of the weapon and a public whipping. Alabama's legislature stated bluntly "that it shall not be lawful for any freedman, mulatto, or free person of color in this State, to own

[15] Halbrook 1999 seems to argue that the Fourteenth Amendment did in fact extend individual rights, most particularly the individual right to gun ownership.

fire-arms, or carry about his person a pistol or other deadly weapon" (Avins 1967, p. 209).[16] Guns were for whites, and that was all there was to it. The editor of the *Charleston Mercury* wrote that if blacks were allowed to bear arms they would become "swaggering buck niggers" and would of course attack white women (Friedman 1970, p. 15). White racists did not wait for the black militia to become familiar with their firearms but launched preemptive strikes (Singletary 1957; Wilson 1965).

Once Congress imposed its national reconstruction in 1867, democratic legislatures (those recognizing the right of blacks to vote) removed the racist legislation limiting the rights of the freedmen. But there were still a number of alternative legislative tactics available to the white elite. Antebellum legislation had hindered the ability of poor whites to hunt while strictly forbidding blacks, slave and free, from that activity. Drawing upon this heritage, the southern legislatures moved to control the labor and activities of the freedmen by the strict regulation of hunting, often under the pretense of preserving "white game" (deer and fowl). States that failed to enforce these restrictions were often criticized for allowing blacks to learn the use of firearms through the "manly sport" of hunting (Hahn 1982; Proctor 1998). In the northern states, hunting laws had the goal of conserving game; in the South these laws intended to preserve hunting for the elite (Kentucky 1809–19; North Carolina 1886-1909; Trefethen 1975; Lund 1980; Tober 1981; Marks 1991; Bean and Rowland 1997; Warren 1997). The U.S. Supreme Court repeatedly upheld the right of states to regulate hunting and fishing as the legislatures saw fit. As Justice Roger Taney explained, the American states came into possession of all the "powers of sovereignty, the prerogatives and regalities which before belonged either to the crown or the parliament," including the authority to pass game laws (*Martin v. Waddell*, 41 U.S. [16 Pet.] 367 [1842], p. 416).[17] So complete was the state's ownership of wildlife that it extended even to interference with interstate commerce (*McCready v. Virginia*, 94 U.S. 391 [1876]; *Manchester v. Commonwealth of Massachusetts*, 139 U.S. 240 [1891]; *Geer v. Connecticut*, 161 U.S. 519 [1896]).

Where legislation would not work to disarm blacks, southern racists turned to violence. In several states the Ku Klux Klan terrorized the

[16] For similar laws in other southern states, see South Carolina 1865; Fleming 1906–7; Wilson 1965.

[17] See also Pollard v. Hagan, 44 U.S. (3 How.) 212 (1845); Smith v. Maryland, 59 U.S. (18 How.) 71 (1855); Sax 1970.

black community, seizing all the guns they could discover in possession of blacks, doing battle with black militia units, and murdering hundreds of freedmen and their white supporters (Wilson 1903; Trelease 1971; Foner 1988; Williams 1996). In the single most notorious instance of such violence, Louisiana's Colfax Massacre of 1873, the Klan killed at least 135 blacks attempting to exercise their right to vote (Tunnell 1984). White racists saw themselves acting to disarm the freedmen in this extralegal fashion precisely because the federal government would not allow the states to do so legally (Waldrep 1998).

When local authorities would not bring murder charges against the whites responsible for the Colfax Massacre, the federal government brought ninety-eight people to trial for violating the 1870 Force Act. Among other arguments, the government insisted that the white mob, in seeking to disarm black citizens, violated their Second Amendment right to possess firearms. In the centennial year of 1876, the U.S. Supreme Court ruled in *U.S. v. Cruikshank* that the right "of bearing arms for a lawful purpose is not a right granted by the Constitution nor is it in any manner dependent upon that instrument for its existence. . . . This is one of the amendments that has no other effect than to restrict the power of the national government." The Fourteenth Amendment, the court explained, "prohibits a State from depriving any person of life, liberty, or property, without due process of law; but this adds nothing to the rights of one citizen as against another" (92 U.S. 542 [1876]). Since private persons had acted to deprive individuals of their rights, there was nothing the federal government could do; protecting individual rights remained the purview of state authority.

The irony of the *Cruikshank* decision is that it reaffirmed the framers' conception of the Second Amendment while insuring that it would be ignored. The Court found no individual right to gun ownership, as would remain the standard finding of the federal courts from that date forth. Yet private citizens were empowered to use deadly force to attain political ends without fear of prosecution, so long as the state government agreed with their objectives. Since the goal of the southern states was white supremacy, the Supreme Court handed white racists all the legitimization they needed to institute a reign of terror that lasted nearly a hundred years.[18] That terror was backed by the full force of

[18] For more examples of white violence against blacks and their white supporters in these years, see Wilson 1903, pp. 107–88.

the law, as southern legislatures felt justified and unhindered in passing laws depriving blacks of the right to own firearms. Most race-based gun regulation in the South remained extralegal but backed by the full authority of the law (Berry 1971; Ayers 1984).

B. West

Utah aside, the western part of the United States was settled under the oversight of the federal government. As John Phillip Reid has so ably demonstrated, western migrants did not leave behind either their respect for law or their laws (Reid 1980, 1997). It is within this context of a desire for well-ordered communities that we should view the struggles of western communities to control the perceived ill effects of the easy availability of firearms in the immediate aftermath of the Civil War. Robert Dykstra's studies have convincingly indicated that many towns instituted strict limitations on the carrying of firearms, requiring that guns be checked with the local sheriff or locked in storage. Such proactive enforcement kept murder rates in western towns remarkably low; the towns in Dykstra's studies averaged 1–1.5 murders per year through the period usually identified as "the Wild West" (Dykstra 1968, 1996, 1999). Other western scholars have found higher rates of homicide in the western towns with large concentrations of well-armed young men. These scholars argue that the presence of so many firearms produced a higher rate of personal violence (McGrath 1984; Boessenecker 1988; McKanna 1997). Several scholars have insisted that the real story of western violence is found not in cases of individual homicide but in vigilante actions, which were usually race or class based (Hollon 1974; Nobles 1997; Carrigan 1999).

In addition, many western states and several cities passed concealed weapons acts. Unlike today's acts of the same name, this nineteenth-century legislation forbade the carrying of concealed firearms. For instance, Oklahoma's 1890 law outlawed the carrying of any handgun, Bowie knife, dirk, sword cane, metal knuckles, or spear concealed or openly. The only weapons permitted were shotguns and rifles intended for hunting or militia drills; the only other reason they could be carried in public is if they were being transported for repair. It was also illegal to sell guns of any kind to minors, and only police officers could bring a weapon into any sort of public gathering except a militia muster. And even police officers could only carry weapons while on duty (Oklahoma 1891). The law in Arizona Territory was nearly identical, with the added criminalization of the drawing or exhibition of any deadly weapon in a "rude, angry, or threatening manner" in the presence of two or more people (Arizona 1887, p. 726).[19] Western boosters hoped the gun would vanish as their towns became more civilized. Even Wild Bill Hickock, marshal of Abilene at the time, had proclaimed that "there's no bravery in carrying revolvers in a civilized community. Such a practice is well enough and perhaps necessary among Indians or other barbarians, but among white people it ought to be discontinued" (Rosa 1969, p. 63).

Obviously a concealed weapons act is meaningless if it is not enforced. Dykstra's study of Kansas indicates that sheriffs and marshals took these acts seriously and regularly prosecuted those who broke the law (Dykstra 1968). No scholarly study indicates that police agencies lacked public support in the enforcement of these acts passed by the people's representatives. As a further indication of popular concern in the West over the carrying of firearms in public places, most states also had laws against "exhibiting dangerous weapons." These acts were intended to prevent individuals from intimidating others by waving guns around as an implied threat. Between 1865 and 1889, Washington Territory successfully prosecuted 110 men for violating this law. In nearly every instance, the defendant insisted that he did not intend to commit or even imply an act of violence by displaying his gun. Yet in each instance the judge or jury dismissed this defense as irrelevant and found that the public display of a firearm constituted a threat to the public order (Washington 1853–89).

State firearms legislation received a major boost in 1886 with the Supreme Court's decision in *Presser v. Illinois* (116 U.S. 252 [1886]). Illinois had prohibited the parading in arms by any group other than the official state militia. Herman Presser challenged this law on behalf of his fraternal organization, charging that the law violated both the Second and Fourteenth Amendments. Writing for the entire court, Justice William B. Woods rejected this reasoning, insisting that the Second Amendment "is a limitation only upon the power of Congress and the National government, and not upon that of the States." Justice Woods could find no part of the Constitution or statute law that allowed Presser "to associate with others as a military company, and to drill and parade with arms. . . . The Constitution and laws of the United States will be searched in vain for any support to the view that these rights are privileges and immunities of citizens of the United

[19] See also Kentucky 1871; New Mexico 1880; North Dakota 1896.

States independent of some specific legislation on the subject." If Presser and the other members of his club desired a right to parade with firearms, they would have to convince their fellow citizens to change the law (*Presser v. Illinois*).

C. North

The gun industry found itself caught between public concerns over the relative danger of its product and the need to stay in business. American manufacturers hoped to retain the pleasurable profits of the Civil War years, avoiding the bankruptcy that overtook such prominent firms as Spencer Firearms. However, the 1870s witnessed the near universal adoption of the safety on firearms, culminating with the hugely popular Smith and Wesson Safety Hammerless of 1877, the promotion of gun racks with locks, and the introduction of childproof guns such as Smith and Wesson's safety grip. Many gun makers focused their advertising on the safety of their handguns. Advertisements for the Iver Johnson Revolver Company, whose slogan was "accidental discharge impossible," showed a small girl playing with her doll and a revolver over the caption, "Daddy says this gun is absolutely safe."

To remain profitable and successful, the gun makers promoted the handgun as essential to personal protection in the modern urban environment. In 1875 the gun industry put out a little book titled *The Pistol as a Weapon of Defence in Its Home and on the Road.* This work praised the pistol as an equalizer that "renders mere physical strength of no account, and enables the weak and delicate to successfully resist the attacks of the strong and brutal." The book optimistically did not consider the possibility that the gun could be used for attack as well as defense and baldly stated that "there can be no objections to it [a pistol] on moral or prudential grounds" (*The Pistol as a Weapon of Defence* 1875).

Many urban city councils disagreed with this estimation of the gun's moral neutrality, often as a result of their police having no alternative but to become more gun conscious. Several urban police forces, some carrying guns for the first time, found themselves in an arms race against well-armed criminals. In the 1870s New Orleans issued Winchester repeating rifles to its police (though it was still illegal for them to carry concealed weapons). Nashville, Philadelphia, and Boston all issued revolvers to their police for the first time in the early 1880s (Lane 1967; Rousey 1996). Many police and public officials sought to respond to the spread of handguns through the more forceful enforcement of concealed weapons acts. In Louisiana, the state supreme court upheld the legality of these acts and the state legislature stiffened the punishments for carrying concealed weapons (*State [of Louisiana] v. Lucy Bias*, 37 La. Ann. 259 [1885]; Louisiana 1898). Atlanta legislators called for the banning of all handguns, one stating that it would be "like exterminating vipers" to remove pistols from public places (Rousey 1996, p. 187).

New York City best exemplifies the concerns of many cities. In the fifteen years after the war ended, the newspapers were packed with debates over the threat posed to public safety by the wide availability of cheap handguns. After all, New York had first allowed its police to carry pistols after the murder of officer Eugene Anderson in 1857 and did not make them standard issue until after the Draft Riot of 1863. There were many calls, including by the chief of police, for returning to the antebellum norm of police armed only with billy clubs ("Table Talk" 1870; Balch 1882). The state's Concealed Weapons Act of 1866 had made the carrying of "sling shot, billy, sand-club or metal knuckles and any dirk or dagger, or sword cane or air gun" a felony, but it did not include pistols (New York State 1866, 2:1523). The first effort by the city's representatives to persuade the state legislature to add pistols to that list in 1874 failed; its opponents claimed that such a restriction would affect only the law-abiding. In 1877, following a noticeable rise in the city's homicide rate, the legislature added handguns to the list of proscribed weapons, though an infraction was treated as a misdemeanor (New York State 1881).[20]

The debate persisted, the *New York Tribune* taking the lead in calling for more restrictive legislation. The *Tribune* editorialized often about the danger posed by the large number of guns in evidence in New York City and the willingness of people to fire them despite an 1835 statute outlawing the firing of firearms within the city limits (New York City 1851). The *Tribune* expressed particular trepidation over the inability of most men to shoot accurately. Drawing on the classic scenario justifying the carrying of firearms, the mad dog, the *Tribune* held that if one hundred men fired at a mad dog, that ninety-nine would miss and ten would hit a bystander as "the average New Yorker who carries a pistol cannot hit anything with it." The paper was also troubled by the rising suicide rate, fueled, they charged, by the easy

[20] For discussions of the rising homicide rate and the perceived need to change the laws, see *New York Tribune* (February 22, 1878), p. 4; (January 30, 1881), p. 7; (March 24, 1895), p. 6.

availability of cheap .22 caliber pistols. "But generally speaking, the twenty-two calibre may be said to lack emphasis; it cannot command the respect accorded to the thirty-two calibre, nor rivet the attention like the thirty-eight calibre, nor depopulate the neighborhood as can the forty-four and forty-five calibre" (*New York Tribune* 1892).

Calls for gun control had no necessary relation to political position in the period after the Civil War. The liberals and conservatives of the day united in perceiving a need for a safer society. A danger that particularly frightened members of the elite was the working-class gun club. Thus, the editors of the conservative *Army and Navy Journal* could call for limitations on gun ownership by noting that "it is never safe for any community to have irregular bodies of armed men patrolling the streets and practicing with firearms" (*Army and Navy Journal* 1867). The *New York Times* found enough to fear in the unorganized poor. "They rush eagerly into quarrels and fights, and at the first opportunity draw their weapons and fire promiscuously about them." The streets were becoming unsafe as "sudden passion and ready pistols lead to homicides almost innumerable" (*New York Times* 1866). From another direction, Anthony Comstock, the great moral reformer, attacked the spread of cheap firearms, especially fraudulent copies of elite guns, warning that these weapons could be more dangerous to the possessor than to the target (Comstock 1880).

However, there was an obvious increase in the demand for firearms and a spreading acceptance of the gun as a necessary part of American life. Guns were becoming ever less expensive, reaching the low price of the notorious "$5 specials," particularly poorly made revolvers that could fit in the front pants pocket. Advertisements encouraged fathers to teach their sons the true meaning of being an American and a male by giving them a gun for Christmas, while promotions of all kind, including for a religious magazine, offered pistols as premiums. Most observers agreed that the carrying of pistols had become almost routine in eastern cities despite concealed weapons acts. The police still issued citations for carrying concealed guns without a license, but the sheer numbers in the eastern cities made their job very difficult (Gilmore 1974).

Arms regulation took many shapes. Several states attempted to decrease the number of handguns by increasing their cost with high licensing fees. Alabama passed such legislation in 1892 (Alabama 1897); in 1907 Texas imposed a 50 percent tax on pistols (Texas 1928); Oregon in 1913 required a permit backed up by two written affidavits of "good moral character" in order to own a pistol (Oregon 1913, p. 497). Popular opinion seemed broadly in favor of some sort of regulation, no matter what form it took. As a 1907 editorial in *The Nation* stated, guns are "the costliest type of luxury" (*Nation* 1907). Speaking to the Wisconsin State Bar Association in 1910, U.S. District Court Judge George C. Holt said that "the repeating pistol is the greatest nuisance in modern life" (Holt 1910, p. 280).

Efforts to control inexpensive handguns came to a head in 1911 with the passage of the Sullivan Act in New York. An ethnic bias lurked behind this act. There had long been an association in New York of Italians and crime, and, starting in 1903, the police routinely denied Italians permits for the carrying of pistols. In 1905 the state legitimated this bias by outlawing the possession of firearms in any public place by the foreign born (New York State 1905).[21] The police wanted more authority to prevent the carrying of concealed handguns. Even with the existing weak legislation, the police seized 10,567 handguns between 1907 and 1910, or seven a day. The assassination attempt against Mayor William J. Gaynor in 1910 riveted the city's attention and brought renewed calls for the regulation of handguns. Particularly notable for most of those calling for stricter laws was the fact that several people saw the attacker carrying the gun, and even twirling it around his finger, yet did not think it unusual and said nothing to the police (Van Loan 1912). These news stories were capped by a report in 1911 from the city's coroner's office that the number of gun-related homicides had increased by 50 percent in 1910. The Coroner's Clerk, George P. Lebrun, recommended "severe measures for the regulation of the indiscriminate sale and carrying of firearms" (*New York Tribune* 1911).

A new Democratic member of the state senate from New York City, Timothy D. Sullivan, immediately proposed legislation regulating the purchase, possession, and carrying of firearms throughout the state. That "Big Tim" Sullivan, one of Tammany Hall's most prominent figures, would promote such legislation seems a sure indication of its popularity. The only hostile testimony came, not surprisingly, from gun manufacturers and sellers. The bill received broad support from

[21] Pennsylvania's law forbidding foreign-born residents from killing any animal was upheld by the U.S. Supreme Court in Pastone v. Pennsylvania, 232 U.S. 138 (1914).

the cultural and economic elite of New York, which saw it as a necessary part of the civilizing process. The Senate passed the Sullivan Act by a vote of 37 to 5 and the House by 123 to 7, and Governor John A. Dix signed it into law on May 29, 1911 (Weller 1962). The Sullivan Act reinforced older legislation on weapons other than firearms (slingshots and such) and limitations on the ownership and carrying of firearms by aliens and minors. The Sullivan Act instituted three additions to existing firearms acts: it added pistols to section 1897 of the criminal code, making it a felony to carry concealed weapons; required residents of cities to get a permit to carry concealable firearms—though failure to do so only constituted a misdemeanor; and required those who sold pistols to first examine a permit and to keep a record of the sale recording the purchaser and firearm. In an effort to contain the spread of the "$5 specials," the cost of these permits was fixed at $10. The bill also retained the prohibition of firearm possession by aliens (New York State 1911). Based on letters and editorials in the leading newspapers, the public reaction was overwhelmingly positive.

The Sullivan Act had been represented in the Assembly as responding to the concerns and needs of the state's police, and several officers and chiefs had spoken in its support. The easily concealed pistol had been labeled a particular threat to the safety of law enforcement, with police adding further justification on the grounds that it would allow them to arrest armed miscreants before they committed serious crimes, or those who had avoided apprehension for other crimes. Police demonstrated their support through vigorous enforcement, especially in New York City, where five arrests were made on the first day of the act (September 1, 1911). The first person convicted under the Sullivan Act was a career criminal named Giuseppe Costabile, an alleged chief of the Black Hand (*New York Times* 1911).

The New York City police rated the act a great success.[22] Raids on "criminal centers" initially produced vast numbers of firearms, though later searches of suspected gangster hangouts discovered few guns. However, commentators disagreed over the Sullivan Act's impact as reflected in the homicide rates. In 1910 there had been 108 homicides

[22] Perhaps the first scholarly examination of the Second Amendment appeared in the midst of the debate over the Sullivan Act's value. Lucilius Emery concluded his article with a list of people, including "Women, young boys, the blind, tramps, persons non compos mentis or dissolute of habits," who "may be prohibited from carrying weapons" (Emery 1915, p. 476).

committed with firearms in New York; in 1912, there were 113, with little change over the next ten years. Some observers insisted that this lack of change proved that the Sullivan Act was meaningless, while others insisted that the act halted the steady rise in homicide that had occurred between 1895 and 1911 (Van Loan 1912).

Many states followed New York's example; a few even anticipated its legislation. For instance, the Florida legislature voted in 1893 to require a license in order to carry a handgun; revised, stricter versions followed in 1901 and 1906 (Florida 1906). In 1923 Arkansas required registration of all handguns (Arkansas 1923); Michigan followed suit in 1925 (Michigan 1925). In 1910, South Carolina outlawed the manufacture and sale of any pistol less than twenty inches long and three pounds in weight. Such a gun would have been very difficult to conceal, which was the point, and none of that nature was manufactured in the United States at that time (South Carolina 1910).

D. A National Problem

The federal government's role in gun regulation remained ambiguous in the early twentieth century. Congress effectively terminated the state militia with the passage of the National Militia Act in 1903 (known as the Dick Act), its first reform of the militia since the original 1792 Militia Act. President Theodore Roosevelt had pushed for the nationalization of the militia, stating that the American "militia law is obsolete and worthless" (Richardson 1897–1917, 9:6670). The Dick Act recognized what George Washington had noted during the American Revolution, that the defense of the United States could not rest on amateur soldiers. The Dick Act aimed to create a cadre of well-trained citizen soldiers who could support the U.S. Army in times of emergency. Toward that end the act mandated that the federal government arm and train the new National Guard (32 U.S. Stat. 775–80 [1903]). The 1916 National Defense Act further clarified this professionalization of the militia by bringing the National Guard under the direct supervision of the army (39 U.S. Stat. 166 [1916]).

The Dick Act can be read as putting an end to the legitimate need for common citizens to arm themselves in anticipation of service in their nation's defense (Spitzer 1998). However, Theodore Roosevelt, who certainly did not want just anyone owning guns, feared what would happen if red-blooded American boys stopped shooting for pleasure. He therefore encouraged Congress to make a National Board for the Promotion of Rifle Practice part of the Dick Act. Officially, the board's justification was that young Americans needed to be trained in the use of firearms so that they could move easily into military service in case of need. But the board attained this end by becoming the main prop for the almost defunct National Rifle Association (NRA) (Serven and Trefethen 1967; Gilmore 1974). Beginning in 1905 and continuing through 1979, the board ordered the sale of surplus military weapons and ammunition at very low prices to members of the NRA. These sales reached a peak of half a million guns between 1959 and 1964 (Spitzer 1998). Occasionally, as in 1910, these guns were given as free gifts to members of the NRA. The federal government even paid for the NRA's target shooting contests, which have usually been held on federal lands (Kennett and Anderson 1975; Leff and Leff 1981; Davidson 1993). These efforts indicate a long effort on the part of the central government to keep a large number of Americans armed.

There were so many state and local firearms regulations, many in direct contradiction, that successive U.S. Postmasters General complained that the post office was "compelled to carry firearms" in defiance of "local laws and regulations prohibiting the purchase and possession" of guns. Postmasters repeatedly called for federal legislation ending the right to mail firearms through the mail, but such efforts failed to pass both houses (Postmaster General 1925, p. 65).[23] The most significant of these efforts began in 1915. That year Tennessee senator John K. Shields introduced a bill to prohibit the interstate shipment of any but service revolvers (Tennessee had long prohibited the carrying of any gun except a service revolver). Shields saw a simple distinction between "big pistols" useful in home defense, and little guns intended for concealment by criminals, and he sought to terminate the popularity of the latter. Shields introduced his bill every year for twelve years, without success. The Shields Bill reached the hearing level just once, in June 1921. The Judiciary Committee's deliberations were widely covered by the newspapers, especially the appearance of S. M. Stone of Colt Firearms, who insisted that regulation was up to the states and only the states. The Shields Bill, Stone charged, would discourage armaments inventors, to the detriment of America's national defense. Shields was guaranteed unfriendly reception by the presence on the Judiciary Committee of Senator Frank Brandegee of Connecticut, which was still the center of arms manufacture in the

[23] See also Postmaster General 1911, 1926.

United States. Brandegee insured that the Shields proposal never left the committee (United States Congress 1921).[24]

Representative John F. Miller of Washington succeeded Shields as the prime mover of national gun control in 1924, when he first introduced a bill to ban pistols from the public mail. At that time the leading opponent of Miller's bill was Thomas Blanton of Texas, who summarized perfectly the deterrence argument in seeing firearms as the best defense against every imaginable form of aggression. "I hope that every American boy. . . will know how to use a six-shooter. I hope he will learn from his hip to hit a dime twenty paces off. It would be their only means of defense in combating that deadly art of jiu jitsu in close quarters should war ever face them with such danger. It is not brave men who know how to shoot straight that violate laws or carry concealed weapons. I hope every woman in America will learn how to use a revolver. . . . It will be for her safety; it will safeguard her rights. . . . That is what the framers of this Constitution had in mind when they said the Congress should never infringe upon the right to keep firearms in the home" (United States Congress 1922, 66:727–28). Blanton succeeded in stalling the bill until 1926, when it passed the House but did not come up for a vote in the Senate. The following year Miller's bill finally passed both houses of Congress and was signed into law by President Coolidge (United States Congress 1927).

Throughout the 1920s, criminologists, law enforcement officials, editorialists, and politicians debated the efficacy of gun regulation, with the majority of these individuals calling for further legislation and at the federal level. In 1924, former New York police commissioner William G. McAdoo briefly captured public attention with his book on guns and crime. McAdoo argued that local communities could not combat the spread of firearms on their own; the federal government had to step in under its right to regulate interstate commerce to halt what he saw as a gun epidemic. "The pistol is the curse of America, and they are as common as lead pencils," McAdoo wrote (McAdoo 1927, p. 419). Frederick L. Hoffman, a leading statistician working for insurance companies, found that firearms were involved in three-fourths of all homicides. He concluded that new, federal gun laws were a necessity (Hoffman 1925). Many others went further and recom-

[24] Connecticut's congressmen continued to represent the interests of the gun industry for the next twenty years at least, amending the Fordney-McCumber Tariff of 1922 and the Hawley-Smoot Tariff of 1930 to place high imposts on foreign-made firearms (United States Congress 1922, 1929).

mended outlawing the production of pistols. In 1922, the American Bar Association resolved, "We recommend that the manufacture and sale of pistols and of cartridges designed to be used in them, shall be absolutely prohibited, save as such manufacture shall be necessary for governmental and official use under legal regulation and control" (Swaney et al. 1922, p. 591).

Almost everyone agreed that there was an obvious problem in the lack of uniformity in state gun legislation and enforcement. Throughout the 1920s, New York's attorney general called upon New Jersey to pass a Sullivan Law, with New Jersey responding by making it even simpler to buy guns in that state. In 1917 the Chicago police began enforcing the city's ban on carrying concealed weapons, making three arrests a day in 1921 for concealed weapons violations. But the police quickly discovered that those who could not buy guns in the city could do so in nearby towns and by mail order. A Chicago businessman, John R. Thompson, placed ads around the country offering a $1,000 reward "to anyone who would give one good reason why the revolver manufacturing industry should be allowed to exist and enjoy the facilities of the mails" (Beman 1926). The city received a negative response from the state's appellate court, which ordered that Chicago police had to respect permits issued elsewhere in the state, even from gangster-dominated Cicero. Eventually Chicago's law was declared void precisely because it was in conflict with other laws within the state, the same fate that awaited a Chattanooga statute (*City of Chicago v. Thomas*, 228 Ill. App. 65 [1923]).[25]

Reacting to what they perceived as a problem that could be addressed only on the national level, many state attorneys general joined in calling for a national Uniform Firearms Act. Olympic pistol champ Karl T. Frederick had first proposed the Uniform Firearms Act in his capacity as executive officer of the United States Revolver Association. Seventeen states passed major legislation regulating firearms modeled on Frederick's proposal during the 1920s (Imlay 1926, 1930; Bakal 1966).

But in the mid-1920s gun manufacturers and their supporters fought back with the deterrence argument, maintaining that armed people did not have as much to fear from armed criminals. This logic was disputed by the testimony of sixteen police chiefs before the National

[25] See also The People v. O'Donnell, 223 Ill. App. 161 (1921); Glasscock v. City of Chattanooga, 157 Tenn. 518 (1928).

Crime Committee in 1927; they "gave it as their unanimous opinion that nothing could be gained by allowing citizens to arm themselves against bandits" ("Battle to Disarm" 1927). Nonetheless, the deterrence argument proved psychologically satisfying and effective in defeating firearms regulation in Arkansas and Michigan, and in moving the Bar Association in 1926 to abandon its support for the Uniform Firearms Act (Adams 1926; American Bar Association 1926). The New York legislature almost joined the trend in passing the appropriately named Hanley-Fake Bill, which would have superseded the Sullivan Act with a weak version of the Uniform Firearms Act. Governor Franklin D. Roosevelt vetoed the law as a threat to public safety and called for more federal regulation (*New York Times* 1932). The following year Roosevelt was in a position to deliver on his summons for federal laws.

E. Federal Regulation

State and federal courts consistently upheld gun regulation in the century after the end of the Civil War. Any questioning of such regulation in light of an individual reading of the Second Amendment met the same response that the Supreme Court had voiced in its *Cruikshank* decision: the Second Amendment was about the militia. Such reasoning held in every region of the country. Thus, in *English v. The State of Texas* (35 Tex. 473 [1872]), that state's highest court ruled that "the word 'arms' in the connection we find it in the Constitution of the United States refers to the arms of a militiaman or soldier, and the word is used in its military sense." Courts in Georgia, Arkansas, West Virginia, Kansas, Oklahoma, and California used the same reasoning.[26] Most state courts added to this judicial analysis the simple logic of public safety. As the California Supreme Court ruled in *People v. Camperlingo* (69 Cal. 466 [1924]), "It is clear that, in the exercise of the police power of the state, that is, for public safety or the public welfare generally, such right [to bear arms] may be either regulated or, in proper cases, entirely destroyed." The Illinois Supreme Court ruled in *Biffer v. City of Chicago* (278 Ill. 562 [1917]) that "the sale of deadly weapons may be absolutely prohibited."

Members of Congress cited the logic of these court decisions in pro-

[26] Fife v. State, 31 Ark. 455 (1876); Hill v. State, 53 Ga. 472 (1874); State v. Workman, 35 W. Va. 367, 14 S.E. 9 (1891); City of Salina v. Blaksley, 72 Kan. 230, 83 P. 619 (1905); Ex parte Thomas, 21 Okla. 770, 97 P. 260 (1908); In re Application of Rameriz, 193 Cal. 633, 226 P. 914 (1924).

posing national gun legislation during the 1920s. In 1924 alone, thirteen firearm regulation acts were introduced in the House of Representatives, all of which died in committee. One of these proposals, Kansas Senator Arthur Capper's version of the Uniform Firearms Act, nearly passed after Senator Frank Greene of Vermont suffered a serious wound when caught in the crossfire during a battle between police and criminals on a Washington street. But the Capper Act, which was ultimately limited to Washington, D.C., did not pass until 1932 (United States 1932).

The year 1934 witnessed a dramatic and significant shift in public attitudes toward firearms. Many critics saw a connection between the increased violence of America's cities and the accelerating violence in Hollywood's movies. Of particular concern to many Americans was what they saw as a glorification of gangsters exemplified in such films as *Little Caesar* (1930), *The Public Enemy* (1931), and *Scarface* (1932) (Cook 1996). The latter film was especially disturbing in its near adulation of the machine gun. In 1933 Henry James Forman published *Our Movie Made Children*, a summary of the three-year Payne Fund Studies that suggested that movies were making young Americans more violent (Forman 1933). With the Catholic Church threatening a national boycott, the Motion Picture Producers and Distributors of America imposed a Production Code on all films made in the United States. Among other limitations placed on filmmakers, the code forbade the depiction of the details of any firearms, the display of submachine guns or other illegal weapons, the discussion of such weapons, and even the sound of such weapons offscreen. In addition, no criminal could be shown killing a police officer, and all criminal activities had to result in an appropriate punishment (Cook 1996). A 1938 amendment to the code specified that "frequent presentations of murder tend to lessen regard for the sacredness of life" (Cook 1999, p. 133).

In 1934 Attorney General Homer Cummings became concerned about the increasing availability of machine guns. The Irish Republican Army had placed the first large private order for Thompson submachine guns. However, U.S. customs agents had seized these guns before they left the country, much to the anger of Colt Firearms Company. Evoking this sale to the IRA, Cummings sought to prevent the spread of firearms to criminals through a National Firearms Act. The proposed act would use federal tax powers to require nationwide registration of a variety of firearms, including pistols above .22 caliber, shotguns and rifles with barrels under eighteen inches, machine guns and fully automatic weapons, silencers, and concealed trick weapons (e.g., canes with firing mechanisms). Cummings's bill also required a federal license to manufacture, sell, or import the listed weapons; fingerprinting; and a tax of from $1 for pistols to $200 for machine guns at every transfer of the title to a weapon. And, most dramatically, every gun, like every car, would bear a title of ownership. Those already owning such weapons were to be given four months to register them, though, oddly, there was no penalty for violation of this latter provision (Helmer 1969).

Attorney General Cummings framed these proposals as part of a national anticrime crusade, setting the standard that would be followed with future regulatory efforts. In a national radio address in 1935, Cummings warned that "our great American underworld is armed to the teeth." Particularly dangerous were the machine guns. "There is no legitimate reason on earth for an individual to have possession of a machine gun; nor do I believe that any honest citizen should object to having all classes of lethal weapons placed under registrations. To permit the present situation to continue indefinitely amounts to a disclaimer of national intelligence." Cummings called for a national system of firearms registration, which he insisted would be no more complicated than registering a car. "Show me the man who does not want his gun registered and I will show you a man who should not have a gun" (Cummings 1939, pp. 82, 89).[27]

Senator Royal S. Copeland of New York altered Cummings's proposal and introduced a pair of alternatives. Copeland approached gun regulation from the direction of interstate commerce. Under his version of the act, only manufacturers could ship a concealable firearm and only to registered gun dealers. His bill also banned the interstate shipment of machine guns, required manufacturers to keep one bullet fired by every gun they made, with each bullet required to bear a code on its base denoting the IRS district in which it was sold. Congress initially seemed supportive of the Copeland proposal (United States Congress 1934).[28]

General M. A. Reckford, the executive vice-president of the Na-

[27] President Franklin Roosevelt also saw gun registration as part of a larger anticrime effort. See his address to the Conference on Crime, December 10, 1934, in Roosevelt 1938–50.

[28] Frederick L. Hoffman provided the committee with statistical evidence that 250,000 people had been killed with firearms in the previous twenty years in homicides, suicides, and accidents (United States Congress 1934).

tional Rifle Association, spoke in favor of a Uniform Firearms Act, assuring the Senate Commerce Committee that the NRA had no objection to the regulation of machine guns and any other "gangster type" weapons. "You can be just as severe with machine guns and sawed-off shotguns as your desire, and we will go along with you" (United States Congress 1934, p. 30). Yet the committee, apparently guided by some influential gun manufacturers, crafted a watered-down version of Copeland's bill that avoided the national registration of firearms while banning the sale and transportation of certain weapons. Congress rapidly considered and passed the National Firearms Act of 1934, and President Roosevelt signed it into law (United States 1934). In 1938, Copeland succeeded in further regulating the movement of firearms with the National Firearms Act of 1938, which included a general licensing and record-keeping procedure for gunmakers, with a $1 fee paid by the dealer. More important, no arms were to be shipped across state lines contrary to state law (United States Congress 1937; United States 1938). That same year the Gallup organization asked for the first time what people thought about gun regulation. Of those surveyed, 84 percent agreed with the statement that "all owners of pistols and revolvers should be required to register with the government"—not that public opinion polls have ever had the slightest relevance to the politics of gun regulation (Gallup 1972, 1:99–100).

A challenge to the National Firearms Act of 1934 reached the U.S. Supreme Court in 1939. Jack Miller and Frank Layton, who both had criminal records, had been convicted in the Arkansas District Court of transporting a sawed-off shotgun across state lines. The Supreme Court issued its opinion in *United States v. Miller* on May 15, 1939 (307 U.S. 174 [1939]). Justice James C. McReynolds linked the Second Amendment with Article 1, Section 8, of the U.S. Constitution in writing for a unanimous court that the "obvious purpose" of the Second Amendment was "to assure the continuation and render possible the effectiveness" of the militia. The Second Amendment "must be interpreted and applied with that end in view." McReynolds added that he could find no contradiction of the purposes of the National Firearms Act with any state legislation. The court could therefore find no reason why outlawing the sale and transportation of sawed-off shotguns interfered with "the preservation or efficiency of a well regulated militia," as guaranteed by the Second Amendment.

Succeeding federal cases would continue to use the logic of *United States v. Miller*. For instance, in 1942, a former New Jersey felon,

Frank Tot, appealed his conviction for owning a Colt automatic capable of being fitted with a silencer. Tot's lawyers argued that the state had violated his Second Amendment rights. But the Third Circuit court rejected this logic, ruling that the Second Amendment "was not adopted with individual rights in mind, but as a protection for the States in the maintenance of their militia organizations against possible encroachments by federal power" (*United States v. Tot,* 131 F. 2d 261 [3d Cir. 1942]). That same year, the First Circuit court offered a similar Constitutional reading in *Cases v. United States* (131 F. 2d 916 [1st Cir. 1942]).

In the seventy years after the end of the Civil War, local and state governments attempted to ameliorate what they saw as the potentially harmful effects of the widespread ownership of firearms. In the case of the southern states, many of these efforts were focused on keeping firearms out of the hands of black Americans. Other efforts aimed at preventing the concealment of guns in public places as posing an obvious danger to public peace and order. Finally, in the 1930s Congress joined in these regulatory efforts with an attempt to prevent the acquisition of certain types of firearms. The right of these governments to exercise this sovereign power was not overturned by the nation's court system. In the case of firearms, there was a broad consensus, joined in by the National Rifle Association, that some types of dangerous items fell within the purview of the state's police powers.

IV. Contested Ground

In the 1960s opponents of gun regulation in the United States began insisting that there were already 20,000 gun laws in the country. The origins of this number remain shrouded in obscurity, but the number has been repeated over the past four decades with unvarying exactness. Even to inquire as to the accuracy of this figure is to bring down a storm of condemnation, including in academic circles.[29] But the general acceptance of this number reflects well the deep-seated conviction among many gun owners that their rights are under attack. Anyone who has been to a gun shop or gun show, however, may find the prop-

[29] Based on my experience on h-law, a listserve for legal history. No one could identify the source of this number, but several were certain that it must be accurate. As one person wrote, "In asking this question you imply that there are not 20,000 gun laws and that we have room for more. I warn you not to try to take away my guns." I have no intention of attempting to take away this person's guns. For a listing of gun legislation (which falls far short of 20,000), see http://www.atf.treas.gov/firearms/statelaws/index.htm (Bureau of Alcohol, Tobacco and Firearms 2000).

osition that access to firearms is in any way seriously constrained a bit overstated. As recently as 1997 the National Rifle Association invited its members to take part in their "Jackpot O' Guns" sweepstakes, with $40,000 worth of guns up for grabs. The reality of gun laws in the second half of the twentieth century is not open to easy generalization, as the issue has become fiercely political. But it seems safe to say that localities, states, and the federal government are pulling in many contrary directions and that the country currently operates under a notable inconsistency in its regulatory legislation.

In the immediate aftermath of World War II gun laws faded from public consciousness in the United States. There were still concealed weapons acts and limitations on the right to own automatic weapons in every state, and the Federal Firearms Acts of 1934 and 1938 were still on the books; yet the issue vanished from legislative consideration. For the most part, it was possible for any adult to walk into a pawn shop or sporting goods store and walk out minutes later with a pistol, rifle, or shotgun and ammunition. There is some evidence that southern blacks still found it difficult to acquire firearms and were often intimidated when they attempted to purchase them. In one notable instance in the 1950s the National Rifle Association revoked the charter of a South Carolina gun club when it discovered that it served as an African American protective organization against Klan violence (Pascoe 1999). However, it was an easy matter for anyone to purchase a gun through the mail. It was not until the mid-1960s that some Americans began to question the wisdom of this laissez-faire attitude toward firearms. The rapid increase in violent crimes in the 1960s combined with the series of riots in America's cities convinced many people on both sides of the political spectrum that unhindered access to firearms is not always the best policy for preserving public order (Serven and Trefethen 1967; Spitzer 1998).

The modern controversy over gun regulation began on November 22, 1963. Lee Harvey Oswald purchased the Mannlicher-Carcano he used to kill the president of the United States through an advertisement in the NRA's official publication, *American Rifleman.* This upset many members of Congress, who moved to regulate the sale of firearms through the U.S. Postal Service. In 1965 the NRA called upon its core constituency to crush this effort. Members of Congress reported that they had never received so many letters on a single issue, as thousands of NRA members wrote in condemning the effort to terminate the convenience of buying guns through the mail (Serven and Trefethen 1967; Spitzer 1998).

The proposed legislation did not leave the committee room until 1968, when the assassinations of Martin Luther King, Jr., and Robert Kennedy inspired the Gun Control Act of 1968. In addition to banning the interstate shipment of guns and ammunition, the act also ended the sale of firearms to minors, drug addicts, convicted felons, and mental incompetents (United States 1968; Zimring 1975). While there is some evidence that the prohibition on firearms sales to minors was effectively enforced until 1984, the act's overall impact seems to have been negligible.[30]

One of the more significant consequences of the Gun Control Act of 1968 was the transformation of the National Rifle Association. The NRA had long attracted a wide diversity of gun owners, from target shooters to hunters to gun collectors, and their focus had traditionally been on the recreational uses of firearms rather than on politics. But in 1968 Executive Vice-President Franklin Orth indicated that some sorts of gun regulation might be appropriate, immediately antagonizing an activist core of gun-rights absolutists who saw any compromise as total surrender. At the NRA's 1977 convention, this group, led by Harlon Carter, took over the NRA (Davidson 1993; LaPierre 1994), instituting what Robert Spitzer calls "issue purity" (Spitzer 1998, p. 85). From 1977, the NRA has opposed nearly all proposed gun regulation and become one of the most effective lobbying groups in American history.

Much has happened in relation to gun regulation since 1977, but those developments are more in the realm of public policy or political science than history. Gun control advocates overcame the resistance of the National Rifle Association on a number of occasions, persuading the Congress to enact restrictions on the availability of some kinds of semiautomatic weapons, and achieving enactment of the Brady Bill, which imposed a five-day waiting period on gun purchases. At the state level, gun control opponents persuaded many legislatures to revise state law to permit broader possession and carrying of concealed

[30] In 1984, 4.8 percent of the homicides in the United States involved people under the age of eighteen. After the 1968 Gun Control Act was gutted in 1984, that percentage began to increase, reaching 9.9 percent in 1993, with nearly 20 percent of the homicides involving people under the age of twenty-one (Zimring and Hawkins 1997; Zimring 1998).

weapons than theretofore was legal and successfully persuaded some states to change their state constitutions expressly to create an affirmative right to private possession of firearms. Gun control advocates continued their efforts, expressed in such things as strict liability suits by municipalities against gun manufacturers for the sale of inherently dangerous instruments, and gun control opponents resisted by persuading state legislatures to enact legislation forbidding such lawsuits. Where it will all end remains to be seen. What is clear, however, from historical sources, is that gun regulation has never been far from the policy agendas of American governments or of their English predecessors.

V. The Legal History of the Gun in America

Until the very end of the twentieth century, federal courts repeatedly accepted the reasoning in *United States v. Miller.*[31] One of the more interesting of these cases was *United States v. Warin*, argued before the Sixth Circuit court in 1976. James Warin purchased but did not register a machine gun. Though he violated federal law in failing to register this purchase, Warin, backed by the Second Amendment Foundation, insisted that Ohio's militia law and the Second Amendment granted him an unhindered right to own any military weapon. The court found it an "erroneous supposition that the Second Amendment is concerned with the rights of individuals," for the "Second Amendment guaranteed a collective rather than an individual right." Striving to leave no doubt of the state's right to protect itself, the court explained that "there can be no question that an organized society which fails to regulate the importation, manufacture and transfer of the highly sophisticated lethal weapons in existence today does so at its peril" (*United States v. Warin*, 530 F. 2d 103 [6th Cir. 1976]).

The *Warin* decision was followed by a number of supportive cases that seemed close to clarifying the meaning of the Second Amendment in American law. In 1980, the Supreme Court ruled in *Lewis v. United States* that there were no constitutionally protected liberties infringed

[31] Cases v. United States, 131 F. 2d 916 (1st Cir. 1942); Love v. Pepersack, 47 F. 3d 120 (4th Cir. 1995); United States v. Synnes, 438 F. 2d 764 (8th Cir. 1971); United States v. Oakes, 564 F. 2d 384 (10th Cir. 1977); Quilici v. Village of Morton Grove, 695 F. 2d 261 (7th Cir. 1982); Hickman v. Block, 81 F. 3d 98 (9th Cir. 1996); United States v. Ryber, 103 F. 3d 273 (3d Cir. 1996); United States v. Wright, 117 F. 3d 1265 (11th Cir. 1997); United States v. Scanio, No. 97-1584, 1998 U.S. App. LEXIS 29415 (2d Cir. 1998); United States v. Henson, 1999 U.S. Dist. LEXIS 8987 (S.D. W. Va. 1999); Fraternal Order of Police v. United States, 173 F. 3d 898 (D.C. Cir. 1999).

by federal gun regulations (100 S. Ct. 915, 921 [1980]). In 1990, the Court held that the National Guard was the only legitimate inheritor of the militia mantle (*Perpich v. Department of Defense*, 110 S. Ct. 2418 [1990]). As the Eighth Circuit Court of Appeals stated, the federal courts had consistently "analyzed the Second Amendment purely in terms of protecting state militias, rather than individual rights" (*United States v. Nelson*, 859 F. 2d 1318 [8th Cir. 1988]). As recently as 1996 the Supreme Court refused to review a Ninth Circuit decision that the Second Amendment did not protect the private ownership of firearms (*Hickman v. Block*, 81 F. 3d 98 [9th Cir. 1996]). In 1999, the Supreme Court refused to hear two challenges to its previous rulings that the Second Amendment is about a "well regulated militia" and that states and the federal government both have the authority to regulate gun production and ownership.

Given this judicial history, it was little wonder that opponents of gun regulation turned their logic to the Tenth Amendment. In 1997, opponents of the Brady Bill succeeded in having a provision of that act overturned by the Supreme Court on Tenth Amendment grounds. In *Printz v. United States*, 138 L. Ed. 2d 914 (1997), five members of the court ruled that Congress had exceeded its authority in requiring that local police conduct background checks on prospective gun buyers. Though Congress called on law enforcement to make a "reasonable effort to ascertain within 5 business days whether receipt or possession would be in violation of the law" and contained no mechanism for punishing those police who failed in this duty, the court found that the very request of such assistance was an effort to "conscript" local officials to enforce a federal law. The Court seems to have read the Brady Bill's discretionary checking system as mandatory. *Printz v. United States* signaled that the Supreme Court might be open to reversing direction on gun legislation, if not on the Second Amendment itself.

But a case arising out of the North Texas District Court in 1999 provided the high court with an opportunity to rethink its historic understanding of the Second Amendment. In *United States v. Emerson*, U.S. Dist. LEXIS 4700 (N.D. Tex. 1999), District Judge Sam R. Cummings drew upon the writings of the "standard model" scholars to argue that the Second Amendment grants an absolute individual right to gun ownership. "A historical examination of the right to bear arms, from English antecedents to the drafting of the Second Amendment, bears proof that the right to bear arms has consistently been, and should still be, construed as an individual right." *United States v. Emerson* came before the court at its October 2000 session.

As Judge Cummings's decision indicates, much of the debate over the meaning of the Second Amendment hinges on a very narrowly defined range of interpretation: what precisely that single sentence means. Far too often it appears as though the different interpretations of this amendment come down to whether one reads the first or second part of the sentence. Much of the scholarship is more sophisticated than that, but until very recently there has been a notable lack of interest in fixing the precise context in which the Second Amendment became part of the Constitution. Efforts to fix the original intent of the Second Amendment generally founder on an inability to appreciate how different a world was the United States in the 1790s. Federalists and antifederalists shared fears that the fragile new republic could collapse in the face of domestic insurrection. Radicals or separatists could send the country spinning into anarchy, while conservatives or nationalists could drive the nation toward a dictatorship. Adding to the uncertainty was the constant threat of slave insurrection, with the leaders of the southern states particularly terrified of a generalized uprising. Thus, the antifederalists worried that in the absence of government arms, the people would remain unarmed, evoking a federalist pledge to find the formula that would arm reliable citizens while keeping guns out of the hands of the dangerous classes. The Second Amendment promised to attain that goal, guaranteeing that, should the national government fail in its constitutional mandate to arm, organize, and train the militia, the states could step into the breach.

Even when legal scholars move beyond the immediate period in which the Constitution and Bill of Rights were written, they have a tendency to treat texts as little more than repositories of useful quotations. A good example of that proclivity is evident in a favorite quotation employed by those favoring the individualist reading of the Second Amendment. In his classic *Commentaries on the Constitution of the Unites States,* Justice Joseph Story famously stated that "the right of the citizens to keep and bear arms has justly been considered as the palladium of the liberties of a republic, since it offers a strong moral check against the usurpation and arbitrary power of rulers, and will generally, even if these are successful in the first instance, enable the people to resist and triumph over them." Rarely quoted are the next two sentences, which complicate the matter considerably. "And yet, though this truth would seem so clear, and the importance of a well-regulated militia would seem so undeniable, it cannot be disguised that, among the American people, there is a growing indifference to any system of militia discipline, and a strong disposition, from a sense of its burdens, to be rid of all regulations. How it is practicable to keep the people duly armed without some organization it is difficult to see" (Story 1851, 2:620–21).

While it is important to finish reading the paragraph from which a quotation is lifted, for historians it is even more vital to appreciate how such a quotation fits into the pattern of a speaker's life. Postmodernists speak of the "fallacy of authorial intent," maintaining that the author's own purposes, beliefs, actions, and social context are irrelevant. Fortunately, historians still insist on all these factors for a complete analysis. It is therefore necessary in this instance to know that the militia appears a minor issue in Joseph Story's life and thought; in fact there is no reference to it in any collection of his works or biographies, and Story never served in the militia himself (Bellesiles 1999).

But consider also a quotation often used by those on the collectivist side (and referenced above). In *Aymette v. Tennessee*, that state's supreme court ruled that whereas "the object, then, for which the right of keeping and bearing arms is secured is the defence of the public," that the legislature retains "a right to prohibit the wearing or keeping weapons dangerous to the peace and safety of the citizens." This single quotation is definitely in keeping with the general thrust of this decision. "To hold that the Legislature could pass no law upon this subject by which to preserve the public peace, and protect our citizens from the terror which a wanton and unusual exhibition of arms might produce, . . . would be to pervert a great political right to the worst of purposes, and to make it a social evil of infinitely greater extent to society than would result from abandoning the right itself" (21 Tenn. 154, 1840 WL 1554, 2 Hum. 15).

But even while Judge Green upheld the state's power to limit gun ownership and use, he still insisted that the people retained a right to bear arms for the defense of the state. This carefully constrained reading of that right is in keeping with section 26 of the state's declaration of rights: "The free white men of this state have a right to keep and bear arms for their common defence." The right to own guns was limited to white men for a simple reason: the greatest threat to the state, in the eyes of most whites, came from blacks. Thus, taking this single quotation as establishing a clear pattern of a collectivist right to gun ownership ignores the circumscribed nature of that collectivity: it applies to white men only. But even then, the white elite of the South consistently feared that poor whites would make common cause with the blacks, convincing many legislatures to maintain a cautious curb on arms possession (Waldrep 1998). A consideration of the exact environment of the antebellum South highlights legislative efforts to preserve a three-sided balance between the state's need to maintain order while keeping whites armed yet also preventing blacks and possible white supporters from accessing arms.

If law review articles have erred (in my opinion) in not paying far more attention to the complexities of context, it seems fair to cast some calumny on historians as well. Historical scholarship is just catching up with the public's and legal community's interest in firearms and firearms legislation. There has been surprisingly little research into America's fascination with firearms and nearly none on its history of gun legislation. Far too many historians have been content to repeat without attempting to validate accepted generalities. Popular attitudes toward guns and gun laws are assumed but seldom demonstrated. The absence of public response to gun regulation through much of the nineteenth century could indicate either agreement or indifference; at the moment no one has attempted to determine which was the case. Even the twentieth century remains largely unexplored on these issues beyond public opinion polls and assertions often informed by a dogmatically held political position.

The history of the law is more complex than a collection of quotations or, admittedly, simply a listing of legislation. The essence of law is enforcement. In order to understand a precise social and legal context it is therefore necessary to examine the enforcement of laws. The study of gun laws in America is really in its infancy. There are some initial indications that some gun laws were taken seriously and regularly and rigorously enforced. However, there has not yet been a systematic examination of the enforcement of gun laws or of their impact. Such a study would prove a valuable addition to the historical literature and would go a long way toward indicating the substance of public attitudes toward gun ownership in America.

REFERENCES

Adams, Lynn G. 1926. "Adequate and Proper Restrictions on Sale and Ownership of Firearms." *Annals of the American Academy of Political and Social Science* 125:153–57.

Alabama. 1897. *The Code of Alabama, Adopted by Act of the General Assembly.* Compiled by William L. Martin. Atlanta: Foote & Davies.

American Bar Association. 1926. "Denver Meeting of Association Breaks All Attendance Records." *American Bar Association Journal* 12:527–32, 560–72.

Anderson, Fred. 2000. *Crucible of War: The Seven Years' War and the Fate of Empire in British North America, 1754–1766.* New York: Knopf.

Arizona. 1887. *Revised Statutes of Arizona.* Edited by Cameron H. King. Prescott, Ariz.: Prescott Courier Print.

Arkansas. 1923. *Acts of the Arkansas Legislature.* N.p.

Army and Navy Journal. 1867. Editorial. April 13.

Avins, Alfred, ed. 1967. *The Reconstruction Amendments' Debates: The Legislative History and Contemporary Debates in Congress on the Thirteenth, Fourteenth, and Fifteenth Amendments.* Richmond: Virginia Commission on Constitutional Government.

Ayers, Edward L. 1984. *Vengeance and Justice: Crime and Punishment in the Nineteenth Century American South.* New York: Oxford University Press.

Bailyn, Bernard. 1967. *The Ideological Origins of the American Revolution.* Cambridge, Mass.: Harvard University Press.

Bakal, Carl. 1966. *The Right to Bear Arms.* New York: McGraw-Hill.

Balch, William R. 1882. "The Police Problem." *International Review* 13:507–17.

Banning, Lance. 1995. *The Sacred Fire of Liberty: James Madison and the Founding of the Federal Republic.* Ithaca, N.Y.: Cornell University Press.

Barlow, Joel. 1956. *Advice to the Priveleged Orders of Europe.* Ithaca, N.Y.: Cornell University Press. (Originally published 1792.)

Barnett, Randy E., and Don B. Kates. 1996. "Under Fire: The New Consensus on the Second Amendment." *Emory Law Journal* 45:1139–1259.

Batey, Robert. 1986. "Strict Construction of Firearms Offenses: The Supreme Court and the Gun Control Act of 1968." *Law and Contemporary Problems* 49:163–98.

"The Battle to Disarm the Gunman." 1927. *Literary Digest* 92(February 19):9.

Bean, Michael J., and Melanie J. Rowland. 1997. *The Evolution of National Wildlife Law.* 3d ed. Westport, Conn.: Praeger.

Bellesiles, Michael A. 1996. "The Origins of Gun Culture in the United States, 1760–1865." *Journal of American History* 83:425–55.

———. 1998. "Gun Laws in Early America: The Regulation of Firearms Ownership, 1607–1794." *Law and History Review* 16:567–89.

———. 1999. "Suicide Pact: New Readings of the Second Amendment." *Constitutional Commentary* 16:247–62.

———. 2000. *Arming America: The Origins of a National Gun Culture.* New York: Knopf.

Beman, Lamar T., ed. 1926. *Outlawing the Pistol.* New York: Wilson.

Berger, Raoul. 1977. *Government by Judiciary: The Transformation of the Fourteenth Amendment.* Cambridge, Mass.: Harvard University Press.

Berry, Mary Frances. 1971. *Black Resistance, White Law: A History of Constitutional Racism in America.* New York: Appleton-Century-Crofts.

Blackmore, Howard L. 1986. *A Dictionary of London Gunmakers, 1350–1850.* Oxford: Shumway.

Blackstone, William. 1979. *Commentaries on the Laws of England.* 4 vols. Chicago: University of Chicago Press.

Boessenecker, John. 1988. *Badge and Buckshot: Lawlessness in Old California.* Norman: University of Oklahoma Press.

Bowling, Kenneth R., and Helen E. Veit, eds. 1988. *The Diary of William Maclay and Other Notes on Senate Debates.* Baltimore: Johns Hopkins University Press.

Breen, T. H., and Stephen Innes. 1980. *"Myne Owne Ground": Race and Freedom on Virginia's Eastern Shore, 1640–1676.* New York: Oxford University Press.

Brundage, Lyle D. 1958. "The Organization, Administrations, and Training of the United States Ordinary and Volunteer Militia, 1792–1861." Ph.D. dissertation, University of Michigan.

Bureau of Alcohol, Tobacco and Firearms. 2000. Federal Firearms Regulations Reference Guide. http://www.atf.treas.gov/pub/2000 ref.htm.

Burn, Richard. 1836. *The Justice of the Peace, and Parish Officer.* Revised by Edward Vaughan Williams and Thomas D'Oyly. 5 vols. London: Williams & D'Oyly.

Calhoon, Robert M. 1965. *The Loyalists in Revolutionary America, 1760–1781.* New York: Harcourt Brace.

Carp, E. Wayne. 1984. *"To Starve the Army at Pleasure": Continental Army Administration and American Political Culture, 1775–1783.* Chapel Hill: University of North Carolina Press.

Carrigan, William D. 1999. "Between South and West: Race, Violence, and Power in Central Texas, 1836–1916." Ph.D. dissertation, Emory University.

Commissioners of the Indian Trade. 1710–18. *Journals of the Commissioners of the Indian Trade, Sept. 20, 1710–August 29, 1718.* Edited by W. L. McDowell. Columbia: South Carolina Archives, 1955.

Comstock, Anthony. 1880. *Frauds Exposed; or, How the People Are Deceived and Robbed, and Youth Corrupted.* New York: Patterson Smith.

Connecticut. 1850–90. *The Public Records of the Colony of Connecticut.* Edited by J. Hammond Trumbull et al. 15 vols. Hartford, Conn.: Hartford Lockwood & Brainard.

Continental Congress. 1774–89. *Journals of the Continental Congress, 1774–1789.* Edited by Worthington C. Ford et al. 34 vols. Washington, D.C.: Government Printing Office.

Cook, David A. 1996. *A History of Narrative Film.* 3d ed. New York: Norton.

———. 1999. "Ballistic Balletics: Styles of Violent Representation in *The Wild Bunch* and After." In *Sam Peckinpah's "The Wild Bunch,"* edited by Stephen Prince. Cambridge: Cambridge University Press.

Cooper, John S. 1993. *For Commonwealth and Crown: English Gunmakers of the Seventeenth Century.* Gillingham: Wilson Hunt.

Cornell, Saul. 1999. "Commonplace or Anachronism: The Standard Model, the Second Amendment, and the Problem of History in Contemporary Constitutional Theory." *Constitutional Commentary* 16:221–46.

Crane, Verner S. 1956. *The Southern Frontier.* Ann Arbor: University of Michigan Press.

Cress, Lawrence Delbert. 1982. *Citizens in Arms: The Army and the Militia in*

American Society to the War of 1812. Chapel Hill: University of North Carolina Press.

Cummings, Homer. 1939. *Selected Papers of Homer Cummings: Attorney General of the United States, 1933–1939.* Edited by Carl B. Swisher. New York: Scribner's.

Davidson, Osha Gray. 1993. *Under Fire: The NRA and the Battle for Gun Control.* New York: Holt.

diGiacomantonio, William C., Kenneth R. Bowling, Charlene Bangs Bickford, and Helen E. Veit, eds. 1996. *Documentary History of the First Federal Congress.* Vol. 14, *Debates in the House of Representatives Third Session, December 1790–March 1791.* Baltimore: Johns Hopkins University Press.

Dykstra, Robert R. 1968. *The Cattle Towns.* New York: Knopf.

———. 1996. "Field Notes: Overdosing on Dodge City." *Western Historical Quarterly* 27:505–14.

———. 1999. "To Live and Die in Dodge City: Body Counts, Law and Order, and the Case of *Kansas v. Gill.*" In *Lethal Imagination: Violence and Brutality in American History,* edited by Michael A. Bellesiles. New York: New York University Press.

Elkins, Stanley, and Eric McKitrick. 1993. *The Age of Federalism.* New York: Oxford University Press.

Ellis, Richard E. 1987. "The Persistence of Antifederalism after 1789." In *Beyond Confederation: Origins of the Constitution and American National Identity,* edited by Richard Beeman, Stephen Botein, and Edward C. Carter II. Chapel Hill: University of North Carolina Press.

Emery, Lucilius. 1915. "The Constitutional Right to Bear Arms." *Harvard Law Review* 28:473–77.

Farrand, Max, ed. 1937. *The Records of the Federal Convention of 1787.* 4 vols. New Haven, Conn.: Yale University Press.

Finkelman, Paul. 1987. "Slavery and the Constitutional Convention: Making a Covenant with Death." In *Beyond Confederation: Origins of the Constitution and American National Identity,* edited by Richard Beeman, Stephen Botein, and Edward C. Carter II. Chapel Hill: University of North Carolina Press.

Fleming, Walter L., ed. 1906–7. *Documentary History of Reconstruction: Political, Military, Social, Religious, Educational and Industrial, 1865 to the Present Time.* 2 vols. Cleveland: Clark.

Flick, Alexander C. 1901. *Loyalism in New York during the American Revolution.* New York: Columbia University Press.

Florida. 1866. *Acts and Resolutions of the General Assembly, 1865, 1866.* Tallahassee, Fla.: C. H. Walton.

———. 1906. *Laws of the State of Florida.* Tallahassee, Fla.: Capital.

Foner, Eric. 1988. *Reconstruction: America's Unfinished Revolution, 1863–1877.* New York: Harper & Row.

Forman, Henry James. 1933. *Our Movie Made Children.* New York: Macmillan.

Friedman, Lawrence J. 1970. *The White Savage: Racial Fantasies in the Postbellum South.* Englewood Cliffs, N.J.: Prentice-Hall.

Gallup, George H., ed. 1972. *The Gallup Poll.* 3 vols. Wilmington, Del.: Scholarly Resources.

Georgia. 1851. *Digest of Statute Laws of Georgia, 1851.* Athens, Ga.: Christy, Kelsea & Burke.

Gilmore, Russell S. 1974. "Crack Shots and Patriots: The National Rifle Association and America's Military-Sporting Tradition, 1871–1929." Ph.D. dissertation, University of Wisconsin.

Gilmour, Ian. 1992. *Riot, Risings and Revolution: Governance and Violence in Eighteenth-Century Britain.* London: Pimlico.

Greener, W. W. 1967. *The Gun and Its Development.* New York: Bonanza Books. (Originally published 1910.)

Hahn, Steve. 1982. "Hunting Fishing, and Foraging: Common Rights and Class Relations in the Postbellum South." *Radical History Review* 26:37–64.

Halbrook, Stephen P. 1986. "What the Framers Intended: A Linguistic Analysis of the Right to 'Bear Arms.'" *Law and Contemporary Problems* 49:151–62.

———. 1999. *Freedmen, the Fourteenth Amendment, and the Right to Bear Arms, 1866–1876.* Westport, Conn.: Praeger.

Hamilton, Alexander. 1961–87. *The Papers of Alexander Hamilton.* Edited by Harold C. Syrett and Jacob E. Cooke. 27 vols. New York: Columbia University Press.

Hamilton, Alexander, James Madison, and John Jay. 1787–88. *The Federalist, or the New Constitution.* Norwalk, Conn.: Easton Press, 1979.

Hatley, Thomas. 1993. *The Dividing Paths: Cherokees and South Carolinians through the Era of Revolution.* New York: Oxford University Press.

Hayward, J. F. 1962. *The Art of the Gunmaker.* 2 vols. London: Barrie & Rockliff.

Helmer, William J. 1969. *The Gun That Made the Twenties Roar.* New York: Gun Room Press.

Higginbotham, Don. 1998. "The Federalized Militia Debate: A Neglected Aspect of Second Amendment Scholarship." *William and Mary Quarterly* 55:39–58.

———. 1999. "The Second Amendment in Historical Context." *Constitutional Commentary* 16:263–68.

Hoffman, Frederick L. 1925. *The Homicide Problem.* Newark, N.J.: Prudential.

Hollon, W. Eugene. 1974. *Frontier Violence: Another Look.* New York: Oxford University Press.

Holt, George C. 1910. "Address to the Wisconsin State Bar Association." *Independent* 11(August):278–83.

Illinois. 1833. *The Revised Laws of Illinois, Containing All Laws of a General and Public Nature.* Vandalia, Ill.: Greiner & Sherman.

Imlay, Charles V. 1926. "The Uniform Firearms Act." *American Bar Association Journal* 12:767–69.

———. 1930. "Uniform Firearms Act Reaffirmed." *American Bar Association Journal* 16:799–801.

Jensen, Merrill, John P. Kaminski, and Gaspare J. Saladino, eds. 1976–95. *The Documentary History of the Ratification of the Constitution.* 18 vols. Madison: State Historical Society of Wisconsin.

Jordan, Philip D. 1970. *Frontier Law and Order: Ten Essays.* Lincoln: University of Nebraska Press.

Juricek, John T. 1964. "The Westo Indians." *Ethnohistory* 11:134–73.

Kalman, Laura. 1996. *The Strange Career of Legal Liberalism.* New Haven, Conn.: Yale University Press.

Kennett, Lee, and James L. Anderson. 1975. *The Gun in America.* Westport, Conn.: Greenwood.

Kentucky. 1809–19. *The Statute Laws of Kentucky.* Edited by William Littell. 5 vols. Frankfort, Ky.: William Hunter.

———. 1835. *Digest of the Statute Laws of Kentucky.* Edited by C. S. Morehead and Mason Brown. 2 vols. Frankfort, Ky.: A. G. Hodges.

———. 1871. *Kentucky Acts, Adjourned Session, 1871.* Frankfort, Ky.: State Journal Co.

Kirby, C. H. 1932. "The English Game Law System." *American Historical Review* 38:240–62.

Lambert, Robert S. 1987. *South Carolina Loyalists in the American Revolution.* Columbia: University of South Carolina Press.

Lane, Roger. 1967. *Policing the City: Boston, 1822–1885.* Cambridge, Mass.: Harvard University Press.

LaPierre, Wayne. 1994. *Guns, Crime and Freedom.* Washington, D.C.: Regnery.

Leff, Carol S., and Mark H. Leff. 1981. "The Politics of Ineffectiveness: Firearms Legislation, 1919–38." *Annals of the American Academy of Political and Social Science* 455:60–61.

Leibiger, Stuart. 1993. "James Madison and Amendments to the Constitution, 1787–1789: 'Parchment Barriers.'" *Journal of Southern History* 59:441–68.

Levinson, Sanford. 1989. "The Embarrassing Second Amendment." *Yale Law Journal* 99:636–59.

Levy, Leonard. 1988. *Original Intent and the Framers' Constitution.* New York: Macmillan.

Lott, John R., Jr. 1998. *More Guns, Less Crime: Understanding Crime and Gun-Control Laws.* Chicago: University of Chicago Press.

Louisiana Advertiser. 1834. Editorial. February 14.

Louisiana. 1813. *Acts of Louisiana, 1813.* N.p.

———. 1841. *Louisiana Digest, 1804–1841.* Compiled by Meinrad Greiner. New Orleans: B. Levy.

———. 1855. *Annual Report of the Attorney General to the Legislature of the State of Louisiana, 1855.* New Orleans: E. LaSere.

———. 1876. *The Revised Statute Laws of the State of Louisiana from the Organization of the Territory to the Year 1869.* Edited by Albert Voorhies. New Orleans: B. Bloomfield.

———. 1898. *Acts of Louisiana, 1898.* New Orleans: F. F. Hansell.

Lund, Thomas A. 1980. *American Wildlife Law.* Berkeley: University of California Press.

Macfarlane, Alan. 1981. *The Justice and the Mare's Ale: Law and Disorder in Seventeenth-Century England.* Oxford: Blackwell.

Malcolm, Joyce Lee. 1994. *To Keep and Bear Arms: The Origins of an Anglo-American Right.* Cambridge, Mass.: Harvard University Press.

Manning, Roger B. 1993. *Hunters and Poachers: A Cultural and Social History of Unlawful Hunting in England, 1485–1640.* Oxford: Clarendon Press.

Marks, Stuart A. 1991. *Southern Hunting in Black and White: Nature, History, and Ritual in a Carolina Community.* Princeton, N.J.: Princeton University Press.

Maryland. *Archives of Maryland.* 1883–1972. Edited by William H. Browne et al. 72 vols. Baltimore: Maryland Historical Society.

Massachusetts. 1836. *Militia Laws of the United States and Massachusetts.* Boston: Young & Minns.

———. 1853–54. *Records of the Governor and Company of the Massachusetts Bay.* Edited by Nathaniel B. Shurtleff. 5 vols. Boston: W. White.

———. 1856. *Annual Report of the Adjutant General of the Commonwealth of Massachusetts for the Year Ending Dec. 31, 1855.* By Ebenezer Stone. Boston: White & Potter.

Matthews, Richard K. 1995. *If Men Were Angels: James Madison and the Heartless Empire of Reason.* Lawrence: University Press of Kansas.

Mayton, William T. 1984. "Seditious Libel and the Lost Guarantee of a Freedom of Expression." *Columbia Law Review* 84:91–142.

McAdoo, William G. 1927. "Crime and Punishment: Causes and Mechanisms of Prevalent Crimes." *Scientific Monthly* 24:415–25.

McDonald, Forrest. 1965. *E Pluribus Unum: The Formation of the American Republic, 1776–1790.* Boston: Houghton Mifflin.

———. 1985. *Novus Ordo Seclorum: The Intellectual Origins of the Constitution.* Lawrence: University Press of Kansas.

McGrath, Roger D. 1984. *Gunfighters, Highwaymen, and Vigilantes: Violence on the Frontier.* Berkeley: University of California Press.

McKanna, Clare V. 1997. *Homicide, Race, and Justice in the American West, 1880–1920.* Tucson: University of Arizona Press.

Memphis City Council. 1857. *Digest of the Ordinances of the City Council of Memphis, 1826–1857.* Memphis, Tenn.: Eagle & Enquirer Steam Press.

Michigan. 1925. *Laws of the State of Michigan.* Lansing, Mich.: The Library.

Millis, Walter. 1956. *Arms and Men: A Study in American Military History.* New York: Putnam.

Minnesota. 1859. *Public Statutes of the State of Minnesota, 1849–1858.* Edited by Moses Sherburne and William Hollinshead. St. Paul, Minn.: Pioneer Printing.

Minor, William T. 1856. *Message of His Excellency William T. Minor, Governor of Connecticut.* New Haven, Conn.

Mooney, Chris. 2000. "Showdown." *Lingua Franca* 10(February):26–34.

Morgan, Edmund S. 1975. *American Slavery, American Freedom: The Ordeal of Colonial Virginia.* New York: Norton.

Morison, Samuel E., ed. 1929. *Sources and Documents Illustrating the American Revolution.* 2d ed. New York: Oxford University Press.

Munsche, P. B. 1981. *Gentlemen and Poachers: The English Game Laws, 1671–1831.* Cambridge: Cambridge University Press.

Nation. 1907. Editorial. July 25, p. 161.

Neal, W. Keith, and D. H. L. Back. 1984. *Great British Gunmakers, 1540–1740*. Norwich: Historical Firearms.

Nebraska. 1867. *The Statutes of Nebraska, Embracing all of the General Laws of the State*. Edited by Experience Estabrook. Chicago: Culver, Page & Hoyne.

New Mexico. 1880. *General Laws of New Mexico*. Edited by L. Bradford Price. Albany, N.Y.: W. C. Little.

New York City. 1851. *Rules and Regulations for the Government of the Police Department of the City of New-York*. New York: MoSpedon & Baker.

New York State. 1866. *Laws of the State of New York*. 2 vols. Albany, N.Y.: Joel Munsell.

———. 1881. *Laws of the State of New York*. 3 vols. Albany, N.Y.: L. K. Strouse.

———. 1905. *Laws of the State of New York*. 3 vols. Albany, N.Y.: M. Bender.

———. 1911. *Laws of the State of New York*. Albany, N.Y.: M. Bender.

New York Times. 1866. Editorial. August 16.

———. 1911. (September 28), p. 8.

———. 1932. (March 21), p. 4.

New York Tribune. 1892. Editorial. April 20, p. 18.

———. 1911. (January 30), p. 3.

Nobles, Gregory H. 1997. *American Frontiers: Cultural Encounters and Continental Conquest*. New York: Hill & Wang.

North Carolina. 1886. *Colonial Records of North Carolina*. Edited by William Saunders. 6 vols. Raleigh, N.C.: Hale & Daniels.

———. 1886–1909. *The State Records of North Carolina*. Edited by Walter Clark. 30 vols. Goldsboro, N.C.: Nash.

North Dakota. 1896. *Revised Codes of North Dakota*. Bismarck: State of North Dakota.

Novak, William J. 1992. "Salus Populi: The Roots of Regulation in America, 1787–1873." Ph.D. dissertation, Brandeis University.

Ohio. 1833–35. *The Statutes of Ohio and the Northwest Territory, Adopted or Enacted from 1788 to 1833 Inclusive*. Edited by Salmon P. Chase. 3 vols. Cincinnati: R. P. Donogh & Co.

Ohio General Assembly. 1859. *Ohio Acts, Fifty-Third General Assembly, 2d sess., January, 1859*. Columbus, Ohio: Follett, Foster.

Oklahoma. 1891. *Statutes of Oklahoma, 1890*. Edited by Will T. Little. Guthrie, Okla.: Co-operative Publishing Co.

Oliver, Benjamin L. 1970. *The Rights of an American Citizen; With a Commentary on State Rights*. Freeport, N.Y.: Books for Libraries. (Originally published 1832.)

Oregon. 1913. *Laws of the State of Oregon*. Portland, Oreg.: Bledsoe.

Pascoe, Craig. 1999. "The Monroe Rifle Club: Finding Justice in an 'Ungodly and Social Jungle Called Dixie.'" In *Lethal Imagination: Violence and Brutality in American History*, edited by Michael A. Bellesiles. New York: New York University Press.

Patterson, Stephen E. 1993. "The Federalist Reaction to Shays's Rebellion."

In *Debt to Shays: The Bicentennial of an Agrarian Rebellion*, edited by Robert A. Gross. Charlottesville: University Press of Virginia.

Pennsylvania. 1903. *The Statutes at Large of Pennsylvania.* Edited by James T. Mitchell and Henry Flanders. Philadelphia: T. & J. W. Johnson.

Peterson, Harold L. 1956. *Arms and Armor in Colonial America, 1526–1783.* Harrisburg, Pa.: Stackpole.

The Pistol as a Weapon of Defence in the House and on the Road. 1875. New York: Industrial Publishing Co.

Pitcavage, Mark. 1995. "An Equitable Burden: The Decline of the State Militias, 1783–1858." Ph.D. dissertation, Ohio State University.

Pocock, J. G. A. 1957. *The Ancient Constitution and the Feudal Law: A Study of English Historical Thought in the Seventeenth Century.* Cambridge: Cambridge University Press.

Postmaster General. 1911. *Post Office Department Annual Reports for the Fiscal Year Ended June 30, 1910.* Washington, D.C.: Government Printing Office.

———. 1925. *Annual Report of the Postmaster General for the Fiscal Year Ended June 30, 1925.* Washington, D.C.: Government Printing Office.

———. 1926. *Annual Report of the Postmaster General for the Fiscal Year Ended June 30, 1926.* Washington, D.C.: Government Printing Office.

Powell, H. Jefferson. 1987. "Rules for Originalists." *Virginia Law Review* 73:673–84.

Proctor, Nicolas Wolfe. 1998. "Bathed in Blood: Hunting in the Antebellum South." Ph.D. dissertation, Emory University.

Rakove, Jack N. 1997. *Original Meanings: Politics and Ideas in the Making of the Constitution.* New York: Knopf.

———. 1998. *Declaring Rights: A Brief History with Documents.* Boston: Bedford Books.

———. 2000. Comments, Second Amendment Conference, Chicago-Kent Law School.

Rakove, Jack N., ed. 1990. *Interpreting the Constitution: The Debate over Original Intent.* Boston: Northeastern University Press.

Reid, John Phillip. 1980. *Law for the Elephant: Property and Social Behavior on the Overland Trail.* San Marino, Calif.: Huntington Library.

———. 1986. *The Authority of Rights.* Madison: University of Wisconsin Press.

———. 1997. *Policing the Elephant: Crime, Punishment, and Social Behavior on the Overland Trail.* San Marino, Calif.: Huntington Library.

Reynolds, Glenn Harlan. 1995. "A Critical Guide to the Second Amendment." *Tennessee Law Review* 62:461–512.

Richardson, James, comp. 1897–1917. *A Compilation of the Messages and Papers of the Presidents.* 11 vols. New York: Bureau of National Literature.

Robertson, John. 1985. *The Scottish Enlightenment and the Militia Movement.* Edinburgh: Donald.

Roosevelt, Franklin D. 1938–50. *The Public Papers and Addresses of Franklin D. Roosevelt.* Compiled by Samuel I. Rosenman. 13 vols. New York: Random.

Rosa, Joseph G. 1969. *The Gunfighter: Man or Myth?* Norman: University of Oklahoma Press.

Rousey, Dennis C. 1996. *Policing the Southern City: New Orleans, 1805–1889.* Baton Rouge: Louisiana State University Press.

Russell, Carl P. 1957. *Guns on the Early Frontiers.* Berkeley: University of California Press.

Sax, Joseph L. 1970. "The Public Trust Doctrine in Natural Resource Law: Effective Judicial Intervention." *Michigan Law Review* 68:471–566.

Scalia, Antonin. 1997. *A Matter of Interpretation: Federal Courts and the Law.* Princeton, N.J.: Princeton University Press.

Schwoerer, Lois G. 1974. *"No Standing Armies!": The Anti-army Ideology in Seventeenth-Century England.* Baltimore: Johns Hopkins University Press.

———. 1981. *The Declaration of Rights, 1689.* Baltimore: Johns Hopkins University Press.

Serven, James E., and James B. Trefethen, eds. 1967. *Americans and Their Guns: The National Rifle Association Story through Nearly a Century of Service to the Nation.* Harrisburg, Pa.: Stackpole.

Shalhope, Robert E. 1982. "The Ideological Origins of the Second Amendment." *Journal of American History* 69:599–614.

———. 1999. "To Keep and Bear Arms in the Early Republic." *Constitutional Commentary* 16:269–82.

Shea, William L. 1983. *The Virginia Militia in the Seventeenth Century.* Baton Rouge: Louisiana State University Press.

Singletary, Otis A. 1957. *Negro Militia and Reconstruction.* Austin: University of Texas Press.

South Carolina. 1836–41. *The Statutes at Large of South Carolina.* Edited by Thomas Cooper and David J. McCord. 10 vols. Columbia, S.C.: A. S. Johnston.

———. 1865. *Reports and Resolutions of the General Assembly of the State of South Carolina Passed at the Annual Session of 1865.* Columbia, S.C.: Julian Selby.

———. 1910. *Acts of the Legislature of South Carolina.* Columbia, S.C.: The State Co.

South Carolina Commons. 1925. *Journal of the Commons House of the Assembly of South Carolina.* Edited by A. S. Salley. Columbia, S.C.: State Printing Co.

Spitzer, Robert J. 1998. *The Politics of Gun Control.* 2d ed. New York: Chatham.

St. Louis. 1843. *St. Louis, Revised Ordinances . . . Revised and Digested by the Fifth City Council.* St. Louis: E. Dupre.

———. 1846. *St. Louis, Revised Ordinances . . . 1835–1836.* St. Louis: E. Dupre.

Stern, Walter M. 1954. "Gunmaking in Seventeenth-Century London." *Journal of the Arms and Armour Society* 1:55–100.

Story, Joseph. 1851. *Commentaries on the Constitution of the United States: With a Preliminary Review of the Constitutional History of the Colonies and States, before the Adoption of the Constitution.* 2 vols. Boston: Little, Brown. (Originally published 1833.)

Swaney, William, Marcus Kavanagh, Charles Whitman, Wade Ellis, and Charles Farnham. 1922. "For a Better Enforcement of the Law." *American Bar Association Journal* 8:588–91.

Szatmary, David P. 1980. *Shays' Rebellion: The Making of an Agrarian Insurrection.* Amherst: University of Massachusetts Press.

"Table-Talk." 1870. *Appleton's Journal* 4:291, 382.

Taylor, Robert J. 1954. *Western Massachusetts in the Revolution.* Providence, R.I.: Brown University Press.

Tennessee. 1821. *Laws of the State of Tennessee: Including Those of North Carolina Now in Force in This State, from 1715 to 1820, Inclusive.* Compiled by Edward Scott. 2 vols. Knoxville, Tenn.: Heiskell & Brown.

Texas. 1928. *Complete Texas Statutes.* Kansas City, Mo.: Vernon Law Book Co.

Thompson, E. P. 1976. *Whigs and Hunters: The Origins of the Black Act.* New York: Pantheon.

Tober, James A. 1981. *Who Owns the Wildlife? The Political Economy of Conservation in Nineteenth-Century America.* Westport, Conn.: Praeger.

Trefethen, James B. 1975. *An American Crusade for Wildlife.* New York: Winchester.

Trelease, Allen W. 1971. *White Terror: The Ku Klux Klan Conspiracy and Southern Reconstruction.* New York: Harper & Row.

Tunnell, Ted. 1984. *Crucible of Reconstruction: War, Radicalism, and Race in Louisiana, 1862–1877.* Baton Rouge: Louisiana State University Press.

United Kingdom. 1764. *Statutes at Large.* Edited by Danby Pickering. 10 vols. London: H. Lintot.

United States. 1853. *The Public Statutes at Large of the United States of America.* Edited by Richard Peters. 8 vols. Boston: Little, Brown.

———. 1932. *Statutes at Large.* Washington, D.C.: Government Printing Office.

———. 1934. *Statutes at Large.* Washington, D.C.: Government Printing Office.

———. 1938. *Statutes at Large.* Washington, D.C.: Government Printing Office.

———. 1968. *Statutes at Large.* Washington, D.C.: Government Printing Office.

United States Congress. 1921. *Congressional Record.* Washington, D.C.: Government Printing Office.

———. 1922. *Congressional Record.* Washington, D.C.: Government Printing Office.

———. 1927. *Congressional Record.* Washington, D.C.: Government Printing Office.

———. 1929. *Congressional Record.* Washington, D.C.: Government Printing Office.

———. 1934. *Congressional Record.* Washington, D.C.: Government Printing Office.

———. 1937. *Congressional Record.* Washington, D.C.: Government Printing Office.

VanAlstyne, William. 1994. "The Second Amendment and the Personal Right to Arms." *Duke University Law Journal* 43:1236–55.

Van Loan, Charles E. 1912. "Disarming New York." *Munsey's Magazine* 46: 686–91.

Veit, Helen E., et al., eds. 1991. *Creating the Bill of Rights: The Documentary Record from the First Federal Congress.* Baltimore: Johns Hopkins University Press.

Virginia. 1809–23. *The Statutes at Large, Being a Collection of All the Laws of Virginia.* Edited by William W. Hening. 13 vols. Richmond, Va.: Hening.

———. 1961. *Virginia Colonial Abstracts.* Edited by Beverly Fleet. 34 vols. Baltimore: Genealogical Publishing, 1961.

Virginia House of Burgesses. 1619–1658/59. *Journal of the House of Burgesses of Virginia, 1619–1658/59.* Edited by H. R. McIlwaine and J. P. Kennedy. 13 vols. Richmond, Va.: Waddey, 1905–15.

Waldrep, Christopher. 1998. *Roots of Disorder: Race and Criminal Justice in the American South, 1817–80.* Urbana: University of Illinois Press.

Warren, Louis S. 1997. *The Hunter's Game: Poachers and Conservationists in Twentieth-Century America.* New Haven, Conn.: Yale University Press.

Washington, George. 1745–99. *The Writings of George Washington from the Original Manuscript Sources, 1745–1799.* Edited by John C. Fitzpatrick. 39 vols. Washington, D.C.: Government Printing Office, 1931–44.

Washington. 1853–89. Court records of Washington Territory, 1853–1889. Office of the Secretary of State, special collections, University of Washington, Seattle.

Weller, Jack. 1962. "The Sullivan Law." *American Rifleman* 110:33–36.

White, John T. 1978. "Standing Armies in Time of War: Republican Theory and Military Practice during the American Revolution." Ph.D. dissertation, George Washington University.

Williams, Joseph D. 1858. *Annual Report of the Adjutant General of the State of Connecticut for the Year 1857.* Hartford, Conn.: Case, Lockwood.

Williams, Lou Falkner. 1996. *The Great South Carolina Ku Klux Klan Trials, 1871–1872.* Athens: University of Georgia Press.

Wills, Garry. 1999. *A Necessary Evil: A History of American Distrust of Government.* New York: Simon & Schuster.

Wilson, Frederick T. 1903. *Federal Aid in Domestic Disturbances, 1787–1903.* Washington, D.C.: U.S. Congress.

Wilson, Theodore B. 1965. *The Black Codes of the South.* Birmingham: University of Alabama Press.

Wood, Gordon S. 1969. *The Creation of the American Republic, 1776–1787.* New York: Norton.

Wood, Peter. 1974. *Black Majority: Negroes in Colonial South Carolina from 1670 through the Stono Rebellion.* New York: Norton.

Zimring, Franklin E. 1975. "Firearms and Federal Law: The Gun Control Act of 1968." *Journal of Legal Studies* 4:133–43.

———. 1998. *American Youth Violence.* New York: Oxford University Press.

Zimring, Franklin E., and Gordon Hawkins. 1997. *Crime Is Not the Problem: Lethal Violence in America.* New York: Oxford University Press.

Grant T. Harris, Tracey A. Skilling, and Marnie E. Rice

The Construct of Psychopathy

ABSTRACT

As a psychological construct, psychopathy has undergone recent change, and there is still disagreement as to its fundamental character. Nevertheless, it can be reliably and validly measured with such behaviors as callousness, impulsivity, sensation seeking, dishonesty, emotional detachment, extreme selfishness, antisociality, belligerence, juvenile delinquency, and sexual promiscuity. Hare's Psychopathy Checklist-Revised is the best available assessment. Psychopathy exists in women, men, children, and in all racial and ethnic groups examined. No one knows whether some psychopaths function successfully without committing serious offenses. Among institutionalized offender samples, psychopathy is the strongest predictor of violent recidivism and differential response to treatment yet discovered. Although psychopaths can exhibit subtle neurological, physiological, and cognitive differences compared with other people, it is unclear whether these differences constitute defective brain function or the execution of a viable life strategy.

Psychopathy is a real phenomenon (essentially a restriction of that described as antisocial personality), and psychopaths comprise a discrete natural class of individuals (even though the boundaries of this class may be indistinct). Psychopathy is a lifelong persistent condition characterized, in males at least, by aggression beginning in early childhood, impulsivity, resistance to punishment, general lack of emotional at-

Grant Harris is research psychologist at the Mental Health Centre, Penetanguishene, Ontario. Tracey Skilling is research psychologist at the Centre for Addiction and Mental Health, Toronto. Marnie Rice is director of research at the Mental Health Centre, Penetanguishene, Ontario. We gratefully acknowledge our research collaboration on this topic with Zoe Hilton, Martin Lalumière, and Vernon Quinsey.

0192-3234/2001/0028-0004$02.00

tachment or concern for others, dishonesty and selfishness in social interactions, and high levels of promiscuous and uncommitted sexual behavior. The available evidence suggests that psychopathy is substantially heritable and mediated, in part at least, by genes that modulate some neuroanatomical structures and monoamine oxidase-type A (MAO) neurotransmitters. The evidence indicates that psychopathy exists in both sexes and in all racial and ethnic groups, though the expression and prevalence vary systematically. The concept of psychopathy is of paramount importance in the assessment and treatment of serious offenders (especially violent offenders). When measured optimally, psychopathy is the strongest indicator of treatment response and risk for violence yet discovered for such offender populations. The best available measure of psychopathy for forensic populations is Hare's (1991) Psychopathy Checklist-Revised. Finally, we believe that psychopathy's prevalence in the human population is a result of being an evolutionarily stable reproductive strategy maintained at relatively low frequencies.

Most serious crime is committed by a small proportion of the criminal population. In longitudinal studies, about 5 percent of criminally active subjects are responsible for over half the offenses recorded (e.g., Wolfgang, Figlio, and Sellin 1972; Farrington et al. 1988). Although the proportion of these persistent offenders who would be identified as psychopathic is unknown, many of the most serious and persistent offenders would be identified as psychopathic. Nagin, Farrington, and Moffitt (1995) describe three groups of offenders in a sample of 403 British males who were followed from ages eight to thirty-two (see Farrington and West 1993 for a complete description of the data set). One group was labeled "high-level chronics." This group offended at a high rate throughout the observation period. They were much more likely to have started their criminal careers at an early age (many by age ten–eleven years) and at ages fourteen and eighteen had conviction rates well above the other groups. Similarly, Wolfgang and colleagues (Wolfgang, Thornberry, and Figlio 1987) reported that among their group of persistent offenders (those arrested both before and after age eighteen), those that started offending early (by age eleven–twelve) had the highest average number of arrests per offender. The most serious violent offenses were committed by these persistent offenders during their adult years. Many members of these groups, who have also often been referred to as sociopathic or antisocial personality disordered, would be considered psychopathic by today's standards.

Research on adult offenders has shown that psychopathic offenders are responsible for a disproportionate amount of crime (Hare and Jutai 1983; Kosson, Smith, and Newman 1990). They are more difficult to manage in correctional and institutional settings (Hare and McPherson 1984; Wong 1984; Forth, Hart, and Hare 1990). They reoffend and violate conditions of release faster and more often and are at higher risk to reoffend violently than other offenders (Hare 1981; Hare and McPherson 1984; Wong 1984; Hart, Kropp, and Hare 1988; Rice, Harris, and Quinsey 1990; Serin, Peters, and Barbaree 1990; Harris, Rice, and Cormier 1991; Serin 1991). Before discussing the literature, we describe some of our own work that demonstrates how profoundly the construct of psychopathy has influenced our thinking and illustrates its centrality for criminal justice systems.

We examined the violent recidivism of men released from a maximum security institution after either an insanity acquittal or conviction for a violent offense (Harris, Rice, and Cormier 1991). Of the over fifty variables we examined, the score on the Psychopathy Checklist-Revised (PCL-R; Hare 1991) was the single best predictor of violent recidivism. We had previously suspected that psychopathy was merely a euphemism for a lengthy history of officially recorded criminal conduct. To test this idea, we examined the ability of psychopathy scores to predict outcomes after the four best predictors reflecting criminal history had been entered first in a multiple regression solution. Even such a conservative test showed a unique effect of psychopathy in the prediction of violent recidivism. Among nonpsychopaths there was an age-related decline in the likelihood of violent recidivism, but this was not true for psychopaths. In another study, psychopaths scored much higher on a measure of prior alcohol abuse than nonpsychopaths, but alcohol abuse added to the prediction of violent recidivism only among nonpsychopaths (Rice and Harris 1995). These results convinced us that psychopathy was a real phenomenon not subsumed by criminality per se and that violent criminal behavior was different among psychopaths than among nonpsychopaths.

Our research has revealed another interesting interaction with psychopathy in the prediction of recidivism. Among sex offenders released from maximum security confinement, those who were both psychopathic and sexually deviant (measured using phallometric testing; see Harris and Rice 1996) exhibited a drastically greater likelihood of sexual recidivism compared with all the other offenders (Rice and Harris 1997*a*). This suggests that if the term "sexual predator" has any scientifically relevant meaning, it refers to this small but extremely dangerous group of offenders (Harris, Rice, and Quinsey 1998). This interaction again implied that the psychopath-nonpsychopath distinction must be of fundamental importance.

For many years, our institution ran a therapeutic community program for violent offenders that was thought to be especially effective for psychopaths (Harris, Rice, and Cormier 1994; Weisman 1995). After its demise we evaluated the program by comparing its participants to a matched group of offenders who had been imprisoned (Rice, Harris, and Cormier 1992) over a mean ten-year follow-up. The program had little overall effect on violent recidivism, but there was a remarkable interaction with psychopathy. Among nonpsychopaths, there was a significant negative association between participation and violent recidivism, while among psychopaths the association was significantly positive. The data suggested that the "treatment" made the psychopaths more dangerous. Moreover, even though they behaved much worse than nonpsychopaths during therapy, psychopaths were just as successful at convincing the clinicians to recommend them for discharge and to give them leadership roles in the program (Rice, Harris, and Cormier 1992). This was (and still is) the most profound effect of a psychological variable on treatment response we have seen, convincing us yet again how fundamentally different psychopaths are from other people, including other serious offenders (Quinsey et al. 1998).

Psychopathy has been studied most thoroughly in North American offender populations. In male forensic populations prevalence rates vary from approximately 10 to 30 percent depending on the setting (forensic psychiatric facility; minimum, medium, or maximum security prison; see Hare [1991] for a review). Similar estimates have been given for North American female forensic populations with prevalence estimates varying depending on security levels (Neary 1990; Strachan 1993; Loucks 1996). Recent estimates from the American correctional system put the prevalence of psychopathy in female offenders at about 15 percent (Salekin, Rogers, and Sewell 1997; Salekin et al. 1998). The prevalence of psychopathy has also been estimated in forensic samples of North American adolescents. In secure settings for incarcerated young offenders, the prevalence of psychopathy is typically reported at about 30 percent (Forth, Hart, and Hare 1990; Forth 1995; Brandt et al. 1997).

Outside North America, studies examining this construct in forensic populations are also underway. The prevalence estimates for psychopathy have varied depending on the country and the type of population examined. Estimates range from a low of 3 percent in Scottish prisons

(Cooke 1997) to approximately 15 percent in Portugal's and Spain's prison systems (Gonçalves 1999; Moltó, Poy, and Torrubia 2000) and up to 30 percent in English forensic hospitals (Hobson and Shine 1998; Reiss, Grubin, and Meux 1999). We return to the topic of cross-cultural differences below.

An accurate estimation of the prevalence of psychopathy in the general population is not available. Hare (1996, 1998) suggests that the rate may be around 1 percent, but this is an educated guess, possibly based on a study by Forth et al. (1996). In this study of university undergraduates, the prevalence of psychopathy was estimated to be 1 percent among a sample of Caucasian male students. The rate of antisocial personality disorder (American Psychiatric Association 1994) in the general population has been assessed through epidemiological studies. The prevalence of this disorder in North American males typically ranges from 1.5 to 5.5 percent (Compton et al. 1991). Because, as we will discuss later, only a subset of individuals with antisocial personality disorder are psychopathic, it is likely that the prevalence of psychopathy is lower than 5 percent in the general population (see Hare 1983, 1985). We return to the question of prevalence in a later section of this review.

Our research studies described earlier exemplify two other important aspects of the scientific literature on psychopathy. First, the phenomenon itself has undergone swift conceptual change, and only quite recently have investigators established that it can be measured with scientific adequacy. Indeed, this latter development is so recent that scholars still disagree somewhat about the fundamental properties of psychopathy. At first blush, this might seem a fatal limitation—how can psychopathy be studied scientifically when scientists do not agree on who is a psychopath and who is not? Scientific endeavors, however, usually progress by overlapping and converging operations so that the final definition of a phenomenon occurs in parallel with its explanation. For example, the fundamental meaning of "species" underwent several revisions as scientists, in attempting to understand how species arise and change, learned more about population and molecular genetics.

Second, much of the research on psychopathy comes from male convicted criminals and institutionalized forensic psychiatric patients in North America and Western Europe. How can useful conclusions be drawn based on such selected samples? As we discuss at length later, there has been research on psychopathy in women, adolescents, and children, but it is true that there has been little research on psychopathy in non-Western societies or on noncriminal psychopaths. However, when the concept of psychopathy has been examined in non-Western societies (Bhojak et al. 1997; Howard, Payamal, and Neo 1997; Sakuta and Fukushima 1998) or used with populations not selected due to criminality (civil psychiatric patients; see e.g., Steadman et al. 2000), it has been shown to be empirically valuable. In addition, it is likely that the majority of this essay's readers can apply the available work on psychopathy in exactly the same populations in which the work was done—criminal offenders or forensic patients in Western countries.

Here is how this essay is organized. We begin in Section I with a brief description of the concept's history followed by discussion of some diagnostic puzzles—psychopathy among children, female psychopathy, racial and ethnic difference in psychopathy, and noncriminal psychopaths. In Section II we address the heritability of psychopathy and the proximal neurophysiological, cognitive, or personality mechanisms that might underlie the condition. In Section III we examine the fundamental nature of psychopathy and how it is best measured. In Section IV we examine evidence relating to seven different mechanisms that have been hypothesized to underlie psychopathy, and in Section V we consider the hypothesis that psychopathy is not a pathology but instead a trait that is the product of natural selection. Our next topic in Section VI is the application of this work on psychopathy to criminal justice policy and practice. We discuss the importance of this concept in the assessment and treatment of offenders especially pertaining to risk appraisal, criminal responsibility, sentencing, and preventive detention. Finally, in Section VII, we speculate about the future directions of scientific research on this topic.

I. What Is the History of This Construct?

At the beginning of the nineteenth century, the term "psychopathic" meant no more than that someone was psychologically damaged or had a psychological defect. Pritchard (1835) popularized the concept of psychopathy as a disorder of moral capabilities, coining the phrase "moral insanity" to refer to a perversion of temper, affective, and moral disposition without disorder or defect of the intellect. Walker and McCabe (1973) concluded that he meant nothing more by the term "moral" than "psychological" or "emotional," and was thus referring more to psychosis than what today is called psychopathy. Maudsley (1879) used the term "moral insanity" to describe psychopathy as a failure in the development of a moral sense or moral responsibility, using the term in much the same way as modern clinicians do. As early as 1885, psychopathy became related to antisocial behavior and by the mid-twentieth century was used as an equivalent of personality disorder (Walker and McCabe 1973). Since then, the association of psychopathy with antisocial behavior has strengthened, and there has been some clinical agreement regarding the affective, interpersonal, and behavioral attributes of the construct, whether labeled psychopathy, antisocial personality disorder, or sociopathy (Hare 1996).

Cleckley's (1941) *The Mask of Sanity* described the author's experience with nonforensic psychopathic patients. His identification of psychopathy's core attributes had a major impact on the field. These features included superficial charm and good intelligence, absence of delusions and other signs of irrational thinking, absence of "nervousness" or other neurotic manifestations, unreliability, untruthfulness and insincerity, lack of remorse and shame, inadequately motivated antisocial behavior, poor judgment and failure to learn by experience, pathological egocentricity and incapacity for love, general poverty in major affective reactions, specific loss of insight, unresponsiveness in interpersonal relations, fantastic and uninviting behavior, suicide rarely carried out, sex life impersonal, and failure to follow any plan. Cleckley viewed psychopaths as lacking life's normal emotions. In his view, morality is learned, and this learning is guided and enforced by the emotions. Thus, moral feelings are the mechanisms of socialization among nonpsychopaths. Cleckley compared psychopathy with semantic aphasia, a condition in which brain-injured patients can speak in coherent sentences but do not grasp the meaning of words. Generally, however, there is little evidence that psychopaths cannot experience emotion (Steuerwald and Kosson, forthcoming). There is evidence that they feel anger, satisfaction, happiness, and other common emotions (Lykken 1995).

Robert Hare built on Cleckley's work by studying the construct of psychopathy in institutionalized adult male offenders. He expanded Cleckley's sixteen characteristics to twenty-two in the Psychopathy Checklist (Hare 1980), then refined that list to twenty in the Psychopathy Checklist-Revised (Hare 1991). Without question, Hare has had the largest theoretical and empirical impact in the area of psychopathy research. His greatest contribution has been development of a measure of the phenomenon that has remarkably good reliability and validity (see Hart and Hare 1989; Hare 1991; Salekin, Rogers, and Sewell

1996). Hare's theoretical contribution has also been significant. Hare's research on the measurement of psychopathy has profoundly affected current thinking. Based on factor analysis, for example, Hare and his colleagues (Harpur, Hakstian, and Hare 1988) identified two related aspects of psychopathy: an affective/interpersonal dimension characterized by shallowness, callousness, remorselessness, and dishonesty; and a behavioral, lifestyle component characterized by juvenile delinquency, criminal versatility, irresponsibility, sensation seeking, and impulsivity (Hare 1996). These components have often been summarized as reflecting personality traits and behavioral dispositions, respectively, although others have argued that such a distinction is elusive (Widiger and Lynam 1998). Nevertheless, following Hare and colleagues' reports of two correlated factors (a Pearson *r* of about .5), considerable theoretical and empirical debate ensued. The most hotly debated issues concerned whether diagnosis should be based on personality or behavior (e.g., Lilienfield 1994), whether the personality factor predicted violent recidivism better than the behavioral factor (e.g., Salekin, Rogers, and Sewell 1996), whether measurement of the first factor yielded better psychometric properties than the second (e.g., Cooke and Michie 1997, 1999), and whether some particular psychophysiological measure is more related to one factor than the other (e.g., Patrick 1994). Even though Hare has now abandoned this two-factor characterization in favor of three factors (Hare 1999), interest in this idea of two related psychopathic subcomponents drove much of the research through the 1990s. No published work exists evaluating the usefulness of Hare's three-factor characterization, and it remains an open question as to whether it will further our understanding of the construct.

Somewhat overlapping with psychopathy (as defined by Cleckley or Hare) is the concept of antisocial personality disorder (APD; American Psychiatric Association 1994), a pattern of irresponsible and antisocial behavior beginning in childhood or early adolescence. Successive editions of the American Psychiatric Association's Diagnostic and Statistical Manual (DSM) have radically changed the construct. The features described as defining APD in DSM II (American Psychiatric Association 1968) were undersocialization, selfishness, callousness, lack of guilt, irresponsibility, impulsiveness, and failure to learn from experience. No explicit diagnostic criteria were described. The DSM III (American Psychiatric Association 1980) and DSM-III-R (American Psychiatric Association 1987) revised the criteria in light of research on childhood conduct disorder and emphasized observable behavior in line with Robins's (1978) research and recommendations. The DSM IV (American Psychiatric Association 1994) made minor changes to the behavioral criteria. Although DSM IV equates antisocial personality to psychopathy, sociopathy, and dissocial personality disorder, and the accompanying discussion refers to core personality traits, there are no guidelines on how to take account of the personality traits separately from the behavioral criteria.

Dissocial personality disorder listed in the tenth edition of the World Health Organization's "International Classification of Diseases" (1996) appears to be a very similar diagnosis to APD. The criteria for this diagnosis include pervasive, enduring, and destructive callousness; irresponsibility and violation of social norms; ease in establishing but inability to maintain relationships; low tolerance for frustration, irritability, and aggression; lack of guilt and inability to learn from punishment; and proneness to blame others combined with failure to take responsibility. Although seemingly quite similar to the construct of psychopathy, we are aware of no research on this diagnostic category relevant to criminal justice policy.

Despite its long history, almost all of the research on psychopathy has been conducted on adult males in prison, and most of the research has been done in North America. If psychopathy is the fundamental construct we believe it to be, this focus leaves many crucial unanswered questions.

A. Do Child Psychopaths Exist?

Although there is agreement among researchers that a core feature of psychopathy is a lifelong pattern of behavior that is evident in childhood or early adolescence (e.g., Hare 1991; Forth, Kosson, and Hare, forthcoming), few researchers have investigated the psychopathy construct specifically in youth. Only recently have measures of adolescent and childhood psychopathy (Psychopathy Checklist Youth Version [PCL-YV]: Forth, Kosson, and Hare, forthcoming; Psychopathy Screening Device: Frick and Hare, forthcoming) become available. Concerns have been raised regarding the application of psychopathy to children (see Quay 1987) because, for example, it is unknown what implications childhood psychopathy has for the life course of an individual. It is also unknown whether the negative treatment outcomes associated with psychopathic adults also apply to children. Moreover, we are not now able reliably to identify that subgroup of children who will continue with antisocial behavior and go on to be adult psychopaths. Accurate identification of this subgroup seems crucial for understanding the etiology of psychopathy and designing effective treatments.

There is good evidence that psychopathy in adolescence is similar to psychopathy in adulthood. Although the evidence produced by Frick and his colleagues (Christian et al. 1997; Barry et al., 2000) suggests that something very similar to adult psychopathy occurs in a small subgroup of antisocial children, the data are somewhat less clear because its measurement appears to be less precise among children than among adults and adolescents. Forth and Mailloux (2000) have noted that there is relatively low interrater agreement between parent and teacher ratings on the callous/unemotional factor and that some of the items thought to be core personality features of psychopathy do not load onto this factor among children as expected from the adult and adolescent literature. Longitudinal studies will tell whether children and youth identified as psychopathic follow the life course of adult psychopaths.

Many studies have examined children diagnosed as conduct disordered based on evidence that the child is engaging in frequent and persistent antisocial behavior (American Psychiatric Association 1994). However, fewer than half of all children with this diagnosis go on to be severely antisocial in adulthood (Robins 1978) or to be considered psychopathic. Loeber (1982) outlined four factors predictive of chronic delinquency following a diagnosis of conduct disorder: frequent childhood antisocial behaviors, a variety of antisocial behaviors, early age of onset, and the presence of antisocial behavior in more than one setting. These are also predisposing factors for adult Antisocial Personality Disorder (Robins, Tipp, and Przybeck 1991). These criteria may identify children at risk for adult psychopathy. Due to the lack of a common metric, however, the issue remains an empirical question.

The PCL-YV (Forth, Kosson, and Hare, forthcoming) is a modification of the PCL-R that has been developed for adolescent offenders. The eighteen-item measure has shown evidence of reliability and validity (Forth, Hart, and Hare 1990; Brandt et al. 1997; Forth and Burke 1998; Forth and Mailloux 2000). With respect to reliability, indices of internal consistency and interrater reliability are high, and evidence for all aspects of validity are substantial. For example, in studies of incarcerated adolescent offenders (Forth, Hart, and Hare 1990; Forth 1995; Brandt et al. 1997), scores on the PCL-YV were significantly related to having committed more acts of violent and nonviolent delinquent behavior as well as to violence and aggression in the prison setting, institutional charges, recidivism, and shorter lengths of time to reoffending. Moreover, treatment did not prevent future offenses. These data suggest that youths identified as psychopathic are already engaging in a great deal of serious antisocial behavior and that psychopathic traits are clearly evident and entrenched by midadolescence (Forth and Mailloux 2000).

Frick and colleagues (Frick et al. 1994) have used another modification of the PCL-R—the Psychopathy Screening Device (PSD) (Frick and Hare, forthcoming)—to examine psychopathy in elementary school–aged children, yielding a two-factor structure similar to that found in some adult samples of offenders (Hare 1991). One factor reflected impulsivity/conduct problems highly associated with traditional measures of antisocial behavior. The other reflected callous/unemotional traits, characterized by lack of guilt or empathy, superficial charm, and sensation seeking. Similar results were obtained in a community sample of elementary school–aged children (Frick, Barry, and Bodin, forthcoming), although, in this latter sample, three factors emerged.

Using the PSD, Blair (1999) has examined the psychophysiological responsiveness of children to distress cues, threatening stimuli, and neutral stimuli. He found that, relative to controls, children who scored high on the measure of psychopathy showed reduced electrodermal responses to distress cues and threatening stimuli but did not differ in responses to neutral stimuli. Blair (1997) has also reported that children with psychopathic tendencies respond less sensitively than control children on tasks dealing with emotional attribution and with moral/conventional distinctions. Christian et al. (1997) examined whether callous and unemotional traits in combination with conduct disorder resulted in particularly serious problems. They found that this combination of traits resulted in a greater number and variety of conduct problems, more police contacts, and a stronger parental history of antisocial personality disorder than occurred without the combination.

There have been many attempts to define homogenous subgroups of conduct-disordered children (e.g., Quay 1986; Achenbach et al. 1989; Hinshaw, Lahay, and Hart 1993; Loeber et al. 1993; Moffitt 1993; Frick et al. 1994), but none has gained widespread acceptance. Recently, Lynam (1996) proposed that children who exhibit a combination of conduct disorder and hyperactivity are "fledgling" psychopaths. It has recently been argued by some researchers, however, that a more restrictive definition may be needed because the conduct disorder and hyperactivity group might be too large a group. Frick and his colleagues (Frick et al. 1994; Christian et al. 1997; Frick and Ellis 1999), in their studies of clinic-referred children, have focused on two approaches to achieve this more refined subset of high-risk children. The first approach divides children with conduct disorder into two groups, those with childhood onset and those with adolescent onset of antisocial behavior. The second subdivides the group with childhood onset further, based on the idea that the most chronic and severe antisocial behavior is likely to characterize those children closest to the adult conceptualization of psychopathy.

A recent study (Barry et al. 2000) supports the idea that within the conduct disorder plus hyperactivity group, it is the children who also exhibit callousness and emotional unreactivity that are most like adult psychopaths (i.e., exhibit a lack of emotional distress, a preference for thrill-seeking activities, and a reward-oriented response style). Frick and Ellis (1999) propose that this group of children owe their antisocial behavior to a temperament characterized by low behavioral inhibition. They maintain that the diagnostic criteria for conduct disorder lack sufficient clarity to identify these severely affected children (Frick, Barry, and Bodin 2000).

B. *Are There Women Psychopaths?*

Psychopathy seems to exist in females, but more research is needed to confirm the validity of the construct (Zinger and Forth 1998). There appear to be three main differences between male and female inmate samples. First, psychopathy is less prevalent in women. Second, psychopathy appears to have somewhat different symptoms in women; in particular, it appears to have a later onset and entail less aggressive antisocial acts in childhood. Third, there is more overlap between psychopathy and other personality disorders in women (Rutherford et al. 1996).

Research attempting to measure psychopathy in women began only in the early 1990s, and thus few data are available. Nevertheless, the data suggest that the phenomenon can be identified successfully in female offenders (Neary 1990; Strachan 1993; Loucks 1996; Salekin, Rogers, and Sewell 1997; Salekin et al. 1998). Some studies have found, for example, that scores on measures of psychopathy are reliable and distributed much as they are for male offenders but that some items are not relevant to female offenders (e.g., juvenile delinquency and revocation of conditional release; Neary 1990; Strachan 1993). Others (Rutherford et al. 1996) have reported that women yielded lower mean scores than those found in male prison populations and also reported that several items were not related to total scores (juvenile delinquency, grandiosity, and failure to accept responsibility). A more recent study (Rutherford, Cacciola, and Alterman 1999) examined the prevalence of psychopathy and antisocial personality disorder in cocaine-dependent, mostly African-American, unemployed, unmarried women. Most (almost 80 percent) had undergone psychiatric treatment but were not institutionalized at the time of the study. Mean psychopathy scores in this sample were lower than those of male prisoners.

Salekin, Rogers, and Sewell (1997) examined psychopathy in female inmates using a multitrait-multimethod approach and concluded that there was strong evidence for its existence and applicability to female offenders. However, they reported that the current conceptualization of psychopathy based on males may not be completely adequate for females. Scores were lower than those usually reported among male samples. Furthermore, total score on the psychopathy measure did not correlate with any measures of antisocial behavior. Only scales with a behavioral emphasis evidenced modest correlations with external criteria. There is only one study to date examining the relationship between psychopathy and recidivism in females (Salekin et al. 1998). Although total score on the psychopathy measure was not significantly related to recidivism over the one-year follow-up, scores on some specific items were.

C. Are There Ethnic and Racial Differences in Psychopathy?

Recent evidence supports the conclusion that the psychopathy construct is cross-racially valid and that psychopathy exists in many cultures, although its frequency and expression may vary. Systematic differences in the patterns of variation in frequency and expression could provide valuable opportunities to test etiological theories.

Kosson, Smith, and Newman (1990) evaluated the validity of the psychopathy construct in black and white male offenders. Overall, they found more similarities than differences between these two groups. For example, they reported that psychopaths of both races showed deficits in learning to inhibit responses when both punishment and reward were associated with a behavior. Black inmates did, however, have slightly higher psychopathy scores. In both races, psychopaths were charged with more violent and nonviolent offenses than nonpsychopaths. Some researchers (Newman, Schmitt, and Voss 1997; Newman and Schmitt 1998; Schmitt and Newman 1999) have reported that theoretically predicted results (in modulating responses in the presence of salient reward) found in white inmates were not replicated in black offenders. Racial differences have also been examined in adolescent offenders (Brandt et al. 1997). There were no racial differences in mean scores, reliabilities, or criterion variable relationships found in that sample.

The North American conceptualization of psychopathy has not been widely accepted in the United Kingdom and the rest of Europe (Cooke 1997). This may be due to the long-standing use of the term outside North America to refer to legally defined classes of offenders often different from those defined by the scientific use of the term. The result has been a clinical tradition that questions the validity of the construct of psychopathy (e.g., Blackburn 1988). Demonstrating cross-cultural generalizability is an important test of a construct's viability. Researchers have recently begun this task (e.g., Cooke 1995*a*, 1995*b*, 1996). The use of consistent diagnostic criteria (e.g., the PCL-R) across settings can greatly aid communication between researchers from different cultures and facilitate cross-cultural comparisons. If cultural variation is confirmed, it may lead to a better understanding of the etiology of psychopathy (Cooke 1995*b*).

Although its prevalence may vary across cultures, psychopathy appears to be recognized in both industrialized and nonindustrialized countries (Cooke 1996). For example, Murphy's (1976) description of the Inuit term *kunlangeta*, referring to someone who lies, cheats, steals, takes advantage of people both sexually and nonsexually, and ignores reprimands or punishment, sounds very much like the prototypical psychopath.

Item-response analyses (Cooke and Michie 1999) have been conducted comparing PCL-R scores from North American and Scottish samples of mostly male, mostly Caucasian institutionalized offenders. The purpose of this study was to determine the extent to which the North American conceptualization of psychopathy could be generalized to Scotland. The results suggested that the construct underlying psychopathy as measured by the PCL-R can be generalized from North America to Scotland. Furthermore, Cooke and Michie's results suggested that psychopathic characteristics have the same relevance in both places, although the range of expression on some may differ. Cooke and Michie (1999) argued that these differences may be due to differences in the value cultures attach to certain traits, thereby affecting their prevalence. Cooke (1996) also argued that collectivist societies that value group loyalty and responsibility over self-expression and assertion should be less likely to produce psychopaths. In addition, cultures that encourage male competitiveness and low paternal investment should favor the expression of antisocial traits. There is no direct empirical evidence on these questions, but the rate of antisocial personality disorder in Chinese societies (considered collectivistic) appears to be lower than in individualistic North American societies (see Compton et al. 1991). It has also been suggested that the prevalence of psychopathy is lower in Scottish compared with English prisons, perhaps because psychopaths migrate to the larger English cities. Cooke (1997) reported that the Scottish offenders from his prison sample who had higher psychopathy scores were more likely to have one or more convictions in England and Wales.

A few recent studies conducted in England reported rates of psychopathy similar to those in North America but higher than those found in Scotland (Hobson and Shine 1998; Reiss, Grubin, and Meux 1999). In both of the latter studies, subjects were referred to the institutions studied because they had already been assessed as personality disordered or psychopathic, which may have obviated comparisons regarding prevalence rates.

Recently, attempts at examining psychopathy have begun in Portugal (Gonçalves 1999) and in Spain (Moltó, Poy, and Torrubia 2000). In the Portugese study, the PCL-R was administered to a sample of 150 male inmates from local and central prisons. The psychopathic offenders in the sample perpetrated more crimes, more crimes against persons, and a wider variety of crimes than the nonpsychopaths in this sample. Moreover, the psychopaths committed more apparently casual and remorseless murders against strangers. Likewise, the psychopathic sex offenders tended to choose strangers as victims for rape (Gonçalves 1999).

In the Spanish study (Moltó, Poy, and Torrubia 2000), the PCL-R was administered to 117 adult male prisoners. The interrater reliability and internal consistency coefficients for the PCL-R were high, and there was evidence of construct validity from correlational data. Psychopathic inmates in the sample were younger at first arrest, had a higher number of convictions, and were more likely to have convictions for rape and armed robbery. Furthermore, the psychopathic offenders displayed a greater number of violent and aggressive behaviors in prison and were more likely than other offenders to violate temporary absences and to commit a new offense while on these temporary absences.

D. Are There Noncriminal Psychopaths?

The scarce evidence to date on this topic suggests there are few, if any, adult psychopaths who have not engaged in substantial criminal behavior and few, if any, who would meet socioeconomic definitions of success. Of course, the answer to this question somewhat hinges on decisions about just what are the key, fundamental diagnostic characteristics of psychopathy. We return to that conundrum later in this essay.

Given the negative impact psychopaths have on society, it is reasonable to wonder whether there are psychopaths living in the community without contact with the criminal justice system. Hare (1993, 1996, 1998), for example, has speculated that psychopaths "form a significant proportion of persistent criminals, drug dealers, spouse and child abusers, swindlers and con men, mercenaries, *corrupt politicians, unethical lawyers and doctors*" and "they are well represented in the business and corporate world" and "some psychopaths ply their trade with few formal or serious contacts with the law" (our emphasis; see, e.g., Hare 1998, p. 104). There is very little evidence to support this position, however. Psychopathy has very rarely been studied in persons who have not had significant criminal involvement.

Babiak (1995) presented a case study of a "psychopath" working in an industrial organization who received a very high score on a standardized measure of psychopathy, the Psychopathic Checklist: Screening Version (the PCL:SV). Babiak suggests that an "industrial" psychopath is someone with psychopathic personality characteristics without the typical progression of increasing antisocial behavior and deviant lifestyle: "much of the success of subcriminal psychopaths is attributed to their ability to evade apprehension" (p. 176). Thus, the issue may really be one of the detection of antisocial behavior as opposed to its absence. Babiak's (1995) subject was offensive, disruptive, irresponsible, dishonest, manipulative, unreliable, promiscuous, and aggressive, and he engaged in illegal behavior. In actuality, he seems to have been a prototypical psychopath (Hare 1991), albeit with a higher-level education and a "white-collar" job. Babiak (2000) suggested that psychopaths flourish in workplace environments characterized by chaos associated with the currently popular trends of "downsizing" and "rightsizing," although there are no hard data to support this assertion.

Other researchers have tried recruiting psychopaths from the community (e.g., Widom 1977; Widom and Newman 1985), but it is unclear whether these participants would meet diagnostic criteria for psychopathy. In addition, two-thirds of the subjects reported in Widom (1977) had been arrested, and half had been incarcerated. Furthermore, Widom (1977) reported that the socioeconomic status of the community sample was not substantially higher than that of psychopaths in prison. It was, therefore, unclear how "successful" these subjects were. In a replication study, Widom and Newman (1985) reported that community-recruited psychopaths had low socioeconomic status and serious financial problems, and almost all had been arrested. They had held a large number of short-term jobs, had frequently been on welfare and unemployed, and had lower reported occupational levels than the nonpsychopaths in the sample. In other studies (Belmore and Quinsey 1994; Lalumière and Quinsey 1996), where community-recruited subjects clearly met the criteria for psychopathy, the men appeared to have been between prison sentences when assessed. Again, it seems unlikely that these men would be considered successful, noncriminal members of the general community.

Clearly, even if they exist, methodological difficulties make it hard to study socioeconomically successful psychopaths. It is unlikely that corporate executives would respond to newspaper advertisements, offers of payment, or other feasible recruitment methods. Forth et al. (1996) recruited male and female university undergraduates and reported a prevalence for psychopathy of 1 percent—the two psychopaths in the sample were males who reported serious antisocial behavior as children, but it was unclear whether they had always avoided detection by justice authorities.

Lynam's (1996) review of psychopathy strongly suggests it is very unlikely that there are many highly successful psychopaths. Children who are most likely to be "fledgling" psychopaths are comorbid for conduct and attention deficit disorders, a combination not associated with academic and vocational success. The recent work by Frick and his colleagues also leads to the same conclusion. Cleckley (1976) noted that psychopaths have "a history of unexplained failure" because they are reckless, dishonest, imprudent, and exploitative. These traits would be associated with low socioeconomic status regardless of the circumstances of the family of origin. Similarly, adult psychopaths invest little in their children, have very unstable marriages, and are more likely than others to have been raised by single mothers with the higher risk of poverty that entails (Lykken 1995).

II. Is Psychopathy Inherited?

The evidence supporting a heritable component to lifelong, persistent antisociality is indisputable but complex. It is also almost certain that there is a heritable component to psychopathy per se, even though behavioral genetic studies using well-validated measures of psychopathy have yet to be done.

Many studies have examined the heritability of antisocial behavior, and the evidence for a genetic influence is overwhelming (see Lykken 1995). Twin studies have confirmed that antisocial personality, juvenile delinquency, conduct disorder, and criminality all have a genetic component. An example from Rutter (1996) provides a simple illustration of the genetic influence on antisocial conduct. He demonstrates a declining resemblance in antisocial conduct going from identical or monozygotic twins (within-pair correlation of .81), to fraternal or dizygotic twins and full siblings, to half siblings, and finally to unrelated siblings reared together (within-pair correlation of .27). The correlation among unrelated siblings provides an estimate for the effects of shared environment. Carey and Goldman (1997) reviewed behavioral genetic studies of antisocial behavior. Of seventeen twin studies, all but one found evidence for a genetic effect. Antisocial behavior was defined in various ways, including officially recorded offenses, self-reported offenses, antisocial personality symptoms, and conduct disorder symptoms. Similarly, Carey and Goldman identified twenty-nine modern adoption studies of antisocial behavior, almost all of which identified a genetic effect. We review some of the most relevant studies here.

Mednick, Gabrielli, and Hutchings (1984) used all extrafamilial adoptions in Denmark between 1924 and 1947 for whom the biological parents were known. Biological fathers, followed by their adopted-away sons, were the most frequently convicted of crimes; the females in this sample showed the same relationship at a much lower rate. Criminality of the biological parents, but not of adoptive parents, was associated with adoptees' convictions. There was a positive correlation between the number of convictions of the biological parent and the number of the offspring's convictions for boys whose adoptive parents were noncriminals. Almost all of these convictions were for property crimes. There was no relationship between parental (biological or adoptive) criminality and violent crime. A small proportion (4 percent) of the adoptees contributed 69 percent of the convictions. Adoptees whose biological parents had three or more convictions but whose adoptive parents had none were twice as likely to have three or more convictions than adoptees with noncriminal biological parents.

Moffitt (1987) used the same database to examine biological parents' psychiatric hospitalization. Of 5,659 male adoptees for whom the biological parents were known, and whose adoptive parents had neither criminal nor psychiatric histories, psychiatric hospitalization of a biological parent was associated with a son's convictions just slightly less than was criminality of a biological parent. There was no effect of biological parent hospitalization on the adoptee's likelihood of being a chronic offender, but the combination of parental multiple convictions and hospitalization (for alcohol abuse or personality disorder) was significant (but small). Neither biological parent hospitalization nor multiple convictions alone were related to adoptive sons' convictions for violent offenses (the base rate was about 4 percent). The combination of these variables doubled the rate, but the difference was not significant. More recent data from the same cohort (Brennan, Mednick, and Jacobsen 1996) suggested heritability for violence but that the same heritable characteristic that increases risk for violence in biological fathers also increases risk for schizophrenia in adopted-away offspring.

There is evidence for genetic-environment interaction in the etiology of violence. Bohman (1996) examined criminal careers among 913 female and 862 male Swedish adoptees. Two types of male criminal careers were identified. One type involved alcohol abusers who exhibited repeated crimes of violence, and the second type involved petty property crime. Overall, petty criminals were likely to have genetic parents who were also involved in petty crime. The risk of criminality in the alcohol abusers increased with the severity of alcohol abuse. Unstable preadoptive placement increased the risk of both petty criminality and alcohol abuse. Neither low socioeconomic status nor genetic influence alone led to petty criminality, but their combination did. A similar genetic-environment interaction has recently been found in the etiology of aggression and conduct disorder (Cadoret et al. 1996) in which an adverse adoptive home environment was associated with aggression and conduct disorder only among adoptees whose biological parents exhibited antisocial personality disorder.

Eley (1998) has reported findings from several large twin data sets. Of particular interest are data pertaining to the aggression and delinquency subscales of the Achenbach Child Behavior Checklist (Achenbach 1991). These subscales correlated .55 with each other. Sixty-five percent of the variance in aggression scores was attributable to genetic influence, 5 percent to shared environment, and 30 percent to nonshared environmental influence. In contrast, 40 percent of the variance in delinquency scores was due to genetic influence, 30 percent to shared environment, and 30 percent to nonshared environmental factors. Fifty percent of the shared variance in the combination of these traits was due to genetic factors, 40 percent to shared environment, and 10 percent to nonshared environment.

Recently, there have been dramatic advances in molecular genetics, offering the possibility that individual genes contributing to antisocial behavior may be identified. With respect to psychopathy, this work is only in its infancy. We consider some of the most promising work in this area when we discuss heritability again in the section on the future of research on psychopathy. We are aware of no behavioral genetic studies of psychopathy as measured by an instrument such as the Psychopathy Checklist. However, conduct disorder, a developmental precursor to psychopathy, shows substantial heritability, as does antisocial personality that empirically and conceptually overlaps with psychopathy. In addition, all personality domains so far investigated have shown substantial heritability, especially, for present purposes, impulsive aggressivity and sensation seeking. Finally, there are substantial heritable components to persistent criminal behavior and alcohol abuse, both behaviors common in psychopaths. Consequently, although the size of the genetic contribution is unknown, it is, in our opinion, almost certain that psychopathy itself has a heritable component. Of course, it is equally certain that not all of the variability in psychopathy is genetic.

The heritability of psychopathy raises the question of whether it is a genetic disorder or whether it is some other heritable condition. We discuss the issue of ultimate causation later. Next, however, we examine the question of the proximal mechanisms underlying psychopathy.

III. How Should Psychopathy Be Measured?

A formal definition of psychopathy has not been agreed upon, and consensus on this issue is imperative if meaningful comparisons are to be made across studies. There seem to be fundamental disagreements among researchers regarding the central features of psychopathy. At worst, it is not always clear that researchers in this field are talking about the same people. As mentioned earlier, there is debate over whether to define psychopathy in terms of abnormal behavior or personality (e.g., Coid 1993).

The twenty-item revised Psychopathy Checklist (PCL-R; Hare 1991) is a continuous measure that allows an assessment of the extent that someone matches a prototypical psychopath. The PCL-R has yielded high interrater reliability and test-retest reliability on prisoners and forensic psychiatric patients. Internal consistency has been reported to be .87; the intraclass correlation was .83 for single ratings and .91 for the average of two ratings (Hart, Hare, and Harpur 1992). Even more important with respect to validity, the PCL-R score is among the most efficient predictors of recidivism among various populations of offenders and, except for actuarial measures such as the *Violence Risk Appraisal Guide* that include PCL-R score (see Quinsey et al. 1998), is the best predictor of violent recidivism among criminal and psychiatric populations (Hemphill, Hare, and Wong 1998; Steadman et al. 2000).

Disagreements about the fundamental nature of psychopathy notwithstanding, the foregoing discussion makes it abundantly clear that the PCL-R has been a major advance in the study of this phenomenon. Scientific investigation using a common measurement tool has facilitated progress that would not otherwise have occurred. One cannot help but be impressed at the astuteness of Cleckley's original clinical observations and Hare's operationalization of them in the PCL-R. As we discuss in the next section, essentially every credible current theory about the proximal mechanisms underlying psychopathy leads to several PCL-R items, and there are very few clinical characteristics implied by any theory that are not represented in the PCL-R. Future scientific work on psychopathy will be advanced if, whenever possible, researchers report PCL-R scores, whatever other theoretically motivated measures they also use. Hare, Hart, and Harpur (1991) suggested that the American Psychiatric Association should discard its diagnostic criteria for APD and adopt a version of the PCL-R, a position also advocated by others (e.g., Mealey 1995).

Would the best measurement tool resemble antisocial personality criteria or the PCL-R? The most straightforward way to address such questions about the key features of a hypothetical construct is to revisit the empirical question—do the various approaches to measurement actually show the disagreement implied by the theoretical controversy? If the operationalizations motivated by different theoretical positions actually agree, the controversy is probably more apparent than real. If, however, one theoretical approach leads to operationalizations that are more highly related to phenomena (e.g., violent crime) to which they should be related (and not related to phenomena to which they should not be related), the field is likely to regard both those measures and their theoretical underpinnings as superior. It is known, for example, that scores on the PCL-R are highly predictive of both treatability (Rice, Harris, and Cormier 1992; Seto and Barbaree 1999) and general and violent recidivism among serious male offenders (Hemphill, Hare, and Wong 1998). Moreover, Hare, Hart, and Harpur (1991) demonstrated that the PCL-R was a better predictor of such outcomes than DSM-III-R diagnoses of antisocial personality.

Antisocial personality scored in a categorical manner has substantial overlap with psychopathy scored using the PCL-R, but the relationship is asymmetric: 50–75 percent of inmates meet the criteria for APD, but only 15–25 percent exceed the customary (though nonempirical) PCL-R cutoff of thirty for psychopathy (Hare 1983, 1985). However, from a psychometric perspective, reliability is improved by using continuous scales, whether or not the underlying trait is categorical. We scored the Antisocial Personality Disorder criteria from both DSM-III-R and DSM-IV by scoring each of the items as nonapplicable (0), uncertain (1), or present (2), and then correlated the total with PCL-R scores on the same subjects (Skilling et al. 2000). Whether the PCL-R was scored from files alone or from files and interviews, the correlations were extremely high (when corrected for attenuation due to imperfect reliability, the correlations approached unity). These results have implications for future efforts to develop measurement tools and diagnostic criteria.

Progress may be aided by moving toward indicators that are easily observed at a young age. We suggest that chronic antisocial behavior beginning in early childhood is the most diagnostic feature of psychopathy and that aggression, risk taking, and callousness, especially that apparent before adolescence (if adequate information can be obtained), may be good indicators of the underlying construct. Perhaps juvenile behaviors can be reliably observed before the individual begins to disguise them in adulthood. In addition, these behaviors might simply be more easily detected than so-called affective traits that are just as "central" to psychopathy but more difficult to measure (Robins 1978). Almost by definition, manipulativeness, lying, and conning ought to be harder to detect than childhood behavior problems, for example. We wonder whether the best indicators have already been identified and, in the discussion of mechanisms underlying psychopathy, discuss the implications each theory has for improved methods of measurement and diagnosis. And, because there is extensive evidence that psychopathy is substantially heritable, behavioral genetic studies offer another promising method of identifying its core features.

IV. What Mechanisms Underlie Psychopathy?

Each of seven of the most influential hypotheses put forward to explain the nature and proximal causes of psychopathy has considerable evidence to support it, but none is entirely satisfactory. Laboratory findings about psychopathy are sometimes surprisingly subtle given the clinical findings showing its stubborn persistence over time and circumstances. Moreover, the responsiveness of psychopaths to seemingly minor manipulations in laboratory research stands in stark contrast to their current intractability with respect to treatment. Ultimately, it may turn out that each of these hypotheses has something to contribute to a comprehensive theory of psychopathy.

A. Hare's Lateralization Theory

Subtle differences in processing the affective aspects of language have been demonstrated between psychopaths and others (Williamson, Harpur, and Hare 1991). Hare and his colleagues (e.g., Jutai and Hare 1983; Hare and McPherson 1984; Hare and Jutai 1988) have tried to identify specific differences in how psychopaths process language, especially emotive language. This program of research initially involved lateralization studies—targeting the right visual field, which connects more directly to the left hemisphere of the brain that is specialized, generally, for processing language.

An early study by Hare (1979) did not support the hypothesis that psychopaths would show a left hemisphere (where linguistic processing primarily occurs) deficit—both psychopaths and nonpsychopaths showed left hemisphere superiority. Similar studies (Hare and Jutai 1983, 1988) showed, at best, weak support for the idea that psychopaths could not process emotional information as well as nonpsychopaths. However, in subsequent studies (e.g., Williamson, Harpur, and Hare 1991), the task was changed to the identification of words with emotional connotations. This research demonstrated that psychopaths yielded smaller physiological responses than nonpsychopaths to the emotional connotations of descriptive statements or pictures and that nonpsychopaths responded faster to emotional words, whereas psychopaths showed no differences. Moreover, psychopaths showed fewer differences in EEG-evoked potentials between neutral and emotional words than nonpsychopaths. Additional electrocortical research led to the hypothesis that, compared with nonpsychopaths, psychopaths have limited left-hemispheric resources for processing linguistic stimuli. Among nonpsychopaths, there is evidence of a strong right ear advantage, whereas this asymmetry is lacking among psychopaths (Hare and McPherson 1984; Raine et al. 1990).

B. Lykken's Low-Fear Theory

This theory suggests that what psychopaths lack is a normal fear or anxiety response. Because the normal socialization process depends on fear of punishment to inhibit acting on impulses, someone who is fearless is harder to socialize. Lykken (1995) proposed that "fear-quotient" is a stable physiological individual difference that does not, even in the extreme, comprise a qualitative innate neural defect. Lykken (1957) reported that psychopaths were less fearful than other offenders and nonoffenders. He demonstrated in a classical conditioning paradigm that psychopaths showed lower physiological arousal in anticipation of shock than nonpsychopaths, and when shock was contingent on errors, psychopaths showed poorer avoidance learning.

Other studies demonstrated that although psychopaths appeared relatively indifferent to shock, they were not indifferent to other punishments such as losing money. Since Lykken's first experiments in the 1950s, considerable research has replicated the basic finding of poorer passive avoidance but only in the presence of both salient reward and punishment (Newman et al. 1990, Scerbo et al. 1990; Arnett et al. 1993). As well, once psychopaths are engaged in goal-directed behavior, they have difficulty shifting their attention to the processing of peripheral cues (e.g. Newman, Kosson, and Patterson 1992). Similarly, Hare (1978) showed that psychopaths showed less palmar sweating in anticipation of a noxious stimulus (shock, loud noise) and concluded there was hyporeactivity among psychopaths to the anticipation of punishment. Psychopaths, however, exhibited an increase in heart rate when exposed to aversive stimuli. Psychopaths were less likely than nonpsychopaths to inhibit a response for which the reward was immediate and the anticipated punishment delayed. These studies of electrocortical measures suggest that, compared with nonpsychopaths, psychopaths tend to focus on the most salient stimuli in a particular situation and ignore less salient but relevant stimuli. Nevertheless, they were capable of normal responding when sufficiently motivated. Schmitt and Newman (1999) reported that psychopaths did not differ from other prisoners on several self-report measures of anxiety.

C. Fowles-Gray Neurobehavioral Theory

This theory is an updated version of Lykken's low-fear hypothesis. It posits that a hypothetical central behavioral inhibition system (BIS; Gray 1987) is activated by cues associated with fear or frustrative non-reward. A weak BIS would, therefore, lead to low anxiety in fearful or punishing situations, leading to poor passive avoidance learning. Fowles (1980) introduced the idea of the behavioral activation system (BAS) associated with reward or with escape from fear or pain. A person with a strong BAS might find rewards extremely salient. Lykken (1995) proposed that true psychopaths have a weak BIS. On the other hand, offenders he considers to be sociopaths have a strong BAS and a normal BIS—they are impulsive but simultaneously experience fear and anxiety.

More recent research has confirmed that psychopaths do not appear to frighten as easily as nonpsychopaths. Studies of the startle response (Patrick, Bradley, and Lang 1993; Patrick 1994; Patrick, Cuthbert, and Lang 1994) have shown that the emotional valence of pictures modulates the strength of the startle response in nonpsychopaths. Compared to neutral slides, pleasant stimuli produced weaker startle responses, while disturbing stimuli produced frowning and stronger startle responses. Psychopaths, however, did not frown to the negative pictures and showed smaller startle responses to both positive and negative stimuli (compared to neutral stimuli). That is, psychopaths behaved as though the stimuli engaged their interest without causing as much emotional disturbance. Further, Patrick (1994) suggested that low scores on the interpersonal/affective aspects of psychopathy alone were responsible for this "potentiated startle" effect.

Very recent results from this research (Levenston et al. 2000) indicate that the experimental stimuli had very different valence for psychopaths compared to other offenders. That is (based on their potentiated startle responses), nonpsychopaths responded as though "thrilling" stimuli (roller coasters, cliff diving) were unpleasant, while psychopaths' responses to such stimuli were characteristic of pleasant events. Conversely, psychopaths responded as though stimuli depicting mutilation and assault (but not threat) were pleasant. Other results suggested that this pattern was not merely due to superficial processing by the psychopaths. These results imply that psychopaths may experience as much fear as others (Steuerwald and Kosson, forthcoming) but that fear is elicited by different things.

D. Disinhibition Theory—the Frontal Lobe Defect Hypothesis

This hypothesis proposes something dysfunctional in the frontal lobe of psychopaths' brains without implying that psychopaths have suffered neurological damage. The observation that psychopaths act impulsively, or "without thinking," has led to the hypothesis that psychopaths have inadequate inhibitory control. Superficially at least, psychopaths resemble laboratory animals with lesions of the septum and frontal cortex, areas thought to involve the inhibitory control of behavior. In humans, the frontal lobe appears to participate in planning and coordinating complex acts and sustaining goal-directed behavior. Damage to this area results in deficient self-awareness, concrete attitude, and inability to plan or sustain goal directedness (see Kandel and Freed 1989).

Gorenstein (1982) reported that psychopaths persevered more than controls on the Wisconsin Card Sorting Task (a concept formation test). Newman and colleagues have examined this perseveration phenomenon further (e.g., Kosson and Newman 1986; Newman, Patterson, and Kosson 1987; Newman, Kosson, and Patterson 1992; Smith, Arnett, and Newman 1992) but did not find the predicted differences between psychopaths and controls. Belmore and Quinsey (1994) used this same task to study psychopaths and nonpsychopaths, all recruited from the local community. They reported that psychopaths persevered more than nonpsychopaths but were not less successful in a monetary task, implying that nonpsychopaths failed to persevere as long as they should have to maximize their profit. In all of these studies, the requirement to wait five seconds before responding eliminated group differences (see the next section).

Research indicates that although psychopaths may exhibit subtle differences on tasks thought to indicate frontal lobe functioning, psychopaths do not have gross frontal lobe damage. Hare and his colleagues (Hare 1984; Hart, Forth, and Hare 1990) reported no group differences on a variety of psychological tests associated with the clinical detection of gross damage. Sutker and Allain (1987) reported no deficits among psychopaths on measures of frontal lobe integrity, such as concept formation, abstraction, flexibility, planning, and control. Smith and colleagues (1992) reported only weak support for deficient frontal lobe functioning in psychopaths. Patients with frontal lobe damage exhibit some behaviors similar to those of psychopaths, but so far there have been no reports of even very subtle brain damage in psychopaths. Kandel and Freed (1989) identified several problems with this neuropsychological research that have impeded progress: lack of appropriate control for possible substance abuse and institutionalization, inconsistent operational definitions of psychopathy, poor measures of frontal lobe functioning, and lack of corroborating neuroimaging evidence.

A more narrowly focused study by Lapierre, Braun, and Hodgins (1995) concentrated on frontal lobe regions thought to modulate aggressive behavior, verbal identification of olfactory stimuli, and social and self-awareness. Damage to these areas results in preoccupation with sexual matters, promiscuity, choosing immediate over long-term gratification, and abnormally low galvanic responses to stressful stimuli. The precise location responsible for these seemingly psychopathic traits is not entirely clear, inasmuch as these frontal areas are modulated by and modulate areas in completely different parts of the brain. Nevertheless, this well-controlled study, as well as the research on language processing, suggests that psychopaths exhibit subtle neuropsychological differences from nonpsychopaths, albeit without gross abnormalities (Hart, Forth, and Hare 1990).

E. Response Modulation

An ambitious program of experimental research (Newman 1998; Wallace et al. 2000) has implicated subtle differences in response modulation as central to psychopathy. A lengthy experimental series has indicated that psychopaths (defined by the PCL-R) automatically use less nonsalient information to adjust goal-directed behavior. Manipulations that make the information more salient, make the goal less salient, or that introduce a mandatory task delay generally produce equivalency in psychopaths' and nonpsychopaths' performance. The investigators hypothesize that the key difference (between psychopaths and others) is that psychopaths automatically allocate fewer attentional and other resources so that nonsalient information is less available to affect goal-directed activity (Wallace et al. 2000). The authors clearly assume that such a style of resource allocation is disadvantageous to psychopaths. Of course, it remains an empirical question whether this psychopathic style of response modulation affects (or affected) psychopaths' performance in real-world tasks either in the modern world or in the ancestral human environment. Belmore and Quinsey (1994) suggested that perhaps psychopathy is not a response modulation problem, but, rather, the problem is that psychopaths simply allocate fewer attentional resources overall and then become bored more easily than nonpsychopaths. Nevertheless, in the laboratory psychopaths appear hampered by a failure to allocate automaticity optimally (Wallace et al. 2000).

As a general comment, we note that findings on all of these laboratory-based theories of psychopathy often seem somewhat ephemeral. That is, effects seem difficult to obtain and are easily abolished by seemingly minor procedural variations. This observation stands in contrast, for example, to the robustness of findings on the reliability of the Psychopathy Checklist (Hare 1991) and the consistency with which scores on the Psychopathy Checklist predict such important outcomes as violent and criminal recidivism (Salekin, Rogers, and Sewell 1996). Similarly, one might expect that measures of cerebral lateralization, fear in avoidance learning, learning efficiency in the presence of salient reward, startle responses in response to emotionally disturbing material, laboratory response modulation, or neuroimages of the frontal cortex will eventually supplant the Psychopathy Checklist in discriminating psychopaths from other offenders and predicting violent and criminal recidivism in offender samples. To our knowledge, no such results have yet been reported, and, indeed, there has been no research showing that any of these laboratory measures is even related to criminal or violent outcomes. By far the best measurement of psychopathy has been achieved with the clinical assessment of those traits implicated by laboratory tasks—impulsivity, irresponsibility, need for stimulation, proneness to boredom, lack of empathy, callousness, poor behavior controls, shallow affect, lack of remorse, and failure to accept responsibility—all of which are items on the Psychopathy Checklist.

F. *Low-Neurotransmitter Syndromes*

Serotonin is a cerebral neurotransmitter that in nonhuman animals has been related to passive avoidance learning and aggression. In humans, low levels of this neurotransmitter have been found in impulsive-aggressive offenders, but these offenders were also more anxious than other people (see Ellis 1991; Twitchell et al. 1998). Low levels of serotonergic activity have been associated with aggressive, antisocial alcohol abuse (Lappalainen et al. 1998; Hill et al. 1999). Lower dopaminergic activity has also been associated with antisocial alcohol abuse

(Gabel et al. 1993). Monoamine oxidase-type A (MAO) is a neurologically active enzyme that regulates such crucial neurotransmitters as serotonin, dopamine, and epinephrine. Low MAO activity has been linked with psychopathy (Ellis 1991; Alm et al. 1996) and also has a moderate relationship with impulsivity, childhood hyperactivity, childhood aggression, learning disabilities, sensation seeking, and substance abuse (Siever et al. 1984; Brunner et al. 1993; Klinteberg and Oreland 1995; Hallman, von Knorring, and Oreland 1996; Stålenheim, von Knorring, and Oreland 1997). Other studies have suggested that infants with low MAO activity, especially serotonin, are fussier and more active (Clarke, Murphy, and Constantino 1999). And lowered serotonergic activity has been reported in newborns whose first-degree relatives showed high incidence of antisocial personality disorder (Constantino, Morris, and Murphy 1997).

Based on these intriguing findings, one is tempted to conclude that the neurochemical basis for psychopathy has been elucidated—relatively low levels of MAO activity, especially reflected in the neurotransmitter serotonin. In our judgment such a conclusion is premature for several reasons. Very few studies have assessed psychopathy using such established measures as the PCL-R. As well, studies linking serotonin and aggression are fraught with other definitional and methodological problems (Berman, Tracy, and Coccaro 1997). And attempts to associate measures of psychopathy per se with genetic markers known to regulate MAO neurotransmitters have sometimes failed (e.g., Smith et al. 1993). At this point, one can conclude that MAO activity is related to such personality traits as aggressivity (especially in childhood), antisociality, sensation seeking, impulsivity, and resistance to punishment. However, the neurochemical substrate that underlies the particular constellation of traits that corresponds to the discrete natural class we know as psychopathy has not yet been elucidated.

G. *Psychopathy as Variation in Personality*

Many of the clinical features of psychopathy seem to be aspects of agreed-upon personality dimensions. The personality-based approach (Lilienfeld 1994) views psychopathy primarily as a constellation of personality traits with an emphasis on the distinction between psychopathy and antisocial behavior per se. For example, Widiger and Lynam (1998) suggested that psychopathy represents extremely low values especially on the agreeableness and conscientiousness factors of the widely accepted five-factor model of personality. This five-factor model posits that all of the observable variation in human personality can be subsumed by five orthogonal dimensions: introversion/extroversion, openness to experience, emotional stability, agreeableness, and conscientiousness. Theoretically, then, all meaningful variation in personality can be located in a hypothetical space defined by these five dimensions. Although the theory is silent on how the human population is distributed on these dimensions, it is often assumed to be roughly normal.

Similarly, Blackburn (1998) proposed that psychopaths are characterized by high dominance, coerciveness, and hostility in a two-dimensional model of interpersonal relations. Most commonly, those who propose that psychopathy reflects natural variation along personality dimensions assume, implicitly or explicitly, that psychopathy itself must be dimensional in nature. This expectation presumably depends on the idea that humans are distributed more or less normally along these dimensions of personality. If, however, the naturally occurring distribution on some or all of these dimensions of personality were distinctly bimodal (or multimodal), there could exist some discrete types or classes of persons. Existing research on the personality characteristics of psychopaths does not permit a clear conclusion.

Much informal clinical description and some research results imply that psychopathy is a discrete entity and not merely the end of a continuum of natural variation (e.g., Moffitt 1993; Hare 1998; Lykken 1998). Hare stated that "the personality and behavior of offenders diagnosed as psychopathic differ in fundamental ways from other offenders" (1998, p. 99). Many other researchers also believe that psychopaths differ from nonpsychopaths in fundamental ways, but it remains unclear whether the construct of psychopathy should be construed as discrete or continuous, that is, whether people fall into two separate, nonoverlapping classes (psychopaths and nonpsychopaths) or whether people differ in the degree to which they exhibit psychopathic tendencies.

To determine whether psychopathy is better conceptualized as reflecting a natural discrete class or a dimension, Harris, Rice, and Quinsey (1994) examined measures of psychopathy as well as childhood variables reflecting antisocial conduct. Evidence supported the hypothesis that there is a natural class underlying psychopathy. Chronic antisocial behavior beginning in childhood was the most central feature of this class, rather than adult antisociality or affective and personality characteristics typically associated with psychopathy. Most theoretical accounts of psychopathy and all of the empirical evidence point to a genetic or very early environmental diathesis, or both. Therefore, if psychopathy is a natural class, the class should be demonstrable in children. The finding that childhood behavior problems assessed in adulthood were strong indicators of the class suggests that it may be possible to identify psychopaths early in life. There is increasing support for the idea that children who exhibit both early hyperactivity-impulsivity-attention problems and conduct disorder may be "fledgling psychopaths" (Lynam 1996) and may become lifelong persistent criminals.

Skilling, Quinsey, and Craig (forthcoming) conducted a study to determine whether a group of boys who may be on a trajectory of lifelong antisocial behavior could be uncovered in an uncensored community sample of children. Taxometric analyses provided evidence of a discontinuous, discrete entity underlying scores on three different measures of serious antisocial behavior in children—DSM-IV conduct disorder, eight items of the PCL-YV, and the childhood and adolescent indicators previously identified (Harris, Rice, and Quinsey 1994). These findings were consistent with the claim by Harris, Rice, and Quinsey (1994) that psychopathy is a categorical construct rather than a dimensional one. Longitudinal studies are required, however, to determine whether boys so identified are also identified as psychopaths in adulthood. Furthermore, it is important to point out that the idea of psychopathy as a discrete class or type is not, in principle, in conflict with psychopathy as part of the variation in personality.

There have also been studies of the psychometric properties of individual characteristics. For example, items more clearly reflecting impulsivity, antisociality, and exploitative use of others have yielded more accurate predictions of violent recidivism (Salekin, Rogers, and Sewell 1996) than have other traits representing superficiality, dishonesty, and remorselessness.

V. Is Psychopathy a Pathology?

Many psychological, neurological, and behavioral variables are related to psychopathy. Many are candidate proximal underlying mechanisms. For example, psychopathy may be due to a relatively inactive behavioral inhibition system (BIS) or a difference in the ventral frontal area of the brain. But why do these differences exist in the first place? That is, are these differences the result of pathology—a disruption in normal development? Most researchers implicitly or explicitly view psychopathy as a disorder, most commonly, a disorder of personality (e.g.,

Hare 1996; Zinger and Forth 1998). As such, it could be viewed as a functional or psychological disorder with one or more unspecified physiological bases. As well, psychopathy might further be attributed to a brain disorder, perhaps due to injuries or secondary to other medical conditions. A brain disorder could also be the result of a pathological genetic aberration. Some researchers (e.g., Moore and Rose 1995), in accordance with this line of thinking, have argued that the prevalence of psychopathy is comparable to such other forms of psychopathology as mental retardation and schizophrenia.

Criminality, although not psychopathy, has been linked to a variety of neurodevelopmental difficulties. Gualtieri and Hicks (1985) have reviewed the literature on selective male afflictions—those in which the sex ratio markedly "favors" males. These afflictions include such childhood disorders as hyperkinesis; conduct disorder; schizophrenia; autism; cerebral palsy; Down's Syndrome; stuttering; dyslexia; minor physical anomalies; neuromotor deficits, including seizure disorders; and perinatal disorders (e.g., spontaneous abortion, toxemia, pulmonary infection, cerebral birth trauma, and other birth complications; Waldrop et al. 1978; Kandel et al. 1989; Brennan, Mednick, and Mednick 1993; Raine 1993; Raine, Brennan, and Mednick 1994; Raine et al. 1996).

Robins (1966) argued that psychopathy (what she called sociopathy) is a psychiatric disease because "it occurs in children whose fathers have a high incidence of the disease and whose siblings and offspring also appear to have a elevated incidence. The symptoms follow a predictable course, beginning early in childhood with illegal behavior and school discipline problems and continuing into adulthood as illegal behavior, marital instability, social isolation, poor work history, and excessive drinking" (pp. 302–3).

However, not all heritable patterns of behavior that follow a predictable course are diseases or disorders. Perhaps psychopathy exists because it was adaptive during human evolution. Physiological adaptations (including those with psychological effects) were selected because they increased inclusive fitness in ancestral environments. For example, belonging to a cohesive, mutually supportive (i.e., "reciprocally altruistic") group was adaptive, and heritable inclinations favoring group solidarity and adherence to rules have probably been associated with past human reproductive success (Dawkins 1978; Ridley 1993). However, we (Quinsey et al. 1998; see also Mealey 1995) hypothesize that the use of such a general strategy by the majority of ancestral humans created a niche for an alternative cheating strategy that allowed one to take advantage of others. To do this effectively, one would need to be selfish, callous, superficially charming, and lack empathy. If many people were cheaters, though, the strategy would lose its effectiveness because of the difficulty in finding cooperators to exploit and because of the increased vigilance they would employ. Thus, these two strategies would be expected to be frequency dependent, with psychopathy being maintained at low prevalence.

Psychopathy seems to comprise high mating effort (time and energy devoted to attracting, monopolizing, and defending sexual partners). Of course, some items on the PCL-R resemble high mating effort—promiscuous sexual behavior and many short-term marital relationships. In addition, glibness, superficial charm, and lack of empathy, for example, could also have facilitated mating effort.

Aggression could also have been used to deter sexual rivals. Belsky, Steinberg, and Draper (1991) argued that a life strategy emphasizing mating effort is characterized by insecure attachment to parents and childhood behavior problems followed, in turn, by early puberty and precocious sexual behavior and unstable adult pair bonding and low parental investment. Psychopathy might thus represent a genetically determined life strategy that has been maintained in the population through its relationship with reproductive success (Quinsey 1995; Rice 1997; Quinsey et al. 1998). The hypothesized elements of this strategy are short-term mating tactics, selfishness, nonreciprocating and duplicitous tactics in social exchange, and an aggressive and risky approach to achieving social dominance.

The most straightforward version of a selectionist hypothesis of psychopathy would assert that psychopaths are executing a "healthy" (in the biomedical but not moral sense) obligate strategy. Thus, it is expected that psychopaths would exhibit personalities quite different from other people and that these differences would be evident (perhaps, especially) in childhood. Of course, substantial heritability and subtle neuroanatomical and neurochemical influences (without gross lesions) are totally consistent with such a selectionist hypothesis. As well, it is to be expected that special tests would reveal that psychopaths act relatively impulsively, fearlessly, and unempathically; are resistant to punishment only under certain carefully arranged conditions; and do not appear to be grossly or generally disadvantaged, even in the laboratory.

This Darwinian hypothesis would predict that the population prevalence of psychopathy would vary with the size of the ecological niche and that the niche would vary, for example, as a function of the intensity of intergroup conflict and warfare, scarcity of resources, and social stability. We return to other implications of our hypothesis in the last section. This hypothesis asserts that while many adverse medical conditions cause antisocial, violent behavior, they do not cause psychopathy. Thus, psychopathy should be unrelated to these disorders even though they themselves are associated with criminality. By such an account, there may be two quite different paths to serious and chronic criminality. The path associated with psychopathy might not be pathological, and the other path (perhaps associated with less extensive criminal histories) is clearly associated with developmental neuropathology and perhaps competitive disadvantage (Harris, Rice, and Lalumière, forthcoming).

Perhaps surprisingly, the terms "disorder" and "pathology" do not have a consensual meaning in psychology and psychiatry. The most cogent proposed definition (Wakefield 1992, 1999) states that a disorder is a harmful condition that results from the failure of a mechanism to perform its natural (i.e., evolved) function. According to the selectionist account outlined above, psychopathy is not a disorder. Some (e.g., Lilienfeld and Marino 1999), however, have argued that a formal scientific definition of disorder is impossible, and the best one can do is document how the term is used.

In any case, psychopaths do not seem disordered. First, any cogent definition of disorder notwithstanding, it is difficult for us to conceive of a neurocognitive defect that could enhance such qualities as lying, conning, manipulation, glibness, and charm. It seems a logical contradiction to suppose that a disorder could improve cognitive abilities. Second, persons considered "mentally ill" by laypeople are those persons who act against their own inclusive fitness (Daly and Wilson 1988). For example, persons who kill genetic kin are more likely to be found mentally ill than those whose victims are not biologically related. As we shall see below, psychopaths, because they are implicitly perceived as acting in their own interests, are not often found mentally ill or insane.

VI. What Are the Implications for Criminal Justice Policy and Practice?

In this section, we address the direct application of all of this research in the criminal justice system. We conclude that psychopathy is the most important and useful psychological construct yet discovered for criminal justice policies. We discuss its importance for assessing risk among offenders, planning treatment and other interventions for forensic populations, and determining sentences and other criminal sanctions. First, though, we note that the amount of empirical research on psychopathy varies directly with offense severity. That is, there is much more research on incarcerated offenders, felons, institutionalized forensic patients, and maximum security inmates than on probationers, misdemeanants, psychiatric outpatients, and inmates in minimum security. Of course, this is not likely to be regarded as a serious weakness of the empirical literature because, from a practical perspective, it is only among relatively serious offenders that there is the opportunity to make decisions contingent upon an assessment of psychopathy. In addition, measures of psychopathy have been shown to predict future violence in community samples, even among those not charged with criminal offenses (e.g., Steadman et al. 2000).

A. The Assessment of Offenders

Psychopathy has been shown to be highly related to violence, especially predatory, dispassionate, and instrumental violence (Williamson, Hare, and Wong 1987; Meloy and Gacono 1992; Hare 1993; Cornell et al. 1996). Furthermore, psychopathy is a robust predictor of recidivism and violence among criminal, forensic, and psychiatric populations (Hare and McPherson 1984; Hare, McPherson, and Forth 1988; Harris, Rice, and Cormier 1991; Serin 1991; Harris, Rice, and Quinsey 1993; Salekin, Rogers, and Sewell 1996; Rice and Harris 1997*a;* Hemphill, Hare, and Wong 1998; Douglas, Ogloff, and Grant 1999; Grann et al. 1999; Steadman et al. 2000; Tengström et al. 2000). As discussed earlier, the PCL-R is the most reliable and valid current measure of psychopathy. Although scoring the DSM-IV criteria for antisocial personality as a dimension can be reliable, this method of scoring is inconsistent with clinical practice, where diagnosis is the goal and there are more data to support the predictive validity of the PCL-R than APD criteria using any version of the DSM (Harris, Rice, and Quinsey 1993; Gacono and Hutton 1994; Hart and Hare 1997; Zinger and Forth 1998).

Because the Psychopathy Checklist takes considerable time and training to score and because it requires extensive corroborative information, there has been an effort to develop shorter, simpler measures of psychopathy. The screening version of the Psychopathy Checklist, the Hare PCL:SV (Hart, Cox, and Hare 1995) was developed as a short, parallel form (Hare 1998; Cooke et al. 1999) for nonforensic populations and may be a useful screening device for forensic populations (Bodholdt, Richards, and Gacono, forthcoming). Similarly, the Child and Adolescent Taxon Scale (Harris, Rice, and Quinsey 1994; Quinsey et al. 1998) has also been investigated as a possible replacement for the PCL-R in risk assessment. Nevertheless, for criminal populations, the full PCL-R is presently the best-validated test for psychopathy in adults, and it appears that the PCL-YV is the best validated test for use with seriously antisocial adolescents (Forth and Mailloux 2000).

It has been argued that psychopathy is a crucial clinical construct in the criminal justice system, especially for the assessment of risk for recidivism and violence and the selection of appropriate treatment and management programs for offenders (Hare 1996, 1998). This position has not only been argued by Hare but by many other forensic scientists and researchers in the criminal justice system (e.g., Wilson and Herrnstein 1985; Salekin, Rogers, and Sewell 1996). Of course, this means that those who conduct psychopathy assessments and testify on these findings, or report on them for decision-making purposes within the criminal justice system, must meet high standards and acknowledge limitations (Zinger and Forth 1998). For example, it is important to note that criminal samples to date have all used selected incarcerated offenders: none have used representative samples of arrestees, probationers, or representative prison release cohorts. To score psychopathy using any of the empirically valid methods requires extensive record information, and assessments should be postponed or declined if adequate records are not available (Gacono and Hutton 1994). Those who rate psychopathy for clinical purposes must demonstrate the validity of their scoring (Gacono and Hutton 1994; Hare 1998). Furthermore, because therapists have an understandable tendency to perceive their clients positively (especially after treatment), it has been argued that psychopathy assessments should be performed by independent assessors. It has also been argued that scoring for psychopathy should be done independently by two raters and scores averaged to increase accuracy (Gacono and Hutton 1994; Hare 1998).

B. The Treatment of Offenders

The literature on the treatment of psychopathy is pessimistic about positive outcomes, but that pessimism was, until quite recently, based as much on clinical lore as on empirical evidence. Cleckley (1982) had described psychopaths as capable of neither benefiting from experience nor forming the emotional bonds necessary for effective treatment. Although early reports indicated positive effects of psychotherapy (Rodgers 1947; Schmideberg 1949; Lipton 1950; Rosow 1955; Showstack 1956; Corsini 1958; Thorne 1959), more recent critical evaluations of the evidence have concluded that there have been no demonstrations of effective treatment for adult psychopaths (Hare 1970; Cleckley 1982; McCord 1982; Woody et al. 1985). Psychopaths derive little benefit from programs aimed at the development of empathy, conscience, or interpersonal skills. There is evidence that such programs actually increase the risk of recidivism among psychopaths.

As described in the introduction, the violent recidivism of psychopaths and nonpsychopaths who participated in a therapeutic community program inside a maximum security psychiatric hospital was compared to that of matched men who went to prison (Rice, Harris, and Cormier 1992; Harris, Rice, and Cormier 1994). Whereas the rates of violent recidivism in the ten-year follow-up were significantly lower among the treated nonpsychopaths than their nontreated counterparts, the opposite was true for the psychopaths. That is, the treated psychopaths had significantly higher rates of violent recidivism than psychopaths who went to prison. It seemed that both psychopaths and nonpsychopaths in the therapeutic community learned how to perceive the feelings of others, take the perspective of others, and delay gratification, but the psychopaths used these new abilities to facilitate the manipulation and exploitation of others.

Ogloff, Wong, and Greenwood (1990) reported on the behavior of psychopaths and nonpsychopaths (defined according to an early version of the Psychopathy Checklist) in another therapeutic community program. Psychopaths showed less clinical improvement, displayed lower levels of motivation, and were discharged earlier from the program (usually because of lack of motivation or security concerns) than were nonpsychopaths.

Despite the North American evidence that therapeutic communities are contraindicated for psychopaths, they continue to flourish in prisons, secure hospitals, and other psychiatric hospitals in Europe (Dolan 1998). Moreover, they are also still popular in North America for substance abusers (e.g., Wexler, Falkin, and Lipton 1990). In all of these cases, although it is undoubtedly the case that some of the participants would be true psychopaths, as the term is used in this chapter, there are no data to allow a determination of how many would score over a particular score on the PCL-R or meet any other empirical operational definition of psychopathy. Dolan contends that the term "therapeutic community" has been interpreted differently in Canada, the United States, and Europe. Yet, the descriptions of the various programs (e.g., Gunn and Robertson 1982; DeLeon 1984; Weisman 1995) reveal a high degree of similarity in both philosophy and content, although it is also true that there are differences that may have been critical. Methodologically, the U.S. and European studies have been criticized for comparing treatment completers with a comparison group that, although perhaps equivalent prior to treatment to the treatment group, was not a suitable comparison group following treatment because it is likely that the offenders highest in psychopathy would have been the most likely to have dropped out of the program prior to completion (Rice and Harris 1997*b*). As Dolan (1998) concludes, more methodologically rigorous studies are required in order to improve our knowledge about the treatment of psychopaths.

Numerous authors have recommended that intensive cognitive-behavioral programs targeted to criminogenic needs are indicated for psychopaths (e.g., Brown and Gutsch 1985; Andrews and Bonta 1994; Serin and Kuriychuk 1994). Relapse prevention techniques integrated with cognitive-behavioral correctional programming have also been recommended (Hare 1992). This combination of relapse prevention and cognitive-behavioral techniques, however, is very similar to a program for sex offenders recently evaluated by Seto and Barbaree (1999). These investigators predicted that good treatment behavior (measured by in-session behavior, quality of homework, and therapists' ratings of motivation and positive change achieved in treatment) would be associated with parole success and lower recidivism in a large sample of sex offenders. However, men who scored high in psychopathy and who were rated by therapists as showing the most improvement were more likely to reoffend, especially violently, than all the others. These results were surprising because the treatment followed the established principles of good correctional treatment, namely, risk, need, and responsivity (Andrews et al. 1990; Andrews and Bonta 1994). Psychopaths fit into the category of high-risk, high-need individuals with low responsivity (Zinger and Forth 1998), presenting the greatest treatment challenge. The program used in the Seto and Barbaree (1999) study targeted criminogenic needs such as deviant sexual arousal and antisocial attitudes and beliefs (Barbaree and Seto 1998; Barbaree et al. 1998). In addition, the program followed the responsivity principle inasmuch as it was highly structured and cognitive-behavioral, which is generally the mode of service thought to best match the learning style of psychopaths. Aside from the Seto and Barbaree study, there have been few attempts to test whether high doses of treatments that show the most promise for offenders in general will also work for psychopaths (Lösel 1998), although such studies are underway (Serin and Brown 1996). The dismal results regarding treatment of psychopaths to date have led some to suggest that the relation between risk and treatment efficacy is curvilinear rather than linear and that treatability of many very high-risk offenders (i.e., psychopaths) is questionable even with the most intensive and carefully designed programs (Lösel 1998).

The hypothesis that psychopathy is not a disorder implies that there may be little "wrong" with them for therapy to "repair." Of course, this hypothesis says nothing about the possibility of change through environmental intervention, but it is possible that interventions that work for psychopaths could be quite different from those that work for nonpsychopathic (i.e., disordered) offenders. Viewed in the light of a selectionist hypothesis about psychopathy, the findings (Rice, Harris, and Cormier 1992; Harris, Rice, and Quinsey 1994) that those treatments that benefit other offenders actually harm psychopaths is less surprising. Furthermore, the suggestion that psychopaths were actually changed by the intervention (albeit for the worse) supports the idea that psychopaths require very different interventions.

It has been proposed that treatment for psychopaths include teaching them about their particular cognitive processing and about specific situations in which this processing is likely to result in violence (Serin and Kuriychuk 1994; Serin 1995; Wong and Hare, forthcoming). Hare (1992, 1998) suggested that treatment for psychopaths begin by convincing them that, before they can change, they must learn about how they differ from other individuals. Because emotion will always be less important in controlling their behavior than it is for others, psychopaths must develop prosocial behavior patterns based on other motivators. They must comprehend that they are capable of learning more socially appropriate, nonviolent ways to interact, though they are unlikely to become warm and loving. There are, as yet, no data available to tell whether the incorporation of such insight-oriented components into treatment for psychopaths will reduce recidivism.

Certain criminogenic needs among nonpsychopaths might not be criminogenic needs among psychopaths. For example, substance abuse is a very common problem among offenders in general, and substance abuse is commonly recognized as an important criminogenic need to be addressed in treatment (e.g., Andrews et al. 1990). However, some data suggest that among psychopaths, alcohol abuse does not confer additional risk to reoffend (even though psychopaths are more likely to abuse it; Rice and Harris 1995). These findings lead us to question whether targeting alcohol abuse in an intervention to reduce future violence among psychopaths is likely to have the desired effect.

Among sex offenders in general, deviant sexual preferences appear to be an important risk factor for future sex offending (Hanson and Bussière 1998). However, deviant sexual preferences among psychopaths might be an even more important risk factor than among offenders in general. Psychopaths who have deviant sexual preferences were very much more likely to commit a new sexual offense than nondeviant psychopaths and all nonpsychopaths (Rice and Harris 1997*a*). Thus, while sexual deviance increased the risk for specifically sexual recidivism for both psychopaths and nonpsychopaths, it increased the risk for psychopaths much more than it did for nonpsychopaths. This finding leads us to believe that altering deviant sexual preferences is even more important in the treatment of psychopathic sex offenders than it is for other sex offenders.

The idea that psychopathy is an adaptation suggests that violence by psychopaths might be reduced only by careful monitoring and supervision that lowers the payoff for cheating by increasing the odds of detection. The evidence that psychopaths continue to be at high risk to fail for very long periods of time (e.g., Harris, Rice, and Cormier 1991; Rice and Harris 1997*a*) implies that supervision needs to be very long-term and intensive.

C. Psychopathy and Criminal Responsibility

In most jurisdictions, acquittal due to insanity requires, among other things, that the accused suffered from a mental disorder at the time of the offense. Generally, persistent criminality alone is insufficient evidence for mental disorder, and the majority of insanity acquittees have a diagnosis of psychosis. A substantial minority, however, have a primary diagnosis of personality disorder (Lymburner and Roesch 1999). In Canada, for example, it has generally been possible to establish that psychopathy constitutes a "disease of the mind" (Zinger and Forth 1998) for purposes of insanity acquittal. The theory that psychopathy is an adaptation rather than a disorder has obvious implications for the applicability of the insanity defense for psychopaths.

In the United Kingdom, "psychopathic disorder" is a legal category of mental disorder within the English Mental Health Act of 1983. English law recognizes four groups of patients—mentally ill, severely subnormal, subnormal, and psychopathic disorder (Coid 1993). "Psychopaths" were defined as individuals with a personality disorder resulting in abnormally aggressive or seriously irresponsible behavior, who required medical treatment that was "likely to alleviate or prevent a deterioration of" the condition. The treatability qualifications were provided to ensure that hospitals not be obliged to admit these patients unless it was thought that they would benefit from treatment (Bluglas 1990). This legal category has become increasingly controversial (e.g., Grounds 1987; Dell and Robertson 1988; Coid 1993), and again the suggestion that psychopathy is not a disorder calls into question the basis for this legislation. In addition, the research on the treatment of psychopathy establishes that it would, at present, be impossible to establish on empirical grounds that treatment is likely to be effective or even that it can "prevent deterioration." Perhaps because it is becoming difficult for psychopaths to gain admission to security hospitals, these individuals are more likely to be admitted to prison special units (Coid 1993). The meaning of "mental illness" is currently so widely interpreted in law that psychopaths can be detained under that legal category even if they cannot be detained under the "psychopathic disorder" category (Baker and Crichton 1995). Again, however, if psychopathy is not a disorder, this legal category would not apply to psychopaths.

The research on psychopathy has significant implications for release decisions regarding insanity acquittees. Many insanity acquittees who have committed a violent offense (some of whom also have diagnoses associated with other psychiatric disorders) are psychopaths (Harris, Rice, and Cormier 1991). In most jurisdictions, release of insanity acquittees depends upon their being no longer dangerous and no longer mentally ill. The research showing a strong, positive association between psychopathy and violent recidivism and the research showing a negative association between schizophrenia and violent recidivism (Harris, Rice, and Quinsey 1993) suggests that public safety would be enhanced by making release decisions regarding insanity acquittees on the basis of risk of future violence alone rather than on recovery from mental disorder.

D. Sentencing, Parole, and Young Offenders

Psychopathy has often been used as a basis for longer sentences (Zinger and Forth 1998). In Canada, for example, psychopathy is frequently used to increase sentence length on the grounds of public protection (Davis 1982). In the United States, "just deserts" proponents (based on deterrence ideas about criminal sanctions) have pushed for sentences based principally on the severity of the current offense. In practice, prior offense history weighs heavily for all but the most serious violent and drug offenses. Sentencing policies under three strikes laws, for example, allow for an increase of sentences for subsequent offenses up to five or six times that prescribed for a first offense. Nevertheless, the terms "just deserts," "truth in sentencing," "do the crime, do the time," and "three strikes and you're out" all imply that incarceration time be fixed based primarily on the offense history. The empirical data on psychopathy (e.g., Hare 1991), as well as data on the use of actuarial instruments that incorporate psychopathy (Harris, Rice, and Quinsey 1993; Quinsey et al. 1998), strongly suggest that public safety can be increased by basing sentencing and parole decisions on more comprehensive information about offenders, including measures of psychopathy.

Similarly, in some jurisdictions, evidence regarding dangerousness may be introduced in a hearing to decide whether a young person should be tried in adult court, where a longer sentence may be imposed, than in juvenile court. Expert testimony based on diagnoses of psychopathy has been used to justify such decisions (Zinger and Forth 1998). The empirical evidence suggests that this practice is likely to contribute to public safety by contribution to more accurate decisions about which youth are highest risk.

E. Psychopathy and Preventive Detention

Most jurisdictions permit certain very serious offenders to be held in custody indefinitely or for very long periods. In Canada, for example, some are designated "dangerous offenders," which allows for indefinite sentences at the time of conviction. The court considers the likelihood of future serious violence in making a determination about this designation. A Canadian study of "dangerous sexual offenders" (the precursor to the current "dangerous offenders") showed that use of the dangerous sexual offender legislation was inconsistent and not primarily based on factors having to do with actual risk (Wormith and

Ruhl 1987). More recently, assessments of psychopathy have entered into the designation and have affected length of detention (Zinger and Forth 1998). A recent study concluded that it would be possible to improve public safety even more by increasing the emphasis in making decisions on ratings of psychopathy and objective measures of risk but, even so, that those individuals detained recently using the dangerous offender provisions are at high risk for violent recidivism (Bonta et al. 1998). Thus, it appears that the use of objective ratings of psychopathy and risk are being used to increase public safety.

In the United States, many "sexual predator" laws allow for preventive detention of the most dangerous sex offenders with post-criminal-sentence civil commitment statutes that have been greatly criticized by mental health and legal professionals (e.g., La Fond 1992; Wettstein 1992; Brooks 1996). Nevertheless, the U.S. Supreme Court has upheld the one sexual predator law that came to it on appeal (*Kansas v. Hendricks*, 117 S. Ct. 2072 [1997]). Most sexual predator statutes require establishing "dangerousness," typically coupled with a requirement for some mental health condition, which may be called illness, defect, or abnormality (Faigman et al. 1999). However, unlike most other civil commitment laws, and unlike many insanity laws, a diagnosis of "personality disorder" is explicitly included as a possible qualification for the designation. However, some legal commentators have argued that the term has no additional legal meaning beyond dangerousness—that is, a person is "mentally abnormal" because the person is dangerous (Faigman et al. 1999). Again, the evidence showing the predictive accuracy of measures of psychopathy and actuarial instruments that include psychopathy strongly indicate the value of such tools in decisions about commitment of sexual predators.

There is, however, little empirical justification for the application of sexual predator laws at the end of sentence. Whether or not psychopathy is a disorder, it is an enduring aspect of a person, and currently available measures of psychopathy, because they are based on lifelong behavior patterns, cannot be expected to change as a result of either time in prison or treatment. Similarly, almost none of the variables known to predict violent recidivism have yet been shown to be truly dynamic (Quinsey et al. 1998). A truly dynamic prediction implies that scores on the predictor change with treatment or time and that this changed score adds to the prediction possible from the prechange score. Although we and others have searched, and continue to search, for dynamic variables, there is as yet no evidence that predictions of future violence made during incarceration are more accurate than those that could be made at the outset (Quinsey et al. 1997).

As discussed earlier, sexual recidivism rates of psychopaths who also exhibit deviant sexual preferences are so high, that, for all intents and purposes, they meet the legal criteria for sexual predators (Rice and Harris 1999). For example, in one study (Rice and Harris 1997*a*), survival analyses showed that 80 percent of sexually deviant psychopaths had been reconvicted of a sexual offense within six years of release. Thus, in combination with deviant sexual preferences, information about psychopathy is highly relevant to the commitment of sexual predators.

VII. What Is Next for Psychopathy Research?

In this section, we propose avenues for further research. In particular, we focus on the potential for molecular genetics to enhance our understanding of psychopathy; the need for research efforts focused on the effective management of psychopathic offenders; the necessity of expanding our understanding of the construct to populations other than Caucasian, male, North American offenders; and the potential for other theoretical perspectives to increase our knowledge about this group of people. We predict that measures of psychopathy will lead to enhancements in the actuarial prediction of criminal and violent behavior. Research will identify the genetic substrate of such psychopathic traits as lack of emotional attachment, glibness, and manipulativeness and better elucidate its proximal personality and cognitive underpinnings. Innovative therapies will be tested based on these hypothetical proximal mechanisms. The psychopathy construct will be applied cross-culturally, to juveniles and to females, perhaps thereby yielding estimates of population prevalence. Together with our colleagues we will attempt to test our hypothesis that psychopathy is a Darwinian adaptation and not a biomedical disorder.

A. Prediction

Hare's Psychopathy Checklist is the best available tool for the measurement of psychopathy. However, that is not to say that there is no room for improvement. The PCL-R is essentially an atheoretical tool, and it may be that future versions of the PCL-R or other more theoretically based measures of the construct of psychopathy will lead to better identification of true psychopaths.

B. Heritability

The genetic and environmental factors responsible for the development and maintenance of psychopathy are not well understood. Because of success in measuring the heritability of other characteristics, efforts have recently begun to focus on identifying the specific genes responsible for various psychiatric disorders. Studies of this kind on psychopathy are soon to follow. Until recently, investigations of the genetics of behavioral disorders have been guided by the "one gene, one disorder" hypothesis. Unfortunately, this strategy has not been successful in the area of major mental disorders, leading to failures to replicate and withdrawn claims. The principal reason for this lack of success appears to be that the etiology of major mental disorders does not involve single genes of large effect. Therefore, the staple of genetic investigations of psychiatric disorders, pedigree studies of affected kindreds, has not been very informative. The search for many genes of small effect has led to the increasing use of designs in which affected and unaffected individuals are compared regardless of their kinship status. Already, the human genome project has identified a large number of markers on many chromosomes, which means that genes of modest effect size can be identified. Because studies using these association designs are relatively easy to conduct, they will contribute to rapid progress in the study of multigene disorders and other conditions.

Association designs have already been applied to personality characteristics, such as Cloninger's novelty seeking (Sigvardsson, Bohman, and Cloninger 1987), which corresponds to the measures of impulsiveness, sensation seeking, and lack of conscientiousness in other personality measurement systems (Bouchard 1997) and which would seem to bear some relationship to psychopathy. The broad sense heritability of novelty seeking obtained from twin studies is 41 percent, and a gene for a particular dopamine receptor has been linked to novelty seeking (Benjamin et al. 1996; Ebstein et al. 1996; Hamer 1997). One allele of a dopamine receptor gene (DRD4) has been associated with such personality traits as novelty seeking and risk taking (Hamer 1997). Moreover, association analyses have suggested a relationship between DRD4 frequencies and population migration resulting from the effects of natural selection (Chen et al. 1999). Such research offers the promise of identifying the genetic substrate of personality traits even more closely related to psychopathy (conscientiousness and aggressivity, e.g.) and testing hypotheses about their adaptive significance.

Other personality characteristics associated with juvenile delinquency have also been linked to specific genes. Lesch et al. (1996) found that variations in a serotonin-related gene accounted for approximately 8 percent of the inherited variance of a personality scale measure of anxiety, depression, angry hostility, and impulsiveness. Similar results were reported for Cloninger's harm avoidance dimension.

The molecular genetic literature has identified what appear to be "general" genes for psychopathology. Comings (1997) has argued from association studies that polygenes (mutant genes involved in polygenic inheritance) are not specific but are involved in a spectrum of disorders and are fundamentally different from those involved in single-gene disorders. One way they differ is that they have a much milder effect on gene function, and thus the carrier rate in the population can be high. Their deleterious effect comes only when individuals inherit a greater-than-threshold number. These polygenes are thought to cause neurohormonal imbalances that result in a variety of impulsive, compulsive, addictive, anxious, and affective behaviors. Blum et al. (1997) have conducted a detailed review of the molecular genetic studies of alcoholism and other addictions. One dopamine receptor gene locus has been linked to severe alcoholism and polydrug abuse in a large number of studies. A higher frequency of one of the alleles of this gene is associated not only with severe alcoholism but also with a wide variety of other behavioral problems including some that are highly relevant for psychopathy, especially polydrug dependence and conduct disorder.

C. *Treatment*

The results of the Rice, Harris, and Cormier (1992) follow-up showing that treatment made psychopaths worse are discouraging but do at least suggest that their behavior is modifiable. Group therapy and insight-oriented programs may help psychopaths to become more proficient at manipulating and deceiving others and should therefore be considered inappropriate. If effective treatment is to be achieved, the effort and resources required will be very high. However, because psychopaths are responsible for a disproportionate amount of violent crime, small effect sizes can have important public safety implications (Zinger and Forth 1998).

Some interesting biological/neurological findings may lead to new and better treatments. Pharmacotherapy comes to mind as one obvious option. In treating psychopaths, another key may be to alter their perceptions of the cost/benefits to criminal activity, that is, increase the costs, decrease the benefits, and increase the benefits of alternative behaviors. Carefully designed behavioral programs that are faithfully implemented and that are carried on for long periods might prove to be effective in the treatment, or at least the management, of adolescent and adult psychopaths. Such a combination of pharmacotherapy and psychosocial treatment has been attempted but unfortunately without the use of standardized measurement of psychopathy (Kristiansson 1995).

The identification of a subset of children at greatest risk for psychopathy is already under way, and these studies will allow for the determination of the best measure of juvenile psychopathy and what factors are related to the risk of becoming an adult psychopath. This has important implications for prevention, especially since current treatments for adults are ineffective. Some children who are identified as members of the psychopathy class may avoid a life of crime (or violent crime at least), and identification of variables that seem to "innoculate" such individuals will be crucial in providing clues for treatment of psychopaths. Skillful parenting is promoted as the single most important factor in prevention by Lykken (1995, 1998). He suggested a strong parental bond with careful monitoring and patient and consistent intervention, and he cautioned against relying on punishment, especially heavy punishment. Lykken stressed the promotion of a positive self-concept in high-risk children, directing their interest to exciting, constructive activities, and seeking help early if needed. It should be noted, however, that there is evidence that simply promoting high self-esteem may be contraindicated among delinquent or aggressive children. Baumeister, Smart, and Boden (1996) found evidence that high, rather than low, self-esteem was related to violent behavior. Nevertheless, it remains an empirical question whether the more comprehensive type of intervention advocated by Lykken will prevent high-risk children from proceeding on to adult psychopathy.

D. Diagnostic Puzzles

Tremendous progress has been made in the identification of the small subset of male offenders who are psychopathic and the characteristics associated with this group. But much work remains to be done, particularly with populations other than white male offenders. The PCL-R seems to be a reliable tool for identifying psychopathy in females (Neary 1990; Strachan 1993; Loucks 1996), but more work is needed to determine whether it will identify women offenders who are at high risk for both general and violent recidivism. Some evidence suggests that not all of the PCL-R items are relevant to female offenders, and revisions may be needed to optimize its effectiveness for the assessment of dangerousness. Understanding psychopathy in women is crucial in light of recent evidence suggesting that conduct disorder in children is related to maternal antisocial behavior (Frick and Loney, forthcoming).

Researchers have only recently started to employ measures of psychopathy outside of North America. The available data seem to indicate that, as in North America, the PCL-R is a reliable and valid measure. However, it appears that the base rate of psychopathy varies geographically, and such factors as population mobility and community cohesiveness may affect its prevalence. The recent call to researchers (Mealey 1995; Cooke 1996) to use a common label (psychopathy) and metric (the PCL-R) should aid in discovering what community characteristics allow psychopaths to flourish and what ones suppress its expression or motivate psychopaths to move to other localities. Hare (1998) suggested that in "frontier" societies like the American Wild West of the 1800s, psychopathic behavior may not have been considered unusual. Likewise, in societies such as the former Yugoslavia and other countries that are experiencing serious upheaval, psychopaths may be more successful than in more stable societies. On the other hand, in highly structured, close-knit societies without opportunities for exploitation without detection, psychopathy may be a much less successful strategy.

E. *Proximal Mechanisms*

Attempts at identifying gross structural abnormalities in psychopaths have failed, but subtle neurological differences have been reported. Psychopaths experience less emotional disturbance in the face of distress than nonpsychopaths, evidenced by their potentiated startle response, for example. This response may be mediated by differences in levels of serotonin, MAO, or both; a lack of lateralization in linguistic processing; or problems with ventral frontocortical hypoactivation. An increased understanding of brain functioning in this group of offenders may lead to increased accuracy in the prediction of future dangerousness and the possibility of designing pharmacological treatments to prevent future offending.

An intriguing clue about the environmental influences that might affect the expression of psychopathy comes from a study of mothers who experienced severe malnutrition during the first two trimesters of pregnancy (Neugebauer, Hoek, and Susser 1999). Sons born to such mothers showed increased risk for antisocial personality disorder (compared to the risks associated with less serious malnutrition and with malnutrition during the third trimester).

F. Psychopathy as an Adaptation

We and others have proposed that psychopathy is an adaptation and that psychopaths are, in a biomedical sense, healthy and engaged in what has been a reproductively viable strategy. The strongest form of this hypothesis implies, first, that the condition is polygenic. Second, the various genes underlying psychopathy have been maintained in the human population because they have conferred a selective advantage under many conditions. Third, psychopathy is due to a particular combination of genes responsible for behavioral and personality traits. And fourth, psychopathy itself has been a low-frequency, reproductively viable strategy throughout human evolutionary history. Of course, this selectionist hypothesis also implies that the specific expression of psychopathy should be sensitive to the physical and, especially, the interpersonal environment. This idea leads to several other testable hypotheses.

In general, the strongest prediction from this account is that biomedical phenomena known to be related to ill health should not be related to psychopathy. For example, minor physical anomalies include adherent ear lobes, single palmar crease, and curved fifth fingers that result from disruptive influences occurring in utero and are associated with obstetrical complications (Firestone and Prabhu 1983), older maternal age (Rapoport et al. 1977), hyperactivity in boys and inhibition in girls (Waldrop and Goering 1971; Firestone, Leewy, and Douglas 1976; Halverson and Victor 1976; Fogel, Mednick, and Michelsen 1985), and distractibility in boys and girls (reviewed in Bell and Waldrop [1989]). They are also associated with autism and schizophrenia in children (Steg and Rapoport 1975; Campbell et al. 1978), schizophrenia in adults (Guy et al. 1983), and mental retardation and learning disability (Steg and Rapoport 1975; von Hilscheimer and Kurko 1979), lower IQ (reviewed in Bell and Waldrop [1989]), and aggression and impulsivity in boys (Waldrop, Pedersen, and Bell 1968; Waldrop et al. 1978). In some samples, boys have more anomalies than girls (e.g., Waldrop and Goering 1971). As indices of disrupted development, minor physical anomalies and obstetrical complications should not be associated with psychopathy, if the strongest version of the selectionist account of psychopathy is true (Lalumière, Harris, and Rice, forthcoming).

Fluctuating asymmetry (FA) represents "the imprecise expression of underlying developmental design due to developmental perturbations" (Gangestad and Thornhill 1997, p. 72). An organism's degree of bilateral symmetry reflects the stability of its ontogenetic development. Fluctuating asymmetry is measured by comparing the left and right sides of bilateral morphological traits—the degree to which the left and right halves of the body are identical. Research on many different species shows that organisms with low FA grow faster, live longer, and have greater fecundity (Moller 1997). In humans, low-FA men are considered by female raters to be more physically attractive than high-FA men (Gangestad, Thornhill, and Yeo 1994). Compared to high-FA men, low-FA men report having more sexual partners and an earlier age at first intercourse (Thornhill and Gangestad 1994), and their female partners report having more orgasms during sexual intercourse (Thornhill, Gangestad, and Comer 1995). Men who initiate and win fights (Furlow, Gangestad, and Armijo-Prewitt 1998) and boys who are more aggressive (Manning and Wood 1998), especially in response to provocation, have lower FA than men who lose fights or boys who are less aggressive, respectively. There is also evidence that high FA is associated with higher resting metabolic rates (Manning, Koukourakis, and Brodie 1998), schizophrenia (Mellor 1992), birth prematurity (Livshits and Kobyliansky 1991), mental retardation and developmental delay (Naugler and Ludman 1996), lower IQ among university students (Furlow et al. 1997), left-handedness (Yeo, Gangestad, and Daniel 1993), and genetic homozygosity (Livshits and Kobyliansky [1987]; for the relationship between FA and health see Thornhill and Moller [1997]). Again, by the strongest version of the selectionist account, psychopaths should be low in FA compared to those persons with clear mental disorders and other offenders. Indeed, psychopaths' FA appears to be similar to healthy, noncriminal, nonpsychopaths (Lalumière, Harris, and Rice, forthcoming).

As a final example of testable hypotheses, if psychopathy is a viable life strategy, there should be evidence of it from early childhood. For example, it follows that members of the psychopathy class should not show the history of perinatal and obstetrical complications that characterize persons who suffer from major mental illness. Again, psychopaths show fewer signs of developmental instability than do other violent offenders (Lalumière, Harris, and Rice 1999). Coid (1993) found that indicators of neuropsychological abnormality such as perinatal trauma, developmental delay, and history of seizures did not correlate with APD but did correlate with schizotypal and schizoid personalities. This observation suggests that a life-history or nonpathological interpretation may apply to members of the psychopathy class but not to other violent offenders.

G. *Theoretical Integration*

We believe psychopathy is the most important psychological construct relevant to the criminal justice system and that research findings support that belief. These persistently antisocial and violent men represent the greatest public risk and the greatest challenge to supervisory and rehabilitative efforts. Even though the etiology of psychopathy remains unknown, it can be measured with good reliability and validity using the Hare Psychopathy Checklist family of instruments, and these measures comprise the best indices of violence risk and treatment response available to forensic clinicians. Understanding the causes of psychopathy holds the eventual promise of even more accurate risk assessment and effective interventions.

Research in psychopathy could serve as a model for applied psychological research in general. For us, the most striking conclusion of this review is the degree of theoretical and empirical compatability. Whether regarded as a disorder or not, the genetic substrate of psychopathy is likely to be revealed soon. That discovery, however, will not immediately reveal more proximal physiological and psychological mechanisms, in part because the ways in which the environment modulates the expression of psychopathy still must be elucidated. Ongoing research on neuroanatomical, neurophysiological, and neurobehavioral characteristics of psychopathy is entirely compatible with an ultimate genetic diathesis. Ongoing research on the psychological and behavioral characteristics of psychopaths is even more crucial—the association studies required to establish the genetic substrate demand highly valid measures of the phenotype. And, of course, astute clinical observation and clinically relevant research has guided that effort since its inception. We look forward to significant progress that will illuminate fundamental processes and, at the same time, help make the world a safer place.

REFERENCES

Achenbach, T. M. 1991. *Manual for the Child Behavior Checklist and 1991 Profile.* Burlington: University of Vermont, Department of Psychiatry.

Achenbach, T. M., C. K. Conners, H. C. Quay, F. C. Verhulst, and C. T. Howell. 1989. "Replication of Empirically Derived Syndromes as a Basis for Taxonomy of Child/Adolescent Psychopathology." *Journal of Abnormal Child Psychology* 17:299–323.

Alm, P. O., B. af Klinteberg, K. Humble, J. Leppert, S. Sörenson, L. H. Thorell, L. Lidberg, and L. Oreland. 1996. "Psychopathy, Platelet MAO Activity and Criminality among Former Juvenile Delinquents." *Acta Psychiatrica Scandinavica* 94:105–11.

American Psychiatric Association. 1968. *The Diagnostic and Statistical Manual of Mental Disorders.* 2d ed. Washington, D.C.: American Psychiatric Association.

———. 1980. *The Diagnostic and Statistical Manual of Mental Disorders.* 3d ed. Washington, D.C.: American Psychiatric Association.

———. 1987. *The Diagnostic and Statistical Manual of Mental Disorders.* 3d ed. rev. Washington, D.C.: American Psychiatric Association.

———. 1994. *The Diagnostic and Statistical Manual of Mental Disorders.* 4th ed. Washington, D.C.: American Psychiatric Association.

Andrews, D. A., and J. Bonta. 1994. *The Psychology of Criminal Conduct.* Cincinnati: Anderson.

Andrews, D. A., I. Zinger, R. D. Hoge, J. Bonta, P. Gendreau, and F. T. Cullen. 1990. "Does Correctional Treatment Work? A Clinically Relevant and Psychologically Informed Meta-analysis." *Criminology* 28:369–404.

Arnett, P. A., E. W. Howland, S. S. Smith, and J. P. Newman. 1993. "Autonomic Responsivity during Passive Avoidance in Incarcerated Psychopaths." *Personality and Individual Differences* 14:173–94.

Babiak, P. 1995. "When Psychopaths Go to Work." *International Journal of Applied Psychology* 44:171–88.

———. 2000. "Psychopathic Manipulation at Work." In *The Clinical and Forensic Assessment of Psychopathy: A Practitioner's Guide,* edited by C. Gacono. Mahwah, N.J.: Erlbaum.

Baker, E., and J. Crichton. 1995. "Ex Parte A: Psychopathy, Treatability and the Law." *Journal of Forensic Psychiatry* 6:101–19.

Barbaree, H. E., E. J. Peacock, F. Cortini, W. L. Marshall, and M. Seto. 1998. "Ontario Penitentiaries' Program." In *Sourcebook of Treatment Programs for Sexual Offenders,* edited by W. L. Marshall, Y. M. Fernandez, S. M. Hudson, and T. Ward. New York: Plenum.

Barbaree, H. E., and M. C. Seto. 1998. "The Ongoing Follow-Up of Sex Offenders Treated at the Warkworth Sexual Behaviour Clinic." Report prepared for the Correctional Service of Canada, Ottawa.

Barry, C. T., P. J. Frick, T. Grooms, M. G. McCoy, M. Ellis, and B. R. Loney. 2000. "The Importance of Callous-Unemotional Traits for Extending the Concept of Psychopathy in Children." *Journal of Abnormal Psychology* 109: 335–40.

Baumeister, R. F., L. Smart, and J. M. Boden. 1996. "Relation of Threatened Egotism to Violence and Aggression: The Dark Side of High Self-Esteem." *Psychological Review* 103:5–33.

Bell, R. Q., and M. F. Waldrop. 1989. "Achievement and Cognitive Correlates of Minor Physical Anomalies in Early Development." In *Stability and Continuity in Mental Development: Behavioral and Biological Perspectives*, edited by M. N. Bornstein and N. A. Krasnegor. Hillsdale, N.J.: Erlbaum.

Belmore, M. F., and V. L. Quinsey. 1994. "Correlates of Psychopathy in a Non-institutional Sample." *Journal of Interpersonal Violence* 9:339–49.

Belsky, J., L. Steinberg, and P. Draper. 1991. "Childhood Experience, Interpersonal Development, and Reproductive Strategy: An Evolutionary Theory of Socialization." *Child Development* 62:647–70.

Benjamin, J., L. Li, C. Patterson, B. D. Greenberg, D. L. Murphy, and D. H. Hamer. 1996. "Population and Familial Association between the D4 Dopamine Receptor Gene and Measures of Novelty Seeking." *Nature Genetics* 12: 81–84.

Berman, M. E., J. I. Tracy, and E. F. Coccaro. 1997. "The Serotonin Hypothesis of Aggression Revisited." *Clinical Psychology Review* 17:651–65.

Bhojak, M. M., S. Krishnan, S. S. Nathawat, and J. Ali. 1997. "A Comparative Study of Emotional Life and Subjective Well-Being in Drug Addicts and Non-addicts." *Journal of the Indian Academy of Applied Psychology* 23:63–67.

Blackburn, R. 1988. "On Moral Judgements and Personality Disorders: The Myth of Psychopathic Personality Revisited." *British Journal of Psychiatry* 153:505–12.

———. 1998. "Psychopathy and the Contribution of Personality to Violence." In *Psychopathy: Antisocial, Criminal, and Violent Behavior*, edited by T. Millon, E. Simonsen, M. Birket-Smith, and R. D. Davis. New York: Guilford.

Blair, R. J. R. 1997. "Moral Reasoning in the Child with Psychopathic Tendencies." *Personality and Individual Differences* 22:731–39.

———. 1999. "Responsiveness to Distress Cues in the Child with Psychopathic Tendencies." *Personality and Individual Differences* 27:135–45.

Bluglas, R. 1990. "The Mental Health Act 1983." In *Principles and Practice of Forensic Psychiatry*, edited by R. Bluglas and P. Bowden. Edinburgh: Churchill Livingstone.

Blum, K., J. G. Cull, E. R. Braverman, T. J. H. Chen, and D. E. I. Comings. 1997. "Reward Deficiency Syndrome: Neurobiological and Genetic Aspects." In *Handbook of Psychiatric Genetics*, edited by K. Blum and E. P. Noble. New York: CRC Press.

Bodholdt, R. H., H. R. Richards, and C. B. Gacono. Forthcoming. "Assessing Psychopathy in Adults: The Psychopathy Checklist-Revised and Screening Version." In *The Clinical and Forensic Assessment of Psychopathy*, edited by C. B. Cacono. Mahwah, N.J.: Erlbaum.

Bohman, M. 1996. "Predisposition to Criminality: Swedish Adoption Studies in Retrospect." In *Genetics of Criminal and Antisocial Behaviour*, edited by G. R. Bock and J. A. Goode. Ciba Foundation Symposium. Chichester and New York: Wiley.

Bonta, J., I. Zinger, A. Harris, and D. Carrière. 1998. "The Dangerous Offender Provisions: Are They Targeting the Right Offenders?" *Canadian Journal of Criminology* 377–400.

Bouchard, T. J. 1997. "The Genetics of Personality." In *Handbook of Psychiatric Genetics*, edited by K. Blum and E. P. Noble. New York: CRC Press.

Brandt, J. R., W. A. Kennedy, C. J. Patrick, and J. J. Curtin. 1997. "Assessment of Psychopathy in a Population of Incarcerated Adolescent Offenders." *Psychological Assessment* 9:429–35.

Brennan, P. A., B. R. Mednick, and S. A. Mednick. 1993. "Parental Psychopathology, Congenital Factors, and Violence." In *Mental Disorder and Crime*, edited by Sheilagh Hodgins. Newbury Park, Calif.: Sage.

Brennan, P. A., S. A. Mednick, and B. Jacobsen. 1996. "Assessing the Role of Genetics in Crime Using Adoption Cohorts." In *Genetics of Criminal and Antisocial Behaviour*, edited by G. R. Bock and J. A. Goode. Ciba Foundation, vol. 194. Chichester and New York: Wiley.

Brooks, A. D. 1996. The Incapacitation by Civil Commitment of Pathologically Violent Sex Offenders." In *Law, Mental Health, and Mental Disorder*, edited by B. D. Sales and D. W. Shuman. Pacific Grove, Calif.: Brooks/ Cole.

Brown, H. J. D., and K. U. Gutsch. 1985. "Cognitions Associated with a Delay of Gratification Task: A Study with Psychopaths and Normal Prisoners." *Criminal Justice and Behavior* 12:453–62.

Brunner, H. G., M. Nelen, X. O. Breakefield, H. H. Ropers, and B. A. Van Oost. 1993. "Abnormal Behavior Associated with a Point Mutation in the Structural Gene for Monoamine Oxidase A." *Science* 262:578–80.

Cadoret, R. J., W. R. Yates, E. Troughton, G. Woodworth, and M. A. Stewart. 1996. "Genetic-Environmental Interaction in the Genesis of Aggressivity and Conduct Disorders." *Archives of General Psychiatry* 52:916–24.

Campbell, M., B. Geller, A. M. Small, T. A. Petti, and S. H. Ferris. 1978. "Minor Physical Anomalies in Young Psychotic Children." *American Journal of Psychiatry* 135:573–75.

Carey, G., and D. Goldman. 1997. The Genetics of Antisocial Behavior." In *Handbook of Antisocial Behavior*, edited by D. M. Stoff et al. New York: Wiley.

Chen, C., M. Burton, E. Greenberger, and J. Dmitrieva. 1999. "Population Migration and the Variation of Dopamine D4 Receptor (DRD4) Allele Frequencies around the Globe." *Evolution and Human Behavior* 20:309–24.

Christian, R. E, P. J. Frick, N. L. Hill, L. A. Tyler, and D. R. Frazer. 1997. "Psychopathy and Conduct Problems in Children: II. Subtyping Children with Conduct Problems Based on Their Interpersonal and Affective Style." *Journal of the American Academy of Child and Adolescent Psychiatry* 36:233–41.

Clarke, R. A., D. L. Murphy, and J. N. Constantino. 1999. "Serotonin and Externalizing Behavior in Young Children." *Psychiatry Research* 86:29–40.

Cleckley, H. 1941. *The Mask of Sanity*. St. Louis: Mosby.

———. 1976. *The Mask of Sanity: An Attempt to Clarify Some Issues about the So-Called Psychopathic Personality*. 5th ed. St. Louis: Mosby.

———. 1982. *The Mask of Sanity*. Rev. ed. St. Louis: Mosby.

Coid, J. 1993. "Current Concepts and Classifications of Psychopathic Disorder." In *Personality Disorder Reviewed*, edited by P. Tyrer and G. Stein. London: Gaskell.

Comings, D. E. 1997. "Polygenic Inheritance in Psychiatric Disorders." In *Handbook of Psychiatric Genetics*, edited by K. Blum and E. P. Noble. New York: CRC Press.

Compton, W. M., J. E. Helzer, H. G. Hwu, E. K. Yeh, L. McEvoy, J. E. Tipp, and E. L. Spitznagel. 1991. "New Methods in Cross-Cultural Psychiatry: Psychiatric Illness in Taiwan and the United States." *American Journal of Psychiatry* 148:1697–1704.

Constantino, J. N., J. A. Morris, and D. L. Murphy. 1997. "CSF 5-HIAA and Family History of Antisocial Personality Disorder in Newborns." *American Journal of Psychiatry* 154:1771–73.

Cooke, D. J. 1995*a*. "Psychological Disturbance in the Scottish Prison System: A Preliminary Account." In *Psychology, Law and Criminal Justice: International Developments in Research and Practice*, edited by G. Davie, S. Lloyd-Bostock, M. McMurran, and C. Wilson. Berlin: de Grutyer.

———. 1995*b*. "Psychopathic Disturbance and Offending in the Scottish Prison Population." *Psychology, Crime and Law* 2:101–18.

———. 1996. "Psychopathic Personality in Different Cultures: What Do We Know? What Do We Need to Find Out?" *Journal of Personality Disorders* 10:23–40.

———. 1997. "Psychopaths: Oversexed, Overplayed, but Not Over Here?" *Criminal Behaviour and Mental Health* 7:3–11.

Cooke, D. J., and C. Michie. 1997. "An Item Response Theory Analysis of the Hare Psychopathy Checklist-Revised." *Psychological Assessment* 9:3–14.

———. 1999. "Psychopathy across Cultures." *Journal of Abnormal Psychology* 108:58–68.

Cooke, D. J., C. Michie, S. Hart, and R. D. Hare. 1999. "Evaluating the Screening Version of the Hare Psychopathy Checklist–Revised (PCL:SV)." *Psychological Assessment* 11:3–13.

Cornell, D. G., J. Warren, G. Hawk, E. Stafford, G. Oram, and D. Pine. 1996. "Psychopathy in Instrumental and Reactive Violent Offenders." *Journal of Consulting and Clinical Psychology* 64:783–90.

Corsini, R. J. 1958. "Psychodrama with a Psychopath." *Group Psychotherapy* 11: 33–39.

Daly, M., and M. Wilson. 1988. *Homicide*. Hawthorne, N.Y.: de Gruyter.

Davis, R. P. N. 1982. *Canadian Sentencing Digest*. Vol. 1. Toronto: Carswell.

Dawkins, R. 1978. *The Selfish Gene*. London: Paladin.

DeLeon, G. 1984. *The Therapeutic Community: Study of Effectiveness*. Washington, D.C.: Government Printing Office.

Dell, S., and G. Robertson. 1988. *Sentenced to Hospital: Offenders in Broadmoor*. Oxford: Oxford University Press.

Dolan, D. 1998. "Therapeutic Community Treatment for Severe Personality Disorders." In *Psychopathy: Antisocial, Criminal, and Violent Behavior*, edited by T. Millon, E. Simonsen, M. Birket-Smith, and R. D. Davis. New York: Guilford.

Douglas, K. W., J. R. P. Ogloff, and I. Grant. 1999. "Assessing Risk for Violence among Psychiatric Patients: The HCR-20 Violence Risk Assessment Scheme and the Psychopathy Checklist: Screening Version." *Journal of Consulting and Clinical Psychology* 67:917–30.

Ebstein, R. P., O. Novick, R. Unmansky, B. Priel, Y. Osher, D. Blaine, E. R. Bennett, L. Nemanov, M. Katz, and R. H. Belmaker. 1996. "Dopamine D4 Receptor (D4DR) Exon III Polymorphism Associated with the Human Personality Trait of Novelty Seeking." *Nature Genetics* 12:78–80.

Eley, T. C. 1998. "General Genes: A New Theme in Developmental Psychopathology." *Current Directions in Psychological Science* 6:90–95.

Ellis, L. 1991. "Monoamine Oxidase and Criminality: Identifying an Apparent Biological Marker for Antisocial Behavior." *Journal of Research in Crime and Delinquency* 28:631–42.

Faigman, D. L., D. H. Kaye, M. J. Saks, and J. Sanders. 1999. *Modern Scientific Evidence: The Law and Science of Expert Testimony.* St. Paul, Minn.: West Group.

Farrington, D. P., B. Gallagher, L. Morely, R. J. St. Ledger, and D. J. West. 1988. "A 24-Year Follow-Up of Men from Vulnerable Backgrounds." In *The Abandonment of Delinquent Behavior: Promoting the Turnaround,* edited by R. L. Jenkins and W. K. Brown. New York: Praeger.

Farrington, D. P., and D. J. West. 1993. "Criminal, Penal and Life Histories of Chronic Offenders: Risk and Protective Factors and Early Identification." *Criminal Behaviour and Mental Health* 3:492–523.

Firestone, P., F. Leewy, and V. I. Douglas. 1976. "Hyperactivity and Physical Anomalies." *Canadian Psychiatric Association Journal* 21:23–26.

Firestone, P., and A. N. Prabhu. 1983. "Minor Physical Anomalies and Obstetrical Complications: Their Relationship to Hyperactive, Psychoneurotic, and Normal Children and Their Families." *Journal of Abnormal Child Psychology* 11:207–16.

Fogel, C. A., S. A. Mednick, and N. Michelsen. 1985. "Hyperactive Behavior and Minor Physical Anomalies." *Acta Psychiatrica Scandinavica* 72:551–56.

Forth, A. E. 1995. *Psychopathy and Young Offenders: Prevalence, Family Background, and Violence.* Program Branch Users Report. Ottawa: Ministry of the Solicitor General of Canada.

Forth, A. E., S. L. Brown, S. D. Hart, and R. D. Hare. 1996. "The Assessment of Psychopathy in Male and Female Noncriminals: Reliability and Validity." *Personality and Individual Differences* 20:531–43.

Forth, A. E., and H. Burke. 1998. "Psychopathy in Adolescence: Assessment, Violence, and Developmental Precursors." In *Psychopathy: Theory, Research, and Implications for Society,* edited by R. D. Cooke, A. E. Forth, and R. D. Hare. Dordrecht: Kluwer.

Forth, A. E., S. D. Hart, and R. D. Hare. 1990. "Assessment of Psychopathy in Male Young Offenders." *Psychological Assessment: A Journal of Consulting and Clinical Psychology* 2:1–3.

Forth, A. E., D. S. Kosson, and R. D. Hare. Forthcoming. *The Psychopathy Checklist: Youth Version.* Toronto: Multi-Health Systems.

Forth, A. E., and D. L. Mailloux. 2000. "Psychopathy in Youth: What Do We

Know?" In *The Clinical and Forensic Assessment of Psychopathy*, edited by C. B. Gacono. Mahwah, N.J.: Erlbaum.

Fowles, D. C. 1980. "The Three Arousal Model: Implications of Gray's Two-Factor Learning Theory for Heart Rate, Electrodermal Activity, and Psychopathy." *Psychophysiology* 17:87–104.

Frick, P. J., C. T. Barry, and S. D. Bodin. 2000. "Applying the Concept of Psychopathy to Children: Implications for the Assessment of Antisocial Youth." In *The Clinical and Forensic Assessment of Psychopathy*, edited by C. B. Gacono. Mahwah, N.J.: Erlbaum.

Frick, P. J., and M. Ellis. 1999. "Callous-Unemotional Traits and Subtypes of Conduct Disorder." *Clinical Child and Family Psychology Review* 2:149–68.

Frick, P. J., and R. D. Hare. Forthcoming. *The Psychopathy Screening Device.* Toronto: Multi-Health Systems.

Frick, P. J., and B. R. Loney. 1999. "Outcomes of Children and Adolescents with Conduct Disorder and Oppositional Defiant Disorder." In *Handbook of Disruptive Behavior Disorders*, edited by H. C. Quay and A. Hogan. New York: Plenum.

Frick, P. J., B. O'Brien, J. Wootton, and K. McBurnett. 1994. "Psychopathy and Conduct Problems in Children." *Journal of Abnormal Psychology* 103: 700–707.

Furlow, F. B., T. Armijo-Prewitt, S. W. Gangestad, and R. Thornhill. 1997. "Fluctuating Asymmetry and Psychometric Intelligence." *Proceedings of the Royal Society of London B* 264:823–29.

Furlow, F. B., S. W. Gangestad, and T. Armijo-Prewitt. 1998. "Developmental Stability and Human Violence." *Proceedings of the Royal Society of London B* 266:1–6.

Gabel, S., J. Stadler, J. Bjorn, R. Shindledecker, and J. Bowden. 1993. "Dopamine-Beta-Hydroxylase in Behaviorally Disturbed Youth: Relationship between Teacher and Parent Ratings." *Biological Psychiatry* 34:434–42.

Gacono, C. B., and H. E. Hutton. 1994. "Suggestions for Clinical and Forensic Use of the Hare Psychopathy Checklist–Revised (PCL-R)." *International Journal of Law and Psychiatry* 17: 303–17.

Gangestad, S. W., and R. Thornhill. 1997. "The Evolutionary Psychology of Extrapair Sex: The Role of Fluctuating Asymmetry." *Evolution and Human Behavior* 18:69–88.

Gangestad, S. W., R. Thornhill, and R. A. Yeo. 1994. "Facial Attractiveness, Developmental Stability, and Fluctuating Asymmetry." *Ethology and Sociobiology* 15:73–85.

Gonçalves, R. A. 1999. "Psychopathy and Offender Types." *International Journal of Law and Psychiatry* 22:337–46.

Gorenstein, E. E. 1982. "Frontal Lobe Functions in Psychopaths." *Journal of Abnormal Psychology* 91:368–79.

Grann, M., N. Langstrom, A. Tengstrom, and G. Kullgren. 1999. "Psychopathy (PCL-R) Predicts Violent Recidivism among Criminal Offenders with Personality Disorders in Sweden." *Law and Human Behavior* 23:205–18.

Gray, J. A. 1987. *The Psychology of Fear and Stress.* Cambridge: Cambridge University Press.

Grounds, A. T. 1987. "Detention of 'Psychopathic Disorder' Patients in Special Hospitals: Critical Issues." *British Journal of Psychiatry* 151:474–78.

Gualtieri, T., and R. E. Hicks. 1985. "An Immunoreactive Theory of Selective Male Affliction." *Behavioral and Brain Sciences* 8:427–41.

Gunn, J., and G. Robertson. 1982. "An Evaluation of Grendon Prison." In *Abnormal Offenders, Delinquency, and the Criminal Justice System*, edited by J. Gunn and D. P. Farrington. New York: Wiley.

Guy, J. D., L. V. Majorski, C. J. Wallace, and M. P. Guy. 1983. "The Incidence of Minor Physical Anomalies in Adult Male Schizophrenics." *Schizophrenia Bulletin* 9:571–82.

Hallman, J., L. von Knorring, and L. Oreland. 1996. "Personality Disorders according to DSM-III-R and Thrombocyte Monoamine Oxidase Activity in Type 1 and Type 2 Alcoholics." *Journal of Studies on Alcohol* 57:155–61.

Halverson, C. F., and J. B. Victor. 1976. "Minor Physical Anomalies and Problem Behavior in Elementary School Children." *Child Development* 47: 281–85.

Hamer, D. 1997. "The Search for Personality Genes: Adventures of a Molecular Biologist." *Current Directions in Psychological Science* 6:111–14.

Hanson, R. K., and M. T. Bussière. 1998. "Predicting Relapse: A Meta-analysis of Sexual Offender Recidivism Studies." *Journal of Consulting and Clinical Psychology* 66:348–62.

Hare, R. D. 1970. *Psychopathy: Theory and Research.* New York: Wiley.

———. 1978. "Electrodermal and Cardiovascular Correlates of Psychopathy." In *Psychopathic Disorder: Approaches to Research*, edited by R. D. Hare and D. Schalling. Chichester, England: Wiley.

———. 1979. "Psychopathy and Laterality of Cerebral Function." *Journal of Abnormal Psychology* 88:605–10.

———. 1980. "A Research Scale for the Assessment of Psychopathy in Criminal Populations." *Personality and Individual Differences* 1:111–19.

———. 1981. "Psychopathy and Violence." In *Violence and the Violent Individual*, edited by J. R. Hayes, T. K. Roberts, and K. S. Solway. Jamaica, N.Y.: Spectrum.

———. 1983. "Diagnosis of Antisocial Personality Disorder in Two Prison Populations." *American Journal of Psychiatry* 140:887–90.

———. 1984. "Performance of the Psychopath on Cognitive Tasks Related to Frontal Lobe Function." *Journal of Abnormal Psychology* 99:374–79.

———. 1985. "Comparison of Procedures for the Assessment of Psychopathy." *Journal of Consulting and Clinical Psychology* 53:7–16.

———. 1991. *The Hare Psychopathy Checklist-Revised.* Toronto: Multi-Health Systems.

———. 1992. *A Model Treatment Program for Offenders at High Risk for Violence.* Ottawa: Correctional Service of Canada, Research Branch.

———. 1993. *Without a Conscience: The Disturbing World of the Psychopaths among Us.* New York: Pocket.

———. 1996. "Psychopathy: A Clinical Construct Whose Time Has Come." *Criminal Justice and Behavior* 23:25–54.

———. 1998. "The Hare PCL-R: Some Issues concerning Its Use and Misuse." *Legal and Criminological Psychology* 3:99–119.
———. 1999. "Psychopathy and Risk Assessment." Paper presented at the Conference on Risk Assessment and Risk Management: Implications for the Prevention of Violence sponsored by the B.C. Institute Against Family Violence. Vancouver, B.C., November.
Hare, R. D., S. D. Hart, and T. J. Harpur. 1991. "Psychopathy and the DSM-IV Criteria for Antisocial Personality Disorder." *Journal of Abnormal Psychology* 100:391–98.
Hare, R. D., and J. W. Jutai. 1983. "Criminal History of the Male Psychopath: Some Preliminary Data. In *Prospective Studies of Crime and Delinquency*, edited by K. T. Van Dusen and S. A. Mednick. Boston: Kluwer-Nijhoff.
———. 1988. "Psychopathy and Cerebral Asymmetry in Semantic Processing." *Personality and Individual Differences* 9:329–37.
Hare, R. D., and L. M. McPherson. 1984. "Violent and Aggressive Behavior by Criminal Psychopaths." *International Journal of Law and Psychiatry* 7:35–50.
Hare, R. D., L. M. McPherson, and A. E. Forth. 1988. "Male Psychopaths and Their Criminal Careers." *Journal of Consulting and Clinical Psychology* 56: 710–14.
Harpur, T. J., A. R. Hakstian, and R. D. Hare. 1988. "Factor Structure of the Psychopathy Checklist." *Journal of Consulting and Clinical Psychology* 56:741–47.
Harris, G. T., and M. E. Rice. 1996. "The Science in Phallometric Measurement of Male Sexual Interest." *Current Directions in Psychological Service* 5: 156–60.
Harris, G. T., M. E. Rice, and C. A. Cormier. 1991. "Psychopathy and Violent Recidivism." *Law and Human Behavior* 15:223–36.
———. 1994. "Psychopaths: Is a Therapeutic Community Therapeutic?" *Therapeutic Communities* 15:283–300.
Harris, G. T., M. E. Rice, and M. Lalumière. Forthcoming. "Criminal Violence: The Roles of Psychopathy, Neurodevelopmental Insults, and Antisocial Parenting." *Criminal Justice and Behavior.*
Harris, G. T., M. E. Rice, and V. L. Quinsey. 1993. "Violent Recidivism of Mentally Disordered Offenders: The Development of a Statistical Prediction Instrument." *Criminal Justice and Behavior* 20:315–35.
———. 1994. "Psychopathy as a Taxon: Evidence That Psychopaths Are a Discrete Class." *Journal of Consulting and Clinical Psychology* 62:387–97.
———. 1998. "Appraisal and Management of Risk in Sexual Aggressors: Implications for Criminal Justice Policy." *Psychology, Public Policy, and Law* 4: 73–115.
Hart, S. D., D. N. Cox, and R. D. Hare. 1995. *Manual for the Psychopathy Checklist: Screening Version (PCL-SV)*. Toronto: Multi-Health Systems.
Hart, S. D., A. E. Forth, and R. D. Hare. 1990. "Performance of Criminal Psychopaths on Selected Neuropsychological Tests." *Journal of Abnormal Psychology* 99:374–79.

Hart, S. D., and R. D. Hare. 1989. "Discriminant Validity of the Psychopathy Checklist in a Forensic Psychiatric Population." *Psychological Assessment: A Journal of Consulting and Clinical Psychology* 1:211–18.

———. 1997. "Psychopathy: Assessment and Association with Criminal Conduct." In *Handbook of Antisocial Behavior*, edited by D. M. Stoff, J. Brieling, and J. Maser. New York: Wiley.

Hart, S. D., R. D. Hare, and T. J. Harpur. 1992. "The Psychopathy Checklist-Revised (PCL-R): An Overview for Researchers and Clinicians." In *Advances in Psychological Assessment*, edited by J. C. Rosen and P. McReynolds. Vol. 8. New York: Plenum.

Hart, S. D., P. R. Kropp, and R. D. Hare. 1988. "Performance of Male Psychopaths Following Conditional Release from Prison." *Journal of Consulting and Clinical Psychology* 56:227–32.

Hemphill, J. F., R. D. Hare, and S. Wong. 1998. "Psychopathy and Recidivism: A Review." *Legal and Criminological Psychology* 3:139–70.

Hill, E. M., S. F. Stoltenberg, M. Burmeister, M. Closser, and R. A. Zucker. 1999. "Potential Associations among Genetic Markers in the Serotonergic System and the Antisocial Alcoholism Subtype." *Experimental and Clinical Psychopharmacology* 7:103–21.

Hinshaw, S. P., B. B. Lahay, and E. L. Hart. 1993. "Issues of Taxonomy and Comorbidity in the Development of Conduct Disorder." *Development and Psychopathology* 5:31–49.

Hobson, J., and J. Shine. 1998. "Measurement of Psychopathy in a U.K. Prison Population Referred for Long-Term Psychotherapy." *British Journal of Criminology* 38: 504–15.

Howard, R., L. T. Payamal, and L. H. Neo. 1997. "Response Modulation Deficits in Psychopaths: A Failure to Confirm and a Reconsideration of the Patterson-Newman Model." *Personality and Individual Differences* 22:707–17.

Jutai, J. W., and R. D. Hare. 1983. "Psychopathy and Selective Attention during Performance of a Complex Perceptual-Motor Task." *Psychophysiology* 20: 146–51.

Kandel, E., and D. Freed. 1989. "Frontal Lobe Dysfunction and Antisocial Behavior: A Review." *Journal of Clinical Psychology* 45:404–13.

Kandel, E., P. A. Brennan, S. A. Mednick, and N. M. Michelson. 1989. Minor Physical Anomalies and Recidivistic Adult Violent Criminal Behavior." *Acta Psychiatry Scandinavia* 79:103–7.

Klinteberg, F., and L. Oreland. 1995. "Hyperactive and Aggressive Behaviors in Childhood as Related to Low Platelet Monoamine Oxidase (MAO) Activity at Adult Age: A Longitudinal Study of Male Subjects." *Personality and Individual Differences* 19:373–83.

Kosson, D. D., and J. P. Newman. 1986. "Psychopathy and Allocation of Attentional Capacity in a Divided-Attention Situation." *Journal of Abnormal Psychology* 95:257–63.

Kosson, D. S., S. S. Smith, and J. P. Newman. 1990. "Evaluation of the Construct Validity of Psychopathy in Black and White Male Inmates: Three Preliminary Studies." *Journal of Abnormal Psychology* 99:250–59.

Kristiansson, M. 1995. "Incurable Psychopaths?" *Bulletin of the American Academy of Psychiatry and the Law* 23:555–62.

La Fond, J. Q. 1992. "Washington's Sexually Violent Predator Law: A Deliberate Misuse of the Therapeutic State for Social Control." *University of Puget Sound Law Review* 15:655–708.

Lalumière, M. L., G. T. Harris, and M. E. Rice. 1999. "Birth Order and Fluctuating Asymmetry: A First Look." *Proceedings of the Royal Society London* 266:2351–54.

———. Forthcoming. "Psychopathy and Developmental Instability." *Evolution and Human Behavior.*

Lalumière, M. L., and V. L. Quinsey. 1996. "Sexual Deviance, Antisociality, Mating Effort, and the Use of Sexually Coercive Behaviors." *Personality and Individual Differences* 21:33–48.

Lapierre, D., M. J. Braun, and S. Hodgins. 1995. "Ventral Frontal Deficits in Psychopathy: Neuropsychological Test Findings." *Neuropsychologia* 11:139–51.

Lappalainen, J., J. C. Long, M. Eggert, N. Ozaki, R. W. Robin, G. L. Brown, H. Naukkarinen, M. Virkkunen, M. Linnoila, and D. Goldman. 1998. "Linkage of Antisocial Alcoholism to the Serotonin 5-HTIB Receptor Gene in Two Populations." *Archives of General Psychiatry* 55:989–94.

Lesch, K. P., D. Bengel, A. Heils, S. Z. Sabol, B. D. Greenberg, S. Petri, J. Benjamin, C. R. Muller, D. H. Hamer, and D. L. Murphy. 1996. "Association of Anxiety-Related Traits with a Polymorphism in the Serotonin Transporter Gene Regulatory Region." *Science* 274:1527–31.

Levenston, G. K., C. J. Patrick, M. M. Bradley, and P. J. Lang. 2000. "The Psychopath as Observer: Emotion and Attention in Picture Processing." *Journal of Abnormal Psychology* 109:373–85.

Lilienfeld, S. O. 1994. "Conceptual Problems in the Assessment of Psychopathy." *Clinical Psychology Review* 14:17–38.

Lilienfeld, S. O., and L. Marino. 1999. "Essentialism Revisited: Evolutionary Theory and the Concept of Mental Disorder." *Journal of Abnormal Psychology* 108:400–411.

Lipton, H. R. 1950. "The Psychopath." *Journal of Criminal Law and Criminology* 40:584–96.

Livshits G., and E. Kobyliansky. 1987. "Dermatoglyphic Traits as Possible Markers of Developmental Processes in Humans." *American Journal of Medical Genetics* 26:111–22.

———. 1991. "Fluctuating Asymmetry as a Possible Measure of Developmental Homeostasis in Humans: A Review." *Human Biology* 63:441–66.

Loeber, R. 1982. "The Stability of Antisocial and Delinquent Child Behavior: A Review." *Child Development* 53:1431–46.

Loeber, R., P. Wung, K. Keenan, B. Giroux, M. Southhamer-Loeber, W. B. VanKammen, B. Maughan. 1993. "Developmental Pathways in Disruptive Child Behavior." *Development and Psychopathology* 5:103–33.

Lösel, F. 1998. "Treatment and Management of Psychopaths." In *Psychopathy: Theory, Research, and Implications for Society*, edited by D. J. Cooke, R. D. Hare, and A. E. Forth. Dordrecht: Kluwer.

Loucks, A. D. 1996. "Criminal Behavior, Violent Behavior, and Prison Maladjustment in Federal Female Offenders." Unpublished doctoral dissertation. Kingston, Ontario: Queen's University, Department of Psychology.

Lykken, D. T. 1957. "A Study of Anxiety in the Sociopathic Personality." *Journal of Abnormal and Social Psychology* 55:6–10.

———. 1995. *The Antisocial Personalities.* Hillsdale, N.J.: Erlbaum.

———. 1998. "The Case for Parental Licensure." In *Psychopathy: Antisocial, Criminal, and Violent Behavior*, edited by T. Millon, E. Simonsen, M. Birket-Smith, and R. D. Davis. New York: Guilford.

Lymburner, J. A., and R. Roesch. 1999. "The Insanity Defense: Five Years of Research (1993–1997)." *International Journal of Law and Psychiatry* 22:213–40.

Lynam, D. R. 1996. "Early Identification of Chronic Offenders: Who Is the Fledgling Psychopath?" *Psychological Bulletin* 120:209–34.

Manning, J. T., K. Koukourakis, and D. A. Brodie. 1998. "Fluctuating Asymmetry, Metabolic Rate and Sexual Selection in Human Males." *Evolution and Human Behavior* 18:15–21.

Manning, J. T., and D. Wood. 1998. "Fluctuating Asymmetry and Aggression in Boys." *Human Nature* 9:53–65.

Maudsley, H. 1879. *The Physiology and Pathology of Mind.* 3d ed. London: Macmillan.

McCord, J. 1982. "Parental Behavior in the Cycle of Aggression." *Psychiatry* 51:14–23.

Mealey, L. 1995. "The Sociobiology of Sociopathy: An Integrated Evolutionary Model." *Behavioral and Brain Sciences* 18:523–99.

Mednick, S. A., W. Gabrielli, and B. Hutchings. 1984. "Genetic Influences in Criminal Convictions: Evidence from an Adoption Cohort." *Science* 224: 891–93.

Mellor, C. S. 1992. "Dermatoglyphic Evidence of Fluctuating Asymmetry in Schizophrenia." *British Journal of Psychiatry* 160:467–72.

Meloy, J. Reid, and C. B. Gacono. 1992. "The Aggression Response and the Rorschach." *Journal of Clinical Psychology* 48:104–14.

Moffitt, T. E. 1987. "Parental Mental Disorder and Offspring Criminal Behavior: An Adoption Study." *Psychiatry* 50:346–60.

———. 1993. "Adolescence-Limited and Life-Course-Persistent Antisocial Behavior: A Developmental Taxonomy." *Psychological Review* 100:674–701.

Moller, A. P. 1997. "Developmental Stability and Fitness: A Review." *American Naturalist* 5:917–32.

Moltó, J., R. Poy, and R. Torrubia. 2000. "Standardization of the Hare Psychopathy Checklist-Revised in a Spanish Prison Sample." *Journal of Personality Disorder* 14:84–96.

Moore, C., and M. R. Rose. 1995. "Adaptive and Nonadaptive Explanations of Sociopathy." *Behavioral and Brain Sciences* 18:566–67.

Murphy, J. M. 1976. Psychiatric Labeling in Cross-Cultural Perspective: Similar Kinds of Disturbed Behavior Appear to be Labeled Abnormal in Diverse Cultures." *Science* 191:1019–28.

Nagin, D. S., D. P. Farrington, and T. E. Moffitt. 1995. "Life-Course Trajectories of Different Types of Offenders." *Criminology* 33:111–39.

Naugler, C. T., and M. D. Ludman. 1996. "Fluctuating Asymmetry and Disorders of Developmental Origins." *American Journal of Medical Genetics* 66: 15–20.

Neary, A. 1990. "DSM-III and Psychopathy Checklist Assessment of Antisocial Personality Disorder in Black and White Female Felons." Unpublished doctoral thesis. St. Louis: University of Missouri, Department of Psychology.

Neugebauer, R., H. W. Hoek, and E. Susser. 1999. "Prenatal Exposure to Wartime Famine and Development of Antisocial Personality Disorder in Early Adulthood." *Journal of the American Medical Association* 282:455–62.

Newman, J. P. 1998. "Psychopathy: An Information Processing Perspective." In *Psychopathy: Theory, Research, and Implications for Society*, edited by D. J. Cooke, A. E. Forth, and R. D. Hare. London: Kluwer.

Newman, J. P., D. S. Kosson, and C. M. Patterson. 1992. "Delay of Gratification In Psychopathic and Nonpsychopathic Offenders." *Journal of Abnormal Psychology* 101:630–36.

Newman, J. P., C. M. Patterson, and D. S. Kosson. 1987. "Response Perseveration in Psychopaths." *Journal of Abnormal Psychology* 96:145–48.

Newman, J. P., C. M. Patterson, E. W. Howland, and S. L. Nichols. 1990. "Passive Avoidance in Psychopaths: The Effect of Reward." *Personality and Individual Differences* 11:1101–14.

Newman, J. P., and W. A. Schmitt. 1998. "Passive Avoidance in Psychopaths: A Replication and Extension." *Journal of Abnormal Psychology* 107:527–32.

Newman, J. P., W. A. Schmitt, and W. D. Voss. 1997. "The Impact of Motivationally Neutral Clues on Psychopathic Individuals: Assessing the Generalizability of the Response Modulation Hypothesis." *Journal of Abnormal Psychology* 106:563–75.

Ogloff, J., S. Wong, and A. Greenwood. 1990. "Treating Criminal Psychopaths in a Therapeutic Community Program." *Behavioral Sciences and the Law* 8:81–90.

Patrick, C. J. 1994. "Emotion and Psychopathy: Startling New Insights." *Psychophysiology* 31:319–30.

Patrick, C. J., M. M. Bradley, and P. J. Lang. 1993. "Emotion in the Criminal Psychopath: Startle Reflex Modulation." *Journal of Abnormal Psychology* 102: 82–92.

Patrick, C. J., B. N. Cuthbert, and P. J. Lang. 1994. "Emotion in the Criminal Psychopath: Fear Image Processing. *Journal of Abnormal Psychology* 103:523–34.

Pritchard, J. C. 1835. *A Treatise on Insanity and Other Disorders Affecting the Mind.* London: Sherwood, Gilbert & Piper.

Quay, H. C. 1986. "Conduct Disorders." In *Psychopathological Disorders of Childhood*, 3d ed., edited by H. C. Quay and J. S. Werry. New York: Wiley.

———. 1987. "Patterns of Delinquent Behavior." In *Handbook of Juvenile Delinquency*, edited by H. C. Quay. New York: Wiley.

Quinsey, V. L. 1995. "The Prediction and Explanation of Criminal Violence." *International Journal of Law and Psychiatry* 18:117–27.

Quinsey, V. L., G. Coleman, B. Jones, and I. Altrows. 1997. "Proximal Antecedents of Eloping and Reoffending among Mentally Disordered Offenders." *Journal of Interpersonal Violence* 12:794–813.

Quinsey, V. L., G. T. Harris, M. E. Rice, and C. Cormier. 1998. *Violent Offenders: Appraising and Managing Risk.* Washington, D.C.: American Psychological Association.

Raine, A. 1993. *The Psychopathology of Crime: Criminal Behavior as a Clinical Disorder.* San Diego: Academic Press.

Raine, A., P. Brennan, B. Mednick, and S. A. Mednick. 1996. "High Rates of Violence, Crime, Academic Problems, and Behavioral Problems in Males with Both Early Neuromotor Deficits and Unstable Family Environments." *Archives of General Psychiatry* 53:544–49.

Raine, A., P. Brennan, and S. A. Mednick. 1994. "Birth Complications Combined with Early Maternal Rejection at Age 1 Predispose to Violent Crime at Age 18 Years." *Archives of General Psychiatry* 51:984–88.

Raine, A., M. O'Brien, N. Smiley, A. Scerbo, and C. Chan. 1990. "Reduced Lateralization in Verbal Dichotic Listening in Adolescent Psychopaths." *Journal of Abnormal Psychology* 99:272–77.

Rapoport, J. L., C. Pandoni, M. Renfield, C. R. Lake, and M. G. Ziegler. 1977. "Newborn Dopamine-Beta Hydroxylase, Minor Physical Anomalies, and Infant Temperament." *American Journal of Psychiatry* 136:676–79.

Reiss, D., D. Grubin, and C. Meux. 1999. "Institutional Performance of Male 'Psychopaths' in a High-Security Hospital." *Journal of Forensic Psychiatry* 10: 290–99.

Rice, M. E. 1997. "Violent Offender Research and Implications for the Criminal Justice System." *American Psychologist* 52:414–23.

Rice, M. E., and G. T. Harris. 1995. "Psychopathy, Schizophrenia, Alcohol Abuse, and Violent Recidivism." *International Journal of Law and Psychiatry* 18:333–42.

———. 1997*a*. "Cross-Validation and Extension of the Violence Risk Appraisal Guide for Child Molesters and Rapists." *Law and Human Behavior* 21:231–41.

Rice, M. E., and G. T. Harris. 1997*b*. "The Treatment of Adult Offenders." In *Handbook of Antisocial Behavior*, edited by D. M. Stoff, J. Breiling, and J. D. Maser. New York: Wiley.

Rice, M. E., and G. T. Harris. 1999. "Sexual Aggressors." In *Modern Scientific Evidence: The Law and Science of Expert Testimony*, edited by D. L. Faigman, D. H. Kaye, M. J. Saks, and J. Sanders. Vol. 3. St. Paul, Minn.: West.

Rice, M. E., G. T. Harris, and C. Cormier. 1992. "Evaluation of a Maximum Security Therapeutic Community for Psychopaths and Other Mentally Disordered Offenders." *Law and Human Behavior* 15:625–37.

Rice, M. E., G. T. Harris, and V. L. Quinsey. 1990. "A Follow-Up of Rapists Assessed in a Maximum Security Psychiatric Facility." *Journal of Interpersonal Violence* 5:435–48.

Ridley, M. 1993. *The Red Queen: Sex and the Evolution of Human Nature*. New York: MacMillan.

Robins, L. N. 1966. *Deviant Children Grown Up: A Sociological and Psychiatric Study of Sociopathic Personality*. Baltimore: Williams & Wilkins.

Robins, L. N. 1978. "Etiological Implications in Childhood Histories Relating to Antisocial Personality." In *Psychopathic Behavior: Approaches to Research*, edited by R. D. Hare and D. Schalling. Chichester: Wiley.

Robins, L. N., J. Tipp, and T. Przybeck. 1991. "Psychiatric Disorders in America." In *Antisocial Personality Disorder*, edited by L. N. Robins and D. A. Regie. New York: Free Press.

Rodgers, T. C. 1947. "Hypnotherapy in Character Neuroses." *Journal of Clinical Psychopathology* 8:519–24.

Rosow, H. M. 1955. "Some Observations on Group Therapy with Prison Inmates." *Archives of Criminal Psychodynamics* 1:866–97.

Rutherford, M. J., J. S. Cacciola, and A. I. Alterman. 1999. "Antisocial Personality Disorder and Psychopathy in Cocaine Dependent Women." *American Journal of Psychiatry* 156:849–56.

Rutherford, M. J., J. S. Cacciola, A. I. Alterman, and J. R. McKay. 1996. "Reliability and Validity of the Revised Psychopathy Checklist in Women Methadone Patients." *Assessment* 3:145–56.

Rutter, M. 1996. "Introduction: Concepts of Antisocial Behavior, of Cause and of Genetic Influences." In *Genetics of Criminal and Antisocial Behavior*, edited by G. R. Bock and J. A. Goode. Toronto: Wiley.

Sakuta, A., and A. Fukushima. 1998. "Two Skyjacker Case Studies." *International Medical Journal* 5:301–11.

Salekin, R. T., R. Rogers, and K. W. Sewell. 1996. "A Review and Meta-analysis of the Psychopathy Checklist and Psychopathy Checklist-Revised: Predictive Validity of Dangerousness." *Clinical Psychology, Science, and Practice* 3:203–15.

Salekin, R. T., R. Rogers, and K. W. Sewell. 1997. "Construct Validity of Psychopathy in a Female Offender Sample: A Multitrait-Multimethod Evaluation." *Journal of Abnormal Psychology* 106:576–85.

Salekin, R. T., R. Rogers, K. L. Ustad, and K. W. Sewell. 1998. "Psychopathy and Recidivism among Female Inmates." *Law and Human Behavior* 22:109–28.

Scerbo, A., A. Raine, M. O'Brien, C. Chan, C. Rhee, and N. Smiley. 1990. "Reward Dominance and Passive Avoidance in Adolescent Psychopaths." *Journal of Abnormal Child Psychology*, 18:451–63.

Schmideberg, M. 1949. "Psychology and Treatment of the Criminal Psychopath." *International Journal of Psychoanalysis* 20:197.

Schmitt, W. A., and J. P. Newman. 1999. "Are All Psychopathic Individuals Low Anxious?" *Journal of Abnormal Psychology* 108:353–58.

Serin, R. C. 1991. "Psychopathy and Violence in Criminals." *Journal of Interpersonal Violence* 6:423–31.

Serin, R. C. 1995. "Treatment Responsivity in Criminal Psychopaths." *Forum on Corrections Research* 7:23–26.

Serin, R. C., and S. Brown. 1996. "Strategies for Enhancing the Treatment of Violent Offenders." *Forum* 8:45–48.

Serin, R. C., and M. Kuriychuk. 1994. "Social and Cognitive Processing Deficits in Violent Offenders: Implications for Treatment." *International Journal of Law and Psychiatry* 17:431–41.

Serin, R. C., R. D.Peters, and H. E. Barbaree. 1990. "Predictors of Psychopathy and Release Outcome in a Criminal Population." *Psychological Assessment* 2:419–22.

Seto, M. C., and H. Barbaree. 1999. "Psychopathy, Treatment Behavior, and Sex Offender Recidivism." *Journal of Interpersonal Violence* 14:1235–48.

Showstack, N. 1956. "Treatment of Prisoners at the California Medical Facility." *American Journal of Psychiatry* 112:821–24.

Siever, L. J., R. D. Coursey, I. S. Alterman, M. S. Buchsbaum, and D. L. Murphy. 1984. "Impaired Smooth-Pursuit Eye Movement: Vulnerability Marker for Schizotypal Personality Disorder in a Normal Volunteer Population." *American Journal of Psychiatry* 141:1560–66.

Sigvardsson, S., M. Bohman, and C.R. Cloninger. 1987. "Structure and Stability of Childhood Personality: Prediction of Later Social Adjustment." *Journal of Child Psychology and Psychiatry and Allied Disciplines* 28:929–46.

Skilling, T., G. T. Harris, M. E. Rice, and V. L. Quinsey. 2000. "The Assessment of Lifelong Persistent Antisociality." Unpublished manuscript. Penetanguishene, Ontario, Canada: Mental Health Centre.

Skilling, T. A., V. L. Quinsey, and W. M. Craig. Forthcoming. "Evidence of a Taxon Underlying Serious Antisocial Behavior in Boys." *Criminal Justice and Behavior.*

Smith, S. S., P. A. Arnett, and J. P. Newman. 1992. "Neuropsychological Differentiation of Psychopathic and Nonpsychopathic Criminal Offenders." *Personality and Individual Differences* 13:1233–43.

Smith, S. S., J. P. Newman, A. Evans, R. Pickens, J. Wydeven, G. R. Uhl, and D. B. Newlin. 1993. "Comorbid Psychopathy Is Not Associated with Increased D_2 Dopamine Receptor TaqI A or B Gene Marker Frequencies in Incarcerated Substance Abusers." *Society of Biological Psychiatry* 33:845–48.

Stålenheim, E. G., L. von Knorring, and L. Oreland. 1997. "Platelet Monoamine Oxidase Activity as a Biological Marker in a Swedish Forensic Psychiatric Population." *Psychiatry Research* 69:79–87.

Steadman, H. J., E. Silver, J. Monahan, P. S. Appelbaum, P. Clark Robbins, E. P. Mulvey, T. Grisso, L. H. Roth, and S. Banks. 2000. "A Classification Tree Approach to the Development of Actuarial Violence Risk Assessment Tools." *Law and Human Behavior* 24:83–100.

Steg, J. P., and J. L. Rapoport. 1975. "Minor Physical Anomalies in Normal, Neurotic, Learning Disabled, and Severely Disturbed Children." *Journal of Autism and Childhood Schizophrenia* 5:299–307.

Steuerwald, B. L., and D. S. Kosson. Forthcoming. "Emotional Experiences of the Psychopath." In *The Clinical and Forensic Assessment of Psychopathy: A Practitioner's Guide*, edited by C. Gacono. Mahwah, N.J.: Erlbaum.

Strachan, C. 1993. "Assessment of Psychopathy in Female Offenders." Unpublished doctoral thesis. Vancouver: University of British Columbia, Department of Psychology.

Sutker, P. B., and A. N. Allain. 1987. "Cognitive Abstraction, Shifting, and Control: Clinical Sample of Psychopaths and Nonpsychopaths." *Journal of Abnormal Psychology* 96:73–75.

Tengstrom A., M. Grann, N. Langstrom, and G. Kullgren. 2000. "Psychopathy (PCL-R) as a Predictor of Violent Recidivism among Criminal Offenders with Schizophrenia." *Law and Human Behavior* 24:45–58.

Thorne, F. C. 1959. "The Etiology of Sociopathic Reactions." *American Journal of Psychotherapy* 13:319–30.

Thornhill R., and S. W. Gangestad. 1994. "Human Fluctuating Asymmetry and Sexual Behavior." *Psychological Science* 5:297–302.

Thornhill R., S. W. Gangestad, and R. Comer. 1995. "Human Female Orgasm and Mate Fluctuating Asymmetry." *Animal Behaviour* 50:1601–15.

Thornhill R., and A. P. Moller. 1997. "Developmental Stability, Disease and Medicine." *Biological Review* 72:497–548.

Twitchell, G. R., G. L. Hanna, E. H. Cook, H. E. Fitzgerald, K. Y. Little, and R. A. Zucker. 1998. "Overt Behavior Problems and Serotonergic Function in Middle Childhood among Male and Female Offspring of Alcoholic Fathers." *Alcoholism: Clinical and Experimental Research* 22:1340–48.

von Hilscheimer, G., and V. Kurko. 1979. "Minor Physical Anomalies in Exceptional Children." *Journal of Learning Disabilities* 12:462–69.

Wakefield, J. C. 1992. "Disorder as Harmful Dysfunction: A Conceptual Critique of DSM-III-R's Definition of Mental Disorder." *Psychological Review* 99:232–47.

———. 1999. "Evolutionary versus Prototype Analyses of the Concept of Disorder." *Journal of Abnormal Psychology* 108:374–99.

Waldrop, M. F., R. Q. Bell, B. McLaughlin, and C. F. Halverson. 1978. "Newborn Minor Physical Anomalies Predict Short Attention Span, Peer Aggression, and Impulsivity at Age Three." *Science* 199:563–64.

Waldrop, M. F., and J. D. Goering. 1971. "Hyperactivity and Minor Physical Anomalies in Elementary School Children." *American Journal of Orthopsychiatry* 41:602–7.

Waldrop, M. F., F. A. Pedersen, and R. Q. Bell. 1968. "Minor Physical Anomalies and Behavior in Preschool Children." *Child Development* 39:391–400.

Walker, N. and S. McCabe. 1973. *Crime and Insanity in England.* Edinburgh: University of Edinburgh Press.

Wallace, J. F., W. A. Schmitt, J. E. Vitale, and J. P. Newman. 2000. "Experimental Investigations of Information-Processing Deficiencies in Psychopaths: Implications for Diagnosis and Treatment." In *The Clinical and Forensic Assessment of Psychopathy: A Practitioner's Guide*, edited by C. Gacono. Mahway, N.J.: Erlbaum.

Weisman, R. 1995. "Reflections on the Oak Ridge Experiment with Mentally Disordered Offenders, 1965–1968." *International Journal of Law and Psychiatry* 18:265–90.

Wettstein, R. M. 1992. "A Psychiatric Perspective on Washington's Sexually Violent Predators Statute." *University of Puget Sound Law Review* 15:597–634.

Wexler, H. K., G. P. Falkin, and D. S. Lipton. 1990. "Outcome Evaluation of a Prison Therapeutic Community for Substance Abuse Treatment." *Criminal Justice and Behavior* 17:71–92.

Widiger, T. A., and D. R. Lynam. 1998. "Psychopathy and the Five-Factor Model of Personality." In *Psychopathy: Antisocial, Criminal, and Violent Behavior*, edited by T. Millon, E. Simonsen, M. Birket-Smith, and R. D. Davis. New York: Guilford.

Widom, C. S. 1977. "A Methodology for Studying Noninstitutionalized Psychopaths." *Journal of Consulting and Clinical Psychology* 45:674–83.

Widom, C. S., and J. P. Newman. 1985. "Characteristics of Noninstitutionalized Psychopaths." In *Aggression and Dangerousness*, edited by D. P. Farrington and J. Gunn. New York: Wiley.

Williamson, S., R. D. Hare, and S. Wong. 1987. "Violence: Criminal Psychopaths and Their Victims." *Canadian Journal of Behavioral Science* 19:454–62.

Williamson, S., T. J. Harpur, and R. D. Hare. 1991. "Abnormal Processing of Affective Words by Psychopaths." *Psychophysiology* 28:260–73.

Wilson, J. Q., and R. J. Herrnstein. 1985. *Crime and Human Nature*. New York: Simon & Schuster.

Wolfgang, M. E., R. M. Figlio, and T. Sellin. 1972. *Delinquency in a Birth Cohort*. Chicago: University of Chicago Press.

Wolfgang, M. E., T. P. Thornberry, and R. M. Figlio. 1987. *From Boy to Man, from Delinquency to Crime*. Chicago: University of Chicago Press.

Wong, S. 1984. *The Criminal and Institutional Behaviours of Psychopaths*. Ottawa: Ministry of Solicitor General.

Wong, S., and R. D. Hare. Forthcoming. *Program Guidelines for the Institutional Treatment of Violent Psychopathic Offenders*. Toronto: Multi-Health Systems.

Woody, G. E., T. A. McLellan, L. Lubersky, and C. P. O'Brien. 1985. "Sociopathy and Psychotherapy Outcome." *Archives of General Psychiatry* 42:1081–86.

World Health Organization. 1996. *International Classification of Diseases*, 10th rev. Geneva: World Health Organization.

Wormith, J. S., and M. Ruhl. 1987. "Preventive Detention in Canada." *Journal of Interpersonal Violence* 1:399–430.

Yeo, R. A., S. W. Gangestad, and W. F. Daniel. 1993. "Hand Preference and Developmental Instability." *Psychobiology* 21:161–68.

Zinger, I., and A. E. Forth. 1998. "Psychopathy and Canadian Criminal Proceedings: The Potential for Human Rights Abuses." *Canadian Journal of Criminology* 40:237–76.

Richard Harding

Private Prisons

ABSTRACT

Private prisons have become integral to penal administration in the United States, Australia, and the United Kingdom. The principal debate revolves around such tangible matters as regime quality, value for money, public accountability and the efficacy of regulatory procedures, and whether the private sector has improved standards and outcomes in the prison business as a whole. There is clear evidence that the advent of the private sector has stimulated system-wide improvement but also evidence that the private sector can succumb to the same failures as the public sector. When this has happened, it is usually because public authorities have, through neglect or naïveté, been in a sense complicit in the failure. The future of privatization will revolve around the ability of contracting states to achieve effective public accountability and the ability of the private sector to continue to deliver high-quality correctional regimes that provide excellent value for money.

A private prison is one managed by a nongovernment entity on behalf of the state. As Logan states (1990, p. 13), it is "a place of [involuntary justice system] confinement managed by a private company under contract to government." The inmates would otherwise be incarcerated in government operated prisons. The U.K. chief inspector of prisons has said that "so-called 'private prisons' are not private sector prisons but [state] prisons run on contract for the [responsible government department] by a private sector company" (Ramsbotham 1995/96, p. 8). This

Professor Richard Harding is inspector of custodial services for the state of Western Australia. Previously, he was foundation director of the Crime Research Centre at the University of Western Australia. He is author of *Private Prisons and Public Accountability* (New Brunswick, N.J.: Transaction, 1997).

0192-3234/2001/0028-0005$02.00

observation remains true whether the private company manages a state-owned prison or also owns the physical structure itself.

These definitions bring out two crucial points: that authority to hold and deal with prisoners is derived from public law, not private arrangement, and that private prisons are an integral component of the jurisdiction's prison system. It is crucial to emphasize the first point so as to contrast contemporary privatization with the statutorily unregulated deals relating to the leasing of convict labor that first emerged in the United States in the early nineteenth century. The second point highlights that the state, in outsourcing or delegating service delivery, has not in principle surrendered any part of its overall responsibility for system objectives, standards, legality, or equity.

In the jargon of organizational theory, the notion of a "purchaser-provider" relationship is also superimposed—the public sector agency purchasing services and the private sector providing them. However, this terminology tends to obscure that the state, as "purchaser," cannot and does not, by choosing to discharge this function in that way, evade ultimate political, moral, and legal responsibility for what the provider does. The prisoners remain prisoners of the state.

One pressing issue is whether the model actually works that way—whether the accountability mechanisms and regulatory structures are properly designed and effectively applied. Can one say with confidence that the state remains actively and effectively involved as regulator, that the private prisons continue to be part of the dynamic responsibility of the state apparatus, that the companies are fully accountable?

There is a view that, however well regulated, accountable, and successful the particular regime turns out to be—even if its outcomes are better for prisoners and its standards more equitable and its processes more transparent—prison privatization is nevertheless unacceptable. This is the fundamental moral criticism that imprisonment is an intrinsic or core state function that by definition cannot legitimately be delegated in any of its aspects to a nonstate agency without undermining the very notion of the state and its responsibility to and for its citizens (Jung 1990; DiIulio 1991; Christie 1993; Sparks 1994; Ryan 1996). For the proponents of this view, no data or evidence can ever be sufficient to justify privatization.

In this context, however, it is unfortunate that some commentators and operators not infrequently ride roughshod over this sensitivity by describing the two dominant companies—Corrections Corporation of America (CCA) and Wackenhut Corrections Corporation (WCC)—as running prison systems. For example, industry analysts Scott and Stringfellow stated in 1998 that "CCA's prisons now form the sixth largest correctional system in the United States, behind California, Texas, Florida, New York and the Federal Bureau of Prisons" (Prison Privatisation Report International 1998, no. 17, p. 4). This is fundamentally erroneous, suggesting that the company has status and autonomy as principal. Both CCA and WCC and each of the other operators are contracted service providers for the state in the various jurisdictions both within the United States and in other countries where management of prison services has been contracted out.

Since the demise of convict leasing, direct administration of adult prisons by the state was the norm until the late 1970s. That position, however, was quite different in relation to juvenile detention. McDonald et al. (1998, p. 5) state that "private, mostly not-for-profit charities and organizations had played a long and distinguished role in operating facilities for juvenile offenders." McDonald (1992, pp. 370–71) has tabulated the numbers and the populations of both public sector and private juvenile correctional facilities in the United States for the period 1969–89. This revealed increasing private sector penetration, to two-thirds of institutions and two-fifths of the population—a position that subsequently has been maintained and is proportionately far in excess of anything likely to be reached with adult imprisonment.

However, the privatization of adult prisons is numerically far more significant, and it is truly private and for-profit rather than nongovernmental organization or voluntary sector. It is thus a more important criminal justice system issue. When privatization started to re-emerge in its new form in the seventies, it related at first mainly to halfway houses. Later, the Immigration and Naturalization Service began to contract out detention of illegal immigrants to the private sector (McDonald 1992, pp. 381–82). This was little more than short-term warehousing. At this stage the private sector had not yet broken into the serious end of detention—adult prisons. Gradually, however, private sector participation began to spread across the penal continuum (McDonald 1992, pp. 383–84). The breakthrough came in Texas in 1988, when the Department of Corrections announced that it would let contracts for four 500-bed, medium-security prisons for adult males. Two of the contracts were won by CCA, the other two by WCC. The prisons opened in 1989. With these contracts the private companies could be said to have started to establish their "penal legitimacy"—status as operators of "real" prisons.

Thereafter, expansion within the United States has been rapid. By the end of 1989, procurement contracts were in place for forty-four secure adult prisons or jails; they were to be located in fourteen states, and their rated capacity would be 15,000 prisoners. By the end of 1996, the comparable figures were 118 prisons or jails in twenty-five states with a capacity of 78,000 (Harding 1998*a*, p. 633). As of November 1999, these figures had increased further to 162 prisons or jails in thirty-one states, with a capacity of 125,000 (http://web.crim.ufl.edu/pcp/). If all this capacity were filled (and these figures relate to procured capacity), that would mean that about 6 percent of the total incarcerated population of the United States would, at the beginning of the new millennium, be held in private prisons.

In terms of types of prisoner and security ratings, private prisons have still not quite caught up with the public sector. Prisons being a major political risk, governments understandably and prudently had been reluctant to throw operators into the deep end of the pool—maximum security. Thus, although private prisons now cover the whole range of imprisonment situations, in comparison to the public sector, they are underrepresented in terms of maximum security prisoners held and overrepresented in terms of medium- and minimum/low-security prisoners. Some very large facilities (1,000–2,500 prisoners) are now privately operated, however, and the racial mix of prisoners is representative (Austin and Coventry 2000). Private prisons are thus now playing a mature and integral part in American penal administration. They are certainly here to stay (McDonald et al. 1998, pp. 29–32).

The United States having led the way, other nations have followed. To date they are Australia (1990), England and Wales (1992), Scotland (1997), New Zealand (1998), Canada (New Brunswick 1998), the Netherlands Antilles (1999), and South Africa (1999). Australia has the greatest proportion of its prison population in private prisons (about 20 percent); indeed, in one state, Victoria, almost 50 percent of prison accommodation is private. Of course, the numbers in Australia (ca. 4,000) are trivial by U.S. standards. The other most-developed jurisdiction, the United Kingdom, has about 10 percent of its inmates in private prisons.[1]

Active consideration is being given to privatization in other provinces of Canada (particularly Ontario), the remaining Australian states,

[1] The "United Kingdom" as used here refers to England and Wales. Scotland is a separate legal jurisdiction.

the Republic of Ireland, Serbia, South Korea, Taiwan, Tanzania, Thailand, the Philippines, Malaysia, Latvia, Jamaica, Costa Rica, Panama, and several South American countries, including Colombia. The extent to which privatization is likely to spread more widely is discussed later, but it is already apparent that it is taking root. Privatization would now seem to be one of the most important developments in penal administration in the second half of the twentieth century.

Six factors came together to act as catalysts for this new wave of privatization. They were

- exponential increases in incarcerated populations,
- overcrowding and federal court intervention,
- legal and political inhibitions upon capital expenditure by governments,
- concern about recurrent costs,
- growing impatience with the perceived obstructionism of unionized labor, and
- some concern for regime improvement.

The relative weight of these factors has varied across privatization jurisdictions.

A. Incarcerated Populations. The growth in the use of imprisonment in the United States during the last two decades of the twentieth century is a well-known story. In the mid-1970s the rate per 100,000 was still only about 110 (today's mean rate across Europe); by 1985, it was 310 (740,000 inmates); by 1990, 447 (1,150,000 inmates); and at the century's end, it is approximately 700 (1,950,000 inmates). From 1985 onward it would have been necessary to construct three new 500-bed prisons per week merely to keep pace. At a capital cost of $50,000 per bed, that would have involved expenditure of $58 billion.

B. Overcrowding and Federal Court Supervision. Accommodation soon became stretched to the uttermost. With overcrowding came acute difficulties in maintaining tolerable regimes or minimum standards: for example, deteriorating prisoner health; increased death rates, including suicide; partial surrender of management control to the strongest groups of prisoners; and conditions that were inimical to prisoner correction (Paulus 1988). The Civil Rights movement had already succeeded in turning the spotlight onto prison conditions (American Friends Service Committee 1971; Davis et al. 1971; Jackson 1971; Mitford 1971), and there it remained as populations continued to increase.

As the impact of overcrowding became more apparent, challenges under the Bill of Rights (particularly the Eighth Amendment relating to "cruel and unusual punishment") became more frequent. By mid-1988, thirty-nine states, as well as the District of Columbia, Puerto Rico, and the Virgin Islands, were currently subject to court supervisory orders or consent decrees in relation to some or all aspects of their prison system (McDonald et al. 1998, p. 8).

C. Inhibitions on Capital Expenditure. Throughout the industrialized world, the voters of the 1980s and 1990s wanted more services for less tax. In the criminal justice field, resistance to "big-spending big-government" was exacerbated by other factors: public disillusionment with the notion of rehabilitation or improvement, increasing fear of crime and calls for tougher penalties, and the consequential dehumanization and demonization of offenders.

In many U.S. states, governments reached their constitutional debt ceilings, with the consequence that additional capital expenditure on infrastructure projects could only go ahead after voter approval for the issue of state bonds. Prisons were not high on voters' priority lists, and prison construction bond proposals were voted down. The point was reached where politicians, valuing their political skins, were reluctant even to put up such proposals.

A way out was to shift capital expenditure into the recurrent or operational state budget, where no constitutional barriers stood in the way. This could be done if a private sector operator was contracted to design, construct, finance, and manage (DCFM) a prison. The contractor could then recover construction costs by way of a lease/buyback arrangement spread over a long period, typically about twenty years.[2] Although there were complex variants on this, usually designed to attract taxation benefits, the essence was usually the same—that the state would buy the capital asset now and pay for it later. Accordingly, although some of the very earliest private prison arrangements—for example, the Texas ones referred to above—involved only private sector management of prisons built and owned by the state, the typical U.S. situation soon became that of a DCFM contract. McDonald et al. (1998, p. 20) report that fifty of the eighty-four facilities in their 1997 inventory were privately owned and subject to DCFM contracts. This trend is consolidating.

[2] In other jurisdictions, particularly some Australian states and South Africa, this is sometimes described as a "BOOT" contract—build, own, operate, and transfer. However, the DCFM terminology is the most widely used.

However, the DCFM model was not initially adopted in either Australia or the United Kingdom—the states that followed the United States most quickly down the privatization path. Neither jurisdiction was constrained by constitutional considerations from drawing upon the public purse nor yet so inhibited by the prevailing sociopolitical culture. In each case the main leverage they wished to exert by way of privatization related to recurrent costs and labor union control of the workplace. The earliest contracts—at Borallon in Queensland (Australia) and The Wolds in the United Kingdom—were thus management only contracts, relating to prisons designed, constructed, and financed by the public sector (Harding 1992). This pattern continued for the first few contracts in each country, but by the mid-1990s the notion of shifting capital infrastructure costs had taken hold, and the DCFM contract had become standard. This is also the predominant model with newer privatization states, such as South Africa.

D. Recurrent Costs. Operational expenditure was also a matter of concern. The temper of the times was belief that the private sector could almost always carry out service tasks more cost-effectively. Some states embedded this value in legislation so as to make cost reduction a specific objective of privatization. For example, Florida (Fl. Stat. 957.07 [1993]) provided that "the [Correctional Privatization] Commission may not enter into a contract . . . unless [it] determines that the contract will result in cost savings to the state of at least seven percent over the public provision of a similar facility."

A consequence is that an extensive literature has been spawned around the issue of comparative public/private costs. Indeed, there seems to be more debate about this than any other single aspect of privatization. The reports and evaluations have become technical, pedantic, arcane, and self-serving. They have also tended to distract attention from more important aspects of the privatization debate, such as accountability and the overall quality of the regime.

By the standards of other Western democracies, the expenditure per prisoner per day in the United States is quite small. Broadly speaking, for every dollar spent per prisoner per year in the United States, $2 are spent in the United Kingdom and $2.50 in Australia. It could be argued that the United States should really be seeking to spend more, not less, on its prison systems while also obtaining better value for money. To the extent that privatization has insulated governments from having to acknowledge and act upon what seems to be acute underfunding, privatization could perhaps be said to have been a socially regressive development. However, there is nothing in recent history to suggest that this alone is holding back a quantum leap in expenditure and regime quality.

E. Union Labor. The relative weakness of American unions, even in public sector employment, meant that this issue never became as important as in Australia, New Zealand, and the United Kingdom. Obstructionism was well documented there, not merely in terms of workplace practices that artificially enhanced overtime payments and shift penalties but also through resistance to the introduction of rehabilitative and vocational prison programs (Harding 1997, pp. 20, 134–36). Even in the United States, however, the factor of cutting out "management from below" was significant. McDonald's 1997 survey of contracting state agencies found that "the desire to gain operational flexibility" (code for controlling the labor force) was the third most cited reason for a state to have embarked upon privatization (McDonald et al. 1998, pp. 15–16).

F. Regime Improvement. The notion of improving prisons and correctional regimes was not overtly prominent in U.S. debates about privatization. Improvement was seen as a possible and desirable, but not essential, by-product of better and more cost-effective management, getting away from the input-based model of public sector corrections. This model, becoming more entrenched after the "nothing works" philosophy (Martinson 1974) had taken hold, seemed to treat the very existence of the prison system as sufficient justification for everything that happened within it. The output-based model of public administration, on the other hand, required prison systems to identify key performance indicators, measure them, adapt regimes to achieve them, and use human and financial resources in ways that best facilitated these outputs. Privatization was thus "principally an issue of fit between the strategic purposes that society seeks to achieve through imprisonment and the currently available means to do so" (O'Hare 1990, p. 128). Achieving that fit might well improve prisons and conditions, but that was not the main point.

Neither, with one exception (McConville 1987, p. 240), did system-wide improvement seem to enter into calculations, that is, the notion that different and perhaps better private sector regimes might cause beneficial change in the public sector. Yet this is, ultimately, the most cogent justification for privatization.

In summary, prison reform was never a prominent aspect of the U.S. privatization agenda. In other countries—notably Australia, the

United Kingdom, and South Africa—it has been much nearer the surface. Indeed, the 1999 procurement in Western Australia explicitly made system-wide prison reform a principal objective (Harding 2000).

Public sector imprisonment practices, processes, and outcomes do not constitute one of the triumphs of twentieth-century civilization. Nevertheless, because privatization is a departure from the previous norm, any meaningful description or valid evaluation requires that privatization be measured against the known characteristics, strengths, and deficiencies of the public sector.

The remainder of this essay discusses these issues, highlighting the following: Is imprisonment a nondelegable core state function that thus always must be managed directly by the state (Section I)? Is there a danger that the commercial opportunities that imprisonment henceforth may provide will lead to the creation of a powerful penal lobby whose views may distort criminal justice policy (Section II)? Will imprisonment costs really be reduced, and, in any case, will private prison regime standards deteriorate (Section III)? Can the private sector manage the risks of imprisonment as effectively as the public sector (Section IV)? How effective is contract as a mechanism to secure enhanced performance in this complex area of human service (Section V)? Above all, what sort of regulatory systems and accountability mechanisms are required, and what assurance is there that they will be effective (Section VI)? And, will privatization work in such a way as to provide a stimulus for improvement in prison regimes generally (Sections VII and VIII)?

These questions are answered in the remainder of this essay. Apart from the first, they cannot really be kept absolutely distinct from each other. Often one bears upon another, for they all involve the same pivotal question: In terms of penal administration, is privatization progressive or regressive? In broad terms the conclusions are that, fully accountable and properly regulated, the private sector can and does stimulate system-wide improvement; however, there is a real danger of slippage when the public authorities reduce regulatory resources and as cost reduction becomes an increasingly predominant motive for privatization. Finally, (Section IX) the future of prison privatization, both in the present participating states and globally, is briefly considered.

I. A Core State Function?

Many European and American commentators have argued that the imprisonment function is, or should be, nondelegable. For example, in 1988, as privatization got under way, Radzinowicz stated: "In a democracy grounded on the rule of law and public accountability, the enforcement of penal legislation . . . should be the undiluted responsibility of the state" (letter to the *London Times* [September 22, 1988], quoted in Shaw 1992). The Norwegian scholar, Christie (1993, p. 102), sees the issue as one of communitarian responsibility and democratic participation:

> The prison officer is my man. I would hold a hand on his key. . . . He could be a bad officer. And I could be bad. Together we made for a bad system, so well known from the history of punishments. But I would have known I was a responsible part of the arrangement. Chances would also be great that some people in the system were not only bad. They would more easily be . . . mobilized. The guard was their guard, their responsibility, not an employee of a branch of General Motors, or Volvo for that matter. *The communal character of punishments evaporates in the proposals for private prisons.* (My emphasis)

Both Radzinowicz and Christie epitomize a quintessentially European approach to the role of the state, one where "in the continental culture the state is seen as much more than a 'service institution'" (Rosenthal and Hoogenboom 1990, pp. 20–21). It is no surprise that the European state that has come nearest to implementing privatization, France, has adopted a model of prisons *semi-privées*—where the custodial functions remain in the exclusive domain of state authorities and only the "hotel," health, welfare, and program activities have been privatized. It is an awkward model but conforms in the letter if not the spirit with the strict European approach.[3]

Various American commentators endorse the nondelegable core function approach. DiIulio's views (1991, p. 197) are representative: "To remain legitimate and morally significant, the authority to govern behind bars, to deprive citizens of their liberty, to coerce (and even kill) them, must remain in the hands of government authorities. Regardless of which penological theory is in vogue, the message that those who abuse liberty shall live without it is the brick and mortar of every correctional facility—a message that ought to be conveyed by

[3] It is not unique, however. The Mansfield Community Corrections Facility in Texas (which despite its name is a place of incarceration) operates with the same division of functions. For technical legal reasons rather than administrative choice, a somewhat similar model exists in South Australia.

the offended community of law-abiding citizens through its public agents to the incarcerated individual."

Is there a convincing answer to these arguments? The standard one is that there is a distinction between the allocation and the administration of punishment. The first function is irrevocably nondelegable; in the sovereign state, private criminal justice systems are a contradiction in terms. However, the second is delegable, with appropriate safeguards, for it does not involve the imposition of additional state-authorized punishment but, rather, a technical and morally neutral process to ensure that the allocated punishment is carried out according to law and due process.

Sparks (1994, p. 23), among others, finds this argument specious because "it serves rhetorically to insulate the two areas" (the legitimacy of imprisonment and how to carry it out) from one another. In Sparks's view, fundamental issues as to the proper scope and utilization of imprisonment, questions that should never be put aside by society, are inextricably linked with questions of delivery; accordingly, any arrangement should be opposed that permits them to be discussed and implemented as if they were discrete issues. That view seems rather contrived, however. There does not seem to be any insuperable intellectual or practical difficulty about challenging the depth and the scope of imprisonment and pursuing vigorously the question of prison conditions, regimes, and reform.

A more productive line of analysis is whether some of the tasks delegated to the private operators, while purporting to be merely the administration of punishment, are in reality its allocation. In that regard, two areas stand out: disciplinary matters and prisoner classification.

A. Disciplinary Matters

Formally, sanctions for misconduct within prisons are not the allocation of punishment for offenses against the criminal law. In abstract terms, the distinction between the allocation and the administration of punishment is not breached. However, the citizen's status as a prisoner means that he is in a situation where he is subject to greater sanction-backed regulation than are other citizens. New deprivations of liberty, such as loss of remission/good time or restrictions upon privileges or stricter levels of incarceration, are tantamount to the allocation of punishment within that particular sociolegal microcosm.

Accordingly, if the allocation/administration dichotomy is to be preserved, disciplinary matters should be dealt with directly by state authorities. In the United Kingdom this is in fact what happens. In all private prisons, disciplinary charges laid by custodial officers are adjudicated by Home Office (i.e., prison service) "controllers"—governor-grade public sector officials—who work on-site (Harding 1997, p. 90). Adjudications affecting intraprison rights are thus made and internal sanctions allocated with the authority and in the name of the state, according to the same criteria as in every other prison and prisoner within the U.K. system.

This rigorous approach is not widely followed in the United States. In many jurisdictions disciplinary functions for breach of prison rules are carried out directly by the private operator. However, the rules themselves generally replicate those applicable in the public sector prisons or, where they differ in some detail, must be approved by or conform with the standards set by the state authorities. For example, Texas contracts generally contain clauses along the following lines: "Contractor shall impose discipline through rules, regulations and orders pursuant to an offender disciplinary system meeting or exceeding ACA standards, court orders and Texas Department of Criminal Justice policy."

There are a few jurisdictions that maintain the strict allocation/administration dichotomy: for example, Florida. The enabling statute has laid down the abstract principle that state Department of Corrections classification officers should have overall responsibility for adjudications, and the contracts have brought it alive with site-specific applications (Harding 1997, p. 91).

Of course, the operator has to manage the prison in a day-to-day sense and cannot constantly be second-guessed by the public authority. Inevitably, this will involve imposition of minor management sanctions, such as temporary segregation of prisoners, limitation upon visiting rights, suspension of work privileges, withdrawal from a program, and so on. For practical reasons, the operator must be able to impose such sanctions directly. There may be, philosophically, a fine line between such matters and the allocation of punishment, but in practical terms the distinction is evident enough.

In Australia also the full significance of this dichotomy has become blurred. Two states, Western Australia and South Australia, require that disciplinary charges be externally adjudicated. In the other states, the working of the disciplinary system is simply one of the regular reporting items required from the private operator as part of the overview of the contractual arrangements.

B. Prisoner Classification

Prisoner classification and its corollary, sentence planning, drive the prison experience for prisoners. There can be a world of difference between the quality of life in maximum security and at a prison farm, and the rate of progress through the custodial continuum is a crucial matter. That being so, systems that delegate initial or follow-up classification to the private sector would seem to be flawed. The principled position is that the private sector supplies a regime of a particular custodial type and the public authorities assign and subsequently reassign prisoners to and from that prison, according to classifications done by and in the name of the state.

By and large, in the United States and elsewhere this point has been recognized. However, there are some striking exceptions. In Queensland (Australia) the initial classification and sentence planning of sentenced prisoners is carried out by the private sector (Moyle 2000), though subject to the nominal supervision of the public sector. And in the United States there are examples where private prisons have been allowed in effect to select their own prisoners through carrying out their own classifications. The most common criticism is that private prisons have managed to influence procedures so that they receive prisoners who are easiest to manage. The example that follows is peculiar through being the converse—choosing to receive prisoners who are the most difficult to manage.

This came about as follows. The Northeast Ohio Correctional Center (NEOCC) at Youngstown is a 2,000-bed medium-security "spec" prison (i.e., one built without any prior commitment by or contractual arrangement with a governmental authority that prisoners will be supplied to the operator) built and owned by CCA. The company entered into a contract with the Department of Corrections of Washington, D.C., to accommodate medium- to medium-high security prisoners. However, maximum-security prisoners were also sent, including many who required segregation. These assignments were initially an error on the part of the D.C. Department of Corrections, but under the contract CCA had the right and the obligation to screen out unsuitably classified inmates. In other words, the determinative classification was carried out by the CCA itself. For whatever reason—and the financial incentive cannot be entirely discounted—the company chose to treat these prisoners as if their security classification were medium high. Subsequently, there were many violent incidents, including the murders of two inmates by other prisoners. An official inquiry (Clark 1998) found that this was substantially attributable to the inappropriate mixing of different security level prisoners, a finding confirmed by the outcomes of subsequent litigation against CCA (Prison Privatisation Report International 1999, no. 29, p. 4).

In summary, the debate about "core state functions" relates above all to values. No amount of debate or evidence will change the minds of those who see privatization as fundamentally objectionable on this basis. However, in the United States this debate has been lost; indeed, it has barely got off the ground. A more productive line of analysis revolves around the question of the allocation and the administration of punishment, where the issues are tangible and improved accountability is attainable.

II. The Creation of a Penal Lobby

It is said that prison privatization is irredeemably expansionist. "It is unconvincing, indeed even inconsistent, for advocates of privatization to argue that their position is not wedded to growth in the prison system" (Sparks 1994, p. 24). This is a superficial observation. There is no documented case of any jurisdiction contracting for a private prison in order to enable it to expand its prisoner population. Quite the contrary: in the United States privatization has almost invariably been a response to increases in prisoner numbers that have already occurred. This response is also driven by other factors such as fiscal constraints, the existence of court orders, and so on, but the key point remains that it is only after the state's criminal justice policies and practices have put the prison situation under stress that privatization has occurred.

In some jurisdictions, other motivations have been at work. For instance, in Victoria (Australia) the three-prison privatization program that commenced in 1994 had as one of its explicit objectives the facilitation of the closure of a fetid and decrepit institution (Pentridge) and a deeply demoralized women's prison (Fairlea). These closures actually occurred.[4] In Western Australia, privatization of a new prison avowedly proceeded on the basis that, as well as relieving chronic overcrowding in prisons whose security ratings were out of kilter with prisoner needs, the new regime would act as a lever for prison reform

[4] Motives are seldom straightforward. The government of the time had a pathological distaste for public sector activity of almost any kind, leading it to pursue privatization uncritically and without adequate regard for regulatory balance. The ideological drive happened to coincide with a correctional imperative.

(Harding 2000). This had also been the case in Queensland (Kennedy 1988).

In South Africa, privatization has been initiated by a cabinet virtually all of whose members had spent time behind bars during the apartheid era. They, above all, were in a position to recognize the deplorable conditions of existing prison accommodations, amounting to an abuse of human rights standards. Coming to office, they realized that public expenditure on the infrastructure needs of the nation in relation to education, housing, and health were entitled to priority over prison infrastructure. Yet a beginning simply had to be made—particularly in light of the burgeoning prison population—to the business of improving prisons. Realistically, this could only be achieved by involving the private sector.

Nevertheless, there are four areas where private sector operators sometimes behave in ways that give cause for concern. These areas are "spec" prison construction, the related notions of exporting prisoners and "bed renting," offers to take over whole systems, and stock market factors.

A. "Spec" Prisons

The normal pattern of privatization is as follows: the state identifies the need for new prison accommodation; decides whether to utilize public sector resources or to invite the private sector to bid; if the latter, sets in motion all the usual procurement processes and draws up a request for proposals (RFP) that specifies the type of structure and regime it requires; evaluates RFPs; selects the successful bidder; negotiates the fine details of the contract; and brings into operation an effective regulatory and accountability system. With that sort of sequence, a new prison does not get built on a whim; it is tied in with the ascertainable penal needs of the state.

"Spec" prisons are quite different. Although McDonald et al. (1998, p. vi) note that in the early stages of privatization "some small firms that speculated by building facilities in the absence of contracts with an agency" went bankrupt, the bigger operators have not been vulnerable in this way. To some extent this has been because they have carefully identified both a need and a potential contracting agency; in other words, they have anticipated the procurement process. For example, CCA has followed this practice in relation to the prison at Youngstown, Ohio, mentioned above, as well as a prison at California City, near Los Angeles, California. This 2,300-bed "spec" prison has subsequently received a contract from the Federal Bureau of Prisons (FBOP). Nevertheless, the ultimate user's correctional needs are something of an afterthought, having to be fitted within the architectural design or correctional strategy of an already existing prison structure.

A recent variant of this is the development of "spec" prisons offering niche services, in particular for sick or geriatric prisoners, who are now a burgeoning component of the U.S. prison population. For example, in 1998 Just Care Inc. of Alabama opened a 326-bed private medical prison in South Carolina. The company has marketed itself across the United States with local, county, and state authorities. However, in its first six months of operation it received only a dozen prisoner-patients, well short of the 100-bed occupancy per day average required to break even.

In Australia, the United Kingdom, New Zealand, Canada, or South Africa, "spec" prisons simply could not spring up. Whatever the correctional arguments, it is the land-use planning issues that would prevail. In none of those countries would the applicable governmental body permit a prison to be built except by governmental endorsement. "Spec" prisons do seem to distort somewhat both privatization and prisonization policy in the United States. This is starting to be recognized; for example, in 1997 Texas legislated that companies must have in place a contract with a city or county or the state Department of Corrections before building a prison.

B. Exporting Inmates and "Bed Renting"

Northeast Ohio Correctional Center at Youngstown accommodated out-of-state prisoners. Other documented examples of out-of-state imprisonment include the following: Washington, D.C., prisoners to Minnesota and Ohio; North Dakota and Hawaii prisoners to Minnesota; Montana and New Mexico prisoners to Texas and Arizona; Oklahoma, North Carolina, Utah, and Missouri prisoners to Texas; Wisconsin prisoners to Oklahoma and Tennessee; Alaska prisoners to Arizona. These arrangements are not only inimical to prisoners' best interests in terms of family visits, but they also stretch the chain of accountability beyond breaking point. The state of origin of the prisoners has no standing to regulate or supervise what happens within the private prison. Five such contracts have been cancelled by "exporting" states (McDonald et al. 1998, p. 53), and in each case belated recognition of their own regulatory impotence has been a factor.

But at least in such arrangements there is some structure, there has been some direct negotiation between service provider and inmate supplier. More worrying than this, however, is the U.S. practice (again, found nowhere else) of "bed renting" or "bed brokering." This practice involves finding a prison bed somewhere, anywhere, for prisoners whom the home state cannot accommodate. Several agencies have sprung up, such as Inmate Placement Services of Nashville—motto, "a bed for every inmate and an inmate for every bed"—and these agencies negotiate space on a flat-fee-per-bed basis.[5]

The structure of the private sector is particularly well adapted for involvement in this commerce, but it should be emphasized that the public sector is no less involved as both exporter and importer of inmates. Out-of-state bed renting is a misconceived concept of imprisonment, weakening the concept of state responsibility. To the extent that prison privatization facilitates this practice, the U.S. model seems flawed.

McDonald et al. (1998, pp. 66–67) rightly identify both of these areas as ones of major legal risk. They cite Texas and Ohio as desirable 1998 examples of legislative regulation, such as the right of the state of location to prescribe minimum standards, carry out inspections, and so on. However, this does not really address the problem, identified above, of the stress on the chain of accountability to the state by whose authority the prisoner is serving a sentence. The authors presciently suggest that "more such legislation can be expected in coming years." In 1999 California enacted a statute entirely prohibiting, not merely regulating, the housing of out-of-state prisoners in private prisons within the borders of California (Bill 1222 of 1999). The passage of this legislation seems to have been one of the factors that caused CCA to cease construction of a "spec" prison that it had already commenced at Mendota, California. North Carolina enacted similar legislation—"prohibition on private prisons housing out-of-state inmates"—on June 30, 2000.

C. System Takeover

Privatization began with a bid by CCA in 1985 to take over the whole of the Tennessee prison system. This offer was repeated in 1997, with a promise that the state would thereby be enabled to save $100 million per annum. In neither case did the legislature let the of-

[5] The main source for this information is the regular reports found in Prison Privatisation Report International; see also McDonald et al. 1998, pp. 10–12.

fers get far. But the fact that a private company was prepared to make them arguably shows a lack of sensitivity to the principles that lie behind a politically appropriate model of privatization. The state must retain and be able actually to exercise "step-in" rights—that is, to reclaim any privatized part of its prison system—and to do this it needs to have ongoing capacity and skill levels of its own. This can only be done if it remains a direct service provider in relation to some part, at least, of its prisoner population. Also, a totally privatized system would cut across the allocation/administration of punishment dichotomy.

D. *Stock Market Factors*

A prominent strand of the antiprivatization movement is encapsulated in the phrase, "no profit from punishment." This argument is in many ways a naive one, for there is no aspect of the public sector prison system that is somehow quarantined from monetary exchange. Workers earn their wages, service providers (e.g., food suppliers) earn revenues from which they pay wages to their employees, construction companies pay dividends to shareholders from profits partly derived from building and maintaining prisons, and so on. However, the legitimate thrust of the argument is that a selfish profit motive should not be allowed to distort and degrade regime standards, as was the case with the leasing of convict labor. But safeguarding that is a matter for contract, regulatory arrangements, and accountability mechanisms, rather than a decisive reason for not privatizing at all.

For better or worse, the commercial side of private prisons is now irreversibly part of the agenda. The whole paraphernalia of big business—mergers, takeovers, executive stock options, making lazy assets work harder, splitting off noncore activities, downsizing administrative staffing levels, tax minimization schemes, and so on—is now part of the scene. With hindsight, this was inevitable. But it does not stop it from being somewhat disturbing to those who are more used to the context where, conventionally, penal administration decisions have been made within a closed box of supposedly abstract and altruistic principles relating to correctional policy.

If the private sector companies do not constitute a penal lobby (and it is still my view that as yet they do not), it is not difficult to see how they might already be perceived this way or might evolve into such a role. Of course, the public sector itself is a remarkably powerful lobby for certain types of penal policy or practice—something that tends to get overlooked in the lobbying debate.

III. Costs

United States privatization avowedly set out to switch capital funding into the private sector, as well as to reduce recurrent costs. However, when surveyed subsequently, agencies rated the cost factor as only the fourth most important motivation (McDonald et al. 1998, p. 16). This is not entirely reconcilable with the contemporaneous rhetoric and may represent a retrospective attempt to put a better public face on things.

Be that as it may, an enormous amount of time and energy has gone into essentially accountancy arguments. Protagonists on both sides (but especially on the antiprivatization side) seem to think that if they can demonstrate that private prisons are more expensive/cheaper, then ipso facto they have won/lost the debate.

McDonald et al. (1998, p. iv) have cogently stated the difficulties and ambiguities inherent in evaluating true costs on a prison-to-prison basis:

> Comparing public and private prisons' costs is complicated for a variety of reasons. Comparable public facilities may not exist in the same jurisdiction. Private facilities may differ substantially from other government facilities in their functions (e.g., the private facility in Arizona houses men and women, or some in Texas are used for drug abuse treatment services or for pre-release populations [who] are placed in halfway houses by other jurisdictions). Or they may differ in age, design, or the security needs of inmates housed, all of which affect the cost of staffing them. Cost comparisons are also difficult because private and public accounting systems were designed for different purposes; that is, public systems were not designed principally for cost accounting. Spending to support imprisonment is often borne and reported by agencies other than the correctional department, and computation of these costs is often difficult for lack of data. The annual costs of "using up" the physical assets are not counted in the public sector, as capital expenditures are generally valued only in the year that they are made, rather than being spread across the life of the assets. Nor is the cost to the taxpayer of contracting readily apparent from tallies of payments to contractors. Governments incur expenses for contract procurement, administration and monitoring; for medical costs above amounts capped by contracts; and for sentence computation, transportation and other activities performed by governments. Cost comparisons often fail to account for such expenditures.

Nevertheless, many prison-to-prison cost comparisons, purportedly controlling for these factors, have been attempted. Nelson (1998) has reviewed the five most detailed of these studies.[6] Her conclusion is as follows:

> In every study that itemized expenditures and adjustments, much of the *reported* difference between public and private sector cost estimates can be traced to differences in the allocated burden of state-allocated overhead costs. If this reported difference is to reflect *actual* cost savings, the privatization must induce cutbacks in state spending on central office operations before taxpayers realize this benefit. (P. 3)

Later she states:

> It is possible to draw some preliminary conclusions. There do appear to be some consistent differences between the public and private facilities. . . . It appears likely that, in privately managed facilities, the wage-bill for non-administrative staff will be lower and prison-level administrative expenses will be higher; that health care costs will be lower; and that the imputed cost of state overhead will be lower. (P. 17)

Pratt and Maahs (1999) ranged more widely, conducting a meta-analysis of thirty-three U.S. cost-effectiveness evaluations. Some derive from a time when costing information was decidedly primitive and were consequently crude methodologically. Nevertheless, reviewing such a large body of literature, the authors felt able to conclude (Pratt and Maahs 1999, p. 367):

> Overall, the results indicate that, regardless of the owner of the facility, it is the economy of scale achieved by the prison, its age, and its security level that largely determine its daily per diem cost. . . . These conclusions have important implications for both correctional policy makers and researchers. First, this analysis provides policy makers with a more realistic and cautious assessment of the relative efficiency (or lack thereof) of private prisons. Although specific privatization policy alternatives may

[6] There is some overlap between her work and the earlier and frequently cited report of the U.S. General Accounting Office (1996), but Nelson's work is more thorough and more recent.

> result in modest cost-savings (e.g., private prison construction and private contracts for specific services such as rehabilitation and medical programs), relinquishing the responsibility for managing prisons to the private sphere is unlikely to alleviate much of the financial burden on state correctional agencies.

Studies such as these have their limitations. The most significant is that they do not draw upon aggregated data analyses, particularly from non-U.S. jurisdictions. What is meant by "aggregated data" in this context is an approach that calculates the overall cost of running prisons or a category of prisons of a comparable type, as opposed to item-by-item and prison-to-prison comparisons. The aggregated data approach epitomizes the United Kingdom and to some extent the Australian approach to cost comparisons.

A sequence of U.K. studies (H.M. Prison Service 1997, 1998*a*, 1998*b*; Woodbridge 1999), each replicating a robust methodology, reveals a picture of gradually decreasing cost savings in the private sector, from a range of 13–22 percent (depending on the measure used) in 1994–95, to 11–16 percent the following year, to 8–15 percent in 1996–97, to minus 2–11 percent in 1997–98. This sequence is important, for it brings out the dynamic public sector response to private sector efficiencies. This in turn emphasizes that the savings we should really be looking for to justify privatization economically are savings in the public sector. Most of the U.S. work misses this crucial point, being stuck at the stage of lining up passive models against each other.

However, the dynamism that is even more important relates to the nature of the prison and correctional regime. This never shows up in the passive costs model. Quality of the correctional regime is a concept that could only be reflected in a "cost-effectiveness" or "correctional value for money" model. It is the most important aspect of the whole privatization debate.

IV. Risks of Prison Regimes

Politicians and administrators still seem to see risks primarily in terms of security and control issues—escapes, riots, assaults, drug use. However, failures in care and well-being are increasingly acknowledged as important risk areas—for example, deaths and self-harm, other health issues such as HIV+ or hepatitis B or C, overcrowding, and equity issues. The question that arises is whether private prisons are more susceptible to such risks and, in any case, how effectively they respond to them.

A threshold problem is the paucity of systematic data. To a large extent information is anecdotal—and story selection criteria operate in such a way that the anecdotes mostly relate to the private sector. This derives from the fact that privatization is still controversial, still under active challenge. For example, a U.K. serial publication, Prison Privatisation Report International (see also http://www.penlex.org.uk), covers the "bad stories" of U.S., as well as international, privatization thoroughly (and, it must be said, very evenhandedly), while never mentioning public sector "bad news" stories nor good news about the private sector. Also, for several years Private Prison Watch News Briefs, covering exclusively U.S. privatization issues and problems, were available on the Internet (ppwatchhotmail.com); a labor union Web site (http://www.cusa.org) also concentrates on "bad news"; and another Web site explicitly identifying itself as "antiprivatization" can be found at http://www.oregonafscme.com/private/.[7]

The real need is for methodologically robust comparative studies of key risk events. A good model is the study of Junee Prison in New South Wales, Australia (Bowery 1999). This private prison, managed by Australian Correctional Management (ACM), a subsidiary of WCC, commenced operations in 1993. A longitudinal study was carried out from the outset with three main objectives: to provide a historical record of how Junee developed from the time it became operational; to identify and illustrate differences in the way it operated compared to the public sector prisons in the state; and to identify those aspects of its operations that were or were not innovative. Key elements involved recording events in custody relating to security and to care. Three public sector prisons were also measured for the same events, with variables being controlled and reliable comparators identified. Aggregated statewide data were also available for comparison, though they were obviously of lesser significance.

With the publication of the four-year (1993–97) overview, data are available that take discussion beyond the point of anecdote. These data relate to such matters as deaths, escapes, self-harm, assaults and fights, disciplinary offenses, prisoner grievances, use of force by officers, posi-

[7] See also http://www.mgl.ca/sroberts/index.html and http://donnasdoc.webjump.com/.

tive urinalysis tests, discovery of home brew alcoholic beverages, time out of cells, and program participation. The availability of such data thus provides a solid basis for making comparative judgments, and in broad terms the private prison emerged creditably by each of the measures. However, the immediate point is not to record conclusions so much as to identify the value of commencing from the outset a reasonably robust evaluation, thus facilitating meaningful analysis.

A. Escapes

Data are patchy and unsystematic. As with all prison bad news, the private facilities tend to receive fuller coverage than the public ones. Thus the escape of six dangerous prisoners from the Northeast Ohio Correctional Center, Youngstown, in July 1998 (all subsequently recaptured) received a great deal of media attention. So have other incidents, such as the escape of eight juveniles from a CCA detention center at Columbia, South Carolina, in 1997. Nevertheless, nothing has so far emerged to suggest that the private sector prisons are generically more porous than public sector ones of a comparable security level.

Some debate has arisen as to whether the private sector should be charged by the state for the expense involved in catching escapees—for example, whether the Bobby Ross Group should pay $1,200 for the cost of a dog team used to track two 1996 escapees. That is hardly a first-order issue. However, it is now starting to be standard practice in some jurisdictions (such as Western Australia and Queensland) for management contracts to contain clauses, akin to exemplary damages, imposing a fixed amount penalty for an escape. An escape symbolizes some presumed misfeasance in the execution of the contractual obligations, and the exemplary penalty is aimed at both deterring the operator and reassuring the public.

B. Riots

There have been several major riots in U.S. private prisons. Youngstown is, once more, the best-known example. The highly accelerated start-up pace was the catalyst for the problems (Clark 1998, pp. 14–15). The start-up schedule is, of course, the responsibility of the public sector purchasers. Officials never seem able to learn from the experience of others (Harding 1997, pp. 123–27), and there is no discernible difference between first-year operations of public sector and private sector prisons. With Youngstown, the public officials (the Washington, D.C., Department of Corrections) had an incentive to export inmates as fast as they could to relieve local political problems, and the company was not reluctant to fill up a "spec" prison so as to increase the flow of occupancy fees. It was an explosive mixture for which the public authority purchaser was no less at fault than the private sector provider.

A similar comment can be made about the 1995 riot at the Immigration and Naturalization Service (INS) detention center at Elizabeth (New Jersey) run by Esmor Correctional Services, Inc. (subsequently reincorporated *sub nom.* Correctional Services Corporation, Inc.). The contract specified that the facility would be occupied and the regime run for short-term (less than thirty days) detainees. Thus the architectural design, the provision of recreational and program opportunities, and the pricing reflected this—little more than human warehousing. At the time the riot occurred—eleven months after the center had first opened—many of the inmates, because of bad planning and resource management within INS, had been there for more than six months; some indeed from the very beginning. A specification that explicitly had acknowledged this possible eventuality would have attracted a quite different bid. So the public authorities were the major contributors to the problem. The *Wall Street Journal* report (July 11, 1995) was scathing: "The real lesson from the riot is that the federal government isn't any better at managing private contracts than it is at the many other things it does poorly. . . . Previous riots involving I.N.S. [Immigration and Naturalization Service] detainees at facilities managed by the federal government have been far more destructive, and they led in part to the I.N.S. deciding to hire private companies to jail detainees. But privatization can be done badly, and the I.N.S. could write the book on how not to write the contract."

However, Esmor itself was not blameless. It became evident that the successful bid had been "lowball," underestimating the true costs of doing the job properly.[8] This had serious consequential effects—inade-

[8] Lowball bids are simply not economic if the specified job is to be done at all. In the early days of privatization such bids were sometimes made to get a foot in the door. There was a view that, once the purchaser is placed in a dependency relationship with the provider, prices may be adjustable upward at the first contract renegotiation. In jurisdictions where RFP evaluations do permit price to be treated as the single most significant selection criterion, lowballing creates a high risk of failure. By and large, lowballing is starting to disappear, though working on low margins is still commonplace with bids in new markets: e.g., it is generally thought that the two South Africa private prison contracts fall into this category.

quately paid and thus poorly qualified guards, insufficient investment in training, high staff turnover, and so on. The subsequent INS inquiry found that the level of salary was not realistic and could not . . . ensure the availability of well-qualified applicants. It is obvious that many of the . . . guards hired by Esmor did not meet the requirements of the contract or were marginally qualified. Consequently, it was no great surprise that, as inmate tensions increased, staff discipline broke down, leading to assaults upon inmates and other forms of mistreatment, which in turn provoked the uprising.

The emerging theme, then, is that riots are seldom monocausal. It will usually be disingenuous to assert that a riot occurred simply because the facility was privately managed (or mismanaged). Just as head office policies and failures often create the preconditions for riots in public sector prisons (Wicker 1976; Dinitz 1981; Weiss 1991; Woolf and Tumim 1991; Adams 1994; Smith, Indermaur, and Boddis 1999), so too they contribute to serious problems in private prisons.

There have been several other major disturbances and riots at private prisons: for example, at Eden Detention Center, Texas (a CCA facility) in 1996; at Dickens County Correctional Center, Texas (a Bobby Ross Group prison) in 1997; at Crowley County Correctional Center, Colorado (a Correctional Services Corporation prison) in 1999; at the Bayamon Detention Center, Puerto Rico (also a CSC facility) in 1999; and at the Guadalupe County Correctional Facility, New Mexico (a WCC prison) in 1999. This list does not purport to be comprehensive. There have also been riots and disturbances at private prisons located outside the United States: for example, Port Phillip in Victoria (Australia), Arthur Gorrie Prison in Queensland (Australia), Parc Prison at Bridgend (United Kingdom), and Doncaster Prison (United Kingdom). Interestingly, each was a postcommissioning riot at prisons whose start-up rates had been pushed too fast. Precisely the same pattern was occurring simultaneously in public sector prisons in those jurisdictions—for example, Woodford (Queensland), Moorland (United Kingdom), and Full Sutton (United Kingdom).

Riots and disturbances are almost always outward manifestations of bad management. The essential issue, therefore, is that of regime quality. It is appropriate that there be an intense media spotlight on any new departure in penal administration, particularly prison privatization. But it is premature to construe these narratives as demonstrating across-the-board inferior regime quality, particularly in light of the fact that only fragmentary information is readily available about public sector prison troubles.

C. *Assaults*

Much the same comment can be made in relation to assaults, whether by staff upon inmates or as an aspect of intimidation and bullying by inmates upon other inmates. Once more, there is no lack of coverage of private prison incidents—but with no comparators by which to evaluate the public sector. The optimum model is a longitudinal study of the sort carried out at Junee (Bowery 1999). That showed, in relation to inmate assaults upon staff, that the private sector prison was doing worse in its first two years' operation in comparison to the established public sector prisons but that, in relation to inmate upon inmate assaults, it was consistently doing better. Those sorts of findings do not, of course, necessarily cross boundaries and cultures. But they suggest that, in this area as virtually every other, it is total system issues with which we are really concerned rather than privatization per se.

D. *Deaths and Self-Harm*

Murders are relatively rare and very serious events. The Youngstown situation, involving two murders, has already been mentioned. The Clark inquiry (1998, pp. 64–65) characterized the second of these events as "a devastating convergence of security lapses. . . . It is very reasonable to conclude that this incident was preventable and should never have occurred." The report concludes: "The incident clearly evidences a combination of major problems which had been allowed to take hold at NEOCC: (1) lack of policy and procedure in critical security areas; (2) inexperience and poor security training of supervisors and line staff; (3) lack of any effective internal management controls at the local or corporate levels. In sum, the most basic security operations were seriously flawed."

Homicides committed by officers are even more serious. There are some documented examples in several privatization jurisdictions. A notable example is found in the United Kingdom with the 1995 death of a prisoner, Alton Manning, at Blakenhurst prison, which is run by U.K. Detention Services, a CCA subsidiary company. The inquest evidence showed staff ignorance or disregard of fairly elementary protocols relating to safe restraint, leading to the prisoner's suffocation. The coroner's jury returned a verdict of "unlawful killing," which under the U.K. system left it to the Crown Prosecution Service to decide whether to bring criminal charges. The company, supported by the Home Office as purchaser of the prison services, had previously resorted to High Court injunctive litigation in an unsuccessful attempt to prevent the coroner from even considering the possibility of such a verdict—a classic case of the purchaser overidentifying with or being captured by the interests of the provider.[9]

These incidents and the official responses are reminiscent of those found in public sector prisons. This point could be illustrated ad nauseam, and reference has already been made to the various inquiries and analyses of the Attica and Santa Fe disasters (Wicker 1976; Dinitz 1981). A more recent example concerns the Corcoran State Prison, California, the location of officially condoned and concealed systematic brutality, including fifty shooting incidents, ten or so of which resulted in prisoner deaths, over a seven-year period (Arax and Gladston 1998). In other jurisdictions, there are similar trends. The Woolf report in the United Kingdom (Woolf and Tumim 1991) illustrates this. In Australia there are numerous documented instances (Nagle 1978; McGivern 1988; Murray 1989), the third of which related to the deaths of five prisoners trapped behind electrically controlled gates during a fire. The coroner concluded with words all too familiar to those versed in public sector corrections: "The Office of Corrections was inept and moribund at every point of observation. It has treated the Coroner as an adversary, both in the courts and by way of personal and public attacks. It has objected, protested and litigated, rather than provide information exclusively within its possession. It has used public resources to protect itself, its interest and its image. It has been prepared to bully, apply pressure and deceive rather than to face the truth. It has placed itself in priority to the community it serves" (Hallenstein, quoted in Murray 1989, p. 63).

The problem of deaths, then, is a problem with prisons—closed systems that are by their nature volatile and high-risk environments. There is nothing so far to suggest that privatization exacerbates the problem.

If, to this point, the evidence concerning homicide is fragmentary and anecdotal, concerning suicide it is much more robust. A recent

[9] The private companies have been quite litigious in their efforts to stem criticism. In Australia there have been several examples of defamation stop writs being used against critics: see Harding 1998*b*, p. 4.

study (Biles and Dalton 1999) has shown that the private sector has no worse a track record and arguably a slightly better one than the public sector. Prisoner suicides have been a much greater problem in Australia than in the United States. They have become inextricably enmeshed with the whole issue of discriminatory criminal justice system practices and general imprisonment rates in relation to the indigenous population. A national inquiry was established into Aboriginal deaths in custody and, while the main focus of its recommendations was upon indigenous needs, a by-product was the collection and analysis of a unique body of information about prisoner suicides generally (Johnston 1991).

Subsequently, there has been widespread recognition in Australia that high suicide and self-harm rates, persisting over a sufficient period of time, constitute a sure indicator of bad prison management (Harding 1999). The United Kingdom has been going down a similar track. The chief inspector of prisons has stated: "This [report] stresses the importance of the total prison environment in amplifying or mitigating suicidal feelings in those who are at risk. . . . The overwhelming conclusion from . . . research is that suicidal behavior is not just a function of individuals' vulnerability and circumstances but is also influenced by the quality of prison regimes and the response of staff" (Ramsbotham 1999*a*, p. 57). The report then goes on to endorse and expound the concept of a "healthy prison," previously formulated by the World Health Organization (1998).

Against that background suicide rates are a good indicator of management quality. The particular context of the Biles and Dalton study was that a new private prison, Port Phillip in Victoria, had been the site of five suicides in little more than a year—a pattern strikingly similar to that of an older private prison (Arthur Gorrie in Queensland) during its first two years of operation (Harding 1997, pp. 129–30). The operators of Port Phillip (Group 4) were consequently the focal point for immense criticism. The Australian study sought to put these matters into context and thus spanned the whole period of privatization in all states. It controlled for risk exposure by calculating prisoner occupancy years and relating this factor to numbers of suicides. These data were then compared with public sector data. In this aggregated form, displayed in table 1, it emerged that the two parts of the system had almost identical performances.

More cogent are the disaggregated data that attempt to compare prisons with similar profiles. Both Arthur Gorrie and Port Phillip are

TABLE 1

Distribution of Suicides in Prison Custody, 1990–99

Type of Prison	Number of Suicides, 1990–99	Suicides per 1,000 Prisoner Years, 1990–99
Private prisons	19	1.51
Public prisons	211	1.57
Total	230	1.56

difficult prisons in terms of functional and inmate mix. They cater for remand, reception (newly sentenced), and protection prisoners, as well as ordinary medium-security inmates. A public sector prison (Silverwater, New South Wales), possessing a comparable profile and being approximately the same size and age, was selected and the three prisons compared. To sharpen the picture, the comparison was made for the first twenty months only of their operation—that being the period during which, by common observation, regimes are at their most volatile, prisoners most vulnerable, and good management most crucial. Table 2 indicates, once more, that the private sector was of fair average quality.

Larger figures or a greater number of comparator prisons would make the data more cogent. Probably they support the view that, during the applicable period, none of the prisons was well managed (Harding 1997, pp. 86–87). However, the point is once more to demonstrate that these failures are not inherent to privatization so much as to "prisonization."

TABLE 2

Comparison of Suicides in Arthur Gorrie, Port Phillip, and Silverwater Prisons

	Arthur Gorrie (June 1992–January 1994)	Port Phillip (September 1997–April 1999)	Silverwater (April 1997–November 1998)
Number of suicides	3	5	7
Suicide rate per 1,000 prisoner years	6.60	5.08	6.03

E. *Summary*

It would be otiose to go through all the remaining risks of the prison situation. It is apparent from the foregoing examples that they are common to the public sector and the private, that to date there is no evidence to suggest that the private sector is any more negligent or incompetent than the public sector, and that the generic questions are, as always, how best to make a closed system accountable and how to put in place effective preventive measures. What also emerges is that data collection is for the most part too fragmented to be useful, though where it has been carried out efficiently it can be seen that the private sector at least meets and quite often exceeds industry standards.

V. Contracts

The prudent model is for states to authorize prison privatization by specific statutory provisions. This was done in Texas, the groundbreaking U.S. state; in Queensland, the first Australian state; and in the United Kingdom. This procedure is prudent not only because it heads off constitutional challenge (a relevant issue in the United States) but also because it enables risk allocation between the state and the contractor to be clarified.

Nevertheless, there are some states that depend upon statutory interpretation, that is, an implied or attributed power arising out of the general authorization to detain prisoners. In the United States, these states include Georgia (seven private prisons), Kansas (two institutions), and North Carolina (three institutions), as well as the territory of Puerto Rico (Thomas, Bolinger, and Badalamenti 1997, pp. 44–45). This is also the case in South Australia. Frustrated in its attempt to get enabling legislation through the upper house of the parliament, the government took the view that, as nothing in the generally applicable Correctional Services Act positively prohibited the delegation of custodial powers, privatization could be justified by reliance on the inherent powers of the executive arm of government to delegate or contract out its functions. However, it was deemed necessary that some of the functions of the prison manager, particularly those involving the exercise of enforcement powers, be done in the name of the superintendent of a neighboring public sector prison—who thus is obliged to visit regularly and be in daily contact. Such an arrangement is cumbersome and constitutes something of a barrier against the very innovation and cultural change that privatization seeks to bring about (Harding 1997, p. 41).

The Western Australian government, negotiating a private prison contract throughout 1999, seemed likely to face a similar dilemma for the same reason—opposition in the upper house. The very detailed attempts to negotiate on this basis brought home graphically that risk transfer is extremely difficult to combine satisfactorily with public accountability in the absence of specific statutory authorization. Providentially, the requisite legislation was passed, enabling the project to proceed without these complications (Harding 2000).

The recent inquiry into prison operations in New Mexico correctional institutions (http://www.legis.state.nm.us/corrections.html) cogently reinforced the point that specific and direct legislation is crucial if privatization is to work smoothly. New Mexico's law authorized privatization of county jails but not state prisons. Two new facilities—Lea County and Guadalupe County Correctional Facilities—were opened pursuant to contracts between the respective counties and WCC. Back-to-back contracts were then made between the counties and the New Mexico Department of Corrections to house state prisoners in those facilities. In fact, no county prisoners were held in either of them. Subsequently, each prison encountered major problems, leading to the setting up of the inquiry. The report stated, "The circumvention of the procurement mode was the most damaging aspect of the approach taken with these two facilities. . . . [I]t cannot be determined who is responsible for many of the inappropriate, confusing, incomplete and costly provisions of the contracts." In the end, the complex contractual arrangements, the unclear facility missions, the need for prison beds, and the involvement of too many agencies and individuals in negotiations resulted in contracts that fall well short of industry standards and create security, programmatic, and fiscal implications for the State (Prison Privatisation Report International 2000, no. 33, pp. 3–4).

A. The Procurement Process

Without benchmarks private procurement is impossible. Entering upon the procurement process with outsiders compels prisons departments to identify precisely what it is they currently purport to achieve, to create process maps, to attempt to attribute accurate costs to specific items, and generally to re-examine their objectives and procedures.[10]

[10] I have been involved in a procurement process on the government side, from the earliest stage of drafting an Expression of Interest document to evaluating responses of short-listed bidders to the RFP to contract finalization. The most revealing aspect of

At the very least, therefore, desired outputs become clearer. There may be various ways of achieving those outputs, and the private sector may have quite different and innovative ways of doing so than the public sector. Often they will be less expensive—perhaps because of greater investment in new technology, or because arcane workplace practices can be avoided, or through the contracting in of specialist services such as health. Or certain aspects may even be more expensive—for example, in the Western Australian context the requirement that culturally appropriate cognitive skills and related programs be developed for the indigenous inmate population.

The procurement process, then, is calculated to throw up varied ideas and approaches, which start to enrich an environment that frequently has become famished. Evaluation of bids by the purchaser is a complex matter in which two matters stand out: probity and price.

i) *Probity.* As to probity, this should encompass all factors that bear, or might be seen to bear, upon conflict of interest. The U.K. and Australian practice, as well as that in most of the U.S. states, is for a "probity auditor" to be present at all key meetings throughout the whole process, to alert participants to possible conflicts or unequal treatment of bidders, and so on, and to sign off at the end that no impropriety has occurred. This serves to switch the focus of commercial groups—traditionally not reluctant to litigate—away from the purchaser.

That is well and good during procurement, but concern has sometimes arisen in the United States and elsewhere that the highest standards of probity may not have been observed before or after the procurement process. For example, the main companies are known to make political donations from time to time in states in which they carry on business, and this can lead to suspicion of favorable treatment. In one case, for example, members of the Wisconsin Assembly Corrections Committee received political donations from CCA sources shortly before the state decided to send an additional 357 Wisconsin prisoners to a CCA prison in Oklahoma (Prison Privatisation Report International 1999, no. 29, p. 3). In another case, CCA won the procurement contract for a juvenile prison in Suffolk, Virgina, even though it had not initially scored best; it later emerged that it had made numerous small political donations to significant players in the

this was the difficulty that the public sector department—charged with benchmarking activities—had in identifying and then sometimes explaining or justifying, what, why, and how it was running its existing prisons in the way it was.

Virginia political world (Prison Privatisation Report International 1997, no. 15, p. 3). There are also documented examples, in both the United States and the United Kingdom, of persons who had been involved in the procurement process from the purchaser side later joining the staff of a successful bidder.

Such practices give the appearance of lack of probity, as indeed they would in any equivalent procurement situation. Political donations are so much a part of U.S. big business culture that it might seem fatuous to urge that they be altogether prohibited. However, this is a particularly sensitive context. As for the subsequent hiring of public sector procurement personnel, smacking as it does of a retrospective reward, the Australian and U.K. practice is to require that successful contractors should not employ specified personnel involved in the procurement process from the government side for a specified period after the opening of the prison—usually one year. In an industry where there always seems to be a shortage of experienced and skilled staff, that may be as far as one can realistically go.

Another probity issue arises when the government itself enters the bidding as a potential provider, while also being the purchaser of the prison services. This comes about in the context of "market testing" or "contestability"—a concept foreign to U.S. prison privatization but familiar in both Australia and the United Kingdom. These labels refer to a procedure in which the public sector provider can bid against the private sector, whether for a new project or in relation to a contract renewal.

Given that one of the principal aims of privatization is to invigorate the public sector through competition, logic requires that the success of this strategy should at some stage be tested in a genuine contest between the public and private sectors. This is significantly different from the process whereby the private sector bids are benchmarked against the notional public sector price and regime—for example, with regard to the 7 percent formula of Florida. Ideally in market-testing situations, the (public sector) purchaser of prison services should not itself be a provider; there should be an arm's length relationship with each of the potential sectors that could provide the services. Unfortunately, this "pure" model of procurement is seldom found.[11] Conse-

[11] An exception was the state of Queensland (Australia), which for a period of two years (1997–99) worked with a purchaser/provider split—the Queensland Corrective Services Commission being the purchaser and Queensland Corrections (QCORR) being the public sector provider (Harding 1998*b*, pp. 2–3). However, this arrangement diluted the political responsibility for prisons in ways that were found unacceptable (Peach

quently, the relevant prisons department or agency, itself the major provider, is in danger of being judge in its own cause—an acute probity issue.

The response in Australia and the United Kingdom has been to create elaborate "Chinese walls"—intended to prevent the bidding group within the public provider from communicating with the evaluation group, to quarantine financial information, and above all to ensure that the public sector bidder has no inkling of the scope of the private sector bids. No matter how fastidious these arrangements seem to be, they do not really command much confidence within the private sector, particularly if the public sector bid is successful. This was what happened in 1994 with respect to a new Queensland prison, Woodford. The public sector provider, in consortium with private sector builders, architects, and bankers, beat both private providers—Australian Correctional Management and Corrections Corporation of Australia. The probity of the outcome came under immediate attack, and although a parliamentary inquiry (Queensland Legislative Assembly 1996) upheld the probity, the mutual trust between the two sectors was badly damaged.

Much the same occurred in the United Kingdom in 1994 in relation to Manchester Prison, where the public sector provider bid successfully against the private sector. Manchester was an old prison that, having been shut down for several years following major riots and arson, was about to reopen. There was widespread cynicism in the marketplace that its management would ever be taken away from the public sector; not only was it one of the biggest in the United Kingdom but it was a stronghold of the labor union. This cynicism was exacerbated less than a year later when the "service level agreement" (an arrangement akin to a private sector contract) was canceled, thus bringing the prison back into the public sector mainstream with regard to funding and many management practices (Harding 1997, pp. 146–47).

The most recent market-testing exercises in the United Kingdom—one won by the private sector and the other by the public sector—have evinced similar cynicism (Prison Privatisation Report International 1999, no. 30, pp. 1–4).

1999). The U.K. arrangement involves a specialist body within the Home Office—the Contracts and Competition Group—making the procurements, but the perception must be that it is too close in its daily operations to the Prison Service itself to be regarded as wholly independent (Harding 1997, p. 50).

Market testing in a genuine contest involving actual pricing and performance undertakings, as opposed to the U.S. model where the superiority of the private sector bid is assessed in a notional comparison of costs and regime quality, is essential if the optimum benefits of privatization are to be obtained. These benefits relate to competition and cross-fertilization, and the only irrefutable way of demonstrating public sector response to the private sector (and vice versa) is by way of rigorous assessment of promised and actual performance. To this point, however, confidence has not yet been established in the probity processes and standards that are applied.

ii) *Price.* The desire to reduce operating costs was one of the main drivers of privatization, and costs evaluation has played a disproportionate role in the debate and research. Lowballing has occurred, and poor performance tends to follow in such circumstances. In that context, it is important to emphasize that, in the majority of procurement systems, the cheapest bid is not ipso facto entitled to be successful.

The typical arrangement is that the procurement agency assigns fixed scores to various items in the proposal. These may be quite broad; for example, in the 1999 Western Australian procurement the weights were 55 percent for operational service requirements, 35 percent for design and construction, 5 percent for the organizational structure and dependability of the consortium, and 5 percent for community acceptability of the total bid. No subweightings were made, though it was specified that each of the various heads within the main categories would carry equal weight. Also, bidders had to obtain an acceptable rating in each category; in other words, a failure even on a 5-percent item such as community acceptability would disqualify a bidder even if the total of all of the items were higher than that of another bidder who had reached an acceptable score on all four categories. Finally, it was stated that the decision would be made on the basis of "value for money," flagging quite clearly that a more expensive bid might well be successful if the additional operational and/or structural value outweighed the higher dollar price.

Broadly speaking, with variations in detail, this is the standard Australian approach. Three of the eight contracts so far awarded in Australia have gone to a bidder who was not the cheapest.

The U.K. approach is not dissimilar. The most complete exposition, amounting in effect to a handbook of procurement best practice, is found in a report by the auditor general relating to the first two

DCFM procurements (National Audit Office 1997). Two key points emerged. First, the criterion of "deliverability" allows some decision-making flexibility to the procurement team (the Contracts and Competition Group), akin to the Australian notion of "value for money." Second, system-wide benefit, going beyond "deliverability" as between the bidders, may be taken into account. In the particular procurements under review, the same bidder was substantially cheaper in each procurement and, had it been awarded both contracts, could have reduced costs even further on the basis of economies of scale. Nevertheless, the Contracts and Competition Group decided not to award both contracts to that bidder, partly on the basis that benefits would be likely to flow to the next procurement by way of enhanced competition if one of the two contracts were awarded to a second bidder. The auditor general considered that this was a defensible decision, not in contravention with any explicit or implicit requirements.

It is doubtful whether this mode of promoting medium-term public interest above the interests of a complying bidder would survive legal challenge in some states of the United States. General procurement laws and practices, as well as the particular protocols applicable to private prisons, tend to be more prescriptive. For example, the Florida Correctional Privatization Commission, in evaluating procurement bids, allocates scores to eighteen separate areas divided, in turn, into 107 subareas. Each has a precise value, some as little as 0.25 percent. The greatest weight is given to price—20 percent. The evaluations are made, the scores added up, and the highest number wins. Thus, the Glades County Correctional Facility contract went to WCC ahead of CCA by a margin of 0.25 percent; no further "subjective" judgment such as "value for money" or "deliverability" could enter into it (Harding 1997, p. 76).

Not all U.S. states are quite as tightly prescriptive as this. For example, Virginia has only nine scoring categories, the final one of which is 10 percent based on interview of the shortlisted candidates. Nevertheless, departure from the numerical scores would only occur very exceptionally.

A threshold criterion adopted by virtually all the U.S. jurisdictions is that the private bid be less expensive than the actual or notional public sector costs of carrying out the same tasks. One approach is to specify a percentage—for example, 7 percent in Florida, 10 percent in Texas and Kentucky—by which the private sector bid must undercut the costs of the public sector. The procurement authority must thus undertake complex calculations—often little better than guesstimates—as to the price at which the public sector could run the planned prison. Contract renewals are typically subject to the same requirement. There does seem to be a law of diminishing returns here. Starting from the low base of expenditure per prisoner per diem in the United States, it is difficult to see how the private sector can go on jumping the price hurdle indefinitely.

The other main approach to pricing is less constraining, looking to quality ahead of price. The Tennessee formula (Tn. Code Ann. Sec. 41-24-105[d]) is typical: "The contract may only be renewed if the contractor is providing at least the same quality of services as the state at a lower cost, or if the contractor is providing services superior to those provided by the state at essentially the same cost." Other states, including Arkansas and Virginia, follow this approach.

A whole literature of research and evaluation of operational costs has been spawned around these requirements. Obviously, a responsible government would not wish to pay the private sector more for a service than it would cost to perform it through its own employees (though the history of privatization generally throws up many examples of imprudent bargains), so cost checking is essential.

B. Specifying Contractual Outputs

A great advantage claimed for private sector contracting is that it has compelled prison authorities to specify what it is they desire should come out of the correctional regime. This relates not only to the primary aim of the secure custody of inmates but also to care and well-being, rehabilitation, and reparation. The avoidance of escapes, deaths, and violence within prisons is a primary objective but so too are good health and nutrition and an equitable regime. Do the purchasers (the state authorities) want to achieve basic literacy rates of 30 percent, or 50 percent, or what for those prisoners illiterate upon receival? Should it be expected that 10 percent or 40 percent of prisoners gain trade qualifications while serving their sentences? What percentage of sex offenders should complete specialist treatment programs, and what does "completion" entail? Is a positive urinalysis rate of 5 percent, or 15 percent, or what acceptable? How many incidents of inmate assaults upon other inmates are tolerable? The list is almost endless.

The input approach, so characteristic of the public sector, was akin to asking, how long is a piece of string? Goals were either not set in advance or, if set, were quite loose. If hepatitis C rates increased within the prison, this was unfortunate but not in itself seen as a sign of unacceptable managerial performance. If literacy rates were improved by 10 percent one year, 25 percent the following year, and 5 percent the year after that, in a context where the staffing and resources inputs had not changed, nothing much turned on it in management terms. The explanation for variance might well be sought, and found, in changing inmate profiles or attitudes.

While the above may, perhaps, be something of a caricature and while, certainly, some aspects of the public sector system were, and are, output focused, nevertheless it is a fair representation of the broad disparity in expectations and attitudes. Contract would change this, it was thought. However, the early contracts did not really provide the mechanisms for doing so, thus lending some support to those who denounced this input/output dichotomy as "gobbledegook" (Ryan 1998, p. 324) or as bespeaking "a dominant form of managerialism" (Sparks 1994, p. 24).

In Australia the original Junee Prison contract provided that "the Correctional Center is to provide access to, and encourage offenders to undertake, a range of educational and vocational programs." While formally this might possibly be construed as output focused, it is so nonprescriptive that it is impossible to say what would or would not constitute compliance. It is indeed exactly the sort of "obligation" that an input-orientated organization would be happy to impose upon itself. This is not really surprising as the contract was written by an input-focused organization, the public sector prisons department, which clearly had not at this early stage woken up to the fact that it was now playing in a new game. Not surprisingly, this clause led to several major disagreements (Harding 1997, p. 67), culminating in its being rewritten.

Much the same problems had been experienced earlier with the Borallon contract in Queensland—the first in Australia. Requirements that the contractor provide "regular" access to various health and dental services, for example, were fraught with the potential and the actuality for dispute. Likewise, a problem with the Victoria contracts of the mid-nineties was that "the private sector outcomes were set on the basis of the average, or in some cases the less than average, results achieved in the outdated prisons which had been identified for replacement" (Auditor General Victoria 1999, p. 2). In other words, in specifying the new regime the public sector providers who were now carrying out the procurement could not escape intellectually from their own experience.

The United States started at a more sophisticated level, but even so some of the early contracts were rather loose. For example, the 1995 Florida/CCA contract relating to a youthful offenders' institution depends a great deal for its meaning on cross-reference to "the standards." This is defined to mean: "ACA Standards; applicable court orders, including but not limited to orders entered into in *Celestino and Costello v. Singletary;* the Health Care Standards, Health Services Bulletins and guidelines and recommendations of the Correctional Medical Authority; and applicable federal, state and local laws, codes and standards."

Important as American Correctional Association (ACA) standards are in maintaining a level of accountability in U.S. corrections, they are primarily processual ("Written policies must provide") and formulaic. Practical, on-the-ground compliance or breach is seldom clear-cut, yet clarity and predictability are crucial for accountability. Moreover, to the extent that ACA standards can be interpreted with sufficient precision, they might well conflict or overlap with the other generalized standards picked up by cross-reference in a clause such as that set out above. Once more, it is difficult to be sure what would or would not amount to compliance.

Australian, U.K., and U.S. contracts have come a long way since then. For example, a 1998 Texas solicitation (the terms of which can be found on Logan's Web site, http://www.ucc.uconn.edu/~logan/) shows modern practice at work. As with virtually all jurisdictions, the terms of the solicitation would be incorporated by reference in the contract or award. It can be seen that the contractor has room to move, to do things its own way, in many program areas. Nevertheless, the problem may here have become that the terms are a little too prescriptive—output focused but based on the assumption that desired outputs can best be achieved by adoption of public sector procedures and inputs. This assumption is shown by the frequency of cross-references to the Texas Department of Criminal Justice Policies and Procedures, which the private prison's own policies and procedures must take into account. This reflects the basic ambivalence governments still have about risk transfer in this politically sensitive area. Nevertheless, the contractor is still left with some room to move.

In Australia, the pattern is not dissimilar. The balance is between encouraging innovation in achieving desired outputs and exercising residual control over how the institution should be run. For example, the 1999 Western Australia contract gives great latitude to the contractor as to what industries should be available for prisoner work and training. The old formula of metalwork, carpentry, leather work, and so on, with workshops purpose-designed for those activities, has been discarded: "The evident failure of traditional prison industry models and practices means that innovation must be found by way of links with suitable business partners and in terms of the design of industry areas. The aim will be to provide industry work experience generating a work habit that will be relevant to post-release employment opportunities" (Western Australian Government 1998, para. 1.6).

In summary, contracts seek to be output based, they look for innovation, they aim to produce measurable compliance or performance criteria, and yet the most recent tendency is that they do not quite transfer the whole risk from the public to the private sector. The days are long gone when the private sector operator could almost write its own contract, for the public authorities are now becoming quite sophisticated in their demands and expectations.[12]

C. *Fee Structures and Compliance Mechanisms*

In DCFM contracts—now the most commonplace—the fee structure will incorporate the capital repayment schedule, and this of course will remain unchanged over whatever is the applicable period. As for management fees, while precise mechanisms vary, the broad objectives are similar: to pay the agreed fee only for full performance and thus to deduct amounts for any aspects of partial or nonperformance. The financial incentive should drive performance in a way that is impossible in the state-funded public sector.

To illustrate the importance of financial leverage: in Victoria (Australia) a maximum fee has been set that is calibrated with actual occupancy, and within that there is a performance-linked fee (PLF) that is only payable to the extent that performance is satisfactorily carried out. The amount of that fee is such that, if it were all lost, the financial return on capital to the operator would make the enterprise marginal. In other words, most of the commercial profit is tied up in the PLF.

[12] The dream of unbridled self-regulation has not yet quite died. A very senior executive of a major company recently lamented in private conversation that governments would still get the best value if they said to the companies, "There's the prison; here's your fee—run it for us as best you can."

In addition, many modern contracts also impose specific penalties for failures of performance in the most sensitive areas—escape, nonnatural death, riot. For example, in Western Australia a penalty of $100,000 is payable for each one of such events.

The corollary is that contracts provide for payment for additional services, usually but not exclusively arising out of such matters as higher occupancy rates or the provision of greater services than previously agreed. For example, in 1997 the fees payable to WCC for the operation of South Bay Correctional Center were increased to take account of the fact that greater numbers of advanced HIV+ prisoners than previously agreed were being sent there.

The very early contracts put great reliance upon the contractor's reporting systems for the purchaser to be able to determine what was payable. This would sometimes be augmented by on-site observation and audit. However, it has become common, but not universal, practice for a contract compliance monitor to work on-site, the purchaser's own records supplementing those made available to it by the contractor. The most recent Australian contracts require that the contractor's books must be available on-line to the contract compliance monitors.

The standard Texas provisions epitomize monitoring practice in most U.S. states:

> TDCJ [Texas Department of Criminal Justice] will designate a contract monitor to review all administrative, non-programmatic, recreational and programmatic requirements of the contract. The Contractor shall provide, at its own expense, a separately keyed private and secure office in the up front Administrative Building for the Contract Monitor. Contractor shall provide all furniture, office equipment, office supplies, and a dedicated telephone and fax line with fax machine and TDCJ mainframe computer connection to the Contract Monitor at Contractor's cost. (Para. C9)
>
> TDCJ in coordination with the Contract Monitor shall, in its discretion, devise its own procedures for monitoring the quality of Contractor's performance under this Contract . . . and the Contractor shall cooperate fully with the TDCJ and the Contract Monitor in obtaining the requisite information. (Para. E3.1)
>
> The Contractor shall be required to maintain acceptable performance standards in various areas as determined by the TDCJ. Contractor's failure to maintain acceptable performance standards shall result in a deduction to the monthly per them as

listed in this section. (Para. G3.5; see Logan's Web site at http://www.ucc.uconn.edu/~logan/)

Of course, a great deal depends upon how the compliance monitoring is actually done. The practices are quite variable, particularly in the United States. At the Lea County and Guadalupe County Correctional Facilities, New Mexico, the state at no stage had any on-site monitoring presence, the Department of Corrections arguing that it could not afford to fund such positions even though they were provided for by contract. The report into the New Mexico corrections system (http://www.legis.state.nm.us/corrections.html) highlighted this failure as an important aspect of the problems that led to the various disorders.

The United Kingdom is resource rich when it comes to monitoring. The key point has been recognized that the more authority is devolved, the greater must be the commitment to regulation and accountability. Consequently, the early recognition of problems and the imposition of sanctions are active components of the privatization structures. The withholding of performance-linked fees is graphically illustrated by the experience at H.M. Prison Parc, in Wales. This started up shakily, with widespread allegations of racism, intimidation, breaches of the duty of care in relation to health and safety matters, and general regime confusion including a malfunctioning electronic security system. In the first six months of 1998, fees totaling about 800,000 pounds (ca. $1.3 million) were withheld from the operators, Securicor Ltd., for failing to meet standard contract requirements. This amount would have accounted for the whole of the operating profit budgeted for that period. By the end of 1999, the chief inspector of prisons (Ramsbotham 1999*b*) was able to report that "Parc has largely overcome many of the problems with which it was beset" (p. 1). While, doubtless, this improvement was driven by additional factors than financial incentive, the normal business concern of a listed company to avoid losses must have played a part.

Withholding fees is the first significant step along the sanctions track, which can culminate in contract cancellation. Harding (1997, p. 48) has postulated that regulatory mechanisms in relation to private prisons are more susceptible to capture—that is, a situation where "regulators come to be more concerned to serve the interests of the industry with which they are in regular contact than the more remote and abstract public interest" (Grabosky and Braithwaite 1986, p. 198)—than in relation to other, more strictly commercial, activities:

"Whenever the principal operator in a public service industry is empowered to contract out or delegate to others some part of its own operational responsibilities, and in so doing takes on the role of regulatory agency in relation to the activities of those delegates, there is a high risk that some degree of capture or co-optation will occur." This is because the failure of the contractor is in effect the failure of the purchasing agency, which is still also wearing the hat of provider of such services.

In Victoria (Australia), this indeed turned out to be the case at Port Phillip. This 600-bed multifunction, medium-security prison commenced operations in 1997. Almost at once the operators, Group 4, ran into all manner of problems—bullying and violence, riot, fire, suicides. The culmination was a major disturbance in March 1998, lasting two days. A task force report stated that "[We have] little confidence in the current management's ability to manage, and believe that this management regime is destined to experience ongoing serious problems; and [we have] concluded that the management of the prison prior to, during and after the incident of 11/12 March 1998 was not and are not able to deliver to a satisfactory standard a range of contracted services" (Auditor General Victoria 1999, chap. 5, p. 22).

Yet no consideration was given to the cancellation of the contract. All that happened was that fees totaling less than 0.2 percent of the annual contracted amount were withheld. A subsequent inquiry (Auditor General Victoria 1999, p. 22) was of the opinion that notice of possible cancellation should have been given. Clearly, the state authorities overidentified with the need to rehabilitate and cushion the operator, and this was partly because of their continued need to ensure that the imprisonment function was carried out on their behalf. As the problems compounded, the authorities appeared unduly reluctant to exercise their full contractual rights: cancellation. Accountability through contract cancellation is something about which United States authorities feel fewer qualms.

D. *Public Access to Contracts*

If contracts remain confidential to the parties, a crucial element of accountability is missing. But if specifications are on the public record, all manner of interested parties can bring pressure to bear upon the contractor as well as the agency whose duty is to ensure compliance. These include prisoners themselves, who are invariably the best informed as to how the regime is functioning; members of legislatures;

the media; and, above all, advocacy groups such as civil liberties and prisoners' support organizations. The latter groups are particularly important in the United States where prisoner litigation is often activated by such bodies.

In the United States, access has not generally been a problem. State procurement laws typically require public access to such contracts. In addition, contracts made by publicly listed companies (a category into which all the market leaders fall) must, under Securities and Exchange Commission rules, be lodged for inspection. Some states, notably Florida, go further, requiring public sessions of the Correctional Privatization Commission to be held at which contract variations are discussed and explained.

In the United Kingdom and Australia, the bureaucratic instinct for secrecy has traditionally been strong. With the early private prison contracts, the authorities in both countries latched on to the notion of "commercial-in-confidence" as a means of trying to prevent public access to any part of the contract. The argument was that the companies were entitled to have their pricing basis protected from the view of their competitors, and that any aspect of contract performance and standards would cast light upon this so that, accordingly, the whole contract should remain secret. This approach produced some remarkable outcomes—for example, in the United Kingdom, the Home Office, as commissioning agency for research into the comparative efficiency of the first private prison and a comparator public prison, withheld the relevant contract from the researchers whom it had commissioned to do the work (Harding 1997, p. 70).

In Australia, this posture soon started to break down (Harding 1997). Nevertheless, the state of Victoria would release only significantly edited versions of its contracts. Public interest litigation was launched under the Freedom of Information Act by the Coburg-Brunswick Legal Referral Center, a group with a strong and enduring interest in prison conditions in both the private and the public sector, and in late 1999 the supreme court ordered the release of all contractual documentation other than the security plans for emergencies. It emerged during the court proceedings that it was the government authorities much more than the contractors who wanted to maintain secrecy (Freiberg 2000).

While this saga worked its way through the courts, the newest privatization state, Western Australia, enacted legislation mandating that the contract and all relevant supporting documentation be tabled in

Parliament within thirty days of signature. In practice, the full contract has also been placed on the government's Web site (http://www.moj.wa.gov.au/offmngt/private.htm). This provision echoed that found in the New Zealand legislation. The U.K. situation remains legally fuzzy, however, with access dependent in practice upon the attitude from time to time of the Home Office.

VI. Regulation and Accountability

Accountability depends upon numerous systems, processes, and values; it is a complex notion of interconnected matters rather than a unitary concept (Harding 1997, pp. 27–31, 158–65). Some key factors are beyond the influence of legislators or administrators, notably the crucially important issue of media exposure and debate. Others are utterly intangible, such as the prevailing attitudes toward crime and offenders. Some accountability factors relate to broad system matters, others to the minutiae of bureaucratic arrangements within the responsible state agencies.

Several issues already discussed fall into the accountability basket. They are whether the delegation of the administration of punishment to the private sector strays over the line into the allocation of punishment; whether the private sector is permitted, or successfully takes upon itself, a privileged and undemocratic role as a penal lobby group; whether the private companies have sufficient capacity to manage prison regime risks lawfully and equitably; whether the processes for letting contracts conform with probity and are applied with integrity; whether the terms of the contract and the processes for ensuring compliance protect the needs of the public authority sufficiently; and, related to this, whether contracts are publicly accessible.

What follows is a discussion of some of the remaining major factors that bear upon accountability. The list cannot be exhaustive; mechanisms and their relative significance vary across time and place. The broad conclusion will be that, in the context of the whole basket of accountability items, the private sector is no less, and arguably somewhat more, accountable than the public sector.

A. The Purchaser/Provider Split and Its Relevance to Accountability

The risk of capture, which is inherent when the regulator of the private sector is itself a public sector provider, has already been raised. The obverse difficulty is antagonism—a determination to find fault. Although this is by no means as well documented, there have been signs of this in New South Wales (Australia), where it was the strong desire of the public correctional authorities to reclaim Junee Prison for the public sector, and also in the United Kingdom in relation to Buckley Hall, a private prison that the state agency seemed determined to return to the public sector.[13]

The best theoretical model is for the purchaser of prison services to be separate from all providers, public or private. This enables true competition, provides a mechanism for a churn rate between sectors, and enables regulatory standards to be applied across the board. Thus, if the state authorities decide that a new prison is required and they have no compelling reason to assign it to the public sector, the purchaser/provider split enables the public sector and the private sector to bid against each other on equal terms in a way that meets probity standards. At the end of the contract period, rebidding can also be open to all comers, with the same advantages including industry confidence in the outcome—something so notably lacking with regard to Manchester, Woodford, and Buckley Hall. Finally, it facilitates the process of applying the same broad regulatory standards to all prisons, regardless of the operator's identity.

However, this model in its "pure" form has only once been used, in Queensland (Australia).[14] The predominant U.S. model is for the public sector prisons authority to be both a provider of services in its own right and also the purchaser of private sector services. This possibly reflects something of the origins of U.S. privatization, which was less about doing a different job more innovatively than doing the same job less expensively. Of course, there are usually distinct work sections within corrections departments administering the private contracts, and many contract monitors are flexible and innovative in overseeing regimes. But the fact remains that the public sector culture and processes are the omnipresent reference point.

[13] Buckley Hall had originally been a public sector prison, then was won from the public sector in a market-testing exercise by Group 4. In 1997 the Prison Service Agency made a declaration that it was in need of "special managerial attention." This was seen in the industry as an early warning of the public sector's determination to reclaim it. Yet the chief inspector of prisons saw the prison as being in many ways a model of best practice and stated, "Not only is the stigma attached to it undeserved, but in view of the large number of prisons which are way below the standard of Buckley Hall but have not been made subject [to such a declaration], it undermines the credibility of the process" (Ramsbotham 1997, preface). Two years later, upon expiry of the private operator's contract, the public sector agency won the bidding for its management—an outcome that was greeted with some cynicism.

[14] See n. 11, above.

Florida broke away from this pattern. From 1985 the Department of Corrections (DOC) had been statutorily empowered "to enter into contracts with private vendors for the provision, operation and maintenance of correctional facilities and the supervision of inmates" (Fla. Stat. 944.105), and the same year county authorities were authorized in similar terms (Fla. Stat. 951.062). The latter soon started to utilize this power, but the state DOC was evidently reluctant to do so. In 1993 the legislature stripped the DOC of this power and established a new organization, the Florida Correctional Privatization Commission, whose sole function was to take charge of privatization at both the state and the county level. Consequently, the line of accountability for private prisons goes to a body that is itself not a provider and not wedded, therefore, to public sector provider patterns and attitudes. That is a good thing, congruent with the ideal model. But the accountability line of the private sector at no point intersects with that of the public sector. This is a flaw in the model. If competition and cross-fertilization occur, it is despite the model, not because of it.

In the United Kingdom, the public sector provider, H.M. Prison Service Agency, contains within it a quasi-autonomous purchasing body known as the Contracts and Competition Group (CCG). Once the government has decided that a private prison should be procured, the CCG sees the whole procurement process through to the point where the contract is ready for the minister to sign. On-site contract compliance managers and controllers (the governor-grade public sector officials responsible for adjudications about disciplinary matters) are appointed by and in theory work for the CCG. However, in practice the dominance of public sector provider interests start to take over at this point, with Prison Service area managers signing off on fee payments or making decisions as to their reduction. Contract rebidding also falls within the CCG's operations. However, the CCG model falls short of what is ideal, for the public sector provider in practice has taken on a significant role in regulating the private sector.

In Victoria (Australia), the Office of the Correctional Services Commissioner was established in 1994, as the state commenced privatization. Its role was to monitor performance in both the public and the private sector. However, its regulatory role was confused and it had no budgetary responsibility for the purchase of services. As the Port Phillip saga showed, it was also unduly diffident in exercising its monitoring role—in particular, by failing to put monitors on-site and by not recommending contract termination.

Queensland, as mentioned, adopted the "pure" model of a purchaser/provider split. Following the industry concern at the award of the Woodford contract by the public sector provider to its own bidders, a purchaser/provider split was legislated. The Queensland Corrective Services Commission (QCSC) became the purchasing, standard-setting, and supervisory body for both the public and the private sector, while Queensland Corrections (QCORR) became the public sector provider. This model lasted only two years, from 1997 until 1999. With a change of government came an inquiry (Peach 1999) and then a much-anticipated change back to a structure where the public sector provider became the regulatory body for the private sector. An autonomous purchaser apparently stripped too much control for their political comfort from a government dependent on support from the labor unions. With the structural change came also an announcement that "market testing" for new prisons would not henceforth occur and a strong industry expectation that not only would there be no new private prisons in the state but also that existing ones might be taken back into the public sector.

In summary, a legislatively mandated purchaser/provider split would tend to facilitate accountable privatization, for it would enable procurements to be made in a way less dominated by the political process. Administrators recognize the importance of this dichotomy, which is crucial in pure commercial privatization, but nevertheless prison privatization has had to go ahead within a public provider-dominated structure that tends to inhibit its development.

B. *The State's Vetting Powers*

The threshold accountability point is the selection stage. It is now so complex and thorough that the state really only has itself to blame if it gets it wrong.[15] Companies often put a great deal of nonrecover-

[15] In the U.K. and Australian experience, "getting it wrong" usually means departing from "correctional value for money principles." Consider the case, e.g., of the problem prison in Victoria—Port Phillip. A tranche of three private prison contracts were being let, and there is some suggestion that the government strongly desired that each of the three main companies—ACM, Corrections Corporation of Australia, and Group 4—should be successful in one bid, this being rather naively seen as a way of enhancing competition. Accordingly, it indicated its preference for the successful bidder to be the one that had not yet won a contract—Group 4. The report of the Auditor General Victoria (1999, paras. 4.53–4.61) makes no reference to these strongly held industry beliefs and records that it is satisfied that the evaluation panel met all probity requirements. However, it did emerge that all three short-listed bids were initially treated as nonconforming and that rebidding was permitted only within the previous base prices. This is an unusual requirement and would certainly seem potentially to open up the opportunity for an unexpected outcome as a consequence, say, of off-the-record government to com-

able money into preparation of a bid—on some estimates for big contracts up to $1 million. After that comes the contract itself—a further opportunity to put into concrete terms what is expected of the operator, and then the contract administration phase involving for the most part on-site monitors.

In addition, a key control and accountability lever relates to the appointment and qualifications of personnel. As McDonald et al. (1998, p. 59) state: "Adequate, quality staffing and training constitute two of the most critical contract provisions public authorities may address in private prison agreements. Both represent likely areas in which private contractors will seek to reduce expenditures, either through the payment of lower wages and benefits, the hiring of less experienced personnel, the deployment of innovative staffing patterns or the introduction of special technology (e.g., specialized surveillance equipment)."

Nevertheless, the U.S. pattern is generally not overprescriptive. Typically, the most invasive level of control is a provision such as that found in Texas contracts: "Contractor will retain no Upper Level Management Personnel for administration of the Facility without prior approval of selection by the Texas Department of Criminal Justice, which approval shall not be unreasonably withheld" (para. I.7: see Logan's Web site: http://www.ucc.uconn.edu/~logan/).

"Upper level management personnel" will have been defined in the request for proposals to meet what the agency sees as its legitimate needs. Moreover, as contracts invariably require ACA accreditation to be obtained, superimposed upon this vetting power is the requirement that managers meet educational and training qualifications expected by those standards. Thus, in the case of wardens, "a bachelor's degree in an appropriate discipline, five years of related administrative experience, and demonstrated administrative ability and leadership" are required (American Correctional Association 1990, 3-4009).

This is also the case with all levels of custodial officers and the training that should be available to them (American Correctional Association 1990, 3-4079–3-4081). However, these provisions stop well short of enabling the state authority to decide for itself whether any particu-

---

pany communication. Subsequently, as Port Phillip failed, the government contributed funds for the redesign and adaptation of parts of the prison. This was thought within the rest of the industry to indicate the bid was probably known to have had a lowball element in it. In the case of Parc Prison in the United Kingdom, the CCG could well have been unduly impressed by the novelty of the footprint of the winning design, which was much smaller than the usual U.K. prison size, and also by the electronic systems. Each of these factors subsequently became a crucial problem.

lar individual is suitable for employment, and they do not empower the agency to dictate training requirements in detail. By contract some states go further: for example, Florida requires that private sector staff undergo the same training as those in the public sector. But for the most part this aspect of the prison function is regarded as within the contractor's management prerogative.

The United Kingdom and Australian approach is quite different. In essence, the state authority not only possesses the power to veto any person at any level for employment or to withdraw authorization subsequently but also must positively authorize private prisons personnel if they are to act in that capacity. No authorization, no employability. The U.K. provisions are found in the Criminal Justice Act 1991. This designates all employees involved in the running of the prison, from the manager or warden to the base-grade uniformed officers, as "prison custody officers": "In this Part 'prison custody officer' means a person in respect of whom a certificate is for the time being in force certifying (*a*) that he has been approved by the [Home Secretary] for the purpose of performing . . . custodial duties; and (*b*) that he is accordingly authorized to perform them" (Criminal Justice Act 1991, Sec. 85[l]).

These personnel thus derive their status and authority not merely from their contract of employment with the private company but also from a certificate granted in the name of the Home Secretary. The statute sets out the qualifying criteria and the circumstances for revocation. A person must be "fit and proper and must have received training to an approved standard"—that is, approved by the state authority. Revocation can occur on the basis that a person has ceased to be, or never was, a fit and proper person. This is very much an administrative process, not reviewable through judicial challenge. The statute has been designed so that the state agency can seek to minimize by its direct intervention one of the management risks—unsuitable personnel—that it is otherwise trying to pass to the contractor.

The U.K. model has been adopted for the most part in Australia: for example, the most recent privatization state, Western Australia, has virtually replicated the U.K. statutory provisions. South Africa has also taken this approach. There is a reason why this is particularly important in non–United States jurisdictions. The private prison industry leaders are CCA, which has approximately 55 percent of the U.S. business, and WCC, with about 22 percent. Each also operates in non-U.S. markets through subsidiary companies that are usually "$2 companies" formally incorporated but not capitalized in the local jurisdiction. In those markets, WCC has 54 percent of the business, CCA 14 percent, and the British/Swedish Group 4 consortium 28 percent.

There is a strong tendency for U.S. companies to believe that the U.S. way of doing things has universal applicability and that American managers are the best choices for starting up new businesses overseas. While this is an understandable belief in relation to, say, motor vehicle manufacture or computer software or pharmaceuticals, it is wrong in relation to prisons. Prisons are as much a manifestation of national culture, identity, priorities, and problems as are schools or sports or dietary habits or religion. For example, a Japanese prison regime—in the broad sense not only of accommodation type and standard but also of less tangible matters such as attitudes of prisoners and staff toward punishment and confinement, acceptance of authority, expectations of privileges, relations with other prisoners, and so on—is completely different from that of, say, a Finnish regime. A French regime is different from a British one, or a Malaysian one from an Australian one. And they are all quite different from the United States. In other words, prison management is not simply a generic skill applicable anywhere on the globe but one that is to a significant degree culture specific. In a closed institutional context, to misread the culture, to fail to pick up the signals could have serious, if not catastrophic, effects.

In fact, this has happened with at least three prisons—Arthur Gorrie and Junee in Australia and Doncaster in the United Kingdom. In each of these cases, statutory power for the agency to withdraw the authorization of senior management personnel to work in the prisons was a strong bargaining chip in discussions with the operating company, leading in two cases to the company's "voluntary" decision to replace U.S. personnel with local managers (Harding 1997, pp. 85–88).

C. *American Correctional Association Accreditation*

It is the invariable practice for U.S. contracts to include a clause requiring the private prison to obtain ACA accreditation within a specified time, usually three years. Even states that do not require accreditation for their own public sector prisons nevertheless impose that requirement upon private prisons (Harding 1997, p. 64). Accreditation works as follows. The ACA, a voluntary association of high-level correctional professionals, has developed and published, through its Commission on Accreditation of Corrections, standards applicable to twenty-one types of corrections, including adult prisons. A state system or an individual institution seeking accreditation will request an audit, and at an agreed date a team of three or four auditors will visit. If standards are acceptable, a certificate will be issued, valid for three years. If the audit is unsatisfactory, deficiencies will be identified and a date for recall set; as long as everything has been rectified, a certificate will then be issued.

Many criticisms have been made of this system. One is that the institution seeking accreditation has to pay for the whole procedure and that the ACA for its part is dependent on these fees. The prisons are "customers," therefore, rather than applicants; a degree of capture is likely. The ACA rejects this criticism, believing that its professionalism is unassailable (Keve 1996, pp. 133–37). Another weakness is the highly structured nature of the visits, with plenty of advance warning. The regulatory literature constantly illustrates this as being a weakness in audit processes. Even more tellingly, perhaps, critics refer to the formulaic and procedural nature of the audit. It is very much dependent on ascertaining what the written procedures of the institution lay down as operational processes, rather than observing whether those processes in fact are followed. An ACA accreditation audit could in principle take place 80 percent in the warden's office and only 20 percent in the prison itself; contact with staff and inmates is something of an afterthought.

McDonald et al. (1998, p. 49) summarize their concerns:

> For the most part, the prevailing professional standards prescribe neither the goals that ought to be achieved nor the indicators that would let officials know if they are making progress toward those goals over time. Two facilities could conform equally to ACA standard by having a written policy on a particular issue, yet they could have diametrically opposite practices and outcomes on that issue.
>
> The effect of these various trends has generally been to conceive of prison performance quite narrowly as conformance to law, state rules and regulations, and professional standards. That is, performance trends tend to be measured according to procedural compliance.

These criticisms possess validity. However, the fact remains that every single private prison has or will soon have ACA accreditation, whereas this is not so with the public sector. Even now, when the accreditation process has been available since 1978, more than 20 percent of public sector facilities have not been accredited. Typically, there is a degree of self-selection at work; prisons that will fall short are located in jurisdictions that choose not to seek accreditation. Privatization marks a distinct step forward, at least symbolically, in the commitment of state agencies to improved standards.

D. Inspection: The U.K. Model

Neither the United Kingdom nor Australia nor any of the other privatization states has an accreditation system. In the United Kingdom the Woolf Report (Woolf and Tumim 1991, 1.186–87, 15.5.6) recommended that such a system should be established, based on precise standards. Procedurally, it would have been tied in with the activities of the chief inspector of prisons, whose inspection reports would form the basis of the accreditation process. The idea met with governmental and bureaucratic resistance, quite possibly because the creation of precise standards carried with it some danger that the courts might construe these as constituting prisoners' rights. The U.K. approach has always basically been that standards, such as the Prison Rules, "do not, either singly or in combination, purport to provide a code of directly enforceable rights in prisoners" (Richardson 1994, p. 80). The United Kingdom—and the Australian—philosophy has been to prevent, as far as possible, the prison regime being judicially overviewed, and there is no Bill of Rights in those countries, as in the United States, to enable prisoners to break down this intransigence and enter through the doors of the courts.

The U.K. inspectorate system performs a related function, however. Until 1981 prison inspections had been very much in-house Prison Service affairs—management reporting for the benefit of management. There was very little continuity in the system; reports were not made public; follow-up actions, if any, thus not able to be logged. These deficiencies led in 1979 to the establishment of a committee to review the process. It recommended that an independent inspectorate be established, within the Home Office but not as part of the Prison Service itself; it should report to the Home Secretary, and its reports would be made public (though not until after the Prison Service had the opportunity to respond to them, its written response being made public simultaneously). The inspectorate would be able to make unannounced, as well as announced, inspections of prisons and also to overview general issues "thematic inspections."

The favored modus operandi is for an inspection team to spend five or more days at a prison. The primary source of information, in contrast to ACA accreditation processes, is direct observation, discussions with prisoners and staff, participation in some programs, follow-up interrogation of management, all this fortified with detailed scrutiny of documentation and records. The two most recent officeholders have created a culture of not pulling their punches, and the findings can be devastating: for example, with Wormwood Scrubs, a "flagship prison" in the U.K. system, the chief inspector characterized his report as "the worst prison report in penal history" (*Times*, June 29, 1999).

The weakness is that no sanctions or other processes necessarily flow from an inspection report, however damning it might be. The reports are advisory and recommendatory only; it is for the Prison Service officials to decide whether to act upon them. Over the years, the low and slow take-up rate has been a source of great frustration to successive chief inspectors.[16] In the context of privatization, however, the great advantage was that it was a ready-to-go, independent body for evaluating the performance of operators in this controversial new area—evaluations that would not merely be self-contained but that would possess a strong comparative element.

This has occurred, with the new private prisons being inspected earlier in their operational lives than was the standard practice with new public sector prisons (Harding 1997, p. 62). By and large, they have emerged with considerable credit. Doncaster prison, run by Premier Prisons, Ltd. (a WCC subsidiary company), was "the most progressive in the country" with regard to its antibullying strategies, its management of young offenders, its care of potentially suicidal prisoners, and several other key functions (Ramsbotham 1996, preface). Blakenhurst Prison (CCA) was "marked by a refreshingly 'can do' attitude amongst staff, demonstrated in their approach to their tasks—an attitude that is, sadly, not found in too many public sector prisons" (Ramsbotham 1998, preface). Altcourse (Group 4) "is by some way the best local prison that we have inspected. . . . It is not the first prison I have left with a feeling of optimism, but never before have I listed forty-five examples of Good Practice in a report" (Ramsbotham 2000, preface, pp. 1–2).

[16] The 1997/98 annual report of the chief inspector of prisons (Ramsbotham 1997/98) epitomizes this frustration, cataloging numerous examples of earlier recommendations that have not been taken up, in each case leading to exacerbation of the identified problem.

The inspectorate model, then, seems very robust for measuring qualitatively, and to some extent quantitatively, the performance of private prisons. It is a model that, unfortunately, is not standard in Australia. For public prisons the pre-1981 U.K. model of in-house inspections or audits is normal. With privatization all states recognized the need to bolster this system, and the relevant statutes all make provision for monitors to be appointed. However, the practice has been to take them off-site after the initial settling-in period (Harding 1997, pp. 42–45) or, in the case of Victoria, only to bring them on-site after trouble has occurred. Visiting audits are now, for the most part, the norm for private as well as public prisons.

However, Western Australia, embarking upon privatization, has seen the inspectorate model as a lever for system-wide reform of penal administration. A major public sector prison riot in 1998 brought the system into crisis (Smith, Indermaur, and Boddis 1999) and revealed the lack of a mechanism either to recognize looming problems or to deal with them after they had occurred. Ostensibly because of the need to ensure accountability of the private sector but no less to bring transparency into the closed public sector system, the opportunity was seized to create a system-wide inspectorate along the U.K. lines. The model is, if anything, a stronger one—the inspector's reports are to be tabled in parliament, not merely presented to the minister of justice, and the inspection function is to extend to police lock-ups and juvenile detention centers. It is an enlightening example of how privatization can bring about system-wide reform.[17]

E. Prisoner Complaints and the Ombudsman System

For public prisons in the United Kingdom, Australia, and other jurisdictions such as New Zealand and Canada, an aspect of accountability is the access of prisoners to an ombudsman to complain about their treatment. This is a crucial part of the accountability jigsaw, for two reasons: first, the inspectorate model, where it exists, is not designed or intended to deal with individual complaints; second, litigation either individually or as part of a class action is seldom possible in a legal context where prison rules do not create prisoners' rights. Without the ombudsman system, therefore, an accountability gap would exist in relation to those manifold day-to-day matters that are the essence of

[17] From August 2000, several months after this article was accepted for publication, the author was appointed as the inaugural inspector of custodial services for Western Australia.—Ed.

prisoner experience and stress. The ombudsman system is no less accessible to prisoners in private as in public sector prisons.

In the United States, the theoretical and practical opportunities for litigation have been much greater either individually or as part of class actions brought not only by prisoners but more typically by external watchdogs such as the American Civil Liberties Union (ACLU). Day-to-day matters tend to be dealt with by on-site mediation procedures of varying procedural quality. The ombudsman model is not generally found. Private prison inmates are, however, on the same ground as public prison inmates. The standard Texas provision exemplifies the position: "*Offender grievance procedure.* Contractor shall provide the resources necessary to implement the offender grievance procedure in the manner detailed in B.P. 03.77, Offender Grievance Procedure Manual, and applicable Court Orders" (C.5.19 at Logan's Web site: http://www.ucc.uconn.edu/logan/).

In recent years both federal and state laws have started to restrict prisoners' access to the courts (Bronstein and Gainsborough 1996). In that context, the ombudsman or the inspectorate model would enhance accountability.

F. Litigation

Actions against public sector prison authorities have led, from time to time, to individual prisons or whole prison systems in no fewer than forty U.S. states being placed under court order. This is usually as a consequence of class actions brought on behalf of prisoners, and the basis is a breach of the Fourth, Fifth, Eighth, or Fourteenth Amendments to the United States Constitution. There is no reason in law or practice why private sector prisons are not susceptible to similar actions. An early example (1997) is an ACLU suit against the Bobby Ross Group for overcrowding in its facility at Karnes City, Texas, to which Colorado prisoners had been sent.

To date, however, most litigation has been aimed at achieving individual compensation in relation to conditions or incidents in particular prisons. (Of course, these cases also may be, and mostly are, brought as class actions.) This litigation is mostly based on 42 U.S. Code 1983—deprivation of constitutional rights under color of state law. To succeed these cases must surmount two hurdles: "state action" (i.e., the defendant must have been acting on behalf of the state rather than privately) and "color of law" (i.e., in purported reliance upon a state or local law or administrative practice). A 1988 decision (*West v. Atkins,*

[1988] S.C.R. 2250) had held that private medical services provided in a public prison by way of contract between the prison authorities and the medical practitioner fell potentially within the liability of 42 U.S. Code (1983). So it was inevitable that direct prison services would also be covered, and in the growing body of subsequent litigation that has not even been questioned.

The Youngstown case has previously been mentioned. Not surprisingly, it soon led to litigation against the operators, CCA, on behalf of all prisoners who had been sent there on or before October 19, 1998. In April 1999 the parties agreed upon a settlement involving the payment of $1.65 million to be distributed among affected prisoners. The settlement also involved CCA agreeing to allow an independent monitor employed by the city of Youngstown to oversee the future operation of the prison.

Litigation by inmates is also in progress in relation to other high profile private sector alleged failures—notably at Columbia, South Carolina, against CCA in relation to staff violence at a juvenile detention center, and at Elizabeth, New Jersey, against Esmor (as it then was) in relation to its running of an INS facility. The companies themselves, not the individual officers, are the defendants in all of these actions. In a public sector context, the individuals would be the nominal defendants—though the state authorities in practice would normally stand behind them in terms of legal and compensation costs. However, as anticipated by Thomas (1991), the Eleventh Amendment provision that nominally insulates state authorities from such actions is not applicable to private sector prison operations. The plaintiff can litigate directly against the companies on the basis of their vicarious liability. In this respect, therefore, the accountability of the private sector by way of litigation is greater than that of state authorities.

Furthermore, the 1997 Supreme Court case of *Richardson v. McNight*, 138 L. Ed. 2d 540 (1997); 521 U.S. 399 (1997), held that there was no qualified immunity for private sector, as opposed to public sector, defendants in 42 U.S. Code (1983) cases. The majority opinion stated:

> Our examination of history and purposes [of prison privatization] thus reveals nothing special enough about the job or about its organizational structure that would warrant providing these private prison guards with a governmental immunity. The job is one that private industry might, or might not, perform; and which history

> shows private firms did sometimes perform without relevant immunities. The organizational structure is one subject to the ordinary competitive pressures that normally help private firms adjust their behavior in response to the incentives that tort suits provide—pressures not necessarily present in government departments. Since there are no special reasons significantly favoring an extension of governmental immunity, . . . we must conclude that private prison guards, unlike those who work directly for the government, do not enjoy immunity from suit in a U.S. Code (1983) case (138 L. Ed. 2d 552 [1997]).

Nevertheless, speaking for the dissentients, Justice Scalia lamented (at p. 559) that this could adversely affect privatized corrections in that "it would artificially raise the costs of privatizing prisons." A preferable perspective would seem to be that it is likely to enhance, albeit marginally, accountability through litigation. In this regard the private sector is thus more accountable than the public sector.

The U.K. and Australian jurisprudence relating to prisoner litigation is, by comparison, stunted and ineffectual. Class actions generally are doomed to fail; this is simply not an actionable matter.[18] Individual actions are for the most part confined to situations involving breaches of the duty of care.

G. Nonrenewal and Cancellation of Contracts and Step-In Rights

Most contracts provide for nonrenewal at the end of the agreed term. This may be by way of unilateral state decision or after the contract has been rebid and a preferable offer accepted. These changes are never straightforward and certainly pose a risk in the prison environment. There is some real reluctance to switch operators, therefore. Nevertheless, as the industry matures, rebidding—whether limited to private companies against each other or involving full "market testing"—is becoming more commonplace, particularly in the United Kingdom and Australia. The U.K. Group 4 recently lost its Buckley

[18] This is epitomized by a decision of the Western Australia Court of Criminal Appeal, *Bekink v. R.* (1999 WASCA 160). A prisoner appealed against sentence on the basis that he had been sent to a prison that was subject to a twenty-three-hour a day lockdown resulting from a riot that had occurred several months before he had been tried and convicted and that these conditions could not have been contemplated by the sentencing court. However, it was held that prison conditions were entirely a question of the manner of administration of punishment and, as such, exclusively within the discretion of the prison authorities. Under the strangulated jurisprudence relating to prisoners' rights, this was the only way in which he could even attempt to raise the issue.

Hall contract to the public sector, and although WCC retained its Doncaster contract against the Prison Service, it also had to beat off at least one private sector competitor. In Australia, the Borallon contract held by CCA for more than ten years will be rebid during 2000, as will the Junee contract currently held by ACM.[19]

In practice, an inhibition against nonrenewal is found when the private operator also owns the prison—as with the standard DCFM contract where the buyback period may be between twenty and forty years. This was a factor in the Group 4/Port Philip case, referred to above. In that regard, the separation of management from real estate ownership assists the process of accountability.

All contracts make provision for cancellation of a subsisting contract and the exercise of step-in rights by the state agency. Normally, a clear hierarchy of sanctions is spelled out—informal caution, formal warning, default notice, notice of intended cancellation. It is usually in the interest of both sides to try to redeem the situation. The withholding of performance-linked fees goes hand in hand with this sequence.

United States authorities have been more willing than their peers in other countries to cancel contracts. McDonald et al. (1998, p. 53) documented the cancellation of five contracts involving the shipment of out-of-state prisoners to private prisons in another state. These related to contracts made by authorities in North Carolina, Oklahoma, Colorado, Utah, and Montana, each with various Texas prisons.

In relation to in-state contracts, there have also been numerous cancellations. Sometimes the threat to do so has been enough to persuade the operator to withdraw voluntarily. To the outsider it is not always readily apparent whether the operator jumped or was pushed. Examples include the INS detention center at Elizabeth, New Jersey, operated by Esmor (1995); a juvenile detention facility at Columbia, South Carolina, operated by CCA (1997); Brazoria County jail, Texas, operated by Capital Corrections Resources, Inc. (1998); the High Plains youth facility, Colorado, operated by Rebound (1998); the Talullah Correctional Center for Youth, Louisiana, run by Trans-American Development Associates, Inc. (1998); North Fork Correctional Center, Oklahoma, run by CCA (1998); and Travis County Community Justice Center, Texas, operated by WCC (1999). The follow-up has varied: sometimes the state has taken over, but more often

[19] The operators of Borallon, CCA, lost the contract to Management Training Corporation.

another private operator has come in on revised terms. The most recent cancellations—in June 2000 of two CCA contracts in North Carolina—involved returning private prisons to public sector management. Whatever the outcome, however, there can be no doubt that cancellation is a significant component of accountability.

In the United Kingdom the only cancellation so far occurred related to the running of the prison workshops at a public sector prison, Coldingley (1999). Operations at both Parc Prison (U.K.) and Port Phillip Prison (Victoria) had provided a suitable trigger for contract cancellation had the authorities chosen to go down that track.[20]

Finally, it should be noted that privatization of a total system—as twice proposed by CCA in Tennessee—seriously weakens accountability by inhibiting cancellation and step-in rights. If the state no longer runs some part of a prison system directly, how can it have the skills and experience to take over a private prison that is in crisis?

VII. Regime Quality

The ultimate question is whether private prisons can and do provide good, or even superior, quality correctional services. Measurement of this is not easy. It may be qualitative, such as the reports of the U.K. chief inspector of prisons; by way of participant observation studies, as with the U.K. evaluation of The Wolds (James et al. 1997); interview based (Carter 2001); or derived vicariously from the evaluations of contract monitors (McDonald et al. 1998). Ideally, there will be a quantitative element also, and sometimes indeed the evaluation will be predominantly quantitative. A seminal attempt, still possessing validity a decade later, is the work of Logan (1992).

A. Logan's Confinement Quality Index

Logan, a pioneer in the academic analysis of prison privatization, saw the need to develop evaluation methods that were objective and measurable. The qualitative approaches inevitably required subjective leaps of interpretation. Consequently, they could not be replicated with any confidence, making it difficult for a reliable corpus of longitudinal research to be established. If the ultimate question were the quality of privatized corrections, a research base was crucial.

In a context where belief in rehabilitation through the imprisonment

[20] In November 2000, the government of Victoria canceled the CCA contract in relation to the women's prison at Melbourne, and the public sector operator took it over.

experience had been destroyed, Logan's aims were quite modest. He stated, "The criteria proposed here for comparative evaluations of prisons are normative, rather than consequentialist or utilitarian. They are based on a belief that individual prisons ought to be judged primarily according to the propriety and quality of what goes on inside their walls—factors over which prison officials may have considerable control" (1992, p. 579).

Yet what goes on inside the walls is, in reality, an important penological matter. The prison experience is notorious for causing further deterioration in offenders' ability to cope upon release into the outside world. Public antagonism or indifference to humanitarian issues and philosophical disillusionment with rehabilitation (Martinson 1974) should not distract from this fundamental point. A penal objective, minimalist enough to suit the temper of our times, would be to try to ensure that prisoners do not undergo further social or character deformation while incarcerated (Cross 1971, pp. 85–86). In that context, "confinement quality," as Logan called it, is a first-order issue.

Logan created a matrix, or index, which addressed eight key aspects of imprisonment: security, safety, order, care, activity, justice, conditions, and management. These notions were amplified by numerous subthemes. The protocols were then applied to three prisons: the new women's prison in Grants, New Mexico, operated by CCA; the men's side of the public prison from which the women had been transferred; and a federal prison for women in West Virginia. The data were gathered from formal institutional records, staff surveys and interviews, and inmate surveys and interviews. "Confinement quality indices" were then constructed, based on 335 separate data items.

Logan's conclusions are worth quoting at length, not because the performances of those three prisons at that historical period are of any current interest but because they bring out the complexity and highlight the countercurrents in any such evaluation:

> The private prison out-performed the state and federal prisons, often by quite substantial margins, across nearly all dimensions. The two exceptions were the dimension of Care, where the state outscored the private by a modest amount, and the dimension of Justice, where the federal and private prisons achieved equal scores. The results varied, however, across the different sources of data. The private prison compared most favorably to the state prison when using data from the staff surveys and consistently,

> but more moderately so, when using data from official records. When inmate surveys provided the data, however, the state prison moderately outscored the private on all dimensions except Activity. . . . Regardless of the data source examined, there were many similarities among the three prisons, and for each one there were large numbers of both positive and negative indicators. Despite a high level of prior performance, however, the weight of the evidence in this study supports the conclusion that by privately contracting for the operation of its women's prison, the state of New Mexico improved the overall quality of that prison while lowering its costs. (Logan 1992, pp. 601–2)

Shichor (1995) and James et al. (1997) have each reviewed Logan's work, as well as the few other empirical studies available at those times. Each criticizes the fact that his broad-brush conclusion ("the private prison outperformed the state and federal prisons" and "the overall quality improved") did not reflect the more complex picture that the data threw up and that he had himself described. His objectivity as a researcher is questioned on this basis. However, there is no sleight of hand; the data are there for all to see. Other researchers may thus interpret and evaluate them for themselves.

A more pertinent comment is that of McDonald et al. (1998, p. 54): "Perhaps the most striking aspect of this research literature is that it is so sparse and that so few government agencies have chosen to evaluate the performance of their contractors formally. Even though there exist over a hundred privately operated secure confinement facilities [in the United States], there have been very few systematic attempts to compare their performance to that of public facilities. Most government agencies have been satisfied with monitoring compliance with the terms of the contracts."

This is true; for the "research-evaluation-modification loop" (Harding 1997, p. 119) is crucial to humane and constructive penal administration, be it public or private. Research outside the United States is more active than McDonald et al. state, however. Apart from the four-year longitudinal study at Junee (Bowery 1999) and the work in the United Kingdom carried out by James, Bottomley, and their team (James et al. 1997), Harding and Rynne have been conducting evaluative research within the Queensland prison system since 1998. The FBOP has now made a welcome entry upon the scene, commissioning evaluation research through the National Institute of Justice at the

WCC facility operated on its behalf at Taft, California (National Institute of Justice 1999).

Logan's approach, though not methodologically flawless, is a very useful model—capable of improvement, strongly quantitative, and possessing the crucial characteristic of being able to be replicated in disparate correctional facilities. It stops short, however, of addressing the most difficult and methodologically hazardous research question: are the outcomes, in particular recidivism rates, better or worse for prisoners who serve their sentences in private prisons?

B. Recidivism Research in Florida

The Florida Correctional Privatization Commission is required to submit an annual report to the legislature that includes "a comparison of recidivism rates for inmates of private correctional facilities to the recidivism rates for inmates of comparable facilities managed by the department" (Fla. Stat. 957.03(4)(c) [1993]). Lanza-Kaduce, Parker, and Thomas (1999) carried out such research on behalf of the commission in relation to matched samples of prisoners released from private and public prisons in the four-month period June 1, 1996–September 30, 1996. The researchers' methodology addresses the problems in controlling key variables that would affect the sample—security classification of inmates, offense, race, prior record, and age. They rigorously deal with competing definitions of what constitutes recidivism. They also differentiate between degrees of seriousness of recidivism, based both on the administrative/legal sanction imposed and, where recidivism consists of reoffending, the nature of the subsequent offense. They readily concede that a twelve-month follow-up period is not ideal, but for this pilot study this short period was dictated by the exigencies of finding a sample from the private prisons, which had only been in operation since mid-1995, and finishing the report in time for it to be tabled as part of the commission's 1997 report.

The one methodological issue they were not able to address satisfactorily relates to whether the prison sentence was served wholly in the public or wholly in the private prison.[21] The concept of "prison of release" does not tell one enough about the correctional inputs relevant

[21] This problem is explicitly acknowledged in the in-house version that is summarized on Web site http://web.crim.ufl.edu/pcp. However, it is handled inadequately, viz., "If inmates were transferred between public and private institutions during the [follow-up] year, the last institution at the time of release was used to determine whether the release was from a private or public facility" (p. 7).

to the inmates' prison experiences. Ideally, the matching samples should be between inmates who have served their whole sentence in a public prison and those who have served it in a private prison or, at the very least, a finite and unbroken period of, say, twelve months immediately preceding release, including the whole of the period during which they are in receipt of correctional programs. Otherwise, there may be "contamination" effects of one prison regime upon the other.

Nevertheless, their conclusions are striking. By all measures except technical breach, public prison releasees were significantly more likely to recidivate, and their recidivism events were significantly more serious in terms of public safety. Time to failure was approximately the same, however. They conclude as follows:

> Our judgment is that recidivism results probably reflect substantive differences between public and private operations in Florida. Whether the lower recidivism among the group of private prison releasees relates to better programming in the privatized facilities needs to be studied in greater depth. . . . The statutory and contractual requirement for private firms doing business in Florida to involve inmates in programming specifically designed to reduce recidivism may have encouraged them to place inmates into appropriate programming. Certainly, our interviews with programming and classification staff at the private facilities indicated their awareness of the importance of this issue. . . . We [also] wonder whether the specific programs may be less important to recidivism than the organizational context within which they are offered. An institution with leadership and an internal culture that supports something other than "warehousing," that effectively coordinates worthwhile programs with other institutional demands, and that mandates involvement of inmates in programming is likely to create an environment that is conducive to attitudinal and behavioral change. (Lanza-Kaduce, Parker, and Thomas 1999, pp. 42–43)

It is to be hoped that this research will be followed up in Florida or elsewhere, with the remaining methodological flaws able to be addressed. It is precisely the kind of fundamental question that needs to be asked about privatization. It is also the kind of question that public prison systems have often been coy about researching and answering in relation to their own operations.

C. Staff Attitudes

In a closed institutional structure, it is extremely difficult to maintain a culture that stresses programs and prisoner development rather than custody and control. There are myriad reasons for this, all interacting with each other: low recruitment qualifications of officers; inadequate training resources; poor pay; senior management's poor appreciation of the role of the custodial officer, with consequential indifference or hostility to the workplace situation; thus, the use of union power to change or control conditions in the workplace, and so on. It can, and frequently does, become a downward spiral, with uniformed staff ultimately coming to stand in the way of the official correctional objectives. This is particularly so in the public sector by dint of, if nothing else, its size and longevity. There is almost endless documentation of this: see, for example, Vinson (1982), DiIulio (1987), Kauffmann (1988), Woolf and Tumim (1991), and Harding (1997, pp. 134–36).

In the United Kingdom, reports of the chief inspector of prisons are an objective and valuable resource for documenting staff attitudes. The 1999 Wandsworth Prison report (Ramsbotham 1999*c*) is notable not only because it is so critical but also because it is so representative.[22] Wandsworth is a 1,300-bed medium- and maximum-security public sector prison located in South London. Making an unannounced inspection, the chief inspector found a "pervasive culture of fear," with up to 14 percent of inmates having recently been assaulted by staff. As for the "filthy segregation unit, never have I had to write about anything so inhuman and reprehensible as the way that prisoners, some of them seeking protection and some of them mentally disordered, were treated" (Ramsbotham 1999*c*, p. 8). These things grew naturally out of the prison culture:

> In no prison that I have inspected has the "culture" . . . caused me greater concern. . . . This is not just because of the grossly unsatisfactory nature of the regimes for many different types of prisoner . . . but because of the insidious nature of what "the Wandsworth way"—as the local "culture" was described to us—represents in terms of the attitude of too many members of the staff to prisoners and their duty of care for them. . . . Many staff do not seem to think that the phrase, "look after prisoners with

[22] That report refers at various points to four other recent inspections—Brixton, Feltham, Wormwood Scrubs, and Holloway—that were no better. Twenty-six prison officers at Wormwood were charged with assaults upon prisoners in June 1999.

> humanity," enshrined at the heart of the Prison Service Statement of Purpose, applies to them, and they continue to apply an agenda which, if it ever was authorized, is not only long out of date but far removed from current and acceptable practice. (Ramsbotham 1999*c*, pp. 6–7)

In his 1997–98 annual report, the chief inspector had alluded in more general terms to staff attitudes: "Some staff exhibit a cynicism for positive programs with prisoners, oppose the need to change long-established work patterns, and continually challenge the authority of the Prison Service. This is more readily apparent, although not exclusively so, amongst older than newer staff whose instincts appear more akin to those demonstrated by staff at private prisons" (Ramsbotham 1997/98, p. 24).

Carter (2001) has picked up on this last comment in conducting a pilot study of staff and prisoner attitudes at a private prison, Altcourse, situated in the north of England (the prison that subsequently was so highly lauded by the chief inspector of prisons). His detailed observations, based on semistructured interviews with staff and inmates, are made against the backdrop of the following hypothesis: "That the new operators of the private sector are contractually obligated in the delivery of the 'secondary roles of imprisonment' [care and well-being] and they may not have the same unbalanced, one-dimensional attitude and historical overemphasis towards security and control [the primary role of imprisonment] as is evident in the public sector." His conclusion is that attitudes, and the whole culture and ethos of the private prison environment, are tangibly different and that this is in a sense "related to the fact that none of [the staff] carry any of the institutional or historical baggage possessed by many of the staff in the public sector."

This is only a pilot study. But it is exactly the sort of research that should be carried out as a matter of course in both the private and public sectors, on an ongoing basis. It is likely, however, that the currently preferable culture of the private sector would tend to come back toward the public sector culture, unless management explicitly support and nurture it. The contractual obligations and the other mechanisms of accountability should act as a catalyst for them to do this.

Carter's observations tie in with two other structural factors. First, the private sector mostly goes out of its way to avoid hiring uniformed or custodial staff with extensive public sector experience. (They are, however, adept at "poaching" the cream of public sector senior management.) Second, their recruitment policies are for the most part gender blind, with the consequence that from the outset the culture develops in a way that does not simply reflect male working-class values. It is difficult to displace those values, once they are established, by affirmative action recruitment policies. Coming into a male culture, female officers tend to survive and prosper by taking on many of those male values.

In summary, the speculation by Lanza-Kaduce that improved recidivism rates in the private sector may have as much to do with the private sector prisons providing a more supportive environment ties in with the observations about staff attitudes. Each of these matters is central to further research and evaluation of private sector prisons.

VIII. Competition and Cross-Fertilization: System-Wide Improvement?

If it could conclusively be shown that the private sector were doing a better job—however that be defined—than the public sector, this by itself would be a sufficient justification for the complexities and controversies involved in privatization. But only just. If we are left with, in effect, two prison systems—a numerically marginal but new and vibrant private sector and a numerically dominant but run-down and demoralized public sector—we have made some, but not much, progress. The justification for privatization ultimately lies in its system-wide impact. In other words, does the public sector change and improve as a consequence of and in response to private sector performance and ideas?

In seeking to answer this question, one should identify two separate but closely interwoven ideas: competition and cross-fertilization. A competitive response may be a decision to do something simply because the competitor does it, to keep up—but without any precise analysis of whether it is a good thing in itself. Cross-fertilization has a connotation of appreciative learning—adopting a new practice because its benefits are apparent. It is not always clear whether a particular change is attributable to one rather than the other; indeed, motives are usually mixed. For the sake of simplicity, the two notions will hereafter be rolled into the single one of cross-fertilization.

One would expect cross-fertilization to start as a one-way process—from the private to the public sector. This is because the public sector practices and standards are the given from which, by definition, it is desired to progress. This model can be called stage 1 cross-fertilization. But a mature model of cross-fertilization would have the private sector likewise responding to initiatives within the public sector, as the latter began to set new standards of its own—stage 2 cross-fertilization. There is, in fact, a paradox of successful cross-fertilization—that, as it occurs, regimes will progressively come to resemble each other. The source of innovation will be harder to pinpoint, and the incentive to innovate may fade away.

A. Examples of Cross-Fertilization

What evidence is there of cross-fertilization? Harding (1997, pp. 134–49) referred to several examples. In the United States, the state of Louisiana required ACA accreditation by its private prison but not for its own public sector prisons. This requirement soon worked its way into the fabric of the public sector system. The mechanism was the individual initiative of a newly appointed director of the state department of corrections, exposed to the issue by his strong professional links with the manager of the private prison.

In the United Kingdom, an example related to the standards required of the private operators of a new remand prison, The Wolds. The mandated minimum standards far exceeded in every component those expected of comparable public prisons: for example, out-of-cell hours, visits, access to showers, out-of-doors time, telephone usage, and so on. While The Wolds was starting up, the Prison Service was developing its new Model Regime for Local Prisons and Remand Centers. The standards approximated those earlier required of the private prison operator—a quantum leap. Commenting on this, Bottomley et al. (1996, p. 3) state that "the threat of market testing [i.e., opening up more remand prisons to private sector operation] . . . acted as a powerful spur to innovation."

In Queensland (Australia) current research being carried out by Harding and Rynne has identified clear cross-fertilization effects with regard to health care, where the standards the public sector required of the private sector were initially far higher than it required of itself. Within a few years the public sector found it necessary to equal those standards. The international flavor of cross-fertilization emerged here, with ACM (aware, doubtless, of United States developments through its links with WCC) adopting the American Medical Association's custodial health manual as a guide in a jurisdiction that hitherto had no manual of its own.

The same research project has also identified substantial cross-fertilization in the area of prisoner programs. Borallon Prison (CCA) avowedly set out to integrate programs into the daily lives of inmates through a unit management approach. The cognitive programs directed at addressing offending behavior were different from anything else found in the public system, and the vocational and educational programs were innovative in their links to outside certifying bodies. These fresh approaches were picked up by the public sector quite quickly.

In the United Kingdom, the Prison Service has commenced the practice of developing Service Delivery Agreements (SDAs) for each public sector prison. An SDA is akin to a private sector contract; it sets out standards and expectations at the level of the individual prison. While the rate of implementation of this development is a little disappointing, it is nevertheless inexorably occurring. The conceptual complication is how to bring financial sanctions to bear for poor performance, for such sanctions are absolutely central to ensuring private sector performance. But how can the state impose a penalty upon itself, without pushing standards down even further during the period the penalty is in effect?

The U.K. chief inspector of prisons has made it a regular practice to log examples of good practice at private prisons. However, he has been disappointed at being unable to see "any direct evidence that the lessons of good practice learned from these private establishments are being applied to the management of establishments run in the Public Service" (Ramsbotham 1996, preface).

The best-documented account of cross-fertilization relates to Junee Prison (Bowery 1999). This report refers to "a substantial exchange of ideas and information between the Department and the ACM staff at Junee." Reference is made to six departmental initiatives "aimed at ensuring inmates receive a consistent level of treatment and access to programs and services" being extended to Junee (stage 2 cross-fertilization). Likewise, four private operator initiatives "were evaluated by departmental staff with regard to their suitability for incorporation into departmental programs" (stage 1 cross-fertilization). Bowery (1999, pp. 79–80) concludes: "Thus, by the end of year four [i.e., mid-1997] opportunities for innovation in inmate management and the provision of programs and services were limited. The only initiative introduced by ACM . . . that remained unique to Junee was the Integration program. . . . Over time a strong working relationship has developed between ACM and the Department, with Junee staff attending some departmental training courses, visiting departmental centers and sharing information with their colleagues in departmental centers." Junee thus epitomizes the paradox of successful cross-fertilization—that regimes progressively become more similar than dissimilar to each other.

B. The Mechanics of Cross-Fertilization

Cross-fertilization does not occur through some sort of organizational osmosis. Someone has to facilitate it. Quite often this will be a committed individual, as in the Louisiana example; sometimes from executive level, as with the U.K. Standards for Remand Centers; sometimes from middle management, as with programs at Borallon. Movement of staff between systems is also important, as they take the seeds of good ideas back and forth. Ramsbotham (1997, preface) has identified a greater willingness of the private sector to pick up good ideas from the public sector (stage 2 cross-fertilization) than vice versa and perhaps that is because many private prison wardens or governors are refugees from the public sector.

The clearest indication that cross-fertilization has occurred—as opposed to recognizing precisely how it occurred—should be found in market testing. This, it will be recalled, means the bidding of the public sector against the private in a genuine contest. This is different from the benchmarking that is required in many jurisdictions as to costs. Four examples have been referred to—Woodford (Queensland), Manchester (U.K.), Buckley Hall (U.K.), and Doncaster (U.K.)—and it will be recalled that outcomes in each of them have for various reasons been treated with some cynicism. But the principle is clear: if the public sector can beat the private sector in a fair bidding contest, it must have learned well from the experience of others. However, market testing does not occur in the most mature market, the United States, while in Australia and the United Kingdom, a transparent process that commands the confidence of all parties has not yet been developed.

To date, then, there has not really been any sustained or systematic attempt in privatization states to build cross-fertilization into the management structures of the prison system as a whole. Cross-sectoral management conferences, though regular in a few jurisdictions, are generally infrequent; mutual in-service training is uncommon. Academic conferences tend to divide into the "anti" and "pro" privatization camps, and this is reflected in the tone of much of the literature.

Industry conferences likewise tend to focus on one side or the other of the prison scene. And market testing still lacks some credibility.

Cross-fertilization is a first-order question in the privatization debate. In some antiprivatization circles, there is skepticism as to whether it is a topic worth pursuing at all. For example, Ward (1999, p. 126) has stated "Harding [argues] that evaluation studies have been asking the wrong question: what we should ask is not whether private prisons are superior to public ones but whether their presence tends to improve the prison system as a whole. There may seem to be a 'heads I win, tails you lose' quality to this argument (if public prisons turn out to do better than private ones, that just proves that competition is good for them!)."

The National Institute of Justice (1999) has recently committed substantial funds to addressing this very question. Congress has directed the FBOP to undertake a prison privatization demonstration project, which will take the form of research and evaluation of the WCC-run Taft Correctional Institution. Cost and performance are to be addressed, and "of special interest is the development of models explicating specifically *how and why*—and not just *whether*—privatization conveys advantages" (1999, p. 1).

In summary, there is evidence that cross-fertilization occurs, but the public and private sectors are still not yet sufficiently at ease with each other for this long-term public interest objective to be realized systematically rather than fortuitously. Further research may point the way.

C. Barriers against Cross-Fertilization

Institutional resistance to cross-fertilization can be quite stubborn, however. Public sector officials, in monitoring private prisons, may not only be captured but, equally, be positively antagonistic. Outstanding performance by an alternative service provider may be threatening to the principal provider, highlighting its own inferior performance. There is also the standard bureaucratic factor of turf wars—what Aldrich (1979) calls domain consensus/dissensus. Of course, there may also be more legitimate reasons, such as to ensure uniformity of standards and equality for prisoners.

Two examples will suffice. In the United Kingdom, head office resistance arose when the Prison Service won a market-testing contest to operate Manchester prison. This involved a service delivery agreement specifying programs and a ring-fenced budget, that is, one quarantined from general Prison Service savings or reductions. However, almost immediately this budgetary arrangement was canceled; Manchester was to be treated just like any other prison and brought within the overall control of the area manager. The opportunity for innovation was thus strangled at birth and with it any chance for cross-fertilization with other parts of the public sector.

In Queensland, Borallon had commenced operations with fresh programs that were picked up by the public prisons. But from 1995 onward it was decided that all programs, even at the private prisons, must be approved by head office personnel, and this soon shaded into a situation where all programs were developed centrally. Innovation has now dried up; there is no cross-fertilization in this area of activity because everything is the same.

D. *Summary*

The whole discussion of cross-fertilization must be seen against the backdrop of current organizational and political theory, in particular the notion of reinventing government (Osborne and Gaebler 1992) and the National Performance Review (1997). Claims that public administration is shifting "from the classical bureaucratic model . . . to a post-bureaucratic paradigm characterized by risk-taking, innovation, empowerment, customer orientation, teamwork, quality, and continuous improvement" (Sims 1998, p. 9) would not yet seem to have been borne out fully in the context of corrections. There is change in the wind, however, and a key measure will be the extent of cross-fertilization between the private and public sectors.

IX. The Future of Privatization

In 1997 blue-sky expansion of existing markets, particularly in the United States, seemed plausible. Thomas, Bolinger, and Badalamenti (1997, p. xxiii) forecast that there would be 276,000 private prison beds occupied or procured in the United States by the end of 2001. However, the exponential growth pattern has flattened out; a figure of 150,000 or so now seems more realistic. In the other main established markets, Australia and the United Kingdom, expansion is likely to be steady but fairly slow, and there are some countercurrents that could hold it back. These are market testing in the United Kingdom and political ideology in Australia, where Labor Party governments have recently been elected in the two largest privatization states.[23]

[23] Labor governments often feel obliged, as part of their election campaigns and upon taking power, to make antiprivatization noises—"we will take private prisons back into the public sector"—because of their trade union links. In Australia and the United King-

Reassessment of privatization is now occurring in the mature markets. Opposition among community groups is more vociferous and far better organized and sophisticated than in the early days. Examples include the following: refusal of planning permission to Youth Services International to build two detention centers in upper New York state (1997); withdrawal by the county commissioners of permission to build a private prison in Nicholas County, South Carolina, after sustained and acrimonious community debate (1997); preemptive objections by community groups in Fallsburg, New York, to the possibility that CCA might seek planning permission for a prison on land it was discovered it had recently purchased (1998); and litigation in Alaska by seven members on behalf of the community to try to prevent a private prison from being built on the site of Fort Greely, a military base scheduled for closure (1999). Extra sophistication is found in the alliances that have sprung up (between middle-class communities and labor unions), the sorts of arguments made (that the particular project has stock market risks), and the means adopted (not just the usual lobbying and small demonstrations but also the opening of Web sites and resort to litigation). These sorts of action add to the ongoing challenges that civil liberties and similar groups (e.g., ACLU), as well as academic bodies, have made against privatization from the outset.

Similar trends have occurred in Australia, and there has from the beginning been a well-informed and vocal opposition in the United Kingdom. However, general community concern there seems to have abated somewhat.

There has also been much more action by labor unions. For example, Corrections USA (CUSA), a coalition of U.S. and Canadian prison officer labor unions, picketed CCA at its corporate headquarters in Nashville, Tennessee, in October 1998, and another coalition known as the Corrections and Criminal Justice Coalition claims to have 200,000 correctional officers supporting its antiprivatization campaign. Another union, the Florida Police Benevolent Union, which despite its

---

dom, public sector prison officer unions are very strong. The U.K. government, which was elected in 1997, made these noises but predictably (Harding 1997, p. 78) resiled from them. The cost of buying out contracts, particularly DCFM, was out of all proportion to the political costs of diverting infrastructure expenditure from other social needs. In Victoria, where a Labor government was elected in October 1999, the incoming minister has made the familiar statements but is likely to find himself politically inhibited exactly as the U.K. Labor government has been. However, the November 1999 incoming Labor government in New Zealand seems likely to terminate the procurement process in relation to all but one of the five adult and seven juvenile private correctional institutions to which its predecessor had been committed.

name represents correctional officers in that state, led the campaign against Charles Thomas of the University of Florida that finally resulted in his deciding to resign from the university (Geis, Mobley, and Shichor 1999). Thomas was regarded as the leading academic supporter of privatization in the United States, so the union campaign to tar him with the conflict of interest brush was symbolically a campaign to delegitimize privatization.

The increase in overt opposition is probably also associated with the fact that the private sector has now had its visible failures, some of them quite dramatic. Harding (1997, p. 156) anticipated that such failures might be difficult for the private sector to absorb:

> What can be predicted . . . is that gross or system-wide repetitive failures by the private sector will cause the debate to be re-located and perhaps to commence all over again. If the chain of private prisons in the UK were ransacked and torched, as was a chain of public prisons in 1990 leading to the Woolf inquiry, it is likely that any review would examine not only what went wrong, not only what to change for the future, but also whether the private sector should be permitted to continue . . . at all. In that regard, the private sector will always be more vulnerable than the public sector whose malfeasance, however negligent or brutal or incompetent, will never lead to its having its prisons taken away from it.

The debate may have started all over again; at the very least the embers have been reignited. While the debate continues, industry growth is likely to be steady at best, rather than spectacular, though the privatization that has so far occurred is most unlikely, particularly in the United States, to be wound back.

As for new markets, at least twenty countries have explored the possibility of privatization, some with greater commitment than others. Bearing in mind the factors associated with privatization—burgeoning prisoner populations, overcrowding, higher state priorities for limited infrastructure outlays, concern about recurrent costs, difficulties with labor unions, and a view of the state as being first and foremost a service provider—it might be thought that Asia, Thailand, the Philippines, and Malaysia could be the most likely to go down that track (and Japan, the People's Republic of China, Hong Kong, Singapore, and, despite its flirtation, South Korea the least likely). The former states of the old Soviet empire, such as Latvia and Serbia, may retain enough of a collectivist view of state responsibilities to hesitate. However, Central and South America seem more likely to look to privatization. Some expansion into new markets over the next five to ten years can be anticipated, therefore, but it is likely to be fragmented.

A. International Standards

As early as 1989, with prison privatization still novel even in the United States, the Cuban representative on the United Nations Commission on Human Rights (Sub-Commission on Prevention of Discrimination and Protection of Minorities) succeeded in setting under way an inquiry into prison privatization. A principal agenda item he wished to have explored was the legality of prison privatization under international human rights law. Assuming it was not illegal, he then sought a further inquiry into the extent of lawful privatization (the administration/allocation of punishment debate coming in through the back door), the development of United Nations standards for private prisons, and identification of an appropriate way for the United Nations to monitor private prisons.

No funds were available for this, so the subcommission sought the appointment of a special rapporteur by the principal commission—in United Nations practice the way of obtaining funding and status for the project. The first such request in 1993 was unsuccessful, and an attempt to reopen the matter in August 1999 was blocked by the United States delegate.

Another United Nations standard that has been invoked is that of the International Labor Organization (ILO) relating to forced labor. An exemption exists for prison labor that is supervised by a public authority. The peak trade union body in Australia took a case to the ILO in which it was argued that labor in private prisons breaches that convention. In a 1999 provisional ruling, the ILO found that the prohibition on the use of forced prison labor for the benefit of private firms was absolute and extended to work done within private prisons even if its nature, pay rates, and conditions were indistinguishable from or better than work done in public prisons in the same state. Such rulings do not have the force of domestic law in Australia, and no consequences have so far followed. These tentative beginnings suggest that privatization may increasingly have to confront challenges based on international law and practice, not merely ones based on state and constitutional law.

B. Research

Prison privatization is a rich field for research. Foremost should be outcomes research, of the sort that Lanza-Kaduce, Parker, and Thomas (1999) piloted in Florida. Cross-fertilization is no less important; the FBOP has picked up this point in its demonstration project at the Taft Correctional Center, California, following Australian leads. Integrated with this is the quality of confinement itself, building upon Logan's (1992) model. None of this can be done without research into staff and inmate attitudes, their interactions, and the bearing of these matters upon correctional programs and outcomes.

Detailed analysis of the effectiveness of accountability mechanisms is also crucial: How do monitors perform? Are they captured on the job or are they antagonistic? Is the level of intimidation and assault, suicide, and self-harm a function of public/private management regimes and the manner in which control mechanisms are exercised? What about the impact of different technologies on order, prisoner movements, drug availability and use within prisons, and general health matters?

The list goes on. Of course, it also contains the indispensable item of costs. However, the point that should have emerged is that this agenda is one for prison research generally, not merely for private prison research. The advent of private prisons has thrown such matters into higher relief and provided that crucial research tool, a good comparator. And, because of the controversial nature of privatization, there is also a stronger incentive than before. Perhaps that may turn out to be the most important contribution of privatization—that it becomes a catalyst for the kind of research that good penology and responsible penal administration must do better than in the past.

X. Conclusion

Private prisons are here to stay. But they will not displace public prisons or even, in terms of available accommodation, become a serious competitor. They have some tangible advantages and benefits but also pose some serious political and humanitarian risks. These risks tend to become greater as the motive of cost reduction becomes increasingly predominant. It is for this reason that, of the three mature private prison jurisdictions, the United States experience is the one that must continue to be scrutinized most closely.

The regulatory systems and accountability mechanisms that govern their operations must ensure that private prisons meet acceptable state and community standards. Governments, when privatizing activities, are often tempted to reduce regulatory resources at the same time. With prisons, above all, this must not be done. In a context where a primary objective has been cost reduction, this is a particular hazard. The cost of effective and responsive regulation is part of the price of privatization.

Self-contained and inward-looking public sector prison systems around the world have in many aspects become degraded and demoralized. There is evidence that, as long as they are properly regulated and publicly accountable, private prisons can stimulate improvement of the total prison system. Modern societies have made huge investments in punishment as a means of crime control and prevention. If private prisons are part of a process that gives society greater value for money, consistent with decent and equitable standards and improved outcomes, they will certainly have justified their existence. Discussion about the proper nature and extent of imprisonment must continue, and nothing in the recent history of prison privatization distorts or contaminates the terms of that debate.

REFERENCES

Adams, R. 1994. *Prison Riots in Britain and the USA.* London: Macmillan.

Aldrich, H. 1979. *Organizations and Environments.* Englewood Cliffs, N.J.: Prentice Hall.

American Correctional Association. 1990. *Standards for Adult Correctional Institutions.* 3d ed. Washington, D.C.: American Correctional Association.

American Friends Service Committee. 1971. *Struggle for Justice: A Report on Crime and Punishment in America.* New York: Hill & Wang.

Arax, M., and M. Gladston. 1998. "State Whitewashed Fatal Brutality and Mismanagement at Corcoran." *Los Angeles Times* (July 5).

Auditor General Victoria. 1999. *Victoria's Prison System: Community Protection and Prisoner Welfare.* http://www.audit.vic.govt.au/sr60/ags6OOl:html.

Austin, J., and G. Coventry. 2000. "The Private Prison Binge." *Current Issues in Criminal Justice* 11(2):177–201.

Biles, D., and V. Dalton. 1999. "Deaths in Private Prisons 1990–99: A Comparative Study." *Trends and Issues in Crime and Justice* no. 120. Canberra: Australian Institute of Criminology.

Bottomley, A. K., A. James, E. Clare, and A. Liebling. 1996. *Wolds Remand Prison: An Evaluation.* Research Findings no. 32. London: Home Office Research and Statistics Unit.

Bowery, M. 1999. *Private Prisons in New South Wales: Junee—a Four-Year Review.* Research Publication no. 42. Sydney: N.S.W. Department of Corrective Services.

Bronstein, A. J., and J. Gainsborough. 1996. "Prison Litigation: Past, Present and Future." *Overcrowded Times* 7(3):1, 15–20.

Carter, K. 2001. "An Infusion of Change: New Staff in the Private Sector" *Current Issues in Criminal Justice* (forthcoming).

Christie, N. 1993. *Crime Control as Industry: Towards GULAGS Western Style?* London: Routledge.

Clark, J. L. 1998. *Report to the Attorney General: Inspection and Review of the Security Procedures, Management Practices and Work Oportunities of the Northeast Ohio Correctional Center.* Washington, D.C.: U.S. Department of Justice.

Cross, R. 1971. *Punishment, Prison and the Public: An Assessment of Penal Reform in Twentieth-Century England by an Armchair Penologist.* London: Stevens & Sons.

Davis, A. Y., R. Magee, the Soledad brothers, and other political prisoners. 1971. *If They Come in the Morning: Voices of Resistance.* London: Orbach & Chambers.

DiIulio J. J. 1987. *Governing Prisons: A Comparative Study of Correctional Management.* New York: Free Press.

———. 1991. *No Escape.* New York: Basic Books.

Dinitz, S. 1981. "Are Safe and Humane Prisons Possible?" *Australian and New Zealand Journal of Criminology* 14(3):13–19.

Freiberg, A. 2000. "Commercial Confidentiality and Public Accountability for the Provision of Correctional Services." *Current Issues in Criminal Justice* 11(2):119–34.

Geis, G., A. Mobley, and D. Shichor. 1999. "Private Prisons, Criminological Research and Conflict of Interest: A Case Study." *Crime and Delinquency* 45(3):358–71.

Grabosky, P., and J. Braithwaite. 1986. *Of Manners Gentle: Enforcement Strategies of Australian Business Regulatory Agencies.* Melbourne: Oxford University Press.

Harding, R. W. 1992. "Private Prisons in Australia." *Trends and Issues in Crime and Justice* no. 36, pp. 1–8. Canberra: Australian Institute of Criminology.

———. 1997. *Private Prisons and Public Accountability.* Milton Keynes, U.K.: Open University Press; Brunswick, N.J.: Transaction Publishers.

———. 1998*a*. "Private Prisons." In *The Handbook of Crime and Punishment,* edited by Michael Tonry. New York: Oxford University Press.

———. 1998*b*. "Private Prisons in Australia: The Second Phase." *Trends and Issues in Crime and Justice* no. 84, pp. 1–6. Canberra: Australian Institute of Criminology.

———. 1999. "Prisons Are the Problem: A Re-examination of Aboriginal and Non-Aboriginal Deaths in Custody." *Australian and New Zealand Journal of Criminology* 32(2):108–23.

———. 2000. "Privatising Justice Support and Prison Administration Functions: A Western Australian Exemplar of Effective Regulation and Accountability." *University of Western Australia Law Review* 29(2):233–50.

H.M. Prison Service. 1997. *Review of Comparative Costs and Performance of Pri-*

vately and Publicly Operated Prisons. Prison Service Research Report Series. London: Home Office.

———. 1998*a*. "Review of Private Financing of New Prison Procurement." Unpublished manuscript. London: Home Office.

———. 1998*b*. "Public and Private Prison Management: Considerations on Returning Privately Managed Prisons to the Public Sector." Unpublished manuscript. London: Home Office.

Jackson, G. 1971. *Soledad Brother: The Prison Letters of George Jackson.* London: Cape.

James, A. L., A. K. Bottomley, A. Liebling, and E. Clare. 1997. *Privatizing Prisons: Rhetoric and Reality.* London: Sage.

Johnston, E. 1991. *Final Report of the Royal Commission into Aboriginal Deaths in Custody.* Canberra: Australian Government Publishing Service.

Jung, H. 1990. "Introductory Report." In *Privatisation of Crime Control,* edited by H. Jung. Collected Studies in Criminological Research, vol. 27. Strasbourg: Council of Europe.

Kauffmann, K. 1988. *Prison Officers and Their World.* Cambridge, Mass.: Harvard University Press.

Kennedy, J. J. 1988. *Final Report of the Commission of Review into Corrective Services in Queensland.* Brisbane: Government of Queensland.

Keve, P. 1996. *Measuring Excellence: The History of Correctional Standards and Accreditation.* Washington, D.C.: American Correctional Association.

Lanza-Kaduce, L., K. Parker, and C. W. Thomas. 1999. "A Comparative Recidivism Analysis of Releasees from Private and Public Prisons." *Crime and Delinquency* 45(1):28–47.

Logan, C. 1990. *Private Prisons: Cons and Pros.* New York: Oxford University Press.

———. 1992. "Well Kept: Comparing Quality of Confinement in Private and Public Prisons." *Journal of Criminal Law and Criminology* 83(3):577–613.

Martinson, R. 1974. "What Works? Questions and Answers about Prison Reform." *Public Interest* 35:22–54.

McConville, S. 1987. "Aid from Industry? Private Corrections and Prison Overcrowding." In *America's Correctional Crisis,* edited by S. D. Goffredson and S. M. Conville. Westport, Conn.: Greenwood.

McDonald, D. C. 1992. "Private Penal Institutions." In *Crime and Justice: An Annual Review of Research,* vol. 16, edited by Michael Tonry. Chicago: University of Chicago Press.

McDonald, D. C., E. Fournier, M. Russell-Einhorn, and S. Crawford. 1998. *Private Prisons in the United States: An Assessment of Current Practice.* Cambridge, Mass.: Abt Associates, Inc.

McGivern, J. 1988. *Report of the Enquiry into the Causes of the Riot, Fire and Hostage-Taking at Fremantle Prison on the 4th/5th January 1988.* Perth: W. A. Department of Corrective Services.

Mitford, J. 1971. *The American Prison Business.* New York: Penguin.

Moyle, P. 2000. "Separating the Allocation of Punishment from Its Administration: Theoretical and Empirical Observations." *Current Issues in Criminal Justice* 11(2):153–74.

Murray, B. L. 1989. *Report on the Behaviour of the Office of Corrections.* Melbourne: Government of Victoria.

Nagle, J. 1978. *Report of an Inquiry into the New South Wales Department of Corrective Services.* Sydney: State Government Printer.

National Audit Office. 1997. *H.M. Prison Service: The PF1 Contracts for Bridgend and Fazarkely Prisons.* London: Stationery Office.

National Institute of Justice. 1999. *Solicitation: The Examination of Privatization in the Federal Bureau of Prisons.* Washington, D.C.: U.S. Department of Justice, Office of Justice Programs.

National Performance Review. 1997. *Vice President Gore's National Performance Review Accomplishments, 1993–1997.* Washington, D.C.: National Performance Review, http://www.npr.gov.accompli/index.html.

Nelson, J. 1998. "Comparing Public and Private Prison Costs." Appendix 1 of McDonald et al. Cambridge, Mass.: Abt Associates, Inc.

O'Hare, N. 1990. "The Privatization of Imprisonment: A Managerial Perspective." In *Private Prisons and the Public Interest,* edited by D. C. McDonald. New Brunswick, N.J.: Rutgers University Press.

Osborne, D., and T. Gaebler. 1992. *Re-inventing Government: How the Entrepreneurial Spirit Is Transforming the Public Sector.* Reading, Mass.: Addison-Wesley.

Paulus, P. 1988. *Prison Crowding: A Psychological Perspective.* New York: Springer.

Peach, F. 1999. *Corrections in the Balance: A Review of Corrective Services in Queensland.* Brisbane: Queensland Government Publications.

Pratt, T. C., and J. Maahs. 1999. "Are Private Prisons More Cost-Effective than Public Prisons? A Meta-Analysis of Evaluation Research Studies." *Crime and Delinquency* 45(3):358–71.

Prison Privatisation Report International. Various years. London: Prison Reform Trust.

Queensland Legislative Assembly. 1996. *Construction of the New Woodford Correctional Centre.* Public Works Committee Report no. 34. Brisbane: Queensland Parliament.

Ramsbotham, D. 1995/96. *Annual Report of H.M. Chief Inspector of Prisons.* London: Home Office.

———. 1996. *Report of H.M. Chief Inspector of Prisons: H.M. Prison and Young Offender Institution Doncaster.* London: Home Office.

———. 1997. *H.M. Chief Inspector of Prisons: H.M.P. Buckley Hall.* London: Home Office.

———. 1997/98. *Annual Report of Her Majesty's Chief Inspector of Prisons for England and Wales, 1997-1998.* London: Home Office.

———. 1998. *H.M. Chief Inspector of Prisons: H.M. Prison Blakenhurst.* London: Home Office.

———. 1999*a*. Suicide Is Everyone's Concern: A Thematic Review by Her Majesty's Chief Inspector of Prisons. London: Home Office.

———. 1999*b*. *H.M. Chief Inspector of Prisons: H.M.P. Parc.* London: Home Office.

———. 1999c. *Her Majesty's Chief Inspector of Prisons: H.M. Prison Wandsworth.* London: Home Office.

———. 2000. *Her Majesty's Chief Inspector of Prisons: H.M. Prison Altcourse.* London: Home Office.

Richardson, G. 1994. "From Rights to Expectations." In *Prisons after Woolf: Reform through Riot,* edited by E. Player and M. Jenkins. London: Routledge.

Rosenthal, U., and B. Hoogenboom. 1990. "Some Fundamental Questions on Privatisation and Commercialisation of Crime Control." In *Privatisation of Crime Control,* edited by H. Jung. Collected Studies in Criminological Research, vol. 27. Strasbourg: Council of Europe.

Ryan, M. 1996. "Prison Privatization in Europe." *Overcrowded Times* 7(2):1, 16–18.

———. 1998. "Review of Harding, R., Private Prisons and Public Accountability." *British Journal of Criminology* 38:324–26.

Shaw, S. 1992. "The Short History of Prison Privatisation." *Prison Service Journal* 87:30–32.

Shichor, D. 1995. *Punishment for Profit: Private Prisons/Public Concerns.* Thousand Oaks, Calif.: Sage.

Sims, R. R. 1998. "Accountability and Change Drivers in the Public Sector." In *Accountability and Radical Change in Public Organizations,* edited by R. R. Sims. Westport, Conn.: Quorum Books.

Smith, L. E., D. Indermaur, and S. Boddis. 1999. *Report of the Inquiry into the Incident at Casuarina Prison on 25 December 1998.* Perth: Ministry of Justice.

Sparks, R. 1994. "Can Prisons Be Legitimate? Penal Politics, Privatization and the Timeliness of an Old Idea." In *Prisons in Context,* edited by R. King and M. Maguire. Oxford: Clarendon.

Thomas, C. W. 1991. "Prisoners' Rights and Correctional Privatization." *Business and Professional Ethics Journal* 10:3–46.

Thomas, C. W., D. Bolinger, and J. L. Badalamenti. 1997. *Private Adult Correctional Facility Census.* 10th ed. Gainesville: Center for Studies in Criminology and Law, University of Florida.

U.S. General Accounting Office. 1996. *Private and Public Prisons: Studies Comparing Operational Costs and/or Quality of Service.* Washington, D.C.: General Accounting Office.

Vinson, T. 1982. *Wilful Obstruction: The Frustration of Prison Reform.* Sydney: Methuen.

Wall Street Journal. 1995. "Prison Lockups" (July 11).

Ward, T. 1999. "Review of Harding, R., Private Prisons and Public Accountability." *Theoretical Criminology* 3(1):125–26.

Weiss, R. 1991. "Attica: 1971–1991. A Commemorative Issue." *Social Justice* 18, no. 3.

Western Australian Government. 1998. *Wooroloo Prison South Project: Request for Proposal.* Perth: Ministry of Justice.

Wicker, T. 1976. *A Time to Die: The Attica Prison Revolt.* London: Bodley Head.

Woodbridge, J. 1999. *Review of Comparative Costs and Performance of Privately and Publicly Operated Prisons.* Home Office Statistical Bulletin Series no. 13/99. London: Home Office.

Woolf, H. K., and S. Tumim. 1991. *Prison Disturbances, April 1990: Report of an Inquiry by the Rt. Hon. Lord Justice Woolf (Parts 1 and 2) and His Honour Judge Stephen Tumim (Part 2).* Cm. 1456. London: Stationery Office.

World Health Organization. 1998. *Consensus Statement on Health Promotion in Prison.* Hague: W.H.O. Regional Office for Europe.

Daniel S. Nagin

Measuring the Economic Benefits of Developmental Prevention Programs

ABSTRACT

Three changes need to be made in economic evaluations of the crime-reductive effects of developmental prevention programs. The changes address three questions concerning the appropriate unit of analysis: Individuals or crimes? Society or government? The crime rate and its social consequences or the criminal event and its consequences for the victim? Concerning the first question, the conclusion that developmental prevention is a cost-effective alternative to criminal sanctions for averting crime events cannot be convincingly sustained. Instead, a more holistic, individual-level approach is necessary that values benefits across multiple domains of individual functioning. Concerning the second question, analyses that have valued more than crime benefits, by and large, measure financial effects on the public treasury. This is too narrow a focus. Finally, estimates of the costs of crime focus on victim consequences rather than on aggregate social consequences. While consequences for victims are important, they do not capture the full effects of crime on society. Estimates of the costs of crime should value tangible consequences to nonvictims and victims alike.

A small but significant literature has emerged that quantifies the economic costs and benefits of crime prevention. The Bureau of Justice Statistics (1997), for example, estimates that the direct monetary cost of operating the justice system—the police, courts, and corrections—exceeds $100 billion, but this is only a small part of the economic impact of crime. Large sums are expended to repair the consequences of victimization and vast investments in money and time are made by

Daniel Nagin is Teresa and H. John Heinz III Professor of Public Policy at the H. John Heinz III School of Public Policy and Management, Carnegie Mellon University. I thank Philip Cook, Steven Durlauf, Mark Kamlet, Lowell Taylor, Michael Tonry, Frank Zimring, and anonymous referees for helpful comments.

0192-3234/2001/0028-0006$02.00

private citizens and businesses to protect themselves from crime. Further, the costs of crime are not limited to actual and potential victims. Criminals themselves commonly lead desperate lives (Irwin 1987; Shover 1996). Gottfredson and Hirschi (1986, p. 218) observe that a criminal career "starts at the bottom and proceeds nowhere." Also, the incarceration of offenders has adverse effects on their families and communities (Hagan and Dinovitzer 1999) that should also be included in a full accounting of the cost of crime.

One segment of the literature relies on estimates by Cohen and colleagues (Cohen 1988; Cohen, Miller, and Rossman 1994; Miller, Cohen, and Wiersma 1996) of the economic cost of various person and property crimes to calculate quantities such as the cost of a high-rate career criminal (Cohen 1998), the average return for each person-year of incarceration (Levitt 1996), the economic return of "right-to-carry" concealed weapon laws (Lott and Mustard 1997; Lott 1998), and the total economic burden of crime (Anderson 1999). Cohen's crime cost estimates, based largely on civil tort awards for criminal acts, are controversial. As a consequence, their application seems to serve only as a rhetorical capstone—either to endorse or oppose some policy position, usually involving incarceration, based on other arguments or evidence.

Another segment focuses on a novel approach for both reducing crime and the cost of operating the criminal justice system—making investments in the cognitive and social development of children early in life toward the end of diverting them from a life of crime. A number of pre-school child development programs have had well-documented and much publicized success in reducing delinquency and even adult criminality among program participants (Karoly et al. 1998; Welsh and Farrington 2000). These studies are of special interest because of their creative application of the methods of economic evaluation to join two seemingly disjointed policy arenas—the health and welfare of children and crime control. This type of economic analysis has the potential to be more than a rhetorical tool in public discussion of crime control policy. By positioning child development policy in the longstanding debate about the effectiveness and justice of punitively oriented crime-control policy, it may change policy in both domains.

This essay focuses on the application of cost-benefit analysis and cost-effectiveness analysis to the evaluation of the social efficacy of early prevention, particularly with regard to crime prevention. Its scope and purpose is different from that of an earlier *Crime and Justice* essay on this topic by Welsh and Farrington (2000). Welsh and

Farrington summarized the findings of all types of studies that examined the monetary costs and benefits of crime prevention programs. These included not only developmental prevention programs but also situational, correctional, and community crime prevention programs. Thus, the scope of studies reviewed was broader than that of this essay. However, this essay moves beyond Welsh and Farrington by probing in more depth the theoretical and practical obstacles to estimating the benefits of developmental prevention programs. In addition, I emphasize the implications that these problems have for crime control policy analysis. Also, with one important exception, I have not critiqued the evaluations of the behavioral effects of the developmental programs that form the basis for the economic assessments that are the subject of this essay. I take the claimed effects as given. My focus is on how best to place an economic value on them.

Economic analysis of early prevention programs is in its infancy. I have tried to recognize this and have avoided criticism about more detailed technical matters of projection and valuation such as what is the "right" interest rate for discounting future benefits or how best to allocate fixed costs or how to forecast benefit streams into the future. Instead, I have tried to focus on broader conceptual issues concerning the overall structure of the analysis. The initial efforts to analyze prevention programs from an economic perspective are likely to set the direction for research to follow primarily because they have been conducted by very able researchers. My objective is to identify aspects of the analytic strategy used to date that in my judgment should not become the de facto standard for conducting future analyses. The exploration of the Pacific Northwest by Lewis and Clark offers an analogy. Their expedition set the stage for settlement of the American West by European Americans. They established that the journey was feasible, but later explorers and settlers used better routes.

This essay recommends three important changes in the way economic evaluations of early prevention studies are conducted. The changes concern three separate questions pertaining to the appropriate unit of analysis: Should the analysis focus on individuals or criminal events? Society or government? and The crime rate and its social consequences or the criminal event and its consequences to the victim? In each case I argue for the first alternative. Concerning the first question, the argument that developmental prevention is a cost-effective alternative to criminal sanctions for averting crime events is attractive, but it cannot be convincingly sustained. Instead, a more holistic, individual-level approach is necessary that values benefits across multiple domains of individual functioning. Concerning the second question, analyses that have valued more than crime benefits have, by and large, measured financial impact on the public treasury. Here again, this is too narrow a focus. Finally, current estimates of the costs of crime focus on victim consequences. While consequences to victims are important, they do not begin to capture the full impact of crime on the functioning of society. Estimates of the cost of crime should value tangible consequences to nonvictims and victims alike.

Here is how this essay is organized. Section I summarizes key findings from developmental criminology and prevention. Section II addresses whether the unit of analysis should be the individual or the criminal event. It begins with an assessment of the limited literature on the costs and benefits and cost-effectiveness of developmental prevention. Section III discusses alternative person-based strategies for benefit estimation. Section IV addresses whether the unit of analysis should be government or society, and Section V addresses whether the unit of analysis should be the crime rate and its social consequences or the criminal event and its consequences to the victim. Section VI summarizes the major points.

I. Key Findings

The emergence of the developmental prevention movement itself reflects the emergence of developmental criminology (LeBlanc and Loeber 1998) as a dominant intellectual force in criminology. Developmental criminology has a rich and varied intellectual tradition that has made important findings about the developmental course of criminal behavior. First, crime is rarely an isolated event in an individual's life. Rather, it is reflective of an ongoing pattern of behavior. Second, persons who are criminal are, in addition, much more likely to be underemployed, abuse drugs and alcohol, and be violent toward their family, friends, and intimates.

The work of Terrie Moffitt and her colleagues—based largely on their analyses of a prospective longitudinal study of an early 1970s birth cohort of more than 1,000 males and females born in Dunedin, New Zealand—nicely illustrates these points. Moffitt (1993, 1997) documents the persistence of conduct problems and antisocial behavior from childhood onward. Other work documents the generality of these conduct problems across domains of behavior. Among the males convicted of a violent crime by age twenty-one, 51 percent also physically abused their partners. For those with no violent convictions their physical abuse rate of partners was smaller by more than a factor of two, 20 percent (Moffitt and Caspi 1999). In another study, Moffitt and colleagues found that rates of violence, whether measured by self-reports or official records, were five to seven times higher for the 40 percent of the cohort diagnosed with some psychiatric disorder (Arseneault et al. 1999). Further analyses revealed that this heightened risk stemmed principally from alcohol and marijuana dependence and from schizophrenia. In still other studies, Moffitt and colleagues have documented the close links between crime and delinquency and alcohol and drug abuse (Poultin et al. 1997), and between joblessness and delinquency and school failure (Caspi et al. 1998).

Another window on the co-occurrence of crime and other dysfunctional outcomes is shown by data from a prospective longitudinal study of about 1,000 Montreal males, conducted by Richard Tremblay and his colleagues. Among the data collected in this study were teacher ratings of physically aggressive behavior at age six and from ages ten to fifteen years old. Tremblay and I (Nagin and Tremblay 1999) found four distinctive developmental trajectories in these data (see fig. 1). A group called "lows" was composed of individuals who rarely displayed physically aggressive behavior to any substantial degree. This group was estimated to compose about 15 percent of the sampled population. A second group, which composed about 50 percent of the population, was labeled "moderate-level desisters." At age six, boys in this group displayed modest levels of physical aggression, but by age ten they had largely desisted. A third group, comprising about 30 percent of the population, was labeled "high-level near desisters." This group started off scoring high on physical aggression at age six, but by age fifteen scored far lower. Finally, there was a small group of "chronics," comprising about 5 percent of the population, who displayed high levels of physical aggression throughout the observation period.

Table 1 compares the mean levels of various behaviors and outcomes for the small group of chronics compared with a large composite group comprising the moderate desisters and lows. At age seventeen, the subjects were questioned about their involvement in various forms of violent delinquency (e.g., gang fighting, carrying or using a deadly weapon). The chronics were more than three times as likely to be in the upper tenth percentile of this self-reported violent delinquency scale—31.6 percent versus 8.7 percent. The chronics were also four times more likely than the combined low/moderate aggression group

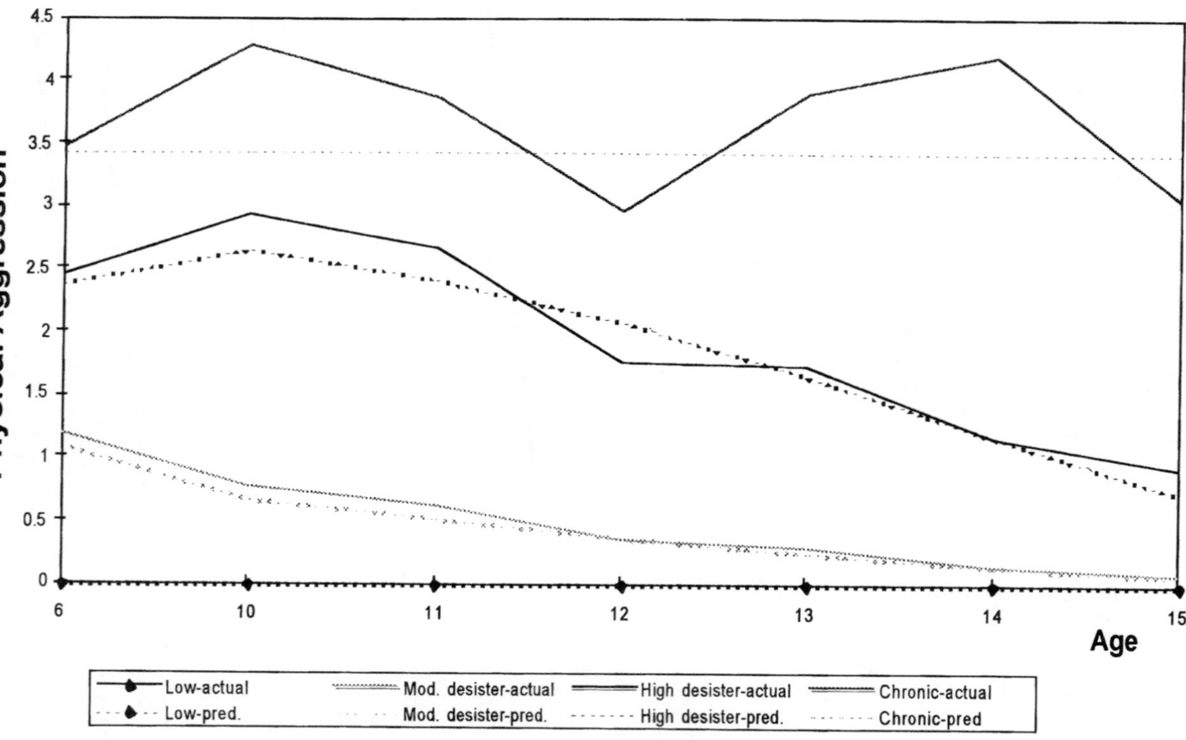

Fig. 1.—Trajectories of physical aggression

TABLE 1

Trajectories of Childhood Physical Aggression and Other Behaviors

Behavior	Trajectory Group	
	Chronic (Percent)	Low–Moderate (Percent)
High violent delinquency at age 17	31.6	8.7
High drug use at age 10	20.0	5.4
School failure by grade 8	93.3	30.7
Accident at age 17	26.3	16.3

to be in the top 10 percent of illicit drug and alcohol usage at age ten. In addition, the chronics experienced an extraordinarily high level of school failure. By the eighth grade, 93 percent had been held back at least one grade, whereas only 31 percent of the low to moderates had been held back. Finally, the chronics were also more accident prone—at age fifteen, 26.3 percent reported having an accident in the past year, compared with 16.3 percent for the low–moderate group.

Table 2 shows summary statistics comparing parental characteristics of the two groups. While all of the boys came from low socioeconomic neighborhoods in Montreal, the high-violence boys disproportionately came from particularly disadvantaged households. They were more than twice as likely to have a mother who began childbearing as a teenager or who had fewer than nine years of education. Family breakup before age five was far more common among the high-violence boys, 43.3 percent versus 23.6 percent.

Turning to the boys' characteristics, the high-violence boys were twice as likely to be in the lowest IQ quartile. They were also much less likely to be judged by teachers to be in the upper quartile of a measure of prosocial behavior at age six. Rather, teachers perceived these boys as more prone to high levels of oppositional behavior. Their inability to get along with others is also reflected in other data not reported here. For example, by age ten the high-violence boys were far less likely to be judged popular by their peers than the low–moderate trajectory boys.

TABLE 2

Predictors of Physical Aggression Trajectory Group Membership

	Trajectory Group	
Behavior	Chronic (Percent)	Low–Moderate (Percent)
Teen mother*	53.3	18.5
Poorly educated mother†	66.7	26.0
Family breakup before age 5	43.3	23.6
Low IQ	43.3	21.9
High opposition	63.3	20.0
High prosociality	10.0	26.7

* Mother began childbearing as a teenager.
† Less than nine years of education.

The data from Montreal and Dunedin mirror findings from all developmental research—antisocial behavior emerges early in life and manifests itself in differing but always undesirable ways over the life course. The prototypical pattern begins with conduct problems in childhood; delinquency, sexual promiscuity, and school failure in adolescence; and crime, partner abuse, unemployment, and substance dependence in adulthood. To be sure, not all troublesome children become antisocial adults. Indeed, most do not. However, as Robins (1978, p. 611) observes, "adult antisocial behavior virtually requires childhood antisocial behavior [yet] most antisocial children do not become antisocial adults." The objective of developmental prevention is to maximize the number of high-risk children who do not become antisocial adults.

II. Should the Unit of Analysis Be the Individual or the Criminal Event?

Analysts who have linked developmental prevention and crime control have generally made the link from a crime control perspective. From that perspective, the natural unit of analysis is the criminal event, whereas from the developmental prevention perspective the natural unit of analysis is the individual. In this section, I argue that in linking developmental prevention and crime control, it is important that the link be person based, not crime based.

A. Review of the Cost-Effectiveness Studies and the Benefit-Cost Studies of Early Prevention Programs

Cost-effectiveness studies compare the effectiveness of early prevention and incarceration in preventing crime. These studies address the question, Is early prevention a cost-effective alternative to imprisonment for averting crime? The metric of analysis is crimes averted per dollar spent. The benefit-cost studies ask a conceptually distinct question: Does the dollar value of the benefits of early prevention programs exceed the dollar value of their cost? The benefit-cost approach is more ambitious because the scope of benefits considered is more than crime control but is also less ambitious, vis-à-vis crime control policy, because it does not compare developmental prevention with conventional crime control measures like imprisonment. This section examines the studies using these alternative analytic strategies for performing economic analysis of early prevention.

B. Cost-Effectiveness Studies

Two studies have compared the effectiveness of early prevention and prison in averting crime: Greenwood et al. (1996) and Donohue and Siegelman (1998). In Greenwood et al., the crime control effectiveness of California's "Three Strikes" statute was compared with two types of early prevention programs: home care/day care programs and parent-training programs. California's Three Strikes statute mandates life imprisonment for the third felony conviction for selected crimes. The metric of comparison was serious crimes averted per dollar spent. Serious crimes included murder, rape, and robbery.

The home care/day care prevention alternative was modeled after two well-publicized prevention programs—the High/Scope Perry Project (Schweinhart, Barnes, and Weikart 1993) and the Prenatal/Early Infancy Project (PEIP) (Olds et al. 1997, 1998). The Perry program, which included both day care and home visit components, was designed to improve the target child's cognitive functioning and social development. The target population was African-American children with low income and low IQ. The Perry intervention was conducted in the mid-1960s.

The more recent PEIP intervention was conducted from 1978 to 1982 and provided home visits to economically disadvantaged first-time mothers and their children. The visits were made by nurse practitioners who counseled mothers on health-related behaviors during pregnancy (e.g., not using drugs or alcohol). After the child's birth, mothers were coached on effective child-rearing practice. The program also aimed to advance the mother's personal development by helping her get access to employment and education programs. The parent-training alternative was modeled after programs such as those of Patterson, DeBaryshe, and Ramsey (1989). These interventions aim to train parents in successful approaches for nurturing prosocial behaviors and outlooks in young children. They emphasize the importance of clear and reasonable rules, close monitoring, and firm, but not hostile, correction for rule breaking.

The Greenwood et al. (1996) analysis suggests that the home visit/day care option is not a cost-effective alternative to Three Strikes in preventing serious crime. The cost-effectiveness of the Three Strikes option is $13,899 per serious crime averted, whereas the counterpart cost for the home visit/day care option is six times greater—$89,035. However, by Greenwood et al.'s calculations, parent-training seems to be a promising alternative. Its cost per serious crime averted is only $6,351. The conclusion of Greenwood and colleagues depends crucially on their extrapolation of the impact of the prevention programs in adult criminality. While their extrapolations have face plausibility, for reasons developed below, they are also highly speculative.

Donohue and Siegelman (1998) took an analytically distinct tack. They compare two states of the world for a contemporary cohort of three-year-olds: one in which by age eighteen they are incarcerated at the per capita as of 1993 and another in which they are incarcerated at a rate that is 50 percent higher. By their estimate, the 50 percent increase would reduce the cohort's index crime rate by 5–15 percent. They then compute the present value of the incremental cost of the 50 percent increase in imprisonment fifteen years "down the road." They calculate this cost at about $6–$8 billion. This sets the stage for the central question of their analysis: Will channeling this $6–$8 billion of incremental cost into prevention programs now lower the crime rate by at least 5–15 percent fifteen years from now? If yes, they argue it is optimal to shift forward this spending because society gets more crime control fifteen years hence at no greater cost in present-value terms.

The Donohue and Siegelman (1998) analysis suggests that, without targeting, early prevention is not a competitive alternative to imprisonment for reducing crime. Specifically, for prevention to be competitive it must be targeted "with sufficient precision to encompass all those three-year-olds who were destined to become the most active 6 percent of delinquents" (Donohue and Siegelman 1998, p. 36). Their analysis suggests that sufficient targeting can be achieved if prevention resources were targeted on black, male children—the prospectively most crime-prone group of the three-year-old cohort. Specifically, Donohue and Siegelman (1998) projected that a Perry preschool–type program will reduce the crime rate by 9.1–20.5 percent. They also projected that a similar Syracuse-based pilot program would produce a comparable crime reduction benefit of 7.1–26.1 percent. Like the analyses of Greenwood and colleagues, this analysis too rests heavily on seemingly plausible, but still highly speculative, estimates of the impact of early prevention on serious criminality.

C. *Critique of the Cost-Effectiveness Analysis Strategy*

My main criticism of the cost-effectiveness analysis strategy is the difficulty of mounting a convincing, as opposed to a plausible, argument that early prevention is a cost-effective alternative to imprisonment for averting crime. The favorable conclusion from the Donohue and Siegelman analysis is based on comparison of prevention to a still higher level of imprisonment than the already historically high rate of 1993. Specifically, two policy options were considered: a 50 percent increase in imprisonment from the 1993 level without a Perry-like program, and holding imprisonment at the 1993 level but with a Perry-like program. Had the analysis been conducted in terms of a 50 percent reduction in 1993 imprisonment levels to the rate that prevailed in about 1984, prevention would not have been a competitive alternative to imprisonment for reducing crime. The reason is attributable to Donohue and Siegelman's use of a constant elasticity model for measuring the impact of imprisonment on crime. With such a model, the increase in crimes attendant to a 50 percent decrease in imprisonment is larger in absolute terms than the reduction in crime from a 50 percent increase in imprisonment. Further, their affirmative conclusion on prevention requires targeting African-American males—a strategy that would likely provoke vocal and strident resistance from both within and outside the African-American community. While such criticism could be diffused by targeting based on community characteristics rather than ethnic characterization per se, this might well undo the degree of targeting that is necessary to maintain the cost-effectiveness argument. Of course, other objectives would be served by non-ethnically based targeting, but this is precisely my point. Cost-effectiveness based only on a crimes-averted metric is an insufficient evaluation criterion.

The Greenwood et al. (1996) analysis supported only the cost-effectiveness of parent training. It did not support home visits/day care. The reason for the difference was entirely due to cost. The present value of the cost of the parent training was estimated at only $3,000 per child, whereas the cost of the home visit/day care alternative was estimated at $26,238 per child. The authors assume that both types of programs were equally effective in reducing serious crime. This assumption is not credible. The home visit/day care alternative includes a parental-training component in addition to other measures. Given the difference in the cost and treatment intensity of these two prevention programs, it is not plausible to assume equal effectiveness. More fundamentally, this assumption reflects the inherently speculative nature of this sort of extrapolation exercise in which the impact of a treatment early in life is related to a very specific behavior later in life. The programs were assumed equally effective because there was no good empirical basis for distinguishing their effects.

Finally, the Greenwood et al. (1996) estimate of the crime control impact of California's Three Strikes law was based solely on crimes averted through incapacitation. If the law also has a deterrent effect, the estimate of the cost-effectiveness of the Three Strikes law was understated.

Reservations about the viability of the cost-effectiveness analysis strategy also involve three generic reservations that extend beyond the specific conclusions and methods of these two studies. One relates to the rarity of serious criminality in the population, the second involves neglect of the broad range of benefits associated with successful early prevention, and the third concerns the disjuncture between the timing of the investment and the realization of the reward.

The first reservation concerns the relative rarity of serious criminality in the population—people who murder, rape, rob, or otherwise inflict serious bodily harm on others. As a society, we have a collective interest in insuring the security of our property. However, threats to personal safety are overwhelmingly more important. The priority status of personal safety, for example, is reflected in criminal sentences. Crimes of violence are punished far more severely than property crimes.

The rarity of serious criminality is emphasized because it is inherently difficult to measure the impact of an intervention on a rare event.

To illustrate, consider the following example. Suppose that in a target population of high-risk two-year-olds who were not offered intervention, 10 percent were destined to engage in serious criminality, but with intervention the rate of serious criminality is cut to 7.5 percent. Thus, in percentage terms the intervention has a large impact—the rate of serious criminality is cut by 25 percent. However, in absolute terms the change is small—only 2.5 percentage points. It is this small absolute change that must be statistically identified in an evaluation. Establishing statistical significance at the 0.05 level would require about 700 individuals each in the treatment and control groups.[1] At the 0.01 level the required sample is even larger, about 1,400 per group. Such large samples are required because, regardless of treatment status, comparatively few from even a high-risk group are destined to be serious criminals. In the above case, with a sample of 700 in both the treatment and control groups, only about 53 and 70 individuals, respectively, would be expected to emerge as serious criminals.

By comparison, the sample sizes in prevention pilots are typically far smaller. In the Perry program, there were about 60 children in each of the treatment and control groups. In the PEIP program, samples were larger (about 100 in the experimental group and 150 in the control group) but still far smaller than the 700 per group calculated above. Given the above power calculation (i.e., the sample that is necessary for demonstrating statistical significance), how then did these programs find significant crime reduction benefits?

Consider the Perry program. For the purposes of estimating crime control effects, this pilot intervention has the best data because subjects were tracked until age 27, a far lengthier evaluation period than for most programs. Reduced criminality accounts for the lion's share of

[1] This power calculation is performed as follows. The test statistic for establishing the statistical significance of the difference in two proportions p_1 and p_2 is

$$z = \frac{\hat{p}_1 - \hat{p}_2}{\sqrt{\frac{2\hat{p}(1 - \hat{p})}{n}}},$$

where n is the sample size used to estimate both p_1 and p_2, the two sample estimates of p_1 and p_2, respectively, and $\hat{p}$ is the average of p_1 and p_2. Solving for n and substituting population values for sample estimate yields

$$n = \frac{(z^2)(2p(1 - p)}{(p_1 - p_2)^2}.$$

The sample size calculations reported above are for $z = 1.65$, $p_1 = .1$, $p_2 = .075$, and $p = .0875$.

the benefit (Barnett 1993, 1996). The program evaluation highlights two findings as evidence of the crime prevention impact (Schweinhart, Barnes, and Weikart 1993). One is that by age nineteen a statistically significant difference existed in the percent arrested for any type of crime, 31 percent for the treatment group and 51 percent for the control group. Compared to the rates of serious criminality used in the above power calculation (10 percent for the nontreated and 7.5 percent for the treated), these rates are very high. This is because the rates from the Perry evaluation include arrests for nonviolent property offenses and for misdemeanors.

The second highlighted finding was a large difference in the percentage of participants with five or more arrests by age twenty-eight. Only 7 percent of the treatment group were chronic arrestees, whereas the counterpart rate for the control group was 35 percent. This implies that the intervention reduced chronic criminality by over 80 percent. The absolute size of the impact explains why it is statistically significant. More detailed breakdowns of the data, reported in Schweinhart, Barnes, and Weikart (1993), suggest that this finding should be interpreted with caution. There is no statistically significant difference in the felony crime arrest rate, personal-violence crime arrest rate, or property crime arrest rate between the treatment and control groups. The only significant difference is for misdemeanor and drug crime arrests. Further, these differences appear to be attributable to the high arrest rates of a small number of individuals.

The second generic concern with crime-based cost-effectiveness is that by construction it ignores other salutary impacts of early prevention programs. The Perry program evaluation found not only statistically significant salutary impacts on crime and delinquency but also on school achievement, employment, and utilization of emergency medical services. Wide-ranging impacts of youth-oriented prevention programs have also been found in other studies. Hawkins et al. (1999) implemented and evaluated a school- and home-based intervention targeted at school-aged children. They found that the intervention not only lowered violent delinquency but also reduced heavy drinking and early sexual behavior and improved school performance. Karoly et al. (1998) summarize the variety of benefits of other early prevention programs and similarly conclude that such programs influence functioning in multiple domains of behavior. This should not be surprising—it is hard to imagine how a program having salutary impacts on social and cognitive development would not have wide-ranging effects on the life course.

The final generic problem that arises from billing developmental prevention as a crime control policy is that it pits a policy option in which benefits are not realized for at least ten years against policies with potential for immediate impact. In reality, developmental prevention does not compete with conventional crime control measures for funding in the political process precisely because of this disjuncture between the timing of the investment and the realization of the benefit. This being the case, it seems misguided to frame the argument for developmental prevention in narrow crime prevention terms when in fact developmental prevention is not directly competing for crime control resources.

Had the analyses of Donohue and Siegelman (1998) and of Greenwood et al. (1996) been successful in making a compelling case that prevention is a cost-effective alternative to imprisonment for crime control, criticism of the narrow focus of the crime-based cost-effectiveness approach arguably would be moot. However, the case, while plausible, is not compelling. Further, the cost-effectiveness approach frames the question of society's use of imprisonment and prevention in a peculiar fashion. It is odd to pose imprisonment as a substitute for prevention. Instead, imprisonment and the criminal justice system (CJS) more generally are necessary social institutions for controlling the behavior of persons for whom socialization has failed. From this perspective, the CJS is a backstop for ineffective prevention, not a substitute.

D. Benefit-Cost Analyses

A small number of valuation studies have considered a broader range of benefits of intervention than crime reduction. However, only Barnett's (1993, 1996) benefit-cost analyses of the Perry program attempt to take a society-wide perspective in its accounting of benefits and costs. Barnett's benefit calculations account not only for reduced crime, but also for lower schooling costs due to reduced use of special education services (Karoly et al. 1998; Olds et al. 1998; Aos et al. 1999), less welfare use, and higher earnings. Other studies measuring more than crime reduction benefits focus on impacts on the government treasury only. These studies are discussed separately in Section IV.

As prelude to a critique of Barnett's evaluation, it is important to make clear what is meant by an economic benefit. An economic benefit accrues when something of value is produced. That something might be tangible, such as a car or house, but it may also be something intangible, such as peace of mind. In economics, the metric of value is willingness to pay. If in principle someone is willing to pay for this good or service, an economic benefit is produced. Thus, for example, producing pork in a strict Jewish or Muslim society produces no economic value because nobody would be willing to pay for it.

The qualifier "in principle" is emphasized because occurrence of an actual transaction to demonstrate such willingness to pay does not affect whether a benefit has been produced. For instance, if police foot patrols make members of a community feel safer, an economic benefit has been produced even though community members did not demonstrate the value of their new-found sense of safety by their purchase of the foot patrol from the police department. Although citizens pay for police services with their tax payments, the provision of police services to a specific community is not based on a direct transaction between the citizens of the community and the police department. Instead, allocation of policing resources is determined administratively.

An economic cost is incurred when something of value is consumed or exhausted. That something may be tangible, like food or a natural resource, but it may also be intangible, like a person's time and energy. The value of a resource is measured by its opportunity cost—its value in its best alternative use. Most commonly, opportunity cost is measured by the price that the resource commands in the marketplace.

By this definition, tax dollars used by government are not necessarily economic costs. Taxes transfer purchasing power from individual citizens to the government. The government in turn uses these funds to achieve collective goals. In some cases, achieving the goal may involve incurring economic costs. An example is the provision of police services. The police officers themselves could be working to provide some other valued good or service, and at the same time the equipment they use to provide public safety has valuable alternative uses. However, other uses of tax funds do not involve the purchase and use of valuable goods and services. Instead, their use simply represents a transfer of purchasing power from one group of citizens to another group of citizens. Examples of such transfers are welfare and social security payments.

My critique of the Perry cost-benefit analysis focuses on the benefit side of the ledger. While a number of tricky technical problems attend the estimation of costs, the real technical hurdles pertain to benefit estimation. Barnett's (1993, 1996) analysis valued four domains of impact: education effects, employment effects, crime effects, and welfare effects. Here, the focus is on the education and employment effects. As noted above, valuing crime effects is discussed separately. Welfare effects are not included in the discussion because welfare is a transfer payment, not an economic cost.

Barnett's evaluation of education effects focused on valuing the cost of educating the experimental and control children. The primary source of benefit was that the children in the preschool program made less use of special education services throughout primary and secondary school. Such services included separate education for mentally handicapped children, speech and language support, compensatory education, and disciplinary education. There are two benefits to decreased use of such services. One is that special education services are more expensive to provide than general education services. The second is that treated children are less likely to suffer from the cognitive or behavioral problems that trigger the provision of these compensatory services. Barnett's analysis measured only the benefit of the former impact and left unvalued what is surely the more important impact, especially for the child.

The importance of capturing and valuing impacts on personal development is exemplified by the Perry program's impact on postsecondary education outcomes. The program had no statistically significant impact on the educational attainment of male participants. However, for the female participants, impacts were large: 84 percent of female program participants achieved a high school education or the equivalent, whereas only 35 percent of the control females achieved the same. As a result, far more of the female participants enrolled in postsecondary education than their control counterparts. Consequently, the valuation of postsecondary education impacts resulted in a debit, not a credit, to the Perry program benefit ledger. Education is costly, but to take account of that cost without valuing the benefits of education is to miss the point of cost-benefit analysis. Another example of this valuation problem is reflected in the salutary impacts of the program on female participants' high school graduation rate. On the margin, this impact also increased the cost of educating program participants, so in this respect it was a cost and not a benefit.

To be fair, Barnett examined one outcome domain in which education pays large returns—earnings. While the program evaluation reported statistically significant earnings impacts for both males and females (Schweinhart, Barnes, and Weikart 1993), Barnett's projections of impacts for lifetime earnings show that only program females had higher earnings than their control counterparts. The present value of the difference, however, was modest, $27,000 for a 3 percent discount rate. For males the estimated impact was actually negative, although small.

How well does the Barnett analysis capture the full benefits of developmental prevention? Should it serve as a template for future analyses? In my judgment the answer to both these questions is no. Karoly et al. (1998) in their discussion of the importance of early childhood observe: "Research and clinical work have found that the experiences of the infant and young child provide the foundation for long-term physical and mental health as well as cognitive development. . . . The period of early childhood development is thus unique—physically, mentally, emotionally, and socially. It is a period of both opportunity and vulnerability" (pp. 2–3). They go on to conclude that, on the whole, developmental programs result in "gains in the emotional or cognitive development, . . . improvements in educational process and outcomes, . . . increased economic self-sufficiency, . . . reduced levels of criminal activity, and improvements in health-related indicators" (p. xv). Programs that have the potential to have such far-reaching impacts must be valued in broader terms rather than focusing on savings on special education services, increased earnings, or lower welfare payments.

Further, the limitations of Barnett's valuation strategy are not easily remedied by including a broader sampling of outcomes in benefit calculations, for example, lower medical costs for treating mental illness or accidents, reduced expenditures for child protective services, and saving for remedial job training. The problem with the broad-based, itemized valuation approach is at least threefold. First, it is difficult and expensive to assemble data to demonstrate such discrete impacts. Many potential impacts such as improved performance in the labor market or lower criminality require years of follow-up to document. Second, valuing discrete impacts is tedious and inevitably highly speculative. The valuation methods used to place a monetary value on discrete events such as an arrest or a year of special education services have not been critiqued, but, not surprisingly, such cost estimates are highly imprecise. Lengthening the list of items valued only increases the speculative content of the analysis. Third, and most important, this approach still does not begin to capture the far-reaching effects of an effective intervention as reflected in Karoly et al.'s observations.

III. An Alternative Approach

The essence of the developmental prevention strategy is captured in a late nineteenth-century temperance print. The left side of the print depicts a socially and personally productive life course. The first panel shows an earnest boy, book in hand, walking to school. In the second panel, the boy is now a young man with his wife and child lovingly looking on as he is hard at work. In the third panel, the focal character is now an old man sitting in a garden with his wife, and being visited by the now grown child. The right side depicts a socially counterproductive, and personally destructive, life course. In the first panel, the boy is drinking and carousing with his mates, in the second, he is abusing his wife in a drunken rage, and in the final panel, he is at hard labor in prison. Minus the Victorian moral undertones of this print, developmental criminology aims to understand the forces that propel people down these very different life paths and developmental prevention aims to use this knowledge to divert individuals from the right-hand to the left-hand life course.

The challenge of placing an economic value on developmental intervention is in identifying a metric that properly values a qualitative improvement in an individual's life chances. The few existing cost-benefit analyses of developmental prevention have approached this task by summing particular benefits and cost. In the prior section, I argued that this approach was flawed because the difference between a socially and personally constructive life course and the destructive counterpart cannot be reduced to balancing items such as lower special education, criminal justice, and welfare costs against items such as higher earnings. Further, the remedy is not a more elaborate accounting scheme including more items on the debit and credit sides of the accounting ledger. The theoretical and philosophical foundations for cost-benefit analysis rest in welfare economics. According to the principles of welfare economics, the value of goods and services can be computed in this fashion, but not the value of a human being. An alternative, more consciously holistic approach is required.

The economics literature on valuing lives and on valuing different states of health provides valuable guidance for formulating such an alternative approach. Consider first the value of life literature. Such estimates, which typically range from \$2 to \$4 million (Viscusi 1993), are not based on a summation of particular benefits and costs such as the present value of economic productivity less the cost of sustaining life. Instead, the theory underlying the economics-based valuation strategy begins with the premise that death is a qualitatively different and inferior state than life, but that living also requires that we take on life-threatening risks. Driving a car, riding a bike, hunting, or even playing golf can have lethal consequences. Still, people regularly engage in these activities. Similarly, some jobs are more dangerous than others, yet people take risky jobs. Certainly, some risks are taken because the risk is inherent to the enjoyment of the activity—mountain climbing and race car driving, for example. However, risk taking just for fun is the exception, not the rule. Most commonly, we take on life-threatening risks because it is a necessary, but undesirable, requirement of living. As Viscusi (1993, p. 1912) observes, "health and safety risks comprise one aspect of our lives that we all want to eliminate."

Economists use evidence of individuals' willingness to pay to avert life-threatening risks or, alternatively, of their requirements for compensation to take on such risks as a basis for inferring the value people place on life. The former valuation strategy uses evidence of people's willingness to pay for safety devices such as seat belts or smoke detectors to draw inferences about value of life. Most commonly, however, value-of-life estimates are inferred from what economists call "compensating wage differentials." Compensating wage differentials refer to the wage premium that in theory is required to lure people into taking risky jobs such as construction or coal mining. For example, if persons demand $1,000 in compensation to take on a task with a risk of death of one in 1,000, the inference is that the 1,000 such persons would collectively pay $1 million to avert this risk. Such an investment would be expected to save one of their lives. It is by this logic that economists would surmise from this hypothetical that the value of human life is $1 million.

Making a determination of the amount of a compensating wage differential is a tricky task both statistically and conceptually. Wages for jobs are based on much more than the life-threatening risk associated with performing those jobs. Some jobs are more onerous or unpleasant. Most people would prefer to work above ground than underground in a cold and wet coal mine. As a result, wages for coal mining also reflect a premium for the unpleasant work environment in addition to any premium for its physical dangers. Alternatively, one of the downsides of vocations with high intrinsic satisfaction, such as the arts or the ministry, is that wages may be lower because part of the compensation comes in the form of job satisfaction. Moreover, other factors determining wages reflect the supply and demand for people with certain skills. In contemporary society, wages for draftsmen are low because of the availability of computer-aided drafting software. Wages for the software developers who create such software are high because of the booming demand for their services. Still, economists have had reasonable success in isolating risk premiums from the other factors determining wages.

An important hurdle to applying the value-of-life methodology to valuing successful developmental interventions is that economists look for value in choices made by individuals themselves. Sometimes choice may be limited to poor options, like taking a dangerous and unpleasant job or having no job at all. Still, the act of choosing reveals preferences even if only between unattractive states. Volitional choice reveals individual preferences, which in economics is the ultimate source of value.

Young children do not make choices about their life course. Their developmental course is largely determined by forces beyond their control: their biological inheritance, their household income, and the social and economic stability of the country in which they live. The early life course is also heavily affected by the choices of others. For example, whether mothers choose to use drugs and alcohol during pregnancy, whether parents choose to invest their time and energy into building a child's personal capital rather than fulfilling their own needs, and whether teachers intervene with help if they observe a developmental delay and respond with encouragement when they detect a special talent can all have developmental consequences. Of course, as time goes on, individuals increasingly take greater control over their lives, but in profound ways life-course outcomes are determined, not chosen.

However, my reading of the developmental criminology literature leads me to conclude that the criminal life course is not one that parents would willingly choose for their children or that in retrospect individuals would choose for themselves. The choices made by individuals with a history of antisocial behavior are tightly circumscribed. They are made within the narrow confines of the life-course trajectory in which they find themselves, not within a trajectory that they have chosen. Except in unusual circumstances, the alternative to a career of crime is a low-wage menial job, not a career in medicine. John Irwin's (1987, p. viii) assessment is even more pessimistic: "Most of those who stay out of prison are 'successes' in only the narrowest, most bureaucratic meaning of the term 'non-recidivism.' Most ex-convicts live menial or derelict lives and many die early of alcoholism or drug use, or by suicide." Retrospective assessments of criminals themselves give testimony to Irwin's conclusion. Neal Shover's book *Great Pretenders* reports on an ethnographic study of career criminals. By the subjects' own accounts their lives are pathetic and wasted. One of Shover's (1996, p. 131) older subjects confided: "I saw myself for what I really was. . . . I could see it just as plain as I'm looking at you now. And I know that what I looked at was a sorry picture of a human being." There is also economic evidence that is directly on point. In an unusual and innovative study, Levitt and Venkatesh (1998) obtained the accounting records of a drug-dealing gang in Chicago. Drug dealing is a very dangerous occupation. Using the economics-based, risk-compensation approach, they calculate that the gang's drug dealers valued their lives at no more than $100,000.

The value-of-life literature provides a useful upper bound of $2–$4 million for valuing an intervention that is successful in diverting a youth from an antisocial to a socially and personally productive life course. Still, it is only an upper bound. However, parental investments in time and money to ameliorate problem behaviors in their children suggest that at least for some parents investments in even highly uncertain treatments to improve their children's life chances are highly valued.

Indeed, analysis of such choices is one promising approach for adapting methods from the value-of-life literature to valuing effective developmental interventions. Most parents make large investments in time and money in their child's intellectual, social, and moral development. A difficult but still tractable analytical and statistical problem is to establish the relationship between these investments and the change in the child's life chances. An alternative, but complementary, approach would rely on survey responses of parents to hypothetical scenarios concerning their willingness to pay for interventions to improve their own child's life chances. For example, they might be asked whether they would be willing to invest $5,000 in some specific psychiatric treatment that would ameliorate the toddler's conduct problems with some probability. The same sort of question could also be framed to assess their willingness to support such a program for all children via increased taxes.

Such analyses would undoubtedly demonstrate large differences in the amount and quality of actual and projected parental investments.

Indeed, the raison d'être for state intervention in the form of targeted child development programs such as Head Start is that some parents lack the capacity or will to make a minimally acceptable investment in their children. This raises the question of what that minimum standard should be.

The literature on educational equality provides some useful guidance. Curren (1995, p. 24) observes, "if one takes the central goal of education to lie beyond immediate results of instruction, to something like the broadening of life options or enhancement of socio-economic status, then one will almost certainly speak of 'equality of educational opportunity,' and take its substance to be something like equalization of life prospects or prospects of middle class status, or more modestly and plausibly, equalization of opportunity to get an education that will improve those prospects." Curren goes on to argue that all children, regardless of background, should have the right to this "threshold of social inclusion" (1995, p. 24). Thus, for Curren the goal of providing the best feasible education is not socially, politically, or economically attainable, but still he argues for the minimal threshold he characterizes in the above statement. In my view, the same standard should be applied for the provision of child development services.

The literature on cost-effective analysis (CEA) in health and medicine offers another useful source of guidance for valuing alternative life courses. In these analyses, alternative medical procedures are valued according to the metric of quality-adjusted life years (QALYs). This analytic strategy attempts to take into account that a medical intervention can return value either by extending the period of life or the quality of life or both. For example, a successful hip replacement procedure may not extend the length of life, but it will certainly improve the quality of life. Alternatively, certain cancer treatments may extend life without improving its quality. Finally, some medical treatments, such as organ transplants, do both.

In medical cost-effectiveness analysis, procedures are ranked according to their efficiency in increasing QALYs on the basis of the criterion of dollar cost per increase in QALYs achieved. This cost-effectiveness approach eschews placing a dollar value on a QALY on the grounds that the economic approach to valuing life depends too heavily on income. Specifically, the conventional economic approach of establishing value based on willingness to pay guarantees that poor people cannot value their lives highly because they lack the income to do so. This fundamental objection has led medical researchers to endorse the QALY approach because it equally values a QALY of the rich and the poor (Gold et al. 1996). Also noteworthy was Gold et al.'s desire to adopt the sort of holistic metric that I have argued is necessary for valuing a developmental intervention program. Gold et al. (1996, p. 8) observe, "The development of QALYs as an outcome measure has made it possible to encompass the diverse effects of a single intervention . . . thus greatly expanding the applicability and usefulness of CEA."

Gold et al. (1996) also summarize the different approaches used to measure QALYs. Various multiattribute scales have been developed and usually include measures of pain, mobility, and social and family life. Weights are estimated through the use of multiattribute utility methods such as time trade-off, standard gamble, and conjoint analysis. For example, in the time trade-off approach respondents are presented with a task of determining how many years of life they would be willing to give up to be in a better versus a poorer health state (Torrance et al. 1972). Other approaches measure welfare relative to changes in state. These methods were developed in response to ideas from prospect theory (Kahneman and Tversky 1983) that emphasize that from a behavioral prospective, utility is commonly measured relative to the status quo.

There are also approaches derived from psychology involving paired-comparison approaches and rating-scale methods. For example, in the paired-comparison approach, respondents might compare which is worse—living for only ten more years in good health or living for twenty years, but with some specified impairment such as serious arthritis.

In differing ways, all of these approaches attempt to assess people's trade-offs between the quality and length of life. With some ingenuity, I am confident that they could be adapted to measuring people's preferences for alternative life courses for themselves, for their children, and for children at large. For example, respondents could be posed with alternative life scenarios that vary both in terms of their length and quality and asked which they prefer. Of special interest would be eliciting people's preferences between a relatively short, but socially and personally productive life and a long but failed life.

IV. Should the Unit of Analysis Be Society or Government?

Studies by Olds et al. (1993), Karoly et al. (1998), and Aos et al. (1999) consider more than just the costs and benefits of crime reduction, but only from the perspective of government spending. Specifically, these studies assessed whether programs had a net positive or negative impact on government expenditures. On the debit side were the expenses to the government of operating the program. On the credit side were items such as reduced expenditures for provision of special education and operation of the criminal justice system and increased tax payments from the mother and later the child. This focus is understandable. The argument that a social program will pay for itself by generating a net positive flow into the public treasury is very attractive politically. Everyone wins—program beneficiaries are better off and the net financial burden of running government for the general public declines.

Olds et al. (1993) estimated the impact of the PEIP program on government spending. The costs to the government were the expense of operating the program—paying the nurse practitioners, transportation costs, and so on. The savings to the government came from a variety of sources that mostly were attributable to the mother. These included a small savings from lower Medicaid expenses for childbearing, because the program mothers were less likely to become pregnant, and from reduced use of child protective services. The mothers also paid more taxes and made less use of Aid for Families with Dependent Children (AFDC) and food stamps because they worked more. Indeed, for the low-income participants, reduced welfare payments accounted for 82 percent of the savings to government.

Karoly et al. (1998) synthesized findings from a number of interventions but gave special attention to the Perry and PEIP programs. Like Olds et al. (1997, 1998), their analysis focused on cash flows into and out of the public treasury. For the PEIP program, the cost side of the ledger in their analysis included the program expense, and the benefit side included estimates of the dollar value of lowered use of health services, increased employment tax payments, reduced welfare costs, and smaller criminal justice system costs. For the Perry program, savings to government were similar—reduced spending on special education services, welfare, and the CJS, as well as more taxes. The major difference is that, for the Perry program, the savings to the government were attributable to the altered future behavior of the child, whereas for the PEIP program the savings were primarily attributable to changes in the labor-force participation of the mother. In addition, Karoly et al. estimate selected nongovernmental benefits, including savings to victims of crimes averted and increases in the child's and mother's future earnings.

Aos et al. (1999) give another analysis that draws from published findings to estimate the costs and benefits of early prevention programs. Unlike Karoly et al., they focus only on crime-related benefits such as reduced costs of processing apprehended offenders through the CJS and avoided victim costs.

The argument that a program has a net positive impact on the public treasury is attractive, but for several reasons it is not an appropriate basis for making the case for developmental prevention programs. It is not that the argument is logically flawed, but it frames the case for developmental prevention too narrowly. Most important, the fiscal impact criterion neglects potential benefits with important consequences for society at large, such as improved public safety, and for the individual who is the target of the program, such as living an effective and productive life. As an example, the principle objective of the PEIP program was to improve the life chances of the target child. Yet, based on the financial analysis reported in Olds et al. (1993), the financial justification for the program rests on the program's impact on the mother's lower welfare use and higher tax payments, not on the child. The result is a fundamental disjuncture between the objectives of the program and the program evaluation criteria.

This disjuncture is avoided by taking the broader societal perspective. In the literature on measuring quality-adjusted life years, the societal perspective is also taken. Gold et al. (1996, p. 7) observe: "The societal perspective does not represent the situation from the viewpoint of particular agents in society, but it is the only perspective that never counts as a gain what is really someone else's loss. If an intervention adopted by an employer reduces the employer's cost for health insurance, but increases costs for Medicare, the societal perspective includes both changes. Beyond the philosophical arguments in its favor, there is value in beginning with a perspective that includes all costs and effects because it provides a background against which to assess results from other perspectives."

Also, the government-centric accounting perspective suggests that the developmental prevention public policy option should be evaluated by a different standard than other options such as increased imprisonment or more police. The social desirability of increased imprisonment and police protection is not judged solely or even primarily by the impact of these social institutions on the public treasury. If this were the case, society would have far fewer police and prisoners because both represent large negative drains on the public treasury.

Finally, a government-based accounting of the effects of developmental prevention depends on other public policies that have no bearing on its social and economic value. Returning again to the PEIP example, the amount of the reduction in welfare payments and the increase in taxes that attended to mothers' increased earnings depend on policies governing the generosity of the welfare system and on tax rates. Thus, for example, the overhaul of the U.S. welfare system prescribed in the Personal Responsibility and Work Opportunity Act of 1996 placed a limit on allowable time on welfare. It is ironic that this change in public policy reduced the value of the PEIP program as measured by its impact on the public treasury, while at the same time it increased its value from the perspective of the mother and child.

V. Should the Unit of Analysis Be the Crime Rate and Its Social Consequences or the Criminal Event and Consequences to the Victim?

A successful developmental intervention not only benefits the individual by improving the quality of his or her life chances, but it also benefits society by averting social harms the individual might otherwise have imposed. Among these is crime. Philip Cook (1983, p. 373) observes, "Crime reduces our standard of living." Certainly, victims bear the direct costs of crime, including physical injury or death, lost or damaged property, and the intangible but still real cost of personal violation, but nonvictims also suffer. For example, they share in the cost of punishing apprehended criminals, but the burden goes well beyond that. As a society, we spend vast sums from both public and private sources to protect ourselves from becoming victims of crime. The criminal justice system not only dispenses justice to those guilty of crime but also prevents crime by some combination of deterrence and incapacitation. In 1993, total U.S. state and federal expenditures for operating the criminal justice system were about $100 billion (Bureau of Justice Statistics 1997). Vast sums are also spent on private self-protection in the form of security guards, alarm systems, and other protective devices (Anderson 1999).

Even this listing of the economic costs of crime is incomplete because it neglects nonmonetary impacts. Fear of victimization diminishes quality of life by causing individuals to alter their routine activities in otherwise undesirable ways. Some people become virtual prisoners in their own homes because they fear venturing out. A less dramatic action is avoiding some places altogether or at certain times

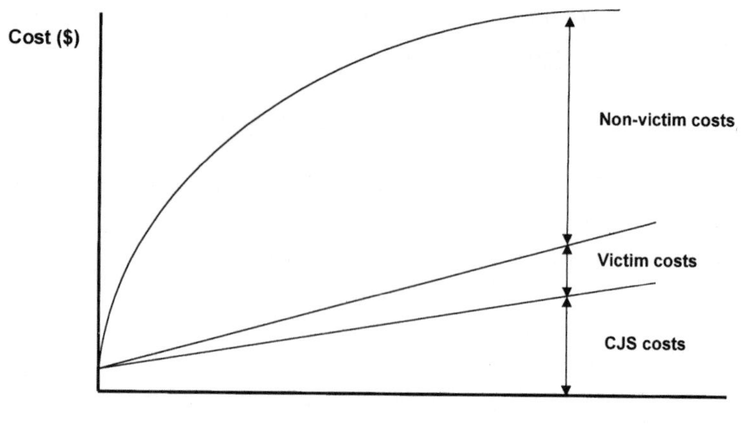

FIG. 2.—The total social cost of crime

because of fear of victimization (e.g., the park on a warm summer night). For the poor, changes in routine activities may have particularly large negative impacts on their quality of life because they lack the resources to purchase security systems or to move to a safer neighborhood. Thus, for them self-protection can be secured only by nonpecuniary means.

Figure 2 is a graphical depiction of these three components of cost: the cost of operating the criminal justice system, victim cost, and nonvictim private costs. The cost of operating the criminal justice system is depicted as growing linearly with the number of crimes committed. However, even with no crime, a positive expenditure is assumed to be required for the purpose of projecting a credible threat of punishment. Victim costs are depicted as growing in strict proportion to the number of crimes, under the assumption that the cost of victimization from the victim's perspective is independent of the total number of people victimized. In addition to victim and criminal justice system-related costs, one must also consider nonvictim private costs. It is assumed that these costs do not grow linearly with the number of crimes. Instead, they are depicted as increasing, but at a decreasing rate with the number of crimes. This implies that even if it were possible to place a dollar value on the total value of nonvictim costs, it could not be surmised that, say, a 10 percent reduction in crime reduces these costs by 10 percent. The reduction would be smaller. How much smaller depends

TABLE 3

Cohen's Estimates of the Cost of Victimization (in Dollars)

Crime	Losses	Suffering	Death	Total
Rape	4,617	43,561	2,880	51,058
Robbery	1,114	7,459	4,021	12,594
Assault	422	4,921	6,685	12,028
Car theft	3,069	...	58	3,127
Burglary	937	317	116	1,372

Source.—Cohen et al. 1994.

on how willing people are "to drop their guard" in response to a reduction in the risk of victimization.

No study has yet attempted to relate the volume of crime to the total social cost of crime. However, the much cited and controversial work of Cohen and colleagues (Cohen 1988; Cohen, Miller, and Rossman 1994; Miller, Cohen, and Wiersma 1996) examined one important component of this total—the cost to victims. In 1988, Mark Cohen published "Pain, Suffering, and Jury Awards: A Study of the Cost of Crime to Victims." Cohen's estimates of victim costs for selected index crimes are reported in table 3. His estimates combined three components of victim cost: direct losses, risk of death, and pain and suffering. Direct losses included lost or damaged property, medical expenses, lost wages, and so on. A rare but very costly outcome of crime is the death of the victim. The risk of death component captured this cost. It is estimated by the product of a crime-specific estimate of the risk of victim fatality and $2 million, the assumed value of life from the economic literature on the value of life. The final component of the cost calculation, pain and suffering, was the focal point of Cohen's analysis.

The procedure Cohen used to estimate the dollar value of pain and suffering is complex and necessarily included idiosyncratic adjustments for specific crimes. In this and later updates of the estimates (Miller, Cohen, and Wiersma 1996), great care is taken to account for as many complexities as possible. However, when stripped to the essentials, the mechanics are straightforward. Based on jury awards in personal injury cases, a regression equation was estimated that related the dollar value of the award for pain and suffering to the amount of the victim's medical expenses and lost wages. Using other sources, Cohen estimated the average dollar value of lost wages and medical expenses for each type of crime. These estimates were applied to the regression equation to estimate the dollar value of pain and suffering reported in table 3.

Cohen's estimates are widely cited and frequently used (cf. Barnett 1993, 1996; Levitt 1996; Lott and Mustard 1997). They have also been much criticized, most forcefully by Zimring and Hawkins (1995). While Zimring and Hawkins praise Cohen for looking beyond out-of-pocket expenses in valuing the cost of crime, they have no praise for his approach to broadening the accounting framework. Concerning the valuation of the risk of fatal consequences, they argue that the use of the $2 million figure for valuing a human life is "unrealistically in excess of the resources that any society would make available to prevent crimes carrying such consequences" (p. 139). On this point, they are joined by Cook and Ludwig (2000), who question whether an estimate based on the lethal risk compensation requirements of generally middle-class samples applies to the typical homicide victim. Homicide victims are not only disproportionately poor but, more fundamentally, they often take risks that exacerbate the risk of their own demise. The conclusion of Levitt and Venkatesh (1998) on the minuscule compensating wage differential demands of drug dealers dramatically illustrates this point. More generally, victim precipitation is a common feature of homicide events with the implication that victims "appear to place relatively little value on their own lives" (Cook and Ludwig 1998, p. 10). Cook and Ludwig also point out that the task of a jury is to set compensation for an identified victim. This amount, they argue, is typically far greater than the amount society is willing to commit to averting the death of a "statistical" victim whose identity is unknown (Cook and Ludwig 1998, p. 5).

Zimring and Hawkins (1995) reserve their main criticism for the pain and suffering cost estimates. They question the validity of using jury awards to measure pain and suffering. Even more fundamentally, they challenge the use of pain and suffering cost estimates in an accounting of the cost of crime. Concerning the first point, they observe, "Pain and suffering damages for personal injury in Anglo-American law are notorious for both their arbitrariness and their inflated size. In fact these findings are the principle target of no-fault insurance reform and a variety of other efforts to displace them in accident compensation plans. Yet, Cohen wants to adopt these measures as appropriate measures for crime costs." They go on to dismiss pain and suffering estimates based on jury awards as "simply adding zeros to the aggregate totals" (Zimring and Hawkins 1995, p. 139).

Cohen (1988, p. 541) rebuts by arguing that juries are instructed to provide "a 'fair' and 'reasonable' amount as compensation for pain and suffering." Still, ample anecdotal evidence shows that juries do not always act as they are instructed. Furthermore, even if the jury is earnest in its desire to follow the judge's instructions, its task is inherently subjective and arguably ill-posed. How can one know someone else's pain and suffering, let alone place a dollar value on it?

A further complication in using data on jury awards is that most damage cases are settled out of court. As Cohen himself acknowledges, those cases that go to jury are not representative. They typically involve larger damage claims and defendants with great financial resources to pay them. These concerns lend further credence to Zimring and Hawkins's claim that Cohen's estimates are too high.

However, on their face, jury awards for pain and suffering do not seem wildly implausible—$12,594 for a robbery, $1,372 for a larceny, or $51,058 for a rape. Hard consideration of the implications of the estimates, however, raises difficult and unsettling issues. Consider the $51,058 estimate (in 1985 dollars) of the average cost of a rape. Of the total cost estimate, 85 percent is for pain and suffering. This too seems plausible. Most rape victims are not seriously injured physically. Rather the injury is psychic—a most intimate personal violation. Surely, this violation has a dollar value equivalent of at least $43,000 (see table 3). This conclusion is not necessarily linked to the logic of the willingness-to-pay criterion for valuing economic costs. For example, one cannot pay what one does not have. A poor woman might not pay $43,000, let alone $51,000, to avoid being raped, not because she is inured to the personal violation, but because she does not have the money.

I raise this uncomfortable reality about the implication of economics-based valuation methods because it speaks to Zimring and Hawkins's second concern about reliance on cost estimates so dominated by two intangibles, pain and suffering and risk of death. They observe, "if one were to construct a list of the harmful consequences experienced by members of society, the aggregate social dollar-cost measures of unpleasant consequences would always far outstrip the aggregate value of the economic output of that society." They go on to conclude that Cohen's estimates "overemphasize what has been quantified," and "wildly overstate the level of resources that could or should be directed at crime in general or at any particular crime" (Zimring and Hawkins 1995, pp. 140–41).

Zimring and Hawkins's criticism may be overly vehement. For too long, crime policy has been made without conscious consideration of costs and benefits. Cohen stepped forward and tried to fill the vacuum. Part of that task involved arguing that the lost or damaged property is only a small part of the cost of crime. The main cost is the threat it poses to the integrity of our lives. Cohen attempted to capture this cost in terms of pain and suffering and risk of death. Zimring and Hawkins acknowledged this point, however grudgingly, when they credited Cohen with expanding his crime-cost estimates to include more than the usual out-of-pocket expense. Still, Zimring and Hawkins made a crucial point. Cost estimates so heavily dominated by intangibles are hard to interpret and subject to abuse. What is needed are cost estimates that reflect the value of tangible actions people take in response to their fear of victimization risk or, alternatively, estimates of willingness to pay to lower the victimization risk by a specified amount.

Using the contingent valuation methodology, Cook and Ludwig (2000) also attempt the latter. In a survey of a nationally representative sample of U.S. households, they asked respondents: "Suppose that you were asked to vote for or against a new program in your state to reduce gun thefts and illegal gun dealers. This program would make it more difficult for criminals and delinquents to obtain guns. It would reduce gun injuries by 30 percent, but taxes would have to be increased to pay for it. If it cost you an extra [$50/$100/$200] in annual taxes would you vote for or against this new program?" (Cook and Ludwig 2000, p. 103).

There are good reasons for being skeptical of responses to a survey question such as this. Because the referendum is not real, respondents might not be candid about their actual vote. Kahneman and Knetsch (1992) wonder whether responses to questions such as this reflect the respondents' desire "to purchase moral satisfaction" rather than actual voting behavior. Possibly, but why this would be so is not clear. Certainly, there are no financial consequences to an affirmative response to a survey question, but in actual balloting it is also true that each individual's vote has no material effect on the eventual outcome.

Another reason for skepticism is that responses are based on, at best, crude impressions of the program's impact. Few voters know the base rate of gun injuries within even a factor of ten, and they probably have even less-well-formed impressions of the distribution of consequences from minor injury to lethal outcome. That said, individuals routinely make decisions involving risks with comparably poor information about base rates and consequences (i.e., consumers choosing among cars with differing safety reputations).

The debate over the validity of the contingent valuation methodology will not be settled soon. For now, applications must be judged case by case. The results of the Cook and Ludwig (2000) application are plausible. Support for the referendum increased when the program cost decreased. Sixty-four percent of the respondents would support a program costing $200 per household. At $25 per household, support increased to 76 percent. Cook and Ludwig also found that support for the initiative increased with the number of children in the household.

The survey was designed to determine maximum willingness to pay for the referendum program. From these responses, Cook and Ludwig estimated that, on average, households would be willing to pay $213 for a program to reduce gunshot injuries by 30 percent. Extrapolated to the United States as a whole, this implies a societal willingness to pay $23 billion, or about $750,000 per averted injury and about $4 million per averted death.

Cook and Ludwig (2000) recognized that their estimates of the value of averted injuries and death seem high given that most survey respondents were at the lower end of the gun-injury risk spectrum. From this, they surmised that respondents place a high value on reduced risks to others, lower tax and insurance rates, and improved quality of life. While this conclusion may be correct, it may also be that the estimates are inflated for the very reasons cited by critics of contingent valuation. That said, it is too early to judge whether contingent valuation will prove to be a productive methodology for understanding how perceptions of the cost of crime varies with the level of crime. More studies like that by Cook and Ludwig will help to reach an informed conclusion.

While Cook and Ludwig's (2000) research suggests that contingent evaluation can provide valuable, highly policy-relevant information on willingness to pay to avert crime, it does not measure how concrete acts of self-protection are linked to the threat of victimization. A better understanding of this link is required for a full and convincing accounting of the various components of cost depicted in figure 2. Two sources of data have promising potential for supporting this type of analysis. One is nationally representative marketing survey data on household expenditures. These surveys are assembled from detailed diaries on spending for all goods and services. Presumably, one spending category is security devices, such as alarm systems. Analyses linking such expenditures to the crime rate in the sampled household's community would be very informative about actual willingness to pay to avert victimization.

A second, even more promising data source is government-sponsored victimization surveys. These surveys provide the basis for linking self-protection measures to measures of both victimization risk and actual victimization experience. Furthermore, unlike marketing surveys, victimization surveys can also provide data on nonpecuniary measures of self-protection. The National Crime Victimization Survey (NCVS) of the United States could provide an ideal platform for such analysis. The sample size is very large (more than 60,000 households), and because the households are interviewed repeatedly over their three-year tenure in the sample, it is possible to examine the connections between victimization and changed behavior. The NCVS, however, lacks the key ingredient for conducting these sorts of analyses. This includes data on pecuniary and nonpecuniary self-protection measures taken by household members. The absence of survey questions on self-protection is a major deficiency in the NCVS that is in urgent need of correction.

VI. Conclusion

For too long, crime policy has been formulated without careful assessment of economic costs and benefits. Recent work has moved toward filling this important gap in policy analysis. The focus of this essay has been economic evaluation of developmental prevention programs. Just as Lewis and Clark demonstrated that overland passage to the Pacific Ocean was possible, the nascent literature on valuing developmental prevention has demonstrated the feasibility and utility of such analysis. However, just as those who succeeded Lewis and Clark found better routes to the Pacific Northwest, future economic valuations of developmental prevention should use different analytic strategies.

The recommended changes were framed in terms of three questions concerning the appropriate unit of analysis: Individuals or criminal events? Society or government? and The crime rate and its social consequences or the criminal event and its consequences to the victim? In each case I argued for the first alternative even though the focus of existing studies was primarily the second alternative.

I have tried to describe in broad outlines a research program that would provide the practical basis for expanding the scope of economic evaluations in a manner that I suggest. Two strategies are suggested for estimating the economic benefit of achieving a qualitative improvement in an individual's life chances. One involves studying the actual decisions that parents make in raising their children, especially when it appears that a child suffers from a conduct problem or cognitive disorder such as attention deficit disorder. A related approach involves using surveys to learn about parental preferences for investing in their own and other children. A second and complementary approach for valuing improvements in life chances that avoids the income dependencies inherent in conventional benefit-cost analysis is to adapt the methods for measuring quality-adjusted life years in the medical domain to valuing developmental interventions.

I have also recommended a parallel research program for measuring the societal benefits of a lower crime rate. One dimension of that program involves further development of the contingent valuation method demonstrated by Cook and Ludwig (1998, 2000; see also Ludwig and Cook 2001). A second dimension would examine actual crime avoidance decisions made by individuals based on household purchase data and on an expanded National Crime Victimization Survey.

Governments spend vast sums to protect their citizens from crime. A comparatively modest investment in methods for better evaluating the effectiveness of these efforts will yield large returns.

REFERENCES

Anderson, David A. 1999. "The Aggregate Burden of Crime." *Journal of Law and Economics* 17:611–42.

Aos, Steve, Polly Phipps, Robert Barnoski, and Roxanne Lieb. 1999. "The Comparative Costs and Benefits of Programs to Reduce Crime: A Review of National Research Findings with Implications for Washington State." Unpublished manuscript. Olympia: Washington State Institute for Public Policy.

Arseneault, Louise, Avshalom Caspi, Terrie E. Moffitt, and Phil A. Silva. 1999. "Half of the Violence in a Cohort Is Accounted for by 3 DSM-III-R Disorders, and Each Disorder Explains Violence for a Different Reason." Working paper. London: Institute of Psychiatry.

Barnett, W. Steven. 1993. "Cost-Benefit Analysis." In *Significant Benefits: The*

High/Scope Perry Preschool Study through Age 27, edited by Lawrence J. Schweinhart, Helen V. Barnes, and David P. Weikart. Ypsilanti, Mich.: High/Scope Press.

———. 1996. *Lives in Balance: Age-27 Benefit-Cost Analysis of the High/Scope Perry Preschool Program.* Ypsilanti, Mich.: High/Scope Press.

Bureau of Justice Statistics. 1997. *Source Book of Criminal Justice Statistics.* Washington, D.C.: U.S. Department of Justice.

Caspi, Avshlom, Terrie E. Moffitt, Bradley R. Entner Wright, and Phil A. Silva. 1998. "Early Failure in the Labor Market: Childhood and Adolescent Predictors of Unemployment in the Transition to Adulthood." *American Sociological Review* 63:424–51.

Cohen, Mark A. 1988. "Pain, Suffering and Jury Awards: A Study of the Cost of Crime to Victims." *Law and Society Review* 22:538–55.

———. 1998. "The Monetary Value of Saving a High-Risk Youth." *Journal of Quantitative Criminology* 14:5–33.

Cohen, Mark A., Ted R. Miller, and Shelli B. Rossman. 1994. "The Costs and Consequences of Violent Behavior in the United States." In *Understanding and Preventing Violence*, vol. 4, *Consequences and Control*, edited by Albert J. Reiss, Jr., and Jeffrey A. Roth. Washington, D.C.: National Academy Press.

Cook, Philip J. 1983. "Costs of Crime." In *Encyclopedia of Crime and Justice*, vol. 1, edited by Sanford Kadish. New York: Macmillan.

Cook, Philip J., and Jens Ludwig. 1998. *A Conceptual Framework for Estimating the Costs of Firearm Injuries.* Mimeo. Durham, N.C.: Duke University.

———. 2000. *Gun Violence.* New York: Oxford University Press.

Curren, Randell. 1995. "Justice and the Threshold of Educational Equality." *Philosophy of Education* 50:239–48.

Donohue, John J., and Peter Siegelman. 1998. "Allocating Resources among Prisons and Social Programs in the Battle against Crime." *Journal of Legal Studies* 27:1–43.

Gold, Marthe R., Joanna E. Siegel, Louise B. Russell, and Milton C. Weinstein. 1996. *Cost-Effectiveness in Health and Medicine.* New York: Oxford University Press.

Gottfredson, Michael, and Travis Hirschi. 1986. "The True Value of Lambda Would Appear to Be Zero: An Essay on Career Criminals, Criminal Careers, Selective Incapacitation, Cohort Studies, and Related Topics." *Criminology* 24:213–34.

Greenwood, Peter W., Karyn E. Model, C. Peter Rydell, and James Chiesa. 1996. *Diverting Children from a Life of Crime: Measuring Costs and Benefits.* Santa Monica, Calif.: RAND.

Hagan, John, and Ronit Dinovitzer. 1999. "Collateral Consequences of Imprisonment for Communities, Children and Prisoners." In *Prisons*, edited by Michael Tonry and Joan Petersilia. Vol. 26 of *Crime and Justice: A Review of Research*, edited by Michael Tonry. Chicago: University of Chicago Press.

Hawkins, David J., Richard F. Catalano, Rick Kosterman, Robert Abbott, and Karl G. Hill. 1999. "Preventing Adolescent Health-Risk Behaviors by Strengthening Protection during Childhood." *Archives of Pediatric and Adolescent Medicine* 153:226–34.

Irwin, John. 1987. *The Felon.* Berkeley: University of California Press.

Kahneman, Daniel, and Jack L. Knetsch. 1992. "Valuing Public Goods: The Purchase of Moral Satisfaction." *Journal of Environmental Economics and Management* 22:57–70.

Kahneman, Daniel, and A. Tversky. 1983. "Choices, Values, and Frames." *American Psychologist* 39:341–50.

Karoly, Lynn A., Peter W. Greenwood, Susan S. Everingham, Jill Hoube, M. Rebecca Kilburn, C. Peter Rydell, Matthew Sanders, and James Chiesa. 1998. *Investing in Our Children: What We Know and Don't Know about the Costs and Benefits of Early Childhood Interventions.* Santa Monica, Calif.: RAND.

LeBlanc, Marc, and Rolf Loeber. 1998. "Developmental Criminology Updated." In *Crime and Justice: A Review of Research*, vol. 23, edited by Michael Tonry. Chicago: University of Chicago Press.

Levitt, Steven D. 1996. "The Effect of Prison Population Size on Crime Rates: Evidence from Prison Overcrowding Litigation." *Quarterly Journal of Economics* 111:319–52.

Levitt, Steven D., and Sudhir Alladi Venkatesh. 1998. "Drug-Selling Gang's Finances." Working Paper no. 6592. Cambridge, Mass.: National Bureau of Economic Research.

Lott, John R., Jr. 1998. *More Guns, Less Crime.* Chicago: University of Chicago Press.

Lott, John R., Jr., and David B. Mustard. 1997. "Crime, Deterrence, and Right-to-Carry Concealed Handguns." *Journal of Legal Studies* 26:1–68.

Ludwig, Jens, and Philip J. Cook. 2001. "The Benefits of Reducing Gun Violence." *Journal of Risk and Uncertainty* 22:207–26.

Miller, Ted R., Mark A. Cohen, and Brian Wiersma. 1996. *Victim Costs and Consequences: A New Look.* National Institute of Justice Research Report. NCJ-155282. Washington, D.C.: National Institute of Justice.

Moffitt, T. E. 1993. "Adolescence-Limited and Life-Course Persistent Antisocial Behavior: A Developmental Taxonomy." *Psychological Review* 100(4): 674–701.

———. 1997. "Adolescent-Limited and Life-Course-Persistent Offending: A Complementary Pair of Developmental Theories." In *Advances in Criminological Theory: Developmental Theories of Crime and Delinquency*, edited by T. Thornberry. London: Transaction Press.

Moffit, T. E., and S. Caspi. 1999. "Findings about Partner Violence from the Dunedin Multidisciplinary Health and Development Study." *National Institute of Justice Research in Brief.* Washington, D.C.: National Institute of Justice.

Nagin, Daniel S., and Richard E. Tremblay. 1999. "Trajectories of Boys' Physical Aggression, Opposition, and Hyperactivity on the Path to Physically Violent and Nonviolent Juvenile Delinquency." *Child Development* 70: 1181–96.

Olds, David L., John Eckenrode, Charles R. Henderson, Harriet Kitzman, Jane Powers, Robert Cole, Kimberly Sidora, Pamela Morris, Lisa M. Pettit, and Dennis Luckey. 1997. "Long-Term Effects of Home Visitation on Maternal Life Course and Child Abuse and Neglect: Fifteen-Year Follow-Up of a Randomized Trial." *Journal of the American Medical Association* 278:637–43.

Olds, David L., Charles R. Henderson, Robert Cole, John Eckenrode, Harriet Kitzman, Dennis Luckey, Lisa M. Pettit, Kimberly Sidora, Pamela Morris, and Jane Powers. 1998. "Long-Term Effects of Nurse Home Visitation on Children's Criminal and Antisocial Behavior: 15-Year Follow-Up of a Randomized Controlled Trial." *Journal of the American Medical Association* 280: 1238–44.

Olds, David L., Charles R. Henderson, Charles Phelps, Harriet Kitzman, and Carole Hanks. 1993. "Effects of Prenatal and Infancy Nurse Home Visitation on Government Spending." *Medical Care* 31:155–74.

Patterson, G. R., B. D. DeBaryshe, and E. Ramsey. 1989. "A Developmental Perspective on Antisocial Behavior." *American Psychologist* 44:329–35.

Poultin, Richie E., Mark Brooke, Terrie E. Moffitt, Warren Stanton, and Phil A. Silva. 1997. "Prevalence and Correlates of Cannabis Use and Dependence in Young New Zealanders." *New Zealand Medical Journal* 110:68–70.

Robins, L. N. 1978. "Sturdy Childhood Predictors of Adult Antisocial Behavior: Replication from Longitudinal Studies." *Psychological Medicine* 8:611–22.

Schweinhart, Lawrence J., Helen V. Barnes, and David P. Weikart. 1993. *Significant Benefits: The High/Scope Perry Preschool Study through Age 27*. Ypsilanti, Mich.: High/Scope Press.

Shover, Neal. 1996. *Great Pretenders: Pursuits and Careers of Persistent Thieves.* Boulder, Colo.: Westview Press.

Torrance, G. W., W. H. Thomas, and D. L. Sacket. 1972. "A Utility Maximization Model for Evaluation of Health Care Programs." *Health Services Research* 7:118–33.

Viscusi, W. Kip. 1993. "The Value of Risks to Human Life." *Journal of Economic Literature* 31:1912–46.

Welsh, Brandon C., and David P. Farrington. 2000. "Monetary Costs and Benefits of Crime Prevention Programs." In *Crime and Justice: A Review of Research*, vol. 25, edited by Michael Tonry. Chicago: University of Chicago Press.

Zimring, Franklin E., and Gordon J. Hawkins. 1995. *Incapacitation: Penal Confinement and Restraint of Crime.* New York: Oxford University Press.

Leena Kurki and Norval Morris

The Purposes, Practices, and Problems of Supermax Prisons

ABSTRACT

At least thirty-four American states in the late 1990s operated supermaximum security prisons or units, providing nearly 20,000 beds and accounting for 1.8 percent of the state prison population. Although conditions vary from state to state, many supermaxes subject inmates to nearly complete isolation and deprivation of sensory stimuli. Surprisingly little is known from research on who is sent to supermaxes, why, and for how long; the effects of supermaxes on security and conditions in other prisons; or the effects of supermax confinement on the mental conditions and social skills of inmates. Deleterious effects are likely to be especially acute for mentally ill and subnormal inmates. The recent proliferation of supermaxes appears premised on a belief that prison disorder is the product primarily of disruptive inmates rather than the characteristics of prison regimes; the best evidence suggests otherwise.

In 1984 there was only one prison in the United States that would now be called a "supermax"—the federal penitentiary at Marion, Illinois, after the October 1983 lockdown. In 1999, by various counts and various definitions, between thirty and thirty-four states had supermax prisons or units, with more building apace (National Institute of Corrections 1997; King 1999).

These prisons are far more expensive to build and enormously more expensive to run than ordinary maximum security prisons, and they impose enormous hardship on many of their inmates. Why this splurge of money and harshness? Have prisoners become more violent, more dangerous? The data do not so suggest. Have the politics of punish-

Leena Kurki is a senior research associate at the Council on Crime and Justice, Minneapolis. Norval Morris is Julius Kreeger Professor of Law and Criminology Emeritus at the University of Chicago.

0192-3234/2001/0028-0007$02.00

ment changed? Probably. It is surprising and disturbing how little reliable information about supermax prisons is available, considering their proliferation and the moral and policy issues they raise. Evaluation literature on various aspects of prison regimes exists, but there is not a single study on supermaxes. Most writings tend to be anecdotal newspaper articles or advocacy statements with little research value. More detailed descriptions exist from three supermaxes: Indiana's Maximum Control Facility (Human Rights Watch 1997), Indiana's Special Housing Unit in the Wabash Valley Correctional Institution (Human Rights Watch 1997), and Virginia's Red Onion (Human Rights Watch 1999). Conditions in Pelican Bay, California, are discussed extensively in *Madrid v. Gomez* (889 F. Supp. 1146 [N.D. Cal. 1995]) and conditions in Texas's Administrative Segregation Units in *Ruiz v. Johnson* (37 F. Supp. 2d 855 [S.D. Tex. 1999]). In addition to these, two surveys give general estimates on the number of supermax facilities and beds and describe some of their typical characteristics (National Institute of Corrections 1997; King 1999), and one study discusses criteria for their operation (Riveland 1999).

In this essay we raise a variety of policy and research questions about supermax prisons, but we are unable to provide definitive answers to them because the research on their operation and their effects on prisoners, staff, or other prisons is scant. Our coverage is also silent on the later conduct of prisoners released from supermax prisons to other prisons or to the free community; data on these subjects are completely lacking, their place taken by anecdotes of staff or prisoners, signifying little. The only available hard data we know of comes from three different sources. David Ward of the University of Minnesota interviewed a large number of transferees and releasees from Alcatraz, Marion, and Florence federal prisons, but his data are as yet unpublished and are not available to us. Results are available from a Home Office evaluation of Close Supervision Centers, which house the most dangerous and disruptive prisoners in England and Wales (Clare and Bottomley 2001). Similarly, we did not have access to data on interviews with prisoners in Oak Park Heights (Minnesota), Colorado State Penitentiary, or Pelican Bay (California), results of which will be published soon by Roy King from the University of Wales Bangor.

We do not discuss case law on the constitutionality—as distinct from the utility and morality—of conditions in supermax prisons or segregation and administrative detention; that case law is of great practical importance but it is fully discussed in a monograph of the National Institute of Corrections (1999). It seemed pointless for us to try to duplicate that study.

Here is how this essay is organized. In Section I we set a frame of reference to consider the evolution of the supermax prison. Section II is a description by Morris of the regime he observed at Tamms, a supermax prison in southern Illinois. Section III compares some of Tamms's characteristics to those observed by Human Rights Watch and federal district court judges in other supermax prisons in California, Indiana, Texas, and Virginia. Because some supermaxes hold prisoners in solitary confinement nearly all the time, and with few contacts with other people, their stresses are likely to be especially challenging to the mentally ill and deficient, of whom there are many in prison (Morris 1982). Accordingly, Section IV concentrates on mentally ill prisoners and the psychiatric effects of solitary confinement. Because removing troublemakers to supermax prisons is commonly justified as necessary for maintaining order, Section V briefly discusses order maintenance in prisons. In Section VI we try to sum up all this material and express our own view of the supermax movement.

I. The Spread of the Supermax

The National Institute of Corrections (1997) reports that as of December 1996, thirty states and the U.S. Bureau of Prisons were operating supermaxes and four states were considering them. At least fifty-seven supermax facilities and special housing units had a capacity to hold more than 13,500 inmates. Updating the National Institute of Corrections findings, King (1999) identified thirty-four states providing a total of 19,630 supermax beds. This accounted for 1.8 percent of the total state prison population, but the use of supermax facilities varied widely from state to state. In eight states and the federal system, 1 percent or less of prison space was designated as supermax. In five states, supermax beds constituted more than 5 percent of the prison capacity. At the high end were Mississippi (12 percent) and Arizona (7.7 percent), and at the low end New Jersey (0.3 percent), Georgia (0.3 percent), and the federal system (0.5 percent) (King 1999).

However, all these figures are at best estimates since lack of a generally accepted definition means that state departments classify very different types of facilities as supermax. For example, Oak Park Heights in Minnesota is generally considered a supermax, although it has little in common with the typical supermax. By contrast, the New York Department of Corrections refuses to acknowledge that any of its special housing units fit the definition of supermax though they clearly do (King 1999).

The National Institute of Corrections (1997) survey defines supermax prisons as facilities or units designated for inmates who have been disruptive or violent while incarcerated and whose behavior can be controlled only by separation, restricted movement, and limited direct access to staff and other inmates, thereby excluding routine disciplinary segregation, protective custody, or other routine purposes. By this definition, a supermax would confine only those prisoners who cannot be controlled by regular disciplinary means in other facilities. However, at least twelve jurisdictions also house protective custody and disciplinary segregation inmates in their supermaxes. In addition, in many supermaxes prisoners can graduate to units that have lower security requirements. For example, the Mississippi Department of Corrections estimates 20 percent of its prison capacity needs to be supermax space, but many inmates in Mississippi supermaxes may in fact be living in conditions that are comparable to regular maximum security prisons in other jurisdictions (National Institute of Corrections 1997).

Another survey published by the National Institute of Corrections (Riveland 1999, p. 6) defines a supermax as a highly restrictive unit or facility "that isolates inmates from the general prison population and from each other due to grievous crimes, repetitive assaultive or violent institutional behavior, the threat of escape or actual escape from high-custody facilities, or inciting or threatening to incite disturbances in a correctional institution."

While these broad definitions describe the goal of separation and the types of inmates that are housed in supermaxes, they fail to indicate the kinds of regimes supermax prisons typically maintain. They have at least four general characteristics.

First, assignment to a supermax prison is long-term, indefinite, and potentially for the rest of the prisoner's life. Confinement is measured in years rather than in months. For example, the average time served in the federal facility in Florence, Colorado, is over three years (Hershberger 1998), the minimum stay in South Carolina's Kirkland special unit is a year and a half (National Institute of Corrections 1997), and transfer from Virginia's Red Onion requires at least two years' confinement with no disruptive behavior (Human Rights Watch 1999).

Second, administrative admission and transfer criteria and procedures typically allow wide discretion to the prison authorities and need not provide even the same attenuated due process protection that must be provided before an inmate can be transferred to punitive segregation (Tachiki 1995; Henningsen, Johnson, and Wells 1999). When transfer to a supermax is being considered, the prisoner has no right to advance written notice or a formal hearing, to present witnesses and evidence, to be represented by an attorney, or to obtain a written decision. An informal opportunity to give the prisoner's statement to the decision maker, within reasonable time after administrative segregation has taken place, is enough to satisfy constitutional requirements (*Hewitt v. Helms*, 459 U.S. 460 [1983]). Common criteria for admission include gang activity or disruption of the orderly operation of a prison, both inclusive catchall criteria. For example, gang affiliation in itself without proof of engaging in an infraction can be considered a severe threat to the safety of others or the security of the prison and form a basis for admission to California's Pelican Bay. Transfer from Pelican Bay back into a conventional prison requires debriefing, meaning that the prisoner reveals his gang history and names of other gang members to the prison authorities (Tachiki 1995). This can often expose prisoners to risks of retaliation by gang members and involves a degree of submission to authority that many prisoners would find demeaning and violative of self-respect.

Third, many supermaxes maintain regimes characterized by nearly complete isolation and deprivation of environmental stimuli—not merely "secure control of inmates" or "limited direct access to staff and other inmates" (see National Institute of Corrections 1997, p. 1). The physical environment is a combination of concrete and steel, cells may lack windows, steel cell doors prohibit any view inside the facility, and the design of exercise yards prohibits any view outside the facility. A principal goal of architectural and technological design is limiting the need for correctional staff to interact with inmates (e.g., Amnesty International 1994). In the majority of facilities, inmates spend about twenty-three hours per day alone in their cells. At least sixteen correctional departments prohibit any interaction between supermax inmates or between inmates and staff (National Institute of Corrections 1997).

Communication with the outside world is also highly restricted. Visits and phone calls, if allowed at all, may be limited to one per month, and if visitors arrive, typically a reinforced glass wall separates them from the prisoner they are visiting. In some supermaxes the "visit" is only through the medium of two video screens.

Fourth, supermaxes typically are characterized by scant or no programmed activities. No work opportunities are offered. Law library, religious, and educational materials are typically delivered to cells and if any substance abuse treatment, vocational training, or the like is available, it is provided through television, correspondence, or written materials (King 1999).

Supermaxes have been described as prisons that "represent the application of sophisticated, modern technology dedicated entirely to the task of social control, and they isolate, regulate, and surveil more effectively than anything that has preceded them" (Haney 1997, p. 428).

The U.S. Constitution requires that medical and mental health care is available for supermax prisoners, although access to services, and quality, vary substantially. Mental health care is typically limited to medication management through antipsychotic or psychotropic drugs; psychiatric treatment is not an option. Psychiatrists are rarely available on a regular basis.

Dynamics of domination, control, subordination, and submission are fundamentally different from those in regular maximum security prisons. Consider Oak Park Heights, Minnesota, a maximum security prison that at the time of its opening in 1982 represented the highest achievement in prison design and technology and was an international model for prison security and management. King (1991) observed life there for four months in 1984. Prisoners were expected to participate in work, education, or treatment programs for seven hours per day and they were able to spend up to fifteen hours per day outside their cells. They could have visitors for sixteen hours per month and keep radios and televisions in their cells. Over one-third of the inmates made phone calls every day. At any time, two correctional officers were in the common areas with prisoners and direct contact between the staff and prisoners was encouraged. King (1991) reports that good and respectful relations between the staff and prisoners seemed genuine and could not have been falsely maintained for the length of his visit.

What changed so much in the United States that a state-of-the-art maximum security prison of the 1980s was not considered secure enough in the 1990s? Proliferation of supermaxes has been justified by changes in criminal justice and sentencing policies from the 1970s on. Thus some portray the supermax as just another symptom of law-and-order punitiveness and disbelief in rehabilitation (e.g., Haney and Zimbardo 1998; Henningsen, Johnson, and Wells 1999). Others say that supermaxes are a political symbol of toughness, because the initiative to build them frequently does not come from corrections departments but from elected officials and is not always based on need projections (Riveland 1999).

However, the most concrete change has been in rhetoric about prisoners. The new "dangerous" prisoner is described as more violent, more disturbed, more disruptive, and, therefore, less likely to adjust to ordinary prison conditions (Haney and Lynch 1997). When correctional departments were asked by the National Institute of Corrections about reasons to develop supermaxes, all but one mentioned the need to manage violent and seriously disruptive inmates better. Seventeen mentioned gang members and their activities (National Institute of Corrections 1997). Prison administrators often describe supermax inmates as "the worst of the worst" (Hershberger 1998, p. 54)—people who have nothing to lose and therefore do not hesitate from "taking a swing at a corrections officer or preying on another inmate" (Johnson 1997, p. A2).

All express goals of supermaxes relate to safety and security. The main purpose is to separate the most disruptive prisoners from one another and from possibly sympathetic or corrupted staff and to create a new kind of double incapacitation: not only to isolate prisoners from the rest of society but to isolate the worst of them from other prisoners and the staff (Harrington 1997). "When we were letting them rec together they were killing each other, so we had to stop" (prison administrator quoted in the *Washington Post*, August 25, 1996, p. C8). Isolation of the most dangerous prisoners reduces their opportunities to violate prison rules and routines but is also said to bring with it some other positive results. One argument is that when the worst are removed, the general prison population is normalized and can enjoy greater freedom of movement and access to educational, vocational, and other correctional programs (Sheppard, Geiger, and Welborn 1996; Hershberger 1998). Another is that supermaxes work as a general deterrent and decrease disruptive behavior in other facilities (Ward 1999). There is, however, only anecdotal evidence to support either of these propositions.

The hypothesis that supermaxes could normalize a prison system has never been evaluated and is judged false by many prison researchers: "What [special subsystems] cannot do is magically to unlock the problem of order for a prison system as whole. Their inherent [trouble] lies in being used as a distraction by those who would argue that just because prison 'control problems' are 'caused' by real individuals they are entirely individual by nature" (Sparks, Bottoms, and Hay 1996, p. 313).

King (1999) notes that prison administrators in other countries have looked to research to understand better the circumstances in which order is maintained in prisons without resort to coercion. In the United States, such research is scarce (see Bottoms 1999).

Since there is practically no empirical research (Ward 1995), it is difficult to be sure who is assigned to supermaxes, why they go, who gets out, when they get out, and how they get out. Some well-informed observers believe that some states overestimated the need for supermax space and have filled it with relatively low-risk inmates (Human Rights Watch 1997, 1999; King 1999).

It has been politically beneficial to ride the bandwagon of supermaxes and perhaps easier to obtain funding for them than for ordinary prisons. Once a supermax is built, there is a tendency to keep it full. Admission criteria typically specify very serious violations (e.g., threatening or injuring other prisoners or staff, possession of a deadly weapon or dangerous drugs, and escape attempts involving injury, threat of life, or use of a deadly weapon) but also leave room for much lesser violations (e.g., disruption of orderly operations; gang influences). Broad assignment criteria may well be used to keep supermaxes full rather than providing safeguards against arbitrary and unnecessary admissions, as was their original purpose. For example, Human Rights Watch (1999) reports that Virginia's Red Onion admits inmates who have no disruptive prison record solely on the basis of the length of their original sentence—a practice generally disapproved of by correctional administrators (Riveland 1999).

Some perspective on the question of who ends up in a supermax can be achieved from abroad. After England and Wales established special disciplinary units for difficult, dangerous, and disruptive prisoners in 1984, attempts were made to determine how this problem population was constructed and identified by prison administrators. Prison wardens were asked to nominate their lists of problem inmates, which then were compared to several other lists, including official records of disciplinary transfers, segregated inmates, and inmates involved in serious incidents. There was little overlap. Those who were identified as troublemakers by prison wardens had typically not experienced sanctions that were designed to deal with dangerous or disruptive behavior (King and McDermott 1990). These findings suggest that different groups of prisoners were identified as administrative problems and as disciplinary problems. As such, the findings support our belief that many prisoners are transferred to supermaxes because they are an administrative nuisance and not because they are particularly dangerous.

Many agree that mentally disordered or retarded inmates often have the most difficulty adjusting to prison routines, rules, and stress (e.g., Uhlig 1976; Toch 1982; Adams 1983; Toch and Adams 1986; Kupers 1999) and, thus, are more likely than other prisoners to be transferred to supermaxes. There are no general estimates on the prevalence of mental illnesses in supermax facilities. However, national (e.g., Veneziano and Veneziano 1996; Petersilia 1997; Powell, Holt, and Fondacaro 1997; Bureau of Justice Statistics 1999) and international studies (e.g., Hodgins and Côté 1991; Birmingham, Mason, and Grubin 1996, 1998; Smith et al. 1996; Bland et al. 1998) repeatedly show that mentally ill, disordered, or retarded persons are overrepresented in prisons and jails. For several reasons, mental health and psychiatric issues may be among the most important and problematic aspects of supermaxes. First, if many prisoners in supermaxes are mentally ill or retarded, should they not be the last, rather than the first, to find themselves in the harshest prison conditions? Second, what are the psychiatric effects of indefinite, long-term isolation on otherwise balanced personalities? Third, what are the effects of such isolation on mentally disordered prisoners?

While there is no proof of positive effects of the supermax on prisoners or on prison systems, evidence of its negative effects is also scant. Views on psychiatric consequences of isolation and sensory deprivation in a prison setting are highly polarized (see Harrington 1997). While some have not found any profound detrimental effects (e.g., Suedfeld et al. 1982; Bonta and Gendreau 1984, 1990; Suedfeld 1984; Rogers 1993), others see definite risks of emotional and psychological damage (e.g., Lucas 1976; Grassian and Friedman 1986; Luise 1989; Haney 1997; Haney and Lynch 1997). However, few studies have focused with any precision on the consequences of long-term isolation in supermax conditions or the effects on mentally ill or retarded inmates (e.g., Grassian 1983).

Because so little systematic evidence, either descriptive or evaluative, is available, we provide here a description of the regime at Tamms supermax in Illinois. In the nature of things, the depiction is subjective. It corresponds closely, however, with similar descriptions provided by Human Rights Watch and by European supermax visitors such as Anthony Bottoms, Roy King, and Rod Morgan.

II. Supermax: The Bad and the Mad

Morris visited the federal supermax at Florence, Colorado, on two occasions and its predecessor at Marion in Illinois several times. Marion was designed to take many prisoners then held in Alcatraz when that institution in the bay of San Francisco was abandoned; and now Florence takes over from Marion. Many states then followed suit.

Tamms is an expensive Illinois investment. It cost over $73 million to build, and it runs at a per prisoner cost of $35,800 per year, roughly twice the per prisoner cost of a maximum security prison in the same state. This is considered inexpensive in Europe. In England, for example, the annual cost per prisoner in a maximum security facility is about twice the cost of a prisoner in Tamms.

There are two categories of prisoners in Tamms—disciplinary detainees and administrative detainees. There are those who come to Tamms while serving a disciplinary sentence for a prison offense in another prison, a term of disciplinary detention imposed on them in the prison from which they came—it is thus for them a prison's prison for offenses that are prison adjudicated. And there are those in the second group who, at the time of their transfer, were not being punished for any prison offense. The Tamms population of 270 is about equally divided between these two groups.

To be legalistic about who goes to Tamms, the pertinent regulation, Section 505.40(b) of the Illinois Administrative Code, reads: "Among other matters, a committed person who the Department has determined has engaged in the following activities or who may be planning to engage in these activities may be referred for placement in the Tamms Correctional Center: escaping or attempting to escape; assaulting staff, inmates or other persons which caused death or serious bodily injury; engaging in dangerous disturbances; having influence in activities of a gang or other unauthorized organization; engaging in non-consensual sexual conduct; or possessing weapons."

That defines the group who may be sent to Tamms. Consider the breadth and elasticity of the phrase "who may be planning to engage in any of these activities," and consider how many prisoners at one time or another "possess weapons" or "engage in dangerous disturbances."

But there are a further six concerns that those responsible for sending a prisoner to Tamms, pursuant to 505.40(d) of the code, must bear in mind: "Placement in the Tamms Correctional Center shall be based upon the following considerations, including but not limited to: the safety and security of the facility, the public, or any person; the committed person's disciplinary and behavioral history; reports and recommendations concerning the committed person; the feasibility of transfer to another facility; medical concerns; and mental health concerns."

Let me now tell you something of the life of a prisoner in Tamms. Your cell measures ten feet by twelve feet. It is made of poured concrete with a steel door—no bars—just a lot of little holes, smaller than the tip of your little finger, punched through it. You have a stainless steel toilet and sink built as a unit that would not be easy to destroy. There is a small window, high and narrow, that lets in a little outside light. There is a mirror made of polished metal, again tending to be indestructible. Your bunk or bed, or whatever you may call it, is also of poured concrete, an integral part of the cell, but you have a slim plastic foam mattress to put on it. There is a well-protected fluorescent light and a light switch. At night, in case you are scared of the dark, the light cannot be turned off entirely; it unrestrainedly gives out a dim light, bright enough for the guards to peer in at you. There is a small trapdoor, low down on the steel door to your cell, through which your food can be pushed to you.

When you are allowed into the exercise yard for an hour, you will find that you are alone in a concrete square, larger than your cell, with a small grating high in the corner of the roof through which you can see the sky. Recently there seems to be some showing of weakness on the part of the Department of Corrections. The exercise yard still has in it no exercise equipment but some prisoners are now allowed to have tough rubber handballs to throw against the walls of the yard.

Your clothing: three jumpsuits (tan), three T-shirts (white), three undershorts (white), three pairs of socks (white), one pair of soft-soled shoes, one knitted cap (blue), two towels (white), one washcloth (white). Provided you remain of good behavior (which really means no bad behavior, since the opportunities for other than promptly conforming behavior are limited) you may also have a wristwatch, a wedding band, a pen, a religious medallion (provided it represents no threat of being converted to a weapon), a dictionary (provided it has only a soft cover), a plastic cup, a coffee cup, and a reasonable supply of paperback books. No picture frames are allowed in your cell but you may have up to fifteen photographs with you.

So much for your cell and your accoutrements. What about contacts with the world outside Tamms? You are given three prestamped envelopes a month and you can pay for more. Depending on your punishment status and your behavior, which I will discuss later, visiting privileges range from once a month to four times a month. But because Tamms is a very long haul from most prisoners' families (many are from Chicago, 350 miles away), visits remain infrequent for all but a very few prisoners. Phone calls are not allowed except in certain emergency situations.

To continue this account of contacts with the world outside the cell, the distinction between the two categories of prisoners in Tamms—disciplinary detainees and administrative detainees—comes into play. The disciplinary detainees, during the term of their disciplinary sentence, receive fewer privileges at Tamms than the administrative detainees, though the differences are not substantial. For the first ninety days, disciplinary detainees receive one shower per week, one hour in the exercise yard per week, and no commissary. After ninety days, if detainees exhibit good behavior, they are allotted one shower per week, five hours per week in the exercise yard, one visit per month, and one commissary per month.

By less-than-sharp contrast, though to prisoners these things matter greatly, administrative detainees for the first ninety days receive one shower per week, two hours in the exercise yard per week, one visit per month, no commissary. After ninety days, if of good behavior, two showers per week, five hours per week in the exercise yard, two visits per month, and one commissary per month; in addition, administrative detainees who have progressed in grade may buy their own television set and watch educational or religious programming.

After six months of good behavior these privileges blossom for both groups into four showers per week, seven hours of exercise per week, four visits per month, two commissary days per month, and they may be allowed a television set in their cell, the available programs of course being centrally controlled.

It bears repetition that these functions—showers, yard, commissary—are not pursued in the company of other prisoners. Going to a shower, the prisoner walks a line, clad in a towel, to the small shower room. He is observed from above by an armed guard looking down on him through a metal grate. The guard can also release a swift-acting disabling gas to discourage any recalcitrance on the way to or from or during the shower. Escorting to the exercise yard normally involves three guards accompanying the prisoner who is heavily shackled until he reaches the exercise yard and one armed guard observer walking above the entourage looking through the steel grating to inhibit any hint of aggression by the prisoner—and likewise on the return journey an hour thereafter.

These few prisoner/staff contacts tend not to be harmonious. Put curtly, they foster a "we/they" relationship of considerable hostility.

All in all, this amounts to solitary confinement far more severe than the solitary confinement imposed in the segregation units of the maximum security prisons—more punitive than "the hole." Prisons thus now have their prisons not just their punishment cells and their withdrawal of congregate and private privileges—thus prisons' prisons' prisons. And the minimum term for all in Tamms is one year—so it is officially predicted and so far enforced.

Visits, when they occur, are your longest flight to a less hostile world. You are taken shackled after an anal search to a small booth and seated facing a thick wall of glass. Your visitor or visitors are seated on the opposite side of that glass. There is no opening in it through which anything can be passed. You talk through microphones on each side of the glass.

Family visits are hard on the visitors. They have to travel long and expensive distances and they must receive specific permission in advance for each visit. As they enter the outer grounds of Tamms and approach the buildings they are likely to be vigorously checked for alcohol, drugs, or nicotine products.

They may be gruffly ordered out of the car that will have brought them to Tamms. The order will be barked by the leader of a team of near riot-clad men. "Barked" is not inappropriate since this team is accompanied by a dog that assists their inspection of visitors and their car by diligently searching, sniffing, and rooting about for contraband. It is, the visitors tell me, an unsettling experience.

Within the building your visitors will be further checked electronically and body searched with a "pat down." Once in the visitors room, communication is not easy. Usually, the prisoner has not much to talk about; he is, after all, denuded of recent experiences other than those occurring within the curtilage of his mind and skin, and typically he is not skilled in light badinage. In the end, visits tend to wane in frequency for all but a very few Tamms prisoners. Visiting privileges, ranging from one to four a month, are for most prisoners a rhetorical flourish rather than a reality.

Visits by your lawyer, if you are fortunate enough to still have such a luxury as a lawyer, are allowed. And if your lawyer actually visits you, rather than merely exchanging letters with you, the meeting will take place in slightly different circumstances. There will be the same glass divider between you and the same microphonic communication, but a prison guard will also sit in a little booth abutting the side of the visiting booths. There will be slots between him and you, and between him and your lawyer visitor, through which documents can be passed under the guard's close observation for contraband.

Without a lawyer for your appeal or for any other legal action, civil or criminal, in which you may be involved, you may wish to seek out the relevant law for yourself. This is possible but difficult. In a long series of cases, the federal courts have established the range of law books that a prison library must contain to facilitate prisoners' access to the courts. In other words, the constitutionally minimally adequate law library has been defined. Tamms has one. Tamms also employs a prisoner to work in the law library to copy whatever extracts from law books you or any prisoner may require. All that sounds very reasonable until one reflects on what little knowledge all but the most exceptional Tamms prisoner has of the law. And the law clerk knows very little more. Nevertheless, it seems clear that Tamms has abided by the legal constitutional requirements.

You are not, of course, isolated from the Tamms staff. The clergyman visits regularly, as do the social worker, the psychologist, the nurse, and various categories of guards who are checking on you or passing your food to you. All these contacts take place through the multiholed steel door. If you need medical attention you will be shackled and escorted, as if going to the exercise yard, by a team of guards. And you will also be shackled to the floor while, for instance, you are talking to the visiting psychiatrist. The medical and dental services are adequately available—there is no desire to have to transport you to an outside hospital.

Should you, as some prisoners have been known to do, throw urine or feces, your food, or anything else at a guard through the little openings in the steel door to your cell, the remedy is easy—a plastic shield is superimposed on the far side of your cell door. This will have a secondary effect. While the steel door remains uncovered it is possible to have some sort of communication with the prisoner in a neighboring cell by shouting loudly. This is seen by many who work in Tamms as a design defect in the building. If the plastic cover goes up, that distant noise of another is effectively inhibited.

Should you or any other prisoner prove recalcitrant at any time, swift action will be taken. For example, suppose you decide to disobey an order to facilitate coming out of your cell, that is, to come forward in the proper manner so that your hands and feet can be shackled without risk to the guards. You will be told again what to do. On your third refusal to obey promptly you will be "extracted" from the cell.

Five men dressed, armed, and protected rather like Darth Vader enter your cell and with a large plastic shield pin you to the wall. This facilitates two of them safely chaining your feet together and your arms together at the wrist behind your back. You are then removed from your cell. The extraction is complete. Extractions are not pleasant to observe; nevertheless all extractions are videotaped so that any allegations of excessive force you care to make can be rebutted.

In one of my visits to Tamms I stumbled upon an extraction. It was not arranged for me to see; I chanced upon it because I went where I wished to go (accompanied by a deputy warden) and spoke to whomever I wished to speak (not overheard by a deputy warden). A gathering of chattering staff in a corridor caught my interest and I joined them. They were there for the entertainment. Five men were dressing in the corridor—big men, ornate apparel, heavy boots, black coveralls cinched at the waist, hoods and gas masks, and garish orange garments covering shoulders, body, and thigh, a startling contrast to the otherwise black accoutrements. This was no swift vestment; details had to be firmly set—one helped another. Heavy gloves were then donned and batons grasped. The lead man who carried a man-sized plastic shield took up his position; the other four formed a unit behind him, all close together like the front and ten legs of a monstrous centipede. In unison, with short, stamping, loud steps they moved forward—left, right, left, right, along the corridor curving to face the first cell in the cell block. A guard with a video camera took up his position behind the centipede. The assembled gapers, myself included, now stood silent, awed by the whole performance.

By now the much less courageous inmate had decided to obey orders. He was told to undress to his underpants and pass his clothes out through the slot in the cell door for weapons inspection. He did so. His clothes were then returned to him and he dressed and put his wrists backward through the slot to be handcuffed together. The lead guard of the five then put down the plastic shield that would have been used to pin the prisoner to the wall after he had been "maced" with a pepper gas. The other four guards would have taken hold of an extremity and continued the extraction. The crowd lost interest. The prisoner was led away. I asked what would happen to him. "Only a month or two extra," said the deputy warden then accompanying me.

The other prisoners on the pod of cells that make up the divisions of the prison also knew of this aborted extraction. Indeed, they have warning of all extractions in their pod since five or so minutes before one commences the fans are turned on so that the pepper gas will be dispersed from other spaces than the cell where it is used.

But in fact the extraction, and certainly not the threat of an extraction that I observed, is not the end of it. Perchance you had precipitated the extraction by throwing food at the guard. Or perchance in the melee of the extraction you had lashed out at or struck a guard assisting in the extraction. If so, it is likely that you will be charged with aggravated battery for that offense—aggravated because it is a guard you struck and not merely a citizen. The preliminary hearings prior to trial will be heard by a visiting judge in a small courtroom deep in the bowels of Tamms adjacent to the state's execution chamber. If you insist on a jury trial, or do not plead guilty in return for a lighter sentence, the trial itself will be held before a jury in a courtroom in a nearby town. You will not find it easy to controvert the video recording of the incident before a jury, most of whom have relatives or friends working in Tamms, or who are appreciative of the business Tamms has brought to this otherwise impoverished region. Acquittal is unlikely and the punishment is likely to be any length from a year of imprisonment up to a maximum of ten years. The extension of your time both in Tamms and, if you are fortunate, in other prisons is far from unlikely. There seems no end to the belief in deterrent controls. Recently, a prisoner who threw water and spat on a guard was offered a plea bargain of eight years.

And yet a further deterrent control has been added to Tamms's armamentarium: the "mealoaf." The mealoaf is designed to be entirely tasteless though sufficiently nutritious; should it be ordered for an infraction it will constitute your only food for a prescribed number of days in order to teach you conformity. The supermax has thus improved on bread and water.

If you manage to avoid such miseries as extractions, how do you stand? Month after month you are thrown back on your own inner resources, a commodity usually not generously present in Tamms prisoners. Is there work to do? Not in Tamms. Education? Entertainment? No and no, other than in the "library's" supply of paperback books, which tend to the western and sickly romantic. You do have a Bible and a dictionary and writing paper, and they help. But, as Churchill said of his brief time in a Boer prison, "The minutes crawl by like constipated centipedes." The consolations and inspirations of religious belief are delivered through the steel door. There are no congregate ceremonies. The insights of professional counseling, such as they are, are also available, but they too are offered through the distance of the steel door.

Misbehavior is swiftly sanctioned. An extraction is a not inconsiderable threat, and to back it up there is the likely prolongation of your residence in Tamms. In any event, you will be in Tamms for a year at minimum and you are on disciplinary segregation until the term of that punishment has expired. But thereafter there is a chance, a realistic chance, of returning to the relative comfort and conviviality of a maximum security prison, unless you have demonstrated undesirable behavior while in Tamms.

All in all, these are harsh conditions for anyone, but it should be appreciated that they are formidably harsh conditions for the mentally ill and those teetering on the brink of serious mental illness—of which there are more than a few in Tamms. For example, on the day I first visited Tamms there were either nine or eleven prisoners taking prescription psychotropic drugs—the visiting psychiatrist was not sure of the number! He did recall that there had been two prisoners transferred to the prison mental hospital run by the Department of Corrections. Many have since been so transferred.

What purposes does this expensive regime at Tamms serve? The warden answers, Two: first, it removes the worst troublemakers from the other prisons and thus makes them safer for staff and prisoners alike; second, by its notorious harshness, a notoriety spread and even exaggerated throughout the entire prison system, it serves as a deterrent to those who otherwise might be troublemakers in the other prisons. Hence you fall for your country in Tamms; you suffer so that many more will not suffer.

A defect in this analysis is that these two purposes are offered as a mantra, as a fixed belief beyond cavil, supported by selected hearsay prison stories. The mantra has never been tested. It is doubtful that it is true. It could be tested empirically. It should be.

But even if it were true, does it justify the degree of adversity visited on the Tamms prisoners? Even in your prison cell in Tamms you will not find that an easy question to answer with any precision. How much suffering by one justifies the avoidance of suffering by others? While you are meditating your answer, let me tell you by what decisional processes of the prison administration you found your way to Tamms.

The courts are, of course, necessary to get you into prison, but judges do not sentence you to serve your term in Tamms. You are sent there by administrative decision not judicial decision. Under the U.S. Constitution, due process is the condition precedent to punishment. If Tamms is a punishment added to your properly imposed prison term, then it attracts this constitutionally sanctified due process. What does due process mean in the context of Tamms?

The Department of Corrections regulations require the warden of Tamms to appoint two of his staff as a "transfer review committee" to advise him on your suitability for detention in Tamms and the wisdom of its continuance. They are directed to interview you within ten days of your arrival at Tamms. Thereafter, every ninety days they must review your record, though there is no requirement that they interview you on these subsequent occasions. Their recommendations go to the warden of Tamms who may recommend to headquarters at Springfield your further detention at or your transfer from Tamms.

For those in administrative detention, as distinct from disciplinary detention, every year you will also be afforded an interview at which you appear in person before the transfer review committee. Of course, the hearing may be held at your cell's door. And if you are thought to be or to have been a member of a street gang, whether in or out of prison, there is an obstacle in even being allowed to seek a hearing before the transfer review committee. You must first petition to perform a "renunciation." A renunciation is described in ambiguous terms in the general order that requires it as a precondition to the hearing by the review committee, but what is involved is an interview by a guard in which the sincerity of your renunciation is tested by your disclosure of the names of those in the street gang (now in prison or on the streets) with whom you were affiliated. Only when thus satisfied of the sincerity of your renunciation will the transfer review committee consider your case. The whole maneuver awards a badge and announces to all that you are an informer, which has obvious and lasting threatening consequences.

To risk a little amateur philosophy: How does one choose between sensory near-isolation for a year for A and a greater risk of violence for B? Surely, in utilitarian terms the choice thus stated is impossible; the two are incommensurable. So it must be a deontological choice.

The answer seems to me clear. Only in the most obvious and extreme cases should the sensory deprivation be imposed. There are such cases, but they are rare indeed. They are certainly not adequately defined by the regulations and procedures that put prisoners in Tamms.

In conscience I cannot omit further discussion of the mentally ill in Tamms. Throughout the United States, the mental health deinstitutionalization movement of the last quarter of the twentieth century and the closure of many mental hospitals had the expansion of community-based treatment and shelter for those evicted from the institutions as its corollary and necessary promise. The promise was not kept. Shelters and community-based care remain in scant supply. What little is available often excludes the indigent mentally ill and has been captured by those with some funds to meet the costs of care. As a result, hundreds of thousands of mentally ill indigent and other-than-wealthy patients found themselves consigned to prison-like hostels, to the streets, to jails, and to prisons. Prison and jail populations swelled as the mental hospitals constricted.

For the time being, this process shows little sign of reversing itself, though a few private institutions do meet the needs of some patients, and some families harbor others. But the political reality is that an increasingly large number of prison and jail slots in this country are occupied by the mentally ill, the weight of their treatment or neglect falling on the prison and jail mental health services. It is a matter lacking precision, but the best current estimate is that 10–20 percent of the population of U.S. prisons and jails suffer diagnosable and treatable serious mental illness; and supermax units hold more than their fair share.

I find it hard to imagine what it must be like for anyone in a Tamms cell at night, isolated from everyone and everything that stimulates life, one's half-sleep filled with terrors and then waking yet again with the mind racing from imaginary conversation to imaginary conversation, none signifying anything, with hopes only for a very distant future, and with thoughts of suicide and its means pervasive. And if you add to that, for the mentally ill, periods of hallucination, of visual and audible stimuli—many of them realistic and powerfully threatening—and their pain becomes more than my empathy can reach.

Of course, psychotropic drugs can reduce the pain and engender a dull shuffling, and a somnolent blankness, but the Tamms regime intensifies even this. All of which leads to the question of whether the mentally ill should be held in Tamms. It seems a merely rhetorical question, requiring an immediate negative reply; but in reality it is more pointed than it seems.

Divide the world of the seriously mentally ill into two parts—clearly a superficial division, but bear with it. One group will be those who are withdrawn into their own fantasy life, deeply depressed, catatonic, passive, and unassertive; they will not normally find their way to Tamms. They are indeed the residue of the seriously mentally ill that are found in our mental hospitals, or homeless on the streets, or in jails, or scraping by in marginal circumstances; but they do not manifest that behavior, whether in or out of prison, that would in prison bring them to Tamms. It is the others, the aggressive, the bizarre, the acting-out mentally ill that can become Tamms inmates.

The problems of causation of human behavior are not easy. In the previous paragraph I introduced the weasel words "seriously mentally ill" as if those words described a clearly diagnosable class. They do not. The line between aggression precipitated by a sense of injustice, and aggression precipitated by mental illness is not clear. Nor is the line between malingering and mentally disturbed hostility. In practice, those who run maximum security prisons tend to see the proper site for the passive seriously mentally ill as in mental hospitals or special medical treatment prisons that now exist in the federal prison system and in some state systems. By contrast, they see the others—the hostile and aggressive—unless their symptoms are particularly bizarre, as properly to be held in prison or in punishment blocks in prisons or in institutions like Tamms.

There is a more insidious aspect of the processes that put the mentally ill in jails, prisons, and supermax prisons. More than the community at large, the criminal justice system and those who serve it rely on deterrence as a system to control human behavior. A substantial proportion of those who suffer from mental illness, or who are marginally retarded, or who tremble on the brink of those conditions tend to respond unfavorably and with increasing resistance to punitive controls. The supposed equilibrium of misbehavior and deterrent punishment is thus ratcheted up step by step so that the inadequate and troubled personality may be jailed for a minor offense and by virtue of an increasing process of deterrent punishment, increased resistance, increased deterrent punishment, yet further increased resistance, the result is a stepping up through the graduated severity of different prisons to the ultimate location in a Tamms.

The Department of Corrections has its rules to exclude the mentally ill from Tamms: when a warden recommends a prisoner for transfer to Tamms, "except in cases of emergency, the medical and master record files" of that prisoner "shall be reviewed by a mental health professional prior to the committed person's placement at Tamms Correctional Center" (Department of Corrections 1999, p. 4). The mental health professional conducting the review shall identify inmates who

> (1) have been on enforced psychotropic medications in the two years preceding the review; (2) have been assigned to the Department's Dixon Psychiatric Unit or committed to a community mental health unit within two years preceding the review; (3) have had serious suicidal attempts within the two years preceding the review; (4) are actively psychotic or are evaluated as having a high probability of decompensating quickly within the near future; (5) have a history of being non-compliant with psychotic medication and exhibiting serious mental illness; (6) display a behavior pattern of frequent and severe and/or bizarre self-mutilation; (7) have been adjudicated Guilty but Mentally Ill; (8) have a recent history of multiple incidents requiring the use of therapeutic restraints, especially when the restraints have been ordered for long periods of time; (9) have exhibited mental health problems during previous placement at Tamms Correctional Center; and (10) present other serious mental health concerns, which would suggest placement at Tamms Correctional Center would be inappropriate. (Department of Corrections 1999)

These regulations do not prohibit a mentally ill person being sent to Tamms. They require merely a notification by a health professional of one or more of the above events.

Apart from the ambiguity of some of the concepts in these ten warning signals, their fatal defect, in my view, is that no face-to-face interview with the patient is required; they rely on records that are notoriously imprecise and often grossly insufficient. Further, the "mental health professional" who scans these records prior to the inmate's transfer to Tamms is defined as a "psychiatrist, physician, psychiatric nurse, clinically trained psychologist, or an individual who has a master's degree in social work and clinical training" (Department of Corrections 1999).

Orders like the above are not self-enforcing. They depend for their efficacy in the first place on the quality of record keeping in prison.

They depend further, up to the prisoner's arrival in Tamms, on the perception of people entirely untrained in the recognition of mental illness.

When the prisoner arrives in Tamms, there is still no mandatory psychiatric examination by anyone trained in that discipline. As a result, certainly at the time of writing, there are several floridly psychotic prisoners in Tamms and several more teetering on the brink of clearly diagnosable psychosis. No prisoner should be placed in Tamms or a prison like it without having been interviewed at reasonable length by a psychiatrist and then again at least quarterly by a psychiatrist whose daily practice is not concerned with that prison.

As to where and how to control the criminal and dangerous mentally ill, the best we can do is to recognize the reality of the pressures of mental illness on human behavior and to provide systems of control, support, and treatment in specialized institutions, a few of which currently exist in the United States and in Europe.

The official, legislatively approved, publicly proclaimed "mission of the Department of Corrections is to protect the public from criminal offenders through a system of incarceration and supervision which securely segregates offenders from society, assures offenders of their constitutional rights and maintains programs to enhance the success of the offender's reentry into society" (Department of Corrections 1999).

Is that what was happening at Tamms? It is hard for anyone who knows the place to so believe, and that skepticism includes some of those leading the Illinois Department of Corrections, including its senior medical staff. Only those who resolutely turn their eyes from reality could so believe and prosper by proclaiming the myth of effective prison control rather than the reality of psychological injury to especially vulnerable human beings.

III. Similarities: Tamms and Other Supermaxes

Many things about Illinois's Tamms are described similarly in other writings about supermaxes in California (*Madrid v. Gomez*, 889 F. Supp. 1146), Indiana (Human Rights Watch 1997), Texas (*Ruiz v. Johnson*, 37 F. Supp. 2d 855), and Virginia (Human Rights Watch 1999). In all five states, supermaxes provide minimum physical necessities (food, warmth, clothes, shelter, hygiene) and attempt to provide other minimum constitutionally mandated necessities (medical and mental health care, religious and legal materials). They deliberately deny other privileges common in prison: work, treatment programs, leisure activities, human interaction, a decent environment.

The physical environment is similar in Tamms, Pelican Bay, Red Onion, and Indiana's and Texas's supermaxes. Cells are a combination of steel and concrete—toilet, sink, and door are steel, the rest is concrete. Exercise yards have concrete floors and walls, lack an outside view, and differ little from cells. They are often empty, although some may have an exercise bar, a basketball hoop and basketball, or a rubber handball. Cells do not have showers or their own exercise yards. When prisoners go to the shower or to the exercise yard, they are handcuffed and shackled and accompanied by several guards. Time and again, the environment is described as "old, hard, and austere" (Human Rights Watch 1997, p. 23) or "dull sameness in design and color" that reinforces detachment from the outside world (*Madrid v. Gomez* at 1228).

Also, there are few differences in privileges between these facilities, for which detailed descriptions are available. Prisoners stay about twenty-three hours each day in their cells. They are allowed three to five showers per week, five to seven hours of exercise per week, and one to four visits per month. Some facilities allow phone calls, televisions, and radios to some of their inmates. In all, visitors stay behind a reinforced glass wall and conversations take place through a telephone. No work, programs, or leisure activities are offered. If social workers, nurses, or priests stop by, they stay behind the steel door. Organization and practice of medical and mental health care vary, but it is often a nurse or a medical technical assistant who screens incoming prisoners and decides whether a prisoner can see a doctor, psychologist, or psychiatrist. Reports on Indiana's supermaxes and Virginia's Red Onion indicate that inmates have real difficulties receiving adequate medical and mental health care (Human Rights Watch 1997, 1999). *Madrid v. Gomez* held that Pelican Bay's health care system was incapable of satisfying minimum constitutional standards and deliberately neglected medical needs of inmates. *Ruiz v. Johnson* found that the medical and psychiatric care systems of Texas prisons were "grossly wanting" (at 907), although not unconstitutional, but only since the present standards for proving unconstitutionality are "inordinately high" (at 892) and "permit inhumane treatment of inmates" (at 907).

Although supermax prisoners are typically isolated from one another, Pelican Bay's special housing unit and Red Onion's general unit double-cell prisoners. It is striking that inmates who are considered too dangerous to live with the general prison population are considered suitable to live with each other all but an hour or two each day. Inmates are forced to live in an intimate and private relationship with another prisoner in a small concrete cube without any power to influence with whom they are sharing their life (Haney 1997). In Pelican Bay, inmates who had previously assaulted their cell mates continued to be double-celled—a practice criticized but not found unconstitutional in *Madrid v. Gomez* because the plaintiffs were not able to show "deliberate indifference" by prison administrators to the risks of these arrangements.

The practice of cell extractions seems to be similar in supermaxes. Relatively nonthreatening disobedience—like a failure to return a food tray or to submit hands for cuffing—may result in a massive maneuver in which four to six officers with special gear, helmets, gloves, and equipment (increasingly including mace and stun guns) enter the cell in order to restrain and remove the prisoner. However, there are differences in the frequency of cell extractions and in the amount of force and weapons used. Pelican Bay had overstepped the constitutional line: multiple weapons of gas gun, mace, taser (shooting darts that give up to 50,000 volt electric shocks), and metal baton were regularly used during cell extractions. There was a pattern of "routinely using the same extremely high level of force" and evidence that "cell extractions at Pelican Bay have too often been considered, not as tools to be used sparingly in response to threats to prison security, but as opportunities to punish and inflict pain" (*Madrid v. Gomez* at 1178).

Observations of relations between the staff and inmates vary from "considerable hostility" in Tamms and "unusually hostile" in Red Onion (Human Rights Watch 1999, p. 20) to an "affirmative management strategy to permit the use of excessive force" in Pelican Bay (*Madrid v. Gomez* at 1199). All the characteristics of supermaxes are more likely than not to create a culture that supports abuse of power. Inmates are labeled as the worst of worst and are isolated from other inmates. The staff have practically unlimited power to control inmates' access to food, possessions, and movement. Any humane relationships between staff and inmates are rare in circumstances where interaction is limited to the most dangerous situations—extracting inmates from cells or escorting shackled and handcuffed inmates to showers, exercise yards, visiting areas, or medical care (Ward 1995). Supermaxes are far removed from the usual sights, sounds, standards, and restrictions of everyday prison life and far removed from the perception of the outside world. The physical and intellectual isolation "helps create a palpable distance from ordinary compunctions, inhibitions, and community norms"—for both the staff and prisoners (*Madrid v. Gomez* at 1160).

No one knows how common abuses of power or the use of excessive force are in supermax prisons. However, many agree that supermax regimes are more likely than other prison regimes to produce abusive and violent behaviors by the staff. Pelican Bay in the early 1990s must have been among the worst examples with a deliberate pattern of violence and excessive force, but unspeakable incidents are also described in *Ruiz v. Johnson* on Texas administrative segregation units and in Human Rights Watch (1997, 1999) reports on Red Onion and Indiana's supermaxes.

Even in Tamms, where staff are rigidly controlled and closely monitored, as an act of personal punishment by a guard a mealoaf was injected with a pepper-like substance to burn a prisoner's mouth; to the credit of the director of corrections and the warden, the guard was immediately and summarily dismissed, the ire of the union notwithstanding.

Quite apart from whether administrative rules exclude mentally ill prisoners from supermaxes, many such prisoners are held in Tamms, Pelican Bay, Red Onion, and Indiana's and Texas's supermaxes. The chief of medical services estimated that 208 prisoners at Pelican Bay in 1990 were either psychotic or psychotic in partial remission (*Madrid v. Gomez* at 1215). Stuart Grassian found that seventeen out of fifty inmates he interviewed in the special housing unit were acutely psychotic and not receiving appropriate treatment (*Madrid v. Gomez* at 1223). The staff of Indiana's special housing unit acknowledged that half to two-thirds of inmates were mentally ill (Human Rights Watch 1997, p. 34). Crisis symptoms of mental illnesses are obvious to everyone: severe self-mutilation, hallucinations, paranoia, panic attacks and anxiety, and impulsive violence (Kupers 1999). Yet descriptions about Tamms, Pelican Bay, Red Onion, and Indiana's and Texas's supermaxes similarly point out that the mental health staff in these supermaxes seemed to be preoccupied with sorting out those inmates they believed were manipulative malingerers who faked their symptoms. All sources describe inmates who suffer serious hallucinations, act absurdly, and are far beyond ordinary human behavior.

Mental health screening and monitoring is characterized as inadequate in all these supermaxes. Evaluations of arriving inmates, if any, are based on written records. Access to a psychologist or psychiatrist is often controlled by a medical assistant or a nurse. For example, in Pelican Bay, staff psychiatrists or psychologists rarely visited the cell blocks. In Red Onion, a psychologist checked in once a week on those inmates who received medication—a short visit behind the cell door was reduced to exchanging everyday pleasantries. *Ruiz v. Johnson* held that Texas's administrative segregation units revealed a "frenzied and frantic state of human despair and desperation" (at 913), were used unconstitutionally to house mentally ill inmates, and confined mentally ill inmates "on conditions that nurture, rather than abate, their psychoses" (at 915).

Although the special characteristics of supermaxes are isolation and sensory deprivation, it is difficult to separate them from the total context of supermax regimes. Concentration of the most dangerous and disruptive inmates in special prisons underlines distance and differences. Since supermaxes are different from other prisons and supermax inmates are different from other inmates, it tends to be accepted that treatment and conditions for supermax inmates can also be different from, and harsher than, those of other inmates.

IV. The Mentally Ill and Effects of Sensory Deprivation

There is both national and international evidence to suggest that mentally disordered and retarded persons are overrepresented in prisons in general. There is much less evidence about supermax prisons, but it is hard to imagine mental illness is less common there than in conventional prisons. Several researchers suggest that solitary confinement in a prison setting does not have detrimental psychiatric effects if three requirements are met: inmates do not have existing mental illnesses, the length of sensory deprivation is days instead of months, and conditions of confinement are humane—requirements that are unfulfilled in a typical supermax.

A. Prevalence of Mental Illnesses

National and international studies repeatedly show that mentally ill or disordered persons are overrepresented in prisons and jails. A literature review of clinical studies from 1970 to 1997 showed that 6–15 percent of jail inmates and 10–15 percent of prison inmates have severe mental illnesses (Lamb and Weinberger 1998). A recent Bureau of Justice Statistics (1999) report estimates that 16.2 percent of state prison inmates, 16.3 percent of local jail inmates, and 7.4 percent of federal prison inmates were mentally ill in 1997. These estimates were based on offender self-reporting and mental illness was defined as current mental or emotional condition or overnight stay in a mental hospital or treatment program. Mentally ill prisoners were more likely than others to be incarcerated for violent offenses, have longer and more violent criminal histories, serve sentences an average twelve months longer, and accumulate disciplinary problems and records (Bureau of Justice Statistics 1999).

Another survey, based on information collected from state and federal prison administrators, found that 7.2 percent of the prison population had psychotic disorders and 12 percent had other psychological disorders (Veneziano and Veneziano 1996). These numbers are probably low because many mental health conditions remain undiagnosed and untreated in prisons. For example, a British study found that 4 percent of male prisoners admitted into Durham Prison in 1995–96 were acutely psychotic and 26 percent had mental disorders, yet routine prison health screening at admission failed to identify more than 75 percent of the mentally ill (Birmingham, Mason, and Grubin 1996, 1998).

A high prevalence of mental disorders was also found in a study based on structured interviews of a random sample of 213 prisoners in a rural northeastern state (Powell, Holt, and Fondacaro 1997), using the Diagnostic Interview Schedule that reveals diagnoses according to the American Psychiatric Association's *Diagnostic and Statistical Manual of Mental Disorders* (American Psychiatric Association 1994). Of all inmates, 3.4 percent were schizophrenic, 9.3 percent suffered from schizoaffective disorder, 23.8 percent had major affective disorders (including bipolar, manic, and depressive disorders), and 37.3 percent had major anxiety disorders (including anxiety, posttraumatic stress, and panic disorders) (Powell, Holt, and Fondacaro 1997, table 4).

A Canadian study (Bland et al. 1998) compared a random sample of male prisoners to a random sample of male Edmonton residents; the prisoners were serving a sentence of less than two years. The results showed that during the preceding six months, 21.1 percent of inmates had experienced affective disorders, 11.7 percent anxiety disorders, and 2.2 percent schizophrenia. The respective prevalences among residents were 6.6 percent, 3.3 percent, and 0.4 percent.

There are no general estimates on the prevalence of mental illnesses in the supermax prisons. However, there is convincing evidence that mentally disordered inmates have the greatest difficulties in adjusting to prison rules and routines and are more likely than other inmates to violate prison order and to accumulate disciplinary records. Toch and Adams (1986) examined prison and mental health records of 9,013 inmates in the New York state prison system and found that mentally ill prisoners had more disciplinary violations than other prisoners; rates were the highest for those suffering from schizophrenia, adjustment disorder (conduct disturbance), and antisocial personality, and the lowest for those with substance abuse disorders. Uhlig (1976) asked key personnel of correctional institutions in New England states to identify special offenders—those who present serious management problems and exhibit repeated, aggressive, acting-out behavior that is disruptive—fitting the characterization of a typical supermax inmate. A total of 365 inmates were nominated by prison administrators; 11.5 percent of them were diagnosed as functionally psychotic and 41.9 percent as having a severe character or personality disorder. Adams (1983) reports a disciplinary infraction rate of 21.6 per 100 for mentally disturbed prisoners (defined as prior mental hospitalization) and 14.0 per 100 for other prisoners in a sample of 3,426 federal prison inmates. However, a study comparing severely disordered Canadian federal prisoners ($N = 36$) with a matched group of nondisordered prisoners ($N = 36$) did not find differences in the amount or types of prison incidents (Porporino and Motiuk 1995).

Human Rights Watch (1997) reviewed inmates' disciplinary records in Indiana's special housing unit and reported that mentally ill inmates were most frequently charged with self-mutilation, refusing orders, making threats, throwing urine and feces, assault, battery, disorderly conduct, physically restricting a staff member, destruction of state property, and insolence and vulgarity—all behaviors that can lead to a supermax (see also Toch 1982).

Few studies have estimated how common mental illnesses are among prisoners in maximum security solitary confinement. Hodgins and Côté (1991) interviewed inmates in two maximum security segregation units in the Quebec region (forty-one inmates were interviewed in the first and thirty-one inmates in the second unit). They reported that 29 percent of inmates in the first unit and 31 percent in the second unit suffered from serious mental disorders. In the majority of cases, these serious mental illnesses existed before inmates were transferred to segregation units (86 percent of inmates in the first and 64 percent in the second unit). The lifetime prevalence of major mental disorders was 46.4 percent in the first and 59.3 percent in the second unit—significantly more than the 29.6 percent prevalence rate among the general

Canadian prison population or the 4.2–11.3 percent prevalence rate among Canadian males generally. The study concluded that mentally disordered inmates were disproportionately isolated in segregation units and did not receive adequate mental care—only two prisoners from the first unit and three prisoners from the second unit had been transferred to a psychiatric hospital.

B. *Psychiatric Effects of Isolation*

Researchers disagree on the effects of isolation and sensory deprivation in a prison setting (Suedfeld and Roy 1975; Lucas 1976; Suedfeld et al. 1982; Grassian 1983; Suedfeld 1984; Harrington 1997). Haney and Lynch (1997, p. 500) assert that "the empirical record compels an unmistakable conclusion: this experience is psychologically painful, can be traumatic and harmful, and puts many of those who have been subjected to it at risk of long-term emotional and even physical damage." By contrast, Bonta and Gendreau (1990, p. 364) write that "the facts are that long-term imprisonment and specific conditions of confinement such as solitary, under limiting and humane conditions, fail to show any sort of profound detrimental effects."

The stark difference in conclusions seems to have more to do with different research methods, designs, and measures than with the effects of solitary confinement. When Bonta and Gendreau (1984, 1990) did not find negative effects of solitary confinement, they referred to studies that used predominantly volunteer substitutes (often college students), limited solitary confinement to ten days or less, and typically excluded from experiments persons with any existing medical, psychiatric, behavioral, or intelligence problems. These studies can tell little about the psychiatric effects of supermaxes, where prisoners with combined medical, psychiatric, behavioral, and intelligence problems are held involuntarily for years. In addition, Bonta and Gendreau separate the effects of sensory deprivation from the context and conditions of isolation. Therefore, they (as well as Suedfeld et al. 1982) conclude that sensory deprivation in itself does not have negative consequences but that this may change depending on the quality of conditions, treatment of inmates, and mental health of inmates.

When Haney and Lynch (1997) found detrimental effects of solitary confinement, they referred to autobiographies, descriptive literature, and other studies based on clinical observations, interviews, and self-reports instead of studies using strong research designs. Haney and Lynch (1997) rely heavily on Grassian's (1983) evaluation of fourteen inmates in solitary confinement at Walpole Maximum Security Facility, a study conducted for a class-action suit against the Massachusetts Department of Corrections (see also Grassian and Friedman 1986). Grassian (1983) found that eleven of the fourteen isolated inmates had become hypersensitive to external stimuli, seven experienced hallucinations and perceptual distortions, ten described acute anxiety reactions, eight had difficulties with memory and concentration, six reported primitive aggressive fantasies and paranoia, and five mentioned lack of impulse control with random violence or self-mutilation. Most of the prisoners denied previously having any of these symptoms, except during previous periods of segregation.

In his book about human breakdowns in prisons, Toch (1992) says that isolated prisoners feel caged, abandoned, and suffocated and react with surges of panic, rage, depression, and emptiness. The uncertain duration of isolation promotes a sense of helplessness in prisoners, their feelings of injustice and victimization evoke panic and, when time goes by, they begin to develop suspicions of persecution and arbitrariness.

Though Bonta and Gendreau (1984, 1990) and Suedfeld et al. (1982) argue that short-term sensory deprivation does not have detrimental effects on prisoners, there is evidence that prolonged solitary confinement increases the risk of psychiatric disorders. Sestoft and colleagues (1998) compared hospitalization of persons in solitary confinement on remand (N = 152; unlimited access to television, radio, books, and newspapers was allowed) to hospitalization of other persons on remand (N = 193) in a large prison in Copenhagen. The admission rate to the prison hospital for psychiatric reasons was similar in both groups, about 12 percent. However, if a person remained in solitary confinement for more than four weeks, the probability of hospitalization increased significantly and was about twenty times higher than for a person detained before trial in the general prison population.

Bonta and Gendreau (1984, p. 474) offer three observations about use of solitary confinement. First, inmates tend to care more about being treated fairly and humanely than about the isolation itself. "Probably the outstanding question in the whole issue begs to be answered, that is, how often are prisoners in solitary abused by their keepers?" Second, they would not recommend long-term solitary confinement that lasts beyond fourteen days of isolation. Third, they urge studies focusing on who cannot tolerate isolation. All three issues are germane to thinking about the psychiatric effects of supermaxes.

Observers of supermaxes regularly see inmates who act absurdly and clearly suffer from serious mental illnesses. In extreme cases, some inmates are ready to mutilate themselves severely in order to be transferred, or they attempt suicide to end their suffering permanently. Interviews with those who do not show obvious symptoms and seem to act within ordinary human limits reveal that their mental states, thought processes, and social abilities are significantly altered as well. Although hard data and controlled clinical studies are lacking, we find it difficult not to believe that prolonged supermax conditions would cause serious psychological and social problems for anyone, whether mentally strong, weak, or something between.

V. How Is Order Maintained in Prisons?

Conditions of confinement in supermaxes bring us back to the initial problem of prison violence and disturbance that supermaxes are supposed to solve. Many prison officials and researchers believe that "the best way of reducing the risk of disruption and disturbance is to improve the regime within a prison and to improve the way prisoners are handled within the prison system" (Woolf and Tumim 1991, p. 317).

The U.S. model of concentrating a large number of prisoners in a separate supermax institution was never fully adopted in Europe, although a small number of dangerous prisoners are held in small special units. Selection procedures and criteria are far more parsimonious and units much more sparsely used in Europe than are supermaxes in the United States (King 1999). There is also more concern in Europe that lack of intellectual and environmental stimulus can damage prisoners' mental and social abilities. The European Committee for the Prevention of Torture—an expert body that makes ad hoc visits to the member states of the Council of Europe to monitor prisons and other institutions of custody—found that a prison regime in which inmates are held for a long period (over a year), spend twenty-two hours each day in their cell, cannot associate with other prisoners, and enjoy limited visits and activities amounts to "inhuman treatment" (Evans and Morgan 1998, p. 251).

More important, the problem of disturbance and violence in prisons in Europe is viewed primarily not as a consequence of disturbed and violent individuals but as a function of the prison system as whole. The idea of supermax prison reduces the problem of order to the idiosyncratic individual prisoner, while many researchers emphasize that prison order is systemic in origin and produced by multiple, complex factors (e.g., Bottoms 1999). While we cannot comprehensively discuss here issues of social organization of prisons and prison management, we mention a few studies to show how order maintenance in supermaxes differs from the best practices suggested by British prison researchers. We rely on an inquiry into the worst prison riots in the modern history of England and Wales at Strangeways Prison in Manchester in April 1990 (Woolf and Tumim 1991), a study on disturbances in two different prison regimes, one characterized as liberal and the other as restrictive (Sparks, Bottoms, and Hay 1996), and an essay that theoretically develops the concept of prison order (Bottoms 1999).

Common to all these works is the notion that the problem of order is best viewed as a systemic issue of justice (Woolf and Tumim 1991) or legitimacy (Sparks, Bottoms, Hay 1996), or a combination of instrumental, normative, and constraining factors (Bottoms 1999).

Lord Justice Woolf's report (Woolf and Tumim 1991) on the 1990 prison riots emphasizes several points that are often disregarded in discussions of supermaxes in the United States. First, the report stresses that the prison riots were not isolated incidents, local disasters, or one-shot events of running out of luck. They rather were symptoms of a series of serious difficulties underlying the prison system as whole. Second, the report identified, as a central goal of all its recommendations, the improvement of relations among management, staff, and inmates, with the aim of ensuring that these relations are based on respect and responsibility. Third, the report concluded that the primary cause of riots was a widely shared sense of injustice among prisoners. Justice in prisons is produced through three main mechanisms—formal quality of life (food, cells, clothes, work, programs, etc.), informal prison life (relations to other prisoners, treatment by staff, connections to outside world), and formal system procedures (grievance and disciplinary procedures)—and they were deficient. Fourth, the report emphasized that the best way to reduce the risk of disturbances is to improve the prison regime, to guarantee fair and respectful treatment of prisoners, and to allow prisoners to contribute to and be informed about the way things are run. In short, "management must make it clear to staff that in a modern Prison Service, the role of the prison officer must not be confined to the unlocking and locking of cells" (Woolf and Tumim 1991, p. 338).

King (1999, p. 183) has suggested the same: "The possibility should at least be examined that the reason for the high levels of violence in American prisons may have as much to do with the way in which prisons have been managed and staffed on the cheap, and the fairness and dignity with which prisoners are treated, as it has with the qualities that criminals bring with them into prison."

In a study of two British maximum security prisons (Sparks, Bottoms, and Hay 1996), Long Lartin is described as valuing choice, responsibility, and self-respect while Albany is described as valuing control, safety, and supervision. The underlying question of the study was, How successful was the staff in legitimating, first, their deployment of power and authority and, second, the techniques and strategies they used? The conclusion was that Long Lartin's more relaxed "social" crime-prevention style produced higher levels of legitimacy and helped to avoid major disturbances, but a small number of prisoners felt more vulnerable.

Bottoms (1999) develops the problem of order further and argues that order in prisons is produced through three different mechanisms that work simultaneously: instrumental factors (incentives and disincentives), normative factors (legitimacy), and constraining factors (individual and structural restrictions). Fairness of the staff and the prison regime becomes essential in producing legitimacy and distributing incentives and disincentives. Supermaxes, however, are based primarily on one mechanism—individual and structural constraints. Respectful and fair treatment of the "worst of the worst" sounds like an oxymoron.

Some defending the regimes in many supermax prisons from arguments like those advanced in this essay have suggested that supermaxes are filled with dangerous men obsessed with hate and with little to lose: have we forgotten, they ask, October 22, 1983, when two guards were killed and four injured by a prisoner in the Control Unit at Marion? This view merits a response.

For several reasons we see the use of power and frequent extractions as a more salient problem in a supermax prison than in other prisons. In the supermax there is less urgency to act at all than in other prisons. The clash of wills between the prisoner and authority in the supermax is confined to the cell and is not a part of a row of cells in which other prisoners are incited and to a degree involved. The prisoner will not be going anywhere from his supermax cell. He can do very little to injure anyone other than himself. There is rarely a necessity to do anything immediately. So he refuses to pass his food tray back through the slot in his cell door, or he throws urine or feces at a guard, or he shouts offensive abuse at a guard, and he refuses to put his hands behind his back and extend them through the slot to be handcuffed. There is a clash of wills. The prisoner has committed a disciplinary offense. It cannot be ignored. But there is no need to do anything at all at that time, let alone an extraction. The supermax does not lack punishments for enforcement of discipline. There is no urgency to impose them—tomorrow will do. A few hours, a day or two, may change a lot. The hands may well then protrude for handcuffing.

If the prisoner is shouting at a decibel level to disturb the rest of the "pod" (the section of cells proximate to his), the plastic shield can be placed over the cell door, and he may shout until his throat is hoarse without too great a disturbance to others. If, of course, the prisoner is injuring himself, there may well be need for immediate action, but otherwise it seems that no violent confrontation has to be precipitated.

Extractions in a supermax have the quality of an organized test of force, defined in immediate time, to prove who has authority, when that issue is not really in doubt. Other prisoners in supermaxes in the cells proximate to that of the recalcitrant prisoner know of the imminence of an extraction some five or so minutes before the arrival, in their words, of "the orange crush." The clash of wills is thus not entirely between prisoner and authority in the supermax, a few other prisoners know of it and its certain result and raise the noise level in the pod accordingly to encourage the prisoner and in the hope of annoying the guards.

In the sparse and punitive atmosphere of the supermax, outbursts of disobedience are even more likely than in other prisons. It seems that the authorities in a supermax are thus even more disinclined to allow any chink in their authority and therefore feel the need to act promptly on any resistance to it.

Videotaped or not, these are powers largely unscrutinized by anyone other than the warden and staff at supermaxes. Unobserved power tends to generate its own misuse. And there is always the excuse, sometimes valid, that injury to the prisoner or others, or immediate disciplinary necessity, justified the extraction. And there is no one with information to contradict the claim, whereas in the ordinary maximum security prison, even in segregation, other prisoners do observe and can report what they have seen.

If we are wrong, if extractions are no more frequent in a supermax prison than in other prisons, even other prisons under lockdown, the records surely exist to find the facts of this matter. But like so much else about a supermax prison, the walls of exclusion of knowledge are here, too, so much higher.

VI. Research and Policy

Before the state supermax prisons were invented, extremely dangerous prisoners were locked down on "nonworking," that is to say, twenty-three-hour confinement, in maximum security cells. They did not work, they did not go to religious services or to educational or other vocational classes, but they were usually held in the same tier of cells as prisoners in disciplinary segregation and they exercised in solitary yards. The basic difference between their regime and the regime in a supermax is that in the supermax one prisoner cannot rationally communicate with another. The ensuing near-totality of sensory deprivation is no minor distinction.

Other distinctions flow from the separateness of the supermax from the rest of the prison system. Everything in a supermax turns on the punitive isolation of all the inmates; not so in a well-run maximum security prison where a wide variety of staff-inmate interactions exist. Working as a guard in a supermax is very different from working as a guard in a maximum security prison. It is a culture built on guard-to-prisoner hostility.

If, in a state system there are some prisoners who cannot be held, as they used to be, the federal supermax at Florence can assist. Such transfers have long been routine.

Gang leaders, who seem to be a main target of state supermax prisons, can be handled by interstate transfers—the Illinois gang leader is rendered far less a threat in prison or to the community outside the prison if held in a Maine or Florida prison rather than an Illinois prison. Again, such interstate transfers are routine.

Otherwise, each prison should take care of its own punishment needs—it has an amplitude of power to do so.

It is boringly common for academic articles to conclude with a plea for research to answer the questions they have just failed to answer; regrettably, this cannot here be avoided since the pattern of need is obvious.

Most of the questions a rational person would ask about supermax prisons remain unanswered. The first set of questions is moral and also applies to other extreme responses to crime, such as the death penalty and civil commitment of sexual offenders: How much harm can be inflicted on one individual in order to produce safety for others? And, more important, how much harm can be inflicted if there is no proof, only surmise, that any safety is achieved? As King (1999, p. 182) has put it, "For the reality is that where prison regimes are so depriving as those offered in most supermax facilities the onus is upon those imposing the regimes to demonstrate this is justified—and demonstration goes considerably beyond simply asserting that the recipients are gang members or the 'worst of the worst.'"

The second set of questions is political. It would be good to know much more about the political conditions and pressures that result in decisions to build a supermax, how states calculate their need for supermax space, and how many supermaxes have been created at the initiative of legislatures or governors and not in response to needs articulated by the state department of corrections.

A third set of questions is practical. In addition to knowing the number of supermax states, facilities, and prisoners, we need to know what happens inside them. How deep is the monotony, solitude, and isolation experienced by a typical prisoner on a typical day in a typical supermax and how often is it disrupted? Are any programs or activities available? Is it true that relations between the staff and prisoners are much worse in supermaxes than in ordinary prisons, as is often suggested? Supermax inmates have few rights, and the staff holds basically unlimited power to distribute benefits and burdens and to control access to food, possessions, and movement. How common are abuses of power and excessive use of force in circumstances that dehumanize prisoners and promote distance between them and the staff? It is axiomatic, as Lord Acton observes, that power corrupts and absolute power corrupts absolutely. In a democracy, few powers of one human being over another come closer to absoluteness than the powers of supermax staff over supermax prisoners. Unspeakable examples of brutality are described, for example, in *Madrid v. Gomez* (889 F. Supp. 1146) and *Ruiz v. Johnson* (37 F. Supp. 2d 855).

The fourth set of descriptive questions is crucial. It is crucial to know the admission and transfer criteria that are applied in practice. Who goes into supermaxes, who gets out, when, and why? Is it true that the most dangerous prisoners are sent to supermaxes or are they just the most annoying and difficult to manage or seriously mentally ill? Likewise, it is essential to know the effects of supermaxes. Does the supermax make other prisons safer? Are inmates getting better or worse, less or more dangerous, less or more mentally ill, and how much time does it take to go one way or the other? If inmates are transferred to ordinary facilities, how long does their good behavior last—if it lasts at all? Is it possible that supermaxes could normalize the general prison population by isolating some and deterring the rest?

A fifth set of questions deserving research attention is more difficult to pursue. What effects does this type of isolation have on the mentally strong, on the mentally ill, and on the rest of us wavering between those two polarities?

All supermax prisons and special housing units functioning as supermaxes now hold some very dangerous prisoners, but they also hold many others who have been identified by the prison authorities as threatening, disruptive, or persistent nuisances. It is clear to us that prison safety and security, the security of an effective and evenhanded prison regime, do not require such harsh and separate conditions of punishment and cruel treatment of prisoners as are typical in most of our supermax prisons.

We have no doubt that supermaxes regularly hold psychotic and seriously mentally ill prisoners. We suspect that many in supermaxes are getting worse, more dangerous, and more psychologically disturbed. It seems clear that many prisoners in supermaxes are deprived of adequate mental health care. We doubt that any state prison system can be rendered safer by building a supermax. And, finally, it is clear to us that many supermax prisons have been built for political reasons rather than to meet correctional needs, the initiative often coming from the legislature rather than the department of corrections.

So long as there is no research-based evidence to show otherwise, we will adhere to our beliefs. It is far past the time when all aspects of our supermax prisons should be evaluated and beliefs such as ours refuted or confirmed. There is a case to be made for a supermax prison for the incorrigibly violent or unmanageable at the federal level. Not one of the state supermax prisons, however, is necessary, and all are a grave error in the sad tale of man's brutality to man.

REFERENCES

Adams, Kenneth. 1983. "Former Mental Patients in a Prison and Parole System." *Criminal Justice and Behavior* 10:358–84.

American Psychiatric Association. 1994. *The Diagnostic and Statistical Manual of Mental Disorders*, 4th ed. Washington, D.C.: American Psychiatric Association.

Amnesty International. 1994. *Conditions for Death Row Prisoners in H-Unit Oklahoma State Penitentiary*. New York: Amnesty International.

Birmingham, Luke, Debbie Mason, and Don Grubin. 1996. "Prevalence of

Mental Disorder in Remand Prisoners: Consecutive Case Study." *British Medical Journal* 313:1521–24.

———. 1998. "A Follow-Up Study of Mentally Disordered Men Remanded to Prison." *Criminal Behaviour and Mental Health* 8:202–13.

Bland, Roger C., Stephen C. Newman, Angus H. Thompson, and Ronald J. Dyck. 1998. "Psychiatric Disorders in the Population and in Prisoners." *International Journal of Law and Psychiatry* 21:273–79.

Bonta, James, and Paul Gendreau. 1984. "Solitary Confinement Is Not Cruel and Unusual Punishment: People Sometimes Are!" *Canadian Journal of Criminology* 26:467–78.

———. 1990. "Reexamining the Cruel and Unusual Punishment of Prison Life." *Law and Human Behavior* 14:347–72.

Bottoms, Anthony. 1999. "Interpersonal Violence and Social Order in Prisons." In *Prisons,* edited by Michael Tonry and Joan Petersilia. Vol. 26 of *Crime and Justice: A Review of Research,* edited by Michael Tonry. Chicago: University of Chicago Press.

Bureau of Justice Statistics. 1999. *Mental Health and Treatment of Inmates and Probationers.* Washington, D.C.: U.S. Department of Justice, Bureau of Justice Statistics.

Clare, Emma, and Keith Bottomley. 2001. *Evaluation of Close Supervision Centres.* Home Office Research Study No. 219. London: Home Office Research, Development and Statistics Directorate.

Department of Corrections. 1999. *Regulations: Administrative Directive No. 05.12.110.* Springfield: Illinois Department of Corrections.

Evans, Malcolm D., and Rod Morgan. 1998. *Preventing Torture: A Study of the European Convention for the Prevention of Torture and Inhuman or Degrading Treatment or Punishment.* Oxford: Clarendon.

Grassian, Stuart. 1983. "Psychopathological Effects of Solitary Confinement." *American Journal of Psychiatry* 140:1450–54.

Grassian, Stuart, and Nancy Friedman. 1986. "Effects of Sensory Deprivation in Psychiatric Seclusion and Solitary Confinement." *International Journal of Law and Psychiatry* 8:49–65.

Haney, Craig. 1997. "'Infamous Punishment': The Psychological Consequences of Isolation." In *Correctional Contexts: Contemporary and Classical Readings,* edited by James W. Marquart and Jonathan R. Sorensen. Los Angeles: Roxbury.

Haney, Craig, and Mona Lynch. 1997. "Regulating Prisons of the Future: A Psychological Analysis of Supermax and Solitary Confinement." *New York University Review of Law and Social Change* 23:477–570.

Haney, Craig, and Philip Zimbardo. 1998. "The Past and the Future of U.S. Prison Policy: Twenty-Five Years after the Stanford Prison Experiment." *American Psychologist* 53:709–27.

Harrington, Spencer. 1997. "Caging the Crazy: 'Supermax' Confinement under Attack." *Humanist* 57:14–19.

Henningsen, Rodney J., W. Wesley Johnson, and Terry Wells. 1999. "Supermax Prisons: Panacea or Desperation?" *Corrections Management Quarterly* 3(2):53–59.

Hershberger, Gregory L. 1998. "To the Max: Supermax Facilities Provide Prison Administrators with More Security Options." *Corrections Today* 60(1): 54–57.

Hodgins, Sheilagh, and Gilles Côté. 1991. "The Mental Health of Penitentiary Inmates in Isolation." *Canadian Journal of Criminology* 33:175–82.

Human Rights Watch. 1997. *Cold Storage: Super-Maximum Security Confinement in Indiana.* New York: Human Rights Watch.

———. 1999. *Red Onion State Prison: Super-Maximum Security Confinement in Virginia.* New York: Human Rights Watch.

Johnson, Kevin. 1997. "American Journal: New Prisons Isolate Worst Criminals." *Detroit News* (August 8), p. 2A.

King, Roy. 1991. "Maximum-Security Custody in Britain and the USA." *British Journal of Criminology* 31:126–52.

———. 1999. "The Rise and Rise of Supermax: An American Solution in Search of a Problem?" *Punishment and Society* 1:163–86.

King, Roy, and Kathleen McDermott. 1990. "'My Geranium Is Subversive': Some Notes on the Management of Trouble in Prisons." *British Journal of Sociology* 41:445–71.

Kupers, Terry A. 1999. *Prison Madness: The Mental Health Crisis Behind Bars and What We Must Do about It.* San Francisco: Jossey-Bass.

Lamb, Richard H., and Linda E. Weinberger. 1998. "Persons with Severe Mental Illness in Jails and Prisons: A Review." *Psychiatric Services* 49:483–92.

Lucas, W. E. 1976. "Solitary Confinement: Isolation as Coercion to Confirm." *Australian and New Zealand Journal of Criminology* 9:153–67.

Luise, Maria A. 1989. "Solitary Confinement: Legal and Psychological Considerations." *New England Journal on Criminal and Civil Confinement* 15:301–30.

Morris, Norval. 1982. *Madness and the Criminal Law.* Chicago: University of Chicago Press.

National Institute of Corrections. 1997. *Supermax Housing: A Survey of Current Practice.* Washington, D.C.: U.S. Department of Justice, National Institute of Corrections.

———. 1999. *Supermax Prisons: Legal Issues and Considerations.* Washington, D.C.: U.S. Department of Justice, National Institute of Corrections.

Petersilia, Joan. 1997. "Justice for All? Offenders with Mental Retardation and the California Corrections System." *Prison Journal* 77:358–80.

Porporino, Frank J., and Laurence L. Motiuk. 1995. "The Prison Careers of Mentally Disordered Offenders." *International Journal of Law and Psychiatry* 18:29–44.

Powell, Thomas A., John C. Holt, and Karen M. Fondacaro. 1997. "Prevalence of Mental Illness among Inmates in a Rural State." *Law and Human Behavior* 21:427–38.

Riveland, Chase. 1999. *Supermax Prisons: Overview and General Considerations.* Washington, D.C.: U.S. Department of Justice, National Institute of Corrections.

Rogers, Robert. 1993. "Solitary Confinement." *International Journal of Offender Therapy and Comparative Criminology* 37:339–49.

Sestoft, Dorte Maria, Henrik Steen Andersen, Tommy Lillebœk, and Gorm Gabrielsen. 1998. "Impact of Solitary Confinement on Hospitalization among Danish Prisoners in Custody." *International Journal of Law and Psychiatry* 21:99–108.

Sheppard, Robert A., Jeffery A. Geiger, and George Welborn. 1996. "Closed Maximum Security: The Illinois SuperMax." *Corrections Today* 58(4):84–87.

Smith, Charles, Helen O'Neill, John Tobin, David Walshe, and Enda Dooley. 1996. "Mental Disorders Detected in Irish Prison Sample." *Criminal Behaviour and Mental Health* 6:177–83.

Sparks, Richard, Anthony Bottoms, and Will Hay. 1996. *Prison and the Problem of Order*. Oxford: Clarendon.

Suedfeld, Peter. 1984. "Measuring the Effects of Solitary Confinement." *American Journal of Psychiatry* 141:1306–8.

Suedfeld, Peter, Carmenza Raminez, John Deaton, and Gloria Baker-Brown. 1982. "Reactions and Attributes of Prisoners in Solitary Confinement." *Criminal Justice and Behavior* 9:303–40.

Suedfeld, Peter, and Chunilal Roy. 1975. "Using Social Isolation to Change the Behaviour of Disruptive Inmates." *International Journal of Offender Therapy and Comparative Criminology* 19:90–99.

Tachiki, Scott N. 1995. "Indeterminate Sentences in Supermax Prisons Based upon Alleged Gang Affiliations: A Reexamination of Procedural Protection and a Proposal for Greater Procedural Requirements." *California Law Review* 83:1115–49.

Toch, Hans. 1982. "The Disturbed Disruptive Inmate: Where Does the Bus Stop?" *Journal of Psychiatry and Law* 10:317–49.

———. 1992. *Mosaic of Despair: Human Breakdowns in Prison*. Washington, D.C.: American Psychological Association.

Toch, Hans, and Kenneth Adams. 1986. "Pathology and Disruptiveness among Prison Inmates." *Journal of Research in Crime and Delinquency* 23:7–21.

Uhlig, Richard H. 1976. "Hospitalization Experience of Mentally Disturbed and Disruptive, Incarcerated Offenders." *Journal of Psychiatry and Law* 4:49–59.

Veneziano, Louis, and Carol Veneziano. 1996. "Disabled Inmates." In *Encyclopedia of American Prisons*, edited by Marilyn D. McShane and Franklin P. Williams. New York: Garland.

Ward, David A. 1995. "A Corrections Dilemma: How to Evaluate Super-max Regimes." *Corrections Today* 57(3):104–8.

———. 1999. "Supermaximum Facilities." In *Prison and Jail Administration: Practice and Theory*, edited by Peter M. Carlson and Judith Simon Garrett. Gaithersburg, Md.: Aspen.

Woolf, Lord Justice, and Stephen Tumim. 1991. *Prison Disturbances, April 1990*. London: H.M. Stationery Office.